LITERARY
REFLECTIONS

LITERARY REFLECTIONS

FOURTH EDITION

WILLIAM R. ELKINS
Emporia State University

JACK L. KENDALL
University of Oklahoma

JOHN R. WILLINGHAM
University of Kansas

McGraw-Hill Book Company
New York St. Louis San Francisco Auckland Bogotá Hamburg
Johannesburg London Madrid Mexico Montreal New Delhi
Panama Paris São Paulo Singapore Sydney Tokyo Toronto

LITERARY REFLECTIONS

4 5 6 7 8 9 0   DODO   8 9 8 7

See Acknowledgments on pages 501–504.
Copyrights included on this page by reference.

This book was set in Vega by Rocappi, Inc.
The editors were Phillip A. Butcher and Barry Benjamin;
the production supervisor was Rosann E. Raspini.
The photo editor was Inge King.
The cover was designed by Robin Hessel;
the cover photograph was taken by
F. J. Dias/Photo Researchers, Inc.
R. R. Donnelley & Sons Company was printer and
binder.

Library of Congress Cataloging in Publication Data

Elkins, William R   comp.
    Literary reflections.

    Includes indexes.
    1. College readers. I. Kendall, Jack L.
II. Willingham, John R. III. Title.
PE1122.E4 1982   808'.0427   80-29006
ISBN 0-07-019232-4

Part Opening Photo Credits:

Part One: Charles Gatewood
Part Two: Bill Stanton/Magnum Photos
Part Three: Ginger Chih/Peter Arnold, Inc.
Part Four: Bruce Davidson/Magnum Photos
Part Five: Wayne Miller/Magnum Photos
Part Six: © Ira Berger 1980/Woodfin Camp & Assoc.

FOR

EILEEN,

JILL,

AND YVONNE

CONTENTS

PART TWO: PROTEST AGAINST RESTRAINT

The Essay

Short Story

PART FOUR: THE PROTEST AGAINST MATERIALISM

PART FIVE: THE SEARCH FOR MODES OF EXPRESSION

PART SIX: IN VIEW OF DEATH

CONTENTS BY LITERARY TYPE

PREFACE

Literary Reflections has always selected for its contents only those literary works which focus sharply on the major human experiences of all time. We have offered a thematic grouping because we believe that the four literary forms within each division maintain a lively dialogue, that they tend to probe and explain each other. Of course, we have reflected our awareness of changing times—from the 1960s into the 1980s. But we have preferred works that transcend the "trendy," the merely "timely," the "faddish"—works that consider the human condition as something quite apart from the transactional ethics of a season or even one decade. The selections for this fourth edition, like those of its predecessors, display that greater vision. And of course the literature need not be read within the thematic order, for the book lends itself readily to the study of literary types.

Our text continues to serve three separate but overlapping purposes. It offers a stimulating insight into the history of ideas. It provides a viable means of identifying, comparing, and contrasting modes of expression. And it challenges students to come to grips with universally relevant ideas and problems, as they recur in literature, and encourages them to work out, carefully and imaginatively, their own formulations of them.

To accomplish our objectives, we have arranged the selections in six thematic units. Each unit is internally structured to present (1) essays that introduce in a relatively familiar prose form the thematic emphasis of the unit; (2) short stories as a logical step from the essay to more imaginative writing; (3) four plays (three of them have only one act) that share some features with fiction but add the impact of visual presentation or imagined production on a stage; and (4) selected poetry that carries students to the most intricate, most compressed, hence most intense form of literary expression. In effect, that movement from type to type within each unit enhances both the understanding of technique and the interest in ideas.

In addition, we have provided brief introductory discussions for each thematic heading to support and guide students' reading. For each selection, we have appended appropriate headnotes, provocative study questions, and suggestions for composition. This fourth edition offers, at the conclusion of each thematic unit, topics for longer compositions; topics that ask the student to draw broadly on the selections and to add other readings and research information that may lead to compositions which evidence considerable depth. A biographical index appears in the fourth edition—brief but pertinent biographical information for each author provides another resource for sorting out questions of *time* and *place* that often bear upon interpretation. All these devices are intended simply to challenge students without in any way preempting their critical judgments. The book, then, contains ample material for a rich encounter with literature and adds, for those who wish it, a framework for purposeful writing about literature. And the thematic organization, keeping faith with each author's general intent and vision, should not hamper the perceptive instructor who chooses his or her own alignment of selections.

Our book's constant features and the additions noted above testify to how much we are aware of our debt to the many colleagues and students whose comments and advice continue to help shape this book. We are especially grateful to Phillip A. Butcher, McGraw-Hill English Editor, for his guidance and cooperation, and to his assistant, Florence Squassi, for her enthusiastic assistance in preparing the manuscript.

William R. Elkins
Jack L. Kendall
John R. Willingham

INTRODUCTION

TO LITERARY TYPES

Critics and scholars have speculated endlessly from the days of Aristotle about the nature and analysis of literature. *Literary Reflections* demonstrates not only the vital relationship between human experience and literary expression but it also directs the reader's attention to the apparently unlimited variety of uses of language in effecting techniques and forms. For any generalization about literature must include statements about the artist's use of words in a certain way to achieve a certain effect. And such statements necessarily must recognize the existence of conventional categories—literary genres or types. In this volume, we encounter four major genres—the essay, the short story, the drama, and the poem. Although the resources of any one of these may be present in the others, we can make some statements which are generally true only for each of the four types.

THE ESSAY

The term essay, as the designation for a type of literary composition, first appeared in English toward the end of the sixteenth century. To the Elizabethans the word meant a kind of literary exploration, an attempt (cf. the French verb *essayer,* "to try") to state something—perhaps a serious argument, sometimes a more or less random reflection upon experience. However or whenever it originally appeared, the essay has always involved exposition of an idea. The author may be relatively uninterested in aesthetic effects, but he or she is always attempting an orderly arrangement of thought. The characteristic mode of the essay, then, is "man thinking" in relatively formal structures. In a well-developed essay, the reader looks for a central idea or thesis, either explicit or implicit. The rest is mainly the arrangement of evidence, of reasons, of illustrations, or whatever amplification the thesis requires. If the author's literary bent permits, he or she may in addition utilize figurative language, narration, description, or dramatic incident as important elements of his thought. The "literary essay," distinguished by its conscious display of style and rhetorical virtuosity, does not enjoy in the twentieth century the favor it enjoyed up through the nineteenth century. Far more familiar today is the "article" which we find in newspapers and magazines, with the writer's ideas set forth in relatively familiar terms. The journalist, such as Vance Packard, with his characteristically simple language and short paragraphs, fills for our day the role which brought honor to such men as Richard Steele, Joseph Addison, Jonathan Swift, Thomas Carlyle, Thomas Babington Macaulay, Ralph Waldo Emerson, and James Russell Lowell. Nevertheless such twentieth-century stylists as George Orwell, Virginia Woolf, Loren Eisley, and Alfred Kazin keep alive the tradition of the essay as a creative literary medium. For discriminating readers, the journey with such representatives of "man thinking" (as Emerson called his ideal "American scholar") can be stimulating and fruitful, whether the author presents himself as an analyst of juvenile delinquency, as a professional sociologist probing the difficulties of love in the modern world, as a scientist advancing his hypothesis about life on Mars, or as a "personal essayist" simply detailing his reactions to old china or recalling his memories of a Creole courtyard in old New Orleans.

THE SHORT STORY

Relatively new as a recognized literary genre, the short story utilizes the mode of narrative. That is, someone recounts for us a plausible, sequential experience. Gertrude Stein may have simplified outrageously the formula for narration. "And after that what changes what changes after that, after that what changes and what changes after that and after that and what changes and after that and what changes after that"; but she emphasized rightly the importance of progression and the relationship of events within imagined time. The writer of fiction further imposes upon his or her narrative a deliberate design by the kind of characters created, the quality and outcome of the situation in which those characters are involved, and the establishment of a viewpoint toward those characters and their situations. Whether the story is told ostensibly by a character deeply involved in the events of the plot, by an outside observer, or even frankly by the author, the method of fiction establishes some meaningful order of events, reveals what of significance the characters did and said, and brings the sequence to a conclusion that implies an attitude toward experience. The order of events may be as straightforward as that outlined by Miss Stein; on the other hand, the narrative may leap backward and forward in time, as it does in Joyce Carol Oates' "An Interior Monologue," making strategic use of what in the movies is called the "flashback." But even when straight chronological order is violated, fiction creates for us a world more or less like the one we have known: the big difference between fiction and life arises from the writer's prerogative to impose upon his or her fictional "world" the kind of order and control the writer desires.

Whereas the essayist restricts his statement to facts, to a report of what he has thought and observed, to his beliefs and an invitation to the reader to accept or at least understand those beliefs, the writer of fiction, particularly in our day, characteristically does not intervene in his narrative with direct, editorial statement. He merely tells his story as artfully as possible and allows the combination of charcterization, plot, theme, imagery, dramatic situation, and condensed narrative to imply as much about his world view as it can. Ivan Bunin does not have to state directly his attitude toward the materialistic values of his nameless "Gentleman from San Francisco"; every juxtaposition of scene and every exchange of dialogue forcibly conveys to us Bunin's judgments. The difference between the "pulp" magazine story or the saccharine tale in a woman's magazine, on the one hand, and the memorable fictional illumination of human experience, on the other, is simply one of insight and artistry, which together distinguish good fiction from escape fiction.

Every student has heard of the pyramid design for plot—in which generating circumstances rise through conflict to *denouement* (literally, the "untying of the knot," or the solution). And ordinarily the pyramid design fits the typical short story rather well. In one way or another, the author of a short story quickly establishes a situation containing the seeds of conflict which rises to a point of crisis or "climax" before descending, perhaps very abruptly, to the resolution or *denouement.* Although the sequence of events may not end happily, it must satisfy the reader's sense of appropriateness in terms of the kind of conflict narrated.

THE DRAMA

Drama, an ancient literary form, was explained by the Greeks with considerable sophistication. Aristotle analyzed the various elements—plot, diction, spectacle— which the dramatist utilizes; and his successors have elaborated endlessly upon theories of the drama. Although much of what we have said about the short story is equally true of the drama (both relate stories, both ask the reader to accept as plausible the sequence of events, and both have a plot design), the writer of fiction tells us in his or her own way *about* certain characters in a certain situation, whereas the dramatist conjures up a world to be created by stage designers and actors and brought to life by actors.

In "Hello Out There," William Saroyan allows considerable leeway for stage design: for the setting, he tells us only, "There is a fellow in a small-town prison cell. . . ." On the other hand, Eugene O'Neill offers relatively precise, often suggestive directions for the stark setting of *Bound East for Cardiff,* for the kind of atmosphere he expects, for the aura of character and incident he envisions. In any of Shakespeare's plays poetry is the only clue to character interpretation, but an imaginative director can find ways to refine those clues. Hamlet can be made as morosely meditative as the director wishes; Macbeth can be made as passive or as aggressive as the vision of actors and production planners can contrive. Beyond an occasional direction like "suddenly" or "almost to himself," Saroyan interferes very little with the possibilities for an actor's interpretation of the Young Man's role. O'Neill, however, specifies the tone and effect he desires from gestures, facial expressions, and speeches.

In any play the characters are interpreted, with the help of such notes and stage directions as the dramatist provides, by directors and by actors who move on and off a stage, speak to each other or to themselves as the script of the play dictates, and seem with the help of lighting, makeup, stage properties, costumes, and gestures to be real people who undergo a span of experience before an audience. One important distinction between drama and fiction is that those segments of imagined experience selected by the playwright as most important are acted out before an audience; moreover, those segments, whether or not divided into acts and scenes, occupy exactly the same time span spent by the audience in watching those segments. To read a play successfully, we must supply through the imagination the staging, the lighting, the direction, the sound effects, and, with such help as we may get from the stage directions, the movements of the actors. Reading a play may be a relatively poor substitute for watching a performance of it, but the reading can be both exciting and profitable nevertheless. We can pause to consider the possible implications of a character's speech, or we may backtrack as often as we wish in order to fathom the emerging form of the drama. And to the extent that drama forces us to attend to each word a character speaks, it requires something of the close reading that we give to poetry.

THE POEM

Like the short story and the novel, the poem may relate a narrative. Or, as in Browning's "The Bishop Orders His Tomb at St. Praxed's Church", the poem may be a drama in miniature: though it is not intended for a performance, its characters simply speak aloud and reveal a dramatic situation. Although it is the most ancient and exalted literary type, poetry is harder than any of the other types to define. We know that poems look different: the poet dictates how his or her work will appear upon the printed page. Its lines, unlike those of prose, tend to be symmetrical, though sentence units are not always completed within the line. Even the poems of an idiosyncratic modern poet like E. E. Cummings, with unconventional uses of typography, have a more formal appearance than any work of prose. But quantitative measures like typography, stanzaic pattern, or meter do not really help much to define poetry. For greeting card "verse" exhibits many of the physical properties of poetry. Qualitative standards, on the other hand, discover for us the presence of poetry. The essential point is that in poetry language is compressed and elevated beyond that of ordinary discourse. Poetry may not always be, as William Wordsworth said, "emotion recollected in tranquillity"; but at least, whether in conventionally metrical or "free" verse or even "prose poems," the conscious ordering of language is all-important. In its compulsion toward rhythmic patterns and selective word sounds, poetry suggests strong relationships to music; in its typical drive to evoke images, poetry suggests comparisons with painting. Perhaps Emerson's witty definition of a poem as a "metre-making argument" comes close enough to a formal definition; but in its combined appeals to emotion and thought through the artful arrangement of words, even the relatively short poem, if it is successful, brings to the reader a sudden illumination of the human condition and a "deliverance" that cannot be obtained through any other literary type. In the twentieth century, poetry probably does not enjoy the prestige it commanded in other ages; on the other hand, more poets write and more experimentation takes place than in any other century.

LITERARY
REFLECTIONS

PART
1

THE SEARCH FOR A PLACE IN SOCIETY

When we speak of man's search for a place in society, we touch upon that side of man's nature that he almost always conceals from others and often conceals from himself. Obviously, the search for a place is both a search for a physical place and a search for an inner sense of identity. In this dual function, only the physical place manifests itself; yet the search is primarily an inner one. Each man, whether or not he admits it, carries within him an ideal image of himself. This self-image is a primary consideration in his attempts to place himself physically within society. In short, the search for a place becomes an attempt of each man to reconcile that ideal image he has of himself not only with his position in society but, also, with the treatment that society accords him. Consequently, writers have found the inner conflict between the *what ought to be* and the *what is* a theme so basic, yet so diverse, that its treatment lends itself to all types of literature.

D. H. Lawrence's essay, "The Spirit of Place," is the first chapter of his book, *Studies in Classic American Literature.* In this essay, Lawrence considers place as a dominant factor in the development of a national character and a national literature. But, in keeping with the dual function of place, Lawrence has much to say about man's inner search for identity and its control of his actions, and the physical place in which he chooses to exercise his actions. Lawrence says, "Men are only free when they are doing what the deepest self likes."

Martin Luther King, Jr., in his famous speech, "I Have a Dream," offers a contemporary statement about the black man's place in American society. Like Lawrence, King sees a potential for the emergence of an American democracy which will destroy the old masters and create equality. But unlike Lawrence, who writes as an observer from a foreign land, King speaks as one who vibrates with a sense of place which, though partially denied, is nevertheless American.

Stephen Crane's short story, "An Experiment in Misery," fictionalizes the plight of the wanderer, the social outcast, whose sense of displacement is only ironically placated when he finds companionship of a kind with those like him. Crane's story, set in nineteenth-century America, offers additional comments by contrasting the emergence of a mighty and wealthy nation with the degradation and deprivation of human dignity.

Degradation and deprivation of human dignity abound in Rudyard Kipling's short story, "The Strange Ride of Morrowbie Jukes." Set in late-nineteenth-century India, the story takes us into a strange world that lies between life and death and, with horrifying detail, introduces us to the attempt to maintain one's inner sense of place; an attempt that is ironic indeed because as Kipling's introductory *Native Proverb* forewarns, "Alive or dead—there is no other way."

Always a pathetic figure is the "exile" who yearns to return from another land,

resisting, for whatever reasons, acceptance of a new place. Such a one is the protagonist in Doris Lessing's short story, "Lucy Grange." Lucy's willingness, albeit somewhat
reluctant, to accept the "second rate" is yet another testimony to the importance a
sense of place holds for the human spirit.

William Saroyan's "Hello Out There" becomes very quickly a dialogue about
"here," "there," and "somewhere." Its specific setting in a dusty West Texas town is,
of course, relatively incidental, though the constant wind and aimless dust of the plains
appropriately mirror the constant frustrations and aimless lives of people who have not
found a "place" that answers to the yearning of the homeless heart. The "rape" that
precedes but generates the situation of the play and the looming "lynching bee" that
closes it hint at the forces which oppose the life that would be liberated for escape to
"Frisco," or wherever the imaginative individual places the location of hope for and
fulfillment of life's possibilities. Significantly and appropriately this first play in a book
thematically structured around important literary avenues for exploring the human condition acknowledges somewhere within its brief scope not only the compulsion to find
and possess a "place" but also all the other five basic motifs—abhorrence of restraint,
the possibilities of love, the ubiquity of materialism, the need for adequate expression,
and the inexorable threat of death.

THE ESSAY

The essay that follows points up the fact that literary classifications should be flexible enough to accommodate the creative talents of the writer. Lawrence's informal approach to what is generally considered a formal area (literary criticism) in essay writing illustrates that the writer of the essay need not be limited by dictates of form in his attempt to reach his reader. Lawrence disarms his reader with a wide variety of unexpected techniques. We should be alert, however, and weigh carefully our reaction to the following:

1 The conversational, bantering tone
2 The use of charged, colorful, idiosyncratic speech forms more characteristic of the orated diatribe than the essay
3 The highly subjective point of view—Lawrence's experience becomes authority for every man's experience
4 The name-calling, blatantly revealing Lawrence's prejudices in such a way as to suggest that they should rightly be every man's prejudices

THE SPIRIT OF PLACE

D. H. Lawrence

We like to think of the old-fashioned American classics as children's books. Just childishness, on our part. The old American art-speech contains an alien quality, which belongs to the American continent and to nowhere else. But, of course, so long as we insist on reading the books as children's tales, we miss all that.

One wonders what the proper high-brow Romans of the third and fourth or later centuries read into the strange utterances of Lucretius or Apuleius or Tertullian, Augustine or Athanasius. The uncanny voice of Iberian Spain, the weirdness of old Carthage, the passion of Libya and North Africa; you may bet the proper old Romans never heard these at all. They read old Latin inference over the top of it, as we read old European inference over the top of Poe or Hawthorne.

It is hard to hear a new voice, as hard as it is to listen to an unknown language. We just don't listen. There is a new voice in the old American classics. The world has declined to hear it, and has babbled about children's stories.

Why?—Out of fear. The world fears a new experience more than it fears anything. Because a new experience displaces so many old experiences. And it is like trying to use muscles that have perhaps never been used, or that have been going stiff for ages. It hurts horribly.

The world doesn't fear a new idea. It can pigeon-hole any idea. But it can't pigeon-hole a real new experience. It can only dodge. The world is a great dodger, and the Americans the greatest. Because they dodge their own very selves.

There is a new feeling in the old American books, far more than there is in the modern American books, which are pretty empty of any feeling, and proud of it. There is a "different" feeling in the old American classics. It is the shifting over from the old psyche to something new, a displacement. And displacements hurt. This hurts. So we try to tie it up, like a cut finger. Put a rag round it.

It is a cut too. Cutting away the old emotions and consciousness. Don't ask what is left.

Art-speech is the only truth. An artist is usually a damned liar, but his art, if it be art, will tell you the truth of his day. And that is all that matters. Away with eternal truth. Truth lives from day to day, and the marvellous Plato of yesterday is chiefly bosh to-day.

The old American artists were hopeless liars. But they were artists, in spite of themselves. Which is more than you can say of most living practitioners.

And you can please yourself, when you read *The Scarlet Letter,* whether you accept what that sugary, blue-eyed little darling of a Hawthorne has to say for himself, false as all darlings are, or whether you read the impeccable truth of his art-speech.

The curious thing about art-speech is that it prevaricates so terribly, I mean it tells such lies. I suppose because we always all the time tell ourselves lies. And out of a pattern of lies art weaves the truth. Like Dostoevsky posing as a sort of Jesus, but most truthfully revealing himself all the while as a little horror.

Truly art is a sort of subterfuge. But thank God for it, we can see through the subterfuge if we choose. Art has two great functions. First, it provides an emotional experience. And then, if we have the courage of our own feelings, it becomes a mine of practical truth. We have had the feelings *ad nauseam.* But we've never dared dig the actual truth out of them, the truth that concerns us, whether it concerns our grandchildren or not.

The artist usually sets out—or used to—to point a moral and adorn a tale. The tale, however, points the other way, as a rule. Two blankly opposing morals, the artist's and the tale's. Never trust the artist. Trust the tale. The proper function of a critic is to save the tale from the artist who created it.

Now we know our business in these studies: saving the American tale from the American artist.

Let us look at this American artist first. How did he ever get to America, to start with? Why isn't he a European still, like his father before him?

Now listen to me, don't listen to him. He'll tell you the lie you expect. Which is partly your fault for expecting it.

He didn't come in search of freedom of worship. England had more freedom of worship in the year 1700 than America had. Won by Englishmen who wanted freedom, and so stopped at home and fought for it. And got it. Freedom of worship? Read the history of New England during the first century of its existence.

Freedom anyhow? The land of the free! This the land of the free! Why, if I say anything that displeases them, the free mob will lynch me, and that's my freedom.

Free? Why, I have never been in any country where the individual has such an abject fear of his fellow countrymen. Because, as I say, they are free to lynch him the moment he shows he is not one of them.

No, no, if you're so fond of the truth about Queen Victoria, try a little about yourself.

Those Pilgrim Fathers and their successors never came here for freedom of worship. What did they set up when they got here? Freedom, would you call it?

They didn't come for freedom. Or if they did, they sadly went back on themselves.

All right then, what did they come for? For lots of reasons. Perhaps least of all in search of freedom of any sort: positive freedom, that is.

They came largely to get *away*—that most simple of motives. To get away. Away from what? In the long run, away from themselves. Away from everything. That's why most people have come to America, and still do come. To get away from everything they are and have been.

"Henceforth be masterless."

Which is all very well, but it isn't freedom. Rather the reverse. A hopeless sort of constraint. It is never freedom till you find something you really *positively want to be.* And people in America have always been shouting about the things they are *not.* Unless, of course, they are millionaires, made or in the making.

And after all there is a positive side to the movement. All that vast flood of human life that has flowed over the Atlantic in ships from Europe to America has not flowed over simply on a tide of revulsion from Europe and from the confinements of the European ways of life. This revulsion was, and still is, I believe, the prime motive in emigration. But there was some cause, even for the revulsion.

It seems as if at times man had a frenzy for getting away from any control of any sort. In Europe the old Christianity was the real master. The Church and the true aristocracy bore the responsibility for the working out of the Christian ideals: a little irregularly, maybe, but responsible nevertheless.

Mastery, kingship, fatherhood had their power destroyed at the time of the Renaissance.

And it was precisely at this moment that the great drift over the Atlantic started. What were men drifting away from? The old authority of Europe? Were they breaking the bonds of authority, and escaping to a new more absolute unrestrainedness? Maybe. But there was more to it.

Liberty is all very well, but men cannot live without masters. There is always a master. And men either live in glad obedience to the master they believe in, or they live in a frictional opposition to the master they wish to undermine. In America this frictional opposition has been the vital factor. It has given the Yankee his kick. Only the continual influx of more servile Europeans has provided America with an obedient labouring class. The true obedience never outlasting the first generation.

But there sits the old master, over in Europe. Like a parent. Somewhere deep in every American heart lies a rebellion against the old parenthood of Europe. Yet no American feels he has completely escaped its mastery. Hence the slow, smouldering patience of American opposition. The slow, smouldering, corrosive obedience to the old master Europe, the unwilling subject, the unremitting opposition.

Whatever else you are, be masterless.

> Ca Ca Caliban
> Get a new master, be a new man.

Escaped slaves, we might say, people the republics of Liberia or Haiti. Liberia enough! Are we to look at America in the same way? A vast republic of escaped slaves. When you consider the hordes from eastern Europe, you might well say it: a vast republic of escaped slaves. But one dare not say this of the Pilgrim Fathers, and the great old body of idealist Americans, the modern Americans tortured with thought. A vast republic of escaped slaves. Look out, America! And a minority of earnest, self-tortured people.

The masterless.

> Ca Ca Caliban
> Get a new master, be a new man.

What did the Pilgrim Fathers come for, then, when they came so gruesomely over the black sea? Oh, it was in a black spirit. A black revulsion from Europe, from the old authority of Europe, from kings and bishops and popes. And more. When you look into it, more. They were black, masterful men, they wanted something else. No kings, no bishops maybe. Even no God Almighty. But also, no more of this new "humanity" which followed the Renaissance. None of this new liberty which was to be so pretty in Europe. Something grimmer, by no means free-and-easy.

America has never been easy, and is not easy to-day. Americans have always been at a certain tension. Their liberty is a thing of sheer will, sheer tension: a liberty of Thou shalt not. And it has been so from the first. The land of Thou shalt not. Only the first commandment is: Thou shalt not presume to be a master. Hence democracy.

"We are the masterless." That is what the American Eagle shrieks. It's a Hen-Eagle.

The Spaniards refused the post-Renaissance liberty of Europe. And the Spaniards filled most of America. The Yankees, too, refused, refused the post-Renaissance humanism of Europe. First and foremost, they hated masters. But under that, they hated the flowing ease of humour in Europe. At the bottom of the American soul was always a dark suspense, at the bottom of the Spanish-American soul the same. And this dark suspense hated and hates the old European spontaneity, watches it collapse with satisfaction.

Every continent has its own great spirit of place. Every people is polarized in some particular locality, which is home, the homeland. Different places on the face of the earth have different vital effluence, different vibration, different chemical exhalation, different polarity with different stars: call it what you like. But the spirit of place is a great reality. The Nile valley produced not only the corn, but the terrific religions of Egypt. China produces the Chinese, and will go on doing so. The Chinese in San Francisco will in time cease to be Chinese, for America is a great melting-pot.

There was a tremendous polarity in Italy, in the city of Rome. And this seems to have died. For even places die. The Island of Great Britain had a wonderful terrestrial magnetism or polarity of its own, which made the British people. For the moment, this polarity seems to be breaking. Can England die? And what if England dies?

Men are less free than they imagine; ah, far less free. The freest are perhaps least free.

Men are free when they are in a living homeland, not when they are straying and breaking away. Men are free when they are obeying some deep, inward voice of religious belief. Obeying from within. Men are free when they belong to a living, organic, *believing* community, active in fulfilling some unfulfilled, perhaps unrealized purpose. Not when they are escaping to some wild west. The most unfree souls go west, and shout of freedom. Men are freest when they are most unconscious of freedom. The shout is a rattling of chains, always was.

Men are not free when they are doing just what they like. The moment you can do just what you like, there is nothing you care about doing. Men are only free when they are doing what the deepest self likes.

And there is getting down to the deepest self! It takes some diving.

Because the deepest self is way down, and the conscious self is an obstinate monkey. But of one thing we may be sure. If one wants to be free, one has to give up the illusion of doing what one likes, and seek what it wishes done.

But before you can do what it likes, you must first break the spell of the old mastery, the old it.

Perhaps at the Renaissance, when kingship and fatherhood fell, Europe drifted into a very dangerous half-truth: of liberty and equality. Perhaps the men who went to America felt this, and so repudiated the old world together. Went one better than Europe. Liberty in America has meant so far the breaking away from *all* dominion. The true liberty will only begin when Americans discover it, and proceed possibly to fulfil it. It being the deepest whole self of man, the self in its wholeness, not idealistic halfness.

That's why the Pilgrim Fathers came to America, then; and that's why we come. Driven by it. We cannot see that invisible winds carry us, as they carry swarms of locusts, that invisible magnetism brings us as it brings the migrating birds to their unforeknown goal. But it is so. We are not the marvellous choosers and deciders we think we are. It chooses for us, and decides for us. Unless, of course, we are just escaped slaves, vulgarly cocksure of our ready-made destiny. But if we are living people, in touch with the source, it drives us and decides us. We are free only so long as we obey. When we run counter, and think we will do as we like, we just flee around like Orestes pursued by the Eumenides.

And still, when the great day begins, when Americans have at last discovered America and their own wholeness, still there will be the vast number of escaped slaves to reckon with, those who have no cocksure, ready-made destinies.

Which will win in America, the escaped slaves, or the new whole men?

The real American day hasn't begun yet. Or at least not yet sunrise. So far it has been the false dawn. That is, in the progressive American consciousness there has been the one dominant desire, to do away with the old thing. Do away with masters, exalt the will of the people. The will of the people being nothing but a figment, the exalting doesn't count for much. So, in the name of the will of the people, get rid of masters. When you have got rid of masters, you are left with this mere phrase of the will of the people. Then you pause and bethink yourself, and try to recover your own wholeness.

So much for the conscious American motive, and for democracy over here. Democracy in America is just the tool with which the old master of Europe, the European spirit, is undermined. Europe destroyed, potentially, American democracy will evaporate. America will begin.

American consciousness has so far been a false dawn. The negative ideal of democracy. But underneath, and contrary to this open ideal, the first hints and revelations, of it. It, the American whole soul.

You have got to pull the democratic and idealistic clothes off American utterance, and see what you can of the dusky body of it underneath.

"Henceforth be masterless."

Henceforth be mastered.

QUESTIONS

1   Why does Lawrence say that the world finds it hard to hear a new voice? In what way does he draw a parallel between the "new voice" and a new experience?
2   How does Lawrence view the intent of the artist in respect to the art that he creates?
3   Lawrence sees the story of America's founding as a myth. What theory does he offer to replace the myth? Is his definition of freedom valid?
4   What does he mean by "Henceforth be masterless"?
5   If we separate Lawrence's hysteria from his subject matter, what three main ideas emerge?

TOPICS FOR COMPOSITION

1   Lawrence's style may obscure many interesting ideas. Write a summary of this essay.
2   The author speaks of a tension in the American idea of freedom. He literally means that Americans constantly work to preserve their concept of freedom. Support this idea by focusing on current events.
3   Investigate the possibilities of complete freedom—the idea of "Henceforth be masterless."

"I Have a Dream" is oratory. As such it provides many insights into techniques of persuasive rhetoric. Although a certain amount of emotionalism is part of an effective appeal, a highly successful work, such as King's speech, relies mainly on carefully chosen appeals that will hold the audience by relating to issues well known to them. As you read this speech, note how King uses:

1   History to provide initial support and as a springboard for his appeal
2   Urgency to add relevancy to his appeal
3   A warning, couched in reasoned terms, to give added emphasis to his statement
4   A prophecy to encompass a vision of hope

"I HAVE A DREAM . . ."

Martin Luther King, Jr.

Five score years ago, a great American, in whose symbolic shadow we stand, signed the Emancipation Proclamation. This momentous decree came as a great beacon light of hope to millions of Negro slaves who had been seared in the flames of withering injustice. It came as a joyous daybreak to end the long night of captivity.

But one hundred years later, we must face the tragic fact that the Negro is still not free. One hundred years later, the life of the Negro is still sadly crippled by the manacles of segregation and the chains of discrimination. One hundred years later, the Negro lives on a lonely island of poverty in the midst of a vast ocean of material prosperity. One hundred years later, the Negro is still languished in the corners of American society and finds himself an exile in his own land. So we have come here today to dramatize an appalling condition.

In a sense we have come to our nation's Capital to cash a check. When the architects of our republic wrote the magnificent words of the Constitution and the Declaration of Independence, they were signing a promissory note to which every American was to fall heir. This note was a promise that all men would be guaranteed the unalienable rights of life, liberty, and the pursuit of happiness.

It is obvious today that America has defaulted on this promissory note insofar as her citizens of color are concerned. Instead of honoring this sacred obligation, America has given the Negro people a bad check; a check which has come back marked "insufficient funds." But we refuse to believe that the bank of justice is bankrupt. We refuse to believe that there are insufficient funds in the great vaults of opportunity of this nation. So we have come to cash this check—a check that will give us upon demand the riches of freedom and the security of justice. We have also come to this hallowed spot to remind America and the fierce urgency of *now*. This is no time to engage in the luxury of cooling off or to take the tranquilizing of gradualism. *Now* is the time to make real the promises of Democracy. *Now* is the time to rise from the dark and desolate valley of segregation to the sunlit path of racial justice. *Now* is the time to open the doors of opportunity to all of God's children. *Now* is the time to lift our nation from the quicksands of racial injustice to the solid rock of brotherhood.

It would be fatal for the nation to overlook the urgency of the moment and to underestimate the determination of the Negro. This sweltering summer of the Negro's legitimate discontent will not pass until there is an invigorating autumn of freedom and equality. 1963 is not an end, but a beginning. Those who hope that the Negro needed to blow off steam and will now be content will have a rude awakening if the nation returns to business as usual. There will be neither rest nor tranquillity in America until the Negro is granted his citizenship rights. The whirlwinds of revolt will continue to shake the foundation of our nation until the bright day of justice emerges.

But there is something that I must say to my people who stand on the warm threshold which leads into the palace of justice. In the process of gaining our rightful place we must not be guilty of wrongful deeds. Let us not seek to satisfy our thirst for freedom by drinking from the cup of bitterness and hatred. We must forever conduct our struggle on the high plane of dignity and discipline. We must not allow our creative protest to degenerate into physical violence. Again and again we must rise to the majestic heights of meeting physical force with soul force. The marvelous new militancy which has engulfed the Negro community must not lead us to a distrust of all white people, for many of our white brothers, as evidenced by their presence here today, have come to realize that their destiny is tied up with our destiny and their freedom is inextricably bound to our freedom. We cannot walk alone.

And as we walk, we must make the pledge that we shall march ahead. We cannot turn back. There are those who are asking the devotees of civil rights, "When will you be satisfied?" We can never be satisfied as long as the Negro is the victim of the unspeakable horrors of police brutality. We can never be satisfied as long as our bodies, heavy with the fatigue of travel, cannot gain lodging in the motels of the highways and the hotels of the cities. We cannot be satisfied as long as the Negro's basic mobility is from a smaller ghetto to a larger one. We can never be satisfied as long as a Negro in Mississippi cannot vote and a Negro in New York believes he has nothing for which to vote. No, no, we are not satisfied, and we will not be satisfied until justice rolls down like waters and righteousness like a mighty stream.

I am not unmindful that some of you have come here out of great trials and tribulations. Some of you have come fresh from narrow jail cells. Some of you have come from areas where your quest for freedom left you battered by the storms of persecution and staggered by the winds of police brutality. You have been the veterans of creative suffering. Continue to work with the faith that unearned suffering is redemptive.

Go back to Mississippi, go back to Alabama, go back to South Carolina, go back to Georgia, go back to Louisiana, go back to the slums and ghettos of our northern cities, knowing that somehow this situation can and will be changed. Let us not wallow in the valley of despair.

I say to you today, my friends, that in spite of the difficulties and frustrations of the moment I still have a dream. It is a dream deeply rooted in the American dream.

I have a dream that one day this nation will rise up and live out the true meaning of its creed: "We hold these truths to be self-evident; that all men are created equal."

I have a dream that one day on the red hills of Georgia the sons of former slaves and the sons of former slaveowners will be able to sit down together at the table of brotherhood.

I have a dream that one day even the state of Mississippi, a desert state sweltering with the heat of injustice and oppression, will be transformed into an oasis of freedom and justice.

I have a dream that my four little children will one day live in a nation where they will not be judged by the color of their skin but by the content of their character.

I have a dream today.

I have a dream that one day the state of Alabama, whose governor's lips are presently dripping with the words of interposition and nullification, will be transformed into a situation where little black boys and black girls will be able to join hands with little white boys and white girls and walk together as sisters and brothers.

I have a dream today.

I have a dream that one day every valley shall be exalted, every hill and mountain shall be made low, the rough places will be made plain, and the crooked places will be made straight, and the glory of the Lord shall be revealed, and all flesh shall see it together.

This is our hope. This is the faith with which I return to the South. With this faith we will be able to hew out of the mountain of despair a stone of hope. With this faith we will be able to transform the jangling discords of our nation into a beautiful symphony of brotherhood. With this faith we will be able to work together, to pray together, to struggle together, to go to jail together, to stand up for freedom together, knowing that we will be free one day.

This will be the day when all of God's children will be able to sing with new meaning

> My country, 'tis of thee,
> Sweet land of liberty,
>   Of thee I sing:
> Land where my fathers died,
> Land of the pilgrims' pride.
> From every mountain-side
>   Let freedom ring.

And if America is to be a great nation this must become true. So let freedom ring from the prodigious hilltops of New Hampshire. Let freedom ring from the mighty mountains of New York. Let freedom ring from the heightening Alleghenies of Pennsylvania!

Let freedom ring from the snowcapped Rockies of Colorado!

Let freedom ring from the curvacious peaks of California!

But not only that; let freedom ring from Stone Mountain of Georgia!

Let freedom ring from Lookout Mountain of Tennessee!

Let freedom ring from every hill and molehill of Mississippi. From every mountain-side, let freedom ring.

When we let freedom ring, when we let it ring from every village and every hamlet, from every state and every city, we will be able to speed up that day when all of God's children, black men and white men, Jews and Gentiles, Protestants and Catholics, will be able to join hands and sing in the words of the old Negro spiritual, "Free at last! free at last! thank God almighty, we are free at last!"

QUESTIONS

1 Granting that King knew well his audience, examine the appropriateness of his word choice, his sentence structure, his use of metaphor and analogy.
2 What is the most prominent structural feature in this speech?

TOPICS FOR COMPOSITION

1 Freedom is an often-used word in both Lawrence's essay and King's speech. Write an essay in which you compare and contrast King's and Lawrence's use of the word in an attempt to arrive at each man's definition of freedom.
2 Write an essay examining King's position in light of today's events.

SHORT STORY

Crane's title, "An Experiment in Misery," is his initial effort to draw the reader into his story, to touch within us those common responses that give its title and its tale meanings broader than its characters, time, and place. Indeed, as the story progresses, it becomes evident that our participation is necessary to the "experiment." Note the following techniques:

1   The forbidding details of the setting: the late night, the cold and storm, and the artificiality of the lighting and the machinery of the city
2   The description of the young man and the response that it brings until he finds those with whom he can superficially identify
3   The progressive pattern of initiation, perhaps only unconsciously understood by the young man, but more fully comprehensible to us

AN EXPERIMENT IN MISERY

Stephen Crane

It was late at night, and a fine rain was swirling softly down, causing the pavements to glisten with hue of steel and blue and yellow in the rays of the innumerable lights. A youth was trudging slowly, without enthusiasm, with his hands buried deep in his trousers' pockets, toward the downtown places where beds can be hired for coppers. He was clothed in an aged and tattered suit, and his derby was a marvel of dust-covered crown and torn rim. He was going forth to eat as the wanderer may eat, and sleep as the homeless sleep. By the time he had reached City Hall Park he was so completely plastered with yells of "bum" and "hobo," and with various unholy epithets that small boys had applied to him at intervals, that he was in a state of the most profound dejection. The sifting rain saturated the old velvet collar of his overcoat, and as the wet cloth pressed against his neck, he felt that there no longer could be pleasure in life. He looked about him searching for an outcast of highest degree that they too might share miseries, but the lights threw a quivering glare over rows and circles of deserted benches that glistened damply, showing patches of wet sod behind them. It seemed that their usual freights had fled on this night to better things. There were only squads of well-dressed Brooklyn people who swarmed towards the bridge.

The young man loitered about for a time and then went shuffling off down Park Row. In the sudden descent in style of the dress of the crowd he felt relief, and as if he were at last in his own country. He began to see tatters that matched his tatters. In

14

Chatham Square there were aimless men strewn in front of saloons and lodging-houses, standing sadly, patiently, reminding one vaguely of the attitudes of chickens in a storm. He aligned himself with these men, and turned slowly to occupy himself with the flowing life of the great street.

Through the mists of the cold and storming night, the cable cars went in silent procession, great affairs shining with red and brass, moving with formidable power, calm and irresistible, dangerful and gloomy, breaking silence only by the loud fierce cry of the gong. Two rivers of people swarmed along the sidewalks, spattered with black mud, which made each shoe leave a scarlike impression. Overhead elevated trains with a shrill grinding of the wheels stopped at the station, which upon its leglike pillars seemed to resemble some monstrous kind of crab squatting over the street. The quick fat puffings of the engines could be heard. Down an alley there were somber curtains of purple and black, on which street lamps dully glittered like embroidered flowers.

A saloon stood with a voracious air on a corner. A sign leaning against the front of the door-post announced "Free hot soup to-night!" The swing doors, snapping to and fro like ravenous lips, made gratified smacks as the saloon gorged itself with plump men, eating with astounding and endless appetite, smiling in some indescribable manner as the men came from all directions like sacrifices to a heathenish superstition.

Caught by the delectable sign the young man allowed himself to be swallowed. A bartender placed a schooner of dark and portentous beer on the bar. Its monumental form upreared until the froth a-top was above the crown of the young man's brown derby.

"Soup over there, gents," said the bartender affably. A little yellow man in rags and the youth grasped their schooners and went with speed toward a lunch counter, where a man with oily but imposing whiskers ladled genially from a kettle until he had furnished his two mendicants with a soup that was steaming hot, and in which there were little floating suggestions of chicken. The young man, sipping his broth, felt the cordiality expressed by the warmth of the mixture, and he beamed at the man with oily but imposing whiskers, who was presiding like a priest behind an altar. "Have some more, gents?" he inquired of the two sorry figures before him. The little yellow man accepted with a swift gesture, but the youth shook his head and went out, following a man whose wondrous seediness promised that he would have a knowledge of cheap lodging-houses.

On the sidewalk he accosted the seedy man. "Say, do you know a cheap place to sleep?"

The other hesitated for a time, gazing sideways. Finally he nodded in the direction of the street, "I sleep up there," he said, "when I've got the price."

"How much?"

"Ten cents."

The young man shook his head dolefully. "That's too rich for me."

At that moment there approached the two a reeling man in strange garments. His head was a fuddle of bushy hair and whiskers, from which his eyes peered with a guilty slant. In a close scrutiny it was possible to distinguish the cruel lines of a mouth which looked as if its lips had just closed with satisfaction over some tender and piteous morsel. He appeared like an assassin steeped in crimes performed awkwardly.

But at this time his voice was tuned to the coaxing key of an affectionate puppy. He looked at the men with wheedling eyes, and began to sing a little melody for charity.

"Say, gents, can't yeh give a poor feller a couple of cents t' git a bed? I got five, and I gits anudder two I gits me a bed. Now, on th' square, gents, can't yeh jest gimme two cents t' git a bed? Now, yeh know how a respecter'ble gentlem'n feels when he's down on his luck, an' I——"

The seedy man, staring with imperturbable countenance at a train which clattered overhead, interrupted in an expressionless voice—"Ah, go t' h——!"

But the youth spoke to the prayerful assassin in tones of astonishment and inquiry. "Say, you must be crazy! Why don't yeh strike somebody that looks as if they had money?"

The assassin, tottering about on his uncertain legs, and at intervals brushing imaginary obstacles from before his nose, entered into a long explanation of the psychology of the situation. It was so profound that it was unintelligible.

When he had exhausted the subject, the young man said to him:

"Let's see th' five cents."

The assassin wore an expression of drunken woe at this sentence, filled with suspicion of him. With a deeply pained air he began to fumble in his clothing, his red hands trembling. Presently he announced in a voice of bitter grief, as if he had been betrayed—"There's on'y four."

"Four," said the young man thoughtfully. "Well, look here, I'm a stranger here, an' if ye'll steer me to your cheap joint I'll find the other three."

The assassin's countenance became instantly radiant with joy. His whiskers quivered with the wealth of his alleged emotions. He seized the young man's hand in a transport of delight and friendliness.

"B' Gawd," he cried, "if ye'll do that, b' Gawd, I'd say yeh was a damned good fellow, I would, an' I'd remember yeh all m' life, I would, b' Gawd, an' if I ever got a chance I'd return the compliment"—he spoke with drunken dignity—"b' Gawd, I'd treat yeh white, I would, an' I'd allus remember yeh."

The young man drew back, looking at the assassin coldly. "Oh, that's all right," he said. "You show me th' joint—that's all you've got t' do."

The assassin, gesticulating gratitude, led the young man along a dark street. Finally he stopped before a little dusty door. He raised his hand impressively. "Look-a-here," he said, and there was a thrill of deep and ancient wisdom upon his face, "I've brought yeh here, an' that's my part, ain't it? If th' place don't suit yeh, yeh needn't git mad at me, need yeh? There won't be no bad feelin', will there?"

"No," said the young man.

The assassin waved his arm tragically, and led the march up the steep stairway. On the way the young man furnished the assassin with three pennies. At the top a man with benevolent spectacles looked at them through a hole in a board. He collected their money, wrote some names on a register, and speedily was leading the two men along a gloom-shrouded corridor.

Shortly after the beginning of this journey the young man felt his liver turn white, for from the dark and secret places of the building there suddenly came to his nostrils strange and unspeakable odors, that assailed him like malignant diseases with wings. They seemed to be from human bodies closely packed in dens; the exhalations from a hundred pairs of reeking lips; the fumes from a thousand bygone debauches: the expression of a thousand present miseries.

A man, naked save for a little snuff-colored undershirt, was parading sleepily along the corridor. He rubbed his eyes, and, giving vent to a prodigious yawn, demanded to be told the time.

"Half-past one."

The man yawned again. He opened a door, and for a moment his form was outlined against a black, opaque interior. To this door came the three men, and as it was again opened the unholy odors rushed out like fiends, so that the young man was obliged to struggle as against an overpowering wind.

It was some time before the youth's eyes were good in the intense gloom within, but the man with benevolent spectacles led him skilfully, pausing but a moment to deposit the limp assassin upon a cot. He took the youth to a cot that lay tranquilly by the window, and showing him a tall locker for clothes that stood near the head with the ominous air of a tombstone, left him.

The youth sat on his cot and peered about him. There was a gas-jet in a distant part of the room, that burned a small flickering orange-hued flame. It caused vast masses of tumbled shadows in all parts of the place, save where, immediately about it, there was a little grey haze. As the young man's eyes became used to the darkness, he could see upon the cots that thickly littered the floor the forms of men sprawled out, lying in deathlike silence, or heaving and snoring with tremendous effort, like stabbed fish.

The youth locked his derby and his shoes in the mummy case near him, and then lay down with an old and familiar coat around his shoulders. A blanket he handled gingerly, drawing it over part of the coat. The cot was covered with leather, and as cold as melting snow. The youth was obliged to shiver for some time on this affair, which was like a slab. Presently, however, his chill gave him peace, and during this period of leisure from it he turned his head to stare at his friend the assassin, whom he could dimly discern where he lay sprawled on a cot in the abandon of a man filled with drink. He was snoring with incredible vigor. His wet hair and beard dimly glistened, and his inflamed nose shone with subdued lustre like a red light in a fog.

Within reach of the youth's hand was one who lay with yellow breast and shoulders bare to the cold drafts. One arm hung over the side of the cot, and the fingers lay full length upon the wet cement floor of the room. Beneath the inky brows could be seen the eyes of the man exposed by the partly opened lids. To the youth it seemed that he and this corpse-like being were exchanging a prolonged stare, and that the other threatened with his eyes. He drew back, watching his neighbor from the shadows of his blanket edge. The man did not move once through the night, but lay in this stillness as of death like a body stretched out expectant of the surgeon's knife.

And all through the room could be seen the tawny hues of naked flesh, limbs thrust into the darkness, projecting beyond the cots; upreared knees, arms hanging long and thin over the cot edges. For the most part they were statuesque, carven, dead. With the curious lockers standing all about like tombstones, there was a strange effect of a graveyard where bodies were merely flung.

Yet occasionally could be seen limbs wildly tossing in fantastic nightmare gestures, accompanied by guttural cries, grunts, oaths. And there was one fellow off in a gloomy corner, who in his dreams was oppressed by some frightful calamity, for of a sudden he began to utter long wails that went almost like yells from a hound, echoing wailfully and weird through this chill place of tombstones where men lay like the dead.

The sound in its high piercing beginnings, that dwindled to final melancholy moans, expressed a red and grim tragedy of the unfathomable possibilities of the man's dreams. But to the youth these were not merely the shrieks of a vision-pierced man: they were an utterance of the meaning of the room and its occupants. It was to him the protest of the wretch who feels the touch of the imperturbable granite wheels, and who then cries with an impersonal eloquence, with a strength not from him, giving voice to the wail of a whole section, a class, a people. This, weaving into the young man's brain, and mingling with his views of the vast and sombre shadows that, like mighty black fingers, curled around the naked bodies, made the young man so that he did not sleep, but lay carving the biographies for these men from his meagre experience. At times the fellow in the corner howled in a writhing agony of his imaginations.

Finally a long lance-point of grey light shot through the dusty panes of the window. Without, the young man could see roofs drearily white in the dawning. The point of light yellowed and grew brighter, until the golden rays of the morning sun came in bravely and strong. They touched with radiant color the form of a small fat man, who snored in stuttering fashion. His round and shiny bald head glowed suddenly with the valor of a decoration. He sat up, blinked at the sun, swore fretfully, and pulled his blanket over the ornamental splendors of his head.

The youth contentedly watched this rout of the shadows before the bright spears of the sun, and presently he slumbered. When he awoke he heard the voice of the assassin raised in valiant curses. Putting up his head, he perceived his comrade seated on the side of the cot engaged in scratching his neck with long finger-nails that rasped like files.

"Hully Jee, dis is a new breed. They've got can-openers on their feet." He continued in a violent tirade.

The young man hastily unlocked his closet and took out his shoes and hat. As he sat on the side of the cot lacing his shoes, he glanced about and saw that daylight had made the room comparatively commonplace and uninteresting. The men, whose faces seemed stolid, serene or absent, were engaged in dressing, while a great crackle of bantering conversation arose.

A few were parading in unconcerned nakedness. Here and there were men of brawn, whose skins shone clear and ruddy. They took splendid poses, standing massively like chiefs. When they had dressed in their ungainly garments there was an extraordinary change. They then showed bumps and deficiencies of all kinds.

There were others who exhibited many deformities. Shoulders were slanting, humped, pulled this way and pulled that way. And notable among these latter men was the little fat man who had refused to allow his head to be glorified. His pudgy form, builded like a pear, bustled to and fro, while he swore in fishwife fashion. It appeared that some article of his apparel had vanished.

The young man attired speedily, and went to his friend the assassin. At first the latter looked dazed at the sight of the youth. This face seemed to be appealing to him through the cloud wastes of his memory. He scratched his neck and reflected. At last he grinned, a broad smile gradually spreading until his countenance was a round illumination. "Hello, Willie," he cried cheerily.

"Hello," said the young man. "Are yeh ready t' fly?"

"Sure." The assassin tied his shoe carefully with some twine and came ambling.

When he reached the street the young man experienced no sudden relief from unholy atmospheres. He had forgotten all about them, and had been breathing naturally, and with no sensation of discomfort or distress.

He was thinking of these things as he walked along the street, when he was suddenly startled by feeling the assassin's hand, trembling with excitement, clutching his arm, and when the assassin spoke, his voice went into quavers from a supreme agitation.

"I'll be hully, bloomin' blowed if there wasn't a feller with a nightshirt on up there in that joint."

The youth was bewildered for a moment, but presently he turned to smile indulgently at the assassin's humor.

"Oh, you're a d——d liar," he merely said.

Whereupon the assassin began to gesture extravagantly, and take oath by strange gods. He frantically placed himself at the mercy of remarkable fates if his tale were not true.

"Yes, he did! I cross m' heart thousan' times!" he protested, and at the moment his eyes were large with amazement, his mouth wrinkled in unnatural glee.

"Yessir! A nightshirt! A hully white nightshirt!"

"You lie!"

"No, sir! I hope ter die b'fore I kin git anudder ball if there wasn't a jay wid a hully, bloomin' white nightshirt!"

His face was filled with the infinite wonder of it. "A hully white nightshirt," he continually repeated.

The young man saw the dark entrance to a basement restaurant. There was a sign which read "No mystery about our hash"! and there were other age-stained and world-battered legends which told him that the place was within his means. He stopped before it and spoke to the assassin. "I guess I'll git somethin' t' eat."

At this the assassin, for some reason, appeared to be quite embarrassed. He gazed at the seductive front of the eating place for a moment. Then he started slowly up the street. "Well, good-bye, Willie," he said bravely.

For an instant the youth studied the departing figure. Then he called out, "Hol' on a minnet." As they came together he spoke in a certain fierce way, as if he feared that the other would think him to be charitable. "Look-a-here, if yeh wanta git some breakfas' I'll lend yeh three cents t' do it with. But say, look-a-here, you've gota git out an' hustle. I ain't goin' t' support yeh, or I'll go broke b'fore night. I ain't no millionaire."

"I take me oath, Willie," said the assassin earnestly, "th' on'y thing I really needs is a ball. Me t'roat feels like a fryin'-pan. But as I can't get a ball, why, th' next bes' thing is breakfast, an' if yeh do that for me, b' Gawd, I say yeh was th' whitest lad I ever see."

They spent a few moments in dexterous exchanges of phrases, in which they each protested that the other was, as the assassin had originally said, "a respecter'ble gentlem'n.'' And they concluded with mutual assurances that they were the souls of intelligence and virtue. Then they went into the restaurant.

There was a long counter, dimly lighted from hidden sources. Two or three men in soiled white aprons rushed here and there.

The youth bought a bowl of coffee for two cents and a roll for one cent. The assassin purchased the same. The bowls were webbed with brown seams, and the tin spoons wore an air of having emerged from the first pyramid. Upon them were black mosslike encrustations of age, and they were bent and scarred from the attacks of long-forgotten teeth. But over their repast the wanderers waxed warm and mellow. The assassin grew affable as the hot mixture went soothingly down his parched throat, and the young man felt courage flow in his veins.

Memories began to throng in on the assassin, and he brought forth long tales, intricate, incoherent, delivered with a chattering swiftness as from an old woman. "——great job out'n Orange. Boss keep yeh hustlin' though all time. I was there three days, and then I went an' ask 'im t' lend me a dollar. 'G-g-go ter the devil,' he ses, an' I lose me job.''

"South no good. Damn niggers work for twenty-five an' thirty cents a day. Run white man out. Good grub, though. Easy livin'.''

"Yas; useter work little in Toledo, raftin' logs. Make two or three dollars er day in the spring. Lived high. Cold as ice, though, in the winter.''

"I was raised in northern N'York. O-a-ah, yeh jest oughto live there. No beer ner whisky, though, way off in the woods. But all th' good hot grub yeh can eat. B'Gawd, I hung around there long as I could till th' ol' man fired me. 'Git t' hell outa here, yeh wuthless skunk, git t' hell outa here, an' go die,' he ses. 'You're a hell of a father,' I ses, 'you are,' an' I quit 'im.''

As they were passing from the dim eating place, they encountered an old man who was trying to steal forth with a tiny package of food, but a tall man with an indomitable moustache stood dragon fashion, barring the way of escape. They heard the old man raise a plaintive protest. "Ah, you always want to know what I take out, and you never see that I usually bring a package in here from my place of business.''

As the wanderers trudged slowly along Park Row, the assassin began to expand and grow blithe. "B'Gawd, we've been livin' like kings,'' he said, smacking appreciative lips.

"Look out, or we'll have t' pay fer it t'night,'' said the youth with gloomy warning.

But the assassin refused to turn his gaze toward the future. He went with a limping step, into which he injected a suggestion of lamblike gambols. His mouth was wreathed in a red grin.

In the City Hall Park the two wanderers sat down in the little circle of benches sanctified by traditions of their class. They huddled in their old garments, slumbrously conscious of the march of the hours which for them had no meaning.

The people of the street hurrying hither and thither made a blend of black figures changing yet frieze-like. They walked in their good clothes as upon important missions, giving no gaze to the two wanderers seated upon the benches. They expressed to the young man his infinite distance from all that he valued. Social position, comfort, the pleasures of living, were unconquerable kingdoms. He felt a sudden awe.

And in the background a multitude of buildings, of pitiless hues and sternly high, were to him emblematic of a nation forcing its regal head into the clouds, throwing no downward glances; in the sublimity of its aspirations ignoring the wretches who may flounder at its feet. The roar of the city in his ear was to him the confusion of strange tongues, babbling heedlessly; it was the clink of coin, the voice of the city's hopes which were to him no hopes.

He confessed himself an outcast, and his eyes from under the lowered rim of his hat began to glance guiltily, wearing the criminal expression that comes with certain convictions.

QUESTIONS

1 An experiment is scientific, thereby objective. How does Crane maintain an objective viewpoint?
2 What instinctual drives motivate the actions of his characters?
3 What realization does the main character reach? What does this realization mean in respect to man's ability to direct his life?

TOPICS FOR COMPOSITION

1 Martin Luther King, Jr. would most likely disagree with Crane's deterministic philosophy. Write an essay in which you examine the precepts of deterministic naturalism in relation to Crane's story and King's speech.
2 If Crane's story is truly universal, "the wanderer" is to some degree a part of our world. Write an essay in which you identify the modern wanderer and his influence on society.

The way an Englishman views Britain's colonial empire is the primary mark of a Rudyard Kipling tale. In the story that follows, we see a British officer in India whose response to a culture foreign to him underscores his sense of his "Britishness." We should be careful not to become so engrossed in the events of the story itself that we overlook the subtleties that give it its true character. As you read, note the following:

1 Kipling's introduction of Jukes, who will tell his story
2 Jukes's reaction to the place, its inhabitants, and especially to Gunga Dass
3 Gunga Dass's constantly changing attitude toward Jukes

THE STRANGE RIDE OF MORROWBIE JUKES

Rudyard Kipling

> Alive or dead—there is no other way.
> —*Native Proverb.*

There is no invention about this tale. Jukes by accident stumbled upon a village that is well known to exist, though he is the only Englishman who has been there. A somewhat similar institution used to flourish on the outskirts of Calcutta, and there is a story that if you go into the heart of Bikanir, which is in the heart of the Great Indian Desert, you shall come across not a village but a town where the Dead who did not die but may not live have established their headquarters. And, since it is perfectly true that in the same Desert is a wonderful city where all the rich money-lenders retreat after they have made their fortunes (fortunes so vast that the owners cannot trust even the strong hand of the Government to protect them, but take refuge in the waterless sands), and drive sumptuous C-spring barouches, and buy beautiful girls and decorate their palaces with gold and ivory and Minton tiles and mother-o'-pearl, I do not see why Jukes's tale should not be true. He is a Civil Engineer, with a head for plans and distances and things of that kind, and he certainly would not take the trouble to invent imaginary traps. He could earn more by doing his legitimate work. He never varies the tale in the telling, and grows very hot and indignant when he thinks of the disrespectful treatment he received. He wrote this quite straightforwardly at first, but he has touched it up in places and introduced Moral Reflections: thus:—

In the beginning it all arose from a slight attack of fever. My work necessitated my being in camp for some months between Pakpattan and Mubarakpur—a desolate sandy stretch of country as every one who has had the misfortune to go there may know. My coolies were neither more nor less exasperating than other gangs, and my work demanded sufficient attention to keep me from moping, had I been inclined to so unmanly a weakness.

On the 23rd December, 1884, I felt a little feverish. There was a full moon at the time, and, in consequence, every dog near my tent was baying it. The brutes assembled in twos and threes and drove me frantic. A few days previously I had shot one loud-mouthed singer and suspended his carcass *in terrorem* about fifty yards from my tent-door, but his friends fell upon, fought for, and ultimately devoured the body: and, as it seemed to me, sang their hymns of thanksgiving afterwards with renewed energy.

The light-headedness which accompanies fever acts differently on different men. My irritation gave way, after a short time, to a fixed determination to slaughter one huge black and white beast who had been foremost in song and first in flight throughout the evening. Thanks to a shaking hand and a giddy head I had already missed him twice with both barrels of my shot-gun, when it struck me that my best plan would be to ride him down in the open and finish him off with a hog-spear. This, of course, was merely the semi-delirious notion of a fever-patient; but I remember that it struck me at the time as being eminently practical and feasible.

I therefore ordered my groom to saddle Pornic and bring him round quietly to the rear of my tent. When the pony was ready, I stood at his head prepared to mount and dash out as soon as the dog should again lift up his voice. Pornic, by the way, had not been out of his pickets for a couple of days; the night air was crisp and chilly; and I was armed with a specially long and sharp pair of persuaders with which I had been rousing a sluggish cob that afternoon. You will easily believe, then, that when he was let go he went quickly. In one moment, for the brute bolted as straight as a die, the tent was left far behind, and we were flying over the smooth sandy soil at racing speed. In another we had passed the wretched dog, and I had almost forgotten why it was that I had taken horse and hog-spear.

The delirium of fever and the excitement of rapid motion through the air must have taken away the remnant of my senses. I have a faint recollection of standing upright in my stirrups, and of brandishing my hog-spear at the great white Moon that looked down so calmly on my mad gallop; and of shouting challenges to the camelthorn bushes as they whizzed past. Once or twice, I believe, I swayed forward on Pornic's neck, and literally hung on by my spurs—as the marks next morning showed.

The wretched beast went forward like a thing possessed, over what seemed to be a limitless expanse of moonlit sand. Next, I remember, the ground rose suddenly in front of us, and as we topped the ascent I saw the waters of the Sutlej shining like a silver bar below. Then Pornic blundered heavily on his nose, and we rolled together down some unseen slope.

I must have lost consciousness, for when I recovered I was lying on my stomach in a heap of soft white sand, and the dawn was beginning to break dimly over the edge of the slope down which I had fallen. As the light grew stronger I saw I was at the bottom of a horseshoe-shaped crater of sand, opening on one side directly on to the shoals of the Sutlej. My fever had altogether left me, and, with the exception of a slight dizziness in the head, I felt no bad effects from the fall over night.

Pornic, who was standing a few yards away, was naturally a good deal exhausted, but had not hurt himself in the least. His saddle, a favourite polo one, was much knocked about, and had been twisted under his belly. It took me some time to put him to rights, and in the meantime I had ample opportunities of observing the spot into which I had so foolishly dropped.

At the risk of being considered tedious, I must describe it at length; inasmuch as an accurate mental picture of its peculiarities will be of material assistance in enabling the reader to understand what follows.

Imagine then, as I have said before, a horseshoe-shaped crater of sand with steeply-graded sand walls about thirty-five feet high. (The slope, I fancy, must have been about 65°.) This crater enclosed a level piece of ground about fifty yards long by thirty at its broadest part, with a rude well in the centre. Round the bottom of the crater, about three feet from the level of the ground proper, ran a series of eighty-three semicircular, ovoid, square, and multilateral holes, all about three feet at the mouth. Each hole on inspection showed that it was carefully shored internally with drift-wood and bamboos, and over the mouth a wooden drip-board projected, like the peak of a jockey's cap, for two feet. No sign of life was visible in these tunnels, but a most sickening stench pervaded the entire amphitheatre—a stench fouler than any which my wanderings in Indian villages have introduced me to.

Having remounted Pornic, who was as anxious as I to get back to camp, I rode round the base of the horseshoe to find some place whence an exit would be practicable. The inhabitants, whoever they might be, had not thought fit to put in an appearance, so I was left to my own devices. My first attempt to "rush" Pornic up the steep sand-banks showed me that I had fallen into a trap exactly on the same model as that which the ant-lion sets for its prey. At each step the shifting sand poured down from above in tons, and rattled on the drip-boards of the holes like small shot. A couple of ineffectual charges sent us both rolling down to the bottom, half choked with the torrents of sand; and I was constrained to turn my attention to the river-bank.

Here everything seemed easy enough. The sand hills ran down to the river edge, it is true, but there were plenty of shoals and shallows across which I could gallop Pornic, and find my way back to *terra firma* by turning sharply to the right or the left. As I led Pornic over the sands I was startled by the faint pop of a rifle across the river; and at the same moment a bullet dropped with a sharp *"whit"* close to Pornic's head.

There was no mistaking the nature of the missile—a regulation Martini-Henry "picket." About five hundred yards away a country-boat was anchored in midstream; and a jet of smoke drifting away from its bows in the still morning air showed me whence the delicate attention had come. Was ever a respectable gentleman in such an *impasse?* The treacherous sand slope allowed no escape from a spot which I had visited most involuntarily, and a promenade on the river frontage was the signal for a bombardment from some insane native in a boat. I'm afraid that I lost my temper very much indeed.

Another bullet reminded me that I had better save my breath to cool my porridge; and I retreated hastily up the sands and back to the horseshoe, where I saw that the noise of the rifle had drawn sixty-five human beings from the badger-holes which I had up till that point supposed to be untenanted. I found myself in the midst of a crowd of spectators—about forty men, twenty women, and one child who could not have been more than five years old. They were all scantily clothed in that salmon coloured cloth which one associates with Hindu mendicants, and, at first sight, gave me the impression of a band of loathsome *fakirs.* The filth and repulsiveness of the assembly were beyond all description, and I shuddered to think what their life in the badger-holes must be.

Even in these days, when local self-government has destroyed the greater part of a native's respect for a Sahib, I have been accustomed to a certain amount of civility from my inferiors, and on approaching the crowd naturally expected that there would be some recognition of my presence. As a matter of fact there was; but it was by no means what I had looked for.

The ragged crew actually laughed at me—such laughter I hope I may never hear again. They cackled, yelled, whistled, and howled as I walked into their midst; some of them literally throwing themselves down on the ground in convulsions of unholy mirth. In a moment I had let go Pornic's head, and, irritated beyond expression at the morning's adventure, commenced cuffing those nearest to me with all the force I could. The wretches dropped under my blows like nine-pins, and the laughter gave place to wails for mercy; while those yet untouched clasped me round the knees, imploring me in all sorts of uncouth tongues to spare them.

In the tumult, and just when I was feeling very much ashamed of myself for having thus easily given way to my temper, a thin, high voice murmured in English from behind my shoulder: "Sahib! Sahib! Do you not know me? Sahib, it is Gunga Dass, the tele-graph-master."

I spun round quickly and faced the speaker.

Gunga Dass (I have, of course, no hesitation in mentioning the man's real name) I had known four years before as a Deccanee Brahmin lent by the Punjab Government to one of the Khalsia States. He was in charge of a branch telegraph-office there, and when I had last met him was a jovial, full stomached, portly Government servant with a marvellous capacity for making bad puns in English—a peculiarity which made me remember him long after I had forgotten his services to me in his official capacity. It is seldom that a Hindu makes English puns.

Now, however, the man was changed beyond all recognition. Caste-mark, stom-ach, slate-coloured continuations, and unctuous speech were all gone. I looked at a withered skeleton, turbanless and almost naked, with long matted hair and deep-set codfish-eyes. But for a crescent-shaped scar on the left cheek—the result of an acci-dent for which I was responsible—I should never have known him. But it was indubita-bly Gunga Dass, and—for this I was thankful—an English-speaking native who might at least tell me the meaning of all that I had gone through that day.

The crowd retreated to some distance as I turned towards the miserable figure, and ordered him to show me some method of escaping from the crater. He held a freshly-plucked crow in his hand, and in reply to my question climbed slowly on a platform of sand which ran in front of the holes, and commenced lighting a fire there in silence. Dried bents, sand-poppies, and driftwood burn quickly; and I derived much consolation from the fact that he lit them with an ordinary sulphur match. When they were in a bright glow, and the crow was neatly spitted in front thereof, Gunga Dass began without a word of preamble:—

"There are only two kinds of men, Sar. The alive and the dead. When you are dead you are dead, but when you are alive you live." (Here the crow demanded his attention for an instant as it twirled before the fire in danger of being burnt to a cinder.) "If you die at home and do not die when you come to the ghât to be burnt you come here."

The nature of the reeking village was made plain now, and all that I had known or read of the grotesque and the horrible paled before the fact just communicated by the ex-Brahmin. Sixteen years ago, when I first landed in Bombay, I had been told by a wandering Armenian of the existence, somewhere in India, of a place to which such Hindus as had the misfortune to recover from trance or catalepsy were conveyed and kept, and I recollect laughing heartily at what I was then pleased to consider a travel-ler's tale. Sitting at the bottom of the sand-trap, the memory of Watson's Hotel, with its swinging punkahs, white-robed servants and the sallow-faced Armenian, rose up in my mind as vividly as a photograph, and I burst into a loud fit of laughter. The contrast was too absurd!

Gunga Dass, as he bent over the unclean bird, watched me curiously. Hindus seldom laugh, and his surroundings were not such as to move him that way. He re-moved the crow solemnly from the wooden spit and as solemnly devoured it. Then he continued his story, which I give in his own words:—

"In epidemics of the cholera you are carried to be burnt almost before you are dead. When you come to the riverside the cold air, perhaps, makes you alive, and then, if you are only little alive, mud is put on your nose and mouth and you die conclusively. If you are rather more alive, more mud is put; but if you are too lively they let you go and take you away. I was too lively, and made protestation with anger against the indignities that they endeavoured to press upon me. In those days I was Brahmin and proud man. Now I am dead man and eat"—here he eyed the well-gnawed breast bone with the first sign of emotion that I had seen in him since we met—"crows, and—other things. They took me from my sheets when they saw that I was too lively and gave me medicines for one week, and I survived successfully. Then they sent me by rail from my place to Okara Station, with a man to take care of me; and at Okara Station we met two other men, and they conducted we three on camels, in the night, from Okara Station to this place, and they propelled me from the top to the bottom, and the other two succeeded, and I have been here ever since two and a half years. Once I was Brahmin and proud man and now I eat crows."

"There is no way of getting out?"

"None of what kind at all. When I first came I made experiments frequently and all the others also, but we have always succumbed to the sand which is precipitated upon our heads."

"But surely," I broke in at this point, "the river-front is open, and it is worth while dodging the bullets; while at night——"

I had already matured a rough plan of escape which a natural instinct of selfishness forbade me sharing with Gunga Dass. He, however, divined my unspoken thought almost as soon as it was formed; and, to my intense astonishment, gave vent to a long low chuckle of derision—the laughter, be it understood, of a superior or at least of an equal.

"You will not"—he had dropped the Sir after his first sentence—"make any escape that way. But you can try. I have tried. Once only."

The sensation of nameless terror which I had in vain attempted to strive against, overmastered me completely. My long fast—it was now close upon ten o'clock, and I had eaten nothing since tiffin on the previous day—combined with the violent agitation of the ride had exhausted me, and I verily believe that, for a few minutes, I acted as one mad. I hurled myself against the sand-slope. I ran round the base of the crater, blaspheming and praying by turns. I crawled out among the sedges of the river-front, only to be driven back each time in an agony of nervous dread by the rifle-bullets which cut up the sand round me—for I dared not face the death of a mad dog among that hideous crowd—and so fell, spent and raving, at the curb of the well. No one had taken the slightest notice of an exhibition which makes me blush hotly even when I think of it now.

Two or three men trod on my panting body as they drew water, but they were evidently used to this sort of thing, and had no time to waste upon me. Gunga Dass, indeed, when he had banked the embers of his fire with sand, was at some pains to throw half a cupful of fetid water over my head, an attention for which I could have fallen on my knees and thanked him, but he was laughing all the while in the same mirthless, wheezy key that greeted me on my first attempt to force the shoals. And so, in a half-fainting state, I lay till noon. Then, being only a man after all, I felt hungry, and said as much to Gunga Dass, whom I had begun to regard as my natural protector.

Following the impulse of the outer world when dealing with natives, I put my hand into my pocket and drew out four annas. The absurdity of the gift struck me at once, and I was about to replace the money.

Gunga Dass, however, cried: "Give me the money, all you have, or I will get help, and we will kill you!"

A Briton's first impulse, I believe, is to guard the contents of his pockets; but a moment's thought showed me of the folly of differing with the one man who had it in his power to make me comfortable; and with whose help it was possible that I might eventually escape from the crater. I gave him all the money in my possession, Rs. 9-8-5—nine rupees, eight annas, and five pie—for I always keep small change as *bakshish* when I am in camp. Gunga Dass clutched the coins, and hid them at once in his ragged loin-cloth, looking round to assure himself that no one had observed us.

"*Now* I will give you something to eat," said he.

What pleasure my money could have given him I am unable to say; but inasmuch as it did please him I was not sorry that I had parted with it so readily, for I had no doubt that he would have had me killed if I had refused. One does not protest against the doings of a den of wild beasts; and my companions were lower than any beasts. While I eat what Gunga Dass had provided, a coarse *chapatti* and a cupful of the foul well-water, the people showed not the faintest sign of curiosity—that curiosity which is so rampant, as a rule, in an Indian village.

I could even fancy that they despised me. At all events they treated me with the most chilling indifference, and Gunga Dass was nearly as bad. I plied him with questions about the terrible village, and received extremely unsatisfactory answers. So far as I could gather, it had been in existence from time immemorial—whence I concluded that it was at least a century old—and during that time no one had ever been known to escape from it. (I had to control myself here with both hands, lest the blind terror should lay hold of me a second time and drive me raving round the crater.) Gunga Dass took a malicious pleasure in emphasising this point and in watching me wince. Nothing that I could do would induce him to tell me who the mysterious "They" were.

"It is so ordered," he would reply, "and I do not yet know any one who has disobeyed the orders."

"Only wait till my servant finds that I am missing," I retorted, "and I promise you that this place shall be cleared off the face of the earth, and I'll give you a lesson in civility, too, my friend."

"Your servants would be torn in pieces before they came near this place; and, besides, you are dead, my dear friend. It is not your fault, of course, but none the less you are dead *and* buried."

At irregular intervals supplies of food, I was told, were dropped down from the land side into the amphitheatre, and the inhabitants fought for them like wild beasts. When a man felt his death coming on he retreated to his lair and died there. The body was sometimes dragged out of the hole and thrown on to the sand, or allowed to rot where it lay.

The phrase "thrown on to the sand" caught my attention, and I asked Gunga Dass whether this sort of thing was not likely to breed a pestilence.

"That," said he, with another of his wheezy chuckles, "you may see for yourself subsequently. You will have much time to make observations."

Whereat, to his great delight, I winced once more and hastily continued the conversation: "And how do you live here from day to day? What do you do?" The question elicited exactly the same answer as before—coupled with the information that "this place is like your European heaven; there is neither marrying nor giving in marriage."

Gunga Dass had been educated at a Mission School, and, as he himself admitted, had he only changed his religion "like a wise man," might have avoided the living grave which was now his portion. But as long as I was with him I fancy he was happy.

Here was a Sahib, a representative of the dominant race, helpless as a child and completely at the mercy of his native neighbours. In a deliberate lazy way he set himself to torture me as a schoolboy would devote a rapturous half-hour to watching the agonies of an impaled beetle, or as a ferret in a blind burrow might glue himself comfortably to the neck of a rabbit. The burden of his conversation was that there was no escape "of no kind whatever," and that I should stay here till I died and was "thrown on to the sand." If it were possible to forejudge the conversation of the Damned on the advent of a new soul in their abode, I should say that they would speak as Gunga Dass did to me throughout that long afternoon. I was powerless to protest or answer; all my energies being devoted to a struggle against the inexplicable terror that threatened to overwhelm me again and again. I can compare the feeling to nothing except the struggles of a man against the overpowering nausea of the Channel passage—only my agony was of the spirit and infinitely more terrible.

As the day wore on, the inhabitants began to appear in full strength to catch the rays of the afternoon sun, which were now sloping in at the mouth of the crater. They assembled by little knots, and talked among themselves without even throwing a glance in my direction. About four o'clock, so far as I could judge, Gunga Dass rose and dived into his lair for a moment, emerging with a live crow in his hands. The wretched bird was in a most draggled and deplorable condition, but seemed to be in no way afraid of its master. Advancing cautiously to the river-front, Gunga Dass stepped from tussock to tussock until he had reached a smooth patch of sand directly in the line of the boat's fire. The occupants of the boat took no notice. Here he stopped, and, with a couple of dexterous turns of the wrist, pegged the bird on its back with outstretched wings. As was only natural, the crow began to shriek at once and beat the air with its claws. In a few seconds the clamour had attracted the attention of a bevy of wild crows on a shoal a few hundred yards away, where they were discussing something that looked like a corpse. Half a dozen crows flew over at once to see what was going on, and also, as it proved, to attack the pinioned bird. Gunga Dass, who had lain down on a tussock, motioned to me to be quiet, though I fancy this was a needless precaution. In a moment, and before I could see how it happened, a wild crow, who had grappled with the shrieking and helpless bird, was entangled in the latter's claws, swiftly disengaged by Gunga Dass, and pegged down beside its companion in adversity. Curiosity, it seemed, overpowered the rest of the flock, and almost before Gunga Dass and I had time to withdraw to the tussock, two more captives were struggling in the upturned claws of the decoys. So the chase—if I can give it so dignified a name— continued until Gunga Dass had captured seven crows. Five of them he throttled at once, reserving two for further operations another day. I was a good deal impressed by this, to me, novel method of securing food, and complimented Gunga Dass on his skill.

"It is nothing to do," said he. "To-morrow you must do it for me. You are stronger than I am."

This calm assumption of superiority upset me not a little, and I answered peremptorily: "Indeed, you old ruffian? What do you think I have given you money for?"

"Very well," was the unmoved reply. "Perhaps not to-morrow, nor the day after, nor subsequently; but in the end, and for many years, you will catch crows and eat crows, and you will thank your European God that you have crows to catch and eat."

I could have cheerfully strangled him for this; but judged it best under the circumstances to smother my resentment. An hour later I was eating one of the crows; and, as Gunga Dass had said, thanking my God that I had a crow to eat. Never as long as I live shall I forget that evening meal. The whole population were squatting on the hard sand platform opposite their dens, huddled over tiny fires of refuse and dried rushes. Death, having once laid his hand upon these men and forborne to strike, seemed to stand aloof from them now; for most of our company were old men, bent and worn and twisted with years, and women aged to all appearance as the Fates themselves. They sat together in knots and talked—God only knows what they found to discuss—in low equable tones, curiously in contrast to the strident babble with which natives are accustomed to make day hideous. Now and then an access of that sudden fury which had possessed me in the morning would lay hold on a man or woman; and with yells and imprecations the sufferer would attack the steep slope until, baffled and bleeding, he fell back on the platform incapable of moving a limb. The others would never even raise their eyes when this happened, as men too well aware of the futility of their fellows' attempts and wearied with their useless repetition. I saw four such outbursts in the course of that evening.

Gunga Dass took an eminently business-like view of my situation, and while we were dining—I can afford to laugh at the recollection now, but it was painful enough at the time—propounded the terms of which he would consent to "do" for me. My nine rupees eight annas, he argued, at the rate of three annas a day, would provide me with food for fifty-one days, or about seven weeks; that is to say, he would be willing to cater for me for that length of time. At the end of it I was to look after myself. For a further consideration—videlicet my boots—he would be willing to allow me to occupy the den next to his own, and would supply me with as much dried grass for bedding as he could spare.

"Very well, Gunga Dass," I replied; "to the first terms I cheerfully agree, but, as there is nothing on earth to prevent my killing you as you sit here and taking everything that you have" (I thought of the two invaluable crows at the time), "I flatly refuse to give you my boots and shall take whichever den I please."

The stroke was a bold one, and I was glad when I saw that it had succeeded. Gunga Dass changed his tone immediately, and disavowed all intention of asking for my boots. At the time it did not strike me as at all strange that I, a Civil Engineer, a man of thirteen years' standing in the Service, and, I trust, an average Englishman, should thus calmly threaten murder and violence against the man who had, for a consideration it is true, taken me under his wing. I had left the world, it seemed, for centuries. I was as certain then as I am now of my own existence, that in the accursed settlement there was no law save that of the strongest; that the living dead men had thrown behind them every canon of the world which had cast them out; and that I had to depend for my own life on my strength and vigilance alone. The crew of the ill-fated *Mignonette* are the only men who would understand my frame of mind. "At present," I argued to myself, "I am strong and a match for six of these wretches. It is imperatively necessary that I should, for my own sake, keep both health and strength until the hour of my release comes—if it ever does."

Fortified with these resolutions, I ate and drank as much as I could, and made Gunga Dass understand that I intended to be his master, and that the least sign of insubordination on his part would be visited with the only punishment I had it in my power to inflict—sudden and violent death. Shortly after this I went to bed. That is to say, Gunga Dass gave me a double armful of dried bents which I thrust down the mouth of the lair to the right of his, and followed myself, feet foremost; the hole running about nine feet into the sand with a slight downward inclination, and being neatly shored with timbers. From my den, which faced the river-front, I was able to watch the waters of the Sutlej flowing past under the light of a young moon and compose myself to sleep as best I might.

The horrors of that night I shall never forget. My den was nearly as narrow as a coffin, and the sides had been worn smooth and greasy by the contact of innumerable naked bodies, added to which it smelt abominably. Sleep was altogether out of the question to one in my excited frame of mind. As the night wore on, it seemed that the entire amphitheatre was filled with legions of unclean devils that, trooping up from the shoals below, mocked the unfortunates in their lairs.

Personally I am not of an imaginative temperament—very few Engineers are—but on that occasion I was as completely prostrated with nervous terror as any woman. After half an hour or so, however, I was able once more to calmly review my chances of escape. Any exit by the steep sand walls was, of course, impracticable. I had been thoroughly convinced of this some time before. It was possible, just possible, that I might, in the uncertain moonlight, safely run the gauntlet of the rifle shots. The place was so full of terror for me that I was prepared to undergo any risk in leaving it. Imagine my delight, then, when after creeping stealthily to the river-front I found that the infernal boat was not there. My freedom lay before me in the next few steps!

By walking out to the first shallow pool that lay at the foot of the projecting left horn of the horseshoe, I could wade across, turn the flank of the crater, and make my way inland. Without a moment's hesitation I marched briskly past the tussocks where Gunga Dass had snared the crows, and out in the direction of the smooth white sand beyond. My first step from the tufts of dried grass showed me how utterly futile was any hope of escape; for, as I put my foot down, I felt an indescribable drawing, sucking motion of the sand below. Another moment and my leg was swallowed up nearly to the knee. In the moonlight the whole surface of the sand seemed to be shaken with devilish delight at my disappointment. I struggled clear, sweating with terror and exertion, back to the tussocks behind me and fell on my face.

My only means of escape from the semicircle was protected with a quicksand!

How long I lay I have not the faintest idea; but I was roused at the last by the malevolent chuckle of Gunga Dass at my ear. "I would advise you, Protector of the Poor" (the ruffian was speaking English) "to return to your house. It is unhealthy to lie down here. Moreover, when the boat returns, you will most certainly be rifled at." He stood over me in the dim light of the dawn, chuckling and laughing to himself. Suppressing my first impulse to catch the man by the neck and throw him on to the quicksand, I rose sullenly and followed him to the platform below the burrows.

Suddenly, and futilely as I thought while I spoke, I asked: "Gunga Dass, what is the good of the boat if I can't get out *anyhow?*" I recollect that even in my deepest trouble I had been speculating vaguely on the waste of ammunition in guarding an already well protected foreshore.

Gunga Dass laughed again and made answer: "*They have the boat only in daytime.* It is for the reason that *there is a way.* I hope we shall have the pleasure of your company for much longer time. It is a pleasant spot when you have been here some years and eaten roast crow long enough."

I staggered, numbed and helpless, towards the fetid burrow allotted to me, and fell asleep. An hour or so later I was awakened by a piercing scream—the shrill, high-pitched scream of a horse in pain. Those who have once heard that will never forget the sound. I found some little difficulty in scrambling out of the burrow. When I was in the open, I saw Pornic, my poor old Pornic, lying dead on the sandy soil. How they had killed him I cannot guess. Gunga Dass explained that horse was better than crow, and "greatest good of greatest number is political maxim. We are now Republic, Mister Jukes, and you are entitled to a fair share of the beast. If you like we will pass a vote of thanks. Shall I propose?"

Yes, we were a Republic indeed! A Republic of wild beasts penned at the bottom of a pit, to eat and fight and sleep till we died. I attempted no protest of any kind, but sat down and stared at the hideous sight in front of me. In less time almost than it takes me to write this, Pornic's body was divided, in some unclean way or other; the men and women had dragged the fragments on to the platform and were preparing their morning meal. Gunga Dass cooked mine. The almost irresistible impulse to fly at the sand walls until I was wearied laid hold of me afresh, and I had to struggle against it with all my might. Gunga Dass was offensively jocular till I told him that if he addressed another remark of any kind whatever to me I should strangle him where he sat. This silenced him till silence became insupportable, and I bade him say something.

"You will live here till you die like the other Feringhi," he said coolly, watching me over the fragment of gristle that he was gnawing.

"What other Sahib, you swine? Speak at once, and don't stop to tell me a lie."

"He is over there," answered Gunga Dass, pointing to a burrow-mouth about four doors to the left of my own. "You can see for yourself. He died in the burrow as you will die, and I will die, and as all these men and women and the one child will also die."

"For pity's sake tell me all you know about him. Who was he? When did he come, and when did he die?"

This appeal was a weak step on my part. Gunga Dass only leered and replied: "I will not—unless you give me something first."

Then I recollected where I was, and struck the man between the eyes, partially stunning him. He stepped down from the platform at once, and, cringing and fawning and weeping and attempting to embrace my feet, led me round to the burrow which he had indicated.

"I know nothing whatever about the gentleman. Your God be my witness that I do not. He was as anxious to escape as you were, and he was shot from the boat, though we all did all things to prevent him from attempting. He was shot here." Gunga Dass laid his hand on his lean stomach and bowed to the earth.

"Well, and what then? Go on!"

"And then—and then, Your Honour, we carried him into his house and gave him water, and put wet cloths on the wound, and he laid down in his house and gave up the ghost."

"In how long? In how long?"

"About half an hour, after he received his wound. I call Vishn to witness," yelled the wretched man, "that I did everything for him. Everything which was possible, that I did!"

He threw himself down on the ground and clasped my ankles. But I had my doubts about Gunga Dass's benevolence, and kicked him off as he lay protesting.

"I believe you robbed him of everything he had. But I can find out in a minute or two. How long was the Sahib here?"

"Nearly a year and a half. I think he must have gone mad. But hear me swear, Protector of the Poor! Won't Your Honour hear me swear that I never touched an article that belonged to him? What is Your Worship going to do?"

I had taken Gunga Dass by the waist and had hauled him on to the platform opposite the deserted burrow. As I did so I thought of my wretched fellow-prisoner's unspeakable misery among all these horrors for eighteen months, and the final agony of dying like a rat in a hole, with a bullet wound in the stomach. Gunga Dass fancied I was going to kill him and howled pitifully. The rest of the population, in the plethora that follows a full flesh meal, watched us without stirring.

"Go inside, Gunga Dass," said I, "and fetch it out."

I was feeling sick and faint with horror now. Gunga Dass nearly rolled off the platform and howled aloud.

"But I am Brahmin, Sahib—a high-caste Brahmin. By your soul, by your father's soul, do not make me do this thing!"

"Brahmin or no Brahmin, by my soul and my father's soul, in you go!" I said, and, seizing him by the shoulders, I crammed his head into the mouth of the burrow, kicked the rest of him in, and, sitting down, covered my face with my hands.

At the end of a few minutes I heard a rustle and a creak; then Gunga Dass in a sobbing, choking whisper speaking to himself; then a soft thud—and I uncovered my eyes.

The dry sand had turned the corpse entrusted to its keeping into a yellow-brown mummy. I told Gunga Dass to stand off while I examined it. The body—clad in an olive-green hunting-suit much stained and worn, with leather pads on the shoulders—was that of a man between thirty and forty, above middle height, with light, sandy hair, long moustache, and a rough unkempt beard. The left canine of the upper jaw was missing, and a portion of the lobe of the right ear was gone. On the second finger of the left hand was a ring—a shield-shaped blood-stone set in gold, with a monogram that might have been either "B. K." or "B. L." On the third finger of the right hand was a silver ring in the shape of a coiled cobra, much worn and tarnished. Gunga Dass deposited a handful of trifles he had picked out of the burrow at my feet, and, covering the face of the body with my handkerchief, I turned to examine these. I give the full list in the hope that it may lead to the identification of the unfortunate man:—

1. Bowl of a briarwood pipe, serrated at the edge; much worn and blackened; bound with string at the screw.

2. Two patent-lever keys; wards of both broken.

3. Tortoise-shell-handled penknife, silver or nickel, name-plated, marked with monogram "B. K."

4. Envelope, postmark undecipherable, bearing a Victorian stamp, addressed to "Miss Mon——" (rest illegible)—"ham'—'nt."

5. Imitation crocodile-skin notebook with pencil. First forty-five pages blank; four and a half illegible; fifteen others filled with private memoranda relating chiefly to three persons—a Mrs. L. Singleton, abbreviated several times to "Lot Single," "Mrs. S. May," and "Garmison," referred to in places as "Jerry" or "Jack."

6. Handle of small-sized hunting-knife. Blade snapped short. Buck's horn, diamond-cut, with swivel and ring on the butt; fragment of cotton cord attached.

It must not be supposed that I inventoried all these things on the spot as fully as I have here written them down. The notebook first attracted my attention, and I put it in my pocket with a view to studying it later on. The rest of the articles I conveyed to my burrow for safety's sake, and there, being a methodical man, I inventoried them. I then returned to the corpse and ordered Gunga Dass to help me to carry it out to the river-front. While we were engaged in this, the exploded shell of an old brown cartridge dropped out of one of the pockets and rolled at my feet. Gunga Dass had not seen it; and I fell to thinking that a man does not carry exploded cartridge-cases, especially "browns," which will not bear loading twice, about with him when shooting. In other words, that cartridge-case had been fired inside the crater. Consequently there must be a gun somewhere. I was on the verge of asking Gunga Dass, but checked myself, knowing that he would lie. We laid the body down on the edge of the quicksand by the tussocks. It was my intention to push it out and let it be swallowed up—the only possible mode of burial that I could think of. I ordered Gunga Dass to go away.

Then I gingerly put the corpse out on the quicksand. In doing so, it was lying face downward, I tore the frail and rotten khaki shooting-coat open, disclosing a hideous cavity in the back. I have already told you that the dry sand had, as it were, mummified the body. A moment's glance showed that the gaping hole had been caused by a gunshot wound; the gun must have been fired with the muzzle almost touching the back. The shooting-coat, being intact, had been drawn over the body after death, which must have been instantaneous. The secret of the poor wretch's death was plain to me in a flash. Some one of the crater, presumably Gunga Dass, must have shot him with his own gun—the gun that fitted the brown cartridges. He had never attempted to escape in the face of the rifle-fire from the boat.

I pushed the corpse out hastily, and saw it sink from sight literally in a few seconds. I shuddered as I watched. In a dazed, half-conscious way I turned to peruse the notebook. A stained and discoloured slip of paper had been inserted between the binding and the back, and dropped out as I opened the pages. This is what it contained: *"Four out from crow-clump; three left; nine out; two right; three back; two left;*

fourteen out; two left; seven out; one left; nine back; two right; six back; four right; seven back.'' The paper had been burnt and charred at the edges. What it meant I could not understand. I sat down on the dried bents turning it over and over between my fingers, until I was aware of Gunga Dass standing immediately behind me with glowing eyes and outstretched hands.

"Have you got it?" he panted. "Will you not let me look at it also? I swear that I will return it."

"Got what? Return what?" I asked.

"That which you have in your hands. It will help us both." He stretched out his long, bird-like talons, trembling with eagerness.

"I could never find it," he continued. "He had secreted it about his person. Therefore I shot him, but nevertheless I was unable to obtain it."

Gunga Dass had quite forgotten his little fiction about the rifle-bullet. I heard him calmly. Morality is blunted by consorting with the Dead who are alive.

"What on earth are you raving about? What it is you want me to give you?"

"The piece of paper in the notebook. It will help us both. Oh, you fool! You fool! Can you not see what it will do for us? We shall escape!"

His voice rose almost to a scream, and he danced with excitement before me. I own I was moved at the chance of getting away.

"Do you mean to say that this slip of paper will help us? What does it mean?"

"Read it aloud! Read it aloud! I beg and I pray to you to read it aloud."

I did so. Gunga Dass listened delightedly, and drew an irregular line in the sand with his fingers.

"See now! It was the length of his gun-barrels without the stock. I have those barrels. Four gun-barrels out from the place where I caught crows. Straight out; do you mind me? Then three left. Ah! Now well I remember how that man worked it out night after night. Then nine out, and so on. Out is always straight before you across the quicksand to the North. He told me so before I killed him."

"But if you knew all this why didn't you get out before?"

"I did *not* know it. He told me that he was working it out a year and a half ago, and how he was working it out night after night when the boat had gone away, and he could get out near the quicksand safely. Then he said that we would get away together. But I was afraid that he would leave me behind one night when he had worked it all out, and so I shot him. Besides, it is not advisable that the men who once get in here should escape. Only I, and *I* am a Brahmin."

The hope of escape had brought Gunga Dass's caste back to him. He stood up, walked about and gesticulated violently. Eventually I managed to make him talk soberly, and he told me how this Englishman had spent six months night after night in exploring, inch by inch, the passage across the quicksand; how he had declared it to be simplicity itself up to within about twenty yards of the river bank after turning the flank of the left horn of the horseshoe. This much he had evidently not completed when Gunga Dass shot him with his own gun.

In my frenzy of delight at the possibilities of escape I recollect shaking hands wildly with Gunga Dass, after we had decided that we were to make an attempt to get away that very night. It was weary work waiting throughout the afternoon.

About ten o'clock, as far as I could judge, when the Moon had just risen above the lip of the crater, Gunga Dass made a move for his burrow to bring out the gun-barrels whereby to measure our path. All the other wretched inhabitants had retired to their lairs long ago. The guardian boat drifted down-stream some hours before, and we were utterly alone by the crow-clump. Gunga Dass, while carrying the gun-barrels, let slip the piece of paper which was to be our guide. I stooped down hastily to recover it, and, as I did so, I was aware that the creature was aiming a violent blow at the back of my head with the gun-barrels. It was too late to turn round. I must have received the blow somewhere on the nape of my neck, for I fell senseless at the edge of the quicksand.

When I recovered consciousness, the Moon was going down, and I was sensible of intolerable pain in the back of my head. Gunga Dass had disappeared and my mouth was full of blood. I lay down again and prayed that I might die without more ado. Then the unreasoning fury which I have before mentioned laid hold upon me, and I staggered inland towards the walls of the crater. It seemed that some one was calling to me in a whisper—"Sahib! Sahib! Sahib!" exactly as my bearer used to call me in the mornings. I fancied that I was delirious until a handful of sand fell at my feet. Then I looked up and saw a head peering down into the amphitheatre—the head of Dunnoo, my dog-boy, who attended to my collies. As soon as he had attracted my attention, he held up his hand and showed a rope. I motioned, staggering to and fro the while, that he should throw it down. It was a couple of leather punkah ropes knotted together, with a loop at one end. I slipped the loop over my head and under my arms; heard Dunnoo urge something forward; was conscious that I was being dragged, face downward, up the steep sand-slope, and the next instant found myself choked and half-fainting on the sand hills overlooking the crater. Dunnoo, with his face ashy gray in the moonlight, implored me not to stay but to get back to my tent at once.

It seems that he had tracked Pornic's footprints fourteen miles across the sands to the crater; had returned and told my servants, who flatly refused to meddle with any one, white or black, once fallen into the hideous Village of the Dead; whereupon Dunnoo had taken one of my ponies and a couple of punkah ropes, returned to the crater, and hauled me out as I have described.

QUESTIONS

1 How does the author give a sense of truth to the story, and why is it important in this particular case?
2 In what ways are the inhabitants' attitudes important?
3 How does Kipling use symbols to add levels of meaning? Think, for instance, about the description of the hole in which each lives, the arrangement of the holes in respect to the place, and the food supply.
4 What does Jukes "learn" from his experience? What does Kipling expect us to "learn"?

TOPICS FOR COMPOSITION

1 Using the story as your reference point, write an essay in which you discuss the ability or inability of an individual from one culture to understand another culture.

2   Write an essay in which you argue for or against the notion that Kipling supports a class-conscious society. You may write a relatively short essay using only evidence from the story, or you may enlarge your perspective by some research into Kipling's viewpoints.

Doris Lessing's story, which follows, is similar to Kipling's in that both deal with a British subject, in this case an Englishwoman, who resides in a British colony, in this case Africa. Lessing, however, is more intent than Kipling in presenting a complex personality in conflict with a sense of displacement. Even more to Lessing's point is the fact that her protagonist is a woman. As you read the story, give special attention to the descriptions of the other women and to Lucy's relationship to them and to her husband.

LUCY GRANGE

Doris Lessing

The farm was fifty miles from the nearest town, in a maize-growing district. The mealie lands began at a stone's throw from the front door of the farmhouse. At the back were several acres of energetic and colourful domestic growth: chicken runs, vegetables, pumpkins. Even on the verandah there were sacks of grain and bundles of hoes. The life of the farm, her husband's life, washed around the house, leaving old scraps of iron on the front step where the children played wagon-and-driver, or a bottle of medicine for a sick animal on her dressing-table among the bottles of Elizabeth Arden.

One walked straight from the verandah of this gaunt, iron-roofed, brick barracks of a house into a wide drawing-room that was shaded in green and orange Liberty linens.

"Stylish?" said the fathers' wives when they came on formal calls, asking the question of themselves while they discussed with Lucy Grange the price of butter and servants' aprons and their husbands discussed the farm with George Grange. They never "dropped over" to see Lucy Grange; they never rang her up with invitations to "spend the day." They would finger the books on child psychology, politics, art; gaze guiltily at the pictures on her walls, which they felt they ought to be able to recognise; and say: "I can see you are a great reader, Mrs. Grange."

There were years of discussing her among themselves before their voices held the good-natured amusement of acceptance: "I found Lucy in the vegetable patch wearing gloves full of cold cream." "Lucy has ordered another dress pattern from town." And later still, with self-consciously straightened shoulders, eyes directly primly before them, discreet non-committal voices: "Lucy is very attractive to men."

One can imagine her, when they left at the end of those mercifully short visits, standing on the verandah and smiling bitterly after the satisfactory solid women with their straight tailored dresses, made by the Dutchwoman at the store at seven-and-six

a time, buttoned loosely across their well-used breasts; with their untidy hair perma-
nent-waved every six months in town; with their femininity which was asserted once
and for all by a clumsy scrawl of red across the mouth. One can imagine her clenching
her fists and saying fiercely to the mealie fields that rippled greenly all around her,
cream-topped like the sea: "I won't. I simply won't. He needn't imagine that I will!"

"Do you like my new dress, George?"

"You're the best-looking woman in the district, Lucy." So it seemed, on the face of
it, that he didn't expect, or even want, that she should . . .

Meanwhile she continued to order cookbooks from town, to make new recipes of
pumpkin and green mealies and chicken, to put skin food on her face at night; she
constructed attractive nursery furniture out of packing-cases enameled white—the
farm wasn't doing too well; and discussed with George how little Betty's cough was
probably psychological.

"I'm sure you're right, my dear."

Then the rich, over-controlled voice: "Yes, darling. No, my sweetheart. Yes, of
course, I'll play bricks with you, but you must have your lunch first." Then it broke, hard
and shrill: "*Don't* make all that noise, darling. I can't stand it. Go on, go and play in the
garden and leave me in peace."

Sometimes, storms of tears. Afterwards: "Really, George, didn't your mother ever
tell you that all women cry sometimes? It's as good as a tonic. Or a holiday." And a lot
of high laughter and gay explanations at which George hastened to guffaw. He liked
her gay. She usually was. For instance, she was a good mimic. She would "take off,"
deliberately trying to relieve his mind of farm worries, the visiting policemen, who
toured the district once a month to see if the natives were behaving themselves, or the
Government agricultural officials.

"Do you want to see my husband?"

That was what they had come for, but they seldom pressed the point. They sat far
longer than they had intended, drinking tea, talking about themselves. They would go
away and say at the bar in the village: "Mrs. Grange is a smart woman, isn't she?"

And Lucy would be acting, for George's benefit, how a khaki-clad, sun-raw youth
had bent into her room, looking around him with comical surprise; had taken a cup of
tea, thanking her three times; had knocked over an ashtray, stayed for lunch and
afternoon tea, and left saying with awkward gallantry: "It's a real treat to meet a lady
like you who is interested in things."

"You shouldn't be so hard on us poor Colonials, Lucy."

Finally one can imagine how one day, when the houseboy came to her in the
chicken runs to say that there was a baas waiting to see her at the house, it was no
sweating policeman, thirsty after fifteen dusty miles on a motorcycle, to whom she
must be gracious.

He was a city man, of perhaps forty or forty-five, dressed in city clothes. At first
glance she felt a shudder of repulsion. It was a coarse face, and sensual; and he
looked like a patient vulture as the keen, heavy-lidded eyes travelled up and down her
body.

"Are you looking for my husband, perhaps? He's in the cowsheds this morning."

"No, I don't think I am. I was."

She laughed. It was as if he had started playing a record she had not heard for a long time, and which started her feet tapping. It was years since she had played this game. "I'll get you some tea," she said hurriedly and left him in her pretty drawing-room.

Collecting the cups, her hands were clumsy. Why, Lucy! she said to herself, archly. She came back, very serious and responsible, to find him standing in front of the picture that filled half the wall at one end of the room. "I should have thought you had sunflowers enough here," he said, in his heavy, over-emphasised voice, which made her listen for meanings behind his words. And when he turned away from the wall and came to sit down, leaning forward, examining her, she suppressed an impulse to apologise for the picture: Van Gogh is obvious, but he's rather effective, she might have said; and she felt that the whole room was that: effective but obvious. But she was pleasantly conscious of how she looked: graceful and cool in her green linen dress, with her corn-coloured hair knotted demurely on her neck. She lifted wide, serious eyes to his face and asked, "Milk? Sugar?" and knew that the corners of her mouth were tight with self-consciousness.

When he left, three hours later, he turned her hand over and lightly kissed the palm. She looked down at the greasy dark head, the red folded neck, and stood rigid, thinking of the raw, creased necks of vultures.

Then he straightened up and said with simple kindliness, "You must be lonely here, my dear"; and she was astounded to find her eyes full of tears.

"One does what one can to make a show of it." She kept her lids lowered and her voice light. Inside she was weeping with gratitude. Embarrassed, she said quickly, "You know, you haven't yet said what you came for."

"I sell insurance. And besides, I've heard people talk of you."

She imagined the talk and smiled stiffly. "You don't seem to take your work very seriously."

"If I may, I'll come back another time and try again?"

She did not reply. He said, "My dear, I'll tell you a secret: one of the reasons I chose this district was because of you. Surely there aren't so many people in this country one can really talk to that we can afford not to take each other seriously?"

He touched her cheek with his hand, smiled, and went.

She heard the last thing he had said like a parody of the things she often said and felt a violent revulsion.

She went to her bedroom, where she found herself in front of the mirror. Her hands went to her cheeks and she drew in her breath with the shock. "Why, Lucy, whatever is the matter with you?" Her eyes were dancing, her mouth smiled irresistibly. Yet she heard the archness of her "Why, Lucy," and thought: I'm going to pieces. I must have gone to pieces without knowing it.

Later she found herself singing in the pantry as she made a cake, stopped herself; made herself look at the insurance salesman's face against her closed eyelids; and instinctively wiped the palms of her hands against her skirt.

He came three days later. Again, in the first shock of seeing him stand at the door, smiling familiarly, she thought, It's the face of an old animal. He probably chose this kind of work because of the opportunities it gives him.

He talked of London, where he had lately been on leave; about the art galleries and the theatres.

She could not help warming, because of her hunger for this kind of talk. She could not help an apologetic note in her voice, because she knew that after so many years in this exile she must seem provincial. She liked him because he associated himself with her abdication from her standards by saying: "Yes, yes, my dear, in a country like this we all learn to accept the second-rate."

While he talked his eyes were roving. He was listening. Outside the window the turkeys were scraping in the dust and gobbling. In the next room the houseboy was moving; then there was silence because he had gone to get his midday meal. The children had had their lunch and gone off to the garden with the nurse.

No, she said to herself. No, no, no.

"Does your husband come back for lunch?"

"He takes it on the lands at this time of the year, he's so busy."

He came over and sat beside her. "Well, shall we console each other?" She was crying in his arms. She could feel their impatient and irritable tightening.

In the bedroom she kept her eyes shut. His hand travelled up and down her back. "What's the matter, little one? What's the matter?"

His voice was a sedative. She could have fallen asleep and lain there for a week inside the anonymous, comforting arms. But he was looking at his watch over her shoulder. "We'd better get dressed, hadn't we?"

"Of course."

She sat naked on the bed, covering herself with her arms, looking at his white hairy body in loathing, and then at the creased red neck. She became extremely gay; and in the living-room they sat side by side on the big sofa, being ironical. Then he put his arm around her, and she curled up inside it and cried again. She clung to him and felt him going away from her; and in a few minutes he stood up, saying, "Wouldn't do for your old man to come in and find us like this, would it?" Even while she was hating him for the "old man," she put her arms around him and said, "You'll come back soon."

"I couldn't keep away." The voice purred caressingly over her head, and she said: "You know, I'm very lonely."

"Darling, I'll come as soon as I can. I've a living to make, you know."

She let her arms drop, and smiled, and watched him drive away down the rutted red-rust farm road, between the rippling sea-coloured mealies.

She knew he would come again, and next time she would not cry; she would stand again like this, watching him go, hating him, thinking of how he had said: In this country we learn to accept the second-rate. And he would come again and again and again; and she would stand here, watching him go and hating him.

QUESTIONS

1 In how many ways in the first ten or so paragraphs does Lessing describe the extent of Lucy's displacement?

2 Why is the description of the insurance salesman important? Why is he nameless?

3 What is the full meaning of Lucy's thinking that "In this country we learn to accept the second-rate"?

TOPICS FOR COMPOSITION

1 Doris Lessing appears to neither condemn nor approve of Lucy Grange's actions. Write an essay in which you deal with the story on similar terms; i.e., argue that the story is a realistic depiction because Lucy's particular personality allows for no other.
2 Write an essay in which you argue the universality of the need to belong by using as examples the main characters in Crane's story, Kipling's story, and Lessing's story.

DRAMA

In "Hello Out There" two lonely people together postulate a place—San Francisco—where the individual is no longer alone or exploited ("raped"). The very title and its recurrence in the dialogue insist upon the urgency of establishing a place beyond the emptiness of Wheeling and Matador, Texas—beyond the Young Man's prison cell and The Girl's equally desolate prison of hopelessness, ridicule, and exploitation. San Francisco becomes, in their mutually stirred imaginations, the *locus* of the ideal—a place of "Cool fog and seagulls," where more people "love somebody" than in a town like Matador, where there is "Nothing . . . but the lonesome wind all the time, lifting the dirt and blowing out to the prairie." In the play's inevitable *dénouement,* the horror of life in a meaningless place is forced upon an indignant husband as well as upon The Girl.

1   The exchanges between the Young Man and The Girl move gradually but insistently from mere banality toward a kind of visionary eloquence. The Girl confesses, "I'm nobody here"; and the Young Man sees his past in terms of "going from one poor little town to another, trying to get in on something good somewhere."
2   The inescapable contrasts between the "Frisco" of the charged imagination, on the one hand, and Wheeling and Matador, Texas, or a jail cell of stark reality, on the other, point up Saroyan's theme of the imperative call of the unfettered life.
3   Everything in the play's context that conspires against the achievement of "place"—including The Woman—reveals itself as an enemy of love and life.

HELLO OUT THERE

William Saroyan

For George Bernard Shaw

CHARACTERS
A YOUNG MAN   TWO OTHER MEN
A GIRL   A WOMAN
A MAN

> *Scene: There is a fellow in a small-town prison cell, tapping slowly on the floor with a spoon. After tapping half a minute, as if he were trying to telegraph words, he gets up and begins walking around the cell. At last he stops, stands at the center of the cell, and doesn't move for a long time. He feels his head, as if it were wounded. Then he looks around. Then he calls out dramatically, kidding the world.*

YOUNG MAN   Hello—out there! *(Pause)* Hello—out there! Hello—out there! *(Long pause)* Nobody out there. *(Still more dramatically, but more comically, too)* Hello—out there! Hello—out there!

(A GIRL'S VOICE is heard, very sweet and soft)

THE VOICE   Hello.

YOUNG MAN   Hello—out there.

THE VOICE   Hello.

YOUNG MAN   Is that you, Katey?

THE VOICE   No—this here is Emily.

YOUNG MAN   Who? *(Swiftly)* Hello out there.

THE VOICE   Emily.

YOUNG MAN   Emily who? I don't know anybody named Emily. Are you that girl I met at Sam's in Salinas about three years ago?

THE VOICE   No—I'm the girl who cooks here. I'm the cook. I've never been in Salinas. I don't even know where it is.

YOUNG MAN   Hello out there. You say you cook here?

THE VOICE   Yes.

YOUNG MAN   Well, why don't you study up and learn to cook? How come I don't get no jello or anything good?

THE VOICE   I just cook what they tell me to. *(Pause)* You lonesome?

YOUNG MAN   Lonesome as a coyote. Hear me hollering? Hello out there!

THE VOICE   Who you hollering to?

YOUNG MAN   Well—nobody, I guess. I been trying to think of somebody to write a letter to, but I can't think of anybody.

THE VOICE   What about Katey?

YOUNG MAN   I don't know anybody named Katey.

THE VOICE   Then why did you say, Is that you, Katey?

YOUNG MAN   Katey's a good name. I always did like a name like Katey. I never *knew* anybody named Katey, though.

THE VOICE   *I* did.

YOUNG MAN   Yeah? What was she like? Tall girl, or little one?

THE VOICE   Kind of medium.

YOUNG MAN   Hello out there. What sort of a looking girl are *you*?

THE VOICE   Oh, I don't know.

YOUNG MAN   Didn't anybody ever tell you? Didn't anybody ever talk to you that way?

THE VOICE   What way?

YOUNG MAN   You know. Didn't they?

THE VOICE   No, they didn't.

YOUNG MAN   Ah, the fools—they should have. I can tell from your voice you're O.K.

THE VOICE   Maybe I am and maybe I ain't.

YOUNG MAN   I never missed yet.

THE VOICE   Yeah, I know. That's why you're in jail.

YOUNG MAN   The whole thing was a mistake.

THE VOICE   They claim it was rape.

YOUNG MAN   No—it wasn't.

THE VOICE   That's what they claim it was.

YOUNG MAN   They're a lot of fools.

THE VOICE   Well, you sure are in trouble. Are you scared?

YOUNG MAN   Scared to death. *(Suddenly)* Hello out there!

THE VOICE   What do you keep saying that for all the time?

YOUNG MAN   I'm lonesome. I'm as lonesome as a coyote. *(A long one)* Hello—out there!

(THE GIRL appears, over to one side. She is a plain girl in plain clothes.)

THE GIRL   I'm kind of lonesome, too.

YOUNG MAN   *(Turning and looking at her)*   Hey—No fooling? Are you?

THE GIRL   Yeah—I'm almost as lonesome as a coyote myself.

YOUNG MAN   Who *you* lonesome for?

THE GIRL   I don't know.

YOUNG MAN   It's the same with me. The minute they put you in a place like this you remember all the girls you ever knew, and all the girls you didn't get to know, and it sure gets lonesome.

THE GIRL   I bet it does.

YOUNG MAN   Ah, it's awful. *(Pause)* You're a pretty kid, you know that?

THE GIRL   You're just talking.

YOUNG MAN   No, I'm not just talking—you *are* pretty. Any fool could see that. You're just about the prettiest kid in the whole world.

THE GIRL   I'm not—and you know it.

YOUNG MAN   No—you are. I never saw anyone prettier in all my born days; in all my travels. I knew Texas would bring me luck.

THE GIRL   Luck? You're in jail, aren't you? You've got a whole gang of people all worked up, haven't you?

YOUNG MAN   Ah, that's nothing. I'll get out of this.

THE GIRL   Maybe.

YOUNG MAN   No, I'll be all right—*now.*

THE GIRL   What do you mean—now?

YOUNG MAN   I mean after seeing you. I got something now. You know for a while there I didn't care one way or another. Tired. *(Pause)* Tired of trying for the best all the time and never getting it. *(Suddenly)* Hello out there!

THE GIRL   Who you calling now?

YOUNG MAN   You.

THE GIRL   Why, I'm right here.

YOUNG MAN   I know. *(Calling)* Hello out there!

THE GIRL   Hello.

YOUNG MAN   Ah, you're sweet. *(Pause)* I'm going to marry you. I'm going away with you. I'm going to take you to San Francisco or some place like that. I *am,* now. I'm going to win myself some real money, too. I'm going to study 'em real careful and pick myself some winners, and we're going to have a lot of money.

THE GIRL   Yeah?

YOUNG MAN   Yeah. Tell me your name and all that stuff.

THE GIRL   Emily.

YOUNG MAN   I know that. What's the rest of it? Where were you born? Come on, tell me the whole thing.

THE GIRL   Emily Smith.

YOUNG MAN   Honest to God?

THE GIRL   Honest. That's my name—Emily Smith.

YOUNG MAN   Ah, you're the sweetest girl in the whole world.

THE GIRL   Why?

YOUNG MAN   I don't know why, but you are, that's all. Where were you born?

THE GIRL   Matador, Texas.

YOUNG MAN   Where's that?

THE GIRL   Right here.

YOUNG MAN   Is this Matador, Texas?

THE GIRL   Yeah, it's Matador. They brought you here from Wheeling.

YOUNG MAN   Is that where I was—Wheeling?

THE GIRL   Didn't you even know what town you were in?

YOUNG MAN   All towns are alike. You don't go up and ask somebody what town you're in. It doesn't make any difference. How far away is Wheeling?

THE GIRL   Sixteen or seventeen miles. Didn't you know they moved you?

YOUNG MAN   How could I know, when I was out—cold? Somebody hit me over the head with a lead pipe or something. What'd they hit me for?

THE GIRL   Rape—that's what they *said*.

YOUNG MAN   Ah, that's a lie. *(Amazed, almost to himself)* She wanted me to give her money.

THE GIRL   Money?

YOUNG MAN   Yeah, if I'd have known she was a woman like that—well, by God, I'd have gone on down the street and stretched out in a park somewhere and gone to sleep.

THE GIRL   Is that what she wanted—money?

YOUNG MAN   Yeah. A fellow like me hopping freights all over the country, trying to break his bad luck, going from one poor little town to another, trying to get in on something good somewhere, and she asks for money. I thought she was lonesome. She *said* she was.

THE GIRL   Maybe she was.

YOUNG MAN   She was *something*.

THE GIRL   I guess I'd never see you, if it didn't happen, though.

YOUNG MAN   Oh, I don't know—maybe I'd just mosey along this way and see you in this town somewhere. I'd recognize you, too.

THE GIRL   Recognize me?

YOUNG MAN   Sure, I'd recognize you the minute I laid eyes on you.

THE GIRL   Well, who would I be?

YOUNG MAN   Mine, that's who.

THE GIRL   Honest?

YOUNG MAN   Honest to God.

THE GIRL   You just say that because you're in jail.

YOUNG MAN   No, I mean it. You just pack up and wait for me. We'll high-roll the hell out of here to Frisco.

THE GIRL   You're just lonesome.

YOUNG MAN   I been lonesome all my life—there's no cure for that—but you and me— we can have a lot of fun hanging around together. You'll bring me luck. I know it.

THE GIRL   What are you looking for luck for all the time?

YOUNG MAN   I'm a gambler. I don't work. I've *got* to have luck, or I'm a bum. I haven't had any decent luck in years. Two whole years now—one place to another. Bad luck all the time. That's why I got in trouble back there in Wheeling, too. That was no accident. That was my bad luck following me around. So here I am, with my head half busted. I guess it was her old man that did it.

THE GIRL   You mean her father?

YOUNG MAN   No, her husband. If I had an old lady like that, I'd throw her out.

THE GIRL   Do you think you'll have better luck, if I go with you?

YOUNG MAN   It's a cinch. I'm a good handicapper. All I need is somebody good like you with me. It's no good always walking around in the streets for anything that might be there at the time. You got to have somebody staying with you all the time— through winters when it's cold, and springtime when it's pretty, and summertime when it's nice and hot and you can go swimming—through *all* the times—rain and snow and all the different kinds of weather a man's got to go through before he dies. You got to have somebody who's right. Somebody who knows you, from away back. You got to have somebody who even knows you're wrong but likes you just the same. I know I'm wrong, but I just don't want anything the hard way, working like a dog, or the *easy* way, working like a dog—working's the hard way and the easy way both. All I got to do is beat the price, always—and then I don't feel lousy and don't hate anybody. If you go along with me, I'll be the finest guy anybody ever saw. I won't be wrong any more. You know when you get enough of that money, you *can't* be wrong any more—you're right because the money says so. I'll have a lot of money and you'll be just about the prettiest, most wonderful kid in the whole world. I'll be proud walking around Frisco with you on my arm and people turning around to look at us.

THE GIRL   Do you think they will?

YOUNG MAN   Sure they will. When I get back in some decent clothes, and you're on my arm—well, Katey, they'll turn around and look, and they'll see something, too.

THE GIRL   Katey?

YOUNG MAN   Yeah—that's your name from now on. You're the first girl I ever called Katey. I've been saving it for you. O.K.?

THE GIRL   O.K.

YOUNG MAN   How long have I been here?

THE GIRL   Since last night. You didn't wake up until late this morning, though.

YOUNG MAN   What time is it now? About nine?

THE GIRL   About ten.

YOUNG MAN   Have you got the key to this lousy cell?

THE GIRL   No. They don't let me fool with any keys.

YOUNG MAN   Well, can you get it?

THE GIRL   No.

YOUNG MAN   Can you *try?*

THE GIRL   They wouldn't let me get near any keys. I cook for this jail, when they've got somebody in it. I clean up and things like that.

YOUNG MAN   Well, I want to get out of here. Don't you know the guy that runs this joint?

THE GIRL   I know him, but he wouldn't let you out. They were talking of taking you to another jail in another town.

YOUNG MAN   Yeah? Why?

THE GIRL   Because they're afraid.

YOUNG MAN   What are they afraid of?

THE GIRL   They're afraid these people from Wheeling will come over in the middle of the night and break in.

YOUNG MAN   Yeah? What do they want to do that for?

THE GIRL   Don't *you* know what they want to do it for?

YOUNG MAN   Yeah, I know all right.

THE GIRL   Are you scared?

YOUNG MAN   Sure I'm scared. Nothing scares a man more than ignorance. You can argue with people who ain't fools, but you can't argue with fools—they just go to work and do what they're set on doing. Get me out of here.

THE GIRL   How?

YOUNG MAN   Well, go get the guy with the key, and let me talk to him.

THE GIRL   He's gone home. Everybody's gone home.

YOUNG MAN   You mean I'm in this little jail all alone?

THE GIRL   Well—yeah—except me.

YOUNG MAN   Well, what's the big idea—doesn't anybody stay here all the time?

THE GIRL   No, they go home every night. I clean up and then I go, too. I hung around tonight.

YOUNG MAN   What made you do that?

THE GIRL   I wanted to talk to you.

YOUNG MAN   Honest? What did you want to talk about?

THE GIRL   Oh, I don't know. I took care of you last night. You were talking in your sleep. You liked me, too. I didn't think you'd like me when you woke up, though.

YOUNG MAN   Yeah? Why not?

THE GIRL   I don't know.

YOUNG MAN   Yeah? Well, you're wonderful, see?

THE GIRL   Nobody ever talked to me that way. All the fellows in town—*(Pause)*

YOUNG MAN   What about 'em? *(Pause)* Well, what about 'em? Come on—tell me.

THE GIRL   They laugh at me.

YOUNG MAN   Laugh at *you?* They're fools. What do they know about anything? You go get your things and come back here. I'll take you with me to Frisco. How old are you?

THE GIRL   Oh, I'm of age.

YOUNG MAN   How old are you?—Don't lie to me! Sixteen?

THE GIRL   I'm seventeen.

YOUNG MAN   Well, bring your father and mother. We'll get married before we go.

THE GIRL   They wouldn't let me go.

YOUNG MAN   Why not?

THE GIRL   I don't know, but they wouldn't. I know they wouldn't.

YOUNG MAN   You go tell your father not to be a fool, see? What is he, a farmer?

THE GIRL   No—nothing. He gets a little relief from the government because he's supposed to be hurt or something—his side hurts, he says. I don't know what it is.

YOUNG MAN   Ah, he's a liar. Well, I'm taking you with me, see?

THE GIRL   He takes the money I earn, too.

YOUNG MAN   He's got no right to do that.

THE GIRL   I know it, but he does it.

YOUNG MAN   *(Almost to himself)*   This world stinks. You shouldn't have been born in this
town, anyway, and you shouldn't have had a man like that for a father, either.

THE GIRL   Sometimes I feel sorry for him.

YOUNG MAN   Never mind feeling sorry for him. *(Pointing a finger)* I'm going to talk to
your father some day. I've got a few things to tell that guy.

THE GIRL   I know you have.

YOUNG MAN   *(Suddenly)*   Hello—out there! See if you can get that fellow with the keys
to come down and let me out.

THE GIRL   Oh, I couldn't.

YOUNG MAN   Why not?

THE GIRL   I'm nobody here—they give me fifty cents every day I work.

YOUNG MAN   How much?

THE GIRL   Fifty cents.

YOUNG MAN   *(To the world)*   You see? They ought to pay money to *look* at you. To
breathe the *air* you breathe. I don't know. Sometimes I figure it never is going to
make sense. Hello—out there! I'm scared. You try to get me out of here. I'm
scared them fools are going to come here from Wheeling and go crazy, thinking
they're heroes. Get me out of here, Katey.

THE GIRL   I don't know what to do. Maybe I could break the door down.

YOUNG MAN   No, you couldn't do that. Is there a hammer out there or anything?

THE GIRL   Only a broom. Maybe they've locked the broom up, too.

YOUNG MAN   Go see if you can find anything.

THE GIRL   All right. *(She goes)*

YOUNG MAN   Hello—out there! Hello—out there! *(Pause)* Hello—out there! Hello—out
there! *(Pause)* Putting me in jail. *(With contempt)* Rape! Rape? *They* rape everything good that was ever born. His side hurts. They laugh at her. Fifty cents a day.
Little punk people. Hurting the only good thing that ever came their way. *(Suddenly)* Hello—out there!

THE GIRL   *(Returning)*   There isn't a thing out there. They've locked everything up for
the night.

YOUNG MAN   Any cigarettes?

THE GIRL   Everything's locked up—all the drawers of the desk, all the closet doors—
everything.

YOUNG MAN   I ought to have a cigarette.

THE GIRL   I could get you a package maybe, somewhere. I guess the drug store's open.
It's about a mile.

YOUNG MAN   A mile? I don't want to be alone that long.

THE GIRL   I could run all the way, and all the way back.

YOUNG MAN   You're the sweetest girl that ever lived.

THE GIRL   What kind do you want?

YOUNG MAN   Oh, any kind—Chesterfields or Camels or Lucky Strikes—any kind at all.

THE GIRL   I'll go get a package. *(She turns to go)*

YOUNG MAN   What about the money?

THE GIRL   I've got some money. I've got a quarter I been saving. I'll run all the way. *(She is about to go.)*

YOUNG MAN   Come here.

THE GIRL *(Going to him)*   What?

YOUNG MAN   Give me your hand. *(He takes her hand and looks at it, smiling. He lifts it and kisses it.)* I'm scared to death.

THE GIRL   I am, too.

YOUNG MAN   I'm not lying—I don't care what happens to me, but I'm scared nobody will ever come out here to this God-forsaken broken-down town and find you. I'm scared you'll get used to it and not mind. I'm scared you'll never get to Frisco and have 'em all turning around to look at you. Listen—go get me a gun, because if they come, I'll kill 'em! They don't understand. Get me a gun!

THE GIRL   I could get my father's gun. I know where he hides it.

YOUNG MAN   Go get it. Never mind the cigarettes. Run all the way. *(Pause, smiling but seriously)* Hello, Katey.

THE GIRL   Hello. What's your name?

YOUNG MAN   Photo-Finish is what they *call* me. My races are always photo-finish races. You don't know what that means, but it means they're very close. So close the only way they can tell which horse wins is to look at a photograph after the race is over. Well, every race I bet turns out to be a photo-finish race, and my horse never wins. It's my bad luck, all the time. That's why they call me Photo-Finish. Say it before you go.

THE GIRL   Photo-Finish.

YOUNG MAN   Come here. (THE GIRL *moves close and he kisses her.)* Now, hurry. Run all the way.

THE GIRL   I'll run. (THE GIRL *turns and runs. The* YOUNG MAN *stands at the center of the cell a long time.* THE GIRL *comes running back in. Almost crying)* I'm afraid. I'm afraid I won't see you again. If I come back and you're not here, I—

YOUNG MAN   Hello—out there!

THE GIRL   It's so lonely in this town. Nothing here but the lonesome wind all the time, lifting the dirt and blowing out to the prairie. I'll stay *here.* I won't *let* them take you away.

YOUNG MAN   Listen, Katey. Do what I tell you. Go get that gun and come back. Maybe they won't come tonight. Maybe they won't come at all. I'll hide the gun and when they let me out you can take it back and put it where you found it. And then we'll go away. But if they come, I'll kill 'em! Now, hurry—

THE GIRL   All right. *(Pause)* I want to tell you something.

YOUNG MAN   O.K.

THE GIRL *(Very softly)* If you're not here when I come back, well, I'll have the gun and I'll know what to do with it.

YOUNG MAN You know how to handle a gun?

THE GIRL I know how.

YOUNG MAN Don't be a fool. *(Takes off his shoe, brings out some currency)* Don't be a fool, see? Here's some money. Eighty dollars. Take it and go to Frisco. Look around and find somebody. Find somebody alive and halfway human, see? Promise me —if I'm not here when you come back, just throw the gun away and get the hell to Frisco. Look around and find somebody.

THE GIRL I don't *want* to find anybody.

YOUNG MAN *(Swiftly, desperately)* Listen, if I'm not here when you come back, how do you know I haven't gotten away? Now, do what I tell you. I'll meet you in Frisco. I've got a couple of dollars in my other shoe. I'll see you in San Francisco.

THE GIRL *(With wonder)* San Francisco?

YOUNG MAN That's right—San Francisco. That's where you and me belong.

THE GIRL I've always wanted to go to *some* place like San Francisco—but how could I go alone?

YOUNG MAN Well, you're not alone any more, see?

THE GIRL Tell me a little what it's like.

YOUNG MAN *(Very swiftly, almost impatiently at first, but gradually slower and with remembrance, smiling, and* THE GIRL *moving closer to him as he speaks)* Well, it's on the Pacific to begin with—ocean water all around. Cool fog and sea-gulls. Ships from all over the world. It's got seven hills. The little streets go up and down, around and all over. Every night the fog-horns bawl. But they won't be bawling for you and me.

THE GIRL What else?

YOUNG MAN That's about all, I guess.

THE GIRL Are people different in San Francisco?

YOUNG MAN People are the same everywhere. They're different only when they love somebody. That's the only thing that makes 'em different. More people in Frisco love somebody, that's all.

THE GIRL Nobody anywhere loves anybody as much as I love you.

YOUNG MAN *(Shouting, as if to the world)* You see? Hearing you say that, a man could die and still be ahead of the game. Now, hurry. And don't forget, if I'm not here when you come back, get the hell to San Francisco where you'll have a chance. Do you hear me? *(*THE GIRL *stands a moment looking at him, then backs away, turns and runs. The* YOUNG MAN *stares after her, troubled and smiling. Then he turns away from the image of her and walks about like a lion in a cage. After a while he sits down suddenly and buries his head in his hands. From a distance the sound of several automobiles approaching is heard. He listens a moment, then ignores the implications of the sound, whatever they may be. Several automobile doors are slammed. He ignores this also. A wooden door is opened with a key and closed, and footsteps are heard in a hall. Walking easily, almost casually and yet arrogantly, a* MAN *comes in. The* YOUNG MAN *jumps up suddenly and shouts at the man, almost scaring him)* What the hell kind of jail-keeper are you, anyway? Why don't you attend to your business? You get paid for it, don't you? Now, get me out of here.

THE MAN   But I'm *not* the jail-keeper.

YOUNG MAN   Yeah, Well, who are you, then?

THE MAN   I'm the husband.

YOUNG MAN   What husband you talking about?

THE MAN   You know what husband.

YOUNG MAN   Hey! *(Pause, looking at* THE MAN*)* Are you the guy that hit me over the head last night?

THE MAN   I am.

YOUNG MAN *(With righteous indignation)*   What do you mean going around hitting people over the head?

THE MAN   Oh, I don't know. What do you *mean* going around—the way you do?

YOUNG MAN *(Rubbing his head)*   You hurt my head. You got no right to hit anybody over the head.

THE MAN *(Suddenly angry, shouting)*   Answer my question! What do you mean?

YOUNG MAN   Listen, you—don't be hollering at me just because I'm locked up.

THE MAN *(With contempt, slowly)*   You're a dog!

YOUNG MAN   Yeah? Well, let me tell you something. You *think* you're the husband. You're the husband of nothing. *(Slowly)* What's more, your wife—if you want to call her that—is a tramp. Why don't you throw her out in the street where she belongs?

THE MAN *(Draws a pistol)*   Shut up!

YOUNG MAN   Yeah? Go ahead, shoot—*(Softly)* and spoil the fun. What'll your pals think? They'll be disappointed, won't they? What's the fun hanging a man who's already dead? *(*THE MAN *puts the gun away.)* That's right, because now you can have some fun yourself, telling me what you're going to do. That's what you came here for, isn't it? Well, you don't need to tell me. I *know* what you're going to do. I've read the papers and I know. They have fun. A mob of 'em fall on one man and beat him, don't they? They tear off his clothes and kick him, don't they? And women and little children stand around watching, don't they? Well, before you go on *this* picnic, I'm going to tell you a few things. Not that that's going to send you home with your pals—the other heroes. No. You've been outraged. A stranger has come to town and violated your women. Your pure, innocent, virtuous women. You fellows have got to set this thing right. You're men, not mice. You're homemakers, and you beat your children. *(Suddenly)* Listen, you—I didn't know she was your wife. I didn't know she was anybody's wife.

THE MAN   You're a liar!

YOUNG MAN   Sometimes—when it'll do somebody some good—but not this time. Do you want to hear about it? *(*THE MAN *doesn't answer.)* All right, I'll tell you. I met her at a lunch counter. She came in and sat next to me. There was plenty of room, but she sat next to me. Somebody had put a nickel in the phonograph and a fellow was singing *New San Antonio Rose.* Well, she got to talking about the song. I thought she was talking to the waiter, but *he* didn't answer her, so after a while *I* answered her. That's how I met her. I didn't think anything of it. We left the place together and started walking. The first thing I knew she said, This is where I live.

THE MAN   You're a dirty liar!

YOUNG MAN   Do you want to hear it? Or not? *(THE MAN does not answer.)* O.K. She asked me to come in. Maybe she had something in mind, maybe she didn't. Didn't make any difference to me, one way or the other. If she was lonely, all right. If not, all right.

THE MAN   You're telling a lot of dirty lies!

YOUNG MAN   I'm telling the truth. Maybe your wife's out there with your pals. Well, call her in. I got nothing against her, or you—or any of you. Call her in, and ask her a few questions. Are you in love with her? *(THE MAN doesn't answer.)* Well, that's too bad.

THE MAN   What do you mean, too bad?

YOUNG MAN   I mean this may not be the first time something like this has happened.

THE MAN   *(Swiftly)* Shut up!

YOUNG MAN   Oh, you know it. You've always known it. You're afraid of your pals, that's all. She asked me for money. That's all she wanted. I wouldn't be here now if I had given her the money.

THE MAN   *(Slowly)* How much did she ask for?

YOUNG MAN   I didn't ask her how much. I told her I'd made a mistake. She said she would make trouble if I didn't give her money. Well, I don't like bargaining, and I don't like being threatened, either. I told her to get the hell away from me. The next thing I knew she'd run out of the house and was hollering. *(Pause)* Now, why don't you go out there and tell 'em they took me to another jail—go home and pack up and leave her. You're a pretty good guy, you're just afraid of your pals. *(THE MAN draws his gun again. He is very frightened. He moves a step toward the YOUNG MAN then fires three times. The YOUNG MAN falls to his knees. THE MAN turns and runs, horrified)* Hello—out there! *(He is bent forward. THE GIRL comes running in, and halts suddenly, looking at him)*

THE GIRL   There were some people in the street, men and women and kids—so I came in through the back, through a window. I couldn't find the gun. I looked all over but I couldn't find it. What's the matter?

YOUNG MAN   Nothing—nothing. Everything's all right. Listen. Listen, kid. Get the hell out of here. Go out the same way you came in and run—run like hell—run all night. Get to another town and get on a train. Do you hear me?

THE GIRL   What's happened?

YOUNG MAN   Get away—just get away from here. Take any train that's going—you can get to Frisco later.

THE GIRL   *(Almost sobbing)* I don't want to go any place without you.

YOUNG MAN   I can't go. Something's happened. *(He looks at her)* But I'll be with you always—God damn it. Always!

(He falls forward. THE GIRL stands near him, then begins to sob softly, walking away. She stands over to one side, stops sobbing, and stares out. The excitement of the mob

outside increases. THE MAN, *with two of his pals, comes running in.* THE GIRL *watches, unseen)*

THE MAN Here's the son of a bitch!
ANOTHER MAN O.K. Open the cell, Harry.

(The THIRD MAN *goes to the cell door, unlocks it, and swings it open.)*

(A WOMAN *comes running in.)*

THE WOMAN Where is he? I want to see him. Is he dead? *(Looking down at him, as the* MEN *pick him up)* There he is. *(Pause)* Yeah, that's him. *(Her husband looks at her with contempt, then at the dead man.)*
THE MAN *(Trying to laugh)* All right—let's get it over with.
THIRD MAN Right you are, George. Give me a hand, Harry. *(They lift the body)*
THE GIRL *(Suddenly, fiercely)* Put him down!
THE MAN What's this?
SECOND MAN What are you doing here? Why aren't you out in the street?
THE GIRL Put him down and go away. *(She runs toward the* MEN. THE WOMAN *grabs her.)*
THE WOMAN Here—where do you think *you're* going?
THE GIRL Let me go. You've got no right to take him away.
THE WOMAN Well, listen to her, will you? *(She slaps* THE GIRL *and pushes her to the floor.)* Listen to the little slut, will you?

(They all go, carrying the YOUNG MAN'S *body.* THE GIRL *gets up slowly, no longer sobbing. She looks around at everything, then looks straight out, and whispers.)*

THE GIRL Hello—out—there! Hello—out there!

QUESTIONS

1 Why does the Young Man compulsively reiterate "Hello out there" not only at the beginning of, but also throughout the play? Do you think The Girl has been waiting for such a seemingly cryptic communication?

2 How do you interpret the Young Man's quickly informing The Girl that she is "a pretty kid" (though Saroyan informs us that "She is a plain girl in plain clothes"), proposing marriage, and promising to take her to "San Francisco or some place like that"? Can these seemingly hasty developments be interpreted as his imaginative perception that neither her native Matador nor his jail cell adequately defines the possibilities of their being?

3 How is the dialogue between the outraged husband (The Man) and the Young Man related to the earlier dialogue of the Young Man and The Girl? Is The Man also a "displaced" person? And does his shooting of the Young Man suggest that he too has gained insight into the inadequacies of "place"?

4 Is the ending of the play, in your opinion, the only really satisfactory solution to the conflict of values? Are the mob also trying to assert their sense of "a place in society"?

TOPICS FOR COMPOSITION

1 Collect all the references to "place" in the play and analyze their relationships and contrasts. Try to find a scheme of classification that will link all the characters to a "place"—not only two small towns in Texas or a celebrated city in California but also more abstract, perhaps even nebulous, human associations with a sense of "place."

2 Compare and contrast the situations of the Young Man and The Girl. Are both the prisoners of a society that tries to circumscribe or to legislate the individual's "search for a place"?

3 Argue for or against the possible proposition that Saroyan suggests symbolic identification of geographical locations with human experience and aspiration.

POETRY

The need for a place in society, because it is part of a larger, very complex need for orientation, finds expression in many ways, as the following poems will amply demonstrate. It is indeed not easy to generalize about a group of works that vary as much in perspective as these do; yet it is possible to make comparisons among them which illuminate their common theme—and at the same time illustrate the range of poetic vision. It is admittedly a far cry, for example, from Alexander Pope's relatively calm reflections on social principles to the powerfully emotional response to social injustice which we find in Claude McKay's "The White House." Yet the larger perspective offered by Pope's discourse should make it easier for us to sympathize with McKay's speaker and to reflect upon the possible social consequences of such angry defiance. And our ultimate emotional response to "The White House," a sense of pity mingled with respect, should in turn make us more receptive to Pope's reasoned optimism. At least we may be led to think what a blessing it would be if self-love and social love should come to be the same, as Pope predicts. Thus our response to each of these works is complicated and enriched by comparison.

Comparison of poems from different periods, moreover, will provide useful historical perspective and food for thought about the effects of changing social conditions. The passage from Shakespeare, for example, reflects almost implicit belief in the necessity of a stable, hierarchical social structure; Pope speaks for the so-called Age of Reason, when faith in rational control of the self and society was in the ascendant; Whitman's "Crossing Brooklyn Ferry" voices the later Romantic hope that imaginative sympathy or a mystical sense of the vital unity of all things would make possible a feeling of free participation that reason alone could not give; Arnold's "A Summer Night," on the other hand, reveals a Romantic sense of alienation which has in some quarters persisted up to the present—we see it in Yeats's "A Prayer for My Daughter," for example, along with some wise reflections upon how it can be overcome, how a place in society may be created even in contentious times. The various contemporary poems, then, will help us to analyze in some depth the special conditions that nowadays affect the search for self-fulfillment through social participation. In reading some of them we should perhaps have uppermost in our minds Matthew Arnold's dictum concerning humanism, since humanism is probably the strongest moral force in operation in current civilization. Arnold says:

> And because men are members of one great whole, and the sympathy which is in human nature will not allow one member to be indifferent to the rest or to have a perfect welfare independent of the rest, the expansion of our humanity, to suit the idea of perfection which culture forms, must be a *general* expansion. Perfection, as culture conceives it, is not possible while the individual remains isolated. The individual is required, under pain of being stunted and enfeebled in his own development if he

disobeys, to carry others along with him in his march towards perfection, to be continually doing all he can to enlarge and increase the volume of the human stream sweeping thitherward.

Once again, it must not be forgotten that these poems can provide not only ideas to be developed or analyzed but also much insight into the nature of language and effective communication. As writers, we would do well to compare carefully the ways in which these poets achieve perspective, emphasis, and unity of thought and tone.

THE WANDERER

Anonymous—translated by Melvin G. Storm

The lonely man ever longs for kindness,
For the mercy of God, but, sorrowing at heart,
He long must row over the rime-cold sea,
He must follow the exile's path, for his fate is firm.
    Mindful of woes, remembering cruel slaughters,   5
Bereft of his kinsmen, thus said the Wanderer:
    "I am bound in the cold of the mornings to lament
My cares alone. No one now lives
To hold in common trust the thoughts of my heart.
I have found it a truth that the noblest warrior   10
Binds fast his feelings, veils his pains,
Locks his sorrows secret in his soul.
    "The soul that is weary is slave to fate;
Fate holds the troubled heart in thrall:
Therefore men eager for glory—though often mournful—   15
Sorrow in silence, conceal their cares.
So then must I, wretched and homeless
And far from kinsmen, fetter my mood;
For long ago, to the grave's dark keeping
I lost my lord, my treasure-giver   20
And set out, sorrowful as winter
To seek the hearth of a friendly chief,
One whose mead-hall would offer me haven,
Whose folk would comfort my heart with friendship.
But cruel sorrow ever walks with the exile,   25
His only mate when his loved friends are gone.
He is held by the turns of the trail he wanders

1: The speaker was, in the days whose passing he laments, a thane, a member of the bodyguard of a lord or king; no social relationship was more highly valued in Anglo-Saxon culture. *23 mead-hall:* the meeting places of the lords and their thanes. Mead is beer made from honey.

And not by the twistings of bright wound gold;
He knows but the frost in his heart, not the fruits of the earth.
Often he remembers jolly companions, the joy of gifts,   30
Remembers his fallow boyhood, when his lord taught him to feast:
All fallen away! He who has long been lonely knows
How often sorrow and sleep join to deceive
And bind in dreams the grieving lone-dweller:
In his mind then he sees his master; he imagines   35
The embrace of happy greeting—sits at his feet
Before the gift-seat in a summer of gladness.
But then the friendless, lordless warrior wakes,
Sees before him only the winter sea-ways—
The sea-birds fold their feathers, dive, and soar again   40
And the hard sky mingles snow with hail.
Then he feels the heart's heavy wound,
Pressed by longing for love, renew its pain
When memories of kinsmen tease his mind.
He smiles at imagined faces,   45
Eagerly greets with joyful welcoming words
The mist-made friends that ever float away
And speak no words in answer. Sorrow is full
To him who sends too often soaring
His weary heart back over the sea in dreams.   50
   "No wonder, then, if I should grieve,
If my spirit should bow to bitter darkness,
When I consider the sad lives of the most courageous—
How quickly they desert the hall in death.
This earth decays: daily it further dies and wastes away.   55
But the wise man needs his winters;
Weary, he barters seasons of pain for wisdom.
He learns the price of patience: learns he must be
Neither too hot of heart nor too hasty of speech,
Nor too frail in battle, nor too overbold,   60
Nor too much a coward, nor too glad, nor too greedy,
Nor too eager to speak in boast before knowing success,
Before seeing the thoughts of his heart take shape in deeds.
   "The wise man finds how fleeting is the world,
Knows how the wealth of earth will waste,   65
As even now throughout this freezing land
Walls stand wind-blown,
Storm-beaten dead dwellings in shrouds of frost.
The wine-halls crumble, lords sleep
In dreamless death; the war-troops have fallen   70
Brave by the wall: battle took many;
One was borne off in pieces by birds

Over the high waves; one fell prey
To the grey wolf's plunder; a sad-faced friend
Covered one in a cave of earth.   75
Thus the Creator of men laid waste his creation,
Relentlessly silenced the sounds of its people,
Made the works of the giants of old stand empty.
    "The one who wisely sees these foundations, wasted walls,
Remembers from distant days cruel deaths,   80
Deeply considers this dark life, and says,
'Where is the horse? Where is the man? Where is the chief?
Where are the feast-seats? Where are the joys of the feasting?
Alas the bright cup! Alas the warrior brilliant in armor!
Alas the prince's power! Those times have passed,   85
Grown dark under night's cloud, as if they never were.
Where stood loved warriors stand now walls alone,
Wondrously high, adorned with serpent shapes.
Ashen spears, ravenous for slaughter,
Took off the earls: hard fate felled them.   90
And now storms beat these cliffs,
Snow binds the earth;
Night shadows darken, and dread winter
Sends from the north fierce hail-showers against men.
    "'Earth's kingdom teems with hardship;   95
Fate changes always the world under heaven.
Here goods vanish, here friends die,
Here men and kinsmen forever pass away,
And fate drains empty the world itself.' "
Thus spoke the man wise in soul, who sat musing apart.   100
He is good who keeps faith and binds fast his distress,
Who reveals not his pain unless he know remedy.
Men longing for mercy must look from the world
And seek help in our heavenly Father, in whom is all strength.

                                            Ca. eighth century

90 earls: warriors.

QUESTIONS

1   This dramatic monologue underscores some of the advantages and disadvantages
    of a small, tightly knit society. What are some of these?
2   Are there in our time any groups that offer social relationships comparable to those
    described in this poem?
3   Does there appear to be, in the culture represented here, a close causal relation-
    ship between social values and religious belief? Would you want to make any gen-
    eralizations on this subject?

ULYSSES' SPEECH ON DEGREE
FROM
TROILUS AND CRESSIDA, I, iii, 75–137

William Shakespeare

Troy, yet upon his basis, had been down,
And the great Hector's sword had lacked a master,
But for these instances.
The specialty of rule hath been neglected.
And look how many Grecian tents do stand   5
Hollow upon this plain, so many hollow factions.
When that the general is not like the hive
To whom the foragers shall all repair,
What honey is expected? Degree being vizarded,
The unworthiest shows as fairly in the mask.   10
The heavens themselves, the planets and this center,
Observe degree, priority, and place,
Insisture, course, proportion, season, form,
Office and custom, in all line of order.
And therefore is the glorious planet Sol   15
In noble eminence enthroned and sphered
Amidst the other, whose medicinable eye
Corrects the ill aspects of planets evil,
And posts like the commandment of a king,
Sans check to good and bad. But when the planets   20
In evil mixture to disorder wander,
What plagues and what portents, what mutiny,
What raging of the sea, shaking of earth,
Commotion in the winds, frights, changes, horrors,
Divert and crack, rend and deracinate,   25
The unity and married calm of states
Quite from their fixture! Oh, when degree is shaked,
Which is the ladder to all high designs,
The enterprise is sick! How could communities
Degrees in schools and brotherhoods in cities,   30
Peaceful commerce from dividable shores,
The primogenitive and due of birth,
Prerogative of age, crowns, scepters, laurels,
But by degree, stand in authentic place?

1: Ulysses is explaining to the Greeks that they have failed to capture Troy because their leader, Agamemnon, has lost his authority. *3 instances:* reasons. *4 rule:* discipline. *9 Degree being vizarded:* rank being obscured, as by a mask. *11 center:* the earth. *13 Insisture:* regularity. *14 Office:* function; *in all line of order:* according to degree of importance. *18:* controls their positions, upon which their influence depended. *25 deracinate:* uproot. *27 fixture:* established place. *32 primogenitive:* the right of the oldest son to inheritance.

Take but degree away, untune that string, 35
And hark what discord follows! Each thing meets
In mere oppugnancy. The bounded waters
Should lift their bosoms higher than the shores,
And make a sop of all this solid globe.
Strength should be lord of imbecility, 40
And the rude son should strike his father dead.
Force should be right, or rather, right and wrong,
Between whose endless jar justice resides,
Should lose their names, and so should justice too.
Then everything includes itself in power, 45
Power into will, will into appetite,
And appetite, a universal wolf,
So doubly seconded with will and power,
Must make perforce a universal prey,
And last eat up himself. Great Agamemnon, 50
This chaos, when degree is suffocate,
Follows the choking.

37 oppugnancy: complete opposition.   *40 imbecility:* weakness.

QUESTIONS

1   What forces, according to Ulysses, come into play when "degree" is neglected?
2   Note the examples of degree mentioned by Ulysses. What kinds of rank or authority
    are most important in our time?
3   Ulysses urges that hierarchical order is the law of nature. How does our conception
    of rightful authority differ?
4   Would people feel more secure if various kinds of authority or distinction were more
    closely defined? Would they be more ambitious, assuming that it was possible to
    rise to higher "places"? Would they be happier, on the whole?

AN ESSAY ON MAN, EPISTLE III, 269–319

Alexander Pope

So drives self-love, through just and through unjust,
To one man's power, ambition, lucre, lust:
The same self-love, in all, becomes the cause
Of what restrains him, government and laws.
For, what one likes if others like as well, 5
What serves one will, when many wills rebel?

1-2: The poet has explained that when reason is obscured by fear, self-love leads to tyranny and
conflict, despite the lesson of interdependence taught by nature.

How shall he keep, what, sleeping or awake,
A weaker may surprise, a stronger take?
His safety must his liberty restrain;
All join to guard what each desires to gain.   10
Forced into virtue thus by self-defence,
Even kings learned justice and benevolence;
Self-love forsook the path it first pursued,
And found the private in the public good.
       'Twas then the studious head or generous mind,   15
Follower of God or friend of humankind,
Poet or patriot, rose but to restore
The faith and moral nature gave before;
Re-lumed her ancient light, not kindled new;
If not God's image, yet his shadow drew;   20
Taught power's due use to people and to kings
Taught nor to slack, nor strain its tender strings;
The less, or greater, set so justly true,
That touching one must strike the other too;
Till jarring interests of themselves create   25
The according music of a well-mixed state.
Such is the world's great harmony, that springs
From order, union, full consent of things;
Where small and great, where weak and mighty, made
To serve, not suffer, strengthen, not invade—   30
More powerful each as needful to the rest,
And, in proportion as it blesses, blessed—
Draw to one point, and to one centre bring
Beast, man, or angel, servant, lord, or king.
       For forms of government let fools contest;   35
Whate'er is best administered is best:
For modes of faith let graceless zealots fight;
His can't be wrong whose life is in the right:
In faith and hope the world will disagree,
But all mankind's concern is charity: 40
All must be false that thwart this one great end
And all of God, that bless mankind or mend.
       Man, like the generous vine, supported lives;
The strength he gains is from the embrace he gives.
On their own axis as the planets run,   45
Yet make at once their circle round the sun;
So two consistent motions act the soul,
And one regards itself, and one the whole.
       Thus God and nature linked the general frame,
And bade self-love and social be the same.   50

1733–1734

QUESTIONS

1 Pope's subject here is social love. What is his thesis? What is his argument?
2 Does Pope indicate precisely enough how social love will express itself? Do you find his definition of love adequate?
3 Consider the structure of this passage. What is the function of the paragraphing? Does each paragraph have a new idea to present? Does each paragraph have a special purpose?
4 Are there any features of Pope's style that might be effective in prose writing? Be able to point out at least one.

A SUMMER NIGHT

Matthew Arnold

In the deserted, moon-blanched street,
How lonely rings the echo of my feet!
Those windows, which I gaze at, frown,
Silent and white, unopening down,
Repellent as the world—but see,   5
A break between the housetops shows
The moon! and, lost behind her, fading dim
Into the dewy dark obscurity
Down at the far horizon's rim,
Doth a whole tract of heaven disclose!   10

And to my mind the thought
Is on a sudden brought
Of a past night, and a far different scene.
Headlands stood out into the moonlit deep
As clearly as at noon;   15
The spring-tide's brimming flow
Heaved dazzlingly between;
Houses, with long white sweep,
Girdled the glistening bay;
Behind, through the soft air,   20
The blue haze-cradled mountains spread away.
That night was far more fair—
But the same restless pacings to and fro,
And the same vainly throbbing heart was there,
And the same bright, calm moon.   25

And the calm moonlight seems to say:
Hast thou then still the old unquiet breast,

Which neither deadens into rest,
Nor ever feels the fiery glow
That whirls the spirit from itself away,   30
But fluctuates to and fro,
Never by passion quite possessed
And never quite benumbed by the world's sway?—
And I, I know not if to pray
Still to be what I am, or yield and be   35
Like all the other men I see.

For most men in a brazen prison live,
Where, in the sun's hot eye,
With heads bent o'er their toil, they languidly
Their lives to some unmeaning taskwork give,   40
Dreaming of naught beyond their prison-wall.
And as, year after year,
Fresh products of their barren labor fall
From their tired hands, and rest
Never yet comes more near,   45
Gloom settles slowly down over their breast;
And while they try to stem
The waves of mournful thought by which they are prest
Death in their prison reaches them,
Unfreed, having seen nothing, still unblest.   50

And the rest, a few,
Escape their prison and depart
On the wide ocean of life anew.
There the freed prisoner, where'er his heart
Listeth, will sail;   55
Nor doth he know how there prevail,
Despotic on that sea,
Trade-winds which cross it from eternity.
Awhile he holds some false way, undebarred
By thwarting signs, and braves   60
The freshening wind and blackening waves,
And then the tempest strikes him; and between
The lightning-bursts is seen
Only a driving wreck,
And the pale master on his spar-strewn deck   65
With anguished face and flying hair
Grasping the rudder hard,
Still bent to make some port he knows not where,

33 sway: control.

Still standing for some false, impossible shore.
And sterner comes the roar   70
Of sea and wind, and through the deepening gloom
Fainter and fainter wreck and helmsman loom,
And he too disappears, and comes no more.

Is there no life, but these alone?
Madman or slave, must man be one?   75

Plainness and clearness without shadow of stain!
Clearness divine!
Ye heavens, whose pure dark regions have no sign
Of languor, though so calm, and, though so great,
Are yet untroubled and unpassionate;   80
Who, though so noble, share in the world's toil,
And, though so tasked, keep free from dust and soil!
I will not say that your mild deeps retain
A tinge, it may be, of their silent pain
Who have longed deeply once, and longed in vain—   85
But I will rather say that you remain
A world above man's head, to let him see
How boundless might his soul's horizons be,
How vast, yet of what clear transparency!
How it were good to abide there, and breathe free;   90
How fair a lot to fill
Is left to each man still!

                                        1852

QUESTIONS

1 The reflections in this poem might be said to revolve around the poet's idea of "the world's sway"—the effect upon the individual spirit of submission to the control of society. This effect is described metaphorically in lines 51–73. Is there anything in your experience of society that would help you if you were asked to explain what the poet is talking about?
2 What, in the poet's view, are the alternatives to submission to the world's sway? What is his own position?
3 Why does the poet use so much sky imagery? What effect does his contemplation of celestial bodies have finally upon his state of mind?

CROSSING BROOKLYN FERRY

Walt Whitman

1
Flood-tide below me! I see you face to face!
Clouds of the west—sun there half an hour high—I see you also face to face.

Crowds of men and women attired in the usual costumes, how curious you
    are to me!
On the ferry-boats the hundreds and hundreds that cross, returning home, are
    more curious to me than you suppose,
And you that shall cross from shore to shore years hence are more to me,
    and more in my meditations, than you might suppose.   5

2
The impalpable sustenance of me from all things at all hours of the day,
The simple, compact, well-join'd scheme, myself disintegrated, every one
    disintegrated yet part of the scheme.
The similitudes of the past and those of the future,
The glories strung like beads on my smallest sights and hearings, on the walk
    in the street and the passage over the river,
The current rushing so swiftly and swimming with me far away,   10
The others that are to follow me, the ties between me and them,
The certainty of others, the life, love, sight, hearing of others.

Others will enter the gates of the ferry and cross from shore to shore,
Others will watch the run of the flood-tide,
Others will see the shipping of Manhattan north and west, and the heights of
    Brooklyn to the south and east,   15
Others will see the islands large and small;
Fifty years hence, others will see them as they cross, the sun half an hour high,
A hundred years hence, or ever so many hundred years hence, others will
    see them,
Will enjoy the sunset, the pouring-in of the flood-tide, the falling-back to the
    sea of the ebb-tide.

3
It avails not, time nor place—distance avails not,   20
I am with you, you men and women of a generation, or ever so many
    generations hence,
Just as you feel when you look on the river and sky, so I felt,
Just as any of you is one of a living crowd, I was one of a crowd,
Just as you are refresh'd by the gladness of the river and the bright flow, I was
    refresh'd,

Just as you stand and lean on the rail, yet hurry with the swift current, I stood
    yet was hurried,   25
Just as you look on the numberless masts of ships and the thick-stemm'd
    pipes of steamboats, I look'd.

I too many and many a time cross'd the river of old,
Watched the Twelfth-month sea-gulls, saw them high in the air floating with
    motionless wings, oscillating their bodies,
Saw how the glistening yellow lit up parts of their bodies and left the rest
    in strong shadow,
Saw the slow-wheeling circles and the gradual edging toward the south,   30
Saw the reflection of the summer sky in the water,
Had my eyes dazzled by the shimmering track of beams,
Look'd at the fine centrifugal spokes of light round the shape of my head in
    the sunlit water,
Look'd on the haze on the hills southward and south-westward,
Look'd on the vapor as it flew in fleeces tinged with violet,   35
Look'd toward the lower bay to notice the vessels arriving,
Saw their approach, saw aboard those that were near me,
Saw the white sails of schooners and sloops, saw the ships at anchor,
The sailors at work in the rigging or out astride the spars,
The round masts, the swinging motion of the hulls, the slender serpentine
    pennants,   40
The large and small steamers in motion, the pilots in their pilot-houses,
The white wake left by the passage, the quick tremulous whirl of the wheels,
The flags of all nations, the falling of them at sunset,
The scallop-edged waves in the twilight, the ladled cups, the frolicsome crests
    and glistening,
The stretch afar growing dimmer and dimmer, the gray walls of the granite
    storehouses by the docks,   45
On the river the shadowy group, the big steam-tug closely flank'd on each side
    by the barges, the hay-boat, the belated lighter,
On the neighboring shore the fires from the foundry chimneys burning high and
    glaringly into the night,
Casting their flicker of black contrasted with wild red and yellow light over
    the tops of houses and down into the clefts of streets.

4
These and all else were to me the same as they are to you,
I loved well those cities, loved well the stately and rapid river,   50
The men and women I saw were all near to me,
Others the same—others who look back on me because I look'd forward
    to them,
(The time will come, though I stop here to-day and to-night.)

5

What is it then between us?
What is the count of the scores or hundreds of years between us?   55

Whatever it is, it avails not—distance avails not, and place avails not,
I too lived, Brooklyn of ample hills was mine,
I too walk'd the streets of Manhattan island, and bathed in the waters around
  it,
I too felt the curious abrupt questionings stir within me,
In the day among crowds of people sometimes they came upon me   60
In my walks home late at night or as ! lay in my bed they came upon me,
I too had been struck from the float forever held in solution,
I too had receiv'd identity by my body,
That I was I knew was of my body, and what I should be I knew I should be
  of my body.

6

It is not upon you alone the dark patches fall,   65
The dark threw its patches down upon me also,
The best I had done seem'd to me blank and suspicious,
My great thoughts as I supposed them, were they not in reality meagre?
Nor is it you alone who knew what it is to be evil,
I am he who knew what it was to be evil,   70
I too knitted the old knot of contrariety,
Blabb'd, blush'd, resented, lied, stole, grudg'd,
Had guile, anger, lust, hot wishes I dared not speak,
Was wayward, vain, greedy, shallow, sly, cowardly, malignant,
The wolf, the snake, the hog, not wanting in me,   75
The cheating look, the frivolous word, the adulterous wish, not wanting,
Refusals, hates, postponements, meanness, laziness, none of these wanting,
Was one with the rest, the days and haps of the rest,
Was call'd my nighest name by clear loud voices of young men as they saw
  me approaching or passing,
Felt their arms on my neck as I stood, or the negligent leaning of their flesh
  against me as I sat,   80
Saw many I loved in the street or ferry-boat or public assembly, yet never told
  them a word,
Lived the same life with the rest, the same old laughing, gnawing, sleeping,
Play'd the part that still looks back on the actor or actress,
The same old role, the role that is what we make it, as great as we like,
Or as small as we like, or both great and small.   85

62 float: dissolved substance.   *78 haps:* happenings.

7

Closer yet I approach you,
What thought you have of me now, I had as much of you—I laid in my stores
    in advance,
I consider'd long and seriously of you before you were born.
Who was to know what should come home to me?
Who knows but I am enjoying this?   90
Who knows, for all the distance, but I am as good as looking at you now, for
    all you cannot see me?

8

Ah, what can ever be more stately and admirable to me than mast-hemm'd
    Manhattan?
River and sunset and scallop-edg'd waves of flood-tide?
The sea-gulls oscillating their bodies, the hay-boat in the twilight, and the
    belated lighter?

What gods can exceed these that clasp me by the hand, and with voices I love
    call me promptly and loudly by my nighest name as I approach?   95

What is more subtle than this which ties me to the woman or man that looks
    in my face?

Which fuses me into you now, and pours my meaning into you?

We understand then do we not?
What I promis'd without mentioning it, have you not accepted?
What the study could not teach—what the preaching could not accomplish
    is accomplish'd, is it not?   100

9

Flow on, river! flow with the flood-tide, and ebb with the ebb-tide!
Frolic on, crested and scallop-edg'd waves!
Gorgeous clouds of the sunset! drench with your splendor me, or the men and
    women generations after me!
Cross from shore to shore, countless crowds of passengers!
Stand up, tall masts of Mannahatta! stand up, beautiful hills of Brooklyn!   105
Throb, baffled and curious brain! throw out questions and answers!
Suspend here and everywhere, eternal float of solution!
Gaze, loving and thirsting eyes, in the house or street or public assembly!
Sound out, voices of young men! loudly and musically call me by my nighest
    name!
Live, old life! play the part that looks back on the actor or actress!   110
Play the old role, the role that is great or small according as one makes it!

Consider, you who peruse me, whether I may not in unknown ways be looking
    upon you;
Be firm, rail over the river, to support those who lean idly, yet haste with the
    hasting current;
Fly on, sea-birds! fly sideways, or wheel in large circles high in the air;
Receive the summer sky, you water, and faithfully hold it till all downcast eyes
    have time to take it from you!

                                                                                      115

Diverge, fine spokes of light, from the shape of my head, or any one's head,
    in the sunlit water!
Come on, ships from the lower bay! pass up or down, white-sail'd schooners,
    sloops, lighters!
Flaunt away, flags of all nations! be duly lower'd at sunset!
Burn high your fires, foundry chimneys! cast black shadows at nightfall! cast
    red and yellow light over the tops of the houses!
Appearances, now or henceforth, indicate what you are,   120
You necessary film, continue to envelop the soul,
About my body for me, and your body for you, be hung our divinest aromas,
Thrive, cities—bring your freight, bring your shows, ample and sufficient rivers,
Expand, being than which none else is perhaps more spiritual,
Keep your places, objects than which none else is more lasting.   125

You have waited, you always wait, you dumb, beautiful ministers,
We receive you with free sense at last, and are insatiate henceforward,
Not you any more shall be able to foil us, or withhold yourselves from us,
We use you,—and do not cast you aside—we plant you permanently within us,
We fathom you not—we love you—there is perfection in you also,   130
You furnish your parts toward eternity,
Great or small, you furnish your parts toward the soul.

                                                            1856–1881

QUESTIONS

1 To whom is the poet speaking?
2 What are the bonds that unite the speaker to other people?
3 What are the two principal metaphors used to describe individual existence? What
   do they mean? How are they related?
4 What is the speaker's view of the relation between the human spirit and the things
   of nature?
5 Why does the poet use so much repetition in the last part of the poem?

A PRAYER FOR MY DAUGHTER

William Butler Yeats

Once more the storm is howling, and half hid
Under this cradle-hood and coverlid
My child sleeps on. There is no obstacle
But Gregory's wood and one bare hill
Whereby the haystack- and roof-leveling wind,   5
Bred on the Atlantic, can be stayed;
And for an hour I have walked and prayed
Because of the great gloom that is in my mind.

I have walked and prayed for this young child an hour
And heard the sea-wind scream upon the tower,   10
And under the arches of the bridge, and scream
In the elms above the flooded stream;
Imagining in excited reverie
That the future years had come,
Dancing to a frenzied drum,   15
Out of the murderous innocence of the sea.

May she be granted beauty and yet not
Beauty to make a stranger's eye distraught,
Or hers before a looking glass, for such,
Being made beautiful overmuch,   20
Consider beauty a sufficient end,
Lose natural kindness and maybe
The heart-revealing intimacy
That chooses right, and never find a friend.

Helen being chosen found life flat and dull   25
And later had much trouble from a fool,
While that great Queen, that rose out of the spray,
Being fatherless could have her way
Yet chose a bandy-leggéd smith for man.
It's certain that fine women eat   30
A crazy salad with their meat
Whereby the Horn of Plenty is undone.

In courtesy I'd have her chiefly learned;
Hearts are not had as a gift but hearts are earned
By those that are not entirely beautiful;   35
Yet many, that have played the fool
For beauty's very self, has charm made wise,

And many a poor man that has roved,
Loved and thought himself beloved,
From a glad kindness cannot take his eyes.   40

May she become a flourishing hidden tree
That all her thoughts may like the linnet be,
And have no business but dispensing round
Their magnanimities of sound,
Nor but in merriment begin a chase,   45
Nor but in merriment a quarrel.
O may she live like some green laurel
Rooted in one dear perpetual place.

My mind, because the minds that I have loved,
The sort of beauty that I have approved,   50
Prosper but little, has dried up of late,
Yet knows that to be choked with hate
May well be of all evil chances chief.
If there's no hatred in a mind
Assault and battery of the wind   55
Can never tear the linnet from the leaf.

An intellectual hatred is the worst,
So let her think opinions are accursed.
Have I not seen the loveliest woman born
Out of the mouth of Plenty's horn,   60
Because of her opinionated mind
Barter that horn and every good
By quiet natures understood
For an old bellows full of angry wind?

Considering that, all hatred driven hence,   65
The soul recovers radical innocence
And learns at last that it is self-delighting,
Self-appeasing, self-affrighting,
And that its own sweet will is Heaven's will;
She can, though every face should scowl   70
And every windy quarter howl
Or every bellows burst, be happy still.

And may her bridegroom bring her to a house
Where all's accustomed, ceremonious;
For arrogance and hatred are the wares   75
Peddled in the thoroughfares.

How but in custom and in ceremony
Are innocence and beauty born?
Ceremony's a name for the rich horn,
And custom for the spreading laurel tree.

1919

QUESTIONS

1   What is meant by "the murderous innocence of the sea"? With what is the sea wind connected? Is innocence meant to suggest mindlessness?
2   The poet asserts in lines 77 and 78 that custom and ceremony give birth to innocence. Is he using "innocence" in a different sense here?

A SUMMER NIGHT, 1933

W. H. Auden

(To Geoffrey Hoyland)

Out on the lawn I lie in bed,
Vega conspicuous overhead
  In the windless nights of June,
As congregated leaves complete
Their day's activity; my feet   5
  Point to the rising moon.

Lucky, this point in time and space
Is chosen as my working-place,
  Where the sexy airs of summer,
The bathing hours and the bare arms,   10
The leisured drives through a land of farms
  Are good to the newcomer.

Equal with colleagues in a ring
I sit on each calm evening
  Enchanted as the flowers   15
The opening light draws out of hiding
With all its gradual dove-like pleading,
  Its logic and its powers

2 Vega: the brightest star in the constellation Lyra.

That later we, though parted then,
May still recall these evenings when   20
    Fear gave his watch no look;
The lion griefs loped from the shade
And on our knees their muzzles laid,
    And Death put down his book.

Now north and south and east and west   25
Those I love lie down to rest;
    The moon looks on them all,
The healers and the brilliant talkers
The eccentrics and the silent walkers,
    The dumpy and the tall.   30

She climbs the European sky,
Churches and power-station lie
    Alike among earth's fixtures:
Into the galleries she peers
And blankly as a butcher stares   35
    Upon the marvellous pictures.

To gravity attentive, she
Can notice nothing here, though we
    Whom hunger does not move,
From gardens where we feel secure   40
Look up and with a sigh endure
    The tyrannies of love:

And, gentle, do not care to know,
Where Poland draws her eastern bow,
    What violence is done,   45
Nor ask what doubtful act allows
Our freedom in this English house,
    Our picnics in the sun.

Soon, soon, through dykes of our content
The crumpling flood will force a rent   50
    And, taller than a tree,
Hold sudden death before our eyes
Whose river dreams long hid the size
    And vigours of the sea.

44 Poland was in 1933 a focal point of the international tensions that finally were resolved by
World War II.

But when the waters make retreat   55
And through the black mud first the wheat
     In shy green stalks appears,
When stranded monsters gasping lie,
And sounds of riveting terrify
     Their whorled unsubtle ears,   60

May these delights we dread to lose,
This privacy, need no excuse
     But to that strength belong,
As through a child's rash happy cries
The drowned parental voices rise   65
     In unlamenting song.

After discharges of alarm
All unpredicted let them calm
     The pulse of nervous nations,
Forgive the murderer in his glass,   70
Tough in their patience to surpass
     The tigress her swift motions.

                              1936

70 The phrase "the murderer in his glass" probably has reference to lines 34–36.

QUESTIONS

1   This poem, of course, is pervaded by an awareness of impending large-scale social
    catastrophe such as many people still dread; yet the speaker, as it seems, manages
    to reconcile himself to this terrible circumstance. Would you call him an escapist, or
    not?
2   The poet here uses an almost chaotic variety of metaphors. Can you think of any
    reason for his doing so?

THE WHITE HOUSE

Claude McKay

Your door is shut against my tightened face,
And I am sharp as steel with discontent;
But I possess the courage and the grace
To bear my anger proudly and unbent.
The pavement slabs burn loose beneath my feet,   5
And passion rends my vitals as I pass,
A chafing savage, down the decent street,
Where boldly shines your shuttered door of glass.
Oh, I must search for wisdom every hour,
Deep in my wrathful bosom sore and raw,   10
And find in it the superhuman power
To hold me to the letter of your law!
Oh, I must keep my heart inviolate
Against the poison of your deadly hate.

1953

QUESTIONS

1   Claude McKay was a black poet. What does the title of the poem mean? Could it
have more than one meaning?
2   The speaker struggles to maintain "grace." What does the effort involve?

COLD-WATER FLAT

Philip Booth

      Come to conquer
this living labyrinth of rock,
      young Theseus of Dubuque
finds he is mazed without a minotaur,
without his Ariadne in the dark.   5

      He dreams beyond
his steelwalled fear to fields grown
      vertical with corn
and hope. Home to this heroic end:
imprisoned in the city of alone;   10

here smog obscures
his visionary victor's world
   and street sounds dulled
with rain reverberate in airshaft hours
where braver conquerors have been felled.   15

   Amazed at night,
stalking the seven maids no sword
   can save, he is devoured
in passageways of reinforced concrete,
trapped by his beast, and overpowered   20

   in sleepless dead-
end dreams. How now, Theseus? How send
   word home you are confined
with neither wings nor lover's thread
in the city that a murderer designed?   25

                 1955

Cold-Water Flat: The poet alludes repeatedly to the following mythic story of the encounter between the Athenian hero Theseus and a monster called the Minotaur. Minos, the ruler of Crete, whose son had perished in an expedition undertaken while he, as a guest of Aegeus, King of Athens, had conquered Athens and demanded that a tribute of seven Athenian maids and seven youths be sent to him every nine years. When the young people reached Crete, they were placed in an inescapable labyrinth, built by the great inventor Daedalus, there to be devoured by the fabulous Minotaur, who was half human, half bull. When he was old enough, Theseus, who was the son of Aegeus, volunteered to be one of the victims, intending to slay the Minotaur by one means or another. By good fortune, Ariadne, the daughter of Minos, saw Theseus when he and the others were paraded toward the labyrinth, and fell in love with him. She sent for him and promised that she would help him escape from the labyrinth if he would promise to take her to Athens and marry her. Upon his readily agreeing, she gave him a device which she had procured from Daedalus himself, a ball of thread. As he was instructed, Theseus fastened one end of the thread by the inside of the door and unwound the ball as he went boldly into the maze to seek out the Minotaur. He found the monster asleep, fell upon him, and battered him to death with his fists. Then he retraced his steps with the aid of the thread, the other intended victims following him. Once outside, they fled quickly to their ship, taking Ariadne with them, and set sail for Athens.

QUESTIONS

1 Reconstruct the story upon which this poem is based. Who is "young Theseus of Dubuque"? Why did he leave Dubuque? What has happened to him?
2 What is the general purpose of the comparison between the young man from Dubuque and Theseus? Do any of the details of that comparison have a special significance?

A BIRD IN SEARCH OF A CAGE

Robert Pack

Said the bird in search of a cage,
This world is even large for wings,
The mindless seasons drive me down
Tormenting me with changing things.

A cage is not escape, but need,   5
And though once in all travel's done,
I'll sing so every bird will know
My wanderings in moon and sun,

And all the crickets will be stilled,
And stilled the summer air and grass,   10
And hushed the secrets of the wind,
For when my final callings pass.

And if a friend should stop to talk,
Reminding me of what is past,
And ask the meaning of my song,   15
I'd say that only cages last.

1955

QUESTIONS

1 This poem, obviously, has something to say about freedom, and it is not, of course, about the nature of birds. What kind of freedom is the poet talking about? What does the cage stand for? Is the poem an allegory?
2 Is there any irony in this poem?
3 What does this poem say about the problem of finding a place in the scheme of things?

EX-BASKETBALL PLAYER

John Updike

Pearl Avenue runs past the high-school lot.
Bends with the trolley tracks, and stops, cut off
Before it has a chance to go two blocks,
At Colonel McComsky Plaza. Berth's Garage

Is on the corner facing west, and there,   5
Most days, you'll find Flick Webb, who helps Berth out.

Flick stands tall among the idiot pumps—
Five on a side, the old bubble-head style,
Their rubber elbows hanging loose and low.
One's nostrils are two S's, and his eyes   10
An E and O. And one is squat, without
A head at all—more of a football type.

Once Flick played for the high-school team, the Wizards.
He was good: in fact, the best. In '46,
He bucketed three hundred ninety points,   15
A county record still. The ball loved Flick.
I saw him rack up thirty-eight of forty
In one home game. His hands were like wild birds.

He never learned a trade, he just sells gas,
Checks oil, and changes flats. Once in a while,   20
As a gag, he dribbles an inner tube,
But most of us remember anyway.
His hands are fine and nervous on the lug wrench.
It makes no difference to the lung wrench, though.

Off work, he hangs around Mae's Luncheonette.   25
Grease-grey and kind of coiled, he plays pinball,
Sips lemon cokes, and smokes those thin cigars;
Flick seldom speaks to Mae, just sits and nods
Beyond her face towards bright applauding tiers
Of Necco Wafers, Nibs and Juju Beads.   30

                                          1957

30 Nibs, Juju Beads: packaged candies.

QUESTIONS

1   What purpose does the brief description of Pearl Avenue serve? Is there any special
    significance in the selection of the details? Does the description help set the tone of
    the poem?
2   Does the ex-basketball player really dribble inner tubes just as a gag?

WE REAL COOL

Gwendolyn Brooks

The Pool Players.
Seven at the Golden Shovel.

We real cool. We
Left school. We

Lurk late. We   5
Strike straight. We

Sing sin. We
Thin gin. We

Jazz June. We
Die soon.   10
            1959

QUESTIONS

1   The word "we" is strongly emphasized by being placed at the end of each line
    except the last. What is the purpose of this emphasis? Why is there no "we" at the
    end of the line?
2   Why "we die soon"?
3   What is the tone of these utterances? Or is there a change in tone?

POINT SHIRLEY

Sylvia Plath

From Water-Tower Hill to the brick prison
The shingle booms, bickering under
The sea's collapse.
Snowcakes break and welter. This year
The gritted wave leaps   5
The seawall and drops onto a bier
Of quahog chips,
Leaving a salty mash of ice to whiten

2 shingle: coarse gravel.   *7 quahog:* a kind of clam.

In my grandmother's sand yard. She is dead,
Whose laundry snapped and froze here, who   10
Kept house against
What the sluttish, rutted sea could do.
Squall waves once danced
Ship timbers in through the cellar window;
A thresh-tailed, lanced   15
Shark littered in the geranium bed—

Such collusion of mulish elements
She wore her broom straws to the nub.
Twenty years out
Of her hand, the house still hugs in each drab   20
Stucco socket
The purple egg-stones: from Great Head's knob
To the filled-in Gut
The sea in its cold gizzard ground those rounds.

Nobody wintering now behind   25
The planked-up windows where she set
Her wheat loaves
And apple cakes to cool. What is it
Survives, grieves
So, over this battered, obstinate spit   30
Of gravel? The waves'
Spewed relics clicker masses in the wind,

Gray waves the stub-necked eiders ride.
A labor of love, and that labor lost.
Steadily the sea   35
East at Point Shirley. She died blessed,
And I come by
Bones, bones only, pawed and tossed,
A dog-faced sea.
The sun sinks under Boston, bloody red.   40

I would get from these dry-papped stones
The milk your love instilled in them.
The black ducks dive.
And though your graciousness might stream,
And I contrive,   45
Grandmother, stones are nothing of home
To that spumiest dove.
Against both bar and tower the black sea runs.

1960

QUESTIONS

1   What does her grandmother's former home stand for in the mind of the speaker? The answer or answers to this question should lead to some comprehension of other symbolic implications.
2   This poem seems to be highly personal even in its symbolism. Can you find any justification for such an approach to the general theme of this section?
3   Do you find any ambivalence here?

ELEANOR RIGBY

John Lennon and Paul McCartney

Ah, look at all the lonely people!
Ah, look at all the lonely people!
Eleanor Rigby picks up the rice
    in the church
Where a wedding has been.   5
Lives in a dream.
Waits at the window, wearing the face
    that she keeps in a jar by the door.
Who is it for?

All the lonely people,   10
    where do they all come from?
All the lonely people,
    where do they all belong?

Father McKenzie writing the words
    of a sermon that no one will hear—   15
No one comes near. Look at him
    working, darning his socks in the night
    when there's nobody there.

All the lonely people,
    where do they all come from?   20
All the lonely people.
    where do they all belong?

Ah, look at all the lonely people!
Ah, look at all the lonely people!
Eleanor Rigby died in the church and   25
    was buried along with her name.
Nobody came.

Father McKenzie wiping the dirt from
    his hands as he walks from the grave.
No one was saved.   30

All the lonely people,
    where do they all come from?
All the lonely people,
    where do they all belong?

                      1966

QUESTIONS

1   What is the answer to the question posed in line 9?
2   Note the three stanzas that serve as a refrain. What is the answer to the question that they ask?
3   What is the importance of Father McKenzie's actions to the main point of the poem? What does it all mean?

TOPICS FOR COMPOSITION

1   Make a case for the proposition that there are people in our own time who might well feel much as the speaker in "The Wanderer" does.
2   Is Pope's conception of social love adequate to explain most social conduct? If you think so, write an essay defending the thesis that self-love and social love are the same. Use Pope's ideas if you wish, but try to draw upon your own experience and knowledge for illustration. If you disagree with Pope, write an essay explaining why. Other poems in this section may provide material for your argument.
3   Write a commentary on the relevance of Arnold's "A Summer Night" to modern times—that is, if you find any.
4   Write a short essay comparing Walt Whitman's response to life in the city to that of Philip Booth.
5   Using Auden's "A Summer Night, 1933" as an aid to reflection, write a commentary on the effect of the threat of nuclear war on social attitudes.
6   "Cold-Water Flat" has to do with the decline of heroism. Have we lost faith in the possibility of heroic living, outside of special circumstances such as war temporarily provides? Write an essay on some points that might be raised in a discussion of the matter. For example, you might address yourself to the question "Are our modern heroes authentic?" and give a tentative answer by examining a typical kind of hero worship.
7   Drawing upon an interpretation of Robert Pack's "A Bird in Search of a Cage," write an essay on the thesis "a cage is not escape but need."
8   We see that John Updike's ex-basketball player, though he does not know it, has been exploited. Are our schools being used unintentionally in other ways to exploit students? Write a commentary on the matter.
9   Comment upon the principal symbolic implications of the descriptive details in John Updike's "Ex-Basketball Player."

10 Convert "A Prayer for My Daughter" into prose.

11 If you have the experience, describe briefly a subculture in the United States.

12 Write a short theme on the connotations of the title "The White House." Make an argument for the reference you think is meant.

TOPICS FOR LONGER COMPOSITIONS

1 Lawrence's essay and King's speech argue that true freedom is not doing whatever one individual wants but is rather the individual's sense of belonging to "place." Structure a paper around this idea by developing the argument implicit in both works (quoting from each). Continue to support the universality of your argument by using material from the short stories by Crane, Kipling, and Lessing. You may also wish to enlarge the scope of your paper by reading and incorporating material from Ralph Ellison's well-known work, *The Invisible Man*.

2 Using any three or four selections from Part One, define "place" by dividing it into several contexts (e.g., starting with "place" as specific landscape or region, moving on to cultural, social, political, mythic, or spiritual implications of "place") and establishing each context by definition and appropriate illustrations from the selections and from your own experience wherever possible.

3 Consider, with all the latitude allowed by Saroyan's text and context, the possibilities that "Hello Out There" traces an archetypal, ever-recurring pattern of human behavior and experience. Consider how convincingly the Young Man and The Girl incarnate human possibilities in an unequal contest with an antagonistic force. If you explore this possibility, you will probably argue that the play acquires, as it moves along, a mythic power which far exceeds the local detail of its surface.

4 Saroyan's focus in "Hello Out There" seems obviously on the lonely, the dispossessed, the outcast. Explain whether or not the play suggests that the antagonists (The Man, Another Man, The Woman) represent American society generally. If so, does the play offer a viewpoint about the predictability of American experience in which the weak move about and have their being at the pleasure of the tyrannical majority?

5 Drawing upon the poems of Part One and others you may know, discuss at some length the evidence that people have always sought, in various ways, to secure a sense of community and social order. Then comment briefly upon the effects of alienation. Finally, assess the modern condition: describe and rate the worth of various current loyalties.

PART
2

THE PROTEST
AGAINST
RESTRAINT

When we approach the problem of protest, we recognize that our problem is neither new nor unique; for, certainly, our world is one where protest is constantly with us. Moreover, man's need to protest the restraint that society places on his individuality takes many forms. The protest may be private, concerned only with an issue one man considers vital to his individuality, remaining hidden from all but the most perceptive observer. Or the protest may be public, concerned with a social or political alignment, involving a kindred segment of mankind and, of course, the public view. The following selections, the products of various times and places, show some of the different ways in which man has responded to threats against his individuality.

Since we live during a time when the question of civil rights is a major issue, we would be hard pressed to find a better introductory selection than Henry David Thoreau's "Civil Disobedience." Thoreau's major point, that a good citizen, when oppressed by a bad law, has a duty to break that law, has become the guiding principle of today's civil protests. But equally important to Thoreau's philosophy is the fact that the citizen's protest must remain passive: nowhere in his essay does Thoreau advocate violent overthrow of existing authority. Thoreau's view, radical during his time, is now considered by some as restraining for its insistence on nonviolence.

Although part of the civil rights' issue but yet distinct are women's rights and the restraints brought about by sexist attitudes that still dominate all facets of society. Gail Rock's essay, "Same Time, Same Station, Same Sexism," first published in *Ms. Magazine,* takes a penetrating look at the TV industry and finds it a prime contributor to perpetuating sexist attitudes.

Richard Rive, a South African black, in his short story, "The Bench," protests the imposed restraint of apartheid. Rive's main character, existing as he does under a system that denies civil liberties to nonwhites, makes an individual bid for human dignity and personal freedom.

"The Life You Save May Be Your Own," by Flannery O'Connor, presents a harsh view of the extent to which individual restraint is a part of everyday life. Her main character uses and abuses personal restraint within the context of relationships where characters struggle to find freedom though they do not fully understand the web of forces that motivate their actions.

"The Conversion of the Jews," by Philip Roth, also concerns an individual protest, by a young Jewish boy, against not only the dogma of his religion, but the insistence by the older generation that he accept the dogma without question. Ozzie's real protest then, as Roth states in the story, is that "what he wanted to know was different."

Shakespeare's *The Tempest* takes us to a strange island, ruled over by a magician-philosopher-lord who will acknowledge no restraints to recover his place in the world, at a strange time, dominated by storm and displacement. Prospero's occult knowledge and skill speed his project to unmask the criminality of those who have restrained him; but in the end, after he has righted ancient wrongs and when heart has overcome head, he offers the vision of a new order, "a brave new world," which will sustain freedom for the pursuits of love, virtue, and wisdom. Casting aside his identity as magician, Prospero frees himself to resume his place in the world and to be a responsible ruler. Throughout the play, however, the world is seen as geared to the fixing of restraints; their removal requires trial and error, diligence, and imagination.

THE ESSAY

Although this essay is probably longer and more involved than those you will write, we can use its length to advantage to illustrate techniques that are common to effective persuasive writing. As you read, notice the abundant variety of support that Thoreau provides. In particular, observe how he supports his controlling techniques of personal observation, personal experience, and appeal to authority with methods of analogy; cause-to-effect relationship; comparison and contrast; narration; definition; description.

CIVIL DISOBEDIENCE

Henry David Thoreau

I heartily accept the motto,—"That government is best which governs least;" and I should like to see it acted up to more rapidly and systematically. Carried out, it finally amounts to this, which also I believe,—"That government is best which governs not at all;" and when men are prepared for it, that will be the kind of government which they will have. Government is at best but an expedient; but most governments are usually, and all governments are sometimes, inexpedient. The objections which have been brought against a standing army, and they are many and weighty, and deserve to prevail, may also at last be brought against a standing government. The standing army is only an arm of the standing government. The government itself, which is only the mode which the people have chosen to execute their will, is equally liable to be abused and perverted before the people can act through it. Witness the present Mexican war, the work of comparatively a few individuals using the standing government as their tool; for, in the outset, the people would not have consented to this measure.

    This American government,—what is it but a tradition, though a recent one, endeavoring to transmit itself unimpaired to posterity, but each instant losing some of its integrity? It has not the vitality and force of a single living man; for a single man can bend it to his will. It is a sort of wooden gun to the people themselves. But it is not the less necessary for this; for the people must have some complicated machinery or other, and hear its din, to satisfy that idea of government which they have. Governments show thus how successfully men can be imposed on, even impose on themselves, for their own advantage. It is excellent, we must all allow. Yet this government never of itself furthered any enterprise, but by the alacrity with which it got out of its way. *It* does not keep the country free. *It* does not settle the West. *It* does not educate.

The character inherent in the American people has done all that has been accomplished; it would have done somewhat more, if the government had not sometimes got in its way. For government is an expedient by which men would fain succeed in letting one another alone; and, as has been said, when it is most expedient, the governed are most let alone by it. Trade and commerce, if they were not made of India-rubber, would never manage to bounce over the obstacles which legislators are continually putting in their way; and, if one were to judge these men wholly by the effects of their actions and not partly by their intentions, they would deserve to be classed and punished with those mischievous persons who put obstructions on the railroads.

But, to speak practically and as a citizen, unlike those who call themselves no-government men, I ask for, not *at once* no government, but *at once* a better government. Let every man make known what kind of government would command his respect, and that will be one step toward obtaining it.

After all, the practical reason why, when the power is once in the hands of the people, a majority are permitted, and for a long period continue, to rule is not because they are most likely to be in the right, nor because this seems fairest to the minority, but because they are physically the strongest. But a government in which the majority rule in all cases cannot be based on justice, even as far as men understand it. Can there be a government in which majorities do not virtually decide right and wrong, but conscience?—in which majorities decide only those questions to which the rule of expediency is applicable? Must the citizen ever for a moment, or in the least degree, resign his conscience to the legislator? Why has every man a conscience, then? I think that we should be men first, and subjects afterward. It is not desirable to cultivate a respect for the law, so much as for the right. The only obligation which I have a right to assume is to do at any time what I think right. It is truly enough said, that a corporation has no conscience; but a corporation of conscientious men is a corporation *with* a conscience. Law never made men a whit more just; and, by means of their respect for it, even the well-disposed are daily made the agents of injustice. A common and natural result of an undue respect for law is, that you may see a file of soldiers, colonel, captains, corporal, privates, powder-monkeys, and all, marching in admirable-order over hill and dale to the wars, against their wills, ay, against their common sense and consciences, which makes it very steep marching indeed, and produces a palpitation of the heart. They have no doubt that it is a damnable business in which they are concerned; they are all peaceably inclined. Now, what are they? Men at all? or small movable forts and magazines, at the service of some unscrupulous man in power? Visit the Navy-Yard, and behold a marine, such a man as an American government can make, or such as it can make a man with its black arts,—a mere shadow and reminiscence of humanity, a man laid out alive and standing, and already, as one may say, buried under arms with funeral accompaniments, though it may be,—

Not a drum was heard, not a funeral note,
  As his course to the rampart we hurried;
Not a soldier discharged his farewell shot
  O'er the grave where our hero we buried.

The mass of men serve the state thus, not as men mainly, but as machines, with their bodies. They are the standing army, and the militia, jailers, constables, posse comitatus, etc. In most cases there is no free exercise whatever of the judgment or of the moral sense; but they put themselves on a level with wood and earth and stones; and wooden men can perhaps be manufactured that will serve the purpose as well. Such command no more respect than men of straw or a lump of dirt. They have the same sort of worth only as horses and dogs. Yet such as these even are commonly esteemed good citizens. Others—as most legislators, politicians, lawyers, ministers, and office-holders—serve the state chiefly with their heads; and, as they rarely make any moral distinctions, they are as likely to serve the Devil, without *intending* it, as God. A very few, as heroes, patriots, martyrs, reformers in the great sense, and *men,* serve the state with their consciences also, and so necessarily resist it for the most part; and they are commonly treated as enemies by it. A wise man will only be useful as a man, and will not submit to be "clay," and "stop a hole to keep the wind away," but leave that office to his dust at least:—

> I am too high-born to be propertied,
> To be a secondary at control,
> Or useful serving-man and instrument
> To any sovereign state throughout the world.

He who gives himself entirely to his fellowmen appears to them useless and selfish; but he who gives himself partially to them is pronounced a benefactor and philanthropist.

How does it become a man to behave toward this American government to-day? I answer, that he cannot without disgrace be associated with it. I cannot for an instant recognize the political organization as *my* government which is the *slave's* government also.

All men recognize the right of revolution; that is, the right to refuse allegiance to, and to resist, the government, when its tyranny or its inefficiency are great and unendurable. But almost all say that such is not the case now. But such was the case, they think, in the Revolution of '75. If one were to tell me that this was a bad government because it taxed certain foreign commodities brought to its ports, it is most probable that I should not make an ado about it, for I can do without them. All machines have their friction; and possibly this does enough good to counterbalance the evil. At any rate, it is a great evil to make a stir about it. But when the friction comes to have its machine, and oppression and robbery are organized, I say, let us not have such a machine any longer. In other words, when a sixth of the population of a nation which has undertaken to be the refuge of liberty are slaves, and a whole country is unjustly overrun and conquered by a foreign army, and subjected to military law, I think that it is not too soon for honest men to rebel and revolutionize. What makes this duty the more urgent is the fact that the country so overrun is not our own, but ours is the invading army. . . .

> A drab of state, a cloth-o'-silver slut,
> To have her train borne up, and her soul trail in the dirt.

Practically speaking, the opponents to a reform in Massachusetts are not a hundred thousand politicians at the South, but a hundred thousand merchants and farmers here, who are more interested in commerce and agriculture than they are in humanity, and are not prepared to do justice to the slave and to Mexico, *cost what it may.* I quarrel not with far-off foes, but with those who, near at home, coöperate with, and do the bidding of, those far away, and without whom the latter would be harmless. We are accustomed to say, that the mass of men are unprepared; but improvement is slow, because the few are not materially wiser or better than the many. It is not so important that many should be as good as you, as that there be some absolute goodness some-where; for that will leaven the whole lump. There are thousands who are *in opinion* opposed to slavery and to the war, who yet in effect do nothing to put an end to them; who, esteeming themselves children of Washington and Franklin, sit down with their hands in their pockets, and say that they know not what to do, and do nothing; who even postpone the question of freedom to the question of free-trade, and quietly read the prices-current along with the latest advices from Mexico, after dinner, and, it may be, fall asleep over them both. What is the price-current of an honest man and patriot to-day? They hesitate, and they regret, and sometimes they petition; but they do noth-ing in earnest and with effect. They will wait, well disposed, for others to remedy the evil, that they may no longer have it to regret. At most, they give only a cheap vote, and a feeble countenance and God-speed, to the right, as it goes by them. There are nine hundred and ninety-nine patrons of virtue to one virtuous man. But it is easier to deal with the real possessor of a thing than with the temporary guardian of it.

All voting is a sort of gaming, like checkers or backgammon, with a slight moral tinge to it, a playing with right and wrong, with moral questions; and betting naturally accompanies it. The character of the voters is not staked. I cast my vote, perchance, as I think right; but I am not vitally concerned that that right should prevail. I am willing to leave it to the majority. Its obligation, therefore, never exceeds that of expediency. Even voting *for the right* is *doing* nothing for it. It is only expressing to men feebly your desire that it should prevail. A wise man will not leave the right to the mercy of chance, nor wish it to prevail through the power of the majority. There is but little virtue in the action of masses of men. When the majority shall at length vote for the abolition of slavery, it will be because they are indifferent to slavery, or because there is but little slavery left to be abolished by their vote. *They* will then be the only slaves. Only *his* vote can hasten the abolition of slavery who asserts his own freedom by his vote.

I hear of a convention to be held at Baltimore, or elsewhere, for the selection of a candidate for the Presidency, made up chiefly of editors, and men who are politicians by profession; but I think, what is it to any independent, intelligent, and respectable man what decision they may come to? Shall we not have the advantage of his wisdom and honesty, nevertheless? Can we not count upon some independent votes? Are there not many individuals in the country who do not attend conventions? But no: I find that the respectable man, so called, has immediately drifted from his position, and despairs of his country, when his country has more reason to despair of him. He forthwith adopts one of the candidates thus selected as the only *available* one, thus proving that he is himself *available* for any purposes of the demagogue. His vote is of no more worth than that of any unprincipled foreigner or hireling native, who may have been bought. O for a man who is a *man,* and, as my neighbor says, has a bone in his back which you cannot pass your hand through! Our statistics are at fault: the population has been returned too large. How many *men* are there to a square thousand miles in this country? Hardly one. Does not America offer any inducement for men to settle here? The American has dwindled into an Odd Fellow,—one who may be known by the development of his organ of gregariousness, and a manifest lack of intellect and cheerful self-reliance; whose first and chief concern, on coming into the world, is to see that the Alms-houses are in good repair; and, before yet he has lawfully donned the virile garb, to collect a fund for the support of the widows and orphans that may be; who, in short, ventures to live only by the aid of the Mutual Insurance company, which has promised to bury him decently.

It is not a man's duty, as a matter of course, to devote himself to the eradication of any, even the most enormous wrong; he may still properly have other concerns to engage him; but it is his duty, at least to wash his hands of it, and, if he gives it no thought longer, not to give it practically his support. If I devote myself to other pursuits and contemplations, I must first see, at least, that I do not pursue them sitting upon another man's shoulders. I must get off him first, that he may pursue his contemplations too. See what gross inconsistency is tolerated. I have heard some of my townsmen say, "I should like to have them order me out to help put down an insurrection of the slaves, or to march to Mexico;—see if I would go;" and yet these very men have each, directly by their allegiance, and so indirectly, at least, by their money, furnished a substitute. The soldier is applauded who refuses to serve in an unjust war by those who do not refuse to sustain the unjust government which makes the war; is applauded by those whose own act and authority he disregards and sets at naught; as if the state were penitent to that degree that it hired one to scourge it while it sinned, but not to that degree that it left off sinning for a moment. Thus, under the name of Order and Civil Government, we are all made at last to pay homage to and support our own meanness. After the first blush of sin comes its indifference; and from immoral it becomes, as it were, *un*moral, and not quite unnecessary to that life which we have made.

The broadest and most prevalent error requires the most disinterested virtue to sustain it. The slight reproach to which the virtue of patriotism is commonly liable, the noble are most likely to incur. Those who, while they disapprove of the character and measures of a government, yield to it their allegiance and support are undoubtedly its most conscientious supporters, and so frequently the most serious obstacles to reform. Some are petitioning the state to dissolve the Union, to disregard the requisitions of the President. Why do they not dissolve it themselves,—the union between themselves and the state,—and refuse to pay their quota into its treasury? Do not they stand in the same relation to the state that the state does to the Union? And have not the same reasons prevented the state from resisting the Union which have prevented them from resisting the state?

How can a man be satisfied to entertain an opinion merely, and enjoy *it?* Is there any enjoyment in it, if his opinion is that he is aggrieved? If you are cheated out of a single dollar by your neighbor, you do not rest satisfied with knowing that you are cheated, or with saying that you are cheated, or even with petitioning him to pay you your due; but you take effectual steps at once to obtain the full amount, and see that you are never cheated again. Action from principle, the perception and the performance of right, changes things and relations; it is essentially revolutionary, and does not consist wholly with anything which was. It not only divides states and churches, it divides families; ay, it divides the *individual,* separating the diabolical in him from the divine.

Unjust laws exist: shall we be content to obey them, or shall we endeavor to amend them, and obey them until we have succeeded, or shall we transgress them at once? Men generally, under such a government as this, think that they ought to wait until they have persuaded the majority to alter them. They think that, if they should resist, the remedy would be worse than the evil. But it is the fault of the government itself that the remedy *is* worse than the evil. *It* makes it worse. Why is it not more apt to anticipate and provide for reform? Why does it not cherish its wise minority? Why does it cry and resist before it is hurt? Why does it not encourage its citizens to be on the alert to point out its faults, and *do* better than it would have them? Why does it always crucify Christ, and excommunicate Copernicus and Luther, and pronounce Washington and Franklin rebels?

One would think, that a deliberate and practical denial of its authority was the only offense never contemplated by government; else, why has it not assigned its definite, its suitable and proportionate penalty? If a man who has no property refuses but once to earn nine shillings for the state, he is put in prison for a period unlimited by any law that I know, and determined only by the discretion of those who placed him there; but if he should steal ninety times nine shillings from the state, he is soon permitted to go at large again.

If the injustice is part of the necessary friction of the machine of government, let it go, let it go: perchance it will wear smooth,—certainly the machine will wear out. If the injustice has a spring, or a pulley, or a rope, or a crank, exclusively for itself, then perhaps you may consider whether the remedy will not be worse than the evil; but if it is of such a nature that it requires you to be the agent of injustice to another, then, I say, break the law. Let your life be a counter friction to stop the machine. What I have to do is to see, at any rate, that I do not lend myself to the wrong which I condemn.

As for adopting the ways which the state has provided for remedying the evil, I know not of such ways. They take too much time, and a man's life will be gone. I have other affairs to attend to. I came into this world, not chiefly to make this a good place to live in, but to live in it, be it good or bad. A man has not everything to do, but something; and because he cannot do *everything,* it is not necessary that he should do *something* wrong. It is not my business to be petitioning the Governor or the Legislature any more than it is theirs to petition me; and if they should not hear my petition, what should I do then? But in this case the state has provided no way: its very Constitution is the evil. This may seem to be harsh and stubborn and unconciliatory; but it is to treat with the utmost kindness and consideration the only spirit that can appreciate or deserve it. So is all change for the better, like birth and death, which convulse the body.

I do not hesitate to say, that those who call themselves Abolitionists should at once effectually withdraw their support, both in person and property, from the government of Massachusetts, and not wait till they constitute a majority of one, before they suffer the right to prevail through them. I think that it is enough if they have God on their side, without waiting for that other one. Moreover, any man more right than his neighbors constitutes a majority of one already.

I meet this American government, or its representative, the state government, directly, and face to face, once a year—no more—in the person of its tax-gatherer; this is the only mode in which a man situated as I am necessarily meets it; and it then says distinctly, Recognize me; and the simplest, the most effectual, and, in the present posture of affairs, the indispensablest mode of treating with it on this head, of expressing your little satisfaction with and love for it, is to deny it then. My civil neighbor, the tax-gatherer, is the very man I have to deal with,—for it is, after all, with men and not with parchment that I quarrel,—and he has voluntarily chosen to be an agent for the government. How shall he ever know well what he is and does as an officer of the government, or as a man, until he is obliged to consider whether he shall treat me, his neighbor, for whom he has respect, as a neighbor and well-disposed man, or as a maniac and disturber of the peace, and see if he can get over this obstruction to his neighborliness without a ruder and more impetuous thought or speech corresponding with his action. I know this well, that if one thousand, if one hundred, if ten men whom I could name,—if ten *honest* men only,—ay, if *one* honest man, in this State of Massachusetts, *ceasing to hold slaves,* were actually to withdraw from this copartnership, and be locked up in the county jail therefor, it would be the abolition of slavery in America. For it matters not how small the beginning may seem to be: what is once well done is done forever. But we love better to talk about it: that we say is our mission. Reform keeps many scores of newspapers in its service, but not one man. If my esteemed neighbor, the State's ambassador, who will devote his days to the settlement of the question of human rights in the Council Chamber, instead of being threatened with the prisons of Carolina, were to sit down the prisoner of Massachusetts, that State which is so anxious to foist the sin of slavery upon her sister,—though at present she can discover only an act of inhospitality to be the ground of a quarrel with her,—the Legislature would not wholly waive the subject the following winter.

Under a government which imprisons any unjustly, the true place for a just man is also a prison. The proper place to-day, the only place which Massachusetts has provided for her freer and less desponding spirits, is in her prisons, to be put out and locked out of the State by her own act, as they have already put themselves out by their principles. It is there that the fugitive slave, and the Mexican prisoner on parole, and the Indian come to plead the wrongs of his race should find them; on that separate, but more free and honorable ground, where the State places those who are not *with* her, but *against* her,—the only house in a slave State in which a free man can abide with honor. If any think that their influence would be lost there, and their voices no longer afflict the ear of the State, that they would not be as an enemy within its walls, they do not know by how much truth is stronger than error, nor how much more eloquently and effectively he can combat injustice who has experienced a little in his own person. Cast your whole vote, not a strip of paper merely, but your whole influence. A minority is powerless while it conforms to the majority; it is not even a minority then; but it is irresistible when it clogs by its whole weight. If the alternative is to keep all just men in prison, or give up war and slavery, the State will not hesitate which to choose. If a thousand men were not to pay their tax-bills this year, that would not be a violent and bloody measure, as it would be to pay them, and enable the State to commit violence and shed innocent blood. This is, in fact, the definition of a peaceable revolution, if any such is possible. If the tax-gatherer, or any other public officer, asks me, as one has done, "But what shall I do?" my answer is, "If you really wish to do anything, resign your office." When the subject has refused allegiance, and the officer has resigned his office, then the revolution is accomplished. But even suppose blood should flow. Is there not a sort of blood shed when the conscience is wounded? Through this wound a man's real manhood and immortality flow out, and he bleeds to an everlasting death. I see this blood flowing now.

I have contemplated the imprisonment of the offender, rather than the seizure of his goods,—though both will serve the same purpose,—because they who assert the purest right, and consequently are most dangerous to a corrupt State, commonly have not spent much time in accumulating property. To such the State renders comparatively small service, and a slight tax is wont to appear exorbitant, particularly if they are obliged to earn it by special labor with their hands. If there were one who lived wholly without the use of money, the State itself would hesitate to demand it of him. But the rich man—not to make any invidious comparison—is always sold to the institution which makes him rich. Absolutely speaking, the more money, the less virtue; for money comes between a man and his objects, and obtains them for him; and it was certainly no great virtue to obtain it. It puts to rest many questions which he would otherwise be taxed to answer; while the only new question which it puts is the hard but superfluous one, how to spend it. Thus his moral ground is taken from under his feet. The opportunities of living are diminished in proportion as what are called the "means" are increased. The best thing a man can do for his culture when he is rich is to endeavor to carry out those schemes which he entertained when he was poor. Christ answered the Herodians according to their condition. "Show me the tribute-money," said he;—and one took a penny out of his pocket;—if you use money which has the image of Cæsar on it, and which he has made current and valuable, that is, *if you are men of the State,* and gladly enjoy the advantages of Cæsar's government, then pay him back some of his own when he demands it. "Render therefore to Cæsar that which is Cæsar's, and to God those things which are God's"—leaving them no wiser than before as to which was which; for they did not wish to know. . . .

I have paid no poll-tax for six years. I was put into a jail once on this account, for one night; and, as I stood considering the walls of solid stone, two or three feet thick, the door of wood and iron, a foot thick, and the iron grating which strained the light, I could not help being struck with the foolishness of that institution which treated me as if I were mere flesh and blood and bones, to be locked up. I wondered that it should have concluded at length that this was the best use it could put me to, and had never thought to avail itself of my services in some way. I saw that, if there was a wall of stone between me and my townsmen, there was a still more difficult one to climb or break through before they could get to be as free as I was. I did not for a moment feel confined, and the walls seemed a great waste of stone and mortar. I felt as if I alone of all my townsmen had paid my tax. They plainly did not know how to treat me, but behaved like persons who are underbred. In every threat and in every compliment there was a blunder; for they thought that my chief desire was to stand the other side of that stone wall. I could not but smile to see how industriously they locked the door of my meditations, which followed them out again without let or hindrance, and *they* were really all that was dangerous. As they could not reach me, they had resolved to punish my body; just as boys, if they cannot come at some person against whom they have a spite, will abuse his dog. I saw that the State was half-witted, that it was timid as a lone woman with her silver spoons, and that it did not know its friends from its foes, and I lost all my remaining respect for it, and pitied it.

Thus the State never intentionally confronts a man's sense, intellectual or moral, but only his body, his senses. It is not armed with superior wit or honesty, but with superior physical strength. I was not born to be forced. I will breathe after my own fashion. Let us see who is the strongest. What force has a multitude? They only can force me who obey a higher law than I. They force me to become like themselves. I do not hear of *men* being *forced* to live this way or that by masses of men. What sort of life were that to live? When I meet a government which says to me, "Your money or your life," why should I be in haste to give it my money? It may be in a great strait, and not know what to do: I cannot help that. It must help itself; do as I do. It is not worth the while to snivel about it. I am not responsible for the successful working of the machinery of society. I am not the son of the engineer. I perceive that, when an acorn and a chestnut fall side by side, the one does not remain inert to make way for the other, but both obey their own laws, and spring and grow and flourish as best they can, till one, perchance, overshadows and destroys the other. If a plant cannot live according to its nature, it dies; and so a man. . . .

When I came out of prison,—for some one interfered, and paid that tax,—I did not perceive that great changes had taken place on the common, such as he observed who went in a youth and emerged a tottering and gray-headed man; and yet a change had to my eyes come over the scene,—the town, and State, and country,—greater than any that mere time could effect. I saw yet more distinctly the State in which I lived. I saw to what extent the people among whom I lived could be trusted as good neighbors and friends; that their friendship was for summer weather only; that they did not greatly propose to do right; that they were a distinct race from me by their prejudices and superstitions, as the Chinamen and Malays are; that in their sacrifices to humanity they ran no risks, not even to their property; that after all they were not so noble but they treated the thief as he had treated them, and hoped, by a certain outward observance and a few prayers, and by walking in a particular straight though useless path from time to time, to save their souls. This may be to judge my neighbors harshly; for I believe that many of them are not aware that they have such an institution as the jail in their village.

It was formerly the custom in our village, when a poor debtor came out of jail, for his acquaintances to salute him, looking through their fingers, which were crossed to represent the grating of a jail window, "How do ye do?" My neighbors did not thus salute me, but first looked at me, and then at one another, as if I had returned from a long journey. I was put into jail as I was going to the shoemaker's to get a shoe which was mended. When I was let out the next morning, I proceeded to finish my errand, and, having put on my mended shoe, joined a huckleberry party, who were impatient to put themselves under my conduct; and in half an hour,—for the horse was soon tackled,—was in the midst of a huckleberry field, on one of our highest hills, two miles off, and then the State was nowhere to be seen. . . .

I have never declined paying the highway tax, because I am as desirous of being a good neighbor as I am of being a bad subject; and as for supporting schools, I am doing my part to educate my fellow-countrymen now. It is for no particular item in the tax-bill that I refuse to pay it. I simply wish to refuse allegiance to the State, to with-draw and stand aloof from it effectually. I do not care to trace the course of my dollar, if I could, till it buys a man or a musket to shoot one with,—the dollar is innocent,—but I am concerned to trace the effects of my allegiance. In fact, I quietly declare war with the State, after my fashion, though I will still make what use and get what advantage of her I can, as is usual in such cases.

If others pay the tax which is demanded of me, from a sympathy with the State, they do but what they have already done in their own case, or rather they abet injustice to a greater extent than the State requires. If they pay the tax from a mistaken interest in the individual taxed, to save his property, or prevent his going to jail, it is because they have not considered wisely how far they let their private feelings interfere with the public good.

This, then, is my position at present. But one cannot be too much on his guard in such a case, lest his action be biased by obstinacy or an undue regard for the opinions of men. Let him see that he does only what belongs to himself and to the hour.

I think sometimes, Why, this people mean well, they are only ignorant; they would do better if they knew how: why give your neighbors this pain to treat you as they are not inclined to? But I think again, This is no reason why I should do as they do, or permit others to suffer much greater pain of a different kind. Again, I sometimes say to myself, When many millions of men, without heat, without ill will, without personal feeling of any kind, demand of you a few shillings only, without the possibility, such is their constitution, of retracting or altering their present demand, and without the possi-bility, on your side, of appeal to any other millions, why expose yourself to this over-whelming brute force? You do not resist cold and hunger, the winds and the waves, thus obstinately; you quietly submit to a thousand similar necessities. You do not put your head into the fire. But just in proportion as I regard this as not wholly a brute force, but partly a human force, and consider that I have relations to those millions as to so many millions of men, and not of mere brute or inanimate things, I see that appeal is possible, first and instantaneously, from them to the Maker of them, and, secondly, from them to themselves. But if I put my head deliberately into the fire, there is no appeal to fire or to the Maker of fire, and I have only myself to blame. If I could convince myself that I have any right to be satisfied with men as they are, and to treat them accordingly, and not according, in some respects, to my requisitions and expec-tations of what they and I ought to be, then, like a good Mussulman and fatalist, I should endeavor to be satisfied with things as they are, and say it is the will of God. And, above all, there is this difference between resisting this and a purely brute or natural force, that I can resist this with some effect; but I cannot expect, like Orpheus, to change the nature of the rocks and trees and beasts.

I do not wish to quarrel with any man or nation. I do not wish to split hairs, to make fine distinctions, or set myself up as better than my neighbors. I seek rather, I may say, even an excuse for conforming to the laws of the land. I am but too ready to conform to them. Indeed, I have reason to suspect myself on this head; and each year, as the tax-gatherer comes round, I find myself disposed to review the acts and position of the general and State governments, and the spirit of the people, to discover a pretext for conformity. . . .

I believe that the State will soon be able to take all my work of this sort out of my hands, and then I shall be no better a patriot than my fellow-countrymen. Seen from a lower point of view, the Constitution, with all its faults, is very good; the law and the courts are very respectable; even this State and this American government are, in many respects, very admirable, and rare things, to be thankful for, such as a great many have described them; but seen from a point of view a little higher, they are what I have described them; seen from a higher still, and the highest, who shall say what they are, or that they are worth looking at or thinking of at all?

However, the government does not concern me much, and I shall bestow the fewest possible thoughts on it. It is not many moments that I live under a government, even in this world. If a man is thought-free, fancy-free, imagination-free, that which *is not* never for a long time appearing *to be* to him, unwise rulers or reformers cannot fatally interrupt him.

I know that most men think differently from myself; but those whose lives are by profession devoted to the study of these or kindred subjects content me as little as any. Statesmen and legislators, standing so completely within the institution, never distinctly and nakedly behold it. They speak of moving society, but have no resting-place without it. They may be men of a certain experience and discrimination, and have no doubt invented ingenious and even useful systems, for which we sincerely thank them; but all their wit and usefulness lie within certain not very wide limits. They are wont to forget that the world is not governed by policy and expediency. Webster never goes behind government, and so cannot speak with authority about it. His words are wisdom to those legislators who contemplate no essential reform in the existing government; but for thinkers, and those who legislate for all time, he never once glances at the subject. I know of those whose serene and wise speculations on this theme would soon reveal the limits of his mind's range and hospitality. Yet, compared with the cheap professions of most reformers, and the still cheaper wisdom and eloquence of politicians in general, his are almost the only sensible and valuable words, and we thank Heaven for him. Comparatively, he is always strong, original, and, above all, practical. Still, his quality is not wisdom, but prudence. The lawyer's truth is not Truth, but consistency or a consistent expediency. Truth is always in harmony with herself, and is not concerned chiefly to reveal the justice that may consist with wrong-doing. He well deserves to be called, as he has been called, the Defender of the Constitution. There are really no blows to be given by him but defensive ones. He is not a leader, but a follower. His leaders are the men of '87. "I have never made an effort," he says, "and never propose to make an effort; I have never countenanced an effort, and never mean to countenance an effort, to disturb the arrangement as originally made, by which the various States came into the Union." Still thinking of the sanction which the Constitution gives to slavery, he says, "Because it was a part of the original compact,—let it stand." Notwithstanding his special acuteness and ability, he is unable to take a fact out of its merely political relations, and behold it as it lies absolutely to be disposed of by the intellect,—what, for instance, it behooves a man to do here in America to-day with regard to slavery,—but ventures, or is driven, to make some such desperate answer as the following, while professing to speak absolutely, and as a private man,—from which what new and singular code of social duties might be inferred? "The manner," says he, "in which the governments of those States where slavery exists are to regulate it is for their own consideration, under their responsibility to their constituents, to the general laws of propriety, humanity, and justice, and to God. Associations formed elsewhere, springing from a feeling of humanity, or any other cause, have nothing whatever to do with it. They have never received any encouragement from me, and they never will."[1]

They who know of no purer sources of truth, who have traced up its stream no higher, stand, and wisely stand, by the Bible and the Constitution, and drink at it there with reverence and humility; but they who behold where it comes trickling into this lake or that pool, gird up their loins once more, and continue their pilgrimage toward its fountain-head.

No man with a genius for legislation has appeared in America. They are rare in the history of the world. There are orators, politicians, and eloquent men, by the thousand; but the speaker has not yet opened his mouth to speak who is capable of settling the much-vexed questions of the day. We love eloquence for its own sake, and not for any truth which it may utter, or any heroism it may inspire. Our legislators have not yet learned the comparative value of free-trade and of freedom, of union, and of rectitude, to a nation. They have no genius or talent for comparatively humble questions of taxation and finance, commerce and manufactures and agriculture. If we were left solely to the wordy wit of legislators in Congress for our guidance, uncorrected by the seasonable experience and the effectual complaints of the people, America would not long retain her rank among the nations. For eighteen hundred years, though perchance I have no right to say it, the New Testament has been written; yet where is the legislator who has wisdom and practical talent enough to avail himself of the light which it sheds on the science of legislation?

The authority of government, even such as I am willing to submit to,—for I will cheerfully obey those who know and can do better than I, and in many things even those who neither know nor can do so well,—is still an impure one: to be strictly just, it must have the sanction and consent of the governed. It can have no pure right over my person and property but what I concede to it. The progress from an absolute to a limited monarchy, from a limited monarchy to a democracy, is a progress toward a true respect for the individual. Even the Chinese philosopher was wise enough to regard the individual as the basis of the empire. Is a democracy, such as we know it, the last improvement possible in government? Is it not possible to take a step further towards recognizing and organizing the rights of man? There will never be a really free and enlightened State until the State comes to recognize the individual as a higher and independent power, from which all its own power and authority are derived, and treats

[1] These extracts have been inserted since the lecture was read.

him accordingly. I please myself with imagining a State at last which can afford to be just to all men, and to treat the individual with respect as a neighbor; which even would not think it inconsistent with its own repose if a few were to live aloof from it, not meddling with it, nor embraced by it, who fulfilled all the duties of neighbors and fellowmen. A State which bore this kind of fruit, and suffered it to drop off as fast as it ripened, would prepare the way for a still more perfect and glorious State, which also I have imagined, but not yet anywhere seen.

QUESTIONS

1   Paraphrase Thoreau's concept of "This American government" in the second paragraph. How accurate is his appraisal of government's function?
2   What is Thoreau's position on majority rule?
3   How does Thoreau see his obligation to government? Summarize the arguments he uses to support his position.
4   Explain Thoreau's paradoxical statement, "He who gives himself entirely to his fellowmen appears to them useless and selfish; but he who gives himself partially to them is pronounced a benefactor and a philanthropist."
5   What does Thoreau think about the average citizen as a force in government? Briefly summarize his examples—voting, selection of officials, military service, eradication of unjust laws.
6   Summarize Thoreau's arguments for "passive resistance." What was his personal experience in implementing his position?
7   Is the concluding paragraph consistent with the rest of the essay? Is it consistent with an ideal concept of man? An ideal concept of democratic government?

TOPICS FOR COMPOSITION

1   Using selected comments from "Civil Disobedience," write an essay applying Thoreau's position to the present-day American scene.
2   Refute Thoreau's essay as impractical and irresponsible in view of man's obligation to mankind.
3   Referring directly to the essay, support or refute the position that Thoreau advocates anarchy.
4   Write a composition, based on personal experience, in which you describe the details of a protest against, or a desire to protest, restraint by governmental authority. Support the validity of your position as you saw it.

The effective writer is one whose commitment to a viewpoint is not just so much rhetoric but is solidly based on support. To put it another way, people do not really write well unless they are deeply involved in the topic and have convincing material to back up that involvement. Gail Rock's essay shows her involvement in her thesis and the attention to supporting material that gives the essay both authority and credibility. Note particularly:

1 Her abundant use of examples
2 Her ability to effectively compare and contrast within her examples to maintain a consistent viewpoint
3 Her use of appropriate statistical evidence

SAME TIME, SAME STATION, SAME SEXISM

Gail Rock

It's no secret that TV is the single most influential medium of communication in American society. American children spend more time in front of the TV set than they do in the classroom. More people watch TV than read books or magazines, or go to the movies. More people get their news from TV than from newspapers.

The television industry, however, is dominated by white, middle-class men, and the information dispensed and the social attitudes presented cannot help but be part of that group's own self-aggrandizing view of the world.

Consider the statistics. During prime evening hours on the three networks, there are 62 shows which have regularly appearing leading performers. Of those 62 shows, 48 have only male protagonists, 8 shows have men and women sharing the leads, and a mere 6 shows have only female protagonists. (This total of 62 does not include news shows which are always anchored by men, or "anthology" series which have no continuing characters. And there is not one woman on a regularly scheduled sports show, not one woman hosting a game show, and not one woman as an evening talk-show host.)

Of the six shows ($9\frac{1}{2}$ percent of the TV schedule) which do star women (51 percent of the population), four—"Here's Lucy," "Diana," "The Mary Tyler Moore Show," and "Maude"—are situation comedy; one—"The Carol Burnett Show"—is musical comedy; and one—"The Snoop Sisters"—is adventure comedy. Ha ha. Aren't we women funny? Well, we're sure as hell not serious—at least not on TV. There are 34 "serious" shows (adventure, drama, and so on) on the tube this season, and not one has a solo woman star. The only one that even has a woman sharing the lead is "The Waltons." But then, "The Waltons" has been an exception to every rule, so one might not be surprised to see it treating women with respect.

Lucille Ball ("Here's Lucy" on CBS) pretty much wrote the rule book for the standard "dumb broad" format that has dominated the TV image of women. Now in her twenty-third TV season, she is still playing the same character: the birdbrained redhead who gets into ridiculous trouble, draws everyone else in with her, and finally gets out by some equally birdbrained scheme. In the old days the plots hinged on her driving Desi Arnaz crazy with her antics and fearfully waiting for his exploding temper. He would scold and discipline her like a child, and finally forgive her. Now she drives Gale Gordon crazy.

The Lucille Ball situation comedy model is a zany child-woman who is dumb and innocent and who has to be patronizingly disciplined by the husband/father/boss. (In situation comedies starring women, there is always a dominant male. Women are never independently in charge of their own lives.) This format depends for much of its comedy on the woman manipulating the man: tricking, deceiving, flirting, coddling, finally admitting she's doing wrong and being forgiven. It is, thankfully, going out of style, though remnants of it still persist in even the most updated shows.

"The Mary Tyler Moore Show," now in its fourth year on CBS, is probably the best example of how things have changed. Mary is over 30, unmarried and not the least in a panic about it, actually appears to have a sex life, and is neither stupid nor helpless. Her show is the most consistently well-written comedy on the air because the people are funny, not the situation, and that's what makes a sitcom work. The comedy evolves from characterization, and not from strained sight gags or unbelievable twists of plot. Moore is the superb straight woman for a terrific bunch of second bananas, and she remains the most realistic and identifiable "heroine" of all the women on the tube. Still, she has her problems.

Mary is supposedly the associate producer, which would make her second in command on her evening news show. Yet she addresses the producer (the dominant male) as Mr. Grant, and he calls her Mary. She takes dictation from him and answers his phone. Would a male associate producer play secretary? No way. It is also interesting to note that though she is second in command and refers to him as Mr. Grant, mere writers on the show call him Lou. They, of course, are men, so it's okay. (Never let a woman get familiar with you; she's in a lower caste.)

There is another character on this show of particular interest to women, and that is Mary's friend Rhoda (played by the excellent Valerie Harper). Rhoda's character began as a rather frumpy, overweight, wisecracking man-chaser. Then at the beginning of last season, Valerie Harper returned, weight off, looking gorgeous, and they had to rewrite her part. She became the very attractive, wisecracking Rhoda who now makes jokes about all the men who are chasing her instead of those who got away. She's just as funny now that she's an attractive woman. (In fact, there is talk of spinning off a new series based on Rhoda herself.) You see? And they said it couldn't be done.

"Diana," on NBC, is producer-director Leonard Stern's attempt to do a rip-off of "The Mary Tyler Moore Show," and he at least had the good sense to get a terrific actress for the part. Diana Rigg is probably the most talented woman any sitcom has to offer, but Stern's brain seems to have turned to mush once he had her sign the contract. He forgot to get a concept for a show and then forgot to get good writers. So we have a very tired "cute" idea about a 30-year-old British designer who comes to New York to work in a department store full of cute sexist men, and she sublets her bachelor brother's cute apartment, not knowing that he has loaned keys to a lot of other cute sexist men.

Any woman with a brain in her head would: (a) get a job where men didn't treat her like a piece of meat, and (b) change the lock on the apartment door. But then Leonard Stern wouldn't have a series, which shows you that he doesn't really have a series in the first place. Rigg plays a divorcée who is, in her words, "not untouched by human hands." Score one for reality, but it ends there. The result is a lot of smirky sex from her boss (the dominant male) and from the assorted creeps who have apartment keys.

If this series makes it, it will be only because Rigg is able to inject some of her own wit and intelligence into this dated idiocy. She deserves better, as reruns of "The Avengers" will prove.

"Maude" is back on CBS for her second year, and we are promised an answer this year to that age-old question, "What does she do all day?" She has no outside job; she has only a five-room house with a maid who comes in to clean and cook, but we never see Maude do anything except yell at everyone. No wonder she's testy; she's bored to death. But she's also very funny. Bea Arthur can get a laugh from just about any old line. Happily, she has a lot to work with, as this is one of the best-written sitcoms on the air.

There is, of course, the dominant male, her husband, who gets the best of her by being calm while she blows up, but once in a while she wins one. Maude is over 40, four times married, and has an apparently happy sex life. She is a sassy, brainy, knee-jerk liberal who now and then mouths a few things about women's rights, but shows no evidence of it in her own lifestyle. The show has had the guts to tackle subjects like abortion and alcoholism head-on, and for that, one must be grateful. Whether the series will reconcile Maude's intelligence and independence of spirit with the life she lives remains to be seen. It's a problem a lot of women have in real life, and ought to be worth a provocative episode or two.

"The Snoop Sisters," on NBC, is a new 90-minute show that appears once every four weeks in rotation with other series. It stars the top-notch Helen Hayes and Mildred Natwick as two sisters who live in luxury in a Gramercy Park town house in New York and meddle in their nephew's police detective work. They, of course, solve all the crimes because Hayes is a mystery writer.

Alan Shayne, the creator of the series, had intended the pair to be two anachronistic characters, one a tweedy anthropology buff (à la Margaret Mead) and the other an elegant diplomat's widow, determined above all else to live life with style and grace. Leonard Stern strikes again. He is producing the series and has watered the characters down, at least in the pilot episode, into cute old ladies doing a lot of shtick that doesn't fit their characters, and bogged down by phony plot details. If the series survives, it will be due, again, to the power of two strong, superb actresses to overcome their material.

Carol Burnett, now in her seventh season on CBS, has a show that seems to improve with age. Burnett is quick to proclaim her admiration for Lucille Ball, but, though Ball has obviously influenced some of her work, she reminds me much more of the great Imogene Coca. Burnett, like Coca, is at her best in sketch comedy, and will do anything for a laugh, which is what endears her to her audiences. The running-gag characters she plays on her show are almost always funny because they are ugly, ridiculous, stupid, haggy, or in some other way grotesque; unfortunately, Burnett's humor epitomizes the idea that a woman can't be attractive while she's being funny. Wit has little to do with it except in Burnett's own ability to kid what she's doing even while she's doing it, a subtlety that is not lost on those of us who have loved her over the years. She is also blessed with the greatest second banana in the business, Harvey Korman, and writers who are able to come up to her talent about 75 percent of the time. For TV, that's not bad.

In addition to the six shows mentioned above, in which women star on their own, there are eight more shows in which they star with men. Half a dozen of them are situation comedies: "Adam's Rib," "Room 222," "The Girl with Something Extra," "Bob & Carol & Ted & Alice," "The Partridge Family," and "The Brady Bunch." The other two shows are a musical comedy, "Sonny and Cher," and the previously mentioned drama "The Waltons."

The most promising of the sitcoms was "Adam's Rib," based on the Tracy-Hepburn movie, and starring as the husband-and-wife lawyers two delightful actors, Blythe Danner and Ken Howard. The scripts seen at this writing did not live up to the promise. The other sitcoms have to do with cute domestic situations between hubby and wife and kids, except for "Room 222," in which Denise Nicholas has the only leading black woman's role in all of prime-time TV, that of a school counselor.

In the 48 remaining shows on the schedule, dominated by male stars, the women's roles are almost all those of housewives, secretaries, nurses, or the male star's girlfriend, mother, child, or ex-wife; women who exist not on their own character contributions to the show, but as appendages to men who are the center of the TV universe.

It matters not that some women have "star" billing in these 48 series. They are not the protagonists. Hope Lange, for instance, who "stars" as Dick Van Dyke's wife, is leaving even if the show is renewed, because all she does is "pour coffee." On "Ironside," the policewoman, played by Elizabeth Baur, has so little to do that one woman who watched two whole episodes thought she was Ironside's secretary.

But then, the "crime drama" format is not very sympathetic to women, and there are 26 of those shows on the tube this season—almost half the schedule. None of them have women protagonists, and what's worse, a recent study at the University of Pennsylvania shows that not only is violence on TV on the increase again, but that women and minorities are increasingly being shown as the victims of that violence. Further, the study shows that this repeated victimization of women and minorities adds to their own feelings of insecurity and to a reduced self-image. Could it be that it's backlash time from all those white middle-class men over there on Broadcast Boulevard?

If what you see on the tube isn't enough to convince you, consider this: there is not one woman executive producer on any of those 62 shows. There is only one woman producer (Cleo Smith; an old friend of Lucille Ball's and producer of her show) and not one regularly scheduled woman director. Out of all 62 shows, there is only one woman script consultant or story editor and only three regularly retained women writers, two of them teamed with their husbands.

If the three commercial networks aren't guilty of discrimination against women, I don't know who is.

QUESTIONS

1 What are the key terms in the thesis? How is each term supported in the essay?
2 Granting that "self-aggrandizing" is a loaded word, is its use justified? Why or why not?
3 Which of Rock's major points have changed in recent years? To what extent?

TOPICS FOR COMPOSITION

1   Using question 3 above, write an update of Rock's essay.
2   Argue either side of the idea that sexism exists in one of the following: schools, employment, sports. Pattern your essay after Rock's, using pertinent examples, statistical evidence, etc.

SHORT STORY

"The Bench" is committed literature. In this sense, its major purpose is to reveal a social and political condition that affects an oppressed or minority group. Karlie's individual protest is, at the same time, an assertion of his dignity and oneness with his race. The story unfolds through Karlie's at first hesitant acceptance of the truth of the words that he hears in stark contrast with the reality of conditions about him.

THE BENCH

Richard Rive

"We form an integral part of a complex society, a society complex in that a vast proportion of the population are denied the very basic privileges of existence, a society that condemns a man to an inferior position because he has the misfortune to be born black, a society that can only retain its precarious social and economic position at the expense of an enormous oppressed proletariat!"

Karlie's eyes shone as he watched the speaker. Those were great words, he thought, great words and true. The speaker paused for a moment and sipped some water from a glass. Karlie sweated. The hot October sun beat down mercilessly on the gathering. The trees on the Grand Parade afforded very little shelter and his handkerchief was already soaked where he had placed it between his neck and shirt collar. Karlie stared round him at the sea of faces. Every shade of colour was represented, from shiny ebony to the one or two whites in the crowd. He stared at the two detectives who were busily making shorthand notes of the speeches, and then turned to stare back at the speaker.

"It is up to us to challenge the rights of any groups who wilfully and deliberately condemn a fellow group to a servile position. We must challenge the rights of any people who see fit to segregate human beings solely on grounds of pigmentation. Your children are denied the rights which are theirs by birth. They are segregated socially, economically. . . ."

Ah, thought Karlie, that man knows what he is speaking about. He says I am as good as any other man, even a white man. That needs much thinking. I wonder if he thinks I have the right to go into any bioscope or eat in any restaurant, or that my children can go to any school? These are dangerous ideas and need much thinking; I wonder what Ou Klaas would say to this. Ou Klaas said God made the white man and the black man separately and the one must always be *"baas"* and the other *"jong."* But this man says different things and somehow they seem true.

Karlie's brow was knitted as he thought. On the platform were many speakers, both white and black, and they were behaving as if there were no difference of colour between them. There was a white woman in a blue dress offering a cigarette to Nxeli. That could never happen at Bietjiesvlei. Old Lategan at the store would have fainted if his Annatjie had offered Witbooi a cigarette. And Annatjie had no such pretty dress. These were new things, and he, Karlie, had to be careful before he accepted them. But why shouldn't he accept them? He was not coloured any more, he was a human being. The speaker had said so. He remembered seeing pictures in the newspaper of people who defied laws which relegated them to a particular class, and those people were smiling as they went to prison. This was a strange world.

The speaker continued and Karlie listened intently. His speech was obviously carefully prepared and he spoke slowly, choosing his words. This is a great man, Karlie thought.

The last speaker was the white lady in the blue dress, who asked them to challenge any discriminatory laws or measures in every possible manner. Why should she speak like that? thought Karlie. She could go to the best bioscopes, and swim at the best beaches. Why, she was even more beautiful than Annatjie Lategan. They had warned him in Bietjiesvlei about coming to the city. He had seen the *Skollies* in District Six and knew what to expect there. Hanover Street held no terrors for him. But no one had told him about this. This was new, this set one's mind thinking, yet he felt it was true. She said one should challenge. He would challenge. He, Karlie, would astound old Lategan and Balie at the dairy farm. They could do what they liked to him after that. He would smile like those people in the newspaper.

The meeting was almost over when Karlie threaded his way through the crowd. The words of the speakers were still milling through his head. It could never happen in Bietjiesvlei, he thought, or could it? The sudden screech of a car pulling to a hurried stop whirled him back to his senses. A white head was angrily thrust through the window. "Look where you're going, you black bastard!"

Karlie stared dazedly at him. Surely this white man had never heard what the speakers had said. He could never have seen the white woman offering Nxeli a cigarette. Karlie could never imagine the white lady shouting those words at him. It would be best to catch a train and think these things over.

He saw the station in a new light. Here was a mass of human beings, some black, some white, and some brown like himself. Here they mixed with one another, yet each mistrusted the other with an unnatural fear. Each treated the other with suspicion, each moved in a narrow, haunted pattern of its own manufacture. One must challenge these things the speaker had said . . . in one's own way. Yet how in one's own way? How was one to challenge? Slowly it dawned upon him. Here was his chance, *the bench.* The railway bench with the legend "Europeans Only" neatly painted on it in white. For one moment it symbolized all the misery of the plural South African society. Here was a challenge to his rights as a man. There it stood, a perfectly ordinary wooden railway bench, like hundreds of thousands of others in South Africa. His challenge. That bench, now, had concentrated in it all the evils of a system he could not understand. It was the obstacle between himself and humanity. If he sat on it he was a man. If he was afraid he denied himself membership as a human in a human society. He almost had visions of righting the pernicious system if only he sat on that bench. Here was his chance. He, Karlie, would challenge.

He seemed perfectly calm when he sat down on the bench, but inside his heart was thumping wildly. Two conflicting ideas now throbbed through him. The one said, "I have no right to sit on this bench"; the other said, "Why have I no right to sit on this bench?" The one voice spoke of the past, of the servile position he had occupied on the farms, of his father and his father's father who were born black, lived like blacks and died like oxen. The other voice spoke of the future and said, "Karlie, you are a man. You have dared what your father would not have dared. You will die like a man!"

Karlie took out a cigarette and smoked. Nobody seemed to notice his sitting there. This was an anti-climax. The world still pursued its monotonous way. No voice shouted "Karlie has conquered!" He was a normal human being sitting on a bench in a busy station, smoking a cigarette. Or was this his victory, the fact that he was a normal human being? A well-dressed white woman walked down the platform. Would she sit on the bench, Karlie wondered. And then that gnawing voice, "You should stand and let the white woman sit." Karlie narrowed his eyes and gripped tighter at his cigarette. She swept past him without the slightest twitch of an eyelid and walked on down the platform. Was she afraid to challenge, to challenge his right to be human? Karlie now felt tired. A third conflicting emotion was now creeping in, a compensatory emotion which said, "You do not sit on this bench to challenge, you sit there because you are tired. You are tired; therefore you sit." He would not move, because he was tired, or was it because he wanted to sit where he liked?

People were now pouring out of a train that had pulled into the station. There were so many people pushing and jostling one another that nobody noticed him. This was his train. It would be quite easy to step into the train and ride off home, but that would be giving in, suffering defeat, refusing the challenge, in fact admitting that he was not a human being. He sat on. Lazily he blew the cigarette smoke into the air, thinking . . . his mind was far from the meeting and the bench, he was thinking of Bietjiesvlei and Ou Klaas, how he had insisted that Karlie should come to Cape Town. Ou Klaas could look so quizzically at one and suck at his pipe. He was wise to know and knew much. He had said one must go to Cape Town and learn the ways of the world. He would spit and wink slyly when he spoke of District Six and the women he knew in Hanover Street. Ou Klaas knew everything. He said God made us white or black and we must therefore keep our places.

"Get off this seat!"

Karlie did not hear the gruff voice. Ou Klaas would be on the land now, waiting for his tot of cheap wine.

"I said get off the bench, you swine!"

Karlie suddenly whipped back to reality. For a moment he was going to jump up, then he remembered who he was and why he was sitting there. Suddenly he felt very tired. He looked up slowly into a very red face that stared down at him.

"Get up! I said. There are benches down there for you!"

Karlie stared up and said nothing. He stared up into very sharp, cold gray eyes.

"Can't you hear me speaking to you, you black swine!"

Slowly and deliberately Karlie puffed at his cigarette. So this was his test. They both stared at each other, challenged with the eyes, like two boxers, each knowing that they must eventually trade blows yet each afraid to strike first.

"Must I dirty my hands on scum like you?"

Karlie said nothing. To speak would be to break the spell, the supremacy he felt he was slowly gaining. An uneasy silence. Then,

"I will call a policeman rather than kick a Hotnot like you! You can't even open your black jaw when a white man speaks to you!"

Karlie saw the weakness. The white youth was afraid to take action himself. He, Karlie, had won the first round of the bench dispute!

A crowd now collected. "Afrika!" shouted one joker. Karlie ignored the remark. People were now milling around, staring at the unusual sight of a black man sitting on a white man's bench. Karlie merely puffed on.

"Look at the black ape! That's the worst of giving these Kaffirs too much rope!"

"I can't understand it, they have their own benches!"

"Don't get up, you have every right to sit there!"

"He'll get hell when a policeman comes!"

"Mind you, I can't see why they shouldn't sit where they please!"

"I've said before, I've had a native servant, and a more impertinent . . ."

Karlie sat and heard nothing. Irresolution had now turned to determination. Under no condition was he going to rise. They could do what they liked.

"So this is the fellow. Hey, get up there! Can't you read?" The policeman was towering over him. Karlie could see the crest on his buttons and the thin wrinkles on his neck. "What is your name and address?"

Karlie still maintained his obstinate silence. It took the policeman rather unawares. The crowd was growing every minute.

"You have no right to speak to this man in such a manner!" It was the white lady in the blue dress.

"Mind your own business! I'll ask your help when I need it. It is people like you who make Kaffirs think they're as good as white people!" Then, addressing Karlie, "Get up, you!"

"I insist that you treat him with proper respect!"

The policeman turned red. "This . . . this . . . ." He was at a loss for words.

"Kick up the Hotnot if he won't get up!" shouted a spectator.

Rudely a white man laid hands on Karlie. "Get up, you bloody bastard!"

Karlie turned to resist, to cling to the bench, his bench. There were more than one man now pulling at him. He hit out wildly and then felt a dull pain as somebody rammed a fist into his face. He was now bleeding and wild-eyed. He would fight for it. The constable clapped a pair of handcuffs round Karlie's wrists and tried to clear a way through the crowd. Karlie was still struggling. A blow or two landed on him. Suddenly he relaxed and slowly struggled to his feet. It was useless fighting any longer. Now it was his turn to smile. He had challenged and won. Who cared at the result?

"Come on, you swine!" said the policeman, forcing Karlie through the crowd.

"Certainly," said Karlie for the first time, and stared at the policeman with the arrogance of one who dared to sit on a "European" bench.

QUESTIONS

1 A knowledge of the full implications of *apartheid* is necessary to understanding Rive's story. Exactly what restrictions does this policy impose on South African nonwhites?
2 What moves Karlie to consider his condition? Does he have doubts about what he hears?
3 What events contribute to his final determination to protest?
4 What does Karlie's sitting on the restricted bench actually accomplish?

TOPIC FOR COMPOSITION

Certainly we recognize that Karlie's assessment of a racially mixed society—the mistrust, the unnatural fear, the suspicion—accurately reflects the events of our time and place. The speaker said, "One must challenge these things . . . in one's own way." Karlie found a way. How can each of us, in our time and place, combat mistrust, unnatural fear, and suspicion?

An old woman, her deaf-mute, retarded daughter, and a drifter form a trio by which Flannery O'Connor explores the conflict between restraint and repressed desire. Old Mrs. Crater wants desperately to "marry-off" Lucynell and gain a man about the place. Tom T. Shiftlet, for all his professed "moral intelligence," is willing to sacrifice the half-witted Lucynell for a small sum of money, a car, and freedom from the restraints of his meager existence. But we should be careful not to oversimplify the artistry of Miss O'Connor's characterization. As you read, you should give careful attention to the motivations and ambiguities her two main characters display.

THE LIFE YOU SAVE MAY BE YOUR OWN

Flannery O'Connor

The old woman and her daughter were sitting on their porch when Mr. Shiftlet came up their road for the first time. The old woman slid to the edge of her chair and leaned forward, shading her eyes from the piercing sunset with her hand. The daughter could not see far in front of her and continued to play with her fingers. Although the old woman lived in this desolate spot with only her daughter and she had never seen Mr. Shiftlet before, she could tell, even from a distance, that he was a tramp and no one to be afraid of. His left coat sleeve was folded up to show there was only half an arm in it and his gaunt figure listed slightly to the side as if the breeze were pushing him. He had on a black town suit and a brown felt hat that was turned up in the front and down in the back and he carried a tin tool box by a handle. He came on, at an amble, up her road, his face turned toward the sun which appeared to be balancing itself on the peak of a small mountain.

The old woman didn't change her position until he was almost into her yard; then she rose with one hand fisted on her hip. The daughter, a large girl in a short blue organdy dress, saw him all at once and jumped up and began to stamp and point and make excited speechless sounds.

Mr. Shiftlet stopped just inside the yard and set his box on the ground and tipped his hat at her as if she were not in the least afflicted; then he turned toward the old woman and swung the hat all the way off. He had long black slick hair that hung flat from a part in the middle to beyond the tips of his ears on either side. His face descended in forehead for more than half its length and ended suddenly with his features just balanced over a jutting steeltrap jaw. He seemed to be a young man but he had a look of composed dissatisfaction as if he understood life thoroughly.

"Good evening," the old woman said. She was about the size of a cedar fence post and she had a man's gray hat pulled down low over her head.

The tramp stood looking at her and didn't answer. He turned his back and faced the sunset. He swung both his whole and his short arm up slowly so that they indicated an expanse of sky and his figure formed a crooked cross. The old woman watched him with her arms folded across her chest as if she were the owner of the sun, and the daughter watched, her head thrust forward and her fat helpless hands hanging at the wrists. She had long pink-gold hair and eyes as blue as a peacock's neck.

He held the pose for almost fifty seconds and then he picked up his box and came on to the porch and dropped down on the bottom step. "Lady," he said in a firm nasal voice, "I'd give a fortune to live where I could see me a sun do that every evening."

"Does it every evening," the old woman said and sat back down. The daughter sat down too and watched him with a cautious sly look as if he were a bird that had come up very close. He leaned to one side, rooting in his pants pocket, and in a second he brought out a package of chewing gum and offered her a piece. She took it and unpeeled it and began to chew without taking her eyes off him. He offered the old woman a piece but she only raised her upper lip to indicate she had no teeth.

Mr. Shiftlet's pale sharp glance had already passed over everything in the yard— the pump near the corner of the house and the big fig tree that three or four chickens were preparing to roost in—and had moved to a shed where he saw the square rusted back of an automobile. "You ladies drive?" he asked.

"That car ain't run in fifteen year," the old woman said. "The day my husband died, it quit running."

"Nothing is like it used to be, lady," he said. "The world is almost rotten."

"That's right," the old woman said. "You from around here?"

"Name Tom T. Shiftlet," he murmured, looking at the tires.

"I'm pleased to meet you," the old woman said. "Name Lucynell Crater and daughter Lucynell Crater. What you doing around here, Mr. Shiftlet?"

He judged the car to be about a 1928 or '29 Ford. "Lady," he said, and turned and gave her his full attention, "lemme tell you something. There's one of these doctors in Atlanta that's taken a knife and cut the human heart—the human heart," he repeated, leaning forward, "out of a man's chest and held it in his hand," and he held his hand out, palm up, as if it were slightly weighted with the human heart, "and studied it like it was a day-old chicken, and lady," he said, allowing a long significant pause in which his head slid forward and his clay-colored eyes brightened, "he don't know no more about it than you or me."

"That's right," the old woman said.

"Why, if he was to take that knife and cut into every corner of it, he still wouldn't know no more than you or me. What you want to bet?"

"Nothing," the old woman said wisely. "Where you come from, Mr. Shiftlet?"

He didn't answer. He reached into his pocket and brought out a sack of tobacco and a package of cigarette papers and rolled himself a cigarette, expertly with one hand, and attached it in a hanging position to his upper lip. Then he took a box of wooden matches from his pocket and struck one on his shoe. He held the burning match as if he were studying the mystery of flame while it traveled dangerously toward his skin. The daughter began to make loud noises and to point to his hand and shake her finger at him, but when the flame was just before touching him, he leaned down with his hand cupped over it as if he were going to set fire to his nose and lit the cigarette.

He flipped away the dead match and blew a stream of gray into the evening. A sly look came over his face. "Lady," he said, "nowadays, people'll do anything anyways. I can tell you my name is Tom T. Shiftlet and I come from Tarwater, Tennessee, but you never have seen me before: how you know I ain't lying? How you know my name ain't Aaron Sparks, lady, and I come from Singleberry, Georgia, or how you know it's not George Speeds and I come from Lucy, Alabama, or how you know I ain't Thompson Bright from Toolafalls, Mississippi?"

"I don't know nothing about you," the old woman muttered, irked.

"Lady," he said, "people don't care how they lie. Maybe the best I can tell you is, I'm a man; but listen lady," he said and paused and made his tone more ominous still, "what is a man?"

The old woman began to gum a seed. "What you carry in that tin box, Mr. Shiftlet?" she asked.

"Tools," he said, put back. "I'm a carpenter."

"Well, if you come out here to work, I'll be able to feed you and give you a place to sleep but I can't pay. I'll tell you that before you begin," she said.

There was no answer at once and no particular expression on his face. He leaned back against the two-by-four that helped support the porch roof. "Lady," he said slowly, "there's some men that some things mean more to them than money." The old woman rocked without comment and the daughter watched the trigger that moved up and down in his neck. He told the old woman then that all most people were interested in was money, but he asked what a man was made for. He asked her if a man was made for money, or what. He asked her what she thought she was made for but she didn't answer, she only sat rocking and wondered if a one-armed man could put a new roof on her garden house. He asked a lot of questions that she didn't answer. He told her that he was twenty-eight years old and had lived a varied life. He had been a gospel singer, a foreman on the railroad, an assistant in an undertaking parlor, and he come over the radio for three months with Uncle Roy and his Red Creek Wranglers. He said he had fought and bled in the Arm Service of his country and visited every foreign land and that everywhere he had seen people that didn't care if they did a thing one way or another. He said he hadn't been raised thataway.

A fat yellow moon appeared in the branches of the fig tree as if it were going to roost there with the chickens. He said that a man had to escape to the country to see the world whole and that he wished he lived in a desolate place like this where he could see the sun go down every evening like God made it to do.

"Are you married or are you single?" the old woman asked.

There was a long silence. "Lady," he asked finally, "where would you find you an innocent woman today? I wouldn't have any of this trash I could just pick up."

The daughter was leaning very far down, hanging her head almost between her knees watching him through a triangular door she had made in her overturned hair; and she suddenly fell in a heap on the floor and began to whimper. Mr. Shiftlet straightened her out and helped her get back in the chair.

"Is she your baby girl?" he asked.

"My only," the old woman said "and she's the sweetest girl in the world. I would give her up for nothing on earth. She's smart too. She can sweep the floor, cook, wash, feed the chickens, and hoe. I wouldn't give her up for a casket of jewels."

"No," he said kindly, "don't ever let any man take her away from you."

"Any man come after her," the old woman said, "'ll have to stay around the place."

Mr. Shiftlet's eye in the darkness was focused on a part of the automobile bumper that glittered in the distance. "Lady," he said, jerking his short arm up as if he could point with it to her house and yard and pump, "there ain't a broken thing on this plantation that I couldn't fix for you, one-arm jackleg or not. I'm a man," he said with a sullen dignity, "even if I ain't a whole one. I got," he said, tapping his knuckles on the floor to emphasize the immensity of what he was going to say, "a moral intelligence!" and his face pierced out of the darkness into a shaft of doorlight and he stared at her as if he were astonished himself at this impossible truth.

The old woman was not impressed with the phrase. "I told you you could hang around and work for food," she said, "if you don't mind sleeping in that car yonder."

"Why listen, lady," he said with a grin of delight, "the monks of old slept in their coffins!"

"They wasn't as advanced as we are," the old woman said.

The next morning he began on the roof of the garden house while Lucynell, the daughter, sat on a rock and watched him work. He had not been around a week before the change he had made in the place was apparent. He had patched the front and back steps, built a new hog pen, restored the fence, and taught Lucynell, who was completely deaf and had never said a word in her life, to say the word "bird." The big rosy-faced girl followed him everywhere, saying "Burrttddt ddbirrrttdt," and clapping her hands. The old woman watched from a distance, secretly pleased. She was ravenous for a son-in-law.

Mr. Shiftlet slept on the hard narrow back seat of the car with his feet out the side window. He had his razor and a can of water on a crate that served him as a bedside table and he put up a piece of mirror against the back glass and kept his coat neatly on a hanger that he hung over one of the windows.

In the evenings he sat on the steps and talked while the old woman and Lucynell rocked violently in their chairs on either side of him. The old woman's three mountains were black against the dark blue sky and were visited off and on by various planets and by the moon after it had left the chickens. Mr. Shiftlet pointed out that the reason he had improved this plantation was because he had taken a personal interest in it. He said he was even going to make the automobile run.

He had raised the hood and studied the mechanism and he said he could tell that the car had been built in the days when cars were really built. You take now, he said, one man puts in one bolt and another man puts in another bolt and another man puts in another bolt so that it's a man for a bolt. That's why you have to pay so much for a car: you're paying all those men. Now if you didn't have to pay but one man, you could get you a cheaper car and one that had had a personal interest taken in it, and it would be a better car. The old woman agreed with him that this was so.

Mr. Shiftlet said that the trouble with the world was that nobody cared, or stopped and took any trouble. He said he never would have been able to teach Lucynell to say a word if he hadn't cared and stopped long enough.

"Teach her to say something else," the old woman said.

"What you want her to say next?" Mr. Shiftlet asked.

The old woman's smile was broad and toothless and suggestive. "Teach her to say 'sugarpie,'" she said.

Mr. Shiftlet already knew what was on her mind.

The next day he began to tinker with the automobile and that evening he told her that if she would buy a fan belt, he would be able to make the car run.

The old woman said she would give him the money. "You see that girl yonder?" she asked, pointing to Lucynell who was sitting on the floor a foot away, watching him, her eyes blue even in the dark. "If it was ever a man wanted to take her away, I would say, 'No man on earth is going to take that sweet girl of mine away from me!' but if he was to say, 'Lady, I don't want to take her away, I want her right here,' I would say, 'Mister, I don't blame you none. I wouldn't pass up a chance to live in a permanent place and get the sweetest girl in the world myself. You ain't no fool,' I would say."

"How old is she?" Mr. Shiftlet asked casually.

"Fifteen, sixteen," the old woman said. The girl was nearly thirty but because of her innocence it was impossible to guess.

"It would be a good idea to paint it too," Mr. Shiftlet remarked. "You don't want it to rust out."

"We'll see about that later," the old woman said.

The next day he walked into town and returned with the parts he needed and a can of gasoline. Late in the afternoon, terrible noises issued from the shed and the old woman rushed out of the house, thinking Lucynell was somewhere having a fit. Lucynell was sitting on a chicken crate, stamping her feet and screaming, "Burrddtt! bddurrddtttt!" but her fuss was drowned out by the car. With a volley of blasts it emerged from the shed, moving in a fierce and stately way. Mr. Shiftlet was in the driver's seat, sitting very erect. He had an expression of serious modesty on his face as if he had just raised the dead.

That night, rocking on the porch, the old woman began her business, at once. "You want you an innocent woman, don't you?" she asked sympathetically. "You don't want none of this trash."

"No'm, I don't," Mr. Shiftlet said.

"One that can't talk," she continued, "can't sass you back or use foul language. That's the kind for you to have. Right there," and she pointed to Lucynell sitting cross-legged in her chair, holding both feet in her hands.

"That's right," he admitted. "She wouldn't give me any trouble."

"Saturday," the old woman said, "you and her and me can drive into town and get married."

Mr. Shiftlet eased his position on the steps.

"I can't get married right now," he said. "Everything you want to do takes money and I ain't got any."

"What you need with money?" she asked.

"It takes money," he said. "Some people'll do anything anyhow these days, but the way I think, I wouldn't marry no woman that I couldn't take on a trip like she was somebody. I mean take her to a hotel and treat her. I wouldn't marry the Duchesser Windsor," he said firmly, "unless I could take her to a hotel and giver something good to eat.

"I was raised thataway and there ain't a thing I can do about it. My old mother taught me how to do."

"Lucynell don't even know what a hotel is," the old woman muttered. "Listen here, Mr. Shiftlet," she said, sliding forward in her chair, "you'd be getting a permanent house and a deep well and the most innocent girl in the world. You don't need no money. Lemme tell you something: there ain't any place in the world for a poor disabled friendless drifting man."

The ugly words settled in Mr. Shiftlet's head like a group of buzzards in the top of a tree. He didn't answer at once. He rolled himself a cigarette and lit it and then he said in an even voice, "Lady, a man is divided into two parts, body and spirit."

The old woman clamped her gums together.

"A body and a spirit," he repeated. "The body, lady, is like a house: it don't go anywhere; but the spirit, lady, is like a automobile: always on the move, always . . ."

"Listen, Mr. Shiftlet," she said, "my well never goes dry and my house is always warm in the winter and there's no mortgage on a thing about this place. You can go to the courthouse and see for yourself. And yonder under that shed is a fine automobile." She laid the bait carefully. "You can have it painted by Saturday. I'll pay for the paint."

In the darkness, Mr. Shiftlet's smile stretched like a weary snake waking up by a fire. After a second he recalled himself and said, "I'm only saying a man's spirit means more to him than anything else. I would have to take my wife off for the weekend without no regards at all for cost. I got to follow where my spirit says to go."

"I'll give you fifteen dollars for a weekend trip," the old woman said in a crabbed voice. "That's the best I can do."

"That wouldn't hardly pay for more than the gas and the hotel," he said. "It wouldn't feed her."

"Seventeen-fifty," the old woman said. "That's all I got so it isn't any use you trying to milk me. You can take a lunch."

Mr. Shiftlet was deeply hurt by the word "milk." He didn't doubt that she had more money sewed up in her mattress but he had already told her he was not interested in her money. "I'll make that do," he said and rose and walked off without treating with her further.

On Saturday the three of them drove into town in the car that the paint had barely dried on and Mr. Shiftlet and Lucynell were married in the Ordinary's office while the old woman witnessed. As they came out of the courthouse, Mr. Shiftlet began twisting his neck in his collar. He looked morose and bitter as if he had been insulted while someone held him. "That didn't satisfy me none," he said. "That was just something a woman in an office did, nothing but paper work and blood tests. What do they know about my blood? If they was to take my heart and cut it out," he said, "they wouldn't know a thing about me. It didn't satisfy me at all."

"It satisfied the law," the old woman said sharply.

"The law," Mr. Shiftlet said and spit. "It's the law that don't satisfy me."

He had painted the car dark green with a yellow band around it just under the windows. The three of them climbed in the front seat and the old woman said, "Don't Lucynell look pretty? Looks like a baby doll." Lucynell was dressed up in a white dress that her mother had uprooted from a trunk and there was a Panama hat on her head with a bunch of red wooden cherries on the brim. Every now and then her placid expression was changed by a sly isolated little thought like a shoot of green in the desert. "You got a prize!" the old woman said.

Mr. Shiftlet didn't even look at her.

They drove back to the house to let the old woman off and pick up the lunch. When they were ready to leave, she stood staring in the window of the car, with her fingers clenched around the glass. Tears began to seep sideways out of her eyes and run along the dirty creases in her face. "I ain't ever been parted with her for two days before," she said.

Mr. Shiftlet started the motor.

"And I wouldn't let no man have her but you because I seen you would do right. Good-by, Sugarbaby," she said, clutching at the sleeve of the white dress. Lucynell looked straight at her and didn't seem to see her there at all. Mr. Shiftlet eased the car forward so that she had to move her hands.

The early afternoon was clear and open and surrounded by pale blue sky. Although the car would go only thirty miles an hour, Mr. Shiftlet imagined a terrific climb and dip and swerve that went entirely to his head so that he forgot his morning bitterness. He had always wanted an automobile but he had never been able to afford one before. He drove very fast because he wanted to make Mobile by nightfall.

Occasionally he stopped his thoughts long enough to look at Lucynell in the seat beside him. She had eaten the lunch as soon as they were out of the yard and now she was pulling the cherries off the hat one by one and throwing them out the window. He became depressed in spite of the car. He had driven about a hundred miles when he decided that she must be hungry again and at the next small town they came to, he stopped in front of an aluminum-painted eating place called The Hot Spot and took her in and ordered her a plate of ham and grits. The ride had made her sleepy and as soon as she got up on the stool, she rested her head on the counter and shut her eyes. There was no one in The Hot Spot but Mr. Shiftlet and the boy behind the counter, a pale youth with a greasy rag hung over his shoulder. Before he could dish up the food, she was snoring gently.

"Give it to her when she wakes up," Mr. Shiftlet said. "I'll pay for it now."

The boy bent over her and stared at the long pink-gold hair and the half-shut sleeping eyes. Then he looked up and stared at Mr. Shiftlet. "She looks like an angel of Gawd," he murmured.

"Hitchhiker," Mr. Shiftlet explained. "I can't wait. I got to make Tuscaloosa."

The boy bent over again and very carefully touched his finger to a strand of the golden hair and Mr. Shiftlet left.

He was more depressed than ever as he drove on by himself. The late afternoon had grown hot and sultry and the country had flattened out. Deep in the sky a storm was preparing very slowly and without thunder as if it meant to drain every drop of air from the earth before it broke. There were times when Mr. Shiftlet preferred not to be alone. He felt too that a man with a car had a responsibility to others and he kept his eye out for a hitchhiker. Occasionally he saw a sign that warned: "Drive carefully. The life you save may be your own."

The narrow road dropped off on either side into dry fields and here and there a shack or a filling station stood in a clearing. The sun began to set directly in front of the automobile. It was a reddening ball that through his windshield was slightly flat on the bottom and top. He saw a boy in overalls and a gray hat standing on the edge of the road and he slowed the car down and stopped in front of him. The boy didn't have his hand raised to thumb the ride, he was only standing there, but he had a small cardboard suitcase and his hat was set on his head in a way to indicate that he had left somewhere for good. "Son," Mr. Shiftlet said. "I see you want a ride."

The boy didn't say he did or he didn't but he opened the door of the car and got in, and Mr. Shiftlet started driving again. The child held the suitcase on his lap and folded his arms on top of it. He turned his head and looked out the window away from Mr. Shiftlet. Mr. Shiftlet felt oppressed. "Son," he said after a minute, "I got the best old mother in the world so I reckon you only got the second best."

The boy gave him a quick dark glance and then turned his face back out the window.

"It's nothing so sweet," Mr. Shiftlet continued, "as a boy's mother. She taught him his first prayers at her knee, she give him love when no other would, she told him what was right and what wasn't, and she seen that he done the right thing. Son," he said. "I never rued a day in my life like the one I rued when I left that old mother of mine."

The boy shifted in his seat but he didn't look at Mr. Shiftlet. He unfolded his arms and put one hand on the door handle.

"My mother was a angel of Gawd," Mr. Shiftlet said in a very strained voice. "He took her from heaven and giver to me and I left her." His eyes were instantly clouded over with a mist of tears. The car was barely moving.

The boy turned angrily in the seat. "You go to the devil!" he cried. "My old woman is a flea bag and yours is a stinking polecat!" and with that he flung the door open and jumped out with his suitcase into the ditch.

Mr. Shiftlet was so shocked that for about a hundred feet he drove along slowly with the door still open. A cloud, the exact color of the boy's hat and shaped like a turnip, had descended over the sun, and another, worse looking, crouched behind the car. Mr. Shiftlet felt that the rottenness of the world was about to engulf him. He raised his arm and let it fall again to his breast. "Oh Lord!" he prayed. "Break forth and wash the slime from this earth!"

The turnip continued slowly to descend. After a few minutes there was a guffawing peal of thunder from behind and fantastic raindrops, like tin-can tops, crashed over the rear of Mr. Shiftlet's car. Very quickly he stepped on the gas and with his stump sticking out the window he raced the galloping shower into Mobile.

QUESTIONS

1   The names Crater and Shiftlet obviously have symbolic significance. How many different meanings do they evoke?
2   What descriptive details give insights to the complex motivations that lead Mrs. Crater to "sacrifice" Lucynell?
3   How do Tom T. Shiftlet's high-sounding preachments and his advice to the young hitchhiker complicate an even assessment of his character?
4   To what degree does the story illustrate the warning that "the life you save may be your own"?

TOPICS FOR COMPOSITION

1   This story deals with the individual's responsibility to other human beings. Write an essay in which you argue the degree to which one's actions and desires are restrained by a sense of responsibility to others.
2   Write an essay in which you set forth and document from the story the relationship between descriptive detail, symbol, and characterization.

☐

Roth's "The Conversion of the Jews" clearly spans multiple levels of meaning, ranging from an examination of youthful inquisitiveness to a plea for religious and social ecumenicity. Several aspects of the story help in understanding Roth's movement through his levels of meaning. Note the following:

1   The language used by Ozzie and Itzie in their opening "theological" discussion
2   The contrast presented between Ozzie's inquiring mind and the learned responses of his mother, the Rabbi, and the custodian
3   Ozzie's reaction to the power of his individual protest
4   The impact of unexpected action on the mass mind

THE CONVERSION OF THE JEWS

Philip Roth

"You're a real one for opening your mouth in the first place," Itzie said. "What do you open your mouth all the time for?"

"I didn't bring it up, Itz, I didn't," Ozzie said.

"What do you care about Jesus Christ for anyway?"

"I didn't bring up Jesus Christ. He did. I didn't even know what he was talking about. Jesus is historical, he kept saying. Jesus is historical." Ozzie mimicked the monumental voice of Rabbi Binder.

"Jesus was a person that lived like you and me," Ozzie continued. "That's what Binder said—"

"Yeah? . . . So what! What do I give two cents whether he lived or not. And what do you gotta open your mouth!" Itzie Lieberman favored closed-mouthedness, especially when it came to Ozzie Freedman's questions. Mrs. Freedman had to see Rabbi Binder twice before about Ozzie's questions and this Wednesday at four-thirty would be the third time. Itzie preferred to keep *his* mother in the kitchen; he settled for behind-the-back subtleties such as gestures, faces, snarls and other less delicate barnyard noises.

"He was a real person, Jesus, but he wasn't like God, and we don't believe he is God." Slowly, Ozzie was explaining Rabbi Binder's position to Itzie, who had been absent from Hebrew School the previous afternoon.

"The Catholics," Itzie said helpfully, "they believe in Jesus Christ, that he's God." Itzie Lieberman used "the Catholics" in its broadest sense—to include the Protestants.

Ozzie received Itzie's remark with a tiny head bob, as though it were a footnote, and went on. "His mother was Mary, and his father probably was Joseph," Ozzie said. "But the New Testament says his real father was God."

"His *real* father?"

"Yeah," Ozzie said, "that's the big thing, his father's supposed to be God."

"Bull."

"That's what Rabbi Binder says, that it's impossible—"

"Sure it's impossible. That stuff's all bull. To have a baby you gotta get laid," Itzie theologized. "Mary hadda get laid."

"That's what Binder says: 'The only way a woman can have a baby is to have intercourse with a man.'"

"He said *that,* Ozz?" For a moment it appeared that Itzie had put the theological question aside. "He said that, intercourse?" A little curled smile shaped itself in the lower half of Itzie's face like a pink mustache. "What you guys do, Ozz, you laugh or something?"

"I raised my hand."

"Yeah? Whatja say?"

"That's when I asked the question."

Itzie's face lit up. "Whatja ask about—intercourse?"

"No, I asked the question about God, how if He could create the heaven and earth in six days, and make all the animals and the fish and the light in six days—the light especially, that's what always gets me, that He could make the light. Making fish and animals, that's pretty good—"

"That's damn good." Itzie's appreciation was honest but unimaginative: it was as though God had just pitched a one-hitter.

"But making light . . . I mean when you think about it, it's really something," Ozzie said. "Anyway, I asked Binder if He could make all that in six days, and He could *pick* the six days he wanted right out of nowhere, why couldn't He let a woman have a baby without having intercourse."

"You said intercourse, Ozz, to Binder?"

"Yeah."

"Right in class?"

"Yeah."

Itzie smacked the side of his head.

"I mean, no kidding around," Ozzie said, "that'd really be nothing. After all that other stuff, that'd practically be nothing."

Itzie considered a moment. "What'd Binder say?"

"He started all over again explaining how Jesus was historical and how he lived like you and me but he wasn't God. So I said I under*stood* that. What I wanted to know was different."

What Ozzie wanted to know was always different. The first time he had wanted to know how Rabbi Binder could call the Jews "The Chosen People" if the Declaration of Independence claimed all men to be created equal. Rabbi Binder tried to distinguish for him between political equality and spiritual legitimacy, but what Ozzie wanted to know, he insisted vehemently, was different. That was the first time his mother had to come.

Then there was the plane crash. Fifty-eight people had been killed in a plane crash at La Guardia. In studying a casualty list in the newspaper his mother had discovered among the list of those dead eight Jewish names (his grandmother had nine but she counted Miller as a Jewish name); because of the eight she said the plane crash was "a tragedy." During free-discussion time on Wednesday Ozzie had brought to Rabbi Binder's attention this matter of "some of his relations" always picking out the Jewish names. Rabbi Binder had begun to explain cultural unity and some other things when Ozzie stood up at his seat and said that what he wanted to know was different. Rabbi Binder insisted that he sit down and it was then that Ozzie shouted that he wished all fifty-eight were Jews. That was the second time his mother came.

"And he kept explaining about Jesus being historical, and so I kept asking him. No kidding, Itz, he was trying to make me look stupid."

"So what he finally do?"

"Finally he starts screaming that I was deliberately simple-minded and a wise guy, and that my mother had to come, and this was the last time. And that I'd never get bar-mitzvahed if he could help it. Then, Itz, then he starts talking in the voice like a statue, real slow and deep, and he says that I better think over what I said about the Lord. He told me to go to his office and think it over." Ozzie leaned his body toward Itzie. "Itz, I thought it over for a solid hour, and now I'm convinced God could do it."

Ozzie had planned to confess his latest transgression to his mother as soon as she came home from work. But it was a Friday night in November and already dark, and when Mrs. Freedman came through the door she tossed off her coat, kissed Ozzie quickly on the face, and went to the kitchen table to light the three yellow candles, two for the Sabbath and one for Ozzie's father.

When his mother lit the candles she would move her two arms slowly towards her, dragging them through the air, as though persuading people whose minds were half made up. And her eyes would get glassy with tears. Even when his father was alive Ozzie remembered that her eyes had gotten glassy, so it didn't have anything to do with his dying. It had something to do with lighting the candles.

As she touched the flaming match to the unlit wick of a Sabbath candle, the phone rang, and Ozzie, standing only a foot from it, plucked off the receiver and held it muffled to his chest. When his mother lit candles Ozzie felt there should be no noise; even breathing, if you could manage it, should be softened. Ozzie pressed the phone to his breast and watched his mother dragging whatever she was dragging, and he felt his own eyes get glassy. His mother was a round, tired, gray-haired penguin of a woman whose gray skin had begun to feel the tug of gravity and the weight of her own history. Even when she was dressed up she didn't look like a chosen person. But when she lit candles she looked like something better; like a woman who knew momentarily that God could do anything.

After a few mysterious minutes she was finished. Ozzie hung up the phone and walked to the kitchen table where she was beginning to lay the two places for the four-course Sabbath meal. He told her that she would have to see Rabbi Binder next Wednesday at four-thirty, and then he told her why. For the first time in their life together she hit Ozzie across the face with her hand.

All through the chopped liver and chicken soup part of the dinner Ozzie cried; he didn't have any appetite for the rest.

On Wednesday, in the largest of the three basement classrooms of the synagogue, Rabbi Marvin Binder, a tall, handsome, broad-shouldered man of thirty with thick strong-fibered black hair, removed his watch from his pocket and saw that it was four o'clock. At the rear of the room, Yakov Blotnik, the seventy-one-year-old custodian, slowly polished the large window, mumbling to himself, unaware that it was four o'clock or six o'clock, Monday or Wednesday. To most of the students Yakov Blotnik's mumbling along with his brown curly beard, scythe nose, and two heel-trailing black cats, made of him an object of wonder, a foreigner, a relic, towards whom they were alternately fearful and disrespectful. To Ozzie the mumbling had always seemed a monotonous, curious prayer; what made it curious was that old Blotnik had been mumbling so steadily for so many years, Ozzie suspected he had memorized the prayers and forgotten all about God.

"It is now free-discussion time," Rabbi Binder said. "Feel free to talk about any Jewish matter at all—religion, family, politics, sports—"

There was silence. It was a gusty, clouded November afternoon and it did not seem as though there ever was or could be a thing called baseball. So nobody this week said a word about that hero from the past, Hank Greenberg—which limited free discussion considerably.

And the soul-battering Ozzie Freedman had just received from Rabbi Binder had imposed its limitation. When it was Ozzie's turn to read aloud from the Hebrew book the rabbi had asked him petulantly why he didn't read more rapidly. He was showing no progress. Ozzie said he could read faster but that if he did he was sure not to understand what he was reading. Nevertheless, at the rabbi's repeated suggestion Ozzie tried, and showed a great talent, but in the midst of a long passage he stopped short and said he didn't understand a word he was reading, and started in again at a drag-footed pace. Then came the soul-battering.

Consequently when free-discussion time rolled around none of the students felt too free. The rabbi's invitation was answered only by the mumbling of feeble old Blotnik.

"Isn't there anything at all you would like to discuss?" Rabbi Binder asked again, looking at his watch. "No questions or comments?"

There was a small grumble from the third row. The rabbi requested that Ozzie rise and give the rest of the class the advantage of his thought.

Ozzie rose. "I forget it now," he said, and sat down in his place.

Rabbi Binder advanced a seat towards Ozzie and poised himself on the edge of the desk. It was Itzie's desk and the rabbi's frame only a dagger's-length away from his face snapped him to sitting attention.

"Stand up again, Oscar," Rabbi Binder said calmly, "and try to assemble your thoughts."

Ozzie stood up. All his classmates turned in their seats and watched as he gave an unconvincing scratch to his forehead.

"I can't assemble any," he announced, and plunked himself down.

"Stand up!" Rabbi Binder advanced from Itzie's desk to the one directly in front of Ozzie; when the rabbinical back was turned Itzie gave it five-fingers off the tip of his nose, causing a small titter in the room. Rabbi Binder was too absorbed in squelching Ozzie's nonsense once and for all to bother with titters. "Stand up, Oscar. What's your question about?"

Ozzie pulled a word out of the air. It was the handiest word. "Religion."

"Oh, now you remember?"

"Yes."

"What is it?"

Trapped, Ozzie blurted the first thing that came to him. "Why can't He make anything He wants to make!"

As Rabbi Binder prepared an answer, a final answer, Itzie, ten feet behind him, raised one finger on his left hand, gestured it meaningfully towards the rabbi's back, and brought the house down.

Binder twisted quickly to see what had happened and in the midst of the commotion Ozzie shouted into the rabbi's back what he couldn't have shouted to his face. It was a loud, toneless sound that had the timbre of something stored inside for about six days.

"You don't know! You don't know anything about God!"

The rabbi spun back towards Ozzie. "What?"

"You don't know—you don't—"

"Apologize, Oscar, apologize!" It was a threat.

"You don't—"

Rabbi Binder's hand flicked out at Ozzie's cheek. Perhaps it had only been meant to clamp the boy's mouth shut, but Ozzie ducked and the palm caught him squarely on the nose.

The blood came in a short, red spurt on to Ozzie's shirt front.

The next moment was all confusion. Ozzie screamed, "You bastard, you bastard!" and broke for the classroom door. Rabbi Binder lurched a step backwards, as though his own blood had started flowing violently in the opposite direction, then gave a clumsy lurch forward and bolted out the door after Ozzie. The class followed after the rabbi's huge blue-suited back, and before old Blotnik could turn from his window, the room was empty and everyone was headed full speed up the three flights leading to the roof.

If one should compare the light of day to the life of man: sunrise to birth; sunset— the dropping down over the edge—to death; then as Ozzie Freedman wiggled through the trapdoor of the synagogue roof, his feet kicking backwards bronco-style at Rabbi Binder's outstretched arms—at that moment the day was fifty years old. As a rule, fifty or fifty-five reflects accurately the age of late afternoons in November, for it is in that month, during those hours, that one's awareness of light seems no longer a matter of seeing, but of hearing: light begins clicking away. In fact, as Ozzie locked shut the trapdoor in the rabbi's face, the sharp click of the bolt into the lock might momentarily have been mistaken for the sound of the heavier gray that had just throbbed through the sky.

With all his weight Ozzie kneeled on the locked door; any instant he was certain that Rabbi Binder's shoulder would fling it open, splintering the wood into shrapnel and catapulting his body into the sky. But the door did not move and below him he heard only the rumble of feet, first loud then dim, like thunder rolling away.

A question shot through his brain. "Can this be *me?*" For a thirteen-year-old who had just labeled his religious leader a bastard, twice, it was not an improper question. Louder and louder the question came to him—"Is it me? Is it me?"—until he discovered himself no longer kneeling, but racing crazily toward the edge of the roof, his eyes crying, his throat screaming, and his arms flying everywhichway as though not his own.

"Is it me? Is it me Me Me Me Me! It has to be me—but is it!"

It is the question a thief must ask himself the night he jimmies open his first window, and it is said to be the question with which bridegrooms quiz themselves before the altar.

In the few wild seconds it took Ozzie's body to propel him to the edge of the roof, his self-examination began to grow fuzzy. Gazing down at the street he became confused as to the problem beneath the question: was it, is-it-me-who-called-Binder-a-Bastard? or, is-it-me-prancing-around-on-the-roof? However, the scene below settled all, for there is an instant in any action when whether it is you or somebody else is academic. The thief crams the money in his pockets and scoots out the window. The bridegroom signs the hotel register for two. And the boy on the roof finds a streetful of people gaping at him, necks stretched backwards, faces up, as though he were the ceiling of the Hayden Planetarium. Suddenly you know it's you.

"Oscar! Oscar Freedman!" A voice rose from the center of the crowd, a voice that, could it have been seen, would have looked like the writing on a scroll. "Oscar Freedman, get down from there. Immediately!" Rabbi Binder was pointing one arm stiffly up at him; and at the end of that arm, one finger aimed menacingly. It was the attitude of a dictator, but one—the eyes confessed all—whose personal valet had spit neatly in his face.

Ozzie didn't answer. Only for a blink's length did he look towards Rabbi Binder. Instead his eyes began to fit together the world beneath him, to sort out people from places, friends from enemies, participants from spectators. In little jagged starlike clusters his friends stood around Rabbi Binder, who was still pointing. The topmost point on a star compounded not of angels but of five adolescent boys was Itzie. What a world it was, with those stars below, Rabbi Binder below . . . Ozzie, who a moment earlier hadn't been able to control his own body, started to feel the meaning of the word control: he felt Peace and he felt Power.

"Oscar Freedman, I'll give you three to come down."

Few dictators give their subjects three to do anything; but, as always, Rabbi Binder only looked dictatorial.

"Are you ready, Oscar?"

Ozzie nodded his head yes, although he had no intention in the world—the lower one or the celestial one he'd just entered—of coming down even if Rabbi Binder should give him a million.

"All right then," said Rabbi Binder. He ran a hand through his black Samson hair as though it were the gesture prescribed for uttering the first digit. Then, with his other hand cutting a circle out of the small piece of sky around him, he spoke. "One!"

There was no thunder. On the contrary, at that moment, as though "one" was the cue for which he had been waiting, the world's least thunderous person appeared on the synagogue steps. He did not so much come out the synagogue door as lean out, onto the darkening air. He clutched at the doorknob with one hand and looked up at the roof.

"Oy!"

Yakov Blotnik's old mind hobbled slowly, as if on crutches, and though he couldn't decide precisely what the boy was doing on the roof, he knew it wasn't good—that is, it wasn't-good-for-the-Jews. For Yakov Blotnik life had fractionated itself simply: things were either good-for-the-Jews or no-good-for-the-Jews.

He smacked his free hand to his in-sucked cheek, gently. "Oy, Gut!" And then quickly as he was able, he jacked down his head and surveyed the street. There was Rabbi Binder (like a man at an auction with only three dollars in his pocket, he had just delivered a shaky "Two!"); there were the students, and that was all. So far it-wasn't-so-bad-for-the-Jews. But the boy had to come down immediately, before anybody saw. The problem: how to get the boy off the roof?

Anybody who has ever had a cat on the roof knows how to get him down. You call the fire department. Or first you call the operator and you ask her for the fire department. And the next thing there is great jamming of brakes and clanging of bells and shouting of instructions. And then the cat is off the roof. You do the same thing to get a boy off the roof.

That is, you do the same thing if you are Yakov Blotnik and you once had a cat on the roof.

When the engines, all four of them, arrived, Rabbi Binder had four times given Ozzie the count of three. The big hook-and ladder swung around the corner and one of the firemen leaped from it, plunging head-long towards the yellow fire hydrant in front of the synagogue. With a huge wrench he began to unscrew the top nozzle. Rabbi Binder raced over to him and pulled at his shoulder.

"There's no fire . . ."

The fireman mumbled back over his shoulder and, heatedly, continued working at the nozzle.

"But there's no fire, there's no fire . . ." Binder shouted. When the fireman mumbled again, the rabbi grasped his face with both hands and pointed it up at the roof.

To Ozzie it looked as though Rabbi Binder was trying to tug the fireman's head out of his body, like a cork from a bottle. He had to giggle at the picture they made: it was a family portrait—rabbi in black skullcap, fireman in red fire hat, and the little yellow hydrant squatting beside like a kid brother, bareheaded. From the edge of the roof Ozzie waved at the portrait, a one-handed, flapping, mocking wave; in doing it his right foot slipped from under him. Rabbi Binder covered his eyes with his hands.

Firemen work fast. Before Ozzie had even regained his balance, a big, round, yellowed net was being held on the synagogue lawn. The firemen who held it looked up at Ozzie with stern, feelingless faces.

One of the firemen turned his head towards Rabbi Binder. "What, is the kid nuts or something?"

Rabbi Binder unpeeled his hands from his eyes, slowly, painfully, as if they were tape. Then he checked: nothing on the sidewalk, no dents in the net.

"Is he gonna jump, or what?" the fireman shouted.

In a voice not at all like a statue, Rabbi Binder finally answered. "Yes, Yes, I think so . . . He's been threatening to . . ."

Threatening to? Why, the reason he was on the roof, Ozzie remembered, was to get away; he hadn't even thought about jumping. He had just run to get away, and the truth was that he hadn't really headed for the roof as much as he'd been chased there.

"What's his name, the kid?"

"Freedman," Rabbi Binder answered. "Oscar Freedman."

The fireman looked up at Ozzie. "What is it with you, Oscar? You gonna jump, or what?"

Ozzie did not answer. Frankly, the question had just arisen.

"Look, Oscar, if you're gonna jump, jump—and if you're not gonna jump, don't jump. But don't waste our time, willya?"

Ozzie looked at the fireman and then at Rabbi Binder. He wanted to see Rabbi Binder cover his eyes one more time.

"I'm going to jump."

And then he scampered around the edge of the roof to the corner, where there was no net below, and he flapped his arms at his sides, swishing the air and smacking his palms to his trousers on the downbeat. He began screaming like some kind of engine, "Wheeeee . . . wheeeee," and leaning way out over the edge with the upper half of his body. The firemen whipped around to cover the ground with the net. Rabbi Binder mumbled a few words to Somebody and covered his eyes. Everything happened quickly, jerkily, as in a silent movie. The crowd, which had arrived with the fire engines, gave out a long, Fourth-of-July fireworks oooh-aahhh. In the excitement no one had paid the crowd much heed, except, of course, Yakov Blotnik, who swung from the doorknob counting heads. "Fier und tsvantsik . . . finf und tsvantsik . . . Oy, Gut!" It wasn't like this with the cat.

Rabbi Binder peeked through his fingers, checked the sidewalk and net. Empty. But there was Ozzie racing to the other corner. The firemen raced with him but were unable to keep up. Whenever Oscar wanted to he might jump and splatter himself upon the sidewalk, and by the time the firemen scooted to the spot all they could do with their net would be to cover the mess:

"Wheeeee . . . wheeeee . . ."

"Hey, Oscar," the winded fireman yelled, "What the hell is this, a game or something?"

"Wheeeee . . . wheeeee . . ."

"Hey, Oscar—"

But he was off now to the other corner, flapping his wings fiercely. Rabbi Binder couldn't take it any longer—the fire engines from nowhere, the screaming suicidal boy, the net. He fell to his knees, exhausted, and with his hands curled together in front of his chest like a little dome, he pleaded, "Oscar, stop it, Oscar. Don't jump, Oscar. Please come down . . . Please don't jump."

And further back in the crowd a single voice, a single young voice, shouted a lone word to the boy on the roof.

"Jump!"

It was Itzie. Ozzie momentarily stopped flapping.

"Go ahead, Ozz—jump!" Itzie broke off his point of the star and courageously, with the inspiration not of a wise-guy but of a disciple, stood alone. "Jump, Ozz, jump!"

Still on his knees, his hands still curled, Rabbi Binder twisted his body back. He looked at Itzie, then, agonizingly, back to Ozzie.

"Oscar, <u>Don't jump! Please, Don't Jump</u> . . . please please . . ."

"Jump!" This time it wasn't Itzie but another point of the star. By the time Mrs. Freedman arrived to keep her four-thirty appointment with Rabbi Binder, the whole little upside down heaven was shouting and pleading for Ozzie to jump, and Rabbi Binder no longer was pleading with him not to jump, but was crying into the dome of his hands.

Understandably Mrs. Freedman couldn't figure out what her son was doing on the roof. So she asked.

"Ozzie, my Ozzie, what are you doing? My Ozzie, what is it?"

Ozzie stopped wheeeeeing and slowed his arms down to a cruising flap, the kind birds use in soft winds, but he did not answer. He stood against the low, clouded, darkening sky—light clicked down swiftly now, as on a small gear—flapping softly and gazing down at the small bundle of a woman who was his mother.

"What are you doing, Ozzie?" She turned towards the kneeling Rabbi Binder and rushed so close that only a paper-thickness of dusk lay between her stomach and his shoulders.

"What is my baby doing?"

Rabbi Binder gaped up at her but he too was mute. All that moved was the dome of his hands; it shook back and forth like a weak pulse.

"Rabbi, get him down! He'll kill himself. Get him down, my only baby . . ."

"I can't," Rabbi Binder said, "I can't . . ." and he turned his handsome head towards the crowd of boys behind him. "It's them. Listen to them."

And for the first time Mrs. Freedman saw the crowd of boys, and she heard what they were yelling.

"He's doing it for them. He won't listen to me. It's them." Rabbi Binder spoke like one in a trance.

"For them?"

"Yes."

"Why for them?"

"They want him to . . ."

Mrs. Freedman raised her two arms upward as though she were conducting the sky. "For them he's doing it!" And then in a gesture older than pyramids, older than prophets and floods, her arms came slapping down to her sides. "A martyr I have. Look!" She tilted her head to the roof. Ozzie was still flapping softly. "My martyr."

"Oscar, come down, *please*," Rabbi Binder groaned.

In a startlingly even voice Mrs. Freedman called to the boy on the roof. "Ozzie, come down, Ozzie. Don't be a martyr, my baby."

As though it were a litany, Rabbi Binder repeated her words. "Don't be a martyr, my baby. Don't be a martyr."

"Gawhead, Ozz—*be* a Martin!" It was Itzie. "Be a Martin, be a Martin," and all the voices joined in singing for Martindom, whatever *it* was. "Be a Martin, be a Martin . . ."

Somehow when you're on a roof the darker it gets the less you can hear. All Ozzie knew was that two groups wanted two new things: his friends were spirited and musical about what they wanted; his mother and the rabbi were even-toned, chanting, about what they didn't want. The rabbi's voice was without tears now and so was his mother's.

The big net stared up at Ozzie like a sightless eye. The big, clouded sky pushed down. From beneath it looked like a gray corrugated board. Suddenly, looking up into that unsympathetic sky, Ozzie realized all the strangeness of what these people, his friends, were asking: they wanted him to jump, to kill himself; they were singing about it now—it made them that happy. And there was an even greater strangeness: Rabbi Binder was on his knees, trembling. If there was a question to be asked now it was not "Is it me?" but rather "Is it us? . . . Is it us?"

Being on the roof, it turned out, was a serious thing. If he jumped would the singing become dancing? Would it? What would jumping stop? Yearningly, Ozzie wished he could rip open the sky, plunge his hands through, and pull out the sun; and on the sun, like a coin, would be stamped Jump or Don't Jump.

Ozzie's knees rocked and sagged a little under him as though they were setting him for a dive. His arms tightened, stiffened, froze, from shoulders to fingernails. He felt as if each part of his body were going to vote as to whether he should kill himself or not—and each part as though it were independent of *him*.

The light took an unexpected click down and the new darkness, like a gag, hushed the friends singing for this and the mother and rabbi chanting for that.

Ozzie stopped counting votes, and in a curiously high voice, like one who wasn't prepared for speech, he spoke.

"Mamma?"

"Yes, Oscar."

"Mamma, get down on your knees, like Rabbi Binder."

"Oscar—"

"Get down on your knees," he said, "or I'll jump."

Ozzie heard a whimper, then a quick rustling, and when he looked down where his mother had stood he saw the top of a head and beneath that a circle of dress. She was kneeling beside Rabbi Binder.

He spoke again. "Everybody kneel." There was the sound of everybody kneeling.

Ozzie looked around. With one hand he pointed towards the synagogue entrance. "Make *him* kneel."

There was a noise, not of kneeling, but of body-and-cloth stretching. Ozzie could hear Rabbi Binder saying in a gruff whisper, ". . . or he'll *kill* himself," and when next he looked there was Yakov Blotnik off the doorknob and for the first time in his life upon his knees in the Gentile posture of prayer.

As for the firemen—it is not as difficult as one might imagine to hold a net taut while you are kneeling.

Ozzie looked around again; and then he called to Rabbi Binder.

"Rabbi?"

"Yes, Oscar."

"Rabbi Binder, do you believe in God."

"Yes."

"Do you believe God can do Anything?" Ozzie leaned his head out into the darkness. "Anything?"

"Oscar, I think—"

"Tell me you believe God can do Anything."

There was a second's hesitation. Then: "God can do Anything."

"Tell me you believe God can make a child without intercourse."

"He can."

"Tell me!"

"God," Rabbi Binder admitted, "can make a child without intercourse."

"Mamma, you tell me."

"God can make a child without intercourse," his mother said.

"Make *him* tell me." There was no doubt who *him* was.

In a few moments Ozzie heard an old comical voice say something to the increasing darkness about God.

Next, Ozzie made everybody say it. And then he made them all say they believed in Jesus Christ—first one at a time, then all together.

When the catechizing was through it was the beginning of evening. From the street it sounded as if the boy on the roof might have sighed.

"Ozzie?" A woman's voice dared to speak. "You'll come down now?"

There was no answer, but the woman waited, and when a voice finally did speak it was thin and crying, and exhausted as that of an old man who has just finished pulling the bells.

"Mamma, don't you see—you shouldn't hit me. He shouldn't hit me. You shouldn't hit me about God, Mamma. You should never hit anybody about God—"

"Ozzie, please come down now."

"Promise me, promise me you'll never hit anybody about God."

He had asked only his mother, but for some reason everyone kneeling in the street promised he would never hit anybody about God.

Once again there was silence.

"I can come down now, Mamma," the boy on the roof finally said. He turned his head both ways as though checking the traffic lights. "Now I can come down . . ."

And he did, right into the center of the yellow net that glowed in the evening's edge like an overgrown halo.

QUESTIONS

1   Part of the design of this story arises from the juxtaposition of the characters. Each of the major characters provides some complementary attitude to each other character. Consider Ozzie, Itzie, Mrs. Freedman, Rabbi Binder, and Yakov Blotnik. What attitude toward religion does each illustrate? How does that attitude react with each other attitude?
2   What point is Roth making about the system of religion? Why is Rabbi Binder's position indicative of the system?
3   Why does Itzie call to Ozzie to jump from the roof? How does Itzie's action and the support it receives reveal the basic dichotomy in the story?
4   What specific statements in the story emphasize Roth's plea for religious ecumenicity?

TOPICS FOR COMPOSITION

1   Sensitivity and inquisitiveness beyond his years are marks of Ozzie's character. Write an essay showing how Roth manages to maintain the balance between Ozzie's youth and the maturity of his question.
2   This story exemplifies the power of action by a minority. Write an essay illustrating the power of minority action as it is evidenced in America.
3   Roth's story poses the need for greater understanding among religions. Investigate a religion with which you have little familiarity. Write an essay explaining how such an investigation has benefited you.

DRAMA

The Tempest—produced quite late in Shakespeare's career and unpublished until 1623—has consistently intrigued audiences and critics. For a comedy, its tone is often somber; for Shakespeare, its restricted time and place of action are unusual; and its thematic implications defy easy formulation. Although the presence of Prospero and Miranda upon their strange island has its genesis in the sordid politics of Milan and Naples a dozen years before the play begins, violent storm and Prospero's carefully orchestrated exposure of his enemies' villainy and his ultimate forgiveness permit social and individual reintegration for all at the end. Throughout the play, of course, Shakespeare has woven many features of sheer romance—fantasy, magic, music and dance, dreamlike states, young love, preternatural creatures and deeds, rewards for virtue, and disarming of vice. Nothing, however, seems out of place on this strange island: the wronged Duke Prospero of Milan has so ordered affairs upon his wilderness-home that we can willingly suspend disbelief. The magician's arts, which can create a tempest upon the seas, can certainly make the deserted isle a seat of judgment for one day, foster marriage for Miranda and Ferdinand, summon Ariel for extravagant tasks, and prepare to take up his ducal responsibilities. *The Tempest* offers numerous perspectives for considering the issues of freedom and restraint:

1   Prospero's eviction from his throne and the long exile with Miranda proceed from his preference for undisturbed study over the restraints imposed by power and responsibility. Wanting only freedom to pursue the occult, he ironically received almost total restraint—isolation on the island, where power can be exercised only upon his daughter, Ariel, and Caliban.
2   Gonzalo's wistful but mindless description of a utopia (II, i, 149–176)—a vision presumably induced by his first exposure to absolute wilderness—offers a startling contrast to the undiluted lust for power expressed by Antonio and Sebastian as soon as authority slumbers. By their intended villainy, Milan and Naples enter Prospero's pastoral landscape, and once more it seems that freedom can encourage disorder and that Gonzalo's longed-for golden age, where restraint was unknown, is merely a pleasant myth which ignores the strength of human depravity, measured by the crimes of mutiny, treason, and plotted fratricide and regicide.
3   Ariel desires freedom from Prospero's control, but the "airy spirit" also asserts with song, especially the beautiful little air about death at sea, and with dance the power of art to transform human suffering and the natural order of things. Such transformation offers the burdened consciousness of humanity freedom from the darkness of death, pervasive evil, and the restraints we lament. Even Caliban, who seems to embody the less attractive side of human nature, has some justice on his side in

accusing Prospero of tyranny. And the young lovers, innocent as they are, are warned by the magician-prince against sexual license before their marriage is solemnized properly. Prospero, representing pure intelligence, acts in short to restrain all the other characters until his scenario for catching his enemies by storm; revelation of vice; forestalling the comic intrigue of Caliban, Stephano, and Trinculo; manipulating Miranda and Ferdinand in the interests of a better future order; grandly forgiving the villains; releasing Ariel; and grandly authorizing his triumphal reentry to Naples and Milan with a chastened retinue, has been duly acted out. Even his final words, in the "Epilogue," entreat the audience to avoid restraint, by its applause, and thus to grant him the freedom, as Prospero, to sail for Naples, and, as actor playing a difficult role, to realize success in his art.

THE TEMPEST

William Shakespeare

CHARACTERS

ALONSO, *King of Naples*
SEBASTIAN, *his brother*
PROSPERO, *the right Duke of Milan*
ANTONIO, *his brother, the usurping Duke of Milan*
FERDINAND, *son to the King of Naples*
GONZALO, *an honest old counselor*
ADRIAN, and FRANCISCO, *Lords*
CALIBAN, *a savage and deformed slave*
TRINCULO, *a jester*
STEPHANO, *a drunken butler*
MASTER OF A SHIP, BOATSWAIN, MARINERS
MIRANDA, *daughter to* PROSPERO
ARIEL, *an airy spirit*
IRIS, CERES, JUNO, NYMPHS, and REAPERS, *Spirits*

Other Spirits attending on PROSPERO

Scene: A ship at sea; Afterwards, an uninhabited island.

[ACT I, SCENE 1] *A ship at sea.*

A tempestuous noise of thunder and lightning heard. Enter a SHIPMASTER *and a* BOATSWAIN.

SHIPMASTER Boatswain!
BOATSWAIN Here, master; what cheer?

5

SHIPMASTER   Good; speak to the mariners: fall to 't,
   yarely, or we run ourselves aground; bestir.   *Exit.*

Enter MARINERS.

BOATSWAIN   Heigh, my hearts! Cheerly, cheerly, my hearts!
   Yare, yare! Take in the topsail. Tend to th' master's whistle.—   10
   Blow till thou burst thy wind, if room enough!

Enter ALONSO, SEBASTIAN, ANTONIO, FERDINAND, GONZALO,
and others.

ALONSO   Good boatswain, have care. Where's the master?
   Play the men.   15
BOATSWAIN   I pray now, keep below.
ANTONIO   Where is the master, boatswain?
BOATSWAIN   Do you not hear him? You mar our labour.
   Keep your cabins; you do assist the storm.
GONZALO   Nay, good, be patient.   20
BOATSWAIN   When the sea is. Hence! What cares these
   roarers for the name of king? To cabin! Silence! Trouble us not.
GONZALO   Good, yet remember whom thou has aboard.
BOATSWAIN   None that I more love than myself. You are a
   counsellor; if you can command these elements to silence, and   25
   work the peace of the present, we will not hand a rope more;
   use your authority. If you cannot, give thanks you have lived so
   long, and make yourself ready in your cabin for the mischance
   of the hour, if it so hap.—Cheerly, good hearts!—Out of our
   way, I say.   *Exit.*   30
GONZALO   I have great comfort from this fellow. Methinks
   he hath no drowning mark upon him; his complexion is perfect
   gallows. Stand fast, good Fate, to his hanging; make the rope of
   his destiny our cable, for our own doth little advantage. If he be
   not born to be hanged, our case is miserable.   *Exeunt.*   35

Re-enter BOATSWAIN.

BOATSWAIN   Down with the topmast! Yare! Lower, lower!
   Bring her to try wi' the maincourse. [*A cry within.*] A plague
   upon this howling! They are louder than the weather or our
   office.   40

Enter SEBASTIAN, ANTONIO, *and* GONZALO.

   Yet again! What do you here? Shall we give o'er and drown?
   Have you a mind to sink?

6 Good: my good fellow.   *7 yarely:* speedily, at once.   *11 Blow . . . enough:* The boatswain here
yells at the storm to blow as hard as it will as long as there is enough room at sea.   *31 Methinks
. . . gallows:* Gonzalo here refers to an old proverb: "He that is born to be hanged will never be
drowned."   *38 Bring . . . maincourse:* Heave the ship to, with the mainsail.   *40 office:* job.

SEBASTIAN   A pox o' your throat, you bawling, blasphemous,
    incharitable dog!   45
BOATSWAIN   Work you, then.
ANTONIO   Hang, cur! hang, you whoreson, insolent noise-
    maker! We are less afraid to be drowned than thou art.
GONZALO   I'll warrant him for drowning though the ship
    were no stronger than a nutshell and as leaky as an unstanched   50
    wench.
BOATSWAIN   Lay her a-hold, a-hold! Set her two courses off
    to sea again; lay her off.

Enter MARINERS, *wet.*

MARINERS   All lost! To prayers, to prayers! All lost!   55
BOATSWAIN   What, must our mouths be cold?
GONZALO   The King and Prince at prayers! Let's assist them,
    For our case is as theirs.
SEBASTIAN   I'm out of patience.
ANTONIO   We are merely cheated of our lives by drunkards.   60
    This wide-chopp'd rascal—would thou mightst lie drowning
    The washing of ten tides!
GONZALO   He'll be hang'd yet,
    Though every drop of water swear against it
    And gape at wid'st to glut him.   65
                [*A confused noise within:* Mercy on us!]
    We split, we split! Farewell, my wife and children!
    Farewell, brother! We split, we split, we split!
ANTONIO   Let's all sink wi' th' King.
SEBASTIAN   Let's take leave of him.   *Exit.*   70
GONZALO   Now would I give a thousand furlongs of sea for
    an acre of barren ground, long heath, brown furze, anything.
    The wills above be done! but I would fain die a dry death.   *Exeunt.*

[ACT I, SCENE 2]   *The island. Before Prospero's cell.*

Enter PROSPERO *and* MIRANDA.

MIRANDA   If by your art, my dearest father, you have
    Put the wild waters in this roar, allay them.
    The sky, it seems, would pour down stinking pitch,   5
    But that the sea, mounting to th' welkin's cheek,
    Dashes the fire out. O, I have suffered
    With those that I saw suffer! a brave vessel
    (Who had, no doubt, some noble creature in her)

---

49 warrant him for: guarantee him against.   *61 wide-chopp'd:* big-jawed.   *65 glut:* swallow.   *72*
heath: heather.   *furze:* spiny shrub that grows on wasteland.   *6 welkin:* sky.   *8 brave:* fine.

Dash'd all to pieces! O, the cry did knock   10
Against my very heart. Poor souls, they perish'd.
Had I been any god of power, I would
Have sunk the sea within the earth or ere
It should the good ship so have swallow'd and
The fraughting souls within her.   15
PROSPERO   Be collected;
No more amazement. Tell your piteous heart
There's no harm done.
MIRANDA   O, woe the day!
PROSPERO   No harm.   20
I have done nothing but in care of thee,
Of thee, my dear one, thee my daughter, who
Art ignorant of what thou art, naught knowing
Of whence I am, nor that I am more better
Than Prospero, master of a full poor cell,   25
And thy no greater father.
MIRANDA   More to know
Did never meddle with my thoughts.
PROSPERO   'T is time
I should inform thee farther. Lend thy hand,   30
And pluck my magic garment from me. So,

                                        [*Lays down his mantle.*]
Lie there, my art. Wipe thou thine eyes; have comfort.
The direful spectacle of the wreck, which touch'd
The very virtue of compassion in thee,   35
I have with such provision in mine art
So safely ordered that there is no soul—
No, not so much perdition as an hair
Betid to any creature in the vessel
Which thou heard'st cry, which thou saw'st sink. Sit down;   40
For thou must now know farther.
MIRANDA   You have often
Begun to tell me what I am; but stopp'd
And left me to a bootless inquisition,
Concluding, "Stay, not yet."   45
PROSPERO   The hour's now come;
The very minute bids thee ope thine ear.
Obey and be attentive. Canst thou remember
A time before we came unto this cell?
I do not think thou canst, for then thou wast not   50
Out three years old.

13 or ere: before. _15 fraughting:_ making up cargo. _16 collected:_ calm. _36 provision:_ foresight.
38 perdition: loss. _51 Out:_ quite.

MIRANDA   Certainly, sir, I can.
PROSPERO   By what? By any other house or person?
    Of anything the image tell me, that
    Hath kept with thy remembrance.   55
MIRANDA   'T is far off
    And rather like a dream than an assurance
    That my remembrance warrants. Had I not
    Four or five women once that tended me?
PROSPERO   Thou hadst, and more, Miranda. But how is it   60
    That this lives in thy mind? What seest thou else
    In the dark backward and abysm of time?
    If thou rememb'rest aught ere thou cam'st here,
    How thou cam'st here thou may'st.
MIRANDA   But that I do not.   65
PROSPERO   Twelve year since, Miranda, twelve year since,
    Thy father was the Duke of Milan and
    A prince of power.
MIRANDA   Sir, are not you my father?
PROSPERO   Thy mother was a piece of virtue, and   70
    She said thou wast my daughter; and thy father
    Was Duke of Milan, and his only heir
    And princess no worse issued.
MIRANDA   O the heavens!
    What foul play had we, that we came from thence?   75
    Or blessed was't we did?
PROSPERO   Both, both, my girl.
    By foul play, as thou say'st, were we heav'd thence,
    But blessedly holp hither.
MIRANDA   O, my heart bleeds   80
    To think o' th' teen that I have turn'd you to,
    Which is from my remembrance! Please you, farther.
PROSPERO   My brother and thy uncle, call'd Antonio—
    I pray thee, mark me—that a brother should
    Be so perfidious!—he whom next thyself   85
    Of all the world I lov'd, and to him put
    The manage of my state; as at that time
    Through all the signories it was the first,
    And Prospero the prime duke, being so reputed
    In dignity, and for the liberal arts   90
    Without a parallel; those being all my study,
    The government I cast upon my brother
    And to my state grew stranger, being transported

---

57 assurance: genuine memory.   *62 backward:* past.   *79 holp:* helped.   *81 teen:* trouble. *turn'd you to:* caused you to recall.   *88 signories:* states (of Italy).

And rapt in secret studies. Thy false uncle—
Dost thou attend me?   95
MIRANDA   Sir, most heedfully.
PROSPERO   Being once perfected how to grant suits,
    How to deny them, who t' advance and who
    To trash for overtopping, new created
    The creatures that were mine, I say, or chang'd 'em,   100
    Or else new form'd 'em; having both the key
    Of officer and office, set all hearts i' th' state
    To what tune pleas'd his ear; that now he was
    The ivy which had hid my princely trunk,
    And suck'd my verdure out on 't. Thou attend'st not.   105
MIRANDA   O, good sir, I do.
PROSPERO   I pray thee, mark me.
    I, thus neglecting worldly ends, all dedicated
    To closeness and the bettering of my mind
    With that which, but by being so retir'd,   110
    O'er-priz'd all popular rate, in my false brother
    Awak'd an evil nature; and my trust,
    Like a good parent, did beget of him
    A falsehood, in its contrary as great
    As my trust was; which had indeed no limit,   115
    A confidence sans bound. He being thus lorded,
    Not only with what my revenue yielded,
    But what my power might else exact,—like one
    Who having into truth, by telling of it,
    Made such a sinner of his memory   120
    To credit his own lie,—he did believe
    He was indeed the Duke: out o' th' substitution,
    And executing the outward face of royalty,
    With all prerogative, hence his ambition growing—
    Dost thou hear?   125
MIRANDA   Your tale, sir, would cure deafness.
PROSPERO   To have no screen between this part he play'd
    And him he play'd it for, he needs will be
    Absolute Milan. Me, poor man!—my library
    Was dukedom large enough—of temporal royalties   130
    He thinks me now incapable; confederates—
    So dry he was for sway—wi' th' King of Naples
    To give him annual tribute, do him homage,
    Subject his coronet to his crown, and bend

---

99 trash for overtopping: check for getting too powerful. *new created:* made his. *109 closeness:* seclusion (for study). *111 O'erpriz'd . . . rate:* was more valuable than people believe. *114 in its contrary:* by contrast. *116 sans:* without. *lorded:* made into the ruler. *129 Absolute Milan:* genuine Duke of Milan.

The dukedom yet unbow'd—alas, poor Milan!—   135
  To most ignoble stooping.
MIRANDA   O the heavens!
PROSPERO   Mark his condition and th' event, then tell me
  If this might be a brother.
MIRANDA   I should sin   140
  To think but nobly of my grandmother.
  Good wombs have borne bad sons.
PROSPERO   Now the condition.
  This King of Naples, being an enemy
  To me inveterate, hearkens my brother's suit;   145
  Which was, that he, in lieu o' th' promises,
  Of homage and I know not how much tribute,
  Should presently extirpate me and mine
  Out of the dukedom, and confer fair Milan
  With all the honours on my brother; whereon,   150
  A treacherous army levied, one midnight
  Fated to th' purpose did Antonio open
  The gates of Milan; and i' th' dead of darkness,
  The ministers for the purpose hurried thence
  Me and thy crying self.   155
MIRANDA   Alack, for pity!
  I, not rememb'ring how I cried out then,
  Will cry it o'er again: it is a hint
  That wrings mine eye to 't.
PROSPERO   Hear a little further,   160
  And then I'll bring thee to the present business
  Which now's upon's, without the which this story
  Were most impertinent.
MIRANDA   Wherefore did they not
  That hour destroy us?   165
PROSPERO   Well demanded, wench;
  My tale provokes that question. Dear, they durst not,
  (So dear the love my people bore me) nor set
  A mark so bloody on the business; but
  With colours fairer painted their foul ends.   170
  In few, they hurried us aboard a bark,
  Bore us some leagues to sea; where they prepared
  A rotten carcass of a butt, not rigg'd,
  Nor tackle, sail, nor mast; the very rats
  Instinctively have quit it. There they hoist us,   175

---

138 event: what happened afterward.   *146 promises:* conditions.   *148 presently:* at once. *extirpate:* banish.   *154 ministers:* officers.   *155 thy crying self:* you as a baby.   *163 impertinent:* meaningless.   *171 In few:* in short.   *173 butt:* cask.

To cry to th' sea that roar'd to us, to sigh
To the winds whose pity, sighing back again,
Did us but loving wrong.

MIRANDA   Alack, what trouble
Was I then to you!   180

PROSPERO   O, a cherubin
Thou wast that did preserve me. Thou didst smile,
Infused with a fortitude from heaven,
When I have deck'd the sea with drops full salt,
Under my burden groan'd; which rais'd in me   185
An undergoing stomach, to bear up
Against what should ensue.

MIRANDA   How came we ashore?

PROSPERO   By Providence divine.
Some food we had and some fresh water that   190
A noble Neapolitan, Gonzalo,
Out of his charity, who being then appointed
Master of this design, did give us, with
Rich garments, linens, stuffs, and necessaries,
Which since have steaded much; so, of his gentleness, 195
Knowing I lov'd my boks, he furnish'd me
From mine own library with volumes that
I prize above my dukedom.

MIRANDA   Would I might
But ever see that man!   200

PROSPERO   Now I arise.   [*Puts on his robe.*]
Sit still, and hear the last of our sea-sorrow.
Here in this island we arriv'd; and here
Have I, thy schoolmaster, made thee more profit
Than other princess can that have more time   205
For vainer hours, and tutors not so careful.

MIRANDA   Heavens thank you for 't! And now, I pray you,
      sir,
For still 't is beating in my mind, your reason
For raising this sea-storm?   210

PROSPERO   Know thus far forth.
By accident most strange, bountiful Fortune,
Now my dear lady, hath mine enemies
Brought to this shore; and by my prescience
I find my zenith doth depend upon   215
A most auspicious star, whose influence
If now I court not but omit, my fortunes

---

183 *Infused:* filled.   186 *undergoing stomach:* courage.   195 *steaded:* been useful.   212 *Fortune:* Lady Fortune.   215 *zenith:* peak of fortune.

Will ever droop. Here cease more questions.
Thou art inclin'd to sleep; 't is a good dulness,
And give it way. I know thou canst not choose.   220

[MIRANDA *sleeps*.]

Come away, servant, come; I am ready now.
Approach, my Ariel; come.

Enter ARIEL.

ARIEL   All hail, great master! grave sir, hail! I come   225
To answer thy best pleasure, be 't to fly,
To swim, to dive into the fire, to ride
On the curl'd clouds. To thy strong bidding task
Ariel and his quality.
PROSPERO   Hast thou, spirit   230
Perform'd to point the tempest that I bade thee?
ARIEL   To every article.
I boarded the king's ship; now on the beak,
Now in the waist, the deck, in every cabin,
I flam'd amazement. Sometime I'd divide,   235
And burn in many places: on the topmast,
The yards and bowsprit, would I flame distinctly,
Then meet and join. Jove's lightning, the precursors
O' th' dreadful thunder-claps, more momentary
And sight-outrunning were not; the fire and cracks   240
Of sulphurous roaring the most mighty Neptune
Seem to besiege, and make his bold waves tremble,
Yea, his dread trident shake.
PROSPERO   My brave spirit!
Who was so firm, so constant, that this coil   245
Would not infect his reason?
ARIEL   Not a soul
But felt a fever of the mad, and play'd
Some tricks of desperation. All but mariners
Plung'd in the foaming brine and quit the vessel,   250
Then all afire with me. The King's son, Ferdinand,
With hair up-staring,—then like reeds, not hair,—
Was the first man that leap'd; cried, "Hell is empty,
And all the devils are here."
PROSPERO   Why, that's my spirit!   255
But was not this nigh shore?
ARIEL   Close by, my master.

229 quality: ability.   *231 to point:* exactly.   *238 Jove:* supreme god (Jupiter).   *241 Neptune:* god
of the sea.   *243 trident:* three-pointed staff of Neptune.   *246 coil:* tumult.   *248 of the mad:* of
insanity.   *252 up-staring:* standing on end.

PROSPERO   But are they, Ariel, safe?

ARIEL   Not a hair perish'd;
   On their sustaining garments not a blemish,   260
   But fresher than before; and, as thou bad'st me,
   In troops I have dispers'd them 'bout the isle.
   The King's son have I landed by himself,
   Whom I left cooling of the air with sighs
   In an odd angle of the isle, and sitting,   265
   His arms in this sad knot.

PROSPERO   Of the King's ship
   The mariners say how thou hast dispos'd,
   And all the rest o' th' fleet.

ARIEL   Safely in harbour   270
   Is the King's ship; in the deep nook, where once
   Thou call'dst me up at midnight to fetch dew
   From the still-vex'd Bermoothes, there she's hid;
   The mariners all under hatches stow'd,
   Who, with a charm join'd to their suffer'd labour,   275
   I have left asleep; and for the rest o' th' fleet,
   Which I dispers'd, they all have met again,
   And are upon the Mediterranean float
   Bound sadly home for Naples,   280
   Supposing that they saw the King's ship wreck'd
   And his great person perish.

PROSPERO   Ariel, thy charge
   Exactly is perform'd; but there's more work.
   What is the time o' th' day?   285

ARIEL   Past the mid season.

PROSPERO   At least two glasses. The time 'twixt six and
     now
   Must by us both be spent most preciously.

ARIEL   Is there more toil? Since thou dost give me pains,   290
   Let me remember thee what thou hast promis'd,
   Which is not yet perform'd me.

PROSPERO   How now? moody?
   What is 't thou canst demand?

ARIEL   My liberty.   295

PROSPERO   Before the time be out? No more!

ARIEL   I prithee,
   Remember I have done thee worthy service,
   Told thee no lies, made thee no mistakings, serv'd

---

260 sustaining: keeping them afloat.   *266 odd angle:* out-of-the-way spot.   *267 knot:* manner (Ariel poses in the dejected manner of the sorrowing Ferdinand).   *273 still-vex'd Bermoothes:* always stormy Bermudas.   *287 two glasses:* two hours (turns of the hourglass) past noon.

Without or grudge or grumblings. Thou did promise   300
   To bate me a full year.
PROSPERO   Dost thou forget
   From what a torment I did free thee?
ARIEL   No.
PROSPERO   Thou dost, and think'st it much to tread the ooze   305
   Of the salt deep,
   To run upon the sharp wind of the north,
   To do me business in the veins o' th' earth
   When it is bak'd with frost.
ARIEL   I do not, sir   310
PROSPERO   Thou liest, malignant thing! Hast thou forgot
   The foul witch Sycorax, who with age and envy
   Was grown into a hoop? Hast thou forgot her?
ARIEL   No, sir.
PROSPERO   Thou hast. Where was she born? Speak; tell me.   315
ARIEL   Sir, in Argier.
PROSPERO   O, was she so? I must
   Once a month recount what thou hast been,
   Which thou forget'st. This damn'd witch Sycorax,
   For mischiefs manifold and sorceries terrible   320
   To enter human hearing, from Argier,
   Thou know'st, was banish'd; for one thing she did
   They would not take her life. Is not this true?
ARIEL   Ay, sir.
PROSPERO   This blue-ey'd hag was hither brought with   325
      child,
   And here was left by th' sailors. Thou, my slave,
   As thou report'st thyself, was then her servant;
   And, for thou wast a spirit too delicate
   To act her earthy and abhorr'd commands,   330
   Refusing her grand hests, she did confine thee,
   By help of her more potent ministers
   And in her most unmitigable rage,
   Into a cloven pine; within which rift
   Imprison'd thou didst painfully remain   335
   A dozen years; within which space she died
   And left thee there, where thou didst vent thy groans
   As fast as mill-wheels strike. Then was this island—
   Save for the son that she did litter here,
   A freckl'd whelp, hag-born,—not honour'd with   340
   A human shape.

301 bate me: lessen (or abate) my term of service.   *312 Sycorax:* a witch whose name is of uncertain origin.   *envy:* malice.   *313 grown into a hoop:* bent double.   *316 Argier:* Algiers.   *325 blue-eyed:* with dark circles under her eyes.   *331 hests:* orders.

ARIEL   Yes, Caliban her son.

PROSPER Dull thing, I say so; he, that Caliban
  Whom now I keep in service. Thou best know'st
  What torment I did find thee in; thy groans   345
  Did make wolves howl, and penetrate the breasts
  Of ever-angry bears. It was a torment
  To lay upon the damn'd, which Sycorax
  Could not again undo. It was mine art,
  When I arriv'd and heard thee, that made gape   350
  The pine, and let thee out.

ARIEL   I thank thee, master.

PROSPERO If thou more murmur'st, I will rend an oak
  And peg thee in his knotty entrails till
  Thou hast howl'd away twelve winters.   355

ARIEL   Pardon, master;
  I will be correspondent to command
  And do my spriting gently.

PROSPERO   Do so, and after two days
  I will discharge thee.   360

ARIEL   That's my noble master!
  What shall I do? say what. What shall I do?

PROSPERO Go make thyself like a nymph o' th' sea; be sub-
   ject
  To no sight but thine and mine, invisible   365
  To every eyeball else. Go take this shape.
  And hither come in 't. Go, hence with diligence! *Exit* ARIEL.
  Awake, dear heart, awake! Thou hast slept well;
  Awake!

MIRANDA The strangeness of your story put   370
  Heaviness in me.

PROSPERO   Shake it off. Come on,
  We'll visit Caliban my slave, who never
  Yields us kind answer.

MIRANDA   'T is a villain, sir,   375
  I do not love to look on.

PROSPERO   But, as 't is,
  We cannot miss him: he does make our fire,
  Fetch in our wood, and serves in offices
  That profit us. What, ho! slave! Caliban!   380
  Thou earth, thou! speak.

CALIBAN [*Within*] There's wood enough within.

---

357 correspondent: obedient. *358 spriting gently:* work as a spirit faithfully. *378 miss:* do without.

PROSPERO   Come forth, I say! there's other business for
    thee.
    Come, thou tortoise! when?   385

Re-enter ARIEL *like a water-nymph.*

    Fine apparition! My quaint Ariel,
    Hark in thine ear. [*Whispers.*]
ARIEL   My lord, it shall be done.   *Exit.*
PROSPERO   Thou poisonous slave, got by the devil himself   390
    Upon thy wicked dam, come forth!

Enter CALIBAN.

CALIBAN   As wicked dew as e'er my mother brush'd
    With raven's feather from unwholesome fen
    Drop on you both! A south-west blow on ye   395
    And blister you all o'er!
PROSPERO   For this, be sure, to-night thou shalt have
    cramps,
    Side-stitches that shall pen thy breath up; urchins
    Shall, for that vast of night that they may work,   400
    All exercise on thee; thou shalt be pinch'd
    As thick as honeycomb, each pinch more stinging
    Than bees that made 'em.
CALIBAN   I must eat my dinner.
    This island's mine, by Sycorax my mother,   405
    Which thou tak'st from me. When thou cam'st first,
    Thou strok'st me and made much of me, wouldst give me
    Water with berries in 't, and teach me how
    To name the bigger light, and how the less,
    That burn by day and night; and then I lov'd thee   410
    And show'd thee all the qualities o' th' isle,
    The fresh springs, brine-pits, barren place and fertile.
    Curs'd be I that did so! All the charms
    Of Sycorax, toads, beetles, bats, light on you!
    For I am all the subjects that you have,   415
    Which first was mine own king; and here you sty me
    In this hard rock, whiles you do keep from me
    The rest o' th' island.
PROSPERO   Thou most lying slave,
    Whom stripes may move, not kindness! I have us'd thee,   420
    Filth as thou art, with human care, and lodg'd thee

---

387 quaint: skilled.   *391 dam:* mother.   *393 wicked:* destructive.   *395 south-west:* unhealthy
(supposedly).   *399 urchins:* goblins.   *400 vast:* desolate time.   *411 qualities:* resources.   *416
sty:* pen up.   *420 stripes:* a whipping.

In mine own cell, till thou didst seek to violate
The honour of my child.

CALIBAN   O ho, O ho! would 't had been done!
Thou didst prevent me; I had peopl'd else   425
This isle with Calibans.

PROSPERO   Abhorred slave,
Which any print of goodness wilt not take,
Being capable of all ill! I pitied thee,
Took pains to make thee speak, taught thee each hour   430
One thing or other: when thou didst not, savage,
Know thine own meaning, but wouldst gabble like
A thing most brutish, I endow'd thy purposes
With words that made them known. But thy vile race,
Though thou didst learn, had that in 't which good natures   435
Could not abide to be with; therefore wast thou
Deservedly confin'd into this rock, who hadst
Deserv'd more than a prison.

CALIBAN   You taught me language; and my profit on 't
Is, I know how to curse. The red plague rid you   440
For learning me your language!

PROSPERO   Hag-seed, hence!
Fetch us in fuel; and be quick, thou'rt best,
To answer other business. Shrug'st thou, malice?
If thou neglect'st or dost unwillingly   445
What I command, I'll rack thee with old cramps,
Fill all thy bones with aches, make thee roar
That beasts shall tremble at thy din.

CALIBAN   No, pray thee.
[*Aside.*] I must obey. His art is of such power   450
It would control my dam's god, Setebos,
And make a vassal of him.

PROSPERO   So, slave; hence!   Exit CALIBAN.

Enter FERDINAND; *and* ARIEL, *invisible, playing and singing.*

ARIEL'S SONG   455

Come unto these yellow sands,
    And then take hands.
Curtsied when you have, and kiss'd
    The wild waves whist,
Foot it featly here and there.   460

---

428 print: impression.   *434 race:* innate quality.   *440 red plague:* bubonic plague. *rid:* destroy.
446 rack: torture.   *451 Setebos:* a Patagonian, hence pagan, deity.   *452 vassal:* slave.   *457
take hands:* (i.e., for dancing).   *459 whist:* quieted.   *460 featly:* skillfully.

And, sweet sprites, the burthen
    bear.

BURTHEN *dispersedly*

Hark, hark! bow-wow,
The watch dogs bark! Bow-wow!   465

ARIEL

Hark, Hark! I hear
The strain of strutting chanticleer
Cry, "Cock-a-diddle-dow."

FERDINAND   Where should this music be? I' th'
    air or th' earth?   470
It sounds no more; and, sure, it waits upon
Some god o' th' island. Sitting on a bank,
Weeping again the King my father's wreck,
This music crept by me upon the waters,
Allaying both their fury and my passion   475
With its sweet air; thence I have follow'd it,
Or it hath drawn me rather. But 't is gone.
No, it begins again.

ARIEL'S SONG

Full fathom five thy father lies;   480
    Of his bones are coral made;
Those are pearls that were his eyes:
    Nothing of him that doth fade
But doth suffer a sea-change
Into something rich and strange,   485
    Sea-nymphs hourly ring his knell:

BURTHEN   Ding-dong.
ARIEL   Hark! now I hear them,—ding-dong, bell.
FERDINAND   The ditty does remember my drown'd father.
This is no mortal business, nor no sound   490
That the earth owes. I hear it now above me.
PROSPERO   The fringed curtains of thine eye advance
And say what thou seest yond.
MIRANDA   What is 't? A spirit?
Lord, how it looks about! Believe me, sir,   495
It carries a brave form. But 't is a spirit.
PROSPERO   No, wench; it eats and sleeps and hath such
    senses

461 *burthen:* burden (i.e., refrain).   463 *dispersedly:* from different sides of the stage.   467 *chanticleer:* rooster.   475 *passion:* grief.   489 *remember:* recall.   491 *owes:* possesses.   492 *advance:* raise.   496 *brave:* handsome.

As we have, such. This gallant which thou seest
Was in the wreck; and, but he's something stain'd   500
With grief, that's beauty's canker, though mightst call him
A goodly person. He hath lost his fellows
And strays about to find 'em.

MIRANDA   I might call him
A thing divine; for nothing natural   505
I ever saw so noble.

PROSPERO   [*Aside.*] It goes on, I see,
As my soul prompts it. Spirit, fine spirit! I'll free thee
Within two days for this.

FERDINAND   Most sure, the goddess   510
On whom these airs attend! Vouchsafe my prayer
May know if you remain upon this island,
And that you will some good instruction give
How I may bear me here: my prime request,
Which I do last pronounce, is, O you wonder!   515
If you be maid or no?

MIRANDA   No wonder, sir,
But certainly a maid.

FERDINAND   My language! heavens!
I am the best of them that speak this speech,   520
Were I but where 't is spoken.

PROSPERO   How? the best?
What wert thou, if the King of Naples heard thee?

FERDINAND   A single thing, as I am now, that wonders
To hear thee speak of Naples. He does hear me;   525
And that he does I weep. Myself am Naples,
Who with mine eyes, never since at ebb, beheld
The King my father wreck'd.

MIRANDA   Alack, for mercy!

FERDINAND   Yes, faith, and all his lords; the Duke of Milan   530
And his brave son being twain.

PROSPERO   [*Aside.*] The Duke of Milan
And his more braver daughter could control thee,
If now 't were fit to do 't. At the first sight
They have chang'd eyes. Delicate Ariel,   535
I'll set thee free for this. [*To* FERDINAND.] A word, good sir;
I fear you have done yourself some wrong; a word.

MIRANDA   Why speaks my father so ungently? This

---

499 gallant: young man.   *501 canker:* worm that destroys.   *511 attend:* do honor.   *512 remain:*
dwell.   *516 maid or no:* human female or not (i.e., supernatural).   *524 single:* lone.   *526 Naples:*
King of Naples.   *527 at ebb:* stopped flowing.   *533 control:* contradict.   *535 chang'd eyes:*
exchanged eyes (metaphor for "fallen in love").   *537 done yourself some wrong:* made a mistake.

Is the third man that e'er I saw, the first
That e'er I sigh'd for. Pity move my father   540
To be inclin'd my way!
FERDINAND   O, if a virgin,
And your affection not gone forth, I'll make you
The Queen of Naples.
PROSPERO   Soft, sir! one word more.   545
[*Aside.*] They are both in either's powers; but this swift business
I must uneasy make, lest too light winning
Make the prize light.—One word more; I charge thee
That thou attend me. Thou dost here usurp
The name thou ow'st not; and hast put thyself   550
Upon this island as a spy, to win it
From me, the lord on 't.
FERDINAND   No, as I am a man.
MIRANDA   There's nothing ill can dwell in such a temple.
If the ill spirit have so fair a house,   555
Good things will strive to dwell with 't.
PROSPERO   Follow me.
Speak not you for him; he's a traitor. Come.
I'll manacle thy neck and feet together.
Sea-water shalt thou drink; thy food shall be   560
The fresh-brook mussels, wither'd roots and husks
Wherein the acorn cradled. Follow.
FERDINAND   No;
I will resist such entertainment till
Mine enemy has more power.   565
                              [*He draws, but is charmed from moving.*]
MIRANDA   O dear father,
Make not too rash a trial of him, for
He's gentle and not fearful.
PROSPERO   What! I say;   570
My foot my tutor? Put thy sword up, traitor,
Who mak'st a show but dar'st not strike, thy conscience
Is so possess'd with guilt, Come from thy ward,
For I can here disarm thee with this stick
And make thy weapon drop.   575
MIRANDA   Beseech you, father.
PROSPERO   Hence! hang not on my garments.
MIRANDA   Sir, have pity;
I'll be his surety.

---

550 ow'st not: do not own.   *566 charmed:* prevented by magic.   *569 fearful:* dangerous.   *571 foot:* subordinate.   *573 ward:* posture for fighting.   *579 surety:* bond, guarantee.

PROSPERO   Silence! one word more   580
   Shall make me chide thee, if not hate thee. What!
   An advocate for an impostor! hush!
   Thou think'st there is no more such shapes as he,
   Having seen but him and Caliban. Foolish wench!
   To th' most of men this is a Caliban,   585
   And they to him are angels.
MIRANDA   My affections
   Are then most humble; I have no ambition
   To see a goodlier man.
PROSPERO   Come on; obey.   590
   Thy nerves are in their infancy again
   And have no vigour in them.
FERDINAND   So they are.
   My spirits, as in a dream, are all bound up.
   My father's loss, the weakness which I feel,   595
   The wreck of all my friends, nor this man's threats,
   To whom I am subdu'd, are but light to me,
   Might I but through my prison once a day
   Behold this maid: all corners else o' th' earth
   Let liberty make use of; space enough   600
   Have I in such a prison.
PROSPERO   [*Aside.*] It works. [*To* FERDINAND.]
    Come on.
   —Thou hast done well, fine Ariel!—Follow me.
   [*To* ARIEL.] Hark what thou else shalt do me.   605
MIRANDA   Be of comfort;
   My father's of a better nature, sir,
   Than he appears by speech. This is unwonted
   Which now came from him.
PROSPERO   [*To* ARIEL.] Thou shalt be as free   610
   As mountain winds; but then exactly do
   All points of my command.
ARIEL   To th' syllable.
PROSPERO   Come, follow.—
   Speak not for him.   *Exeunt.* 615

[ACT II, SCENE 1] *Another part of the island.*

Enter ALONSO, SEBASTIAN, ANTONIO, GONZALO, ADRIAN, FRANCISCO,
and others.

589 *goodlier:* more handsome.   *591 nerves:* sinews.   *608 unwonted:* unaccustomed.   *613 to th'*
syllable: completely.

GONZALO Beseech you, sir, be merry; you have cause,
     So have we all, of joy; for our escape   5
     Is much beyond our loss. Our hint of woe
     Is common; every day some sailor's wife,
     The masters of some merchant, and the merchant
     Have just our theme of woe; but for the miracle,
     I mean our preservation, few in millions   10
     Can speak like us. Then wisely, good sir, weigh
     Our sorrow with our comfort.
ALONSO   Prithee, peace.
SEBASTIAN He receives comfort like cold porridge.
ANTONIO The visitor will not give him o'er so.   15
SEBASTIAN Look, he's winding up the watch of his wit; by
     and by it will strike.
GONZALO Sir,—
SEBASTIAN One. Tell.
GONZALO When every grief is entertain'd that's offer'd,   20
     Comes to the entertainer—
SEBASTIAN A dollar.
GONZALO Dolour comes to him, indeed; you have spoken
     truer than you purposed.
SEBASTIAN You have taken it wiselier than I meant you   25
     should.
GONZALO Therefore my lord,—
ANTONIO Fie, what a spendthrift is he of his tongue!
ALONSO I prithee, spare.
GONZALO Well, I have done. But yet,—   30
SEBASTIAN He will be talking.
ANTONIO Which, of he or Adrian, for a good wager, first
     begins to crow?
SEBASTIAN The old cock.
ANTONIO The cockerel.   35
SEBASTIAN Done. The wager?
ANTONIO A laughter.
SEBASTIAN A match!
ADRIAN Thought this island seem to be desert,—
SEBASTIAN Ha, ha, ha! Antonio! So you're paid.   40
ADRIAN Uninhabitable and almost inaccessible,—
SEBASTIAN Yet,—

---

6 hint: experience. *15 visitor:* visiting priest. *give him o'er so:* let him off easily (i.e., Gonzalo will keep on talking whether Alonso wants to listen or not). *19 Tell:* count (the strokes of the watch). *20 entertain'd:* received. *23 Dolour:* sorrow (with a pun on "dollar"). *25 wiselier:* acutely. *32–33 Which . . . crow?:* We'll bet on who—Gonzalo or Adrian—speaks first. *35 cockerel:* the young rooster (i.e., Adrian). *37 laughter:* The winner may laugh at the loser.

ADRIAN   Yet,—

ANTONIO   He could not miss 't.

ADRIAN   It must needs be of subtle, tender, and delicate   45
   temperance.

ANTONIO   Temperance was a delicate wench.

SEBASTIAN.   Ay, and a subtle; as he most learnedly delivered.

ADRIAN   The air breathes upon us here most sweetly.

SEBASTIAN   As if it had lungs and rotten ones.   50

ANTONIO   Or as 't were perfumed by a fen.

GONZALO   Here is everything advantageous to life.

ANTONIO   True; save means to live.

SEBASTIAN   Of that there's none, or little.

GONZALO   How lush and lusty the grass looks! How green!   55

ANTONIO   The ground indeed is tawny.

SEBASTIAN   With an eye of green in 't.

ANTONIO   He misses not much.

SEBASTIAN   No; he doth but mistake the truth totally.

GONZALO   But the rarity of it is,—which is indeed almost   60
   beyond credit—

SEBASTIAN   As many vouched rarities are.

GONZALO   That our garments, being, as they were, drenched
   in the sea, hold notwithstanding their freshness and glosses,
   being rather new-dyed than stained with salt water.   65

ANTONIO   If but one of his pockets could speak, would it not
   say he lies?

SEBASTIAN   Ay, or very falsely pocket up his report.

GONZALO   Methinks our garments are now as fresh as when
   we put them on first in Afric, at the marriage of the King's fair   70
   daughter Claribel to the King of Tunis.

SEBASTIAN   'T was a sweet marriage, and we prosper well in
   our return.

ADRIAN   Tunis was never graced before with such a paragon
   to their queen.   75

GONZALO   Not since widow Dido's time.

ANTONIO   Widow! a pox o' that! How came that widow in?
   Widow Dido!

SEBASTIAN   What if he had said "widower Aeneas" too?
   Good Lord, how you take it!   80

ADRIAN   "Widow Dido" said you? You make me study of
   that. She was of Carthage, not of Tunis.

GONZALO   This Tunis, sir, was Carthage.

---

46 temperature: climate.   *48 delivered:* reported.   *61 credit:* credibility.   *62 vouched:* sworn.
76 Dido: In Virgil's *Aeneid,* Queen of Carthage and Aeneas's lover until the gods commanded him
to move on to Italy. The widow of Sychaeus, she committed suicide when Aeneas left her.   *79
widower Aeneas:* Aeneas had lost his wife in the sack of Troy.

ADRIAN   Carthage?

GONZALO   I assure you, Carthage.   85

ANTONIO   His word is more than the miraculous harp.

SEBASTIAN   He hath raised the wall and houses too.

ANTONIO   What impossible matter will he make easy next?

SEBASTIAN   I think he will carry this island home in his
    pocket and give it his son for an apple.   90

ANTONIO   And, sowing the kernels of it in the sea, bring
    forth more islands.

GONZALO   Ay.

ANTONIO   Why, in good time.

GONZALO   Sir, we were talking that our garments seem now   95
    as fresh as when we were at Tunis at the marriage of your
    daughter, who is now Queen.

ANTONIO   And the rarest that e'er came there.

SEBASTIAN   Bate, I beseech you, widow Dido.

ANTONIO   O, widow Dido! ay, widow Dido.   100

GONZALO   Is not, sir, my doublet as fresh as the first day I
    wore it? I mean, in a sort.

ANTONIO   That "sort" was well fished for.

GONZALO   When I wore it at your daughter's marriage?

ALONSO   You cram these words into mine ears against   105
    The stomach of my sense. Would I had never
    Married my daughter there! for, coming, thence,
    My son is lost and, in my rate, she too,
    Who is so far from Italy removed
    I ne'er again shall see her. O thou mine heir   110
    Of Naples and of Milan, what strange fish
    Hath made his meal on thee?

FRANCISCO   Sir, he may live.
    I saw him beat the surges under him,
    And ride upon their backs: he trod the water,   115
    Whose enmity he flung aside, and breasted
    The surge most swoln that met him: his bold head
    'Bove the contentious waves he kept, and oared
    Himself with his good arms in lusty stroke
    To th' shore, that o'er his wave-worn basis bowed,   120
    As stooping to relieve him: I not doubt
    He came alive to land.

ALONSO   No, no, he's gone.

SEBASTIAN   Sir, you may thank yourself for this great loss,

---

86 *miraculous harp:* In Ovid's tale, Amphion raised the walls of Thebes by the music of his harp.
99 *Bate:* except.   101 *doublet:* upper outer garment.   *102 in a sort:* in a way.   *108 rate:* estima-
tion.   *115 surges:* waves.   *120 his:* its.   *basis:* beach or sands.

That would not bless our Europe with your daughter,   125
But rather loose her to an African;
Where she at least is banish'd from your eye,
Who hath cause to wet the grief on 't.
ALONSO   Prithee, peace.
SEBASTIAN   You were kneel'd to and impórtun'd otherwise   130
By all of us, and the fair soul herself
Weigh'd between loathness and obedience, at
Which end o' th' beam should bow. We have lost your son,
I fear, for ever: Milan and Naples have
Moe widows in them of this business' making   135
Than we bring men to comfort them.
The fault's your own.
ALONSO   So is the dear'st o' th' loss.
GONZALO   My lord Sebastian,
The truth you speak doth lack some gentleness   140
And time to speak it in. You rub the sore,
When you should bring the plaster.
SEBASTIAN   Very well.
ANTONIO   And most chirurgeonly.
GONZALO   It is foul weather in us all, good sir,   145
When you are cloudy.
SEBASTIAN   Foul weather?
ANTONIO   Very foul.
GONZALO   Had I plantation of this isle, my lord,—
ANTONIO   He'd sow 't with nettle-seed.   150
SEBASTIAN   Or docks, or mallows.
GONZALO   And were the king on 't, what would I do?
SEBASTIAN   Scape being drunk for want of wine.
GONZALO   I' th' commonwealth I would by contraries
Execute all things; for no kind of traffic   155
Would I admit; no name of magistrate;
Letters should not be known; riches, poverty,
And use of service, none; contract, succession,
Bourn, bound of land, tilth, vineyard, none;
No use of metal, corn, or wine, or oil;   160
No occupation; all men idle, all;
And women too, but innocent and pure;
No sovereignty;—

128 *wet:* weep for.   131 *fair soul:* (i.e., Claribel, Alonso's daughter).   132 *weigh'd:* balanced. *loathness and obedience:* distaste for her espousal and duty to her father.   133 *end o' th' beam:* side of the scale.   135 *Moe:* more.   138 *dear'st:* most costly.   141 *time:* proper occasion.   144 *chirurgeonly:* like a surgeon.   149 *plantation:* charge of colonization (Antonio plays with the literal meaning of the word—"planting").   154 *by contraries:* in contrast to the usual procedure.   155 *traffic:* trade.

SEBASTIAN   Yet he would be king on 't.

ANTONIO   The latter end of his commonwealth forgets the   165
    beginning.

GONZALO   All things in common nature should produce
    Without sweat or endeavour: treason, felony,
    Sword, pike, knife, gun, or need of any engine,
    Would I not have; but nature should bring forth,   170
    Of it own kind, all foison, all abundance,
    To feed my innocent people.

SEBASTIAN   No marrying 'mong his subjects?

ANTONIO   None, man; all idle; whores and knaves.

GONZALO   I would with such perfection govern, sir,   175
    T' excel the golden age.

SEBASTIAN   Save his Majesty!

ANTONIO   Long live Gonzalo!

GONZALO   And,—do you mark me, sir?

ALONSO   Prithee, no more; thou dost talk nothing to me.   180

GONZALO   I do well believe your Highness; and did it to
    minister occasion to these gentlemen, who are of such sen-
    sible and nimble lungs that they always use to laugh at nothing.

ANTONIO   'T was you we laughed at.

GONZALO   Who in this kind of merry fooling am nothing to   185
    you: so you may continue and laugh at nothing still.

ANTONIO   What a blow was there given!

SEBASTIAN   An it had not fallen flatlong.

GONZALO   You are gentlemen of brave mettle; you would
    lift the moon out of her sphere, if she would continue in it   190
    five weeks without changing.

Enter ARIEL *invisible, playing solemn music.*

SEBASTIAN   We would so, and then go a bat-fowling.

ANTONIO   Nay, good my lord, be not angry.

GONZALO   No, I warrant you; I will not adventure my dis-   195
    cretion so weakly. Will you laugh me asleep, for I am very
    heavy?

ANTONIO   Go sleep, and hear us.
                [*All sleep except* ALONSO, SEBASTIAN, *and* ANTONIO.]

ALONSO   What, all so soon asleep! I wish mine eyes   200
    Would, with themselves, shut up my thoughts. I find
    They are inclin'd to do so.

---

169 engine: machinery for war. *171 foison:* plenty. *176 golden age:* a mythical time when man lived in such harmony with nature that government was not needed. *182 minister occasion:* give opportunity. *182–83 sensible:* sensitive. *188 An:* If. *flatlong:* by the flat side of the sword. *189 mettle:* spirit.

SEBASTIAN   Please you, sir.
    Do not omit the heavy offer of it.
    It seldom visits sorrow; when it doth,   205
    It is a comforter.
ANTONIO   We two, my lord,
    Will guard your person while you take your rest,
    And watch your safety.
ALONSO   Thank You. Wondrous heavy.   210
                 [ALONSO *sleeps.*]   *Exit* ARIEL.
SEBASTIAN   What a strange drowsiness possesses them!
ANTONIO   It is the quality o' th' climate.
SEBASTIAN   Why
    Doth it not then our eyelids sink? I find not   215
    Myself dispos'd to sleep.
ANTONIO   Nor I; my spirits are nimble.
    They fell together all, as by consent;
    They dropp'd, as by a thunder-stroke. What might,
    Worthy Sebastian, O, what might—? No more;—   220
    And yet methinks I see it in thy face,
    What thou shouldst be: the occasion speaks thee, and
    My strong imagination sees a crown
    Dropping upon thy head.
SEBASTIAN   What, art thou waking?   225
ANTONIO   Do you not hear me speak?
SEBASTIAN   I do; and surely
    It is a sleepy language, and thou speak'st
    Out of thy sleep. What is it thou didst say?
    This is a strange repose, to be asleep   230
    With eyes wide open; standing, speaking, moving,
    And yet so fast asleep.
ANTONIO   Noble Sebastian,
    Thou let'st thy fortune sleep—die, rather; wink'st
    Whiles thou art waking.   235
SEBASTIAN   Thou dost snore distinctly;
    There's meaning in thy snores.
ANTONIO   I am more serious than my custom; you
    Must be so too, if heed me; which to do
    Trebles thee o'er.   240
SEBASTIAN   Well, I am standing water.
ANTONIO   I'll teach you how to flow.

---

222 *Occasion speaks:* opportunity calls.   *228 sleepy:* dreamlike.   *234 wink'st:* shut your eyes.
240 standing water: makes you three times the man you really are.   *241 standing water:* water
between ebb and flow tides.

SEBASTIAN   Do so. To ebb
    Hereditary sloth instructs me.

ANTONIO   O,   245
    If you but knew how you the purpose cherish
    Whiles thus you mock it! how, in stripping it
    You more invest it! Ebbing men, indeed,
    Most often do so near the bottom run
    By their own fear or sloth.   250

SEBASTIAN   Prithee, say on.
    The setting of thine eye and cheek proclaim
    A matter from thee, and a birth indeed
    Which throes thee much to yield.

ANTONIO   Thus, sir: 255
    Although this lord of weak remembrance, this,
    Who shall be of as little memory
    When he is earth'd, hath here almost persuaded—
    For he's a spirit of persuasion, only
    Professes to persuade—the King his son's alive,   260
    'T is as impossible that he's undrown'd
    As he that sleeps here swims.

SEBASTIAN   I have no hope
    That he's undrown'd.

ANTONIO   O, out of that no hope   265
    What great hope have you! No hope that way is
    Another way so high a hope that even
    Ambition cannot pierce a wink beyond,
    But doubt discovery there. Will you grant with me
    That Ferdinand is drown'd?   270

SEBASTIAN   He's gone.

ANTONIO   Then, tell me,
    Who's the next heir of Naples?

SEBASTIAN   Claribel.

ANTONIO   She that is Queen of Tunis; she that dwells   275
    Ten leagues beyond man's life; she that from Naples
    Can have no note, unless the sun were post—
    The man i' th' moon's too slow—till newborn chins
    Be rough and razorable; she that—from whom
    We all were sea-swallow'd, though some cast again,   280
    And by that destiny to perform an act

---

248 *invest:* clothe in robes.   252 *setting:* serious expression.   254 *throes . . . yield:* pains you to bring forth.   256 *remembrance:* memory.   258 *earth'd:* buried.   268 *pierce a wink:* catch a glimpse.   269 *doubt discovery:* question what it sees.   279 *from:* coming from.   280 *cast:* thrown upon shore (as well as "cast" in a drama).

Whereof what's past is prologue, what to come
In yours and my discharge.

SEBASTIAN   What stuff is this! How say you?   285
'T is true, my brother's daughter's Queen of Tunis;
So is she heir of Naples; 'twixt which regions
There is some space.

ANTONIO   A space whose every cubit
Seems to cry out, "How shall that Claribel
Measure us back to Naples? Keep in Tunis,   290
And let Sebastian wake." Say, this were death
That now hath seiz'd them; why, they were no worse
Than now they are. There be that can rule Naples
As well as he that sleeps; lords that can prate
As amply and unnecessarily   295
As this Gonzalo; I myself could make
A chough of as deep chat. O, that you bore
The mind that I do! what a sleep were this
For your advancement! Do you understand me?

SEBASTIAN Methinks I do.   300

ANTONIO   And how does your content
Tender your own good fortune?

SEBASTIAN   I remember
You did supplant your brother Prospero.

ANTONIO   True.   305
And look how well my garments sit upon me;
Much feater than before: my brother's servants
Were then my fellows; now they are my men.

SEBASTIAN But, for your conscience?

ANTONIO Ay, sir, where lies that? If 't were a kibe,   310
'T would put me to my slipper; but I feel not
This deity in my bosom. Twenty consciences,
That stand 'twixt me and Milan, candied be they
And melt ere they molest! Here lies your brother,
No better than the earth he lies upon   315
If he were that which now he's like, that's dead;
Whom I, with this obedient steel, three inches of it,
Can lay to bed for ever; whiles you, doing thus,
To the perpetual wink for aye might put
This ancient morsel, this Sir Prudence, who   320
Should not upbraid our course. For all the rest,
They'll take suggestion as a cat laps milk;

283 discharge: responsibility. *290 measure us:* trace us. *Keep:* let her stay. *297 A chough . . . chat:* A crow that could speak a few words as well as he (i.e., Gonzalo). *302 Tender:* figure. *307 feater:* more becomingly. *310 kibe:* chilblain. *313 candied:* iced over. *319 wink:* sleep (i.e., death)

    They'll tell the clock to any business that
    We say befits the hour.
SEBASTIAN   Thy case, dear friend,   325
    Shall be my precedent; as thou got'st Milan,
    I'll come by Naples. Draw thy sword. One stroke
    Shall free thee from the tribute which thou payest,
    And I the King shall love thee.
ANTONIO   Draw together;   330
    And when I rear my hand, do you the like,
    To fall it on Gonzalo.
SEBASTIAN   O, but one word.   [*They talk apart.*]

Re-enter ARIEL *invisible, with music and song.*

ARIEL   My master through his art foresees the danger   335
    That you, his friend, are in; and sends me forth—
    For else his project dies—to keep them living.
                            [*Sings in* GONZALO'S *ear.*]

    While you here do snoring lie.
    Open-ey'd Conspiracy   340
       His time doth take.
    If of life you keep a care,
    Shake off slumber, and beware:
       Awake, awake!

ANTONIO   Then let us both be sudden.   345
GONZALO   Now, good angels
    Preserve the King.   [*Wakes* ALONSO.]
ALONSO   Why, how now? Ho, awake! Why are you drawn?
    Wherefore this ghastly looking?
GONZALO   What's the matter?   350
SEBASTIAN   Whiles we stood here securing your repose,
    Even now, we heard a hollow burst of bellowing
    Like bulls, or rather lions; did 't not wake you?
    It struck mine ear most terribly.
ALONSO   I heard nothing.   355
ANTONIO   O, 't was a din to fright a monster's ear,
    To make an earthquake! Sure, it was the roar
    Of a whole herd of lions.
ALONSO   Heard you this, Gonzalo?
GONZALO   Upon mine honour, sir, I heard a humming,   360
    And that a strange one too, which did awake me.
    I shak'd you, sir, and cried: as mine eyes open'd,

324 tell the clock to: count the time for.   *341 time:* opportunity.

I saw their weapons drawn: there was a noise,
That's verily. 'T is best we stand upon our guard,
Or that we quit this place. Let's draw our weapons. 365
ALONSO Lead off this ground; and let's make further search
For my poor son.
GONZALO Heavens keep him from these beasts!
For he is, sure, i' th' island.
ALONSO   Lead away. 370
ARIEL Prospero my lord shall know what I have done.
So, King, go safely on to seek thy son.   *Exeunt.*

[ACT II, SCENE 2] *Another part of the island.*

Enter CALIBAN *with a burden of wood. A noise of thunder heard.*

CALIBAN All the infections that the sun sucks up,
From bogs, fens, flats, on Prosper fall and make him
By inch-meal a disease! His spirits hear me 5
And yet I needs must curse. But they'll nor pinch,
Fright me with urchin-shows, pitch me i' th' mire,
Nor lead me, like a firebrand, in the dark
Out of my way, unless he bid 'em; but
For every trifle are they set upon me, 10
Sometime like apes that mow and chatter at me
And after bite me, then like hedgehogs which
Lie tumbling in my barefoot way and mount
Their pricks at my footfall; sometime am I
All wound with adders who with cloven tongues 15
Do hiss me into madness.

Enter TRINCULO.
                              Lo, now lo!
Here comes a spirit of his, and to torment me
For bringing wood in slowly. I'll fall flat; 20
Perchance he will not mind me.
TRINCULO Here's neither bush nor shrub, to bear off any
weather at all, and another storm brewing; I hear it sing i' th'
wind: yond same black cloud, yond huge one, looks like a
foul bombard that would shed his liquor. If it should thunder 25
as it did before, I know not where to hide my head; yond same
cloud cannot choose but fall by pailfuls. What have we here? A
man or a fish? Dead or alive? A fish; he smells like a fish; a very
ancient and fish-like smell; a kind of not-of-the-newest Poor-

---

364 verily: the truth. *5 inch-meal:* inches. *7 urchin-shows:* apparitions of goblins (caused by
Prospero). *8 fire-brand:* will-o'-the-wisp. *11 mow:* make faces. *25 bombard:* large leather tan-
kard. *29–30 Poor-John:* dried salt fish.

John. A strange fish! Were I in England now, as once I was, and   30
had but this fish painted, not a holiday fool there but would
give a piece of silver: there would this monster make a man;
any strange beast there makes a man: when they will not give a
doit to relieve a lame beggar, they will lay out ten to see a dead
Indian. Legged like a man! and his fins like arms! Warm o' my   35
troth! I do now let loose my opinion, hold it no longer: this is
no fish, but an islander, that hath lately suffered by a thunder-
bolt. [*Thunder.*] Alas, the storm is come again! My best way is
to creep under his gaberdine; there is no other shelter here-
about: misery acquaints a man with strange bedfellows. I will   40
here shroud till the dregs of the storm be past.

Enter STEPHANO, *singing: a bottle in his hand.*

STEPHANO   I shall no more to sea, to sea,
                            Here shall I die ashore—   45

This is a very scurvy tune to sing at a man's funeral. Well, here's
my comfort.   [*Drinks. Sings.*]

                    The master, the swabber, the boatswain, and I,
                    The gunner and his mate
                Lov'd Moll, Meg, and Marian, and Margery,   50
                    But none of us car'd for Kate;
                    For she had a tongue with a tang,
                    Would cry to a sailor, Go hang!
                She lov'd not the savour of tar nor of pitch,
                Yet a tailor might scratch her where'er she did itch;   55
                    Then to sea, boys, and let her go hang!

This is a scurvy tune too; but here's my comfort.   [*Drinks.*]
CALIBAN   Do not torment me! Oh!
STEPHANO   What's the matter? Have we devils here? Do
    you put tricks upon 's with savages and men of Ind, ha! I have   60
    not scaped drowning to be afeard now of your four legs; for it
    hath been said, "As proper a man as ever went on four legs can-
    not make him give ground"; and it shall be said so again while
    Stephano breathes at nostrils.
CALIBAN   The spirit torments me! Oh!   65
STEPHANO   This is some monster of the isle with four legs
    who hath got, as I take it, an ague. Where the devil should he
    learn our language? I will give him some relief, if it be but for

---

31 painted: a sign with a painted fish on a booth at the fair.   *32 make a man:* make a man's
fortune.   *34 doit:* a very small Dutch coin.   *35 Indians:* North American Indians frequently exhibited in England.   *39 gaberdine:* cloak.   *57 scurvy:* bad.   *60 Ind:* India.   *67 ague:* chills and
fever.

that. If I can recover him and keep him tame and get to Naples
with him, he's a present for any emperor that ever trod on neat's-
leather.   70

CALIBAN Do not torment me, prithee; I'll bring my wood
home faster.

STEPHANO He's in his fit now and does not talk after the
wisest. He shall taste of my bottle; if he have never drunk wine   75
afore, it will go near to remove his fit. If I can recover him and
keep him tame, I will not take too much for him; he shall pay
for him that hath him, and that soundly.

CALIBAN Thou dost me yet but little hurt; thou wilt anon,
I know it by thy trembling. Now Prosper works upon thee.   80

STEPHANO Come on your ways: open your mouth; here is
that which will give language to you, cat: open your mouth; this
will shake your shaking, I can tell you, and that soundly: you
cannot tell who's your friend: open your chops again.

TRINCULO I should know that voice; it should be—but he   85
is drowned; and these are devils. O defend me!

STEPHANO Four legs and two voices; a most delicate
monster! His forward voice now is to speak well of his friend;
his backward voice is to utter foul speeches and to detract. If all
the wine in my bottle will recover him, I will help his ague.   90
Come. Amen! I will pour some in thy other mouth.

TRINCULO Stephano!

STEPHANO Doth thy other mouth call me? Mercy, mercy!
This is a devil, and no monster. I will leave him; I have no long
spoon.   95

TRINCULO Stephano! If thou beest Stephano, touch me and
speak to me; for I am Trinculo,—be not afeared—thy good
friend Trinculo.

STEPHANO If thou beest Trinculo, come forth. I'll pull thee
by the lesser legs. If any be Trinculo's legs, these are they. Thou   100
art very Trinculo indeed! How cam'st thou to be the siege of
this moon-calf? Can he vent Trinculos?

TRINCULO I took him to be killed with a thunder-stroke. But
art thou not drowned, Stephano? I hope now thou art not
drowned. Is the storm over-blown? I hid me under the dead   105
moon-calf's gaberdine for fear of the storm. And art thou living,
Stephano? O Stephano, two Neapolitans scaped!

STEPHANO Prithee, do not turn me about; my stomach is
not constant.

70-71 neat's-leather: cowhide. *79 anon:* shortly. *84 chops:* jaws. *94-95 long spoon:* allusion
to an old proverb: "He that eats with the devil must have a long spoon." *101 siege:* excrement.
102 moon-calf: monster (because born at the wrong time of the moon). *109 constant:* steady.

CALIBAN [*Aside.*] These be fine things, an if they be not   110
    sprites.
    That's a brave god and bears celestial liquor.
    I will kneel to him.
STEPHANO How didst thou scape? How cam'st thou hither?
    Swear by this bottle how thou cam'st hither,—I escaped upon   115
    a butt of sack which the sailors heaved o'erboard—by this
    bottle, which I made of the bark of a tree with mine own hands
    since I was cast ashore.
CALIBAN I'll swear upon that bottle to be thy true subject;
    for the liquor is not earthly.   120
STEPHANO Here; swear then how thou escap'dst.
TRINCULO Swam ashore, man, like a duck. I can swim like
    a duck, I'll be sworn.
STEPHANO Here, kiss the book. Though thou canst swim
    like a duck, thou art made like a goose.   125
TRINCULO O Stephano, hast any more of this?
STEPHANO The whole butt, man: my cellar is in a rock by
    th' seaside where my wine is hid. How now, moon-calf! how
    does thine ague?
CALIBAN Hast thou not dropp'd from heaven?   130
STEPHANO Out o' th' moon, I do assure thee. I was the man
    i' th' moon when time was.
CALIBAN I have seen thee in her and I do adore thee.
    My mistress show'd me thee and thy dog and thy bush.
STEPHANO Come, swear to that, kiss the book: I will furnish   135
    it anon with new contents. Swear.
TRINCULO By this good light, this is a very shallow monster!
    I afeard of him! A very weak monster! The man i' th' moon! A
    most poor credulous monster! Well drawn, monster, in good
    sooth!   140
CALIBAN I'll show thee every fertile inch o' th' island;
    And I will kiss thy foot. I prithee, be my god.
TRINCULO By this light, a most perfidious and drunken
    monster! When 's god's asleep, he'll rob his bottle.
CALIBAN I'll kiss thy foot. I'll swear myself thy subject.   145
STEPHANO Come on then; down, and swear.
TRINCULO I shall laugh myself to death at this puppy-
    headed monster. A most scurvy monster! I could find in my heart
    to beat him—

---

116 *butt of sack:* barrel of dry white wine (from Spain).   124 *book:* i.e., the bottle from which
Trinculo drinks.   132 *when time was:* once upon a time.   134 *thee . . . bush:* According to an old
story, the man in the moon was banished from earth for collecting wood on Sunday. His dog and
the last thornbush he gathered were sent to the moon with him.   139 *drawn:* drunk.   140 *sooth:*
truth.

STEPHANO   Come, kiss.   150

TRINCULO   But that the poor monster's in drink. An abomi-
    nable monster!

CALIBAN   I'll show thee the best springs; I'll pluck thee
    berries;
    I'll fish for thee and get thee wood enough.   155
    A plague upon the tyrant that I serve!
    I'll bear him no more sticks, but follow thee,
    Thou wondrous man.

TRINCULO   A most ridiculous monster, to make a wonder
    of a poor drunkard!   160

CALIBAN   I prithee, let me bring thee where crabs grow;
    And I with my long nails will dig thee pignuts;
    Show thee a jay's nest and instruct thee how
    To snare the nimble marmoset. I'll bring thee
    To clust'ring filberts and sometimes I'll get thee   165
    Young scamels from the rock. Wilt thou go with me?

STEPHANO   I prithee now, lead the way without any more
    talking. Trinculo, the King and all our company else being
    drowned, we will inherit here. Here! bear my bottle. Fellow
    Trinculo, we'll fill him by and by again.   170

                   [CALIBAN *sings drunkenly:*]
    Farewell, master; farewell, farewell!

TRINCULO   A howling monster; a drunken monster!

CALIBAN   [*Sings.*]   175

        No more dams I'll make for fish;
           Nor fetch in firing
           At requiring;
        Nor scrape trencher, nor wash dish.
           'Ban, 'Ban, Ca—Caliban   180
           Has a new master, get a new man.

    Freedom, hey-day! hey-day, freedom! freedom, hey-day, freedom!

STEPHANO   O brave monster! Lead the way.   *Exeunt.*

[ACT III, SCENE 1]   *Before Prospero's cell.*

Enter FERDINAND, *bearing a log.*

FERDINAND   There be some sports are painful, and their
    labour
    Delight in them sets off; some kinds of baseness   5

---

161 crabs: crabapples.   *162 pignuts:* sometimes called earthnuts.   *164 marmoset:* a small monkey.   *166 scamels:* (may mean "seagulls").   *177 firing:* firewood.   *179 trencher:* wooden plate
or platter.   *5 Delight . . . sets off:* Delight outweighs the effort.

Are nobly undergone, and most poor matters
Point to rich ends. This my mean task
Would be as heavy to me as odious, but
The mistress which I serve quickens what's dead
And makes my labours pleasures. O, she is   10
Ten times more gentle than her father's crabbed,
And he's compos'd of harshness. I must remove
Some thousands of these logs and pile them up,
Upon a sore injunction. My sweet mistress
Weeps when she sees me work, and says such baseness   15
Had never like executor. I forget;
But these sweet thoughts do even refresh my labours,
Most busiest when I do it.

Enter MIRANDA; *and* PROSPERO *at a distance, unseen.*

MIRANDA   Alas, now, pray you,   20
    Work not so hard. I would the lightning had
    Burnt up those logs that you are enjoin'd to pile!
    Pray, set it down and rest you. When this burns,
    'T will weep for having wearied you. My father
    Is hard at study; pray now, rest yourself;   25
    He's safe for these three hours.
FERDINAND   O most dear mistress,
    The sun will set before I shall discharge
    What I must strive to do.
MIRANDA   If you'll sit down,   30
    I'll bear your logs the while: pray, give me that;
    I'll carry it to the pile.
FERDINAND   No, precious creature;
    I had rather crack my sinews, break my back,
    Than you should such dishonour undergo,   35
    While I sit lazy by.
MIRANDA   It would become me
    As well as it does you; and I should do it
    With much more ease, for my good will is to it,
    And yours it is against.   40
PROSPERO   Poor worm, thou art infected!
    This visitation shows it.
MIRANDA   You look wearily.
FERDINAND   No, noble mistress; 't is fresh morning with
        me   45
    When you are by at night, I do beseech you—

---

9 quickens: gives life to. *14 injunction:* penalty. *15 baseness:* menial task. *16 like executor:* such a performer. *18 Most . . . it:* When I work at my job most busily. (The meaning of the line is not really clear.)

Chiefly that I might set it in my prayers—
What is your name?

MIRANDA   Miranda.—O my father.
I have broke your hest to say so!   50

FERDINAND   Admir'd Miranda!
Indeed the top of admiration! worth
What's dearest to the world! Full many a lady
I have ey'd with best regard, and many a time
Th' harmony of their tongues hath into bondage   55
Brought my too diligent ear; for several virtues
Have I lik'd several women, never any
With so full soul, but some defect in her
Did quarrel with the noblest grace she ow'd
And put it to the foil; but you, O you,   60
So perfect and so peerless, are created
Of every creature's best!

MIRANDA   I do not know
One of my sex; no woman's face remember,
Save, from my glass, mine own; nor have I seen   65
More that I may call men than you, good friend,
And my dear father: how features are abroad,
I am skilless of; but, by my modesty,
The jewel in my dower, I would not wish
Any companion in the world but you;   70
Nor can imagination form a shape,
Besides yourself, to like of. But I prattle
Something too wildly, and my father's precepts
I therein do forget.

FERDINAND   I am in my condition   75
A prince, Miranda; I do think, a king;
I would, not so!—and would no more endure
This wooden slavery than to suffer
The flesh-fly blow my mouth. Hear my soul speak.
The very instant that I saw you, did   80
My heart fly to your service; there resides,
To make me slave to it; and for your sake
Am I this patient log-man.

MIRANDA   Do you love me?

FERDINAND   O heaven, O earth, bear witness to this sound,   85
And crown what I profess with kind event
If I speak true! if hollowly, invert

---

51 Admir'd Miranda: Ferdinand plays on words, for *miranda* in Latin means "she is to be wondered at." *60 put it to the foil:* conquered or overcame it. *67 abroad:* elsewhere. *68 skilless:*
ignorant. *78 wooden slavery:* menial task of carrying wood. *86 kind event:* favorable result.

What best is boded me to mischief! I
Beyond all limit of what else i' th' world
Do love, prize, honour you.   90
MIRANDA   I am a fool
    To weep at what I am glad of.
PROSPERO [*Apart.*]   Fair encounter
    Of two most rare affections! Heavens rain grace
    On that which breeds between 'em!   95
FERDINAND   Wherefore weep you?
MIRANDA   At mine unworthiness, that dare not offer
    What I desire to give, and much less take
    What I shall die to want. But this is trifling;
    And all the more it seeks to hide itself,   100
    The bigger bulk it shows. Hence, bashful cunning!
    And prompt me, plain and holy innocence!
    I am your wife, if you will marry me;
    If not, I'll die your maid: to be your fellow
    You may deny me; but I'll be your servant,   105
    Whether you will or no.
FERDINAND   My mistress, dearest;
    And I thus humble ever.
MIRANDA   My husband, then?
FERDINAND   Ay, with a heart as willing   110
    As bondage e'er of freedom: here's my hand.
MIRANDA   And mine, with my heart in 't: and now farewell
    Till half an hour hence.
FERDINAND   A thousand thousand!
                      Exeunt FERDINAND *and* MIRANDA *severally.*   115
PROSPERO   So glad of this as they I cannot be,
    Who are surpris'd withal; but my rejoicing
    At nothing can be more. I'll to my book,
    For yet ere supper-time must I perform
    Much business appertaining.   *Exit.*   120

[ACT III, SCENE 2] *Another part of the island.*

Enter CALIBAN, STEPHANO, *and* TRINCULO.

STEPHANO   Tell not me: when the butt is out, we will

---

88 *What . . . boded:* Whatever favorable destiny is assigned me. *mischief:* evil outcome.   *99 want:* lack.   *104 maid:* (as your) maidservant (and possibly also, virgin). *fellow:* equal (companion). *107 mistress:* adored lady.   *114 thousand thousand:* i.e., countless farewells.   *116 this:* their flourishing love.   *117 who:* Ferdinand and Miranda. *surpris'd withal:* taken unawares by love. *120 business appertaining:* things to do to complete Prospero's scheme for the marriage of Ferdinand and Miranda.   *3 butt is out:* bottle is empty.

drink water; not a drop before; therefore bear up, and board
'em. Servant-monster, drink to me.   5
TRINCULO   Servant-monster! the folly of this island! They
say there's but five upon this isle: we are three of them; if th'
other two be brained like us, the state totters.
STEPHANO   Drink servant-monster, when I bid thee. Thy
eyes are almost set in thy head.   10
TRINCULO   Where should they be set else? He were a brave
monster indeed, if they were set in his tail.
STEPHANO   My man-monster hath drowned his tongue in
sack: for my part, the sea cannot drown me; I swam, ere I
could recover the shore, five and thirty leagues off and on. By   15
this light, thou shalt be my lieutenant, monster, or my standard.
TRINCULO   Your lieutenant, if you list; he's no standard.
STEPHANO   We'll not run, Monsieur Monster.
TRINCULO   Nor go neither; but you'll lie like dogs and yet
say nothing neither.   20
STEPHANO   Moon-calf, speak once in thy life, if thou beest
a good moon-calf.
CALIBAN   How does thy honour? Let me lick thy shoe.
I'll not serve him; he is not valiant.
TRINCULO   Thou liest, most ignorant monster! I am in case   25
to justle a constable. Why, thou deboshed fish, thou, was there
ever man a coward that hath drunk so much sack as I to-day?
Wilt thou tell a monstrous lie, being but half a fish and half a
monster?
CALIBAN   Lo, how he mocks me! Wilt thou let him, my lord?   30
TRINCULO   "Lord" quoth he! That a monster should be such
a natural!
CALIBAN   Lo, lo, again! Bite him to death, I prithee.
STEPHANO   Trinculo, keep a good tongue in your head. If
you prove a mutineer,—the next tree! The poor monster's my   35
subject and he shall not suffer indignity.
CALIBAN   I thank my noble lord. Wilt thou be pleas'd
To hearken once again to the suit I made to thee?
STEPHANO   Marry, will I; kneel and repeat it. I will stand,
and so shall Trinculo.   40

Enter ARIEL, *invisible.*

CALIBAN   As I told thee before, I am subject to a tyrant, a
sorcerer, that by his cunning hath cheated me of the island.

4–5 bear up, and board 'em: sailing term for "attack" but he means "Drink up."   *10 set:* gone
down (like the setting sun).   *16 standard:* standard-bearer, a junior officer.   *17 list:* please.   *no
standard:* too unsteady to carry a standard.   *19 go:* walk.   *25 in case:* in condition. *justle:* jostle.
26 deboshed: debauched.   *32 natural:* born fool, idiot.

ARIEL Thou liest.

CALIBAN Thou liest, thou jesting monkey, thou. 45
   I would my valiant master would destroy thee!
   I do not lie.

STEPHANO Trinculo, if you trouble him any more in 's tale,
   by this hand, I will supplant some of your teeth.

TRINCULO Why, I said nothing. 50

STEPHANO Mum, then, and no more. Proceed.

CALIBAN I say, by sorcery he got this isle;
   From me he got it. If thy greatness will
   Revenge it on him,—for I know thou dar'st,
   But this thing dare not,— 55

STEPHANO That's most certain.

CALIBAN Thou shalt be lord of it and I'll serve thee.

STEPHANO How now shall this be compassed?
   Canst thou bring me to the party?

CALIBAN Yea, yea, my lord. I'll yield him thee asleep, 60
   Where thou mayst knock a nail into his head.

ARIEL Thou liest; thou canst not.

CALIBAN What a pied ninny 's this! Thou scurvy patch!
   I do beseech thy greatness, give him blows
   And take his bottle from him. When that's gone 65
   He shall drink nought but brine; for I'll not show him
   Where the quick freshes are.

STEPHANO Trinculo, run into no further danger. Interrupt
   the monster one word further, and, by this hand, I'll turn my
   mercy out o' doors and make a stockfish of thee. 70

TRINCULO Why, what did I? I did nothing. I'll go farther
   off.

STEPHANO Didst thou not say he lied?

ARIEL Thou liest.

STEPHANO Do I so? Take thou that. [*Beats him.*] As you 75
   like this, give me the lie another time.

TRINCULO I did not give the lie. Out o' your wits and hearing too? A pox o' your bottle! this can sack and drinking do.
   A murrain on your monster, and the devil take your fingers!

CALIBAN Ha, ha, ha! 80

STEPHANO Now, forward with your tale. Prithee, stand
   farther off.

---

49 supplant: undo or knock out. *58 compassed:* brought about. *63 pied ninny:* fool in motley (the patched or multi-colored costume worn by fools and jesters). *patch:* jester (wearer of "patched" costume). *67 quick freshes:* living or fresh-water springs. *70 stockfish:* dried cod beaten to soften it before cooking. *76 give . . . the lie:* insult. *78 pox:* venereal disease (the equivalent of today's "To hell with your bottle"). *79 murrain:* plague.

CALIBAN Beat him enough: after a little time I'll beat
    him too.

STEPHANO Stand farther. Come, proceed.   85

CALIBAN Why, as I told thee, 't is a custom with him,
    I' th' afternoon to sleep. There thou mayst brain him,
    Having first seiz'd his books, or with a log
    Batter his skull, or paunch him with a stake,
    Or cut his wezand with thy knife. Remember   90
    First to possess his books; for without them
    He's but a sot, as I am, nor hath not
    One spirit to command: they all do hate him
    As rootedly as I. Burn but his books.
    He has brave utensils,—for so he calls them,—   95
    Which, when he has a house, he'll deck withal.
    And that most deeply to consider is
    The beauty of his daughter: he himself
    Calls her a nonpareil: I never saw a woman
    But only Sycorax my dam and she;   100
    But she as far surpasseth Sycorax
    As great'st does least.

STEPHANO   Is it so brave a lass?

CALIBAN Ay, lord; she will become thy bed, I warrant,
    And bring thee forth brave brood.   105

STEPHANO Monster, I will kill this man: his daughter and
    I will be king and queen,—save our Graces!—and Trinculo
    and thyself shall be viceroys. Dost thou like the plot, Trinculo?

TRINCULO Excellent.

STEPHANO Give me thy hand: I am sorry I beat thee; but,   110
    while thou liv'st, keep a good tongue in thy head.

CALIBAN Within this half hour will he be asleep.
    Wilt thou destroy him then?

STEPHANO   Ay, on mine honour.

ARIEL This will I tell my master.   115

CALIBAN Thou mak'st me merry; I am full of pleasure.
    Let us be jocund. Will you troll the catch
    You taught me but while-ere?

STEPHANO At thy request, monster, I will do reason, any
    reason. Come on, Trinculo, let us sing.   *[Sings.]* 120

        Flout 'em and scout 'em
        And scout 'em and flout 'em;
           Thought is free.

---

89 paunch: stab in the belly. *90 wezand:* windpipe. *95 utensils:* furnishings. *99 nonpareil:* without an equal. *117 troll the catch:* sing the round, or part-song.

CALIBAN   That's not the tune.

                    [ARIEL *plays the tune on a tabor and pipe.*]   125

STEPHANO   What is this same?

TRINCULO   This is the tune of our catch, played by the
    picture of Nobody.

STEPHANO   If thou beest a man, show thyself in thy likeness.
    If thou beest a devil, take 't as thou list.   130

TRINCULO   O, forgive me my sins!

STEPHANO   He that dies pays all debts. I defy thee. Mercy
    upon us!

CALIBAN   Art thou afeard?

STEPHANO   No, monster, not I.   135

CALIBAN   Be not afeard. The isle is full of noises,
    Sounds and sweet airs, that give delight and hurt not.
    Sometimes a thousand twangling instruments
    Will hum about mine ears, and sometime voices
    That, if I then had wak'd after long sleep,   140
    Will make me sleep again; and then, in dreaming,
    The clouds methought would open and show riches
    Ready to drop upon me, that, when I wak'd,
    I cried to dream again.

STEPHANO   This will prove a brave kingdom to me, where   145
    I shall have my music for nothing.

CALIBAN   When Prospero is destroyed.

STEPHANO   That shall be by and by. I remember the story.

TRINCULO   The sound is going away. Let's follow it, and
    after do our work.   150

STEPHANO   Lead, monster; we'll follow. I would I could see
    this taborer; he lays it on.

TRINCULO   Wilt come? I'll follow Stephano.   *Exeunt.*

[ACT III, SCENE 3]   *Another part of the island.*

Enter ALONSO, SEBASTIAN, ANTONIO, GONZALO, ADRIAN,
FRANCISCO, *etc.*

GONZALO   By 'r lakin, I can go no further, sir;
    My old bones aches. Here's a maze trod indeed   5
    Through forthrights and meanders! By your patience,
    I needs must rest me.

ALONSO   Old lord, I cannot blame thee,
    Who am myself attach'd with weariness

---

128 picture of Nobody: an illustration of a man with head, arms, and legs but no body appeared with a printed play called *Nobody and Somebody* in 1606. Perhaps the phrase also means "an invisible musician."   *4 By'r lakin:* By our Ladykin (i.e., the Virgin Mary).   *6 forthrights:* straight paths.   *meanders:* winding paths.   *9 attach'd:* overcome.

To th' dulling of my spirits. Sit down, and rest.   10
Even here I will put off my hope and keep it
No longer for my flatterer: he is drown'd
Whom thus we stray to find, and the sea mocks
Our frustrate search on land. Well, let him go.
ANTONIO   [*Aside to* SEBASTIAN.] I am right glad that he's   15
    so out of hope.
Do not, for one repulse, forego the purpose
That you resolv'd t' effect.
SEBASTIAN   [*Aside to* ANTONIO.] The next advantage
Will we take throughly.   20
ANTONIO   [*Aside to* SEBASTIAN.] Let it be to-night;
For, now they are oppress'd with travel, they
Will not, nor cannot, use such vigilance
As when they are fresh.
SEBASTIAN   [*Aside to* ANTONIO.] I say, to-night. No more.   25

Solemn and strange music; and PROSPERO *on the top invisible.*
Enter several strange shapes, bringing in a banquet; and dance
about it with gentle actions of salutation; and, inviting the King,
etc., to eat, they depart.

ALONSO   What harmony is this? My good friends, hark!   30
GONZALO   Marvellous sweet music!
ALONSO   Give us kind keepers, heavens! What were these?
SEBASTIAN   A living drollery. Now I will believe
That there are unicorns, that in Arabia   35
There is one tree, the phoenix' throne, one phoenix
At this hour reigning there.
ANTONIO   I'll believe both;
And what does else want credit, come to me,
And I'll be sworn 't is true. Travellers ne'er did lie,   40
Though fools at home condemn 'em.
GONZALO   If in Naples
I should report this now, would they believe me?
If I should say, I saw such islanders—
For certes, these are people of the island—   45
Who, though they are of monstrous shape, yet, note,
Their manners are more gentle-kind, than of
Our human generation you shall find
Many, nay, almost any.

11 put off: give up.   *19 advantage:* opportunity.   *26 the top:* the upper stage (of the Elizabethan theater).   *27 banquet:* light refreshments of pastries, fruit, jellies, etc.   *34 living drollery:* live puppet-show.   *35 unicorns:* mythical creatures somewhat like horses, with one horn.   *36 phoenix:* mythical bird which lived for 500 years, died by setting itself afire, and rose again from its own ashes.   *39 wants credit:* lacks belief.   *45 certes:* certainly.

PROSPERO   [*Aside.*] Honest lord,   50
    Thou hast said well; for some of you there present
    Are worse than devils.
ALONSO   I cannot too much muse
    Such shapes, such gesture, and such sound, expressing,
    Although they want the use of tongue, a kind   55
    Of excellent dumb discourse.
PROSPERO   [*Aside.*] Praise in departing.
FRANCISCO   They vanish'd strangely.
SEBASTIAN   No matter, since
    They have left their viands behind, for we have stomachs. 60
    Will 't please you taste of what is here?
ALONSO   Not I.
GONZALO   Faith, sir, you need not fear. When we were boys,
    Who would believe that there were mountaineers
    Dew-lapp'd like bulls, whose throats had hanging at 'em   65
    Wallets of flesh? or that there were such men
    Whose heads stood in their breasts? which now we find
    Each putter-out of five for one will bring us
    Good warrant of.
ALONSO   I will stand to and feed,   70
    Although my last: no matter, since I feel
    The best is past. Brother, my lord the Duke,
    Stand to and do as we.

Thunder and lightning. Enter ARIEL, *like a harpy; claps his*
wings upon the table; and, with a quaint device, the banquet   75
vanishes.

ARIEL   You are three men of sin, whom Destiny,
    That hath to instrument this lower world
    And what is in 't, the never-surfeited sea
    Hath caus'd to belch up you; and on this island   80
    Where man doth not inhabit; you 'mongst men
    Being most unfit to live. I have made you mad;
    And even with such-like valour men hang and drown
    Their proper selves.   [ALONSO, SEBASTIAN, *etc.*, *draw.*]
    You fools! I and my fellows   85
    Are ministers of Fate: the elements,

53 muse: marvel at.   *57 Praise in departing:* an old proverb which advises holding up applause until an entertainment is finished.   *65 Dew-lapp'd:* with loose skin hanging from the throat.   *68 putter-out . . . one:* a traveler who puts up a sum of money before departing on a long voyage as a form of insurance which would give him five times his investment if he returned safely but forfeit the deposit if he failed to return.   *74 harpy:* disgusting mythical creature, half-woman and half-vulture.   *75 quaint device:* ingenious stage machinery.   *78 to instrument:* as its agent.   *79 never-surfeited:* never satisfied.   *84 proper:* own.

Of whom your swords are temper'd, may as well
Wound the loud winds, or with bemock'd-at stabs
Kill the still-closing waters, as diminish
One dowle that's in my plume: my fellow-ministers   90
Are like invulnerable. If you could hurt,
Your swords are now too massy for your strengths
And will not be uplifted. But remember—
For that's my business to you—that you three
From Milan did supplant good Prospero;   95
Expos'd unto the sea, which hath requit it,
Him and his innocent child; for which foul deed
The powers, delaying, not forgetting, have
Incens'd the seas and shores, yea, all the creatures,
Against your peace. Thee of thy son, Alonso,   100
They have bereft; and do pronounce by me.
Ling'ring perdition, worse than any death
Can be at once, shall step by step attend
You and your ways; whose wraths to guard you from—
Which here, in this most desolate isle, else falls   105
Upon your heads—is nothing but heart's sorrow
And a clear life ensuing.

[*He vanishes in thunder; then, to soft music, enter the shapes
again, and dance, with mocks and mows, and carrying out the
table.*]   110

PROSPERO   Bravely the figure of this harpy hast thou
    Perform'd, my Ariel; a grace it had, devouring.
    Of my instruction hast thou nothing bated
    In what thou hadst to say; so, with good life
    And observation strange, my meaner ministers   115
    Their several kinds have done. My high charms work,
    And these mine enemies are all knit up
    In their distractions: they now are in my power;
    And in these fits I leave them, while I visit
    Young Ferdinand, whom they suppose is drown'd,   120
    And his and mine lov'd darling.   *Exit.*
GONZALO   I' th' name of something holy, sir, why stand you
    In this strange stare?

87 *temper'd:* made.   89 *still-closing:* forever advancing.   90 *dowle:* tiny bit of down.   *plume:*
plumage.   92 *massy:* heavy.   95 *supplant:* unseat.   96 *requit:* repaid (i.e., avenged).   99
Incens'd: aroused, angered.   102 *perdition:* punishment.   104–107 *whose wraths . . . life ensu-*
ing: Only by repentance ("heart's sorrow") and a sober ("clear") life afterward can you avoid
such "perdition."   112 *a grace . . . devouring:* the harpy splendidly devoured the banquet.   113
bated: omitted.   114 *with good life:* realistically.   115 *observation strange:* wonderful obedience
(to my instructions). *meaner:* inferior.

ALONSO   O, it is monstrous, monstrous!
    Methought the billows spoke and told me of it;   125
    The winds did sing it to me, and the thunder,
    That deep and dreadful organ-pipe, pronounc'd
    The name of Prosper; it did bass my trespass.
    Therefore my son i' th' ooze is bedded, and
    I'll seek him deeper than e'er plummet sounded   130
    And with him there lie mudded.   *Exit.*
SEBASTIAN   But one fiend at a time,
    I'll fight their legions o'er.
ANTONIO   I'll be thy second.
                    Exeunt SEBASTIAN *and* ANTONIO.   135
GONZALO   All three of them are desperate: their great guilt,
    Like poison given to work a great time after,
    Now gins to bite the spirits. I do beseech you
    That are of suppler joints, follow then swiftly
    And hinder them from what this ecstasy   140
    May now provoke them to.
ADRIAN   Follow, I pray you.
                    Exeunt omnes.

[ACT IV SCENE 1]   *Before Prospero's cell.*

Enter PROSPERO, FERDINAND, *and* MIRANDA.

PROSPERO   If I have too austerely punish'd you,
    Your compensation makes amends, for I
    Have given you here a third of mine own life,   5
    Or that for which I live; who once again
    I tender to thy hand. All thy vexations
    Were but my trials of thy love, and thou
    Hast strangely stood the test. Here, afore Heaven,
    I ratify this my rich gift. O Ferdinand,   10
    Do not smile at me that I boast her off,
    For thou shalt find she will outstrip all praise
    And make it halt behind her.
FERDINAND   I do believe it
    Against an oracle.   15
PROSPERO   Then, as my gift and thine own acquisition
    Worthily purchas'd, take my daughter: but
    If thou dost break her virgin-knot before

---

128 bass my trespass: in deep tones declare my crime.   *130 plummet:* lead weight used to
discover the depth of the sea.   *133 o'er:* one after another.   *140 ecstasy:* madness.   *3 austerely:* sternly.   *5 third:* significant part.   *7 tender:* deliver.   *9 strangely:* unusually well.   *11
boast her off:* praise her so strongly.   *13 halt:* limp.   *15 Against an oracle:* Even if an oracle (of a
god) declared the opposite.

All sanctimonious ceremonies may
With full and holy rite be minister'd,   20
No sweet aspersion shall the heavens let fall
To make this contract grow; but barren Hate,
Sour-eyed Disdain and Discord shall bestrew
The union of your bed with weeds so loathly
That you shall hate it both. Therefore take heed,   25
As Hymen's lamps shall light you.

FERDINAND   As I hope
For quiet days, fair issue, and long life,
With such love as 't is now, the murkiest den,
The most opportune place, the strong'st suggestion   30
Our worser genius can, shall never melt
Mine honour into lust, to take away
The edge of that day's celebration
When I shall think or Phoebus' steeds are founder'd
Or Night kept chain'd below.   35

PROSPERO   Fairly spoke.
Sit then and talk with her; she is thine own.
What, Ariel! my industrious servant, Ariel!

Enter ARIEL.

ARIEL   What would my potent master? Here I am.   40
PROSPERO   Thou and thy meaner fellows your last service
Did worthily perform; and I must use you
In such another trick. Go bring the rabble,
O'er whom I give thee power, here to this place.
Incite them to quick motion; for I must   45
Bestow upon the eyes of this young couple
Some vanity of mine art. It is my promise,
And they expect it from me.

ARIEL   Presently?
PROSPERO   Ay, with a twink.   50
ARIEL
                      Before you can say "come" and "go."
                      And breathe twice and cry "so, so,"
                      Each one, tripping on his toe,
                      Will be here with mop and mow.   55
                      Do you love me, master? No?

---

19 sanctimonious: sacred.   *21 aspersion:* blessing.   *26 Hymen:* god of marriage.   *30 suggestion:* temptation.   *31 worser genius:* evil side of our natures.   *34 Or:* whether.   *Phoebus' steeds:* the horses who pull the chariot of the sun god, Phoebus, across the heavens each day. *founder'd:* made lame.   *35 kept chain'd:* imprisoned (hence, unable to arrive).   *43 rabble:* collection of beings.   *47 vanity:* modest display.   *49 Presently:* immediately.   *50 twink:* twinkling of an eye.   *55 mop and mow:* grimace and gesture.

PROSPERO   Dearly, my delicate Ariel. Do not approach
    Till thou dost hear me call.
ARIEL   Well, I conceive.   *Exit.*
PROSPERO   Look thou be true; do not give dalliance   60
    Too much the rein: the strongest oaths are straw
    To the fire i' th' blood. Be more abstemious,
    Or else, good night your vow!
FERDINAND   I warrant you, sir;
    The white cold virgin snow upon my heart   65
    Abates the ardour of my liver.
PROSPERO   Well.
    Now come, my Ariel! bring a corollary,
    Rather than want a spirit. Appear and pertly!
    No tongue! all eyes! Be silent.   [*Soft music.*]   70

Enter IRIS.

IRIS   Ceres, most bounteous lady, thy rich leas
    Of wheat, rye, barley, vetches, oats, and pease;
    Thy turfy mountains, where live nibbling sheep,
    And flat meads thatch'd with stover, them to keep;   75
    Thy banks with pioned and twilled brims,
    Which spongy April at thy hest betrims
    To make cold nymphs chaste crowns; and thy broom groves,
    Whose shadow the dismissed bachelor loves,
    Being lass lorn; thy pole-clipp'd vineyard;   80
    And thy sea-marge, sterile and rocky-hard,
    Where thou thyself dost air;—the queen o' th' sky,
    Whose watery arch and messenger am I,
    Bids thee leave these, and with her sovereign grace,
    Here on this grass-plot, in this very place,   85
    To come and sport; her peacocks fly amain.
    Approach, rich Ceres, her to entertain.

Enter CERES.

CERES   Hail, many-coloured messenger, that ne'er
    Dost disobey the wife of Jupiter;   90
    Who with thy saffron wings upon my flowers

---

59 conceive: understand.   *60 dalliance:* making love.   *66 liver:* sexual passion (according to the age's treatises on the bodily organs).   *68 corollary:* more than enough.   *69 pertly:* promptly.   *71 Iris:* goddess of the rainbow and messenger of the gods.   *72 Ceres:* goddess of vegetation and harvest. *leas:* meadows.   *75 stover:* fodder.   *76 pioned and twilled brims:* furrowed and heaped banks.   *77 hest:* command.   *78 broom groves:* patches of gorse, a low shrub with yellow flowers in the spring, very common in England.   *79 dismissed:* rejected.   *80 lass lorn:* deprived of his mistress. *pole-clipp'd:* with vine-covered poles.   *82 queen o' th' sky:* Juno, wife of Jupiter.   *83 watery arch:* the rainbow.   *86 peacocks:* sacred birds of Juno who pull her chariot.   *91 saffron:* yellow.

Diffusest honey-drops, refreshing showers,
And with each end of thy blue bow dost crown
My bosky acres and my unshrubb'd down,
Rich scarf to my proud earth; why hath thy queen   95
Summon'd me hither, to this short-grass'd green?
IRIS   A contract of true love to celebrate;
And some donation freely to estate
On the blest lovers.
CERES   Tell me, heavenly bow,   100
If Venus or her son, as thou dost know,
Do now attend the Queen? Since they did plot
The means that dusky Dis my daughter got,
Her and her blind boy's scandal'd company
I have forsworn.   105
IRIS   Of her society
Be not afraid: I met her deity
Cutting the clouds towards Paphos, and her son
Dove-drawn with her. Here thought they to have done
Some wanton charm upon this man and maid,   110
Whose vows are, that no bed-right shall be paid
Till Hymen's torch be lighted; but in vain.
Mars's hot minion is return'd again;
Her waspish-headed son has broke his arrows,
Swears he will shoot no more, but play with sparrows   115
And be a boy right out.   [JUNO *descends.*]
CERES   Highest queen of state,
Great Juno, comes; I know her by her gait.
JUNO   How does my bounteous sister? Go with me
To bless this twain, that they may prosperous be   120
And honored in their issue.
JUNO   [*Sings.*]
                    Honor, riches, marriage-blessing,
                    Long continuance, and increasing,
                    Hourly joys be still upon you!   125
                    Juno sings her blessings on you.

CERES   [*Sings.*]

                    Earth's increase foison plenty,
                    Barns and garners never empty,
                    Vines with clustering bunches growing,   130

---

94 bosky: wooded. *down:* open countryside. *98 donation:* gift. *estate:* present. *101 son:* Cupid. *103 dusky Dis:* Pluto, the dark god of the underworld who abducted the daughter of Ceres, Persephone, and made her queen of his realm. *104 scandal'd:* scandalous. *108 Paphos:* town on Cyprus sacred to Venus. *113 Mars's hot minion:* Venus, the lusty mistress of Mars. *114 waspish-headed son:* quick-tempered Cupid. *128 foison:* plenty.

Plants with goodly burden bowing.
Spring come to you at the farthest
In the very end of harvest!
Scarcity and want shall shun you;
Ceres' blessing so is on you.   135

FERDINAND   This is a most majestic vision, and
    Harmonious charmingly. May I be bold
    To think these spirits?
PROSPERO   Spirits, which by mine art
    I have from their confines call'd to enact   140
    My present fancies.
FERDINAND   Let me live here ever;
    So rare a wonder'd father and a wise
    Makes this place Paradise.
PROSPERO   Sweet, now, silence!   145
    Juno and Ceres whisper seriously.
    There's something else to do; hush, and be mute,
    Or else our spell is marr'd.
             [JUNO and CERES whisper, and send IRIS on employment.]
IRIS   You nymphs, call'd Naiads, of the windring brooks,   150
    With your sedg'd crowns and ever-harmless looks,
    Leave your crisp channels, and on this green land
    Answer your summons; Juno does command.
    Come, temperate nymphs, and help to celebrate
    A contract of true love; be not too late.   155

Enter certain NYMPHS.

    You sunburnt sicklemen, of August weary,
    Come hither from the furrow and be merry.
    Make holiday; your rye-straw hats put on
    And these fresh nymphs encounter every one   160
    In country footing.

Enter certain REAPERS, *properly habited: they join with the*
NYMPHS *in a graceful dance; towards the end whereof* PROSPERO
starts suddenly, and speaks.

PROSPERO   [*Aside.*] I had forgot that foul conspiracy   165
    Of the beast Caliban and his confederates
    Against my life. The minute of their plot

---

143 wonder'd: endowed with wonders.   *150 Naiads:* water nymphs. *windring:* wandering plus
winding.   *151 sedg'd crowns:* garlands of sedge, or water-grass.   *152 crisp:* rippling.   *157 sickle-
men:* reapers, who cut grain with their sickles.   *161 footing:* dancing.

Is almost come. [*To the Spirits.*] Well done! Avoid! No more!
[*To a strange hollow and confused noise, they heavily vanish.*]   170
FERDINAND   This is strange. Your father's in some passion
   That works him strongly.
MIRANDA   Never till this day
   Saw I him touch'd with anger, so distemper'd.
PROSPERO   You do look, my son, in a mov'd sort,   175
   As if you were dismay'd: be cheerful, sir,
   Our revels now are ended. These our actors,
   As I foretold you, were all spirits, and
   Are melted into air, into thin air;
   And, like the baseless fabric of this vision,   180
   The cloud-capp'd towers, the gorgeous palaces,
   The solemn temples, the great globe itself,
   Yea, all which it inherit, shall dissolve
   And, like this insubstantial pageant faded,
   Leave not a rack behind. We are such stuff   185
   As dreams are made on, and our little life
   Is rounded with a sleep. Sir, I am vex'd,—
   Bear with my weakness—my old brain is troubled.
   Be not disturb'd with my infirmity.
   If you be pleas'd, retire into my cell   190
   And there repose: a turn or two I'll walk,
   To still my beating mind.
FERDINAND, MIRANDA   We wish your peace.   *Exeunt.*
PROSPERO   Come with a thought. I thank thee, Ariel; come.

Enter ARIEL.   195

ARIEL   Thy thoughts I cleave to. What's thy pleasure?
PROSPERO   Spirit,
   We must prepare to meet with Caliban.
ARIEL   Ay, my commander. When I presented Ceres,
   I thought to have told thee of it, but I fear'd   200
   Lest I might anger thee.
PROSPERO   Say again, where didst thou leave these varlets?
ARIEL   I told you, sir, they were red-hot with drinking;
   So full of valour that they smote the air
   For breathing in their faces; beat the ground   205
   For kissing of their feet; yet always bending
   Towards their project. Then I beat my tabor;
   At which, like unback'd colts, they prick'd their ears,

---

168 *Avoid:* depart.   169 *heavily:* sadly.   175 *mov'd sort:* troubled mind.   180 *baseless fabric:* unreal substance.   183 *inherit:* inhabit.   185 *rack:* cloud.   187 *rounded:* circled (i.e., surrounded).   199 *presented:* represented, acted the role of.   206 *bending:* inclining mentally.   207 *tabor:* small drum.   208 *unback'd:* never ridden.

Advanc'd their eyelids, lifted up their noses
As they smelt music. So I charm'd their ears   210
That calf-life they my lowing follow'd through
Tooth'd briers, sharp furzes, pricking gorse, and thorns,
Which enter'd their frail shins. At last I left them
I' th' filthy-mantled pool beyond your cell,
There dancing up to th' chins, that the foul lake   215
O'erstunk their feet.
PROSPERO   This was well done, my bird.
Thy shape invisible retain thou still.
The trumpery in my house, go bring it hither,
For stale to catch these thieves.   220
ARIEL   I go, I go,   *Exit.*
PROSPERO   A devil, a born devil, on whose nature
Nurture can never stick; on whom my pains,
Humanely taken, all, all lost, quite lost;
And as with age his body uglier grows,   225
So his mind cankers. I will plague them all,
Even to roaring.

Re-enter ARIEL, *loaden with glittering apparel, etc.*

Come, hang them on this line.

PROSPERO *and* ARIEL *remain, invisible. Enter* CALIBAN, STEPHANO   230
and TRINCULO, *all wet.*

CALIBAN   Pray you, tread softly, that the blind mole may
          not
Hear a footfall; we now are near his cell.
STEPHANO   Monster, your fairy, which you say is a harm-   235
less fairy, has done little better than played the Jack with us.
TRINCULO   Monster, I do smell all horse piss, at which my
          nose is in great indignation.
STEPHANO   So is mine. Do you hear, monster? If I should
          take a displeasure against you, look you,—   240
TRINCULO   Thou wert but a lost monster.
CALIBAN   Good my lord, give me thy favour still.
Be patient, for the prize I'll bring thee to
Shall hoodwink this mischance; therefore speak softly.
All's hush'd as midnight yet.   245
TRINCULO   Ay, but to lose our bottles in the pool,—
STEPHANO   There is not only disgrace and dishonour in
          that, monster, but an infinite loss.

---

214 filthy-mantled: scum-covered.   *219 trumpery:* cheap, flashy clothing.   *220 stale:* bait.   *223
Nurture:* training.   *226 cankers:* grows malignant.   *229 line:* linden tree.   *236 Jack:* knave.   *244
hoodwink:* blind your eyes to.

TRINCULO   That's more to me than my wetting; yet this is
    your harmless fairy, monster!   250
STEPHANO   I will fetch off my bottle, though I be o'er
    ears for my labour.
CALIBAN   Prithee, my king, be quiet. See'st thou here,
    This is the mouth o' th' cell. No noise, and enter.
    Do that good mischief which may make this island   255
    Thine own for ever, and I, thy Caliban,
    For aye thy foot-licker.
STEPHANO   Give me thy hand. I do begin to have bloody
    thoughts.
TRINCULO   O King Stephano! O peer! O worthy Stephano!   260
    Look what a wardrobe here is for thee!
CALIBAN   Let it alone, thou fool; it is but trash.
TRINCULO   O, ho, monster! we know what belongs to a
    frippery. O King Stephano!
STEPHANO   Put off that gown, Trinculo; by this hand, I'll   265
    have that gown.
TRINCULO   Thy Grace shall have it.
CALIBAN   The dropsy drown this fool! what do you mean
    To dote thus on such luggage? Let 't alone.
    And do the murder first. If he awake,   270
    From toe to crown he'll fill our skins with pinches,
    Make us strange stuff.
STEPHANO   Be you quiet, monster. Mistress line, is not this
    my jerkin? Now is the jerkin under the line: now, jerkin, you
    are like to lose your hair and prove a bald jerkin.   275
TRINCULO   Do, do; we steal by line and level, an 't like
    your Grace.
STEPHANO   I thank thee for that jest; here's a garment for 't.
    Wit shall not go unrewarded while I am king of this country.
    "Steal by line and level" is an excellent pass of pate; there's   280
    another garment for 't.
TRINCULO   Monster, come, put some lime upon your fingers,
    and away with the rest.
CALIBAN   I will have none on 't. We shall lose our time,
    And all be turn'd to barnacles, or to apes   285
    With foreheads villanous low.

---

251 fetch off: recover.   *254 good mischief:* i.e., the murder of Prospero.   *264 frippery:* shop for
used clothing.   *268 drown:* choke.   *269 luggage:* bunglesome junk.   *274 jerkin:* jacket.   *276
line and level:* carpenter's instruments (i.e., "on the level").   *an't like:* if it please.   *280 pass of
pate:* stroke of wit.   *282 lime upon your fingers:* birdlime, to make your fingers sticky (like a thief).
285 barnacles: wild geese (who were believed to develop from the barnacles that grow upon
wood submerged in seawater).

STEPHANO   Monster, lay-to your fingers. Help to bear this
    away where my hogshead of wine is, or I'll turn you out of my
    kingdom. Go to, carry this.
TRINCULO   And this.   290
STEPHANO   Ay, and this.

*A noise of hunters heard. Enter divers Spirits, in shape of dogs
and hounds, hunting them about,* PROSPERO *and* ARIEL *setting
them on.*

PROSPERO   Hey, Mountain, hey!   295
ARIEL   Silver! there it goes, Silver!
PROSPERO   Fury, Fury! there, Tyrant, there! hark! hark!
    [CALIBAN, STEPHANO, *and* TRINCULO *are driven out.*]
    Go charge my goblins that they grind their joints
    With dry convulsions, shorten up their sinews   300
    With aged cramps, and more pinch-spotted make them
    Than pard or cat o' mountain.
ARIEL   Hark, they roar!
PROSPERO   Let them be hunted soundly. At this hour
    Lies at my mercy all mine enemies.   305
    Shortly shall all my labours end, and thou
    Shalt have the air at freedom. For a little
    Follow, and do me service.   *Exeunt.*

[ACT V, SCENE 1]   *Before Prospero's cell.*

Enter PROSPERO *in his magic robes, and* ARIEL.

PROSPERO   Now does my project gather to a head.
    My charms crack not; my spirits obey; and Time
    Goes upright with his carriage. How's the day?   5
ARIEL   On the sixth hour; at which time, my lord,
    You said our work should cease.
PROSPERO   I did say so,
    When first I rais'd the tempest. Say, my spirit,
    How fares the King and 's followers?   10
ARIEL   Confin'd together
    In the same fashion as you gave in charge,
    Just as you left them; all prisoners, sir,
    In the line-grove which weather-fends your cell;
    They cannot budge till your release. The King,   15

295–297 Mountain . . . Silver . . . Fury . . . Tyrant: names of the hounds.   *301 pinch-spotted:*
covered with pinches.   *302 pard:* leopard. *cat o' mountain:* wildcat.   *4 crack:* break down.   *5
goes . . . carriage:* does not bend over with what remains to be done.   *14 weather-fends:* protects
against the weather.

His brother, and yours, abide all three distracted,
And the remainder mourning over them,
Brimful of sorrow and dismay; but chiefly
Him that you term'd sir, "The good old lord Gonzalo,"
His tears runs down his beard, like winter's drops 20
From eaves of reeds. Your charm so strongly works 'em
That if you now beheld them, your affections
Would become tender.
PROSPERO   Dost thou think so, spirit?
ARIEL   Mine would, sir, were I human. 25
PROSPERO   And mine shall.
Hast thou, which art but air, a touch, a feeling
Of their afflictions, and shall not myself,
One of their kind, that relish all as sharply
Passion as they, be kindlier mov'd than thou art? 30
Though with their high wrongs I am struck to the quick
Yet with my nobler reason 'gainst my fury
Do I take part: the rarer action is
In virtue than in vengeance: they being penitent,
The sole drift of my purpose doth extend 35
Not a frown further. Go release them, Ariel.
My charms I'll break, their senses I'll restore,
And they shall be themselves.
ARIEL   I'll fetch them, sir.   *Exit.*
PROSPERO   Ye elves of hills, brooks, standing lakes, and 40
        groves,
And ye that on the sands with printless foot
Do chase the ebbing Neptune, and do fly him
When he comes back; you demi-puppets that
By moonshine do the green sour ringlets make, 45
Whereof the ewe not bites; and you whose pastime,
Is to make midnight mushrooms, that rejoice
To hear the solemn curfew; by whose aid,
Weak masters though ye be, I have bedimm'd
The noontide sun, call'd forth the mutinous winds, 50
And 'twixt the green sea and the azur'd vault
Set roaring war; to the dread rattling thunder
Have I given fire, and rifted Jove's stout oak
With his own bolt; the strong-bas'd promontory
Have I made shake, and by the spurs pluck'd up 55

21 eaves of reeds: a thatched roof.   *29 relish all:* feel quite.   *30 Passion:* emotion. *kindlier:* more sympathetically.   *33 rarer:* nobler.   *43 Neptune:* the sea.   *44 demi-puppets:* tiny creatures.   *45 green sour ringlets:* circles supposedly made by dancing fairies at night in the wild grass, which was sour to cattle.   *51 azur'd vaults:* blue heavens.   *53 rifted:* split.   *55 spurs:* roots.

The pine and cedar; graves at my command
Have wak'd their sleepers, op'd, and let 'em forth
By my so potent art. But this rough magic
I here abjure, and, when I have requir'd
Some heavenly music, which even now I do,   60
To work mine end upon their senses that
This airy charm is for, I'll break my staff,
Bury it certain fathoms in the earth,
And deeper than did ever plummet sound
I'll drown my book.   [*Solemn music.*] 65

Here enters ARIEL *before; then* ALONSO, *with a frantic gesture,*
attended by GONZALO; SEBASTIAN *and* ANTONIO *in like manner,*
attended by ADRIAN *and* FRANCISCO. *They all enter the circle*
which PROSPERO *had made, and there stand charmed; which*
PROSPERO *observing, speaks.*   70

A solemn air and the best comforter
To an unsettled fancy cure thy brains,
Now useless, boil'd within thy skull! There stand,
For you are spell-stopp'd.
Holy Gonzalo, honourable man,   75
Mine eyes, ev'n sociable to the show of thine,
Fall fellowly drops. The charm dissolves apace,
And as the morning steals upon the night,
Melting the darkness, so their rising senses
Begin to chase the ignorant fumes that mantle   80
Their clearer reason. O good Gonzalo,
My true preserver, and a loyal sir
To him thou follow'st! I will pay thy graces
Home both in word and deed. Most cruelly
Did thou, Alonso, use me and my daughter.   85
Thy brother was a furtherer in the act.
Thou art pinch'd for 't now, Sebastian. Flesh and blood,
You, brother mine, that entertain'd ambition,
Expell'd remorse and nature, whom, with Sebastian,
Whose inward pinches therefore are most strong,   90
Would here have kill'd your king, I do forgive thee,
Unnatural though thou art. Their understanding
Begins to swell, and the approaching tide
Will shortly fill the reasonable shore
That now lie foul and muddy. Not one of them   95

65 *book:* book of magic spells. 66 *frantic gesture:* disturbed manner. 71 *air:* melody. 73 *boil'd:* over-stimulated. 76 *sociable:* sympathetic. 80 *mantle:* hide. 84 *Home:* fully. 89 *remorse:* pity. *nature:* human nature. 94 *reasonable shore:* consciousness.

That yet looks on me, or would know me! Ariel,
Fetch me the hat and rapier in my cell;
I will discase me, and myself present
As I was sometime Milan: quickly, spirit;
Thou shalt ere long be free.   100

[ARIEL *sings and helps to attire him.*]

ARIEL
                   Where the bee sucks, there suck I.
                   In a cowslip's bell I lie;
                   There I couch when owls do cry.   105
                   On the bat's back I do fly
                   After summer merrily.
              Merrily, merrily shall I live now
              Under the blossom that hangs on the bough

PROSPERO   Why, that's my dainty Ariel! I shall miss thee;   110
But yet thou shalt have freedom. So, so, so.
To the King's ship, invisible as thou art;
There shalt thou find the mariners asleep
Under the hatches. The master and the boatswain
Being awake, enforce them to this place,   115
And presently, I prithee.
ARIEL   I drink the air before me, and return
Or ere your pulse twice beat.   *Exit.*
GONZALO   All torment, trouble, wonder, and amazement
Inhabits here. Some heavenly power guide us   120
Out of this fearful country!
PROSPERO   Behold, sir King,
The wronged Duke of Milan, Prospero.
For more assurance that a living prince
Does now speak to thee, I embrace thy body;   125
And to thee and thy company I bid
A hearty welcome.
ALONSO   Whe'er thou be'st he or no,
Or some enchanted trifle to abuse me,
As late I have been, I not know. Thy pulse   130
Beats as of flesh and blood; and, since I saw thee,
Th' affliction of my mind amends, with which,
I fear, a madness held me: this must crave,
And if this be at all, a most strange story.
Thy dukedom I resign and do entreat   135
Thou pardon me my wrongs. But how should Prospero
Be living and be here?

98 discase me: remove my magician's robes.   *99 As . . . Milan:* as I was when I was ruler of Milan.
129 trifle: hallucination.   *134 be at all:* is real.

PROSPERO   First, noble friend,
  Let me embrace thine age, whose honour cannot
  Be measur'd or confin'd.   140
GONZALO   Whether this be
  Or be not, I'll not swear.
PROSPERO   You do yet taste
  Some subtleties o' the isle, that will not let you
  Believe things certain. Welcome, my friends all!   145
  [*Aside to* SEBASTIAN *and* ANTONIO.] But you, my brace of lords,
      were I so minded,
  I here could pluck his Highness' frown upon you
  And justify you traitors. At this time
  I will tell no tales.   150
SEBASTIAN   [*Aside.*] The devil speaks in him.
PROSPERO   No.
  For you, most wicked sir, whom to call brother
  Would even infect my mouth, I do forgive
  Thy rankest fault; all of them; and require   155
  My dukedom of thee, which perforce, I know,
  Thou must restore.
ALONSO   If thou be'st Prospero,
  Give us particulars of thy preservation,
  How thou hast met us here, whom three hours since   . 160
  Were wreck'd upon this shore, where I have lost—
  How sharp the point of this remembrance is!—
  My dear son Ferdinand.
PROSPERO   I am woe for 't, sir.
ALONSO   Irreparable is the loss, and Patience   165
  Says it is past her cure.
PROSPERO   I rather think
  You have not sought her help, of whose soft grace
  For the like loss I have her sovereign aid
  And rest myself content.   170
ALONSO   You the like loss!
PROSPERO   As great to me as late, and, supportable
  To make the dear loss, have I means much weaker
  Than you may call to comfort you, for I
  Have lost my daughter.   175
ALONSO   A daughter?
  O heavens, that they were living both in Naples,
  The King and Queen there! That they were, I wish

---

143 taste: feel.   *144 subtleties:* magical qualities.   *146 brace:* pair (usually of fowls).   *149 justify:*
prove.   *156 perforce:* necessarily.   *169 sovereign:* omnipotent.   *172 late:* recent.

Myself were muddled in that oozy bed
Where my son lies. When did you lose your daughter? 180
PROSPERO In this last tempest. I perceive, these lords
At this encounter do so much admire
That they devour their reason and scarce think
Their eyes do offices of truth, their words
Are natural breath; but, howsoe'er you have 185
Been justled from your senses, know for certain
That I am Prospero and that very duke
Which was thrust forth of Milan, who most strangely
Upon this shore, where you were wreck'd, was landed,
To be the lord on 't. No more yet of this; 190
For 't is a chronicle of day by day,
Not a relation for a breakfast nor
Befitting this first meeting. Welcome, sir;
This cell's my court. Here have I few attendants,
And subjects none abroad: pray you, look in. 195
My dukedom since you have given me again,
I will requite you with as good a thing;
At least bring forth a wonder, to content ye
As much as me my dukedom.

[Here PROSPERO *discovers* FERDINAND *and* MIRANDA *playing* 200
at chess.]

MIRANDA Sweet lord, you play me false.
FERDINAND   No, my dearest love,
I would not for the world.
MIRANDA Yes, for a score of kingdoms you should wrangle, 205
And I would call it fair play.
ALONSO   If this prove
A vision of the island, one dear son
Shall I twice lose.
SEBASTIAN   A most high miracle! 210
FERDINAND Though the seas threaten, they are merciful;
I have curs'd them without cause.   [*Kneels.*]
ALONSO   Now all the blessings
Of a glad father compass thee about!
Arise, and say how thou cam'st here. 215
MIRANDA   O, wonder!
How many goodly creatures are there here!
How beauteous mankind is! O brave new world,
That has such people in 't!

---

182 admire: marvel. *186 justled:* jostled. *195 abroad:* in other places (on this island). *197 requite:* repay. *200 discovers:* reveals. *208 vision:* illusion.

PROSPERO   'T is new to thee.   220
ALONSO   What is this maid with whom thou wast at play?
        Your eld'st acquaintance cannot be three hours.
        Is she the goddess that hath sever'd us,
        And brought us thus together?
FERDINAND   Sir, she is mortal,   225
        But by immortal Providence she's mine.
        I chose her when I could not ask my father
        For his advice, nor thought I had one. She
        Is daughter to this famous Duke of Milan,
        Of whom so often I have heard renown,   230
        But never saw before; of whom I have
        Receiv'd a second life; and second father
        This lady makes him to me.
ALONSO   I am hers.
        But, O, how oddly will it sound that I   235
        Must ask my child forgiveness!
PROSPERO   There, sir, stop.
        Let us not burden our remembrances with
        A heaviness that's gone.
GONZALO   I have inly wept,   240
        Or should have spoke ere this. Look down, you gods,
        And on this couple drop a blessed crown!
        For it is you that have chalk'd forth the way
        Which brought us hither.
ALONSO   I say, Amen, Gonzalo!   245
GONZALO   Was Milan thrust from Milan, that his issue
        Should become Kings of Naples? O, rejoice
        Beyond a common joy, and set it down
        With gold on lasting pillars: in one voyage
        Did Claribel her husband find at Tunis,   250
        And Ferdinand, her brother, found a wife
        Where he himself was lost, Prospero his dukedom
        In a poor isle, and all of us ourselves
        When no man was his own
ALONSO   [To FERDINAND and MIRANDA.] Give me your   255
            hands.
        Let grief and sorrow still embrace his heart
        That doth not wish you joy!
GONZALO   Be it so! Amen!

---

222 *eld'st:* longest possible.   237 *my child:* Miranda (soon to be his "daughter").   239 *heaviness:*
unhappy time.   240 *inly:* inwardly.   244 *chalk'd forth:* shown (by drawing a line as with chalk).
254 *his own:* in control of his senses.

Re-enter ARIEL, *with the Master and Boatswain amazedly*   *260*
following.

    O, look, sir, look, sir! here is more of us.
    I prophesied, if a gallows were on land,
    This fellow could not drown. Now, blasphemy,
    That swear'st grace o'erboard, not an oath on shore?   *265*
    Hast thou no mouth by land? What is the news?
BOATSWAIN   The best news is, that we have safely found
    Our king and company; the next, our ship—
    Which, but three glasses since, we gave out split—
    Is tight and yare and bravely rigg'd as when   *270*
    We first put out to sea.
ARIEL   [*Aside to* PROSPERO.] Sir, all this service
    Have I done since I went.
PROSPERO   [*Aside to* ARIEL.] My tricksy spirit!
ALONSO   These are not natural events; they strengthen   *275*
    From strange to stranger. Say, how came you hither?
BOATSWAIN   If I did think, sir, I were well awake,
    I'd strive to tell you. We were dead of sleep,
    And—how we know not—all clapped under hatches;
    Where but even now with strange and several noises   *280*
    Of roaring, shrieking, howling, jingling chains,
    And moe diversity of sounds, all horrible,
    We were awak'd; straightway, at liberty;
    Where we, in all our trim, freshly beheld
    Our royal, good, and gallant ship, our master   *285*
    Capering to eye her. On a trice, so please you,
    Even in a dream, were we divided from them
    And were brought moping hither.
ARIEL   [*Aside to* PROSPERO.] Was 't well done?
PROSPERO   [*Aside to* ARIEL.] Bravely, my diligence. Thou   *290*
      shalt be free.
ALONSO   This is as strange a maze as e'er men trod;
    And there is in this business more than nature
    Was ever conduct of: some oracle
    Must rectify our knowledge.   *295*
PROSPERO   Sir, my liege,
    Do not infest your mind with beating on

---

264 blasphemy: i.e., the personification of blasphemy. *265 That . . . o'erboard:* That by your
swearing makes the grace of God jump overboard. *269 three glasses:* three hours. *gave out:*
reported as. *270 yare:* shipshape, seaworthy. *274 tricksy:* clever. *275 strengthen:* grow. *279
clapped:* shut away. *280 several:* various. *282 moe:* more. *284 trim:* ship's rigging. *286
Capering:* dancing for joy. *On a trice:* in an instant. *288 Moping:* in a daze. *290 my diligence:*
my diligent one (personification of diligence). *293 nature:* natural explanations. *294 conduct:*
cause. *295 rectify:* straighten out.

The strangeness of this business: at pick'd leisure,
Which shall be shortly, single I'll resolve you,
Which to you shall seem probable, of every   300
These happen'd accidents; till when, be cheerful
And think of each thing well. [*Aside to* ARIEL.] Come hither,
   spirit.
Set Caliban and his companions free;
Untie the spell. [*Exit* ARIEL.] How fares my gracious sir?   305
There are yet missing of your company
Some few odd lads that you remember not.

Re-enter ARIEL, *driving in* CALIBAN, STEPHANO, *and* TRINCULO.
in their stolen apparel.

STEPHANO Every man shift for all the rest, and let no man   310
   take care for himself; for all is but fortune. Coragio, bully
   monster, coragio!
TRINCULO If these be true spies which I wear in my head
   here's a goodly sight.
CALIBAN O Setebos, these be brave spirits indeed!   315
   How fine my master is! I am afraid
   He will chastise me.
SEBASTIAN   Ha, ha!
   What things are these, my lord Antonio?
   Will money buy 'em?   320
ANTONIO   Very like; one of them
   Is a plain fish, and, no doubt, marketable,
PROSPERO Mark but the badges of these men, my lords,
   Then say if they be true. This mis-shapen knave,
   His mother was a witch, and one so strong   325
   That could control the moon, make flows and ebbs,
   And deal in her command without her power.
   These three have robb'd me; and this demi-devil—
   For he's a bastard one—had plotted with them
   To take my life. Two of these fellows you   330
   Must know and own; this thing of darkness I
   Acknowledge mine.
CALIBAN   I shall be pinch'd to death.
ALONSO Is not this Stephano, my drunken butler?
SEBASTIAN He is drunk now. Where had he wine?   335
ALONSO And Trinculo is reeling ripe. Where should they
   Find this grand liquor that hath gilded 'em?

---

299 single: singly. *resolve:* straighten out for. *311 Coragio:* Courage. *313 spies:* eyes. *315
Setebos:* see note I, 2, 451. *323 badges:* emblems of a servant's master. *327 And deal . . .
power:* take over the moon's command of the tides without the moon's aid. *336 reeling ripe:*
drunkenly reeling. *337 gilded:* made them shine (or glow).

How cam'st thou in this pickle?

TRINCULO I have been in such a pickle since I saw you

last that, I fear me, will never out of my bones. I shall not 340

fear fly-blowing.

SEBASTIAN Why, how now, Stephano!

STEPHANO O, touch me not; I am not Stephano, but a

cramp.

PROSPERO You'd be king o' the isle, sirrah? 345

STEPHANO I should have been a sore one then.

ALONSO This is a strange thing as e'er I look'd on.

[*Pointing to* CALIBAN.]

PROSPERO He is as disproportion'd in his manners

As in his shape. Go, sirrah, to my cell; 350

Take with you your companions: as you look

To have my pardon, trim it handsomely.

CALIBAN Ay, that I will; and I'll be wise hereafter

And seek for grace. What a thrice-double ass

Was I, to take this drunkard for a god 355

And worship this dull fool!

PROSPERO   Go to; away!

ALONSO Hence, and bestow your luggage where you found

it.

SEBASTIAN Or stole it, rather. 360

PROSPERO Sir, I invite your Highness and your train

To my poor cell, where you shall take your rest

For this one night; which, part of it, I'll waste

With such discourse as, I not doubt, shall make it

Go quick away,—the story of my life 365

And the particular accidents gone by

Since I came to this isle: and in the morn

I'll bring you to your ship and so to Naples,

Where I have hope to see the nuptial

Of these our dear-belov'd solemnized; 370

And thence retire me to my Milan, where

Every third thought shall be my grave.

ALONSO   I long

To hear the story of your life, which must

Take the ear strangely. 375

PROSPERO   I'll deliver all;

And promise you calm seas, auspicious gales,

339-340 I have been . . . fly-blowing: I have been so full of liquor (i.e., preserved) that I will never have to fear going bad. *345 sirrah:* a variation of "sir," but used only to inferiors to express impatience or contempt. *352 trim it:* straighten it up. *358 luggage:* worthless stuff (their cheap finery). *375 Take:* enchant. *376 deliver:* tell.

And sail so expeditious that shall catch
Your royal fleet far off. [*Aside to* ARIEL.] My Ariel, chick,
That is thy charge. Then to the elements   380
Be free, and fare thou well! Please you, draw near.

                                                        Exeunt omnes.

EPILOGUE

Spoken by PROSPERO

Now my charms are all o'erthrown,
And what strength I have 's mine own,
Which is most faint: now, 't is true,   5
I must be here confin'd by you,
Or sent to Naples. Let me not,
Since I have my dukedom got
And pardon'd the deceiver, dwell
In this bare island by your spell;   10
But release me from my bands
With the help of your good hands.
Gentle breath of yours my sails
Must fill, or else my project fails,
Which was to please. Now I want   15
Spirits to enforce, art to enchant,
And my ending is despair,
Unless I be reliev'd by prayer,
Which pierces so that it assaults
Mercy itself and frees all faults.   20
    As you from crimes would pardon'd be.
    Let your indulgence set me free.   *Exit.*

1 *Epilogue:* a fairly common addition to Elizabethan plays. One of the players conventionally apologizes for the faults of the performance and requests applause from the audience.   *11 bands:* bonds.   *15 Want:* lack.

QUESTIONS

1   What advantages, or liabilities, to the play's action are derived from beginning with a storm at sea? Does the boatswain's indifference to claims of privilege for royalty and nobility suggest that social rank is only relative to the situation?
2   Why does Prospero take such pains to separate Ferdinand from his father? Why does he separate crew and passengers?
3   Does Prospero's delay in informing Miranda of their background seem reasonable in terms of the play's plot and theme? Does the summary he gives her (in I, 2) reveal Prospero's own nature, his approach to complications in the rest of the play, and Miranda's forthcoming role in his plans?
4   Ariel and Caliban are often seen as representations of opposite sides of the human psyche. What evidence seems to support (or deny) this viewpoint? Note that each desires liberty.

5   Why should Ariel seek through his song—"Full fathom five thy father lies"—to utterly deceive Ferdinand? Does the attempt reflect unfavorably upon Prospero's plan? Or since Ferdinand almost immediately sees and falls in love with Miranda, does the whole stratagem simply reveal the brevity of sorrow for youth? Or does the scene simply stress the power of young love to free one from the restraints of sorrow and the fear of death? If the arts of music, dance, and mime, as they appear throughout the play, seem to suggest that the island and its aura encourage the imagination, can this little song be interpreted as a statement about the power of art?

6   Do the conspiracies—one, between Antonio and Sebastian; the other, of Caliban with Stephano and Trinculo—hint that freedom in the human condition may be easily subverted to infringement upon the freedom of others? Although the first plot seems serious enough, how does it come to seem almost as comic as the second within the context of the whole play?

7   Can you offer any justification for Prospero's occasional seeming harshness toward innocence—i.e., Ariel, Ferdinand, and even Miranda?

8   Can you argue that the play takes a dark view of human nature? Does it promise that the future (as represented by the lovers) offers a better prospect than the past? Is Prospero himself a flawed, or merely a wronged, man?

9   What do you make of the apparently elegiac tone of Prospero's speech (IV, 1, 177–187)? What do you think he means by "Our revels," and why should he remind his audience of the ephemeral and transitory course of human life? Has he suddenly been reminded of sadness in the human condition, or has all his speculation been leading toward this speech? Does the recognition of life's brevity and our dreams' fragility fit into the question of protest against restraint?

10 Can you cite evidence that Alonso, Sebastian, and Antonio have really undergone "a sea-change" morally or ethically?

TOPICS FOR COMPOSITION

1   Compare and contrast Prospero's island with the larger world from which he has been expelled and to which he will return. Consider which better fosters the protest against restraint.

2   Explain why Prospero demands submission to his will by all. Is such a demand consistent with his outrage at being wronged?

3   Justify the necessity within The Tempest of the young lovers and their espousal within a few hours after their first meeting.

4   Compare and contrast Ariel and Caliban as exponents of duty and freedom.

5   State why or why not (i.e., a series of developed reasons supporting a general argument) The Tempest affords a reasonable spectrum of humanity.

POETRY

The poems that follow will widen considerably our sampling of modern and relatively modern thought on the question of social restraint and will perhaps help us to proceed to deeper reflections on the subject. The passage from William Cowper's *The Task* and William Blake's famous "London" both present in general—and metaphorical—terms the problem of the tendency of institutions to become ends instead of means, even to the point where people are merely used rather than served by them. Human beings can develop fully only in society, Cowper says; but, he adds, when social organization becomes very complex and specialized, individual development is hampered more than it is aided. Identification with special-interest groups tends to rob a person of perspective and integrity. If one serves such institutions too zealously, one ceases to be a whole person; one becomes instead an instrument and begins to treat others as instruments. If this process continues, imagination, sympathy, and even common sense may be destroyed, and all sorts of oppression rationalized. Such is the state that Blake envisions in his powerful lament. To him the great city of London is the symbol of the complete domination of the human spirit by institutions of its own creating. London is a nightmarish place where people languish in "mind-forg'd manacles," and every face bears "marks of weakness, marks of woe."

Robert Burns's well-known "Address to the Unco Guid" leads us to consideration of a more insidious and, in some ways, even more dangerously oppressive form of restraint (which Blake, it must in fairness be added, also understood well). What Burns is chiefly concerned about—and we should recognize that unpretentiousness is here not incompatible with deep concern—is the tendency of common social sanctions to reflect a puritanical distrust of human nature and to create a purely negative approach to virtue. And the negative spirit of puritanism, to use the term loosely and somewhat unfairly, has assumed many forms in more recent periods—some clearly vicious, like the demagoguery that W. B. Yeats protests against in "The Leaders of the Crowd," some deceptively bland, like the "Greater Community" described in W. H. Auden's "The Unknown Citizen." Yeats believes that not only the followers of the crowd but also the seeming leaders are acting out of insecurity and fear. They do not know that truth flourishes only where "the student's lamp has shone" because they are mortally afraid to face themselves in solitude; to them "that lamp is from the tomb," and they struggle to extinguish it as they would resist physical death. Auden describes a more systematic and sophisticated kind of demagoguery, justified, as it would seem, by a general content produced by material prosperity and psychological conditioning. No one has complained, the impersonal voice of the poem says; surely, then, nothing is wrong. But we surmise that the unknown citizen has been made a modern saint through brainwashing.

Perhaps the most vicious form of restraint is that which results from discrimination on the basis of race or sex and amounts to an open denial of full or even equal human status. The loss of dignity and integrity which it causes is poignantly explored in "Elevators," "We Wear the Mask," and "The Dead Ladies," poems expressive of deep and soul-distorting anger, anguish, frustration, and near-despair. Such restraint has flourished in the last century mainly through the sanction of tradition alone and illustrates the fact that tradition can be a powerfully repressive force. Protest against racism and sexism has been loud in recent years, yet millions and millions of black people and women can attest to the fact that in many more or less insidious ways tradition continues to support an irrational demeaning of our humanity.

There remains to be considered a form of restraint that invites ridicule rather than angry protest: the self-imposed restraint that is involved in mindless or timid conformity. This is the theme of Alistair Reid's "Curiosity," e. e. cummings' "anyone lived in a pretty how town," and Joel Sloman's "Blueprint." Each of these writers insists that adventure is essential to the highest humanity and that a thorough-going conformity is a kind of death in life. This is, of course, a matter for serious consideration. What makes ridicule appropriate is that most successful conformists become unaware that they are missing anything; they are apt to be smug and complacent in their secure and uneventful little worlds. Even ridicule can work its way only with those who have not yet quite "settled in."

THE TASK, BOOK IV

William Cowper

    Man in society is like a flower
Blown in its native bed: 'tis there alone
His faculties, expanded in full bloom,
Shine out; there only reach their proper use.
But man, associated and leagued with man   5
By regal warrant, or self-joined by bond
For interest sake, or swarming into clans
Beneath one head for purposes of war,
Like flowers selected from the rest, and bound
And bundled close to fill some crowded vase,   10
Fades rapidly, and, by compression marred,
Contracts defilement not to be endured.
Hence chartered boroughs are such public plagues;
And burghers men immaculate perhaps,
In all their private functions, once combined,   15
Become a loathsome body, only fit

2 *Blown:* blossomed.   *13 boroughs:* urban corporations having monopolistic control over property.

For dissolution, hurtful to the main.
Hence merchants, unimpeachable of sin
Against the charities of domestic life,
Incorporated, seem at once to lose   20
Their nature; and, disclaiming all regard
For mercy and the common rights of man,
Build factories with blood, conducting trade
At the sword's point, and dyeing the white robe
Of innocent commercial justice red.   25
Hence, too, the field of glory, as the world
Misdeems it, dazzled by its bright array,
With all its majesty of thundering pomp,
Enchanting music, and immortal wreaths,
Is but a school where thoughtlessness is taught   30
On principle, where foppery atones
For folly, gallantry, for every vice.

                                          1785

QUESTIONS

1   What is the difference between "man in society" and man associated with man in
    organizations having special functions? Does Cowper provide a clear conception of
    society in a healthful state? Is the comparison with flowers a good analogy? Is it a
    good metaphor?
2   What three kinds of organization does Cowper specifically condemn? Can you offer
    better instances? Would Cowper condemn unions?

ADDRESS TO THE UNCO GUID, OR THE RIGIDLY RIGHTEOUS

Robert Burns

> My Son, these maxims make a rule,
> An' lump them ay thegither:
> The Rigid Righteous is a fool,
> The Rigid Wise anither:
> The cleanest corn that e'er was dight,
> May hae some pyles o' caff in;
> So ne'er a fellow-creature slight
> For random fits o' daffin.
>   *Solomon (Ecclesiastes 7:16)*

Title: Unco Guid: inordinately good.   *Epigraph: (5) dight:* winnowed.   *(6) caff:* chaff.   *(8) daffin:*
larking, frolicking.

O ye, wha are sae guid yoursel,
    Sae pious and sae holy,
Ye've nought to do but mark and tell
    Your neebour's fauts and folly;
Whase life is like a weel-gaun mill,   5
    Supplied wi' store o' water;
The heapet happer's ebbing still,
    An' still the clap plays clatter!

Hear me, ye venerable core,
    As counsel for poor mortals   10
That frequent pass douce Wisdom's door
    For glaikit Folly's portals:
I for their thoughtless, careless sakes,
    Would here propone defences,—
Their donsie tricks, their black mistakes,   15
    Their failings and mischances.

Ye see your state wi' theirs compared,
    And shudder at the niffer;
But cast a moment's fair regard,
    What makes the mighty differ?   20
Discount what scant occasion gave;
    That purity ye pride in;
And (what's aft mair than a' the lave)
    Your better art o' hidin'.

Think, when your castigated pulse   25
    Gies now and then a wallop,
What ragings must his veins convulse,
    That still eternal gallop!
Wi' wind and tide fair i' your tail,
    Right on ye scud your sea-way;   30
But in the teeth o' baith to sail,
    It makes an unco lee-way.

See Social-life and Glee sit down
    All joyous and unthinking,
Till, quite transmugrify'd, they're grown   35
    Debauchery and Drinking:

---

5 weel-gaun: well-going.   *7 heapet happer's:* heaped hopper.   *8 clap:* the clapper, which shakes the hopper to keep the grain moving.   *9 core:* corps, group.   *11 douce:* sweet.   *12 glaikit:* giddy.   *14 propone:* propose.   *15 donsie:* perverse.   *18 niffer:* exchange.   *20 differ:* difference. *23 lave:* rest.   *35 transmugrify'd:* transformed.

O, would they stay to calculate
   Th' eternal consequences,
Or—your more dreaded hell to state—
   Damnation of expenses!   40

Ye high, exalted, virtuous dames,
   Tied up in godly laces,
Before ye gie poor Frailty names,
   Suppose a change o' cases:
A dear-lov'd lad, convenience snug,   45
   A treach'rous inclination—
But, let me whisper i' your lug,
   Ye're aiblins nae temptation.

Then gently scan your brother man,
   Still gentler sister woman;   50
Tho' they may gang a kennin wrang.
   To step aside is human:
One point must still be greatly dark,
   The moving *why* they do it;
And just as lamely can ye mark   55
   How far perhaps they rue it.

Who made the heart, 'tis He alone
   Decidedly can try us:
He knows each chord, its various tone,
   Each spring, its various bias: 60
Then at the balance let's be mute,
   We never can adjust it;
What's done we partly may compute,
   But know not what's resisted.

                          1786

47 lug: ear.   *48 aiblins:* perhaps.   *51 kennin:* a tiny bit.

QUESTIONS

1   What unpleasant traits does the poet see in the "rigidly righteous"?
2   Is the poet denying the moral value of strict regulation of conduct? If so, what basis
    for judging virtue does he give us?
3   Has the poet displayed in this poem the virtue he preaches?

LONDON

William Blake

I wander through each chartered street
Near where the chartered Thames does flow,
And mark in every face I meet
Marks of weakness, marks of woe.

In every cry of every man,   5
In every infant's cry of fear,
In every voice, in every ban,
The mind-forged manacles I hear:

How the chimney-sweeper's cry
Every blackening church appalls,   10
And the hapless soldier's sigh
Runs in blood down palace walls.

But most, through midnight streets I hear
How the youthful harlot's curse
Blasts the new-born infant's tear,   15
And blights with plagues the marriage hearse.

1794

1 chartered: under the monopolistic control of a corporation. *7 ban:* legal prohibition. *15 blasts:* blights.

QUESTIONS

1 Here, Blake attacks certain institutions, that is, organizations and established systems that shape and express general social and moral attitudes. What are they in this case? What, for example, is represented by the palace? What is the connection with the suffering suggested by the soldier's sigh?
2 The poet suggests that the basic cause of the various forms of oppression he mentions is a kind of mental enslavement. Where does he make this statement?
3 Why does the poet use the phrase "marriage hearse"? What kind of plague would be associated with the harlot's curse?

SHE ROSE TO HIS REQUIREMENT

Emily Dickinson

She rose to His Requirement—dropt
The Playthings of Her Life
To take the honorable Work
Of Woman, and of Wife—

If ought She missed in Her new Day,   5
Of Amplitude, or Awe—
Or first Prospective—Or the Gold
In using, wear away,

It lay unmentioned—as the Sea
Develop Pearl, and Weed,   10
But only to Himself—be known
The Fathoms they abide—

1863

QUESTIONS

1 Who is the "She" in this poem?
2 What kind of restraint is in question here?
3 Do you find the sea metaphor appropriate? What are its main implications for you?
   How does its use affect the tone of the poem?

WE WEAR THE MASK

Paul Laurence Dunbar

We wear the mask that grins and lies,
It hides our cheeks and shades our eyes—
This debt we pay to human guile;
With torn and bleeding hearts we smile,
And mouth with myriad subtleties.   5

Why should the world be over-wise,
In counting all our tears and sighs?
Nay, let them only see us, while
    We wear the mask.

We smile, but, O great Christ, our cries   10
To thee from tortured souls arise.
We sing, but oh the clay is vile
Beneath our feet, and long the mile;
But let the world dream otherwise,
    We wear the mask!   15
                  1913

QUESTIONS

1 Paul Laurence Dunbar was a black. Could this poem nevertheless be taken to refer to other groups besides the blacks of this country? If you think so, name one or two.
2 What does wearing the "mask" involve, according to the poem?
3 What motive or motives are given for wearing the "mask"? Do all people at times feel the need to assume a mask?

THE LEADERS OF THE CROWD

William Butler Yeats

They must to keep their certainty accuse
All that are different of a base intent;
Pull down established honor; hawk for news
Whatever their loose phantasy invent
And murmur it with bated breath, as though   5
The abounding gutter had been Helicon
Or calumny a song. How can they know
Truth flourishes where the student's lamp has shone,
And there alone, that have no solitude?
So the crowd come they care not what may come.   10
They have loud music, hope every day renewed
And heartier loves; that lamp is from the tomb.
                  1924

6 Helicon: On Mount Helicon in Greece was a spring sacred to the Muses. *9 that:* The antecedent is "they" in line 7. *12:* That is, the "leaders of the crowd" think so.

QUESTIONS

1 What is the basic motive attributed here to the "leaders of the crowd"? Does the poet have in mind only political demagogues, or social leaders of other kinds as well? Are such leaders as are described here to be found on college campuses?
2 The poet says that truth flourishes only in solitude. Does this imply that all popular opinions are false or that truth can never be generally accepted? Does the poem have a moral?

HURT HAWKS

Robinson Jeffers

I

The broken pillar of the wing jags from the clotted shoulder,
The wing trails like a banner in defeat,
No more to use the sky forever but live with famine
And pain a few days: cat nor coyote
Will shorten the week of waiting for death, there is game without talons.   5
He stands under the oak-bush and waits
The lame feet of salvation; at night he remembers freedom
And flies in a dream, the dawns ruin it.
He is strong and pain is worse to the strong, incapacity is worse.
The curs of the day come and torment him   10
At distance, no one but death the redeemer will humble that head,
The intrepid readiness, the terrible eyes.
The wild God of the world is sometimes merciful to those
That ask mercy, not often to the arrogant.
You do not know him, you communal people, or you have forgotten him;   15
Intemperate and savage, the hawk remembers him;
Beautiful and wild, the hawks, and men that are dying, remember him.

II

I'd sooner, except the penalties, kill a man than a hawk; but the great redtail
Had nothing left but unable misery
From the bone too shattered for mending, the wing that trailed under his talons
    when he moved.   20
We had fed him six weeks, I gave him freedom,
He wandered over the foreland hill and returned in the evening, asking
    for death,
Not like a beggar, still eyed with the old
Implacable arrogance. I gave him the lead gift in the twilight.
What fell was relaxed.   25
Owl-downy, soft feminine feathers; but what
Soared: the fierce rush: the night-herons by the flooded river cried fear
    at its rising
Before it was quite unsheathed from reality.

1927

QUESTIONS

1   What does Jeffers mean by "the wild God of the world"? Why do men that are
dying remember him? Does Jeffers believe in life after death?
2   What kind of mercy does the poet refer to in lines 13–15? Are circumstances really
different for those who ask mercy, or is it a matter of the way things look to them?

3   What, according to Jeffers, does being free mean in human terms? Does freedom depend primarily upon circumstances, or rather upon knowledge and attitude? What is the relation between freedom and suffering? Is belief in mercy consistent with the sense of freedom?

4   The subject and intent of this poem pose a problem in the control of tone. Both bluster and sentimentality must be carefully avoided. Has Jeffers succeeded? What features of his style help especially in gaining the intended effect? Does the style change at any point?

THE UNKNOWN CITIZEN

**(TO JS/07/M378
THIS MARBLE MONUMENT
IS ERECTED BY STATE)**

W. H. Auden

He was found by the Bureau of Statistics to be
One against whom there was no official complaint,
And all the reports on his conduct agree
That, in the modern sense of an old-fashioned word, he was a saint,
For in everything he did he served the Greater Community.   5
Except for the War till the day he retired
He worked in a factory and never got fired,
But satisfied his employers, Fudge Motors Inc.
Yet he wasn't a scab or odd in his views,
For his Union reports that he paid his dues,   10
(Our report on his Union shows it was sound)
And our Social Psychology workers found
That he was popular with his mates and liked a drink.
The Press are convinced that he bought a paper every day
And that his reactions to advertisements were normal in every way.   15
Policies taken out in his name prove that he was fully insured,
And his Health-card shows he was once in hospital but left it cured.
Both Producers Research and High-Grade Living declare
He was fully sensible to the advantages of the Instalment Plan
And had everything necessary to the Modern Man,   20
A phonograph, a radio, a car and a frigidaire.
Our researchers into Public Opinion are content
That he held the proper opinions for the time of year;
When there was peace, he was for peace; when there was war, he went.
He was married and added five children to the population,   25
Which our Eugenist says was the right number for a parent of his generation,

And our teachers report that he never interfered with their education.
Was he free? Was he happy? The question is absurd:
Had anything been wrong, we should certainly have heard.

1940

QUESTIONS

1   Obviously, the poet thinks that such a man as "the unknown citizen" is not free. But was "the unknown citizen" forced to behave in the way he did? What kept him from being free?
2   "Was he happy?" someone asks. Why would he not be? Under what circumstances might he have been happier?
3   What is the difference between the modern and the old-fashioned sense of the word "saint"?
4   What assumption is being satirized in the last two lines of the poem?

anyone lived in a pretty how town

e. e. cummings

anyone lived in a pretty how town
(with up so floating many bells down)
spring summer autumn winter
he sang his didn't he danced his did.

Women and men(both little and small)   5
cared for anyone not at all
they sowed their isn't they reaped their same
sun moon stars rain

children guessed(but only a few
and down they forgot as up they grew   10
autumn winter spring summer)
that noone loved him more by more

when by now and tree by leaf
she laughed his joy she cried his grief
bird by snow and stir by still   15
anyone's any was all to her

someones married their everyones
laughed their cryings and did their dance
(sleep wake hope and then)they
said their nevers they slept their dream   20

stars rain sun moon
(and only the snow can begin to explain
how children are apt to forget to remember
with up so floating many bells down)

one day anyone died i guess   25
(and noone stopped to kiss his face)
busy folk buried them side by side
little by little and was by was

all by all and deep by deep
and more by more they dream their sleep   30
noone and anyone earth by april
wish by spirit and if by yes.

women and men (both dong and ding)
summer autumn winter spring
reaped their sowing and went their came   35
sun moon stars rain

                              1962

QUESTIONS

1   Are "anyone," "noone," and "someones" to be regarded as characters? If so,
    what distinguishes "anyone" from "someones"?
2   What is the difference between "danced his did" (line 4) and "did their dance" (line
    18)?
3   What does "down they forget as up they grow" (line 10) mean?
4   Put in your own words the statements made about "someones."

CURIOSITY

Alastair Reid

may have killed the cat. More likely,
the cat was just unlucky, or else curious
to see what death was like, having no cause
to go on licking paws, or fathering
litter on litter of kittens, predictably.

Nevertheless, to be curious
is dangerous enough. To distrust
what is always said, what seems,

to ask odd questions, interfere in dreams,
smell rats, leave home, have hunches,
does not endear cats to those doggy circles
where well-smelt baskets, suitable wives, good lunches
are the order of things, and where prevails
much wagging of incurious heads and tails.

Face it. Curiosity
will not cause us to die—
only lack of it will.
Never to want to see
the other side of the hill
or that improbable country
where living is an idyll
(although a probable hell)
would kill us all.
Only the curious
have if they live a tale
worth telling at all.

Dogs say cats love too much, are irresponsible,
are dangerous, marry too many wives,
desert their children, chill all dinner tables
with tales of their nine lives.
Well, they are lucky. Let them be
nine-lived and contradictory,
curious enough to change, prepared to pay
the cat-price, which is to die
and die again and again,
each time with no less pain.
A cat-minority of one
is all that can be counted on
to tell the truth; and what cats have to tell
on each return from hell
is this: that dying is what the living do,
that dying is what the loving do,
and that dead dogs are those who never know
that dying is what, to live, each has to do.

1959–1978

QUESTIONS

1   Why does the poet say "A cat minority of one / Is all that can be counted on / To tell the truth"?
2   "To die" and "dying" are used in two different senses in this poem. What are they?
3   How does this poem define the word "curiosity"?

BLUEPRINT

Joel Sloman

I keep thinking of isolated Long Island estates
with rolling lawns, swimming pools and the distant clinking of plates
on the verandah. The people, always seeming to warn
each other of the rules of behavior: how to eat corn
on the cob, how to walk, talk, drink, and deal   5
with the inconvenience of nature, the perfect meal
being a criticism of the accidental arrangement of the universe.
All solemnity in America is perverse,
all sophistication, a labyrinth that looks like a necessary
rationale. An identity a gleaming estate, isolated from class, the incendiary   10
vehicle that makes a true revolution possible. Experience is what we learn
from, not the fantasy of our self-programming, as if only a handful of
        experiences turn
out to be useful. All blueprints are specks in the
eye of history.

QUESTIONS

1   What perspective is established in this poem?
2   What purpose do the rhymes serve here?

ELEVATORS

Barbara Davis

elevators
make me
extremely
racist.
i hate   5
in elevators.
gray old lady
old gray lady
askin me
to hold it   10
parkinson's disease
takes a halfhour to the door
and then

she wanna
talk   15
about it.
buddha-heads
callin the place a slum.
the super wants to know
if my man   20
was invited,
"lots of robberies lately."
goddamnit
I'M
JUST
TRYING   25
TO
GET
TO
MY   30
ROOM
white man,
don't ask me
if i'm cold in my short,
short skirt and   35
try to make me
before the 8th floor
cause i may kill you 'fore the 4th.
                    1973

QUESTIONS

1 The reason for the arrangement of the words of this poem is obvious. Is the arrangement effective? Take into consideration the appropriate inflection of the cap-
   italized words.
2 Why might the choice of subject be considered ironic?
3 What is the point of mentioning the woman afflicted with Parkinson's disease along
   with the less-than-admirable male types?

THE DEAD LADIES

Mary Gordon

for Maureen Sugden

> We can sit down and weep;
> we can go shopping
> *Elizabeth Bishop*

What's to be done with death,
My friend?
      We sit
Cross legged, hating men.

Virginia filled her English skirt   5
With stones.
Always well bred she left behind
Her sensible shoes, her stick
Her hat, her last note
(An apology)   10
And walked in water
'Til it didn't matter.

We speak of Sylvia
Who could not live
For babies or for poetry.   15

You switch on Joplin's blues
The room looms black
With what we know
But are afraid to think.

Too scared to say: "and us?"   20
We leave for work.
Hearts in our mouths.
In love with the wrong men.
          1973

5 *Virginia:* Virginia Woolf, British novelist. 13 *Sylvia:* Sylvia Plath, American poet. 16 *Joplin:* Janis Joplin, the famous singer. All three of these women committed suicide.

QUESTIONS

1. What, as it turns out, does the poet mean by the question with which she begins?
2. Is there any indication why the poet says that she and her friend hate men? Does her statement mean that she is not to be taken literally when she says that they are in love with the wrong men?

TOPICS FOR COMPOSITION

1 Drawing upon Burns's "Address to the Unco Guid" for opinions, write a satirical description of the puritanical character. Or write a description of someone whom you consider to be somewhat puritanical.

2 Express your views on the question of whether virtue is primarily a matter of conduct or of attitude.

3 Defend the thesis that society is still overpuritanical in some important respect. Or, if you prefer, argue that in certain areas of conduct a more puritanical attitude would be beneficial.

4 Advance a general opinion on the question of whether or not legal restraint of private vice is justified. Support your opinion by analyzing a particular problem of this nature.

5 Using Yeats's "The Leaders of the Crowd" as a starting point for reflection, write an essay on good leadership or bad leadership or the principal difference between the two.

6 Alastair Reid says that life is hell for the curious. Write an essay on the relation between curiosity and mental anguish.

7 With Reid's "Curiosity" in mind, write an essay on the possibilities for adventure in the life of a person of average means and with ordinary responsibilities.

8 E. E. Cummings sadly says of children, "down they forget as up they grow." Write an essay on some features of childhood that ought to be carried into adult life.

9 Write an essay on the life-style of any member of a minority group that you happen to be familiar with.

10 Analyze the moral implications of Jeffers' "Hurt Hawks." What kind of human relations would he approve of?

11 Write a description of some "loner" or "character" you have known.

12 Write a reply to the indictment presented in "The Unknown Citizen"—or propose a partial solution to the problem.

13 After reflection upon what you have read in this book so far and upon your own experience, formulate a general statement about the relation between freedom, morality, and happiness. Use the statement as the thesis for an essay developed by the method of exemplification.

14 Analyze the concept of identity implicitly advocated in "Blueprint."

15 Does it seem to you that Emily Dickinson's "She Rose to His Requirement" and Mary Gordon's "The Dead Ladies" are mutually illuminating? If so, explain why.

TOPICS FOR LONGER COMPOSITIONS

1 Shakespeare evidently knew the travel literature of his time, especially that about British explorations and settlements in North America. Presumably this literature reinforced his opposed notions of uncharted places as pastoral garden and as primitive wilderness. Which attitude predominates in *The Tempest*? Or are the two views held in tension and balance? You should consider that Prospero has mastered his occult studies, reared his daughter, and established a kind of order on his island, but also wants to return to Milan. Keep also in mind Gonzalo's response to his surroundings by a description of the utopia he would like to establish (II, 1, 155–176). Can men and women hope "T'excel the golden age"? Will an empty place on earth—the island or the colony of Virginia—inevitably see innocence displaced by evil?

2 Undertake a study of the forms of freedom that are necessary for individual and social well-being. Then, drawing upon the poems of Part Two for illustration, discuss the causes and effects of the forces that restrict freedom unnecessarily (and therefore unjustifiably). Conclude your essay with a recommendation concerning the means by which a suitable amount of freedom can be assured.

3 Thoreau's classic admonition that it is the *duty* of the individual to disobey unjust laws has obviously captured the imagination of many people and has, often, inspired their actions. Use Rive's short story, Thoreau's essay, and relatively recent civil rights issues (which you will research) to structure an essay in which you not only argue the "right" of Thoreau's admonition but also show that change has been brought about by acts of civil disobedience.

PART
3

THE MEANING
OF LOVE

The attempts of many writers to define or at least to describe love reflect the universality of interest in this facet of man's makeup as well as the virtual impossibility of arriving at any one definition of so complex an emotion. In treating the spiritual, emotional, or physical aspects of love, or a combination of these, writers have illuminated the elusiveness and complexity of love and accordingly have generated a central, compulsive literary theme.

In the first essay, Erich Fromm's "The Theory of Love," we encounter the assertion that love is an inherent part of man's being and that he controls the "activity" of love. In other words, Fromm seeks an individual, highly subjective view of man involved in the act of giving—giving as a requisite to loving. On the other hand, Mervyn Cadwallader's "Marriage as a Wretched Institution" assesses love, and marriage in particular, in the light of the pressures of modern, middle-class American society. That Cadwallader's essay is more an indictment of existing conditions than a resolution to the relationship between love and marriage is evident in his concluding sentences, "How do you marry and live like gentle lovers or at least like friendly roommates? Quite frankly, I do not know the answer to that question."

Whether or not we completely accept Fromm's definition of love or Cadwallader's assessment that love and marriage are incompatible in modern society, we can see that their concerns are among those that also motivate fiction writers in their attempts to capture a sense of the meaning of love. In accepting the Nobel Prize in 1950, William Faulkner said that great writing is concerned with "the problems of the human heart in conflict with itself." And we would probably agree that *love* is the most consistent emotion that brings the heart into conflict with itself.

Faulkner illustrates the validity of his statement in his short story, "Two Soldiers." By portraying the love that two brothers have for each other, as we experience, through the nine-year-old protagonist, the realization of a heart in conflict with itself, the author poignantly shows that love is an elemental force.

Irwin Shaw's short story, "Pattern of Love," presents a cast of characters who are experiencing the conflicting and little-understood emotions that grow from early post-puberty awareness of male-female relationships. Shaw's pattern is the age-old love "triangle," acted out with characteristic passion, hatred, and confusion.

"An Interior Monologue" by Joyce Carol Oates is a fictional parallel to the "wretchedness" of marriage and its subsequent destructiveness upon the lives of those involved. Her story leaves little doubt that personal wishes heightened by everyday pressures are not conducive to the kind of love that marriage seems to demand.

THE ESSAY

In "The Theory of Love," Fromm naturally finds it necessary to first define love. And, as writers of extended definition often find, one definition leads to many more. Fromm's definition shows both its depth and variety in the following ways:

1   The definition of love as activity leads to a definition of activity which in turn leads to definitions of giving, care, responsibility, respect, and knowledge.
2   Each term shows a variety in methods of defining. Note Fromm's use of synonym, example, analogy, and negation.

THE THEORY OF LOVE

Erich Fromm

Mature *love* is *union under the condition of preserving one's integrity,* one's individuality. *Love is an active power in man;* a power which breaks through the walls which separate man from his fellow men, which unites him with others; love makes him overcome the sense of isolation and separateness, yet it permits him to be himself, to retain his integrity. In love the paradox occurs that two beings become one and yet remain two.

If we say love is an activity, we face a difficulty which lies in the ambiguous meaning of the word "activity." By "activity," in the modern usage of the word, is usually meant an action which brings about a change in an existing situation by means of an expenditure of energy. Thus a man is considered active if he does business, studies medicine, works on an endless belt, builds a table, or is engaged in sports. Common to all these activities is that they are directed toward an outside goal to be achieved. What is *not* taken into account is the *motivation* of activity. Take for instance a man driven to incessant work by a sense of deep insecurity and loneliness; or another one driven by ambition, or greed for money. In all these cases the person is the slave of a passion, and his activity is in reality a "passivity" because he is driven; he is the sufferer, not the "actor." On the other hand, a man sitting quiet and contemplating, with no purpose or aim except that of experiencing himself and his oneness with the world, is considered to be "passive," because he is not "doing" anything. In reality, this attitude of concentrated meditation is the highest activity there is, an activity of the soul, which is possible only under the condition of inner freedom and independence. One concept of activity, the modern one, refers to the use of energy for the achievement of external aims; the other concept of activity refers to the use of man's inherent powers, regardless of whether any external change is brought about. The latter concept of activity has been formulated most clearly by Spinoza. He differentiates among the affects between active and passive affects, "actions" and "passions." In the exercise of an active affect, man is free, he is the master of his affect; in the exercise of a passive affect, man is driven, the object of motivations of which he himself is not aware. Thus Spinoza arrives at the statement that virtue and power are one and the same.[1] Envy, jealousy, ambition, any kind of greed are passions; love is an action, the practice of a human power, which can be practiced only in freedom and never as the result of a compulsion.

Love is an activity, not a passive affect; it is a "standing in," not a "falling for." In the most general way, the active character of love can be described by stating that love is primarily *giving*, not receiving.

What is giving? Simple as the answer to this question seems to be, it is actually full of ambiguities and complexities. The most widespread misunderstanding is that which assumes that giving is "giving up" something, being deprived of, sacrificing. The person whose character has not developed beyond the stage of the receptive, exploitative, or hoarding orientation, experiences the act of giving in this way. The marketing character is willing to give, but only in exchange for receiving; giving without receiving for him is being cheated. People whose main orientation is a non-productive one feel giving as an impoverishment. Most individuals of this type therefore refuse to give. Some make a virtue out of giving in the sense of a sacrifice. They feel that just because it is painful to give, one *should* give; the virtue of giving to them lies in the very act of acceptance of the sacrifice. For them, the norm that it is better to give than to receive means that it is better to suffer deprivation than to experience joy.

For the productive character, giving has an entirely different meaning. Giving is the highest expression of potency. In the very act of giving, I experience my strength, my wealth, my power. This experience of heightened vitality and potency fills me with joy. I experience myself as overflowing, spending, alive, hence as joyous. Giving is more joyous than receiving, not because it is a deprivation, but because in the act of giving lies the expression of my aliveness. . . .

In the sphere of material things giving means being rich. Not he who *has* much is rich, but he who *gives* much. The hoarder who is anxiously worried about losing something is, psychologically speaking, the poor, impoverished man, regardless of how much he has. Whoever is capable of giving of himself is rich. He experiences himself as one who can confer of himself to others. Only one who is deprived of all that goes beyond the barest necessities for subsistence would be incapable of enjoying the act of giving material things. But daily experience shows that what a person considers the minimal necessities depends as much on his character as it depends on his actual possessions. It is well known that the poor are more willing to give than the rich. Nevertheless, poverty beyond a certain point may make it impossible to give, and is so degrading, not only because of the suffering it causes directly, but because of the fact that it deprives the poor of the joy of giving.

[1] Spinoza, *Ethics IV,* Def. 8.

The most important sphere of giving, however, is not that of material things, but lies in the specifically human realm. What does one person give to another? He gives of himself, of the most precious he has, he gives of his life. This does not necessarily mean that he sacrifices his life for the other—but that he gives him of that which is alive in him; he gives him of his joy, of his interest, of his understanding, of his knowledge, of his humor, of his sadness—of all expressions and manifestations of that which is alive in him. In thus giving of his life, he enriches the other person, he enhances the other's sense of aliveness by enhancing his own sense of aliveness. He does not give in order to receive; giving is in itself exquisite joy. But in giving he cannot help bringing something to life in the other person, and this which is brought to life reflects back to him; in truly giving, he cannot help receiving that which is given back to him. Giving implies to make the other person a giver also and they both share in the joy of what they have brought to life. In the act of giving something is born, and both persons involved are grateful for the life that is born for both of them. Specifically with regard to love this means: love is a power which produces love; impotence is the inability to produce love. This thought has been beautifully expressed by Marx: "Assume," he says, "*man* as *man,* and his relation to the world as a human one, and you can exchange love only for love, confidence for confidence, etc. If you wish to enjoy art, you must be an artistically trained person; if you wish to have influence on other people, you must be a person who has a really stimulating and furthering influence on other people. Every one of your relationships to man and to nature must be a definite expression of your *real, individual* life corresponding to the object of your will. If you love without calling forth love, that is, if your love as such does not produce love, if by means of an *expression of life* as a loving person you do not make of yourself a *loved person,* then your love is impotent, a misfortune."[2] But not only in love does giving mean receiving. The teacher is taught by his students, the actor is stimulated by his audience, the psychoanalyst is cured by his patient—provided they do not treat each other as objects, but are related to each other genuinely and productively.

It is hardly necessary to stress the fact that the ability to love as an act of giving depends on the character development of the person. It presupposes the attainment of a predominantly productive orientation; in this orientation the person has overcome dependency, narcissistic omnipotence, the wish to exploit others, or to hoard, and has acquired faith in his own human powers, courage to rely on his powers in the attainment of his goals. To the degree that these qualities are lacking, he is afraid of giving himself—hence of loving.

Beyond the element of giving, the active character of love becomes evident in the fact that it always implies certain basic elements, common to all forms of love. These are *care, responsibility, respect* and *knowledge.*

That love implies *care* is most evident in a mother's love for her child. No assurance of her love would strike us as sincere if we saw her lacking in care for the infant, if she neglected to feed it, to bathe it, to give it physical comfort; and we are impressed by her love if we see her caring for the child. It is not different even with the love for

---

[2] "Nationalökonomie und Philosophie," 1844, published in Karl Marx' *Die Frühschriften,* Alfred Kröner Verlag, Stuttgart, 1953, pp. 300, 301. (My translation, E. F.)

animals or flowers. If a woman told us that she loved flowers, and we saw that she forgot to water them, we would not believe in her "love" for flowers. *Love is the active concern for the life and the growth of that which we love.* Where this active concern is lacking, there is no love. This element of love has been beautifully described in the book of Jonah. God has told Jonah to go to Nineveh to warn its inhabitants that they will be punished unless they mend their evil ways. Jonah runs away from his mission because he is afraid that the people of Nineveh will repent and that God will forgive them. He is a man with a strong sense of order and law, but without love. However, in his attempt to escape, he finds himself in the belly of a whale, symbolizing the state of isolation and imprisonment which his lack of love and solidarity has brought upon him. God saves him, and Jonah goes to Nineveh. He preaches to the inhabitants as God has told him, and the very thing he was afraid of happens. The men of Nineveh repent their sins, mend their ways, and God forgives them and decides not to destroy the city. Jonah is intensely angry and disappointed; he wanted "justice" to be done, not mercy. At last he finds some comfort in the shade of a tree which God made to grow for him to protect him from the sun. But when God makes the tree wilt, Jonah is depressed and angrily complains to God. God answers: "Thou hast had pity on the gourd for the which thou has not labored neither madest it grow; which came up in a night, and perished in a night. And should I not spare Nineveh, that great city, wherein are more than sixscore thousand people that cannot discern between their right hand and their left hand; and also much cattle?" God's answer to Jonah is to be understood symbolically. God explains to Jonah that the essence of love is to "labor" for something and "to make something grow," that love and labor are inseparable. One loves that for which one labors, and one labors for that which one loves.

Care and concern imply another aspect of love; that of *responsibility*. Today responsibility is often meant to denote duty, something imposed upon one from the outside. But responsibility, in its true sense, is an entirely voluntary act; it is my response to the needs, expressed or unexpressed, of another human being. To be "responsible" means to be able and ready to "respond." Jonah did not feel responsible to the inhabitants of Nineveh. He, like Cain, could ask: "Am I my brother's keeper?" The loving person responds. The life of his brother is not his brother's business alone, but his own. He feels responsible for his fellow men, as he feels responsible for himself. This responsibility, in the case of the mother and her infant, refers mainly to the care for physical needs. In the love between adults it refers mainly to the psychic needs of the other person.

Responsibility could easily deteriorate into domination and possessiveness, were it not for a third component of love, *respect*. Respect is not fear and awe; it denotes, in accordance with the root of the word (*respicere* = to look at), the ability to see a person as he is, to be aware of his unique individuality. Respect means the concern that the other person should grow and unfold as he is. Respect, thus, implies the absence of exploitation. I want the loved person to grow and unfold for his own sake, and in his own ways, and not for the purpose of serving me. If I love the other person, I feel one with him or her, but with him *as he is,* not as I need him to be as an object for my use. It is clear that respect is possible only if *I* have achieved independence; if I can stand and walk without needing crutches, without having to dominate and exploit anyone else. Respect exists only on the basis of freedom: "l'amour est l'enfant de la liberté" as an old French song says; love is the child of freedom, never that of domination.

To respect a person is not possible without *knowing* him; care and responsibility would be blind if they were not guided by knowledge. Knowledge would be empty if it were not motivated by concern. There are many layers of knowledge; the knowledge which is an aspect of love is one which does not stay at the periphery, but penetrates to the core. It is possible only when I can transcend the concern for myself and see the other person in his own terms. I may know, for instance, that a person is angry, even if he does not show it overtly; but I may know him more deeply than that; then I know that he is anxious, and worried; that he feels lonely, that he feels guilty. Then I know that his anger is only the manifestation of something deeper, and I see him as anxious and embarrassed, that is, as the suffering person, rather than as the angry one.

Knowledge has one more, and a more fundamental, relation to the problem of love. The basic need to fuse with another person so as to transcend the prison of one's separateness is closely related to another specifically human desire, that to know the "secret of man." While life in its merely biological aspects is a miracle and a secret, man in his human aspects is an unfathomable secret to himself—and to his fellow man. We know ourselves, and yet even with all the efforts we may make, we do not know ourselves. We know our fellow man, and yet we do not know him, because we are not a thing, and our fellow man is not a thing. The further we reach into the depth of our being, or someone else's being, the more the goal of knowledge eludes us. Yet we cannot help desiring to penetrate into the secret of man's soul, into the innermost nucleus which is "he."

There is one way, a desperate one, to know the secret: it is that of complete power over another person; the power which makes him do what we want, feel what we want, think what we want; which transforms him into a thing, our thing, our possession. The ultimate degree of this attempt to know lies in the extremes of sadism, the desire and ability to make a human being suffer; to torture him, to force him to betray his secret in his suffering. In this craving for penetrating man's secret, his and hence our own, lies an essential motivation for the depth and intensity of cruelty and destructiveness. In a very succinct way this idea has been expressed by Isaac Babel. He quotes a fellow officer in the Russian civil war, who has just stamped his former master to death, as saying: "With shooting—I'll put it this way—with shooting you only get rid of a chap. . . . With shooting you'll never get at the soul, to where it is in a fellow and how it shows itself. But I don't spare myself, and I've more than once trampled an enemy for over an hour. You see, I want to get to know what life really is, what life's like down our way."[3]

In children we often see this path to knowledge quite overtly. The child takes something apart, breaks it up in order to know it; or it takes an animal apart; cruelly tears off the wings of a butterfly in order to know it, to force its secret. The cruelty itself is motivated by something deeper: the wish to know the secret of things and of life.

[3] I. Babel, *The Collected Stories,* Criterion Books, New York, 1955.

The other path to knowing "the secret" is love. Love is active penetration of the other person, in which my desire to know is stilled by union. In the act of fusion I know you, I know myself, I know everybody—and I "know" nothing. I know in the only way knowledge of that which is alive is possible for man—by experience of union—not by any knowledge our thought can give. Sadism is motivated by the wish to know the secret, yet I remain as ignorant as I was before. I have torn the other being apart limb from limb, yet all I have done is to destroy him. Love is the only way of knowledge, which in the act of union answers my quest. In the act of loving, of giving myself, in the act of penetrating the other person, I find myself, I discover myself, I discover us both, I discover man.

QUESTIONS

1 Fromm makes an initial distinction between passions and actions. What other words does he use that are synonymous with "passions" and "actions"?
2 How is the act of giving related to character development? What assumption would Fromm make about a person incapable of loving?
3 Fromm supports his definition of love by assigning certain basic characteristics. How does each support his definition? Is his list complete, or would you add other characteristics?

TOPICS FOR COMPOSITION

1 Write your own view of the meaning of love. Carefully define your terms, using Fromm's essay as your model.
2 Consider the overworked use of the term *love*. Write an essay in which you argue that the term *love* has been so misused that no clear definition is possible. Support your argument with examples and anecdotes.

By recognizing that Cadwallader's full thesis is that marriage is a wretched institution because it is unable to bear the pressures of contemporary American middle-class society, we are better able to uncover the salient points by which he structures support for his thesis. Notice the progressive nature of the following:

1 The function of marriage in the past
2 The changes brought about by an industrialized society
3 The creation of an adolescent culture and the trend toward marriage at an earlier age
4 The paradox inherent in existing mores: those that insist on stability in marriage while encouraging permissiveness in related human interaction

MARRIAGE AS A WRETCHED INSTITUTION

Mervyn Cadwallader

Our society expects us all to get married. With only rare exceptions we all do just that. Getting married is a rather complicated business. It involves mastering certain complex hustling and courtship games, the rituals and the ceremonies that celebrate the act of marriage, and finally the difficult requirements of domestic life with a husband or wife. It is an enormously elaborate round of activity, much more so than finding a job, and yet while many resolutely remain unemployed, few remain unmarried.

Now all this would not be particularly remarkable if there were no question about the advantages, the joys, and the rewards of married life, but most Americans, even young Americans, know or have heard that marriage is a hazardous affair. Of course, for all the increase in divorce, there are still young marriages that work, unions made by young men and women intelligent or fortunate enough to find the kind of mates they want, who know that they want children and how to love them when they come, or who find the artful blend between giving and receiving. It is not these marriages that concern us here, and that is not the trend in America today. We are concerned with the increasing number of others who, with mixed intentions and varied illusions, grope or fling themselves into marital disaster. They talk solemnly and sincerely about working to make their marriage succeed, but they are very aware of the countless marriages they have seen fail. But young people in particular do not seem to be able to relate the awesome divorce statistics to the probability of failure of their own marriage. And they rush into it, in increasing numbers, without any clear idea of the reality that underlies the myth.

Parents, teachers, and concerned adults all counsel against premature marriage. But they rarely speak the truth about marriage as it really is in modern middle-class America. The truth as I see it is that contemporary marriage is a wretched institution. It spells the end of voluntary affection, of love freely given and joyously received. Beautiful romances are transmuted into dull marriages, and eventually the relationship becomes constricting, corrosive, grinding, and destructive. The beautiful love affair becomes a bitter contract.

The basic reason for this sad state of affairs is that marriage was not designed to bear the burdens now being asked of it by the urban American middle class. It is an institution that evolved over centuries to meet some very specific functional needs of a nonindustrial society. Romantic love was viewed as tragic, or merely irrelevant. Today it is the titillating prelude to domestic tragedy, or, perhaps more frequently, to domestic grotesqueries that are only pathetic.

Marriage was not designed as a mechanism for providing friendship, erotic experience, romantic love, personal fulfillment, continuous lay psychotherapy, or recreation. The Western European family was not designed to carry a lifelong load of highly emotional romantic freight. Given its present structure, it simply has to fail when asked to do so. The very idea of an irrevocable contract obligating the parties concerned to a lifetime of romantic effort is utterly absurd.

Other pressures of the present era have tended to overburden marriage with expectations it cannot fulfill. Industrialized, urbanized America is a society which has lost the sense of community. Our ties to our society, to the bustling multitudes that make up this dazzling kaleidoscope of contemporary America, are as formal and superficial as they are numerous. We all search for community, and yet we know that the search is futile. Cut off from the support and satisfactions that flow from community, the confused and searching young American can do little but place all of his bets on creating a community in microcosm, his own marriage.

And so the ideal we struggle to reach in our love relationship is that of complete candor, total honesty. Out there all is phony, but within the romantic family there are to be no dishonest games, no hypocrisy, no misunderstanding. Here we have a painful paradox, for I submit that total exposure is probably always mutually destructive in the long run. What starts out as a tender coming together to share one's whole person with the beloved is transmuted by too much togetherness into attack and counterattack, doubt, disillusionment, and ambivalence. The moment the once-upon-a-time lover catches a glimpse of his own hatred, something precious and fragile is shattered. And soon another brave marriage will end.

The purposes of marriage have changed radically, yet we cling desperately to the outmoded structures of the past. Adult Americans behave as though the more obvious the contradiction between the old and the new, the more sentimental and irrational should be their advice to young people who are going steady or are engaged. Our schools, both high schools and colleges, teach sentimental rubbish in their marriage and family courses. The texts make much of a posture of hard-nosed objectivity that is neither objective nor hard-nosed. The basic structure of Western marriage is never questioned, alternatives are not proposed or discussed. Instead, the prospective young bride and bridegroom are offered housekeeping advice and told to work hard at making their marriage succeed. The chapter on sex, complete with ugly diagrams of the male and female genitals, is probably wedged in between a chapter on budgets and life insurance. The message is that if your marriage fails, you have been weighed in the domestic balance and found wanting. Perhaps you did not master the fifth position for sexual intercourse, or maybe you bought cheap term life rather than a preferred policy with income protection and retirement benefits. If taught honestly, these courses would alert the teen-ager and young adult to the realities of matrimonial life in the United States and try to advise them on how to survive marriage if they insist on that hazardous venture.

But teen-agers and young adults do insist upon it in greater and greater numbers with each passing year. And one of the reasons they do get married with such astonishing certainty is because they find themselves immersed in a culture that is preoccupied with and schizophrenic about sex. Advertising, entertainment, and fashion are all designed to produce and then to exploit sexual tension. Sexually aroused at an early age and asked to postpone marriage until they become adults, they have no recourse but to fill the intervening years with courtship rituals and games that are supposed to be sexy but sexless. Dating is expected to culminate in going steady, and that is the beginning of the end. The dating game hinges on an important exchange. The male wants sexual intimacy, and the female wants social commitment. The game involves bartering sex for security amid the sweet and heady agitations of a romantic entanglement. Once the game reaches the going-steady stage, marriage is virtually inevitable. The teen-ager finds himself driven into a corner, and the one way to legitimize his sex play and assuage the guilt is to plan marriage.

Another reason for the upsurge in young marriages is the real cultural break between teen-agers and adults in our society. This is a recent phenomenon. In my generation there was no teen culture. Adolescents wanted to become adults as soon as possible. The teen-age years were a time of impatient waiting, as teen-age boys tried to dress and act like little men. Adolescents sang the adults' songs ("South of the Border," "The Music Goes Round and Round," "Mairzy Doats"—notice I didn't say anything about the quality of the music), saw their movies, listened to their radios, and waited confidently to be allowed in. We had no money, and so there was no teen-age market. There was nothing to do then but get it over with. The boundary line was sharp, and you crossed it when you took your first serious job, when you passed the employment test.

Now there is a very definite adolescent culture, which is in many ways hostile to the dreary culture of the adult world. In its most extreme form it borrows from the beats and turns the middle-class value system inside out. The hip teen-ager on Macdougal Street or Telegraph Avenue can buy a costume and go to a freak show. It's fun to be an Indian, a prankster, a beat, or a swinging troubadour. He can get stoned. That particular trip leads to instant mysticism.

Even in less extreme forms, teen culture is weighted against the adult world of responsibility. I recently asked a roomful of eighteen-year-olds to tell me what an adult is. Their deliberate answer, after hours of discussion, was that an adult is someone who no longer plays, who is no longer playful. Is Bob Dylan an adult? No, never! Of course they did not want to remain children, or teens, or adolescents; but they did want to remain youthful, playful, free of squares, and free of responsibility. The teen-ager wants to be old enough to drive, drink, screw, and travel. He does not want to get pushed into square maturity. He wants to drag the main, be a surf bum, a ski bum, or dream of being a bum. He doesn't want to go to Vietnam, or to IBM, or to buy a split-level house in Knotty Pines Estates.

This swing away from responsibility quite predictably produces frictions between the adolescent and his parents. The clash of cultures is likely to drive the adolescent from the home, to persuade him to leave the dead world of his parents and strike out on his own. And here we find the central paradox of young marriages. For the only way the young person can escape from his parents is to assume many of the responsibilities that he so reviles in the life-style of his parents. He needs a job and an apartment. And he needs some kind of emotional substitute, some means of filling the emotional vacuum that leaving home has caused. And so he goes steady, and sooner rather than later, gets married to a girl with similar inclinations.

When he does this, he crosses the dividing line between the cultures. Though he seldom realizes it at the time, he has taken the first step to adulthood. Our society does not have a conventional "rite of passage." In Africa the Masai adolescent takes a lion test. He becomes an adult the first time he kills a lion with a spear. Our adolescents take the domesticity test. When they get married they have to come to terms with the system in one way or another. Some brave individuals continue to fight it. But most simply capitulate.

The cool adolescent finishing high school or starting college has a skeptical view of virtually every institutional sector of his society. He knows that government is corrupt, the military dehumanizing, the corporations rapacious, the churches organized hypocrisy, and the schools dishonest. But the one area that seems to be exempt from his cynicism is romantic love and marriage. When I talk to teen-agers about marriage, that cool skepticism turns to sentimental dreams right out of *Ladies' Home Journal* or the hard-hitting pages of *Reader's Digest*. They all mouth the same vapid platitudes about finding happiness through sharing and personal fulfillment through giving (each is to give 51 percent). They have all heard about divorce, and most of them have been touched by it in some way or another. Yet they insist that their marriage will be different.

So, clutching their illusions, young girls with ecstatic screams of joy lead their awkward brooding boys through the portals of the church into the land of the Mustang, Apartment 24, Macy's, Sears, and the ubiquitous drive-in. They have become members in good standing of the adult world.

The end of most of these sentimental marriages is quite predictable. They progress, in most cases, to varying stages of marital ennui, depending on the ability of the couple to adjust to reality; most common are (1) a lackluster standoff, (2) a bitter business carried on for the children, church, or neighbors, or (3) separation and divorce, followed by another search to find the right person.

Divorce rates have been rising in all Western countries. In many countries the rates are rising even faster than in the United States. In 1910 the divorce rate for the United States was 87 per 1000 marriages. In 1965 the rate had risen to an estimated figure of well over 300 per 1000 in many parts of the country. At the present time some 40 percent of all brides are between the ages of fifteen and eighteen; half of these marriages break up within five years. As our population becomes younger and the age of marriage continues to drop, the divorce rate will rise to significantly higher levels.

What do we do, what can we do, about this wretched and disappointing institution? In terms of the immediate generation, the answer probably is, not much. Even when subjected to the enormous strains I have described, the habits, customs, traditions, and taboos that make up our courtship and marriage cycle are uncommonly resistant to change. Here and there creative and courageous individuals can and do work out their own unique solutions to the problem of marriage. Most of us simply suffer without understanding and thrash around blindly in an attempt to reduce the acute pain of a romance gone sour. In time, all of these individual actions will show up as a trend away from the old and toward the new, and the bulk of sluggish moderates in the population will slowly come to accept this trend as part of social evolution. Clearly, in middle-class America, the trend is ever toward more romantic courtship and marriage, earlier premarital sexual intercourse, earlier first marriages, more extramarital affairs, earlier first divorces, more frequent divorces and remarriages. The trend is away from stable lifelong monogamous relationships toward some form of polygamous male-female relationship. Perhaps we should identify it as serial or consecutive polygamy, simply because Americans in significant numbers are going to have more than one husband or more than one wife. Attitudes and laws that make multiple marriages (in sequence, of course) difficult for the romantic and sentimental among us are archaic obstacles that one learns to circumvent with the aid of weary judges and clever attorneys.

Now, the absurdity of much of this lies in the fact that we pretend that marriages of short duration must be contracted for life. Why not permit a flexible contract perhaps for one to two or more years, with periodic options to renew? If a couple grew disenchanted with their life together, they would not feel trapped for life. They would not have to anticipate and then go through the destructive agonies of divorce. They would not have to carry about the stigma of marital failure, like the mark of Cain on their foreheads. Instead of a declaration of war, they could simply let their contract lapse, and while still friendly, be free to continue their romantic quest. Sexualized romanticism is now so fundamental to American life—and is bound to become even more so—that marriage will simply have to accommodate itself to it in one way or another. For a great proportion of us it already has.

What of the children in a society that is moving inexorably toward consecutive plural marriages? Under present arrangements in which marriages are ostensibly lifetime contracts and then are dissolved through hypocritical collusions or messy battles in court, the children do suffer. Marriage and divorce turn lovers into enemies, and the child is left to thread his way through the emotional wreckage of his parents' lives. Financial support of the children, mere subsistence, is not really a problem in a society as affluent as ours. Enduring emotional support of children by loving, healthy, and friendly adults is a serious problem in America, and it is a desperately urgent problem in many families where divorce is unthinkable. If the bitter and poisonous denouement of divorce could be avoided by a frank acceptance of short-term marriages, both adults and children would benefit. Any time husbands and wives and ex-husbands and ex-wives treat each other decently, generously, and respectfully, their children will benefit.

The braver and more critical among our teen-agers and youthful adults will still ask, But if the institution is so bad, why get married at all? This is a tough one to deal with. The social pressures pushing any couple who live together into marriage are difficult to ignore even by the most resolute rebel. It can be done, and many should be encouraged to carry out their own creative experiments in living together in a relationship that is wholly voluntary. If the demands of society to conform seem overwhelming, the couple should know that simply to be defined by others as married will elicit married-like behavior in themselves, and that is precisely what they want to avoid.

How do you marry and yet live like gentle lovers, or at least like friendly roommates? Quite frankly, I do not know the answer to that question.

QUESTIONS

1 What, according to Cadwallader, is the ideal that we try to reach in a love relationship?
2 How have the purposes of marriage changed?

3 Early in his essay, Cadwallader says that urbanized America has lost its "sense of community." What precisely does he mean and how accurate is his statement?
4 About a decade has passed since this essay appeared. Is its indictment still accurate?

TOPICS FOR COMPOSITION

1 In his essay, Cadwallader offers some alternatives to the long-term marriage contract. Write an essay supporting or refuting the advisability of his alternatives.
2 Research current marriage and divorce statistics. Use your research to predict the success or failure of marriage in this decade.

SHORT STORY

"Two Soldiers" is an outstanding example of William Faulkner's fictional mastery. In fact, it is an outstanding example of many of the techniques that create the art of fiction. Consider, as you read, that the narrator is a boy almost nine years old, and that, through him, Faulkner captures the language of rural Mississippi; describes an array of characters, ranging from the boy's family to sophisticated residents of Memphis; comments on a variety of behavior; and, through it all, makes us believe in and take part in the boy's journey into understanding.

TWO SOLDIERS

William Faulkner

Me and Pete would go down to Old Man Killegrew's and listen to his radio. We would wait until after supper, after dark, and we would stand outside Old Man Killegrew's parlor window, and we could hear it because Old Man Killegrew's wife was deaf, and so he run the radio as loud as it would run, and so me and Pete could hear it plain as Old Man Killegrew's wife could, I reckon, even standing outside with the window closed.

And that night I said, "What? Japanese? What's a pearl harbor?" and Pete said, "Hush."

And so we stood there, it was cold, listening to the fellow in the radio talking, only I couldn't make no heads nor tails neither out of it. Then the fellow said that would be all for a while, and me and Pete walked back up the road to home, and Pete told me what it was. Because he was nigh twenty and he had done finished the Consolidated last June and he knowed a heap: about them Japanese dropping bombs on Pearl Harbor and that Pearl Harbor was across the water.

"Across what water?" I said. "Across that Government reservoy up at Oxford?"

"Naw," Pete said. "Across the big water. The Pacific Ocean."

We went home. Maw and pap was already asleep, and me and Pete laid in the bed, and I still couldn't understand where it was, and Pete told me again—the Pacific Ocean.

"What's the matter with you?" Pete said. "You're going on nine years old. You been in school now ever since September. Ain't you learned nothing yet?"

"I reckon we ain't got as fer as the Pacific Ocean yet," I said.

We was still sowing the vetch then that ought to been all finished by the fifteenth of November, because pap was still behind, just like he had been ever since me and Pete had knowed him. And we had firewood to git in, too, but every night me and Pete would go down to Old Man Killegrew's and stand outside his parlor window in the cold and listen to his radio; then we would come back home and lay in the bed and Pete would tell me what it was. That is, he would tell me for a while. Then he wouldn't tell me. It was like he didn't want to talk about it no more. He would tell me to shut up because he wanted to go to sleep, but he never wanted to go to sleep.

He would lay there, a heap stiller than if he was asleep, and it would be something, I could feel it coming out of him, like he was mad at me even, only I knowed he wasn't thinking about me, or like he was worried about something, and it wasn't that neither, because he never had nothing to worry about. He never got behind like pap, let alone stayed behind. Pap give him ten acres when he graduated from the Consolidated, and me and Pete both reckoned pap was durn glad to get shut of at least ten acres, less to have to worry with himself; and Pete had them ten acres all sowed to vetch and busted out and bedded for the winter, and so it wasn't that. But it was something. And still we would go down to Old Man Killegrew's every night and listen to his radio, and they was at it in the Philippines now, but General MacArthur was holding um. Then we would come back home and lay in the bed, and Pete wouldn't tell me nothing or talk at all. He would just lay there still as a ambush and when I would touch him, his side or his leg would feel hard and still as iron, until after a while I would go to sleep.

Then one night—it was the first time he had said nothing to me except to jump on me about not chopping enough wood at the wood tree where we was cutting—he said, "I got to go."

"Go where?" I said.

"To that war," Pete said.

"Before we even finish gettin' in the firewood?"

"Firewood, hell," Pete said.

"All right," I said. "When we going to start?"

But he wasn't even listening. He laid there, hard and still as iron in the dark. "I got to go," he said. "I jest ain't going to put up with no folks treating the Unity States that way."

"Yes," I said. "Firewood or no firewood, I reckon we got to go."

This time he heard me. He laid still again, but it was a different kind of still.

"You?" he said. "To a war?"

"You'll whup the big uns and I'll whup the little uns," I said.

Then he told me I couldn't go. At first I though he just never wanted me tagging after him, like he wouldn't leave me go with him when he went sparking them girls of Tull's. Then he told me the Army wouldn't leave me go because I was too little, and then I knowed he really meant it and that I couldn't go nohow noways. And somehow I hadn't believed until then that he was going himself, but now I knowed he was and that he wasn't going to leave me go with him a-tall.

"I'll chop the wood and tote the water for you-all then!" I said. "You got to have wood and water!"

Anyway, he was listening to me now. He wasn't like iron now.

He turned onto his side and put his hand on my chest because it was me that was laying straight and hard on my back now.

"No," he said. "You got to stay here and help pap."

"Help him what?" I said. "He ain't never caught up nohow. He can't get no further behind. He can sholy take care of this little shirttail of a farm while me and you are whupping them Japanese. I got to go too. If you got to go, then so have I."

"No," Pete said. "Hush now. Hush." And he meant it, and I knowed he did. Only I made sho from his own mouth. I quit.

"So I just can't go then," I said.

"No," Pete said. "You just can't go. You're too little, in the first place and in the second place——"

"All right," I said. "Then shut up and leave me go to sleep."

So he hushed then and laid back. And I laid there like I was already asleep, and pretty soon he was asleep and I knowed it was the wanting to go to the war that had worried him and kept him awake, and now that he had decided to go, he wasn't worried any more.

The next morning he told maw and pa. Maw was all right. She cried.

"No," She said, crying. "I don't want him to go. I would rather go myself in his place, if I could. I don't want to save the country. Them Japanese could take it and keep it, so long as they left me and my family and my children alone. But I remember my brother Marsh in that other war. He had to go to that one when he wasn't but nineteen, and our mother couldn't understand it then any more than I can now. But she told Marsh if he had to go, he had to go. And so, if Pete's got to go to this one, he's got to go to it. Jest don't ask me to understand why."

But pap was the one. He was the feller. "To the war?" he said. "Why, I just don't see a bit of use in that. You ain't old enough for the draft, and the country ain't being invaded. Our President in Washington, D.C., is watching the conditions and he will notify us. Besides, in that other war your ma just mentioned, I was drafted and sent clean to Texas and was held there nigh eight months until they finally quit fighting. It seems to me that that, along with your Uncle Marsh who received a actual wound on the battlefields of France, is enough for me and mine to have to do to protect the country, at least in my lifetime. Besides, what'll I do for help on the farm with you gone? It seems to me I'll get mighty far behind."

"You been behind as long as I can remember," Pete said. "Anyway, I'm going. I got to."

"Of course he's got to go," I said. "Them Japanese——"

"You hush your mouth!" maw said, crying. "Nobody's talking to you! Go and get me a armful of wood! That's what you can do!"

So I got the wood. And all the next day, while me and Pete and pap was getting in as much wood as we could in that time because Pete said how pap's idea of plenty of wood was one more stick laying against the wall that maw ain't put on the fire yet, maw was getting Pete ready to go. She washed and mended his clothes and cooked him a shoe box of vittles. And that night me and Pete laid in the bed and listened to her packing his grip and crying, until after a while Pete got up in his nightshirt and went back there, and I could hear them talking, until at last maw said, "You got to go, and so I want you to go. But I don't understand it, and I won't never, and so don't expect me to." And Pete come back and got into the bed again and laid again still and hard as iron on his back, and then he said, and he wasn't talking to me, he wasn't talking to nobody: "I got to go. I just got to."

"Sho you got to," I said. "Them Japanese——" He turned over hard, he kind of surged over into his side, looking at me in the dark.

"Anyway, you're all right," he said. "I expected to have more trouble with you than all the rest of them put together."

"I reckon I can't help it neither," I said. "But maybe it will run a few years longer and I can get there. Maybe someday I will jest walk in on you."

"I hope not," Pete said. "Folks don't go to wars for fun. A man don't leave his maw crying just for fun."

"Then why are you going?" I said.

"I got to," he said. "I just got to. Now you go on to sleep. I got to ketch that early bus in the morning."

"All right," I said. "I hear tell Memphis is a big place. How will you find where the Army's at?"

"I'll ask somebody where to go to join it," Pete said. "Go on to sleep now."

"Is that what you'll ask for? Where to join the Army?" I said.

"Yes," Pete said. He turned onto his back again. "Shut up and go to sleep."

We went to sleep. The next morning we et breakfast by lamplight because the bus would pass at six o'clock. Maw wasn't crying now. She jest looked grim and busy, putting breakfast on the table while we et it. Then she finished packing Pete's grip, except he never wanted to take no grip to the war, but maw said decent folks never went nowhere, not even to a war, without a change of clothes and something to tote them in. She put in the shoe box of fried chicken and biscuits and she put the Bible in, too, and then it was time to go. We didn't know until then that maw wasn't going to the bus. She jest brought Pete's cap and overcoat, and still she didn't cry no more, she jest stood with her hands on Pete's shoulders and she didn't move, but somehow, and jest holding Pete's shoulders, she looked as hard and fierce as when Pete had turned toward me in the bed last night and tole me that anyway I was all right.

"They could take the country and keep the country, so long as they never bothered me and mine," she said. Then she said, "Don't never forget who you are. You ain't rich and the rest of the world outside of Frenchman's Bend never heard of you. But your blood is good as any blood anywhere, and don't you never forget it."

Then she kissed him, and then we was out of the house, with pap toting Pete's grip whether Pete wanted him to or not. There wasn't no dawn even yet, not even after we had stood on the highway by the mailbox, a while. Then we seen the lights of the bus coming and I was watching the bus until it come up and Pete flagged it, and then, sho enough, there was daylight—it had started while I wasn't watching. And now me and Pete expected pap to say something else foolish, like he done before, about how Uncle Marsh getting wounded in France and that trip to Texas pap taken in 1918 ought to be enough to save the Unity States in 1942, but he never. He done all right too. He jest said, "Good-by, son. Always remember what your ma told you and write her whenever you find the time." Then he shaken Pete's hand, and Pete looked at me a minute and put his hand on my head and rubbed my head durn nigh hard enough to wring my neck off and jumped into the bus, and the feller wound the door shut and the bus began to hum, then it was moving, humming and grinding and whining louder and louder; it was going fast, with two little red lights behind it that never seemed to get no littler, but just seemed to be running together until pretty soon they would touch and jest be one light. But they never did, and then the bus was gone, and even like it was, I could have pretty nigh busted out crying, nigh to nine years old and all.

Me and pap went back to the house. All that day we worked at the wood tree, and so I never had no good chance until about middle of the afternoon. Then I taken my slingshot and I would have liked to took all my bird eggs, too, because Pete had give me his collection and he holp me with mine, and he would like to git the box out and look at them as good as I would, even if he was nigh twenty years old. But the box was too big to tote a long ways and have to worry with, so I just taken the shikepoke egg, because it was the best un, and wropped it up good into a matchbox and hid it and the slingshot under the corner of the barn. Then we et supper and went to bed, and I thought then how if I would 'a' had to stayed in that room and that bed like that even for one more night, I jest couldn't 'a' stood it. Then I could hear pap snoring, but I never heard no sound from maw, whether she was asleep or not, and I don't reckon she was. So I taken my shoes and drapped them out the window, and then I clumb out like I used to watch Pete do when he was still jest seventeen and pap held that he was too young yet to be tomcatting around at night, and wouldn't leave him out, and I put on my shoes and went to the barn and got the slingshot and the shikepoke egg and went to the highway.

It wasn't cold, it was jest durn confounded dark, and that highway stretched on in front of me like, without nobody using it, it had stretched out half again as fer just like a man does when he lays down, so that for a time it looked like full sun was going to ketch me before I had finished them twenty-two miles to Jefferson. But it didn't. Day-break was jest starting when I walked up the hill into town. I could smell breakfast cooking in the cabins and I wished I had thought to brought me a cold biscuit, but that was too late now. And Pete had told me Memphis was a piece beyond Jefferson, but I never knowed it was no eighty miles. So I stood there on that empty square, with daylight coming and coming and the street lights still burning and that Law looking down at me, and me still eighty miles from Memphis, and it had took me all night to walk jest twenty-two miles, and so, by the time I got to Memphis at that rate, Pete would 'a' done already started for Pearl Harbor.

"Where do you come from?" the Law said.

And I told him again. "I got to git to Memphis. My brother's there."

"You mean you ain't got any folks around here?" the Law said. "Nobody but that brother? What are you doing way off down here and your brother in Memphis?"

And I told him again, "I got to git to Memphis. I ain't got no time to waste talking about it and I ain't got time to walk it. I got to git there today."

"Come on here," the Law said.

We went down another street. And there was the bus, just like when Pete got into it yestiddy morning, except there wasn't no lights on it now and it was empty. There was a regular bus dee-po like a railroad dee-po, with a ticket counter and a feller behind it, and the Law said, "Set down over there," and I set down on the bench, and the Law said, "I want to use your telephone," and he talked in the telephone a minute and put it down and said to the feller behind the ticket counter, "Keep your eye on him. I'll be back as soon as Mrs. Habersham can arrange to get herself up and dressed." He went out. I got up and went to the ticket counter.

"I want to go to Memphis," I said.

"You bet," the feller said. "You set down on the bench now. Mr. Foote will be back in a minute."

"I don't know no Mr. Foote," I said. "I want to ride that bus to Memphis."

"You got some money?" he said. "It'll cost you seventy-two cents."

I taken out the matchbox and unwropped the shikepoke egg. "I'll swap you this for a ticket to Memphis," I said.

"What's that?" he said.

"It's a shikepoke egg," I said. "You never seen one before. It's worth a dollar. I'll take seventy-two cents fer it."

"No," he said, "the fellers that own that bus insist on a cash basis. If I started swapping tickets for bird eggs and livestock and such, they would fire me. You go and set down on the bench now, like Mr. Foote——"

I started for the door, but he caught me, he put one hand on the ticket counter and jumped over it and caught up with me and reached his hand out to ketch my shirt. I whupped out my pocketknife and snapped it open.

"You put a hand on me and I'll cut it off," I said.

I tried to dodge him and run at the door, but he could move quicker than any grown man I ever see, quick as Pete almost. He cut me off and stood with his back against the door and one foot raised a little, and there wasn't no other way to get out. "Get back on that bench and stay there," he said.

And there wasn't no other way out. And he stood there with his back against the door. So I went back to the bench. And then it seemed like to me that dee-po was full of folks. There was that Law again, and there was two ladies in fur coats and their faces already painted. But they still looked like they had got up in a hurry and they still never liked it, a old one and a young one, looking down at me.

"He hasn't got a overcoat!" the old one said. "How in the world did he ever get down here by himself?"

"I ask you," the Law said. "I couldn't get nothing out of him except his brother is in Memphis and he wants to get back up there."

"That's right," I said. "I got to git to Memphis today."

"Of course you must," the old one said. "Are you sure you can find your brother when you get to Memphis?"

"I reckon I can," I said. "I ain't got but one and I have knowed him all my life. I reckon I will know him again when I see him."

The old one looked at me. "Somehow he doesn't look like he lives in Memphis," she said.

"He probably don't," the Law said. "You can't tell though. He might live any-where, overhalls or not. This day and time they get scattered overnight from he——

hope to breakfast; boys and girls, too, almost before they can walk good. He might have been in Missouri or Texas either yestiddy, for all we know. But he don't seem to have any doubt his brother is in Memphis. All I know to do is send him up there and leave him look.''

"Yes,'' the old one said.

The young one set down on the bench by me and opened a hand satchel and taken out a artermatic writing pen and some papers.

"Now, honey,'' the old one said, "we're going to see that you find your brother, but we must have a case history for our files first. We want to know your name and your brother's name and where you were born and when your parents died.''

"I don't need no case history neither,'' I said. "All I want is to git to Memphis. I got to git there today.''

"You see?'' the Law said. He said it almost like he enjoyed it. "That's what I told you.''

"You're lucky, at that, Mrs. Habersham,'' the bus feller said. "I don't think he's got a gun on him, but he can open that knife da—— I mean, fast enought to suit any man.''

But the old one just stood there looking at me.

"Well,'' she said. "Well. I really don't know what to do.''

"I do,'' the bus feller said. "I'm going to give him a ticket out of my own pocket, as a measure of protecting the company against riot and bloodshed. And when Mr. Foote tells the city board about it, it will be a civic matter and they will not only reimburse me, they will give me a medal too. Hey, Mr. Foote?''

But never nobody paid him no mind. The old one still stood looking down at me. She said "Well,'' again. Then she taken a dollar from her purse and give it to the bus feller. "I suppose he will travel on a child's ticket, won't he?''

"Wellum,'' the bus feller said, "I just don't know what the regulations would be. Likely I will be fired for not crating him and marking the crate Poison. But I'll risk it.''

Then they were gone. Then the Law come back with a sandwich and give it to me.

"You're sure you can find that brother?'' he said.

"I ain't yet convinced why not,'' I said. "If I don't see Pete first, he'll see me. He knows me too.''

Then the Law went out for good, too, and I et the sandwich. Then more folks come in and bought tickets, and then the bus feller said it was time to go, and I got into the bus just like Pete done, and we was gone.

I seen all the towns. I seen all of them. When the bus got to going good, I found out I was jest about wore out for sleep. But there was too much I hadn't never saw before. We run out of Jefferson and run past fields and woods, then we would run into another town and out of that un and past fields and woods again, and then into another town with stores and gins and water tanks, and we run along by the railroad for a spell and I seen the signal arm move, and then I seen the train and then some more towns, and I was jest about plumb wore out for sleep, but I couldn't risk it. Then Memphis begun. It seemed like, to me, it went on for miles. We would pass a patch of stores and I would think that was sholy it and the bus would even stop. But it wouldn't be Memphis yet and we would go on again past water tanks and smokestacks on top of the mills, and if they was gins and sawmills, I never knowed there was that many and I never seen any that big, and where they got enough cotton and logs to run um I don't know.

Then I see Memphis. I knowed I was right this time. It was standing up into the air. It looked like about a dozen whole towns bigger than Jefferson was set up on one edge in a field, standing up into the air higher than ara hill in all Yoknapatawpha County. Then we was in it, with the bus stopping ever' few feet, it seemed like to me, and cars rushing past on both sides of it and the street crowded with folks from ever'where in town that day, until I didn't see how there could 'a' been nobody left in Mis'sippi a-tall to even sell me a bus ticket, let alone write out no case histories. Then the bus stopped. It was another bus dee-po, a heap bigger than the one in Jefferson. And I said, "All right. Where do folks join the Army?"

"What?" the bus feller said.

And I said it again, "Where do folks join the Army?"

"Oh," he said. Then he told me how to get there. I was afraid at first I wouldn't ketch on how to do in a town big as Memphis. But I caught on all right. I never had to ask but twice more. Then I was there, and I was durn glad to git out of all them rushing cars and shoving folks and all that racket for a spell, and I thought, It won't be long now, and I thought how if there was any kind of a crowd there that had done already joined the Army, too, Pete would likely see me before I seen him. And so I walked into the room. And Pete wasn't there.

He wasn't even there. There was soldier with a big arrerhead on his sleeve, writing, and two fellers standing in front of him, and there was some more folks there, I reckon. It seems to me I remember some more folks there.

I went to the table where the soldier was writing, and I said, "Where's Pete?" and he looked up and I said, "My brother. Pete Grier. Where is he?"

"What?" the soldier said. "Who?"

And I told him again. "He joined the Army yestiddy. He's going to Pearl Harbor. So am I. I want to ketch him. Where you all got him?" Now they were all looking at me, but I never paid them no mind. "Come on," I said. "Where is he?"

The soldier had quit writing. He had both hands spraddled out on the table. "Oh," he said. "You're going, too, hah?"

"Yes," I said. "They got to have wood and water. I can chop it and tote it. Come on. Where's Pete?"

The soldier stood up. "Who let you in here?" he said. "Go on. Beat it."

"Durn that," I said. "You tell me where Pete——"

I be dog if he couldn't move faster than the bus feller even. He never come over the table, he come around it, he was on me almost before I knowed it, so that I jest had time to jump back and whup out my pocketknife and snap it open and hit one lick, and he hollered and jumped back and grabbed one hand with the other and stood there cussing and hollering.

One of the other fellers grabbed me from behind, and I hit at him with the knife, but I couldn't reach him.

Then both of the fellers had me from behind, and then another soldier come out of a door at the back. He had on a belt with a britching strop over one shoulder.

"What the hell is this?" he said.

"That little son cut me with a knife!" the first soldier hollered. When he said that, I tried to get at him again, but both them fellers was holding me, two against one, and the soldier with the backing strop said, "Here, here. Put your knife up, feller. None of us are armed. A man don't knife-fight folks that are barehanded." I could begin to hear him then. He sounded jest like Pete talked to me. "Let him go," he said. They let me go. "Now what's all the trouble about?" And I told him. "I see," he said. "And you come up to see if he was all right before he left."

"No," I said. "I came to——"

But he had already turned to where the first soldier was wropping a handkerchief around his hand.

"Have you got him?" he said. The first soldier went back to the table and looked at some papers.

"Here he is," he said. "He enlisted yestiddy. He's in a detachment leaving this morning for Little Rock." He had a watch stropped on his arm. He looked at it. "The train leaves in about fifty minutes. If I know country boys, they're probably all down there at the station right now."

"Get him up here," the one with the backing strop said. "Phone the station. Tell the porter to get him a cab. And you come with me," he said.

It was another office behind that un, with jest a table and some chairs. We set there while the soldier smoked, and it wasn't long; I knowed Pete's feet soon as I heard them. Then the first soldier opened the door and Pete come in. He never had no soldier clothes on. He looked jest like he did when he got on the bus yestiddy morning, except it seemed to me like it was at least a week, so much had happened, and I had done had to do so much traveling. He come in and there he was, looking at me like he hadn't never left home, except that here we was in Memphis, on the way to Pearl Harbor.

"What in durnation are you doing here?" he said.

And I told him, "You got to have wood and water to cook with. I can chop it and tote it for you-all."

"No," Pete said. "you're going back home."

"No, Pete," I said. "I got to go too. I got to. It hurts my heart, Pete."

"No," Pete said. He looked at the soldier. "I jest don't know what could have happened to him, lootenant," he said. "He never drawed a knife on anybody before in his life." He looked at me. "What did you do it for?"

"I don't know," I said. "I jest had to. I jest had to git here. I jest had to find you."

"Well, don't you never do it again, you hear?" Pete said. "You put that knife in your pocket and you keep it there. If I ever again hear of you drawing it on anybody, I'm coming back from wherever I am at and whup the fire out of you. You hear me?"

"I would pure cut a throat if it would bring you back to stay," I said. "Pete," I said. "Pete."

"No," Pete said. Now his voice wasn't hard and quick no more, it was almost quiet, and I knowed now I wouldn't never change him. "You must go home. You must look after maw, and I am depending on you to look after my ten acres. I want you to go back home. Today. Do you hear?"

"I hear," I said.

"Can he get back home by himself?" the soldier said.

"He come up here by himself," Pete said.

"I can get back, I reckon," I said. "I don't live in but one place. I don't reckon it's moved."

Pete taken a dollar out of his pocket and give it to me. "That'll buy your bus ticket right to our mailbox," he said. "I want you to mind the lootenant. He'll send you to the bus. And you go back home and you take care of maw and look after my ten acres and keep that durn knife in your pocket. You hear me?"

"Yes, Pete," I said.

"All right," Pete said. "Now I got to go." He put his hand on my head again. But this time he never wrung my neck. He just laid his hand on my head a minute. And then I be dog if he didn't lean down and kiss me, and I heard his feet and then the door, and I never looked up and that was all, me setting there, rubbing the place where Pete kissed me and the soldier throwed back in his chair, looking out the window and coughing. He reached into his pocket and handed something to me without looking around. It was a piece of chewing gum.

"Much obliged," I said. "Well, I reckon I might as well start back. I got a right fer piece to go."

"Wait," the soldier said. Then he telephoned again and I said again I better start back, and he said again, "Wait. Remember what Pete told you."

So we waited, and then another lady come in, old, too, in a fur coat, too, but she smelled all right, she never had no artermatic writing pen nor no case history neither. She come in and the soldier got up, and she looked around quick until she saw me, and come and put her hand on my shoulder light and quick and easy as maw herself might 'a' done it.

"Come on," she said. "Let's go home to dinner."

"Nome," I said. "I got to ketch the bus to Jefferson."

"I know. There's plenty of time. We'll go home and eat dinner first."

She had a car. And now we was right down in the middle of all them other cars. We was almost under the busses, and all them crowds of people on the street close enough to where I could have talked to them if I had knowed who they was. After a while she stopped the car. "Here we are," she said, and I looked at it, and if all that was her house, she sho had a big family. But all of it wasn't. We crossed a hall with trees growing in it and went into a little room without nothing in it but a nigger dressed up in a uniform a heap shinier than them soldiers had, and the nigger shut the door, and then I hollered, "Look out!" and grabbed, but it was all right; that whole little room jest went right on up and stopped and the door opened and we was in another hall, and the lady unlocked a door and we went in, and there was another soldier, a old feller, with a britching strop, too, and a silver-colored bird on each shoulder.

"Here we are," the lady said. "This is Colonel McKellogg. Now, what would you like for dinner?"

"I reckon I'll jest have some ham and eggs and coffee," I said.

She had done started to pick up the telephone. She stopped. "Coffee?" she said. "When did you start drinking coffee?"

"I don't know," I said. "I reckon it was before I could remember."

"You're about eight, aren't you?" she said.

"Nome," I said. "I'm eight and ten months. Going on eleven months."

She telephoned then. Then we set there and I told them how Pete had jest left that morning for Pearl Harbor and I had aimed to go with him, but I would have to go back home to take care of maw and look after Pete's ten acres, and she said how they had a little boy about my size, too, in a school in the East. Then a nigger, another one, in a short kind of shirttail coat, rolled a kind of wheelbarrer in. It had my ham and eggs and a glass of milk and a piece of pie, too, and I thought I was hungry. But when I taken the first bite I found out I couldn't swallow it, and I got up quick.

"I got to go," I said.

"Wait," she said.

"I got to go," I said.

"Just a minute," she said. "I've already telephoned for the car. It won't be but a minute now. Can't you drink the milk even? Or maybe some of your coffee?"

"Nome, " I said. "I ain't hungry. I'll eat when I git home." Then the telephone rung. She never even answered it.

"There," she said. "There's the car." And we went back down in that 'ere little moving room with the dressed-up nigger. This time it was a big car with a soldier driving it. I got into the front with him. She give the soldier a dollar. "He might get hungry," she said. "Try to find a decent place for him."

"O.K., Mrs. McKellogg," the soldier said.

Then we was gone again. And now I could see Memphis good, bright in the sunshine, while we was swinging around it. And first thing I knowed, we was back on the same highway the bus run on this morning—the patches of stores and them big gins and sawmills, and Memphis running on for miles, it seemed like to me, before it begun to give out. Then we was running again between the fields and woods, running fast now, and except for that soldier, it was like I hadn't never been to Memphis a-tall. We was going fast now. At this rate, before I knowed it we would be home again, and I thought about me riding up to Frenchman's Bend in this big car with a soldier running it, and all of a sudden I begun to cry. I never knowed I was fixed to, and I couldn't stop it. I set there by that soldier, crying. We was going fast.

QUESTIONS

1   How do we initially know that the narrator's relationship to his brother is closer than any other that he has?
2   What points in the journey parallel the narrator's symbolic journey into understanding? What does he come to understand?

TOPIC FOR COMPOSITION

Write a narrative essay, based on an experience you had by which you learned something about yourself. Make certain that your reader's impression of the experience is vivid and that the reader clearly sees that what you learned is an outgrowth of the experience.

Irwin Shaw's story, "Pattern of Love," presents the confusions that plague each of us as we become aware of our own sexuality. Shaw seems to say that such awareness is archetypal and that it manifests another pattern, more often than not, that is also archetypal. The latter pattern, of course, is the "eternal triangle." Note how each of the three main characters reacts to the first pattern and how Harold and Charley react to the second.

PATTERN OF LOVE

Irwin Shaw

"I'll go into a nunnery," Katherine said, holding her books rigidly at her side, as they walked down the street toward Harold's house. "I'll retire from the world."

Harold peered uneasily at her through his glasses. "You can't do that," he said. "They won't let you do that."

"Oh, yes, they will." Katherine walked stiffly, looking squarely in front of her, wishing that Harold's house was ten blocks farther on. "I'm a Catholic and I can go into a nunnery."

"There's no need to do that," said Harold.

"Do you think I'm pretty?" Katherine asked. "I'm not looking for compliments. I want to know for a private reason."

"I think you're pretty," Harold said. "I think you're about the prettiest girl in school."

"Everybody says so," Katherine said, worrying over the "about," but not showing it in her face. "Of course I don't really think so, but that's what everybody says. You don't seem to think so, either."

"Oh, yes," said Harold. "Oh, yes."

"From the way you act," Katherine said.

"It's hard to tell things sometimes," Harold said, "by the way people act."

"I love you," Katherine said coldly.

Harold took off his glasses and rubbed them nervously with his handkerchief. "What about Charley Lynch?" he asked, working on his glasses, not looking at Katherine. "Everybody knows you and Charley Lynch . . ."

"Don't you even like me?" Katherine asked stonily.

"Sure. I like you very much. But Charley Lynch . . ."

"I'm through with him." Katherine's teeth snapped as she said it. "I've had enough of him."

"He's a very nice fellow," Harold said, putting his glasses on. "He's the captain of the baseball team and he's the president of the eighth grade and . . ."

"He doesn't interest me," Katherine said, "any more."

They walked silently. Harold subtly increased his speed as they neared his house.

"I have two tickets to Loew's for tonight," Katherine said.

"Thanks," said Harold. "I've got to study."

"Eleanor Greenberg is giving a party on Saturday night." Katherine subtly slowed down as she saw Harold's house getting nearer, "I can bring anyone I want. Would you be interested?"

"My grandmother's," Harold said. "We're going to my grandmother's on Saturday. She lives in Doylestown, Pennsylvania. She has seven cows. I go there in the summertime. I know how to milk the cows and they . . ."

"Thursday night," Katherine said, speaking quickly. "My mother and father go out on Thursday night to play bridge and they don't come home till one o'clock in the morning. I'm all alone, me and the baby, and the baby sleeps in her own room. I'm all alone," she said in harsh invitation. "Would you like to come up and keep me company?"

Harold swallowed unhappily. He felt the blush come up over his collar, surge under his glasses. He coughed loudly, so that if Katherine noticed the blush, she'd think it came from the violence of his coughing.

"Should I slap you on the back?" Katherine asked eagerly.

"No, thank you," Harold said clearly, his coughing gone.

"Do you want to come up Thursday night?"

"I would like to very much," Harold said, "but my mother doesn't let me out at night yet. She says when I'm fifteen . . ."

Katherine's face set in grim lines. "I saw you in the library at eight o'clock at night, Wednesday."

"The library's different," Harold said weakly. "My mother makes an exception."

"You could tell her you were going to the library," Katherine said. "What's to stop you?"

Harold took a deep, miserable breath. "Every time I lie my mother knows it," he said. "Anyway, you shouldn't lie to your mother."

Katherine's lip curled with cold amusement. "You make me laugh," she said.

They came to the entrance to the apartment house in which Harold lived, and halted.

"In the afternoons," Katherine said, " a lot of times nobody's home in the afternoons but me. On your way home from school you could whistle when you pass my window, my room's in front, and I could open the window and whistle back."

"I'm awful busy," Harold said, noticing uneasily that Johnson, the doorman, was watching him. "I've got baseball practice with the Montauk A.C. every afternoon and I got to practice the violin a hour a day and I'm behind in history, there's a lot of chapters I got to read before next month and . . ."

"I'll walk home every afternoon with you," Katherine said. "From school. You have to walk home from school, don't you?"

Harold sighed. "We practice in the school orchestra almost every afternoon." He stared unhappily at Johnson, who was watching him with the knowing, cynical expression of doormen who see everyone leave and everyone enter and have their own opinions of all entrances and exits. "We're working on 'Poet and Peasant' and it's very hard on the first violins and I never know what time we'll finish and . . ."

"I'll wait for you," Katherine said, looking straight into his eyes, bitterly, not hiding anything. "I'll sit at the girl's entrance and I'll wait for you."

"Sometimes," said Harold, "we don't get through till five o'clock."

"I'll wait for you."

Harold looked longingly at the doorway to the apartment house, heavy gilt iron and cold glass. "I'll admit something," he said "I don't like girls very much. I got a lot of other things on my mind."

"You walk home from school with Elaine," Katherine said. "I've seen you."

"O.K.," Harold shouted, wishing he could punch the rosy, soft face, the large, coldly accusing blue eyes, the red, quivering lips. "O.K.!" he shouted, "I walk home with Elaine! What's it to you? I like to walk home with Elaine! Leave me alone! You've got Charley Lynch. He's a big hero, he pitches for the baseball team. I couldn't even play right field. Leave me alone!"

"I don't want him!" Katherine shouted. "I'm not interested in Charley Lynch! I hate you!" she cried, "I hate you! I'm going to retire to a nunnery!"

"Good!" Harold said. "Very good!" He opened the door of the apartment house. Johnson watched him coldly, unmoving, knowing everything.

"Harold," Katherine said softly, touching his arm sorrowfully, "Harold—if you happen to pass my house, whistle 'Begin the Beguine.' Then I'll know it's you. 'Begin the Beguine,' Harold . . ."

He shook her hand off, went inside. She watched him walk without looking back at her, open the elevator door, go in, press a button. The door closed finally and irrevocably behind him. The tears nearly came, but she fought them down. She looked miserably up at the fourth-story window behind which he slept.

She turned and dragged slowly down the block toward her own house. As she reached the corner, her eyes on the pavement before her, a boy spurted out and bumped her.

"Oh, excuse me," said the boy. She looked up.

"What do you want, Charley?" she asked coldly.

Charley Lynch smiled at her, forcing it. "Isn't it funny, my bumping into you? Actually bumping into you. I wasn't watching where I was going, I was thinking of something else and . . ."

"Yeah," said Katherine, starting briskly toward home. "Yeah."

"You want to know what I was thinking about?" Charley asked softly, falling in beside her.

"Excuse me," Katherine said, throwing her head back, all tears gone, looking at a point thirty feet up in the evening sky. "I'm in a hurry."

"I was thinking of that night two months ago," Charley said quickly. "That party Norah O'Brien gave. That night I took you home and I kissed your neck. Remember that?"

"No," she said. She walked at top speed across the street corner, down the row of two-story houses, all alike, with the children playing potsy and skating and leaping out from behind stoops and going, "A-a-a-a-a-h," pointing pistols and machine guns at each other. "Pardon me, I've got to get home and mind the baby; my mother has to go out."

"You weren't in a hurry with Harold," Charley said, his eyes hot and dry, as he matched her step for step. "You walked slow enough with him."

Katherine looked briefly and witheringly at Charley Lynch. "I don't know why you think that's your business," she said. "It's my own affair."

"Last month," Charley said, "you used to walk home with me."

"That was last month," Katherine said loudly.

"What've I done?" Pain sat clearly on Charley Lynch's face, plain over the freckles and the child's nose with the bump on it where a baseball bat had once hit it. "Please tell me what I've done, Katie."

"Nothing," said Katherine, her voice bored and businesslike. "Absolutely nothing."

Charley Lynch avoided three small children who were dueling seriously with wooden swords that clanged on the garbage-pail cover shields with which they protected themselves. "I must have done something," he said sorrowfully.

"Nothing!" Katherine's tones were clipped and final.

"Put 'em up, Stranger!" a seven-year-old boy said right in front of Charley. He had a pistol and was pointing it at a boy who had another pistol. "This town ain't big enough for you and me, Stranger," said the first little boy as Charley went around him, keeping his eyes on Katherine. "I'll give you twenty-four hours and then come out shooting."

"Oh, yeah?" said the second little boy with the pistol.

"Do you want to go to the movies tonight?" Charley asked eagerly, rejoining Katherine, safely past the Westerners. "Cary Grant. Everybody says it's a very funny picture."

"I would love to go," said Katherine, "but I've got to catch up on my reading tonight."

Charley walked silently among the dueling, wrestling, gun-fighting children. Katherine walked slightly head of him, head up, pink and round and rosy-kneed, and Charley looked at the spot on her neck where he had kissed her for the first time and felt his soul drop out of his body.

He laughed suddenly, falsely. Katherine didn't even look at him. "I was thinking about that feller," Charley said. "That Harold. What a name—Harold! He went out for the baseball team and the coach threw him out the first day. The coach hit three balls at him and they went right through his legs. Then he hit another one at him and it bounced and smacked him right in the nose. You should've seen the look on that Harold's face." Charley chuckled shrilly. "We all nearly died laughing. Right square in the nose. You know what all the boys call him? 'Four-eyed Oscar.' He can't see first base from home plate. 'Four-eyed Oscar.' Isn't that funny?" Charley asked miserably.

"He's very nice about you," Katherine turned into the vestibule of her own house. "He tells me he admires you very much; he thinks you're a nice boy."

The last trace of the manufactured smile left Charley's face. "None of the other girls can stand him," Charley said flatly. "They laugh at him."

Katherine smiled secretly, remembering the little girls' conversations in the wardrobes and at recess.

"You think I'm lying!" Charley shouted. "Just ask."

Katherine shrugged coolly, her hand on the inner door leading to her house. Charley moved close to her in the vestibule gloom.

"Come to the movies with me," he whispered. "Please, Katie, please . . ."

"As I told you," she said, "I'm busy."

He put his hand out gropingly, touched hers. "Katie," he begged.

She pulled her hand away sharply, opened the door. "I haven't the time," she said loudly.

"Please, please . . ." he whispered.

Katherine shook her head.

Charley spread his arms slowly, lunged for Katherine, hugged her, tried to kiss her. She pulled her head savagely to the side, kicked him sharply in the shins. "Please . . ." Charley wept.

"Get out of here!" Katherine slapped his chest with her hands.

Charley backed up. "You used to let me kiss you," he said. "Why not now?"

"I can't be bothered," Katherine pulled down her dress with sharp, decisive, warning movements.

"I'll tell your mother," Charley shouted desperately. "You're going around with a Methodist! With a Protestant!"

Katherine's eyes grew large with fury, her cheeks flooded with blood, her mouth tightened. "Now get out of here!" she said. "I'm through with you! I don't want to talk to you. I don't want you to follow me around!"

"I'll walk wherever I goddamn please!" Charley yelled.

"I heard what you said," Katherine said. "I heard the word you used."

"I'll follow whoever I goddam please!" Charley yelled even louder. "This is a free country."

"I'll never talk to you as long as I live," Katherine stamped for emphasis, and her voice rang off the mailboxes and doorknobs of the vestibule. "You bore me! I'm not interested in you. You're stupid! I don't like you. You're a big idiot! Go home!"

"I'll break his neck for him!" Charley shouted, his eyes clouded, his hands waving wildly in front of Katherine's face. "I'll show him! A violin player! When I get through with him you won't be so anxious to be seen with him. Do you kiss him?"

"Yes!" Katherine's voice clanged triumphantly. "I kiss him all the time. And he really knows how to kiss! He doesn't slobber all over a girl, like you!"

"Please," Charley whimpered, "please . . ." Hands out gropingly, he went toward Katherine. She drew back her arm coldly, and with all her round, solid, well-nourished eighty-five pounds, caught him across the face, turned, and fled up the stairs.

"I'll kill him!" Charley roared up the stairwell. "I'll kill that violinist with my bare hands!"

The door slammed in answer. . . .

"Please tell Mr. Harold Pursell," Charley said soberly to Johnson, the doorman, "that a certain friend of his is waiting downstairs; he would like to see him, if it's convenient."

Johnson went up in the elevator and Charley looked with grim satisfaction around the circle of faces of his eight friends, who had come with him to see that everything was carried out in proper order.

Harold stepped out of the elevator, walked toward the boys grouped at the doorway. He peered curiously and short-sightedly at them, as he approached, neat, clean, white-fingered, with his glasses.

"Hello," Charley stepped out and faced Harold. "I would like to talk to you in private."

Harold looked around at the silent ring of faces, drained of pity, brimming with punishment. He sighed, realizing what he was in for.

"All right," he said, and opened the door, holding it while all the boys filed out.

The walk to the vacant lot in the next block was performed in silence, broken only by the purposeful tramp of Charley Lynch's seconds.

"Take off your glasses," Charley said when they reached the exact center of the lot.

Harold took off his glasses, looked hesitantly for a place to put them.

"I'll hold them," Sam Rosenberg, Charley's lieutenant, said politely.

"Thanks," Harold said, giving him the glasses. He turned and faced Charley, blinking slowly. He put up his hands. "O.K." he said.

Charley stood there, breathing deeply, his enemy, blinking, thin-armed, pale, twenty pounds lighter than Charley, before him. A deep wave of exultation rolled through Charley's blood. He put up his hands carefully, stepped in and hit Harold square on the eye with his right hand.

The fight did not take long, although it took longer than Charley had expected. Harold kept punching, advancing into the deadly fire of Charley's fists, the most potent and sharp and brutal in the whole school. Harold's face smeared immediately with blood, and his eye closed, and his shirt tore and the blood soaked in down his clothes. Charley walked in flat-footed, not seeking to dodge or block Harold's weak punches. Charley felt his knuckles smashing against skin and bone and eye, and running with blood, half-delirious with pleasure, as Harold reeled and fell into the cruel, unpitying fists. Even the knuckles on his hands, and the tendons in Charley's fists, carrying the shock of the battle up to his shoulders, seemed to enjoy the pitiless administration of punishment.

From time to time Harold grunted, when Charley took time off from hitting him in the head to hit him, hooking upward from his ankles, in the belly. Except for that, the battle was conducted in complete quiet. The eight friends of Charley watched soberly, professionally, making no comment, finally watching Harold sink to the ground, not unconscious, but too exhausted to move a finger, and lie, spread out, his bloody face pressed harshly, but gratefully, into the dust and rubble of the vacant lot.

Charley stood over the fallen enemy, breathing heavily, his fists tingling joyfully, happy to see the weak, hated, frail figure face down and helpless on the ground, sorry that the pleasure of beating that figure was over. He watched in silence for a minute until Harold moved.

"All right," Harold said, his face still in the dirt. "That's enough." He lifted his head, slowly sat up, then, with a trembling hand, pulled himself to his feet. He wavered, his arms out from his sides and shaking uncontrollably, but he held his feet. "May I have my glasses?" he asked.

Silently, Sam Rosenberg, Charley's lieutenant, gave Harold his glasses. Harold fumblingly, with shaking hands, put them on. Charley watched him, the incongruously undamaged glasses on the damaged face. Suddenly Charley realized that he was crying. He, Charley Lynch, victor in fifty more desperate battles, who had shed no tear since the time he was spanked at the age of four, was weeping uncontrollably, his body shaken with sobs, his eyes hot and smarting. As he wept, he realized that he had been sobbing all through the fight, from the first righthand to the eye until the final sinking, face-first, of the enemy into the dirt. Charley looked at Harold, eye closed, nose swollen and to one side, hair sweated and muddy, mouth all gore and mud, but the face, the spirit behind it, calm, unmoved. Harold wasn't crying then, Charley knew, as he sobbed bitterly, and he wouldn't cry later, and nothing he, Charley Lynch, could ever do would make him cry.

Harold took a deep breath and slowly walked off, without a word.

Charley watched him, the narrow, unheroic, torn and bedraggled back, dragging off. The tears swelled up in a blind flood and Harold disappeared from view behind them.

QUESTIONS

1 How can we explain the inconsistency in Katherine's attitudes toward Harold and Charley?
2 D. H. Lawrence once observed that girls comprehend their own sexuality at an earlier age than boys. Is there evidence of that in Shaw's story?
3 Why does Charley fight? Why does Harold fight?
4 What does the fight resolve? What does Charley's crying mean?

TOPIC FOR COMPOSITION

Using Fromm's definition of love—giving, caring, etc.—as your basis, argue that Shaw's characters illustrate a formative stage of love that as yet has nothing to do with Fromm's definition.

☐

Through her narrator's consciousness, fragmented in time and place, Joyce Carol Oates structures a story of agonized love, casual indifference, marital bliss, and marital "wretchedness." Thus a literary device, which uses the "stream of consciousness" of a character seemingly free of its author's control, becomes the apt title of Miss Oates's story. "An Interior Monologue" is an *interior monologue,* appropriate in technique and subject matter because, as the story implies, love is not easily verbalized. It is, at best, sensory and illusory.

AN INTERIOR MONOLOGUE

Joyce Carol Oates

I am fascinated with that woman. I am a chemist and fascination comes hard with me. I am thirty-one years old, I live alone, my hours are spent concentrating on the cool reality of beakers and statistics, plastics of various types, the icy fuzz of sweat on tubes, the low mysterious hum of machines. Sitting at my workbench, I sometimes glance down at my fingertips, imagining a fine fuzz of ice on them. There is no ice. My fingers are long and lean. I have the idea that they are artistic-looking, though I am not an artist. If I were, I would do something with this laboratory, paint a picture of it, the way it looks at six o'clock in the evening, at quarter after six—glass, enamel, rubber tubes, stoppers, the terrible, powerful pull of vibrations from cooling machines, the terrible power of shadows moving slowly over everything, over me running right down to my fingertips.

THE MEETING

She and X met in a library. They talk about that meeting often. Out with X in a bar once—where I had only a Coke, since I don't drink—he talked about it in a kind of drunken frenzy, giving me details. "Don't stop, tell me everything!" I wanted to cry out to him. X is a gentle, dark-browed young man, about my age. I say about my age: he is really twenty-eight. His hair falls down onto his forehead when he gets excited.

The essential factor that changed our lives, the lives of all three of us, was that meeting.

She sat at a table, her books sprawled out around her. I can picture that. She is sloppy, self-conscious and a little vain about it—she can get away with being sloppy, other girls can't. All right. She seats herself at the table. She is wearing something light, a cotton dress maybe (they don't give me enough details and I must fill in my own) and her charm bracelet, jingling with silver charms. She takes out her reading glasses and fools around with them, holding them up to the light. Very smudged. Her hair is the color of honey, that vain girl. I hate her hair, her white silly teeth, her nitwit's forehead with its flecks of bangs, all so wearily pretty. . . . Still, she is sitting there. I have to prod myself to keep this vision going. She is sitting there, sitting there, sitting there . . . and X comes in, a stranger, sits across from her, his eyes raw from reading, staying up all night, wasting his young life in bars around the University that are dark at eleven o'clock in the morning. He sits down. He lets his books fall beside him. Aching, his eyes ache, his shoulders ache, his very brain aches with precocious weariness, a young man twenty-three years old and already a few years too old for his classmates, feeding upon sophisticated crap in Philosophy 1A with a hunger they don't share. He notices the girl across from him. He can see right through her, through her head, to the periodical shelf behind her, where magazines from *Review of English Studies* to *Studies in Existential Psychology* are displayed.

Not suave, X, but brilliant and plodding; not glamorous, the young woman, but of a full, essential body and a teasing but kindly smile. They meet. They fall in love. They marry.

A TENNIS MATCH

She is not athletic, even with her frame, and is bored by tennis. X and I play tennis on Sunday mornings, in place of church. He was once a very devout Catholic and, falling away from it, saw the world turn to water, saw gnats swimming through it, lay awake weeping at night with his teeth chattering so that he had to bite the pillowcase to keep all his anguish secret from his family. When I broke away it was easier. I don't think I am less deep than X, but still it affected me less; a few ripples, nothing more. We play tennis on Sunday mornings, in place of church. I like the aggressive swing of an over-hand serve, I like the spots of perspiration on my shirt, I like a certain cool freshness to the air, even if this is Detroit's Palmer Park and the junk from last week's picnics lies everywhere. Don't look. Why look? X and I play tennis, calling out our scores. *She* sometimes comes along, carrying the baby. She reads magazines, sitting at a bench, her legs crossed. She wears cotton slacks. She sometimes has her hair brushed back, indifferent, sloppy, a twenty-five-year-old dowdy housewife. No matter: a few strokes of cheap makeup and her cheeks glow again, a few swipes of lipstick and there she is, Miss America, Miss Class of '65, sharp and quick and bright and given to flirting sloppily with me, so casual as to insult me, what does she care? "Here, my love, let me fix your collar behind. This little button—it's broken in half—isn't through the button-hole." And, while I perspire, standing very straight and forcing myself to think of test tubes, beakers, the cool clean perspiration of metal, she nonchalantly buttons that little button.

NONCHALANTLY

She drives me to use that word! I never use it myself. It isn't one of my words. Nothing is nonchalant with me. I received my Ph.D. degree in chemistry at the University of Michigan, 1964. Back in high school I was considered something of a genius—my chemistry teacher gave me a year's subscription to *Scientific American*. I dress casually but neatly, I try for a quiet, correct, uneventful look; I don't want to stick in any-one's eye.

I'M STILL HERE . . .

She is always there, always there! At the back of my mind, lounging. She was already a woman at the age of twelve, obviously. Knowing everything! Knowing everything at the age of eleven, at ten! Her honey-clear eyes, her curly hair, her sweet stupid smile . . . a little queen of the playground, taunting the boys. Oh, would I like to jet back in time to see her ascend the playground slide, pausing at the top with her queenly intolerant look, and setting herself down like a precious substance, precocious woman, and giving herself a push downward . . . . To rise up from under that slide, leering, an eagle of revenge, to grab hold of her legs at that halfway hump and pull her off! Or, instead, better yet, instead to tip the slide over—a giant heavy rusty thing, falling very slowly, falling on top of her. So much for that.

I'm still here. . . . Yes, I hear her cooing in my mind as I lie awake desperately thinking of ways to mend my life. *Her* life needs no mending. The other night when they had me over to dinner, a spaghetti supper, she said, right in front of X, "Out in California the divorce rate has finally caught up with the marriage rate. I was thinking about divorce, theoretically. I was thinking about how it would shake everything loose, make us see ourselves plainly and terribly. . . ." But she is only toying, only toying with X. She will never divorce him. He will never divorce her.

Or are they both toying with me?

I see her sideways grin, at me. She seems to wink. But she says only, innocently, "Alan, have some more more salad. I made this dressing especially for you."

LANDSCAPE OF NEUTRAL COLORS

She and I are in the supermarket, met by accident. She wears white shorts, the baby is fixed somehow in the shopping cart, pudgy legs stuck through the wire basket. Slight signs of fatigue under her eyes. Freckles on her upper arms, probably on her shoulders and back. Not many on her face: powdered over? There is fine, very fine fuzz on her upper lip, hardly worth mentioning. The small muscles of her arms and legs terrify me.

"Yes, I saw that Bergman movie, I hated it," she says.

"Why? Does madness frighten you?"

"Madness like that, on the screen, is terrible because . . . because you can't get away from it, even if you shut your eyes the sound is still there, and the feeling of madness . . . . It isn't like reading a book, you can close the book up. No. I hated it."

"Is it something personal, do you think?"

"Maybe."

"You could have walked out of the theater."

"I never walk out of theaters—not after I've paid to get in!"

"Did Bob like it?"

"Oh, you know Bob—" with a slight pleased shrug, of course *I don't really know Bob*—"He'll sit through anything. He sits through old late movies on television, James Cagney and Ginger Rogers, all that old crap—he's a very sentimental person."

"But why are you afraid of madness?" I say, pushing my cart along nimbly as I push the conversation back to this topic, feeling myself very much in control and very clever. "Isn't that a certain weakness in you? Shouldn't people want to experience as much as they can?"

"Oh hell."

"Should we turn our backs on any kind of experience?"

Too contemptuous to reply, she flashes me her cool schoolgirl's sideways smile, a smile that could suck my front teeth out, so venomous and delicious and unknowing! I'd like to buy her a balloon, a great pink and white striped balloon, I'd like to dress her up in the long, puffed-out dresses women wore in the paintings of Monet and Manet and Renoir, I'd like to paint very carefully over her cheeks, pinkening them, darkening the blue of her eyes, outlining her stubborn little eyebrows, giving her the glamor of a real woman—someone ageless, ancient, worthy of a man's death. I'd like to—no—make the balloon a giant balloon, put a little wicker carrier beneath it for her to step into, carrying a picnic basket, all blues and pinks and yellows, her pale handsome arms exposed but her legs all covered up modestly—her long brown hair done up in a comely bun, a little frayed, prettily frayed—oh, let her set that sure-footed self into a wicker carrier and I will untie the rope, I'll cut the rope with a giant scissors, and let balloon, carrier, and woman float up into the painted blue sky!

Out in the parking lot, helping her with her groceries—I as dutiful a husband as X, and as casually thanked—I notice that the pavement is gray, the sidewalk gray, the sky gray, my trousers gray, my hands gray, graying. When I get back to my three-room apartment, in an expensive building with a canopy, overlooking the river, with a door-man, but still only three rooms, I run to the bathroom and look at myself, wanting to weep, yes, for my graying fair hair.

How can I live my life without committing an act with a giant scissors?

CONJUGAL LOVE

There they are, it's after midnight. They sit in their sleazy little living room. X is pursuing his Ph.D. in English but having a slow, dull time of it, his eyes sore again; *she* is dawdling her life away in yawns and complaints, with a shrewd eye for her girl friends' houses in the suburbs, very jealous, with great slovenly strides walking all over his body, grinding her heel in his soft lungs, giving him a wink. It makes me laugh, this marriage! Marriage! My head aches suddenly, after midnight, and I get out of bed to take an aspirin, and suddenly, very clearly, I can see those six miles across town to *their* little living room, where they sit, a mess of crackers on the sofa between them, crumbs and bits of cheese, X getting a little fat with the relief of *her* pulling through the pregnancy, *she* getting sharp-eyed and restless with his thinning hair. Oh, she knows too much! She reads *Cosmopolitan* and the lead article is "How To Get Your Sec-ond—Third—Fourth Husbands!" and, frowning, severe, she skims through the article to *find out* where life is being lived, what the details of a remote, secret life must be. Shouldn't I buy her that balloon, really? And set her majestically free up into the sky?

The other evening I dropped in on them, after going to a movie alone, and she scurried around to straighten things up—not knowing how much I wanted to see the mess they lived in ordinarily, being hungry for what they live in *ordinarily*—and I sud-denly wanted to embrace her hips, in those unclean unpressed cotton slacks, I wanted to cry out to her, *Have mercy on me!* But instead I talked X into playing a game of chess. She hates chess; women hate chess. X is good-natured and likes to waste time, he can be talked into nearly anything, so he is talked into a long, subtle game, dragging on past one o'clock—oh, my good luck!—and she yawns and complains about the baby, what a bother, and finally goes off to the bedroom, walking heavily. I can hear her in there, in the other room. And in the bathroom. A fine icy fuzz seems to form at the tips of my fingers and around my nostrils as I listen to her, listening deeply, sighing with the effort of such listening, imagining her opening the medicine cabinet door—the

mirror swinging back, framing her high-colored, bored, puffy face and then losing it—
her reaching for a pair of eyebrow tweezers, maybe, or a big jar of cold cream. No: she
wouldn't. She'd throw off her clothes and fall into bed, a lazy weight, she'd sleep at
once and forget about us. Here we sit out in the living room, bent over a coffee table,
worrying about tiny pieces of red and black plastic—the game of chess! X's hair is
getting a little thin, yes. He has a grateful, ironic look, a very sensitive young man but
coarsening with married life, slack around the middle. I imagine him loitering around a
railroad yard as a teen-ager, seeing what he could see. I imagine him with a group of
other boys, fooling around at a beach, at an amusement park, with hard, stony faces
pursuing girls, united in their pursuit. I imagine him at the back of his classroom, trying
to keep awake tomorrow morning, reworking this chess game in his mind, and perhaps
evoking me, my several remarks of despair, which seemed to trouble him—

"I wish you wouldn't talk like that," he said to me seriously. He looked at me. "You
know you're not going to kill yourself, so why talk about it?"

"I know. I'm sorry."

"You've got everything to live for—a good job, freedom, everything you want—
you can go on vacations whenever you want, you can do anything—" But here he
began to falter, casting his mind about: what do I do with my life? What do I, his best
friend, do in my lonely life?

So, to help him out, I say quickly, "I know it, I'm sorry. I must sound very self-
pitying."

"No, but it's just a surprise. . . . Don't ever talk like that around *her*," he said,
giving an abrupt jerk of his head to indicate her, sleeping soundly in that double bed.
"She wouldn't understand. She's so, you know, so healthy and impatient . . . she gets
mad when I'm sick, even. God! She's really something!" And grimly, fondly, he began
to think about her and stopped thinking about me, about my desire to die, oh how real,
how deep is my desire to die! and so the game continued.

They sit in their little living room, night after night. They go into their little bedroom.
Everything is crowded in there—furniture piled together—I saw the room once, helping them move in. I was pleased that they asked me to help them. Afterward we all
went out for a pizza; they bought mine for me. No baby then. I think she was pregnant,
though—how else to explain certain small jokes and smirks between the two of them?
She wore yellow, a yellow sweater. She takes off the sweater in that little bedroom.
Their closet must be a mess, with *her* sharing it. X is very neat, like me. Essentially he
is neat. He complained once about her clothes crowding his out, wrinkling his. He had
lived alone for years. I have lived alone for years, since I left my parents' house. I wake
up at a quarter to one, with a headache. I take an aspirin, a simple and innocent act.
And suddenly I see them—I imagine them—lying in an embrace, the sheet carelessly
over them, X up on one elbow and joking with her and her joking back, nothing is
serious or sacred between them, they are in love, in love, in love; I am six miles away
suddenly nauseated, living alone.

Fire, flood, earthquake, all the classic types of sorrow—molten lava flowing from
faucets—the earth itself turned to a giant griddle—a blast furnace of cities burning,
enough to melt the painted rubber of high-sailing balloons—

How am I to be good? How am I to be saved?

I AM NOT THINKING . . .

I am not thinking of her mouth, his mouth. I am not thinking of their child growing into a human being of its own. I am sitting in the park, Palmer Park. Shouts from kids nearby playing shuffleboard . . . slamming the things around, lyric with violence. A man with a sharp stick wanders by picking up papers. A sharp stick! Picking up papers! I want to say to him, "Why are you looking at me, you old fool?" But he is not looking at me. I want to say to him, "You think I'm strange or something, sitting here?—what do you plan on doing, reporting me? Just who am I harming here? Isn't this a public park?"

I am not thinking of the cancerous cells that may be in her womb, her elastic womb. I am not thinking of the skid her car went into—a whole evening she dramatized it for me, almost frightening me, while X shook his head with a small strained smile and had to think, *had to think,* of how close she had come to dying and leaving him alone. "You should drive more carefully," I told her. I know how she drives: I was with her once and she nearly ran into a boy on a bicycle. Talking all the time, fooling around with her hair. No wonder she almost had an accident. No, I am not thinking of her mangled in a car wreck, her body is too lithe in spite of its disorder for a fate like that. I am not thinking of the rather prominent veins in her throat. I am thinking instead . . . of smooth, taffy-colored sandbanks, untouched by human footprints, unsoiled, virginal and lovely, molded by the wind into flowing tides, blending into the dusty sky; I am thinking of slow, silent caravans of camels crossing the sands, with men on them dressed in glaring, absolute white, swaying on the humps of those ugly sleeping beasts, the men's faces veiled, their eyes dark and their brows dark, seeing everything. I am thinking of delicate drops of music, like drops of water. Falling precisely onto my forehead. A drop of crystal reflecting the sand, and each grain of sand pregnant with camels, men in white, swaying veils, the terrible brute power of hidden limbs and trunks and the muscles of both men and camels, blended . . .

Night comes to the desert all at once, as if someone turned off a light. We are alone. We sleep peacefully.

A STAIRWAY TO THE GALLOWS

In a junk store, an antique store, is a small staircase, four steps high. "A stairway taken from an authentic gallows," says the dealer, a small unconvincing man with a sour line of a mouth. It doesn't look as if *I* would buy such junk! But I linger by it, running my fingers on it, almost hoping for a splinter, thinking, *Yet men have probably walked on these steps who are now dead. . . .*

Later that night I drop in on them. Something in the air, tension? A quarrel? She sits on the sofa, the child is shredding a doll, X is in the alcove of a dining room, at the table, trying to study. They are strangely quiet tonight. I lean over X's shoulder, sympathetic but ironic; he is reading Chaucer. "What of Chaucer's are you reading?" I ask him. He says, "Oh, nothing, it wouldn't interest you," and closes the book. This is a little surprising; but he seems to mean nothing by it. We go into the kitchen. He gets a can of beer for himself and some soda pop for me. Ice falling into the glasses from his fingers. Their ice tray is always a mess. I clean it out for them, put fresh water in it, stick it back in the freezer. Their freezer is always a mess. This gives me time to glance around the kitchen—yes, supper dishes in the sink, a smear of something red on one plate, probably they had nothing better than spaghetti, a frequent dish for them.

Out in the living room we sit and make conversation. *She* is long-legged and sullen. X looks tired. "Is something wrong?" I ask them finally. I am very nervous. "Well, the genius here flunked his German exam today," she says. Bitter and triumphant. I turn to X, flushed with relief, wanting to comfort him. But his face is turned off; no comfort wanted; he sucks at his beer. "Oh, go to hell," he says to her. "I thought you were the genius in this family."

We sit in silence. The little girl frets, has to be taken to bed. X asks me about new records I've bought, pretending interest. I have several thousand records in my apartment, all catalogued and cross-catalogued. I tell him about a new string quartet by a composer he has never heard of. All the time I am aware of *her* padding around in the other room. Finally she comes out, seems to burst upon us, buttoning her coat.

"Walk me to the drugstore, Alan. I've got to get a prescription filled."

I stand at once, such is her power. I follow her out, trying to indicate to X that she has called me, I can't help but obey; she seems to be choosing me over him, to insult him for having failed a foolish German exam; where is love in all this, love, love, love? what does marriage mean?—but he fails to catch my look. She and I go outside. It is November, fairly cold. She walks fast. She says, panting in the cold air, "Why don't you get married yourself? What are you waiting for?"

I am embarrassed. "So many people ask me that. . . ."

"All right, what are you waiting for?"

"A perfect love, I suppose." I smile ironically, to show that this is a joke. She is too grim, too vain to catch the smile.

"Remember that time you and I talked for so long?" she says. Yes, I remember. We talked for hours. I had dropped in late in the afternoon while X was at his Milton seminar, drowsing through that seminar, and we talked seriously, with a very youthful, naive honesty, about the meaning of life without God. She had said that it lay in human love, in marriage. I had said that each person must find his own meaning. The dialogue, the duet, had stretched out for hours; we had tugged back and forth, this exquisite, powerful, venomous woman, a married woman, the wife of my friend X, and I, rather thin-armed in my sports shirt and no match for her, no match. A few days later I gave her a paperback book, *Psychoanalytic Explorations in Art;* it must have been related to our discussion. She never mentioned it afterward, must not have read it. I would have thought she had forgotten about that talk.

"My life, my life with Bob, is very complicated and very strange," she said. "I think I'm going to have another baby. But I don't think it's his . . . isn't that funny? You know us both, you're our closest friend and practically our only friend, you know that we both love you, sort of . . . I mean we really do love you. . . . But my life is in pieces that haven't fallen apart yet and what's so strange is that I'm very happy, and Bob is happy too, though I'm sure he knows . . . everything. I wanted to tell you this. I don't know why."

Stunned, I am stunned. Frightened. At the drugstore I turn away from her—but she is turning away from me. She dabs at her eyes. She has been crying, this woman! While she goes to the prescription counter, I try to get control of myself. My heart is frightened, in a mild shock; why has she such power over me? I imagine her and X entwined in bed, their bodies entwined, and her soft pink tongue prodding his ear, telling him about the mysterious caresses of her womb, breaking him down and turning him golden again, my friend X, short broken veins in the whites of his eyes. And I imagine her lazily unbuttoning a blouse, dropping it over the back of a chair, and turning to embrace another lover, who is not a friend of mine and whom I don't know, I don't know. . . .

She is putting change in her billfold, walking vaguely toward me, looking down. She carries a small paper bag—pills of some kind, what kind? But I can't ask. That's too intimate. She glances up at me and our eyes meet and I am filled, suddenly, with a terrible rage. It has something to do with this healthy happy woman striding through a drugstore, a store built just for her, taking her pick of its phony crazy pills, its sugary pills, getting exactly what she wants. Always. Why won't she decide, whimsically, to divorce X? Why won't X decide, in despair and distraction, to move in with me—until "everything is settled"? Why won't she take a false step outside and be thrown fifteen, twenty, thirty feet down the street by a car full of teen-agers. Why not, why not? A fever rises in me. My eyes are feverish. Out on the street I want to scream at her, *Let him go! Isn't one man enough for you?* But I say nothing. I am drowning, suffocating in the heat of my rage. She is speaking lightly to me in a foreign language, I can't understand any of it, chatter, chatter, light and light-brained as a bird, this American woman grown out of an American girl, her own fever leading her on a tightrope of woven gold, stretched out taut and safe for her size-9 golden feet, so skillful. I could scrape that rather ugly mole off her arm and put a culture of cerebral cancer in it, a small neat culture, tape it down, let it set for a few weeks and see what hatches . . . but she chatters on beside me like a woman in a musical comedy. Happy. She is happy and X is happy. They are happy together. I feel as if I am walking suddenly upstairs, up a stairs, struggling with gravity, my heart and my lungs ready to burst, my face filled to bursting with a fever of blood, my brain in a fury to shout at them, *You are predictable, you too! You are statistics! You very nearly don't exist! What does it matter, your loves and your adulteries and your drooling adorable children, your quarrels, your spaghetti suppers, your stained sofas? What does any of it matter?*

THE MACHINE. THE GODDESS.

I stay late every night in the laboratory, working. The hum of a machine is like music beneath my breath. Later on tonight, oh, not too early, but as if by accident, I will drop by at their apartment. It's been a week now; they must think I am offended. They must wonder if something offended me. I will drop by, maybe around ten, ten-thirty, as if by accident, on my way home . . . I will give *her* a tiny charm for her bracelet that I happened to find in a little shop, thinking at once of her, a tiny silver figure of a female skater. Confident, muscled, a kind of goddess, looking wise and militant, able to skate over land and water as well as ice, and over our knuckles, our pulsing hearts. . . . It is all there, in that tiny figure. Women skating over men. Skating over our bare chests, our legs. I will give it to her, a wife, and I will sit on their sofa, in the currents of their marriage, curious and detached and in love, buffeted about, like seaweed or droplets of water, waiting to see what gifts the future may bring me.

QUESTIONS

1 Who or what is the "they" in the parenthetical "(they don't give me enough details and I must fill in my own)" in paragraph 3 following the heading "The Meeting"?
2 Why does the narrator refer to the husband as X?
3 Since this story is structurally an interior monologue, how many levels of consciousness does its narrator reveal?
4 Why are the part headings important to the structure?
5 How does the fragmentation of time contribute to the effectiveness of the story?
6 How well do we "know" the woman, her husband, the narrator?

TOPICS FOR COMPOSITION

1 Using major points from Cadwallader's and Fromm's essays, argue that the marriage and the narrator's love display both the good and the "wretched" sides of love and marriage.
2 In this part, three short stories have treated love in different ways. Write an essay comparing and contrasting the methods used by the three authors.

POETRY

Everyone knows that for centuries love and poetry have been almost inseparable. What is perhaps not as well known is that some of the finest love poetry offers much more than a lyrical expression of romantic emotion. Poets have thought deeply about the relation between romantic love and the purpose of life, and a wide variety of reflective poems have done much to reveal the meaning of love—and its mysteries as well.

Perhaps the main preoccupation of reflective love poetry has been the controversial relationship between physical and spiritual love. Inevitably, special attention has been given to the effect of time upon love and to the question whether or not duration is the best test of the quality of love. The poems of this section can be regarded as an excited exchange of opinions on these matters. We see, for example, that Edmund Spenser wishes to link love of physical beauty, which must yield to time, with love of virtue and thereby love of God, the unchanging source of all beauty. In attempting to do so, he draws upon an ancient philosophical concept. The seventeenth-century poet William Cartwright names and defines that concept in "No Platonic Love." But Cartwright also repudiates the concept, declaring that the pursuit of such "thin love" is a waste of time. The whole question receives almost classical expression in Andrew Marvell's "To His Coy Mistress," where ironic treatment of the old *carpe diem* (seize the day) theme leads the poet to a fierce desire to believe in love as a life-giving, world-making force working against the inexplicable natural process that shrinks each man's world to the size of a tomb.

As we might expect, our poetic debate is anything but dryly intellectual. In every instance, argument is supported by powerful appeals to experience, effected by the use of emotion-charged imagery, usually involving metaphor and symbol, and by various tonal devices. Shakespeare uses the contrasting metaphors of the guiding star and the court jester to affirm the union of true love with the unchanging order of the mind. The exultant lover in John Donne's "The Anniversary" is scarcely content to compare himself to a prince, and deliberately does so casually and parenthetically; for a moment, at least, he feels almost godlike as, secure in the possession of a love that will outlive death, he serenely envisions "all kings, and all their favorites" drawing to their destruction. With equal zest and comparable overstatement the modern poet Theodore Roethke celebrates the raptures of a love that is both earthly and earthy. The would-be seducer in Browning's poem "Two in the Campagna" combines the metaphor of tracing a thread with images suggestive of the endless fertility of nature in his vain effort to convince his companion (and himself) that indulgence in passion is the best way to be at ease with the ghost of Rome—that is, to counteract depressing thoughts about the limits time imposes upon all human desire. Closely comparable in almost every respect is Rossetti's use of nature imagery in his beautiful "Silent Noon," and with that fact as a clue even the unpracticed reader can hardly fail to see and feel poignantly the significance of the dragonfly that "hangs like a blue thread loosed from the sky."

At this point one is tempted to try to generalize about the ways in which views of romantic love have changed throughout the centuries. There is much to be said on this score; yet as, with that purpose in mind, we contemplate the contemporary poems that conclude this section, we may well be most impressed by the fact that after all that has been said about it, love seems to remain to the most discerning minds both a mystery and something of a miracle. Perhaps most remarkable is its range and variety in all times, a glimpse of which we receive in comparing the two modern poems "Anniversary" and "Living in Sin."

AMORETTI, SONNET 79

Edmund Spenser

Men call you fayre, and you doe credit it,
    for that your selfe ye dayly such doe see:
    but the trew fayre, that is the gentle wit,
    and vertuous mind, is much more praysd of me.
For all the rest, how ever fayre it be,   5
    shall turne to nought and loose that glorious hew:
    but onely that is permanent and free
    from frayle corruption, that doth flesh ensew.
That is true beautie: that doth argue you
    to be divine and borne of heavenly seed: 10
    deriv'd from that fayre Spirit, from whom al true
    And perfect beauty did at first proceed.
He onely fayre, and what he fayre hath made,
    all other fayre lyke flowres untymely fade.

1595

2 *that:* because. 3 *fayre:* fairness, beauty. *wit:* mind, disposition. 8 *ensew:* overtake. 11 *Spirit:* God.

QUESTIONS

1 Is the poet making a sharp distinction between beauty and goodness, or is goodness merely a higher degree of beauty? What is the relation between love and virtue?

2 Do the last two lines mean that God did not make all things? If not, what is the meaning?

SONNET 116

William Shakespeare

Let me not to the marriage of true minds
Admit impediments: Love is not love
Which alters when it alteration finds,
Or bends with the remover to remove.
Oh, no! it is an ever-fixéd mark   5
That looks on tempests and is never shaken;
It is the star to every wandering bark,
Whose worth's unknown, although his height be taken.
Love's not Time's fool, though rosy lips and cheeks
Within his bending sickle's compass come;   10
Love alters not with his brief hours and weeks,
But bears it out even to the edge of doom.
  If this be error and upon me proved,
  I never writ, nor no man ever loved.

1609

2 impediments: "Impediments" is taken from the Marriage Ceremony in *The Book of Common Prayer:* "If either of you know any impediment, why ye may not be lawfully joined together in Matrimony." *4 bends:* inclines. *remover:* restless, changeful person. *8 height:* altitude (for navigational purposes). *9 fool:* court jester. *10:* come within the reach of Time's curved scythe. *12 to the edge of doom:* to the Last Judgment.

QUESTIONS

1 Shakespeare is saying, of course, that true love is unaffected by changes in the physical appearance of the loved one. Does he also mean that true love endures even though the loved one is inconstant? Is such faithfulness understandable? What would be the point of it? (In a marriage of two true minds, of course, this kind of alteration would not be a consideration.)
2 What do the principal metaphors of the poem suggest about the relation between love and the whole conduct or meaning of life?

THE ANNIVERSARY

John Donne

  All kings, and all their favorites,
  All glory of honors, beauties, wits,
The sun itself, which makes times, as they pass,
Is elder by a year, now, than it was
When thou and I first one another saw: 5

3 times: seasons.

All other things to their destruction draw,
   Only our love hath no decay;
This, no tomorrow hath, nor yesterday,
Running it never runs from us away,
But truly keeps his first, last, everlasting day.   10

   Two graves must hide thine and my corse,
     If one might, death were no divorce.
Alas! as well as other princes, we
(Who prince enough in one another be)
Must leave at last in death, these eyes, and ears,   15
Oft fed with true oaths, and with sweet salt tears;
   But souls where nothing dwells but love
(All other thoughts being inmates) then shall prove
This, or a love increaséd there above,
When bodies to their graves, souls from their graves remove.   20

   And then we shall be throughly blest,
     But we no more than all the rest;
Here upon earth, we are kings, and none but we
Can be such kings, nor of such subjects be.
Who is so safe as we? where none can do   25
Treason to us, except one of us two.
   True and false fears let us refrain,
Let us love nobly, and live, and add again
Years and years unto years, till we attain
To write threescore: this is the second of our reign.   30

                     1633

18 *inmates:* temporary lodgers.   *prove:* experience.   21 *throughly:* thoroughly.

QUESTIONS

1 Why is the speaker sure that his love is immortal?
2 Why will the lovers, while they remain on earth, be better off even than kings?
3 What will the lovers lose by death? How important is the loss to their relationship with each other? In this connection, what is the significance of the contradictory phrase "sweet salt tears"? Will death change the lovers' status relative to others? Why?
4 Question 3 and the related questions will have suggested what the true fears are that the speaker refers to in line 27. What are the "false fears"?

NO PLATONIC LOVE

William Cartwright

Tell me no more of minds embracing minds,
    And hearts exchanged for hearts;
That spirits meet, as winds do winds,
    And mix their subt'lest parts;
That two unbodied essences may kiss,   5
And then like Angels, twist and feel one Bliss.

I was that silly thing that once was wrought
    To practice this thin love;
I climb'd from sex to soul, from soul to thought;
    But thinking there to move,   10
Headlong I rolled from thought to soul, and then
From soul I lighted at the sex again.

As some strict down-looked men pretend to fast,
    Who yet in closets eat;
So lovers who profess they spirits taste,   15
    Feed yet on grosser meat;
I know they boast they souls to souls convey,
Howe'r they meet, the body is the way.

Come, I will undeceive thee; they that tread
    Those vain aerial ways,   20
Are like young heirs and alchemists misled
    To waste their wealth and days,
For searching thus to be for ever rich,
They only find a med'cine for the itch.

1635

6 Bliss: i.e., a pure, impersonal happiness. *7 wrought:* persuaded. *9:* In Platonic love the search for beauty is supposed to lead from the sensual to the ideal, or purely abstract. "Soul" here may be taken to mean something like imagination. *10:* i.e., to move in a higher sphere or orbit.

QUESTIONS

1 In the first stanza, Cartwright illustrates the language of spiritual love, but not quite fairly. What are the elements that make for parody?
2 Does "thinking," in the tenth line, have the same sense as "thought," in the ninth? What is the effect of the repetition of the word?
3 What is the "itch" that motivates Platonic lovers? How does the "medicine" work?

TO HIS COY MISTRESS

Andrew Marvell

Had we but world enough, and time,
This coyness, lady, were no crime.
We could sit down and think which way
To walk, and pass our long love's day.
Thou by the Indian Ganges' side   5
Should'st rubies find; I by the tide
Of Humber would complain. I would
Love you ten years before the Flood,
And you should, if you please, refuse
Till the conversion of the Jews.   10
My vegetable love should grow
Vaster than empires, and more slow.
An hundred years should go to praise
Thine eyes, and on thy forehead gaze,
Two hundred to adore each breast,   15
But thirty thousand to the rest.
An age at least to every part,
And the last age should show your heart.
For, lady, you deserve this state,
Nor would I love at lower rate.   20
    But at my back I always hear
Time's winged chariot hurrying near;
And yonder all before us lie
Deserts of vast eternity.
Thy beauty shall no more be found,   25
Nor in thy marble vault shall sound
My echoing song; then worms shall try
That long preserved virginity,
And your quaint honor turn to dust,
And into ashes all my lust.   30
The grave's a fine and private place,
But none, I think, do there embrace.
    Now therefore, while the youthful hue
Sits on thy skin like morning dew,
And while thy willing soul transpires   35
At every pore with instant fires,
Now let us sport us while we may;

7 complain: sing plaintive songs of love. The Humber is in England.   *10 conversion of the Jews:*
popularly supposed to take place just before the end of the world.   *19 state:* dignified treatment.

And now, like am'rous birds of prey,
Rather at once our time devour,
Than languish in his slow-chapped power, 40
Let us roll all our strength, and all
Our sweetness, up into one ball;
And tear our pleasures with rough strife
Through the iron gates of life.
Thus, though we cannot make our sun 45
Stand still, yet we will make him run.
1681

QUESTIONS

1 Is this poem a satire? If so, what is being satirized?
2 Does the tone change? If it does, why?
3 Do you consider the metaphors of the last part of the poem to be appropriate for a
love poem? Does the way the speaker talks about love suggest an attitude toward
life in general? Is his attitude toward love—or life—one that can be found in our
own time? Does this poem describe a search for personal values?

STANZAS: COULD LOVE FOREVER

George Gordon, Lord Byron

Could Love for ever
Run like a river,
And Time's endeavor
    Be tried in vain—
No other pleasure 5
With this could measure;
And like a treasure
    We'd hug the chain.
But since our sighing
Ends not in dying, 10
And, formed for flying,
    Love plumes his wing;
Then for this reason
Let's love a season;
But let that season be only Spring. 15

When lovers parted
Feel broken-hearted,

And, all hopes thwarted,
   Expect to die;
A few years older,   20
Ah! how much colder
They might behold her
   For whom they sigh!
When linked together,
In every weather,   25
They pluck Love's feather
   From out his wing—
He'll stay for ever,
But sadly shiver
Without his plumage, when past the Spring.   30

   Like chiefs of Faction,
   His life is action—
   A formal paction
      That curbs his reign,
Obscures his glory,   35
Despot no more, he
Such territory
   Quits with disdain.
Still, still advancing,
With banners glancing,   40
His power enhancing,
   He must move on—
Repose but cloys him,
Retreat destroys him,
Love brooks not a degraded throne.   45

   Wait not, fond lover!
Till years are over,
And then recover
   As from a dream.
While each bewailing   50
The other's failing,
With wrath and railing,
   All hideous seem—
While first decreasing,
Yet not quite ceasing,   55
Wait not till teasing
   All passion blight:

31 Faction: a political party or clique.   *33 paction:* contract.

If once diminished,
Love's reign is finished—
Then part in friendship—and bid good night.   60

So shall Affection
To recollection
The dear connection
    Bring back with joy:
You had not waited   65
Till, tired or hated,
Your passions sated
    Began to cloy.
Your last embraces
Leave no cold traces—   70
The same fond faces
    As through the past:
And eyes, the mirrors
Of your sweet errors,
Reflect but rapture—not least though last.   75

True, separations
Ask more than patience;
What desperations
    From such have risen!
But yet remaining,   80
What is't but chaining
Hearts which, once waning,
    Beat 'gainst their prison?
Time can but cloy love
And use destroy love: 85
The wingéd boy, Love,
    Is but for boys—
You'll find it torture,
Though sharper, shorter,
To wean, and not wear out your joys.   90

1819

QUESTIONS

1 What evidence do you find that Byron is trying to mock some of his readers? What notions, specifically, is he making fun of? Are they still current?
2 We may disagree with Byron's recommendation and disapprove of his tone, yet still find in the poem a statement or two worthy of serious consideration. Do you find this to be true?

TWO IN THE CAMPAGNA

Robert Browning

I wonder do you feel today
   As I have felt since, hand in hand,
We sat down on the grass, to stray
   In spirit better through the land,
This morn of Rome and May   5

For me, I touched a thought, I know,
   Has tantalized me many times
(Like turns of thread the spiders throw
   Mocking across our path) for rhymes
To catch at and let go.   10

Help me to hold it! First it left
   The yellowing fennel, run to seed
There, branching from the brickwork's cleft,
   Some old tomb's ruin; yonder weed
Took up the floating weft,   15

Where one small orange cup amassed
   Five beetles—blind and green they grope
Among the honey-meal; and last,
   Everywhere on the grassy slope
I traced it. Hold it fast!   20

The champaign with its endless fleece
   Of feathery grasses everywhere!
Silence and passion, joy and peace,
   An everlasting wash of air—
Rome's ghost since her decease.   25

Such life here, through such lengths of hours,
   Such miracles performed in play,
Such primal naked forms of flowers,
   Such letting nature have her way
While heaven looks from its towers!   30

How say you? Let us, O my dove,
   Let us be unashamed of soul,

Campagna: the setting is the expanse of open country around Rome. The poet calls it Rome's ghost because it once contained cities, only ruins of which are now left.   *15 weft:* thread which forms part of a fabric.   *21 champaign:* the poet refers to the Campagna.

As earth lies bare to heaven above!
   How is it under our control
To love or not to love?   35

I would that you were all to me,
   You that are just so much, no more.
Nor yours nor mine, nor slave nor free!
   Where does the fault lie? What the core
O' the wound, since wound must be?   40

I would I could adopt your will,
   See with your eyes, and set my heart
Beating by yours, and drink my fill
   At your soul's springs—your part my part
In life, for good and ill.   45

No. I yearn upward, touch you close,
   Then stand away. I kiss your cheek,
Catch your soul's warmth—I pluck the rose
   And love it more than tongue can speak—
Then the good minute goes.   50

Already how am I so far
   Out of that minute? Must I go
Still like the thistle-ball, no bar,
   Onward, whenever light winds blow,
Fixed by no friendly star?   55

Just when I seemed about to learn!
   Where is the thread now? Off again!
The old trick! Only I discern—
   Infinite passion, and the pain
Of finite hearts that yearn.

                              1855

QUESTIONS

1 Although this monologue begins as a clever attempt at seduction, passion in the usual sense is not its main theme. How would you state that theme? It might help to consider the following question.
2 Why is the Campagna an appropriate setting for introduction of the poem's central theme?
3 The term *thread* is used in more than one metaphor here. What is the implication of each?

NEUTRAL TONES

Thomas Hardy

We stood by a pond that winter day,
And the sun was white, as though chidden of God,
And a few leaves lay on the starving sod;
    —They had fallen from an ash, and were gray.
Your eyes on me were as eyes that rove   5
Over tedious riddles of years ago;
And some words played between us to and fro
    On which lost the more by our love.

The smile on your mouth was the deadest thing
Alive enough to have strength to die;   10
And a grin of bitterness swept thereby
    Like an ominous bird a-wing. . . .

Since then, keen lessons that love deceives,
And wrings with wrong, have shaped to me
Your face, and the God-curst sun, and a tree,
    And a pond edged with grayish leaves.

1867

QUESTIONS

1 It would seem that the speaker in this poem only later fully understood that "grin of
    bitterness" (line 11). Has this later awareness done him any good? Is he now more
    capable of loving, would you say, or less? Does the poem have a moral?
2 What might be the significance of the title of the poem?

SILENT NOON

Dante Gabriel Rossetti

Your hands lie open in the long fresh grass,—
The finger-points look through like rosy blooms:
Your eyes smile peace. The pasture gleams and glooms
'Neath billowing skies that scatter and amass.
All round our nest, far as the eye can pass,   5
Are golden kingcup-fields with silver edge
Where the cow-parsley skirts the hawthorn-hedge.
'Tis visible silence, still as the hour-glass.
Deep in the sun-searched growths the dragonfly

Hangs like a blue thread loosed from the sky:— 10
So this winged hour is dropped to us from above.
Oh! clasp we to our hearts, for deathless dower,
This close-companioned inarticulate hour
When twofold silence was the song of love.

1881

12 *dower:* dowry.

QUESTIONS

1   This sonnet seeks to convey the idea of fulfillment, utter content. However, there are several indications that the speaker is aware that the experience he describes is transitory. How many can you find?
2   The oblique allusions to the passage of time create an element of irony in the poem. What is the effect of this upon the tone?

I KNEW A WOMAN

Theodore Roethke

I knew a woman, lovely in her bones,
When small birds sighed, she would sigh back at them;
Ah, when she moved, she moved more ways than one;
The shapes a bright container can contain!
Of her choice virtues only gods should speak, 5
Or English poets who grew up on Greek
(I'd have them sing in chorus, cheek to cheek).

How well her wishes went! She stroked my chin,
She taught me Turn, and Counter-turn, and Stand;
She taught me Touch, that undulant white skin; 10
I nibbled meekly from her proffered hand;
She was the sickle; I, poor I, the rake,
Coming behind her for her pretty sake
(But what prodigious mowing we did make).

Love likes a gander, and adores a goose: 15
Her full lips pursed, the errant note to seize;
She played it quick, she played it light and loose;
My eyes, they dazzled at her flowing knees;
Her several parts could keep a pure repose,
Or one hip quiver with a mobile nose 20
(She moved in circles, and those circles moved).

Let seed be grass, and grass turn into hay:
I'm martyr to a motion not my own;
What's freedom for? To know eternity.
I swear she cast a shadow white as stone. 25
But who would count eternity in days?
These old bones live to learn her wanton ways:
(I measure time by how a body sways).

1954

QUESTIONS

1   What kind of love does this poem celebrate? Is the poet serious? Try to define his attitude.
2   "I Knew a Woman" is full of overstatement couched in lyrical language. Pick out some examples.
3   In line 9 the poet refers to the movements of a Greek chorus performing an ode, a form of poetry which treated serious themes with great dignity. What is the purpose of comparing his poem with an ode? Is he satirizing himself?
4   Is there any nonsense verse in this poem?
5   Is this poem chauvinistic?

ANNIVERSARY

R. S. Thomas

Nineteen years now
Under the same roof
Eating our bread,
Using the same air;
Sighing, if one sighs, 5
Meeting the other's
Words with a look
That thaws suspicion.

Nineteen years now
Sharing life's table, 10
And not to be first
To call the meal long
We balance it thoughtfully
On the tip of the tongue,
Careful to maintain 15
The strict palate.

Nineteen years now
Keeping simple house,
Opening the door
To friend and stranger;   20
Opening the womb
Softly to let enter
The one child
With his huge hunger.

1954

QUESTIONS

1 What does the language of this poem convey about the quality of the married
   relationship described? Is a comparison with the language of Theodore Roethke's
   "I Knew a Woman" significant?
2 Would you say that this poem describes a relationship that has been relatively
   serene? Are there any signs of discontent?
3 Why does the poet say that they are "Careful to maintain /The strict palate"? Is he
   talking about the simplest kind of enjoyment?
4 What does the poet mean by saying that the one child had a huge hunger? What
   would you say is the tone of his statement?

IN CONSOLATION

Vassar Miller

Do I love you? The question might be well
Rephrased, What do I love? Your face?
Suppose it twisted to a charred grimace.
Your mind? But if it turned hospital cell,
Though pity for its inmate might compel   5
Sick calls from time to time, I should embrace
A staring stranger whom I could not place.
So, cease demanding what I cannot tell

Till He who made you shows me where He keeps you,
And not some shadow of you I pursue   10
And, having found, have only flushed a wraith.
Nor am I Christ to cleave the dark that steeps you.
He loves you then, not I—Or if I do,
I love you only by an act of faith.

1960

QUESTIONS

1   In this poem reflections on "romantic" love lead to thoughts about religion. What relationship between the two do you think the poet wants to suggest?
2   Consider carefully the manner of speaking used here and try to account for it.

WEDDING-WIND

Philip Larkin

The wind blew all my wedding-day,
And my wedding-night was the night of the high wind;
And a stable door was banging, again and again,
That he must go and shut it, leaving me
Stupid in candlelight, hearing rain,   5
Seeing my face in the twisted candlestick,
Yet seeing nothing. When he came back
He said the horses were restless, and I was sad
That any man or beast that night should lack
The happiness I had.

                    Now in the day   10
All's ravelled under the sun by the wind's blowing.
He has gone to look at the floods, and I
Carry a chipped pail to the chicken-run,
Set it down, and stare. All is the wind
Hunting through clouds and forests, thrashing   15
My apron and the hanging cloths on the line.
Can it be borne, this bodying-forth by wind
Of joy my actions turn on, like a thread
Carrying beads? Shall I be let to sleep
Now this perpetual morning shares my bed?   20
Can even death dry up
These new delighted lakes, conclude
Our kneeling as cattle by all-generous waters?

                         1962

QUESTIONS

1   How would you characterize the woman of this poem? Is the poet suggesting that love has a special meaning for her because of the kind of person she is?
2   "Wedding-Wind" might be called a dramatic monologue. Is it realistic?

ONE FLESH

Elizabeth Jennings

Lying apart now, each in a separate bed,
He with a book, keeping the light on late,
She like a girl dreaming of childhood,
All men elsewhere—it is as if they wait
Some new event: the book he holds unread,   5
Her eyes fixed on the shadows overhead.

Tossed up like flotsam from a former passion,
How cool they lie. They hardly ever touch,
Or if they do it is like a confession
Of having little feeling—or too much.   10
Chastity faces them, a destination
For which their whole lives were a preparation.

Strangely apart, yet strangely close together,
Silence between them like a thread to hold
And not wind in. And time itself's a feather   15
Touching them gently. Do they know they're old,
These two who are my father and my mother
Whose fire from which I came, has now grown cold?

1967

One Flesh: from Genesis 2:24.   *7 flotsam:* floating debris.

QUESTIONS

1   The speaker in this poem, observing the seeming remoteness of her parents from
    each other, thinks at first that they must feel at least vaguely bored and frustrated.
    Would you agree, if you were in her place?
2   It is as if, the speaker says, the silence between the couple is "a thread to hold/
    And not wind in." She does not understand. Do you?

LIVING IN SIN

Adrienne Rich

She had thought the studio would keep itself;
no dust upon the furniture of love.
Half heresy, to wish the taps less vocal,
the panes relieved of grime. A plate of pears,
a piano with a Persian shawl, a cat   5

stalking the picturesque amusing mouse
had risen at his urging.
Not that at five each separate stair would writhe
under the milkman's tramp; that morning light
so coldly would delineate the scraps   10
of last night's cheese and three sepulchral bottles;
that on the kitchen shelf among the saucers
a pair of beetle-eyes would fix her own—
Envoy from some village in the moldings . . .
Meanwhile, he, with a yawn,   15
sounded a dozen notes upon the keyboard,
declared it out of tune, shrugged at the mirror,
rubbed at his beard, went out for cigarettes;
while she, jeered by the minor demons,
pulled back the sheets and made the bed and found   20
a towel to dust the table-top,
and let the coffee-pot boil over on the stove.
By evening she was back in love again,
though not so wholly but throughout the night
she woke sometimes to feel the daylight coming   25
like a relentless milkman up the stairs.

1974

QUESTIONS

1 "Living in Sin" portrays the middle of a romantic affair. Supply a beginning and an
   end.
2 Why is it "half heresy" to wish the taps less vocal? Heresy is "dissent from a
   dominant theory or opinion." What theory is in question here?
3 "By evening she was back in love again . . ." What does the poet intend by this?
   Is she really in love?
4 What is the tone of this poem?

TOPICS FOR COMPOSITION

1 With Spenser's definition in mind, write a critical essay on the modern idea of
   feminine desirability. As a way of getting into the subject, consider the following
   questions. Do people nowadays overvalue physical beauty in women? Is the feminine image still a vital symbol of moral beauty, as it was in the last century? Does
   the modern concept of personality involve what might be called spiritual qualities?
   Do the national and international beauty contests provide adequate criteria for the
   assessment of "true" beauty?
2 Write an essay on the subject of idealism based on love between man and woman.
   Can such love be an adequate basis for moral motivation? Can a person achieve
   an adequate degree of moral motivation without such love? Do people tend to be
   too idealistic about marriage or too cynically realistic? Use one of these questions
   or a similar one as a means of focusing your discussion.
3 Platonic love in the religious sense is an outmoded doctrine, but it was once an

important source of motivation. If you are philosophically inclined, try to explain in a short essay why such a relatively sophisticated concept is unacceptable to modern taste.

4   Defend or attack the attitude expressed in Marvell's "To His Coy Mistress."
5   If you feel so inclined, make a case for taking Byron's advice (in "Stanzas: Could Love Forever") seriously.
6   Does Thomas Hardy's "Neutral Tones" have a moral? Say what you think it is, and explain what led you to your conclusion.
7   Compare the attitudes expressed in Rossetti's "Silent Noon" with those in Hardy's "Neutral Tones."
8   Compare the attitudes toward married love expressed in "Wedding-Wind," "In Consolation," and "Anniversary." Which attitude is healthiest? Support your opinion in an essay.
9   Write a response to the speaker in Elizabeth Jenning's "One Flesh."
10 Write an essay on the ideal attitude toward love, drawing freely upon the ideas and sentiments expressed in the poems of this unit.
11 It has become quite common for unmarried couples to live together. Consider in an essay the possible advantages and disadvantages of such a relationship.
12 Write an essay on the importance of humor in love and/or marriage.
13 Discuss the relationships between love of self and love of others.
14 Discuss love as a developing, changing thing.

TOPICS FOR LONGER COMPOSITIONS

1   Cadwallader tells us that our society fails to give young people a realistic view of marriage. Explain how the narrator in Joyce Carol Oates's story has been conditioned to view marriage and how that conditioning fails or succeeds as he observes the marriage of "X" and "she" (as he designates them). Does the narrator ever recognize that he has been conditioned? All of these statements and questions offer the basis for considering Oates's story against the relatively objective approach of Cadwallader.
2   Select a number of poems that express various attitudes toward love between men and women. Analyze the attitude in each and make an assessment taking into consideration when the poem was written and the national origin of the poet (some facts should be relevant). Conclude your paper by posing the elements of an ideal relationship drawn from your analysis; i.e., regardless of time or place, what seems consistent?
3   Love, according to Erich Fromm, has certain definable qualities which give it the possibility of enduring. But we recognize that modern ideas about love do not always lead to enduring relationships. Using Fromm's essay as your focal point, write an essay, drawing on your experience and observation, and on research, which argues that enduring love relationships are threatened by a technological, media-oriented society. Or, argue that these latter forces have no real effect on love relationships.
4   Utilize the methodology of Gail Rock's "Same Time, Same Station, Same Sexism" (in Part Two) by conducting an intensive study of the way in which love is depicted on television soap operas, sitcoms, dramatic series, etc. The study will require you to view and take notes from a wide variety of TV programs. Note that you are using Rock's essay only as a model for your assessment of TV's presentation of the qualities of love.

PART

4

THE PROTEST AGAINST MATERIALISM

Society is often rebuked for its emphasis on material gain, in the caricature of the "status-seeker," for example. Yet a complete rejection of material gain appears impractical. This is the paradox we face: on the one hand, material gain corrupts society; on the other hand, society progresses in proportion to man's ambition. Ambition, in the popular sense, is motivated by a desire for gain, material gain, for the most part. Where do we draw the line? Obviously, the question has no simple answer. But, because proper emphasis on materialistic value creates a dilemma as it touches social, moral, and spiritual behavior, we see that writers have generally taken a position of protest. The selections in this unit represent some varying ways writers have protested materialism's influence on society.

The first essay, "Thrift as a Duty," by Andrew Carnegie was initially published in *The Youth's Companion* (September 1900). Carnegie, a multimillionaire philanthropist, while obviously extolling the merits of a capitalistic society is also "teaching" that thrift is not only the duty of rich men but the responsibility of all men. Even though we may argue with his overly enthusiastic description of the saving man as a "temperate man, a good husband and father, a peaceful, law-abiding citizen," we can perhaps agree that his essay touches upon issues central to man's participation in a materialistic society.

For a quarter-century or so, Vance Packard, the author of the second essay, "Molding Super Consumers. . .," has written about the effects of the advertising industry on the materialistic attitudes of American consumers. The present essay is part of Chapter 9 of Packard's book, *The People Shapers* (1977). As the title of the essay suggests, Packard believes that the advertising industry creates excessive materialistic desires which, at times, seriously impinge on the consumer's freedom of choice and sense of values.

D. H. Lawrence's short story, "The Rocking-Horse Winner," combines materialistic desires and the need for love in a story that dramatically illustrates the destructive effect of material greed on human love and sensitivity. Lawrence tells a story that seems almost sacrificial: it is the young, the innocent, who pay the ultimate price for the greed of their elders.

"Goodwood Comes Back," by Robert Penn Warren, also pursues the problems that arise from the inability to manage one's personal life when faced with sudden fame and affluence. Goodwood, a small-town boy who makes it into big-league baseball, loses all, and ironically "comes back" because, as he says, "Being raised in a town like this . . . a fellow don't know what to do with real money."

The value of money weighed against the value of true art is only a part of B. Traven's view of a Yankee businessman in contention with a simple, yet enigmatic, Mexican Indian artist. "Assembly Line" questions the value of art, the sanctity of a culture, and the logic of illogic.

THE ESSAY

Carnegie's essay, written first as advice to youth, was later included in a collection of his writings called *The Empire of Business.* Read in this latter context, Carnegie's purpose is to persuade everyday working people that their savings are important to their welfare and to the economics of an industrialized society. As such, it allows us to examine his use of the kinds of appeals that mark persuasive writing.

1 He equates the ability to save with the distinction between civilized man and the savage.
2 He parallels the importance of collective savings with production of material things and subsequent creation of jobs.
3 He extols the happiness that comes with job security and economic independence.
4 He appeals to man's humanitarian instincts; that is, to his ability to contribute to the general good of the community, to take care of the needy, and to provide for his family.

THRIFT AS A DUTY

Andrew Carnegie

The importance of the subject is suggested by the fact that the habit of thrift constitutes one of the greatest differences between the savage and the civilized man. One of the fundamental differences between savage and civilized life is the absence of thrift in the one and the presence of it in the other. When millions of men each save a little of their daily earnings, these petty sums combined make an enormous amount, which is called capital, about which so much is written. If men consumed each day of each week all they earned, as does the savage, of course there would be no capital—that is, no savings laid up for future use.

Now, let us see what capital does in the world. We will consider what the shipbuilders do when they have to build great ships. These enterprising companies offer to build an ocean greyhound for, let us say, £500,000, to be paid only when the ship is delivered after satisfactory trial trips. Where or how do the shipbuilders get this sum of money to pay the workmen, the wood merchant, the steel manufacturer, and all the people who furnish material for the building of the ship? They get it from the savings of civilized men. It is part of the money saved for investment by the millions of industrious people. Each man, by thrift, saves a little, puts the money in a bank, and the bank lends it to the shipbuilders, who pay interest for the use of it. It is the same with the building of a manufactory, a railroad, a canal, or anything costly. We could not have had anything more than the savage had, except for thrift.

THRIFT THE FIRST DUTY

Hence, thrift is mainly at the bottom of all improvement. Without it no railroads, no canals, no ships, no telegraphs, no churches, no universities, no schools, no newspapers, nothing great or costly could we have. Man must exercise thrift and save before he can produce anything material of great value. There was nothing built, no great progress made, as long as man remained a thriftless savage. The civilized man has no clearer duty than from early life to keep steadily in view the necessity of providing for the future of himself and those dependent upon him. There are few rules more salutary than that which has been followed by most wise and good men, namely, ''that expenses should always be less than income.'' In other words, one should be a civilized man, saving something, and not a savage, consuming every day all that which he has earned.

The great poet, Burns, in his advice to a young man, says:

> To catch Dame Fortune's golden smile,
> Assiduous wait upon her:
> And gather gear by every wile
> That's justified by honour.

> Not for to hide it in a hedge,
> Not for a train attendant;
> But for the glorious privilege
> Of being independent.

That is sound advice, so far as it goes, and I hope the reader will take it to heart and adopt it. No proud, self-respecting person can ever be happy, or even satisfied, who has to be dependent upon others for his necessary wants. He who is dependent has not reached the full measure of manhood and can hardly be counted among the worthy citizens of the republic. The safety and progress of our country depend not upon the highly educated men, nor the few millionaires, nor upon the greater number of the extreme poor; but upon the mass of sober, intelligent, industrious and saving workers, who are neither very rich nor very poor.

THRIFT DUTY HAS ITS LIMIT

As a rule, you will find that the saving man is a temperate man, a good husband and father, a peaceful, law-abiding citizen. Nor need the saving be great. It is surprising how little it takes to provide for the real necessities of life. A little home paid for and a few hundred pounds—a very few—make all the difference. These are more easily acquired by frugal people than you might suppose. Great wealth is quite another and a far less desirable matter. It is not the aim of thrift, nor the duty of men to acquire millions. It is in no respect a virtue to set this before us as an end. Duty to save ends when just money enough had been put aside to provide comfortably for those dependent upon us. Hoarding millions is avarice, not thrift.

Of course, under our industrial conditions, it is inevitable that a few, a very few men, will find money coming to them far beyond their wants. The accumulation of millions is usually the result of enterprise and judgment, and some exceptional ability for organization. It does not come from savings in the ordinary sense of that word. Men who in old age strive only to increase their already great hoards, are usually slaves of the habit of hoarding formed in their youth. At first they own the money they have made and saved. Later in life the money owns them, and they cannot help themselves, so overpowering is the force of habit, either for good or evil. It is the abuse of the civilized saving instinct and not its use, that produces this class of men.

No one need be afraid of falling a victim to this abuse of the habit if he always bears in mind that whatever surplus wealth may come to him is to be regarded as a sacred trust, which he is bound to administer for the good of his fellows. The man should always be master. He should keep money in the position of a useful servant. He must never let it master and make a miser of him.

A man's first duty is to make a competence and be independent. But his whole duty does not end here. It is his duty to do something for his needy neighbours who are less favoured than himself. It is his duty to contribute to the general good of the community in which he lives. He has been protected by its laws. Because he has been protected in his various enterprises he has been able to make money sufficient for his needs and those of his family. All beyond this belongs in justice to the protecting power that has fostered him and enabled him to win pecuniary success. To try to make the world in some way better than you found it, is to have a noble motive in life. Your surplus wealth should contribute to the development of your own character and place you in the ranks of nature's noblemen.

It is no less than a duty for you to understand how important it is, and how clear your duty is, to form the habit of thrift. When you begin to earn, always save some part of your earnings, like a civilized man, instead of spending all, like the poor savage.

QUESTIONS

1 What distinctions does Carnegie make between the savings of ordinary people and the accumulated wealth of the rich? Are they valid?
2 How prevalent are Carnegie's views today?

TOPICS FOR COMPOSITION

1 Banks, savings and loan institutions, credit unions, and the like continually advertise through every media outlet. Using a number of these current advertisements, relate their approaches to the appeals made by Carnegie.
2 The introduction to this unit states that materialistic desire is one of man's paradoxes. Using Carnegie's essay and current advertising techniques, examine the paradox.

☐

"Molding Super Consumers . . ." is an example of the judicious use of researched material. Packard cites and refers to a wide variety of material that appears to provide highly authoritative support for his thesis. Note particularly that, in keeping with his theme of behavior molding, he presents the work of sociologists and psychologists and offers us an "inside" look at how the advertising industry adapts sociological and psychological research into its advertising philosophy. Observe also how Packard keys the reader to the importance of his major points through the use of subdivision headings.

MOLDING SUPER CONSUMERS . . .

Vance Packard

> *To make people feel or act in a certain way is not manipulating them.*
> —Alvin A. Achenbaum, marketing expert

Mr. Achenbaum was testifying before the United States Federal Trade Commission. The subject of the hearings was "Can Advertising Manipulate Consumers?" A great variety of advertising practices were scrutinized. Federal Trade Commissioner Paul Rand Dixon treated with skepticism Mr. Achenbaum's disavowal that any manipulation was involved.

Whether specific advertising practices are manipulative can be argued. What cannot be argued is that advertising in general is a manipulative force. It has become a major instrument of social control in much of the Western world. Advertisers spend close to $33 billion a year to shape the consuming habits of Americans. That averages out to nearly $600 for each family in the land.

Some ads just announce the availability of a locksmith. But many of the messages are designed to modify life-style and attitudes. They seek to make people more hedonistic, more narcissistic, more status-conscious, more prone to live against the future. The goal is to create more insatiable consumers. And this is starting to be seen as functional in highly technological societies. Some years ago the sociologist Clark Vincent, in making his presidential address to the National Council on Family Relations, said that the family is no longer just a production unit. It was adjusting to a new challenge, that of being a "viable consuming unit."

The massiveness of the behavior-molding effort of advertising can be seen in the viewing of television commercials. By the time young people in the United States are eighteen they have seen and heard about eighteen hundred hours of commercial messages on TV. If you divide that up into thirty-five-hour workweeks you find that they have spent a full year of time listening just to commercials. Adding in radio commercials would take them well into a second year of time.

Since 1950 many hundreds of behavioral scientists have worked to enhance advertising effectiveness. Some have worked for consulting firms. These often are called motivation-research firms. A recent issue of *Bradford's Directory* included 124 of them. The list was not complete. Other social scientists have worked directly for advertising agencies. Still others have worked for companies trying to sell the products.

I have described in previous books a great many strategies devised by these consultants to modify consumer behavior.[1] A more recent and typical approach by one of the marketing-research pioneers was concerned with overcoming consumer resistance to a hair dressing for women. Sales had not risen in proportion to the massiveness of the advertising. This producer had been very successful in selling male hair dressings. The famed psychological consultant Ernest Dichter was called in. His interviewers talked with prospective users about the dressing. They seemed uneasy about its milky color and texture, and talked about the fact that the producer made products for men. Dichter advised his client that the male image of the producing company led women unconsciously to associate the feminine product with male semen. This caused them to feel that it was not for them. He recommended far more feminizing in the product's name and promotion.

Dichter advises clients that nowadays it is not enough to praise a product. First you must remove the customer's feeling that "I don't need it." Need, he explains, is a psychological phenomenon. As he sees it, the great majority of the services and products we use are not needed in a purely utilitarian sense. "Thus, in selling a man another suit you do some psychological selling 'on the pleasures of renewal of yourself.'"

Resistance now is being encountered by cosmetics manufacturers who have for so long been promising women an interesting sexual conquest. There have been so many disappointments that now, Dichter says, it often is better to focus on the fun and narcissistic pleasure of applying cosmetics, even if nothing happens.

In recent years the marketing journals have handled tough subjects with erudition. The *Journal of Marketing* carried a long presentation titled "Fear: The Potential of an Appeal Neglected by Marketing." (I didn't know fear had been neglected.) The principal author was a social psychologist who had been retained by a major advertising agency. He and his colleague reviewed ninety studies of fear to prove that advertisers had been too squeamish about boring in on it.

With an array of charts they demonstrated what levels of fear are most effective in selling such things as insurance, mouthwashes, dietetic foods, and safety features in automobiles to various groups. At the end he and his colleague raised the question of ethics. Was it possible that using the amount of fear necessary for optimum sale of the products might have "deleterious consequences for those high anxiety persons who happen to be in the message audience?" They immediately dismissed this by contending that the level of fear that is effective in marketing would not be high enough to be even remotely unethical.

The matter of sex in advertising received scholarly treatment by two other psychologists in the *Journal of Advertising Research*. The title: "Who Responds to Sex in Advertising?" They explained at the outset that their paper applied both Q-analysis and a heuristic clustering method to the same set of data to find out how various individuals

---

[1] Vance Packard, *The Hidden Persuaders* (New York: David McKay Co., 1957); *The Status Seekers* (New York: David McKay Co., 1959); *The Waste Makers* (New York: David McKay Co., 1960).

interpret sex appeal in advertising. Heuristic clustering analysis proved to be superior in breaking down sex in advertising into its principal components and showed how "one group of individuals differ from another in their responses to sex in advertising." Three hundred advertisements were rated by several hundred young men and women.

A principal finding: the suggestiveness of the copy is a much more important variable in ads for women than for men, contrary to traditional thinking. And women proved to be more sexually aroused by nudity in ads than men. The study also identified groups who had sex fetishes concerning certain of the products seen.

ZEROING IN ON THE BEST PROSPECTS

In recent years the behavioral specialists who advise marketers have put the heaviest stress on identifying the best prospects for products. Vast amounts of research have been done and computers have been heavily used.

Identifying the likeliest prospects is achieved by "segmenting" the universe of consumers. First, you divide people up on the basis of "demographics." That is, you segment by age, income, education, occupation, ethnic background, size of family, and so on. But demographics have no *feeling* for people and their new life-styles. Today many ambitious marketers consider demographics just the beginning. They call next for "psychographics." Enter the behavioral specialists.

The word psychographics was coined by Emanuel Demby, the amiable, bearded head of Motivation Programmers, Inc. It made motivation research sound more precise—and new. It was more measurable, thus more scientific. With psychographics you build psychological profiles within the groups targeted by demographics. People are analyzed by interests, life-styles, status aspirations, self concepts and attitudes (including fears and biases). The aim is to arrive at groups with similar psychological profiles. One facet of a Demby study was to find, within the world of car buyers, the kinds of people who would consider buying a certain brand of car.

A rival of Demby's, the Commercial Analysts, studied at considerable length four thousand people on 360 psychographic dimensions. The computer came up with eight predominant life-styles for each sex.[2] Women readers may find some overlap. For women:

> The self-righteous social conformist
> The family-oriented churchgoer
> The downtrodden salvation seeker
> The happy materialist
> The blithe-spirited natural woman
> The romance and beauty seeker
> The fulfilled suburban matron
> The liberated career seeker

[2] "The New Sex," *Media Decisions* (May, 1973), pp. 68–76.

The eight categories for men:

> The inconspicuous social isolate
> The silent conservative
> The embittered resigned worker
> The highbrow puritan
> The rebellious pleasure seeker
> The work-hard, play-hard executive
> The masculine hero emulator
> The sophisticated cosmopolitan

A major advertising agency, Benton & Bowles, Inc., came up with somewhat different psychographic profiles from a panel of two thousand housewives it was studying. They were asked 214 questions about their attitudes. They were also asked about the products they bought. One clear area of interest to the researchers was concern about germs. Many product promoters thrive on germ anxiety. This study came up with six categories as "most meaningfully classifying" the housewives:

> Outgoing Optimists
> Conscientious Vigilants
> Apathetic Indifferents
> Self-Indulgents
> Contented Cows
> Worriers

It was discovered, for example, that the Conscientious Vigilants and the Worriers were more likely to be receptive to products that promised to kill germs. Contented Cows were described as "relaxed, not worried, relatively unconcerned about germs and cleanliness, not innovative or outgoing, strongly economy-oriented, not self-indulgent." (In short not promising prospects.) The study produced clues on how to appeal to each category of housewife in selling messages for various kinds of products.

One enthusiast of psychographics, Alan R. Nelson, contends that psychographics is "light years" away from other methods in moving consumers into action. He heads Alan R. Nelson Research. Nelson conducted a research effort involving several thousand consumers to find the best way to sell decorated toilet paper, and similarly decorated facial tissue. His group tested thirty-two selling themes in relation to nineteen "life-style value systems." One finding: "Guests instinctively study bathrooms for messages about their hosts. . . . If we have any minor weaknesses, they are most likely to be betrayed by our bathrooms. . . . That's why we are so anxious to 'look good' in them." Decorated toilet paper was concluded to be one good solution to this dilemma of modern life.

Perhaps the most interesting psychographic study by Demby's Motivation Programmers, Inc., involved spotting people who are likely to be "aggressive" buyers of *new* kinds of products. Such people are called "creative" consumers. They are contrasted with drudges who are "passive" consumers. The research group found that lots of rich people with college educations are very slow in taking to new concepts in products. An example would be the electric blender. Other affluent people with identical demographics are three and a half times as likely to buy electric blenders, food liquefiers, and the like. And these others are seven times as likely to buy electric hot trays.

How do they differ? They differ in psychographics. For the kinds of products mentioned above, the heavy buyers lead a more outgoing, socialized way of life. They are joiners. Their life-style is directed outward, aimed toward contacts with other people. In contrast, the equally affluent but dreary prospects lead a life-style that is directed inward. Their important activities tend to be those that "involve the individual, the family and close friends."

MACHINES TO PROBE MOODS

Admen are constantly searching for a better way to get inside our minds. For one thing they want to know how much we are moved by their handiwork. Knowing our reaction beforehand to their persuasive efforts, they can make adjustments before launching a worldwide campaign that can make additional millions of dollars from sales for their clients.

A large part of their analysis involves our reaction to pictures and words: pictures and words in the media; pictures on cans and packages. In the early 1960's a German-born psychologist, Eckhard Hess, came up with what seemed to be a breakthrough. He developed a culture-free device that instantly revealed how much we were interested in a picture. The device was a pupillometer. It measures the pupil, that round spot in the middle of the eye. As the pupil expands (dilates) or contracts while looking at a picture, it purportedly reveals something. Hess had found that the degree of dilation is a measure of how intently we are examining a picture.

Many of the major advertising agencies plunged into pupillometrics, as did many university laboratories. The admen mistakenly leaped to the conclusion that their machines were giving them a yes-or-no answer on whether the beholding eye liked or disliked their ad. It turned out that the machine could not reveal likes and dislikes, and some admen became disgruntled. What the machine did reveal, though, was intensity of interest and concentration. And that was something. You can't either like or dislike a message until you get interested in it.

The machine also couldn't tell them what it was in the ad—the handsome man or the girl admiring the diamond ring being offered—that was causing the beholder's eyes to dilate. Another complication was that the pupil is more likely to dilate at the sight of dark colors than light colors.

In recent years both of these problems have been largely solved as the machines have become more sophisticated—and expensive (up to $20,000). Today's better pupillometers can show exactly what part of the picture is causing the pupil to react. Two psychologists who assessed the state of the art for *Psychology Today* have concluded: "Although the pupil is no panacea, it can play a substantial role in exploring the emotional and mental functions of man."[3]

Different kinds of machinery are used on a large scale to pretest television commercials and TV shows that advertisers have been invited to sponsor. People are brought in off the street. Their reactions are registered by turning dials or pushing buttons. For light entertainment, the previewers' fingers may be attached to electrodes measuring skin reaction. The skin of a person who is enjoying himself throws off less sweat than the skin of a fidgety person.

Viewer interest is also measured by the squirm test. The TV previewers sit in chairs wired to record movement. The assumption is that the more the buttocks move in a chair, the less the interest in what is being shown on the screen.

Recently the researchers have shifted from the buttocks to the brain in searching for clues to viewer interest and selling effectiveness. The *Journal of Advertising Research* reported a test of brain-wave response to advertising. One finding has been that people show much more mental alertness (beta waves) when they read an ad than when they listen to a commercial on TV. Here the more relaxed alpha waves predominate.

In 1975 a researcher at the Brain-Behavior Research Center at the Sonoma State Hospital in California reported that he had been testing reactions to a variety of TV shows. To his subjects' heads he affixed electrodes leading to a computer. He found that the brain-wave patterns of people really interested in what they were watching were clearly different from those of people who had "little interest" in the program being watched.

This brain-tapping presumably is the wave of the future in shaping messages for maximum behavior-shaping impact on the marketplace.

THE SCIENTIFIC SEDUCTION OF CHILDREN

In applying strategies and using machines to determine maximum sales impact the advertisers have focused in particular on one group: children. From the age of three up. Children consume at least $75 billion worth of goods and services in the U.S.A. alone. And they are influential in the adult purchase of many billions of dollars worth of additional items. An adman was quoted in *Advertising Age* as observing:

"If you truly want big sales, you will use the child as your assistant salesman. He sells, he nags, until he breaks down the sales resistance of his mother or father."

The average youngster sees more than twenty thousand television commercials a year. Corporations spend nearly a half-billion dollars on these commercials. Billions in profits are at stake. And most marketers think they are now learning how to get their money's worth. An economist for the Federal Communications Commission says: "Children's programming is the most profitable area of television programming."

Across the land there are dozens of motivation-oriented consulting firms that specialize in probing children's reactions to commercials, programs, and products. The

[3] Michel Pierre Janisse and W. Scott Peavler, "Pupillary Research Today: Emotion in the Eye," *Psychology Today* (Feb. 1974), p. 63.

findings are used to make modifications that will cause child viewers in general to be more eager users and hawkers of the sponsor's product.

Audience Studies, Inc., in Los Angeles runs a small theater for testing commercials and pilot programs. Children are tested apart from adults. Each year about four thousand children man the "interest machine." By turning a dial they can indicate five degrees of enthusiasm.

But the real probing occurs in the more intimate play-area laboratories. Usually these are inside motivation-research firms. Some years ago I visited one up the Hudson from New York where hundreds of children in the area were serving as reactors. About a dozen at a time were probed for their reactions. The playroom wall had a one-way mirror. Behind the mirror were cameras, tape recorders, and chairs for client observers.

Recently an editor for *Human Behavior* made a study of such laboratories under a pledge of confidentiality.[4] One was in a West Coast suburb. The children's responses are tested by pupil-dilation measurement machines, finger sensors, and so on.

She reported that after the children had viewed a commercial a child psychologist questioned each one closely about his reactions. Each group of child-reactors were requested to make drawings about each part of the commercial. These would be analyzed later by specialists. The analysts also drew upon Stanislavski dramatic techniques. Teams of children were organized to act out how they thought their parents would respond to their request for the product. Also they acted out what pitches they themselves would use to sell it to adults. And they were probed on how their playmates would feel about the product.

This honing of sales appeals for maximum exploitation of the child market unquestionably is felt in the home. A survey at Michigan State University of several hundred preschoolers revealed that 80 percent of the children acknowledged that they had urged their parents to buy toys they had seen advertised on television. About the same proportion had appealed to their parents to buy cereals they had seen advertised on television. Many of these cereals are so loaded with sugar (the tooth-decay producer) that they could pass for breakfast candy. Until recently, at least, several drug companies have pushed vitamins to children with the appeal that they were wonderfully sweet.

In a book called *The Youth Market* two advertising executives reported a survey of mothers. How much more did the mothers buy in the supermarket as a result of urgings from their children to buy specific products or brands? The responses would indicate that for U.S. mothers as a whole the cost would come close to $4 billion a year in addition to their grocery bills.

SLIPPING MESSAGES INTO OUR MINDS

In the late 1950's there was a hullabaloo in much of the Western world when it was discovered that hidden messages were being tucked into TV, radio, and motion picture

[4] Marilyn Elias, "How to Win Friends and Influence Kids on Television," *Human Behavior* (Apr. 1974), pp. 16, 17.

shows. Much of the tucking was being done by advertisers. The technique was called subliminal stimulation. It was based on findings by psychologists that the brain can receive quickly flashed images and whispered sounds below our level of conscious awareness.

In 1957 there was an announcement that a firm in New Orleans called Precon Process and Equipment Corporation was in the business of placing subliminal images in movies, on billboards, and in taverns. The firm was set up by a psychologist and a neurologist with engineering training. They said they had been experimenting for several years and had applied for patents. Later they claimed to have doubled the consumption of a beverage advertised subliminally on the premises where it was for sale.

In New York City, James Vicary, the head of a motivation-research firm, called a press conference. The purpose was to demonstrate subliminal stimulation and to announce that he had set up a separate firm, the Subliminal Projection Company. Clients were being solicited. Patents were being sought.

Soon after the unveiling of Precon and of the Vicary enterprise, television and radio stations across the country began trying out the technique. A Chicago radio station for four months broadcast "subaudible" messages at $1,000 for four hundred messages. At least two motion pictures were made using subliminal images of ghosts, blood, and skulls to enhance dramatic impact.

Meanwhile, a public uproar over this hidden seduction arose. (And my first book of social comment, *The Hidden Persuaders,* happily for me, was caught up in the uproar.) The *New Yorker* deplored the fact that minds were being "broken and entered." *Newsday* called it the most alarming invention since the atomic bomb. The *Saturday Review* devoted an editorial page to deploring it. Congressmen and senators joined in, and introduced a number of bills. (Nothing happened on them.) A few state legislatures passed laws outlawing subliminal stimulation. Great Britain banned it. Precon and the Subliminal Projection Company were having problems getting patent rights. (Precon finally got a patent in 1962.)

Broadcasters became nervous. The United States National Association of Television and Radio Broadcasters, which includes the three networks and a majority (but not all) of the nation's TV and radio stations, banned its use. Admen began calling it a terrible idea.

Subliminal stimulation disappeared from the news.

Several years later, in 1967, the political scientist Alan Westin speculated on what "probably would have happened had the protests not been so widespread." He said it was most likely that TV sponsors, display advertisers, theater owners, filmmakers and political advertisers would have tested the technique thoroughly and advertisers would have been arriving at a "costs against presumed return-in-sales" picture. Political users would have been reaching a similar judgment. "Subliminals would have then become part of the communication arsenal."[5]

As a matter of fact, interest in subliminal stimulation has continued, but much more quietly. I have reports on fourteen studies that have been made in recent years, and references to quite a few more. The psychologist James McConnell in his new, widely

[5] Alan F. Westin, *Privacy and Freedom* (New York: Atheneum Publishers, 1967), pp. 295–296.

adopted textbook *Understanding Human Behavior* devotes a chapter to "Subliminal Perception." The *Journal of Marketing Research* has carried an article on the effects of subliminal stimulation on brand preferences.[6] The article told of experiments involving ninety-six people in which messages were subliminally flashed. The results indicated that "a simple subliminal stimulus can serve to arouse a basic drive such as thirst." The author concluded that "the field of marketing should maintain an *active* interest in this area."

Researchers have now developed more precise information on what works and what does not work, subliminally. Words with a high emotional overtone—such as "whore," "raped," "bitch," "penis"—can be flashed twice as fast as neutral words like "river" and still be remembered later. A person must be already motivated to make use of even the weakest hunches suddenly felt. (That is, you must be at least vaguely hungry to accept a subthreshold suggestion that you go buy popcorn.)

A few years ago *Advertising Age* reported matter-of-factly that Toyota Motor Sales U.S.A. was using subliminal images to enhance the impact of its commercials.

In the pre-Christmas season of 1973 the producer of a packaged family game called Husker Du launched a nationwide TV campaign involving subliminal stimulation. Starting on November 26, its minute-long commercial appeared on hundreds of television stations. Many appeared in hours when child-watching was heavy. Four times during the commercial the command "Get It!" was flashed subliminally.

A technician at one of the stations noticed the flickered commands. Within a week the Television Code Authority of the National Association of Broadcasters alerted its member stations that the commercial was in violation of the code. The code prohibits "any technique whereby an attempt is made to convey information to the viewer by transmitting messages below the threshold of normal awareness." Apparently, most members of the association snipped out the "Get It!" commands. But many major stations are not members of the code organization. The manager of the company distributing the commercial contended that the subliminal commands had slipped past him because of the Christmas rush and asked stations to delete them. Weeks later, a few days short of Christmas Eve, a number of stations in large cities were still carrying the subliminal messages.

There are reports that the flashing of messages subliminally is being outmoded by a new technique. The message stays on the screen throughout the movie or TV show, but it is so dim that you are not consciously aware of it. Since you are continuously exposed to the message, it is considered by some to be more effective. And it may be harder to detect than the flashed message.

In 1973 Wilson Bryan Key reported in his book *Subliminal Seduction* the results of inquiries made to commercial research firms in New York, Chicago, and Toronto. Thirteen of the firms were prepared to offer some sort of mechanically induced, subliminal message service to advertisers.

There are still no rules forbidding the use of subliminal images in motion pictures or in supermarkets or taverns. And there are very few legal prohibitions against any kind of subliminal stimulation. It is principally fear of wrath that limits its use.

---

[6] Del Hawkins, "The Effects of Subliminal Stimulation on Drive Level and Brand Preference," *Journal of Marketing Research* (Aug. 1970), p. 322.

I would guess that its greatest potential is not as a huckster's tool in democracies but rather as a conditioning tool for authoritarian regimes.

PUSH-BUTTON BUYING IN THE LIVING ROOM

The great dream of TV advertisers is to find a way to clinch sales immediately. Catch the prospect while he is relaxed in his own living room, perhaps with a drink in hand. Close the sale while his desire is aroused and the product is clearly in his mind. Then you won't have to wait until some future date when he happens to be near a shop where the product or service is available.

That is the dream. And the reality is being tested. The reality is two-way cable television. A push-button console sits near the TV set where you the listener obey the commands or appeals of the salesman on the screen. The device is easier to operate than a pocket calculator. Just push three or four buttons. The machine that makes ice cubes, the electric leg shaver, the mahogany backgammon set, or that ten-speed bike Junior is hollering for will be at your door next morning. Pay later.

Cable television installations are growing rapidly in the United States. As of late 1976 there were about eleven million installations. And by law those now installed in most metropolitan areas must have a two-way capability.

The Advertising Research Foundation has been carrying on an intensive analysis of the potential of push-button selling on two-way cable TV in El Segundo, California. Subscribers can order instantly products and services offered in commercials. They can also order sports, theater, or travel tickets. They can buy items from mail-order catalogues as the items are being demonstrated. They can even ask for a demonstrator to call.

In El Segundo the TV merchandisers have a pretty good idea of whom they are trying to sell to. They are provided with important information about each subscriber who is reached by that two-way cable TV system. This includes not only the standard demographic stuff but psychological characteristics, type of residence, reading and broadcast listening behavior, buying habits—and possessions already owned.

El Segundo is just one place where push-button selling has been occurring. Two-way merchandising systems have been established in Akron, Ohio; Irving, Texas; Mesa, Arizona; Orlando, Florida; Overland Park, Kansas—to mention only a few places. The current costs of apparatus are still a factor causing hesitation.

Some enthusiasts are saying that two-way TV is the most significant development in social communications since Samuel Morse first transmitted his code over wires. Buying is just one thing a subscriber can do with two-way TV. He can see an instant printout of the news. He can see today's menu at a local restaurant. He can arrange that sensors report a fire or burglary while he is away. And political and marketing pollsters can get back his reactions instantly.

Most of the strategies cited above for building super consumers will of course intensify problems already besetting advanced societies. The pressures to keep sales soaring will aggravate the growing shortage of energy and many irreplaceable minerals. The pressures will also lead to increased desecration, pollution, and preoccupation with finding fulfillment through consumption.

QUESTIONS

1 List the techniques that advertisers use to mold consumer behavior. To how many can you attach product names?
2 What are psychographic profiles? Do you agree with the classifications? Why or why not? Can you add to the classifications?
3 Explain subliminal advertising. What instances from your experience can you describe? Is it, as Packard suggests, outmoded? Give examples of the "newer" technique.
4 Do you agree with Packard's conclusion and its warning? Can you support his predictions with recent evidence?

TOPIC FOR COMPOSITION

Leo Tolstoy, the great Russian writer, wrote a story entitled "How Much Land Does a Man Need?" in which he warned Russian peasants about the evils of excessive materialism. Drawing upon Packard's views, write an essay about materialism today simply entitled, "How Much Does Man Need?" Tolstoy's story is readily available. Read the story (thereby finding the answer to his title) and use material from it to enlarge your essay.

SHORT STORY

In Lawrence's story, materialism takes an absurd shape in the form of a child's rocking-horse. Moreover, the child becomes a pathetic pleader for love in the face of materialistic force. When, however, the rocking-horse and its rider move together, the absurd and the pathetic merge to form a monstrous grotesque which overrides all notions of human sensitivity. As you read the story, observe how Lawrence weaves together symbol and characterization by:

1 Showing the mother's inability to love because of her overwhelming materialistic desires
2 Showing Paul's sensitivity to his mother's needs and his desire to be loved for his efforts
3 Showing the tension that exists in every aspect of the family relationships

THE ROCKING-HORSE WINNER

D. H. Lawrence

There was a woman who was beautiful, who started with all the advantages, yet she had no luck. She married for love, and the love turned to dust. She had bonny children, yet she felt they had been thrust upon her, and she could not love them. They looked at her coldly, as if they were finding fault with her. And hurriedly she felt she must cover up some fault in herself. Yet what it was that she must cover up she never knew. Nevertheless, when her children were present, she always felt the centre of her heart go hard. This troubled her, and in her manner she was all the more gentle and anxious for her children, as if she loved them very much. Only she herself knew that at the centre of her heart was a hard little place that could not feel love, no, not for anybody. Everybody else said of her: "She is such a good mother. She adores her children." Only she herself, and her children themselves, knew it was not so. They read it in each other's eyes.

There were a boy and two little girls. They lived in a pleasant house, with a garden, and they had discreet servants, and felt themselves superior to anyone in the neighbourhood.

Although they lived in style, they felt always an anxiety in the house. There was never enough money. The mother had a small income, and the father had a small income, but not nearly enough for the social position which they had to keep up. The

287

father went in to town to some office. But though he had good prospects, these prospects never materialized. There was always the grinding sense of the shortage of money, though the style was always kept up.

At last the mother said: "I will see if *I* can't make something." But she did not know where to begin. She racked her brains, and tried this thing and the other, but could not find anything successful. The failure made deep lines come into her face. Her children were growing up, they would have to go to school. There must be more money, there must be more money. The father, who was always very handsome and expensive in his tastes, seemed as if he never *would* be able to do anything worth doing. And the mother, who had a great belief in herself, did not succeed any better, and her tastes were just as expensive.

And so the house came to be haunted by the unspoken phrase: *There must be more money! There must be more money!* The children could hear it all the time, though nobody said it aloud. They heard it at Christmas, when the expensive and splendid toys filled the nursery. Behind the shining modern rocking-horse, behind the smart doll's-house, a voice would start whispering: "There *must* be more money! There *must* be more money!" And the children would stop playing, to listen for a moment. They would look into each other's eyes, to see if they had all heard. And each one saw in the eyes of the other two that they too had heard. "There *must* be more money! There *must* be more money!"

It came whispering from the springs of the still-swaying rocking-horse, and even the horse, bending his wooden, champing head, heard it. The big doll, sitting so pink and smirking in her new pram, could hear it quite plainly, and seemed to be smirking all the more self-consciously because of it. The foolish puppy, too, that took the place of the teddy bear, he was looking so extraordinarily foolish for no other reason but that he heard the secret whisper all over the house: "There *must* be more money!"

Yet nobody ever said it aloud. The whisper was everywhere, and therefore no one spoke it. Just as no one ever says: "We are breathing!" in spite of the fact that breath is coming and going all the time.

"Mother," said the boy Paul one day, "why don't we keep a car of our own? Why do we always use uncle's, or else a taxi?"

"Because we're the poor members of the family," said the mother.

"But why *are* we, mother?"

"Well—I suppose," she said slowly and bitterly, "it's because your father has no luck."

The boy was silent for some time.

"Is luck money, mother?" he asked rather timidly.

"No, Paul. Not quite. It's what causes you to have money."

"Oh!" said Paul vaguely. "I thought when Uncle Oscar said *filthy lucker*, it meant money."

"*Filthy lucre* does mean money," said the mother. "But it's lucre, not luck."

"Oh!" said the boy. "Then what *is* luck, mother?"

"It's what causes you to have money. If you're lucky you have money. That's why it's better to be born lucky than rich. If you're rich, you may lose your money. But if you're lucky, you will always get more money."

"Oh! Will you? And is father not lucky?"

"Very unlucky, I should say," she said bitterly.

The boy watched her with unsure eyes.

"Why?" he asked.

"I don't know. Nobody ever knows why one person is lucky and another unlucky."

"Don't they? Nobody at all? Does *nobody* know?"

"Perhaps God. But He never tells."

"He ought to, then. And aren't you lucky either, mother?"

"I can't be, if I married an unlucky husband."

"But by yourself, aren't you?"

"I used to think I was, before I married. Now I think I am very unlucky indeed."

"Why?"

"Well—never mind! Perhaps I'm not really," she said.

The child looked at her, to see if she meant it. But he saw, by the lines of her mouth, that she was only trying to hide something from him.

"Well, anyhow," he said stoutly, "I'm a lucky person."

"Why?" said his mother, with a sudden laugh.

He stared at her. He didn't even know why he had said it.

"God told me," he asserted, brazening it out.

"I hope He did, dear!" she said, again with a laugh, but rather bitter.

"He did, mother!"

"Excellent!" said the mother, using one of her husband's exclamations.

The boy saw she did not believe him; or, rather, that she paid no attention to his assertion. This angered him somewhat, and made him want to compel her attention.

He went off by himself, vaguely, in a childish way, seeking for the clue to "luck." Absorbed, taking no heed of other people, he went about with a sort of stealth, seeking inwardly for luck. He wanted luck, he wanted it, he wanted it. When the two girls were playing dolls in the nursery, he would sit on his big rocking-horse, charging madly into space, with a frenzy that made the little girls peer at him uneasily. Wildly the horse careered, the waving dark hair of the boy tossed, his eyes had a strange glare in them. The little girls dared not speak to him.

When he had ridden to the end of his mad little journey, he climbed down and stood in front of his rocking-horse, staring fixedly into its lowered face. Its red mouth was slightly open, its big eye was wide and glassy-bright.

"Now!" he would silently command the snorting steed. "Now, take me to where there is luck! Now take me!"

And he would slash the horse on the neck with the little whip he had asked Uncle Oscar for. He *knew* the horse could take him to where there was luck, if only he forced it. So he would mount again, and start on his furious ride, hoping at last to get there. He knew he could get there.

"You'll break your horse, Paul!" said the nurse.

"He's always riding like that! I wish he'd leave off!" said his elder sister Joan.

But he only glared down on them in silence. Nurse gave him up. She could make nothing of him. Anyhow he was growing beyond her.

One day his mother and his Uncle Oscar came in when he was on one of his furious rides. He did not speak to them.

"Hallo, you young jockey! Riding a winner?" said his uncle.

"Aren't you growing too big for a rocking-horse? You're not a very little boy any longer, you know," said his mother.

But Paul only gave a blue glare from his big, rather close-set eyes. He would speak to nobody when he was in full tilt. His mother watched him with an anxious expression on her face.

At last he suddenly stopped forcing his horse into the mechanical gallop, and slid down.

"Well, I got there!" he announced fiercely, his blue eyes still flaring, and his sturdy long legs straddling apart.

"Where did you get to?" asked his mother.

"Where I wanted to go," he flared back at her.

"That's right, son!" said Uncle Oscar. "Don't you stop till you get there. What's the horse's name?"

"He doesn't have a name," said the boy.

"Gets on without all right?" asked the uncle.

"Well, he has different names. He was called Sansovino last week."

"Sansovino, eh? Won the Ascot. How did you know his name?"

"He always talks about horse-races with Bassett," said Joan.

The uncle was delighted to find that his small nephew was posted with all the racing news. Bassett, the young gardener, who had been wounded in the left foot in the war and had got his present job through Oscar Cresswell, whose batman he had been, was a perfect blade of the "turf." He lived in the racing events, and the small boy lived with him.

Oscar Cresswell got it all from Bassett.

"Master Paul comes and asks me, so I can't do more than tell him, sir," said Bassett, his face terribly serious, as if he were speaking of religious matters.

"And does he ever put anything on a horse he fancies?"

"Well—I don't want to give him away—he's a young sport, a fine sport, sir. Would you mind asking him himself? He sort of takes a pleasure in it, and perhaps he'd feel I was giving him away, sir, if you don't mind."

Bassett was serious as a church.

The uncle went back to his nephew and took him off for a ride in the car.

"Say, Paul, old man, do you ever put anything on a horse?" the uncle asked.

The boy watched the handsome man closely.

"Why, do you think I oughtn't to?" he parried.

"Not a bit of it! I thought perhaps you might give me a tip for the Lincoln."

The car sped on into the country, going down to Uncle Oscar's place in Hampshire.

"Honour bright?" said the nephew.

"Honour bright, son!" said the uncle.

"Well, then, Daffodil."

"Daffodil! I doubt it, sonny. What about Mirza?"

"I only know the winner," said the boy. "That's Daffodil."

"Daffodil, eh?"

There was a pause. Daffodil was an obscure horse comparatively.

"Uncle!"

"Yes, son?"

"You won't let it go any further, will you? I promised Bassett."

"Bassett be damned, old man! What's he got to do with it?"

"We're partners. We've been partners from the first. Uncle, he lent me my first five shillings, which I lost. I promised him, honour bright, it was only between me and him; only you gave me that ten-shilling note I started winning with, so I thought you were lucky. You won't let it go any further, will you?"

The boy gazed at his uncle from those big, hot, blue eyes, set rather close together. The uncle stirred and laughed uneasily.

"Right you are, son! I'll keep your tip private. Daffodil, eh? How much are you putting on him?"

"All except twenty pounds," said the boy. "I keep that in reserve."

The uncle thought it a good joke.

"You keep twenty pounds in reserve, do you, you young romancer? What are you betting, then?"

"I'm betting three hundred," said the boy gravely. "But it's between you and me, Uncle Oscar! Honour bright?"

The uncle burst into a roar of laughter.

"It's between you and me all right, you young Nat Gould," he said, laughing. "But where's your three hundred?"

"Bassett keeps it for me. We're partners."

"You are, are you! And what is Bassett putting on Daffodil?"

"He won't go quite as high as I do, I expect. Perhaps he'll go a hundred and fifty."

"What, pennies?" laughed the uncle.

"Pounds," said the child, with a surprised look at his uncle. "Bassett keeps a bigger reserve than I do."

Between wonder and amusement Uncle Oscar was silent. He pursued the matter no further, but he determined to take his nephew with him to the Lincoln races.

"Now, son," he said. "I'm putting twenty on Mirza, and I'll put five for you on any horse you fancy. What's your pick?"

"Daffodil, uncle."

"No, not the fiver on Daffodil!"

"I should if it was my own fiver," said the child.

"Good! Good! Right you are! A fiver for me and a fiver for you on Daffodil."

The child had never been to a race-meeting before, and his eyes were blue fire. He pursed his mouth tight, and watched. A Frenchman just in front had put his money on Lancelot. Wild with excitement, he flayed his arms up and down, yelling *"Lancelot! Lancelot"* in his French accent.

Daffodil came in first, Lancelot second, Mirza third. The child, flushed and with eyes blazing, was curiously serene. His uncle brought him four five-pound notes, four to one.

"What am I to do with these?" he cried, waving them before the boy's eyes.

"I suppose we'll talk to Bassett," said the boy. "I expect I have fifteen hundred now; and twenty in reserve; and this twenty."

His uncle studied him for some moments.

"Look here, son!" he said. "You're not serious about Bassett and that fifteen hundred, are you?"

"Yes, I am. But it's between you and me, uncle. Honour bright!"

"Honour bright all right, son! But I must talk to Bassett."

"If you'd like to be a partner, uncle, with Bassett and me, we could all be partners. Only, you'd have to promise, honour bright, uncle, not to let it go beyond us three. Bassett and I are lucky, and you must be lucky, because it was your ten shillings I started winning with. . . ."

Uncle Oscar took both Bassett and Paul into Richmond Park for an afternoon, and there they talked.

"It's like this, you see, sir," Bassett said. "Master Paul would get me talking about racing events, spinning yarns, you know, sir. And he was always keen on knowing if I'd made or if I'd lost. It's about a year since, now, that I put five shilling on Blush of Dawn for him—and we lost. Then the luck turned, with that ten shillings he had from you, that we put on Singhalese. And since that time, it's been pretty steady, all things considering. What do you say, Master Paul?"

"We're all right when we're sure," said Paul. "It's when we're not quite sure that we go down."

"Oh, but we're careful then," said Bassett.

"But when are you *sure*?" smiled Uncle Oscar.

"It's Master Paul, sir," said Bassett, in a secret, religious voice. "It's as if he had it from heaven. Like Daffodil, now, for the Lincoln. That was as sure as eggs."

"Did you put anything on Daffodil?" asked Oscar Cresswell.

"Yes, sir. I made my bit."

"And my nephew?"

Bassett was obstinately silent, looking at Paul.

"I made twelve hundred, didn't I, Bassett? I told uncle I was putting three hundred on Daffodil."

"That's right," said Bassett, nodding.

"But where's the money?" asked the uncle.

"I keep it safe locked up, sir. Master Paul he can have it any minute he likes to ask for it."

"What, fifteen hundred pounds?"

"And twenty! And *forty*, that is, with the twenty he made on the course."

"It's amazing!" said the uncle.

"If Master Paul offers you to be partners, sir, I would, if I were you; if you'll excuse me," said Bassett.

Oscar Cresswell thought about it.

"I'll see the money," he said.

They drove home again, and sure enough, Bassett came round to the garden-house with fifteen hundred pounds in notes. The twenty pounds reserve was left with Joe Glee, in the Turf Commission deposit.

"You see, it's all right, uncle, when I'm *sure!* Then we go strong, for all we're worth. Don't we, Bassett?"

"We do that, Master Paul."

"And when are you sure?" said the uncle, laughing.

"Oh, well, sometimes I'm *absolutely* sure, like about Daffodil," said the boy; "and sometimes I have an idea; and sometimes I haven't even an idea, have I, Bassett? Then we're careful, because we mostly go down."

"You do, do you! And when you're sure, like about Daffodil, what makes you sure, sonny?"

"Oh, well, I don't know," said the boy uneasily. "I'm sure, you know, uncle; that's all."

"It's as if he had it from heaven, sir," Bassett reiterated.

"I should say so!" said the uncle.

But he became a partner. And when the Leger was coming on, Paul was "sure" about Lively Spark, which was a quite inconsiderable horse. The boy insisted on putting a thousand on the horse, Bassett went for five hundred, and Oscar Cresswell two hundred. Lively Spark came in first, and the betting had been ten to one against him. Paul had made ten thousand.

"You see," he said, "I was absolutely sure of him."

Even Oscar Cresswell had cleared two thousand.

"Look here, son," he said, "this sort of thing makes me nervous."

"It needn't, uncle! Perhaps I shan't be sure again for a long time."

"But what are you going to do with your money?" asked the uncle.

"Of course," said the boy, "I started it for mother. She said she had no luck, because father is unlucky, so I thought if *I* was lucky, it might stop whispering."

"What might stop whispering?"

"Our house. I *hate* our house for whispering."

"What does it whisper?"

"Why—why"—the boy fidgeted—"why, I don't know. But it's always short of money, you know, uncle."

"I know it, son, I know it."

"You know people send mother writs, don't you, uncle?"

"I'm afraid I do," said the uncle.

"And then the house whispers, like people laughing at you behind your back. It's awful, that is! I thought if I was lucky . . ."

"You might stop it," added the uncle.

The boy watched him with big blue eyes, that had an uncanny cold fire in them, and he said never a word.

"Well, then!" said the uncle. "What are we doing?"

"I shouldn't like mother to know I was lucky," said the boy.

"Why not, son?"

"She'd stop me."

"I don't think she would."

"Oh!"—and the boy writhed in an odd way—"I *don't* want her to know, uncle."

"All right, son! We'll manage it without her knowing."

They managed it very easily. Paul, at the other's suggestion, handed over five thousand pounds to his uncle, who deposited it with the family lawyer, who was then to inform Paul's mother that a relative had put five thousand pounds into his hands, which sum was to be paid out a thousand pounds at a time, on the mother's birthday, for the next five years.

"So she'll have a birthday present of a thousand pounds for five successive years," said Uncle Oscar. "I hope it won't make it all the harder for her later."

Paul's mother had her birthday in November. The house had been "whispering" worse than ever lately, and, even in spite of his luck, Paul could not bear up against it. He was very anxious to see the effect of the birthday letter, telling his mother about the thousand pounds.

When there were no visitors, Paul now took his meals with his parents, as he was beyond the nursery control. His mother went into town nearly every day. She had discovered that she had an odd knack of sketching furs and dress materials, so she worked secretly in the studio of a friend who was the chief "artist" for the leading drapers. She drew the figures of ladies in furs and ladies in silk and sequins for the newspaper advertisements. This young woman artist earned several thousand pounds a year, but Paul's mother only made several hundreds, and she was again dissatisfied. She so wanted to be first in something, and she did not succeed, even in making sketches for drapery advertisements.

She was down to breakfast on the morning of her birthday. Paul watched her face as she read her letters. He knew the lawyer's letter. As his mother read it, her face hardened and became more expressionless. Then a cold, determined look came on her mouth. She hid the letter under the pile of others, and said not a word about it.

"Didn't you have anything nice in the post for your birthday, mother?" said Paul.

"Quite moderately nice," she said, her voice cold and absent.

She went away to town without saying more.

But in the afternoon Uncle Oscar appeared. He said Paul's mother had had a long interview with the lawyer, asking if the whole five thousand could not be advanced at once, as she was in debt.

"What do you think, uncle?" said the boy.

"I leave it to you, son."

"Oh, let her have it, then! We can get some more with the other," said the boy.

"A bird in the hand is worth two in the bush, laddie!" said Uncle Oscar.

"But I'm sure to *know* for the Grand National; or the Lincolnshire; or else the Derby. I'm sure to know for *one* of them," said Paul.

So Uncle Oscar signed the agreement, and Paul's mother touched the whole five thousand. Then something very curious happened. The voices in the house suddenly went mad, like a chorus of frogs on a spring evening. There were certain new furnishings, and Paul had a tutor. He was *really* going to Eton, his father's school, in the following autumn. There were flowers in the winter, and a blossoming of the luxury Paul's mother had been used to. And yet the voices in the house, behind the sprays of mimosa and almond blossom, and from under the piles of iridescent cushions, simply trilled and screamed in a sort of ecstasy: "There *must* be more money! Oh-h-h; there *must* be more money. Oh, now, now-w! Now-w-w—there *must* be more money!—more than ever! More than ever!"

It frightened Paul terribly. He studied away at his Latin and Greek with his tutors. But his intense hours were spent with Bassett. The Grand National had gone by: he had not "known," and had lost a hundred pounds. Summer was at hand. He was in agony for the Lincoln. But even for the Lincoln he didn't "know," and he lost fifty pounds. He became wild-eyed and strange, as if something were going to explode in him.

"Let it alone, son! Don't you bother about it!" urged Uncle Oscar. But it was as if the boy couldn't really hear what his uncle was saying.

"I've got to know for the Derby! I've got to know for the Derby!" the child reiterated, his big blue eyes blazing with a sort of madness.

His mother noticed how overwrought he was.

"You'd better go to the seaside. Wouldn't you like to go now to the seaside, instead of waiting? I think you'd better," she said, looking down at him anxiously, her heart curiously heavy because of him.

But the child lifted his uncanny blue eyes.

"I couldn't possibly go before the Derby, mother!" he said. "I couldn't possibly!"

"Why not?" she said, her voice becoming heavy when she was opposed. "Why not? You can still go from the seaside to see the Derby with your Uncle Oscar, if that's what you wish. No need for you to wait here. Besides, I think you care too much about these races. It's a bad sign. My family has been a gambling family, and you won't know till you grow up how much damage it has done. But it has done damage. I shall have to send Bassett away, and ask Uncle Oscar not to talk racing to you, unless you promise to be reasonable about it; go away to the seaside and forget it. You're all nerves!"

"I'll do what you like, mother, so long as you don't send me away till after the Derby," the boy said.

"Send you away from where? Just from this house?"

"Yes," he said, gazing at her.

"Why, you curious child, what makes you care about this house so much, suddenly? I never knew you loved it."

He gazed at her without speaking. He had a secret within a secret, something he had not divulged, even to Bassett or to his Uncle Oscar.

But his mother, after standing undecided and a little bit sullen for some moments, said:

"Very well, then! Don't go to the seaside till after the Derby, if you don't wish it. But promise me you won't let your nerves go to pieces. Promise you won't think so much about horse-racing and *events,* as you call them!"

"Oh, no," said the boy casually. "I won't think much about them, mother. You needn't worry. I wouldn't worry, mother, if I were you."

"If you were me and I were you," said his mother, "I wonder what we *should* do!"

"But you know you needn't worry, mother, don't you?" the boy repeated.

"I should be awfully glad to know it," she said wearily.

"Oh, well, you *can,* you know. I mean, you *ought* to know you needn't worry," he insisted.

"Ought I? Then I'll see about it," she said.

Paul's secret of secrets was his wooden horse, that which had no name. Since he was emancipated from a nurse and a nursery-governess, he had had his rocking-horse removed to his own bedroom at the top of the house.

"Surely, you're too big for a rocking-horse!" his mother had remonstrated.

"Well, you see, mother, till I can have a *real* horse, I like to have *some* sort of animal about," had been his quaint answer.

"Do you feel he keeps you company?" she laughed.

"Oh, yes! He's very good, he always keeps me company, when I'm there," said Paul.

So the horse, rather shabby, stood in an arrested prance in the boy's bedroom.

The Derby was drawing near, and the boy grew more and more tense. He hardly heard what was spoken to him, he was very frail, and his eyes were really uncanny. His mother had sudden strange seizures of uneasiness about him. Sometimes, for half-an-hour, she would feel a sudden anxiety about him that was almost anguish. She wanted to rush to him at once, and know he was safe.

Two nights before the Derby, she was at a big party in town, when one of her rushes of anxiety about her boy, her first-born, gripped her heart till she could hardly speak. She fought with the feeling, might and main, for she believed in common-sense. But it was too strong. She had to leave the dance and go downstairs to telephone to the country. The children's nursery-governess was terribly surprised and startled at being rung up in the night.

"Are the children all right, Miss Wilmot?"

"Oh, yes, they are quite all right."

"Master Paul? Is he all right?"

"He went to bed as right as a trivet. Shall I run up and look at him?"

"No," said Paul's mother reluctantly. "No! Don't trouble. It's all right. Don't sit up. We shall be home fairly soon." She did not want her son's privacy intruded upon.

"Very good," said the governess.

It was about one o'clock when Paul's mother and father drove up to their house. All was still. Paul's mother went to her room and slipped off her white fur cloak. She had told her maid not to wait up for her. She heard her husband downstairs, mixing a whisky-and-soda.

And then, because of the strange anxiety at her heart, she stole upstairs to her son's room. Noiselessly she went along the upper corridor. Was there a faint noise? What was it?

She stood, with arrested muscles, outside his door, listening. There was a strange, heavy, and yet not loud noise. Her heart stood still. It was a soundless noise, yet rushing and powerful. Something huge, in violent, hushed motion. What was it? What in God's name was it? She ought to know. She felt that she knew the noise. She knew what it was.

Yet she could not place it. She couldn't say what it was. And on and on it went, like a madness.

Softly, frozen with anxiety and fear, she turned the door-handle.

The room was dark. Yet in the space near the window, she heard and saw something plunging to and fro. She gazed in fear and amazement.

Then suddenly she switched on the light, and saw her son, in his green pyjamas, madly surging on the rocking-horse. The blaze of light suddenly lit him up, as he urged the wooden horse, and lit her up, as she stood, blonde, in her dress of pale green and crystal, in the doorway.

"Paul!" she cried. "Whatever are you doing?"

"It's Malabar!" he screamed, in a powerful, strange voice. "It's Malabar!"

His eyes blazed at her for one strange and senseless second, as he ceased urging his wooden horse. Then he fell with a crash to the ground, and she, all her tormented motherhood flooding upon her, rushed to gather him up.

But he was unconscious, and unconscious he remained, with some brain-fever. He talked and tossed, and his mother sat stonily by his side.

"Malabar! It's Malabar! Bassett, Bassett, I *know!* It's Malabar!"

So the child cried, trying to get up and urge the rocking-horse that gave him his inspiration.

"What does he mean by Malabar?" asked the heart-frozen mother.

"I don't know," said the father stonily.

"What does he mean by Malabar?" she asked her brother Oscar.

"It's one of the horses running for the Derby," was the answer.

And, in spite of himself, Oscar Cresswell spoke to Bassett, and himself put a thousand on Malabar: at fourteen to one.

The third day of the illness was critical: they were waiting for a change. The boy, with his rather long, curly hair, was tossing ceaselessly on the pillow. He neither slept nor regained consciousness, and his eyes were like blue stones. His mother sat, feeling her heart had gone, turned actually into a stone.

In the evening, Oscar Cresswell did not come, but Bassett sent a message, saying could he come up for one moment, just one moment? Paul's mother was very angry at the intrusion, but on second thought she agreed. The boy was the same. Perhaps Bassett might bring him to consciousness.

The gardener, a shortish fellow with a little brown moustache, and sharp little brown eyes, tip-toed into the room, touched his imaginary cap to Paul's mother, and stole to the bedside, staring with glittering, smallish eyes, at the tossing, dying child.

"Master Paul!" he whispered. "Master Paul! Malabar came in first all right, a clean win. I did as you told me. You've made over seventy thousand pounds, you have; you've got over eighty thousand. Malabar came in all right, Master Paul."

"Malabar! Malabar! Did I say Malabar, mother? Did I say Malabar? Do you think I'm lucky, mother? I knew Malabar, didn't I? Over eighty thousand pounds! I call that lucky, don't you, mother? Over eighty thousand pounds! I knew, didn't I know I knew? Malabar came in all right. If I ride my horse till I'm sure, then I tell you, Bassett, you can go as high as you like. Did you go for all you were worth, Bassett?"

"I went a thousand on it, Master Paul."

"I never told you, mother, that if I can ride my horse, and *get there,* then I'm absolutely sure—oh, absolutely! Mother, did I ever tell you? I *am* lucky!"

"No, you never did," said the mother.

But the boy died in the night.

And even as he lay dead, his mother heard her brother's voice saying to her: "My God, Hester, you're eighty-odd thousand to the good, and a poor devil of a son to the bad. But, poor devil, poor devil, he's best gone out of a life where he rides his rocking-horse to find a winner."

QUESTIONS

1   What does each of the main characters in the story—the mother, Paul, Bassett, and Uncle Oscar—symbolize? How is the characterization of each appropriate to what he symbolizes?
2   What different meanings are attached to the word, *luck?*
3   How is Paul's "winning" part of the ironic conflict?
4   How does Lawrence use description to heighten the grotesque events in his story?
5   How is the final statement consistent with Lawrence's view of the destructive effect of materialistic greed?

TOPICS FOR COMPOSITION

1   Many segments of our society would agree with Lawrence that the emphasis on materialism is a primary destructive force. In fact, our polluted environment stands as testimony to Lawrence's point. Write an essay arguing that modern society has embraced materialism to the detriment of human values.
2   Write an essay in which you persuasively present a balance between man's basic drive for material acquisition and his sense of human values.

That Robert Penn Warren's main character cannot cope with sudden fame and affluence is true. But we should also recognize that Luke Goodwood's inability to adjust was unique and not merely the logical outcome of his small-town background. For instance, the narrator and others react differently to the same background. Taking a larger perspective, we can better understand the depth of Warren's characterization if we see Luke's problems as facets of other themes seen in other parts of this book. As you read this story, consider how Luke's behavior is motivated by the following:

1   His search for his place in society
2   His lack of personal restraint
3   His confused, seemingly indifferent attitude toward the meaning of love

GOODWOOD COMES BACK

Robert Penn Warren

Luke Goodwood always could play baseball, but I never could, to speak of. I was little for my age then, but well along in my studies and didn't want to play with the boys my size; I wanted to play with the boys in my class, and if it hadn't been for Luke, I never would have been able to. He was a pitcher then, like he has always been, and so he would say, "Aw, let him field." When he was pitching, it didn't matter much who was fielding, anyway, because there weren't going to be any hits to amount to anything in the first place. I used to play catcher some, too, because I had the best mitt, but he pitched a mighty hard ball and it used to fool the batter all right, but it fooled me too a good part of the time so I didn't hold them so good. Also, I was a little shy about standing close up to the plate on account of the boys flinging the bat the way they did when they started off for first base. Joe Lancaster was the worst for that, and since he almost always played on the other side, being a good hitter to balance off Luke's pitching, I had to come close, nearly getting scared to death of him braining me when he did get a hit. Luke used to yell, "For Christ sake get up to that plate or let somebody else catch for Christ sake that can!"

Joe Lancaster wasn't much bigger than I was, but he was knotty and old-looking, with a white face and hair that was almost white like an old man's, but he wasn't exactly an albino. He was a silent and solemn kind of boy, but he could sure hit; I can remember how he used to give that ball a good solid crack, and start off running the bases with his short legs working fast like a fox terrier's trying to catch up with something, but his face not having any expression and looking like it was dead or was thinking about something else. I've been back home since and seen him in the restaurant where he works behind the counter. I'm bigger than he is now, for he never did grow much. He says hello exactly like a stranger that never saw you before and asks what you want. When he has his sleeves rolled up in the summertime, and puts an order on the counter for you, his arms are small like a boy's, still, with very white skin you can see the veins through.

It was Joe hit me in the head with a bat when I was catching. Luke ran up toward the plate, yelling, "You've killed him!"—for the bat knocked me clean over. It was the last time I played catcher; the next time I came out bringing my mitt, which was a good one, Luke said, "Gimme that mitt." He took it and gave it to another boy, and told me to go play field. That was the only thing I didn't like about Luke, his taking my mitt.

I stayed at the Goodwood house a lot, and liked it, even if it was so different from my own. It was like a farmhouse, outside and inside, but the town was growing out toward it, making it look peculiar set so far back off the street with barns and chicken yards behind it. There was Mr. Goodwood, who had been a sheriff once and who had a bullet in his game leg, they said, a big man one time, but now with his skin too big for him and hanging in folds. His mustache was yellow from the chewing tobacco he used and his eyes were bloodshot; some people said he was drinking himself to death, but I'll say this for him, he drank himself to death upstairs without making any fuss. He had four boys, and drink was their ruination. They say it was likker got Luke out of the big league, and none of the Goodwoods could ever leave the poison alone. Anyway, the Goodwood house was a man's house with six men sitting down to the table, counting the grandfather, and Mrs. Goodwood and her daughter going back and forth to the kitchen with sweat on their faces and their hair damp from the stove. There would be men's coats on the chairs in the living room, sometimes hunting coats with the old blood caked on the khaki, balls of twine and a revolver on the mantel-piece, and shotguns and flyrods lying around, even on the spare bed that was in the living room. And the bird dogs came in the house whenever they got good and ready. At my house everything was different, for men there always seemed to be just visiting.

Luke took me hunting with him, or sometimes one of his big brothers took us both, but my mother didn't like for me to go with the grown boys along, because she believed that their morals were not very good. I don't suppose their morals were much worse than ordinary for boys getting their sap up, but hearing them talk was certainly an education for a kid. Luke was as good a shot as you ever hope to see. He hunted a lot by himself, too, for my folks wouldn't let me go just all the time. He would get up before day and eat some cold bread and coffee in the kitchen and then be gone till after dark with his rifle or his shotgun. He never took anything to eat with him, either, for when he was hunting he was like they say the Indians were in that respect. Luke reminded you of an Indian, too, even when he was a boy and even if he was inclined to be a blond and not a brunette; he was long and rangy, had a big fine-cut nose, and looked to be setting his big feet always carefully on the ground, and came up on his toes a little, like a man testing his footing. He walked that way even on a concrete walk, probably from being in the woods so much. It was no wonder with all his hunting he never did study or make any good use and profit of his mind, which was better than most people's, however. The only good grades he made were in penmanship, copybooks still being used then in the grammar school part of school. He could make his writing look exactly like the writing at the top of the page, a Spencerian hand tilted forward, but not too much like a woman's. He could draw a bird with one line without taking the pencil off the paper once, and he'd draw them all afternoon in school sometimes. The birds all looked alike, all fine and rounded off like his Spencerian writing, their beaks always open, but not looking like any birds God ever made in this world. Sometimes he would put words coming out of a bird's bill, like "You bastard," or worse; then he would scratch it out, for he might just as well have signed his name to it, because the teachers and everybody knew how well he could draw a bird in that way he had.

Luke didn't finish high school. He didn't stop all at once, but just came less and less, coming only on bad days most of the time, for on good days he would be off hunting or fishing. It was so gradual, him not coming, that nobody, maybe not even the teachers, knew when he really stopped for good. In the summer he would lie around the house, sleeping out in the yard on the grass where it was shady, stretched out like a cat, with just a pair of old pants on. Or he would fish or play baseball. It got so he was playing baseball for little town teams around that section, and he picked up some change to buy shells and tackle.

That was the kind of life he was living when I finished school and left town. We had drifted apart, you might say, by that time, for he didn't fool around with the school kids any more. I never found out exactly how he broke into real baseball and got out of what you call the sand lot. My sister wrote me some big man in the business saw Luke pitch some little game somewhere and Luke was gone to pitch for a team up in Indiana somewhere. Then the next year he got on the sport page in the papers. My sister, knowing I would be interested in the boy that was my friend, you might say, used to find out about the write-ups and send me clippings when the home paper would copy stories about Luke from the big papers. She said Luke was making nine thousand dollars playing for the Athletics, which was in Philadelphia. The papers called him the Boy Wizard from Alabama. He must have been making a lot of money that year to judge from the presents he sent home. He sent his mother a five-hundred-dollar radio set and a piano, and I admired him for the way he remembered his mother, who had had a hard time and no doubt about it. I don't know why he sent the piano, because nobody at his house could play one. He also fixed up the house, which was in a bad shape by that time. Mr. Goodwood was still alive, but according to all reports he was spending more time upstairs than ever, and his other three boys never were worth a damn, not even for working in the garden, and didn't have enough git-up-and-git to even go fishing.

The next year Luke pitched in the World Series, for the team that bought him from the Athletics, in Philadelphia, and he got a bonus of three thousand dollars, plus his salary. But he must have hit the skids after that, drink being the reason that was reported to me. When he was home on vacation, my sister said he did some fishing and hunting, but pretty soon he was drunk all the time, and carousing around. The next year he didn't finish the season. My sister sent me a clipping about it, and wrote on the margin, "I'm sure you will be sorry to know this because I know you always liked Luke. I like Luke too." For a matter of fact, I never saw a woman who didn't like Luke, he was so good-looking and he had such a mixture of wildness and a sort of embarrassment around women. You never saw a finer-looking fellow in your life than he was going down the street in summer with nothing on except old khaki pants and underwear tops and his long arms and shoulders near the color of coffee and his blondish hair streaked golden color with sunburn. But he didn't have anything to do with girls, that is, decent girls, probably because he was too impatient. I don't suppose he ever had a regular date in his life.

But the next year he was back in baseball, but not in such a good team, for he had done some training and lived clean for a while before the season opened. He came back with great success, it looked like at first. I was mighty glad when I got a clipping from my sister with the headlines, *Goodwood Comes Back*. He was shutting them out right and left. But it didn't last. The drink got him, and he was out of the big time game for good and all, clean as a whistle. Then he came back home.

It was on a visit home I saw him after all that time. I was visiting my sister, who was married and lived there, and I had taken a lawn mower down to the blacksmith shop to get it fixed for her. I was waiting out in front of the shop, leaning against one side of the door and looking out in the gravel street, which was sending up heat-dazzles. Two or three old men were sitting there, not even talking; they were the kind of old men you find sitting around town like that, who never did amount to a damn and whose names even people in town can't remember half the time. I saw Luke coming up the road with another boy, who didn't strike me as familiar right off because he was one of those who had grown up in the meantime. I could see they were both nearly drunk, when they got under the shade of the shed; and I noticed Luke's arms had got pretty stringy. I said hello to Luke, and he said, "Well, I'll be damned, how you making it?" I said, "Fine, how's it going?" Then he said, "Fine."

After they stood there a while I could see the other boy wasn't feeling any too good with the combination of whisky and the heat of the day. But Luke kept kidding him and trying to make him go up to the Goodwood house, where he said he had some more whisky. He said he had kept it under a setting hen's nest for two weeks to age, and the other boy said Luke never kept any whisky in his life two days, let alone two weeks, without drinking it up. It was bootleg whisky they were drinking, because Alabama was a dry state then, according to the law, even after repeal; Luke must have been kidding too, because he ought to know if anybody does, whisky don't age in glass whether it's under a setting hen or not. Then he tried to make the boy go up to Tangtown, which is what they call nigger town because of the immoral goings-on up there, where they could get some more whisky, he said, and maybe something else. The other boy said it wasn't decent in the middle of the afternoon. Then he asked me to go, but I said no thanks to the invitation, not ever having approved of that, and Tangtown especially, for it looks like to me a man ought to have more self-respect. The old men sitting there were taking in every word, probably jealous because they weren't good for drinking or anything any more.

Finally Luke and the other boy started up the road in the hot sun, going I don't know where, whether to his house or off to Tangtown in the middle of the afternoon. One of the old men said, "Now, ain't it a shame the way he's throwed away his chances." One of the others said likker always was hard on the Goodwoods. Luke, not being any piece off and having good ears even if he was drinking, must have heard them, for he stooped down and scooped up a rock from the road like a baseball player scooping up an easy grounder, and yelled, "Hey, see that telephone pole?" Then he threw the rock like a bullet and slammed the pole, which was a good way off. He turned around, grinning pretty sour, and yelled, "Still got control, boys!" Then the two of them went off.

It was more than a year before I saw him again, but he had been mentioned in letters from my sister, Mrs. Hargreave, who said that Luke was doing better and that his conduct was not so outrageous, as she put it. His mother's dying that year of cancer may have quieted him down some. And then he didn't have any money to buy whisky with. My sister said he was hunting again and in the summer pitching a little ball for the town team that played on Saturday and Sunday afternoons with the other teams from the towns around there. His pitching probably was still good enough to make the opposition look silly. But maybe not, either, as might be judged from what I heard the next time I saw him. I was sitting on the front porch of my sister's house, which is between the Goodwood house and what might be called the heart of town. It stands close up to the street without much yard like all the houses built since the street got to be a real street and not just a sort of road with a few houses scattered along it. Some men were putting in a concrete culvert just in front of the house, and since it was the middle of the day, they were sitting on the edge of the concrete walk eating their lunch and smoking. When Luke came along, he stopped to see what they were doing and got down in the ditch to inspect it. Although it was getting along in the season, there were still enough leaves on the vine on my sister's porch to hide me from the street, but I could hear every word they said. One of the workmen asked Luke when the next game would be. He said Sunday with Millville. When they asked him if he was going to win, he said he didn't know because Millville had a tough club to beat all right. I noticed on that trip home that the boys talked about their ball club, and not their ball team. It must have been Luke's influence. Then one of the men sitting on the curb said in a tone of voice that sounded righteous and false somehow in its encouragement, "We know you can beat 'em, boy!" For a minute Luke didn't say anything; then he said, "Thanks," pretty short, and turned off down the street, moving in that easy yet fast walk of his that always seemed not to be taking any effort.

It was a couple of days later when I was sitting in my sister's yard trying to cool off, that he came by and saw me there and just turned in at the gate. We said hello, just like we had been seeing each other every day for years, and he sat down in the other chair without waiting to be asked, just like an old friend, which he was. It wasn't long before he got out of the chair, though, and lay on the grass, just like he always used to do, lying relaxed all over just like an animal. I was a little bit embarrassed at first, I reckon, and maybe he was, too, for we hadn't sort of sat down together like that for near fifteen years, and he had been away and been a big league pitcher, at the top of his profession almost, and here he was back. He must have been thinking along the same lines, for after he had been there on the grass a while he gave a sort of laugh and said, "Well, we sure did have some pretty good times when we were kids going round this country with our guns, didn't we?" I said we sure did. I don't know whether Luke really liked to remember the times we had or whether he was just being polite and trying to get in touch with me again, so to speak.

Then he got to talking about the places he had been and the things he had seen. He said a man took him to a place in some city, Pittsburgh I believe it was, and showed him the biggest amount of radium there is in the world in one place. His mother having died of cancer not much more than a year before that day we were talking must have made him remember that. He told me how he shot alligators in Florida and went deep-sea fishing. That was the only good time he had away from home, he said, except the first year when the Athletics farmed him out to a smaller team. I was getting embarrassed when he started to talk about baseball, like you will when somebody who has just had a death in the family starts talking natural, like nothing had happened, about the departed one. He said his first year in Pennsylvania he got six hundred dollars a month from the club he was pitching for, plus a little extra. "Being raised in a town like this," he said, "a fellow don't know what to do with real money." So he wrote home for them to crate up his bird dogs and express them to him; which they did. He leased a farm to put his dogs on and hired somebody to take care of them for him, because he couldn't be out there all the time, having his job to attend to. Then he bought some more dogs, for he always was crazy about dogs, and bought some Chinese ring-neck pheasants to put on his farm. He said that was a good time, but it didn't last.

He told me about some other pitchers too. There was one who used to room with him when the club went on the road. Every time they got to a new city, that pitcher made the rounds of all the stores, then the boxes would begin coming to the hotel room, full of electric trains and mechanical automobiles and boats, and that grown man would sit down and play with them and after the game would hurry back so he could play some more. Luke said his friend liked trains pretty well, but boats best, and used to keep him awake half the night splashing in the bathtub. There was another pitcher up in Indiana who went to a roadhouse with Luke, where they got drunk. They got thrown out of the place because that other pitcher, who was a Polak, kept trying to dance with other people's women. The Polak landed on a rock pile and put his hand down and found all the rocks were just the size of baseballs, and him a pitcher. He started breaking windows, and stood everybody off till the cops came. But Luke was gone by that time; so the police called up the hotel to tell Luke there was a guy needed two thousand dollars to get out of jail. So he and three other players went down and put up five hundred apiece to get the fellow out, who was sobered up by that time and wanted to go to bed and get some rest. Luke didn't know that fellow very well and when the Polak went off with the team to play some little game and Luke didn't go, he figured his five hundred was gone too. The fellow didn't come back with the team, either, for he had slipped off, so he figured he had really kissed his five hundred good-bye. But the night before the trial, about three o'clock in the morning, there was a hammering on the hotel room door and before Luke could open it, somebody stuck a fist through the panel and opened it. And there was the Polak, wearing a four-bit tuxedo and patent-leather shoes and a derby hat, and his tie under one ear, drunk. He fell flat on the floor, clutching twenty-three hundred dollars' worth of bills in his hands. That Polak had gone back to the mines, having been a miner before he got in baseball, and had gambled for three days, and there he was to pay back the money as soon as he could. Luke said he wouldn't take money from a man who was drunk because the man might not remember and might want to pay him again when he got sober; so he got his the next morning. The fine and expense of fixing up the roadhouse wasn't as much as you'd expect, and the Polak had a good profit, unless a woman who got hit in the head with a rock and sued him got the rest. Luke didn't know how much she got. He said all pitchers are crazy as hell one way or another.

He told me about things that he saw or got mixed up with, but he said he never had a good time after he had to give up the farm where he had the dogs and the Chinese ring-neck pheasants. He said after that it wasn't so good any more, except for a little time in Florida, shooting alligators and fishing. He had been raised in the coun-try, you see, and had the habit of getting up mighty early, with all that time on his hands till the game started or practice. For a while he used to go to the gymnasium in the mornings and take a work-out, but the manager caught on and stopped that because he wouldn't be fresh for the game. There wasn't anything to do in the mornings after that, he said, except pound the pavements by himself, everybody else still being asleep, or ride the lobbies, and he didn't have a taste for reading, not ever having cultivated his mind like he should. Most of the boys could sleep late, but he couldn't, being used to getting up before sun to go fishing or hunting or something. He said he could have stood the night drinking all right, it was the morning drinking got him down. Lying there on the grass, all relaxed, it didn't look like he gave a damn either.

He had his plans all worked out. If he could get hold of a few hundred dollars he was going to buy him a little patch of ground back in the country where it was cheap, and just farm a little and hunt and fish. I thought of old Mr. Bullard, an old bachelor who lived off in a cabin on the river and didn't even bother to do any farming any more, they said, or much fishing, either. I used to see him come in town on a Saturday afternoon, walking nine miles in just to sit around in the stores looking at people, but not talking to them, or, if the weather was good, just standing on the street. But Luke probably liked to hunt and fish better than Mr. Bullard ever did in his life, and that was something for a man to hold on to. I told Luke I hoped he got his farm, and that now was the time to buy while the depression was on and land was cheap as dirt. He laughed at that, thinking I was trying to make a joke, which I wasn't, and said, "Hell, a farm ain't nothing but dirt, anyway."

After lying there some more, having about talked himself out, he got up and remarked how he had to be shoving on. We shook hands in a formal way, this time, not like when he came in the yard. I wished him luck, and he said, "The same to you," and when he got outside the gate, he said, "So long, buddy."

About six months later he got married, much to my surprise. My sister wrote me about it and sent a clipping about it. His bride was a girl named Martha Sheppard, who is related to my family in a distant way, though Lord knows my sister wouldn't claim any kin with them. And I reckon they aren't much to brag on. The girl had a half-interest in a piece of land out in the country, in the real hoot-owl sticks, you might say, where she lived with her brother, who had the other half-share. I guessed at the time when I read the letter that Luke just married that girl because it was the only way he could see to get the little piece of ground he spoke of. I never saw the girl to my recollection, and don't know whether she was pretty or not.

I have noticed that people living way back in the country like that are apt to be different from ordinary people who see more varieties and kinds of people every day. That maybe accounts for the stories you read in papers about some farmer way back off the road getting up some morning and murdering his whole family before breakfast. They see the same faces every day till some little something gets to preying on their mind and they can't stand it. And it accounts for the way farmers get to brooding over some little falling-out with a neighbor and start bushwhacking each other with shotguns. After about a year Martha Sheppard's brother shot Luke. My sister wrote me the bad blood developed between them because Luke and his wife didn't get along so well together. I reckon she got to riding him about the way he spent his time, off hunting and all. Whatever it was, her brother shot Luke with Luke's own shotgun, in the kitchen one morning. He shot him three times. The gun was a .12-gauge pump gun, and you know what even one charge of a .12-gauge will do at close range like a kitchen.

QUESTIONS

1 Warren takes considerable care in describing the Goodwood place and Luke's father. How do his descriptions foreshadow Luke's character and the eventual outcome?
2 What is the importance of the narrator's position? In other words, is he merely the storyteller?
3 Why does the narrator tell us about Joe Lancaster? Recall that he mentions Joe later in the story.
4 How do we know that baseball isn't really Luke's place?

TOPICS FOR COMPOSITION

1 The notion of "winning" is important in both Lawrence's and Warren's stories. Analyze the emphasis on winning in each story.
2 Organized sports to a large extent dominate the American scene today. What does Warren's story seem to say about the individual and team spirit? Argue the question in light of today's emphasis on sports and its candor about its athletes' personal lives.

We need only read the first paragraph of B. Traven's "Assembly Line" to recognize that the ever-active American businessman is the object of the story's satire. But we should not overlook Traven's concern with the place of art in modern society. As you read, notice how Traven presents:

1 The life of the Indian artist
2 The general reception of his artistic endeavors
3 Winthrop and the confectioner's attitudes toward the value of the baskets
4 The improbability of Winthrop's expectations

ASSEMBLY LINE

B. Traven

Mr. E. L. Winthrop of New York was on vacation in the Republic of Mexico. It wasn't long before he realized that this strange and really wild country had not yet been fully and satisfactorily explored by Rotarians and Lions, who are forever conscious of their glorious mission on earth. Therefore, he considered it his duty as a good American citizen to do his part in correcting this oversight.

In search for opportunities to indulge in his new avocation, he left the beaten track and ventured into regions not especially mentioned, and hence not recommended, by travel agents to foreign tourists. So it happened that one day he found himself in a little, quaint Indian village somewhere in the State of Oaxaca.

Walking along the dusty main street of this pueblecito, which knew nothing of pavements, drainage, plumbing, or of any means of artificial light save candles or pine splinters, he met with an Indian squatting on the earthen-floor front porch of a palm hut, a so-called jacalito.

The Indian was busy making little baskets from bast and from all kinds of fibers gathered by him in the immense tropical bush which surrounded the village on all sides. The material used had not only been well prepared for its purpose but was also richly colored with dyes that the basket-maker himself extracted from various native plants, barks, roots and from certain insects by a process known only to him and the members of his family.

His principal business, however, was not producing baskets. He was a peasant who lived on what the small property he possessed—less than fifteen acres of not too fertile soil—would yield, after much sweat and labor and after constantly worrying over the most wanted and best suited distribution of rain, sunshine, and wind and the changing balance of birds and insects beneficial or harmful to his crops. Baskets he made when there was nothing else for him to do in the fields, because he was unable to dawdle. After all, the sale of his baskets, though to a rather limited degree only, added to the small income he received from his little farm.

In spite of being by profession just a plain peasant, it was clearly seen from the small baskets he made that at heart he was an artist, a true and accomplished artist. Each basket looked as if covered all over with the most beautiful sometimes fantastic ornaments, flowers, butterflies, birds, squirrels, antelope, tigers, and a score of other animals of the wilds. Yet, the most amazing thing was that these decorations, all of them symphonies of color, were not painted on the baskets but were instead actually part of the baskets themselves. Bast and fibers dyed in dozens of different colors were so cleverly—one must actually say intrinsically—interwoven that those attractive designs appeared on the inner part of the basket as well as on the outside. Not by painting but by weaving were those highly artistic effects achieved. This performance he accomplished without ever looking at any sketch or pattern. While working on a basket these designs came to light as if by magic, and as long as a basket was not entirely finished one could not perceive what in this case or that the decoration would be like.

People in the market town who bought these baskets would use them for sewing baskets or to decorate tables with or window sills, or to hold little things to keep them from lying around. Women put their jewelry in them or flowers or little dolls. There were in fact a hundred and two ways they might serve certain purposes in a household or in a lady's own room.

Whenever the Indian had finished about twenty of the baskets he took them to town on market day. Sometimes he would already be on his way shortly after midnight because he owned only a burro to ride on, and if the burro had gone astray the day before, as happened frequently, he would have to walk the whole way to town and back again.

At the market he had to pay twenty centavos in taxes to sell his wares. Each basket cost him between twenty and thirty hours of constant work, not counting the time spent gathering bast and fibers, preparing them, making dyes and coloring the bast. All this meant extra time and work. The price he asked for each basket was fifty centavos, the equivalent of about four cents. It seldom happened, however, that a buyer paid outright the full fifty centavos asked—or four reales as the Indian called that money. The prospective buyer started bargaining, telling the Indian that he ought to be ashamed to ask such a sinful price. "Why, the whole dirty thing is nothing but ordinary petate straw which you find in heaps wherever you may look for it; the jungle is packed full of it," the buyer would argue. "Such a little basket, what's it good for anyhow? If I paid you, you thief, ten centavitos for it you should be grateful and kiss my hand. Well, it's your lucky day, I'll be generous this time, I'll pay you twenty, yet not one green centavo more. Take it or run along.''

So he sold finally for twenty-five centavos, but then the buyer would say, "Now, what do you think of that? I've got only twenty centavos change on me. What can we do about that? If you can change me a twenty-peso bill, all right, you shall have your twenty-five fierros." Of course, the Indian could not change a twenty-peso bill and so the basket went for twenty centavos.

He had little if any knowledge of the outside world or he would have known that what happened to him was happening every hour of every day to every artist all over the world. That knowledge would perhaps have made him very proud, because he would have realized that he belonged to the little army which is the salt of the earth and which keeps culture, urbanity and beauty for their own sake from passing away.

Often it was not possible for him to sell all the baskets he had brought to market, for people here as elsewhere in the world preferred things made by the millions and each so much like the other that you were unable, even with the help of a magnifying glass, to tell which was which and where was the difference between two of the same kind.

Yet he, this craftsman, had in his life made several hundreds of those exquisite baskets, but so far no two of them had he ever turned out alike in design. Each was an individual piece of art and as different from the other as was a Murillo from a Velás-quez.

Naturally he did not want to take those baskets which he could not sell at the market place home with him again if he could help it. In such a case he went peddling his products from door to door where he was treated partly as a beggar and partly as a vagrant apparently looking for an opportunity to steal, and he frequently had to swallow all sorts of insults and nasty remarks.

Then, after a long run, perhaps a woman would finally stop him, take one of the baskets and offer him ten centavos, which price through talks and talks would perhaps go up to fifteen or even to twenty. Nevertheless, in many instances he would actually get no more than just ten centavos, and the buyer, usually a woman, would grasp that little marvel and right before his eyes throw it carelessly upon the nearest table as if to say, "Well, I take the piece of nonsense only for charity's sake. I know my money is wasted. But then, after all, I'm a Christian and I can't see a poor Indian die of hunger since he has come such a long way from his village." This would remind her of something better and she would hold him and say, "Where are you at home anyway, Indito? What's your pueblo? So, from Huehuetonoc? Now, listen here, Indito, can't you bring me next Saturday two or three turkeys from Huehuetonoc? But they must be heavy and fat and very, very cheap or I won't even touch them. If I wish to pay the regular price I don't need you to bring them. Understand? Hop along, now, Indito."

The Indian squatted on the earthen floor in the portico of his hut, attended to his work and showed no special interest in the curiosity of Mr. Winthrop watching him. He acted almost as if he ignored the presence of the American altogether.

"How much that little basket, friend?" Mr. Winthrop asked when he felt that he at least had to say something so as not to appear idiotic.

"Fifty centavitos, patroncito, my good little lordy, four reales," the Indian answered politely.

"All right, sold," Mr. Winthrop blurted out in a tone and with a wide gesture as if he had bought a whole railroad. And examining his buy he added, "I know already who I'll give that pretty little thing to. She'll kiss me for it, sure. Wonder what she'll use it for?"

He had expected to hear a price of three or even four pesos. The moment he realized that he had judged the value six times too high, he saw right away what great business possibilities this miserable Indian village might offer to a dynamic promoter like himself. Without further delay he started exploring those possibilities. "Suppose, my good friend, I buy ten of these little baskets of yours which, as I might as well admit right here and now, have practically no real use whatsoever. Well, as I was saying, if I buy ten, how much would you then charge me apiece?"

The Indian hesitated for a few seconds as if making calculations. Finally he said, "If you buy ten I can let you have them for forty-five centavos each , señorito gentleman."

"All right, amigo. And now, let's suppose I buy from you straight away one hundred of these absolutely useless baskets, how much will cost me each?"

The Indian, never fully looking up to the American standing before him and hardly taking his eyes off his work, said politely and without the slighest trace of enthusiasm in his voice, "In such a case I might not be quite unwilling to sell each for forty centavitos."

Mr. Winthrop bought sixteen baskets, which was all the Indian had in stock.

After three weeks' stay in the Republic, Mr. Winthrop was convinced that he knew this country perfectly, that he had seen everything and knew all about the inhabitants, their character and their way of life, and that there was nothing left for him to explore. So he returned to good old Nooyorg and felt happy to be once more in a civilized country, as he expressed it to himself.

One day going out for lunch he passed a confectioner's and, looking at the display in the window, he suddenly remembered the little baskets he had bought in that faraway Indian village.

He hurried home and took all the baskets he still had left to one of the best-known candy-makers in the city.

"I can offer you here," Mr. Winthrop said to the confectioner, "one of the most artistic and at the same time the most orginal of boxes, if you wish to call them that. These little baskets would be just right for the most expensive chocolates meant for elegant and high-priced gifts. Just have a good look at them, sir, and let me listen."

The confectioner examined the baskets and found them extraordinarily well suited for a certain line in his business. Never before had there been anything like them for originality, prettiness and good taste. He, however, avoided most carefully showing any sign of enthusiasm, for which there would be time enough once he knew the price and whether he could get a whole load exclusively.

He shrugged his shoulders and said, "Well, I don't know. If you asked me I'd say it isn't quite what I'm after. However, we might give it a try. It depends, of course, on the price. In our business the package mustn't cost more than what's in it."

"Do I hear an offer?" Mr. Winthrop asked.

"Why don't you tell me in round figures how much you want for them? I'm not good in guessing."

"Well, I'll tell you, Mr. Kemple: since I'm the smart guy who discovered these baskets and since I'm the only Jack who knows where to lay his hands on more, I'm selling to the highest bidder, on an exclusive basis, of course. I'm positive you can see it my way, Mr. Kemple."

"Quite so, and may the best man win," the confectioner said. "I'll talk the matter over with my partners. See me tomorrow same time, please, and I'll let you know how far we might be willing to go."

Next day when both gentlemen met again Mr. Kemple said: "Now, to be frank with you, I know art on seeing it, no getting around that. And these baskets are little works of art, they surely are. However, we are no art dealers, you realize that of course. We've no other use for these pretty little things except as fancy packing for our French pralines made by us. We can't pay for them what we might pay considering them pieces of art. After all to us they're only wrappings. Fine wrappings, perhaps, but nevertheless wrappings. You'll see it our way I hope, Mr.—oh yes, Mr. Winthrop. So, here is our offer, take it or leave it: a dollar and a quarter apiece and not one cent more."

Mr. Winthrop made a gesture as if he had been struck over the head.

The confectioner, misunderstanding this involuntary gesture of Mr. Winthrop, added quickly, "All right, all right, no reason to get excited, no reason at all. Perhaps we can do a trifle better. Let's say one-fifty."

"Make it one-seventy-five," Mr. Winthrop snapped, swallowing his breath while wiping his forehead.

"Sold. One-seventy-five apiece free at port of New York. We pay the customs and you pay the shipping. Right?"

"Sold," Mr. Winthrop said also and the deal was closed.

"There is, of course, one condition," the confectioner explained just when Mr. Winthrop was to leave. "One or two hundred won't do for us. It wouldn't pay the trouble and the advertising. I won't consider less than ten thousand, or one thousand dozens if that sounds better in your ears. And they must come in no less than twelve different patterns well assorted. How about that?"

"I can make it sixty different patterns or designs."

"So much the better. And you're sure you can deliver ten thousand let's say early October?"

"Absolutely," Mr. Winthrop avowed and signed the contract.

Practically all the way back to Mexico, Mr. Winthrop had a notebook in his left hand and a pencil in his right and he was writing figures, long rows of them, to find out exactly how much richer he would be when this business had been put through.

"Now, let's sum up the whole goddamn thing," he muttered to himself. "Damn it, where is that cursed pencil again? I had it right between my fingers. Ah, there it is. Ten thousand he ordered. Well, well, there we got a clean-cut profit of fifteen thousand four hundred and forty genuine dollars. Sweet smackers. Fifteen grand right into papa's pocket. Come to think of it, that Republic isn't so backward after all."

"Buenas tardes, mi amigo, how are you?" he greeted the Indian whom he found squatting in the porch of his jacalito as if he had never moved from his place since Mr. Winthrop had left for New York.

The Indian rose, took off his hat, bowed politely and said in his soft voice, "Be welcome, patroncito. Thank you, I feel fine, thank you. Muy buenas tardes. This house and all I have is at your kind disposal." He bowed once more, moved his right hand in a gesture of greeting and sat down again. But he excused himself for doing so by saying, "Perdoneme, patroncito, I have to take advantage of the daylight, soon it will be night."

"I've got big business for you, my friend," Mr. Winthrop began.

"Good to hear that, señor."

Mr. Winthrop said to himself, "Now, he'll jump up and go wild when he learns what I've got for him." And aloud he said: "Do you think you can make me one thousand of these little baskets?"

"Why not, patroncito? If I can make sixteen, I can make one thousand also."

"That's right, my good man. Can you also make five thousand?"

"Of course, señor. I can make five thousand if I can make one thousand."

"Good. Now, if I should ask you to make me ten thousand, what would you say? And what would be the price of each? You can make ten thousand, can't you?"

"Of course, I can, señor. I can make as many as you wish. You see, I am an expert in this sort of work. No one else in the whole state can make them the way I do."

"That's what I thought and that's exactly why I came to you."

"Thank you for the honor, patroncito."

"Suppose I order you to make me ten thousand of these baskets, how much time do you think you would need to deliver them?"

The Indian, without interrupting his work, cocked his head to one side and then to the other as if he were counting the days or weeks it would cost him to make all these baskets.

After a few minutes he said in a slow voice, "It will take a good long time to make so many baskets, patroncito. You see, the bast and the fibers must be very dry before they can be used properly. Then all during the time they are slowly drying, they must be worked and handled in a very special way so that while drying they won't lose their softness and their flexibility and their natural brilliance. Even when dry they must look fresh. They must never lose their natural properties or they will look just as lifeless and dull as straw. Then while they are drying up I got to get the plants and roots and barks and insects from which I brew the dyes. That takes much time also, believe me. The plants must be gathered when the moon is just right or they won't give the right color. The insects I pick from the plants must also be gathered at the right time and under the right conditions or else they produce no rich colors and are just like dust. But, of course, jefecito, I can make as many of these canastitas as you wish, even as many as three dozens if you want them. Only give me time."

"Three dozens? Three dozens?" Mr. Winthrop yelled, and threw up both arms in desperation. "Three dozens!" he repeated as if he had to say it many times in his own voice so as to understand the real meaning of it, because for a while he thought that he was dreaming. He had expected the Indian to go crazy on hearing that he was to sell ten thousand of his baskets without having to peddle them from door to door and be treated like a dog with a skin disease.

So the American took up the question of price again, by which he hoped to activate the Indian's ambition. "You told me that if I take one hundred baskets you will let me have them for forty centavos apiece. Is that right, my friend?"

"Quite right, jefecito."

"Now," Mr. Winthrop took a deep breath, "now, then, if I ask you to make me one thousand, that is, ten times one hundred baskets, how much will they cost me, each basket?"

That figure was too high for the Indian to grasp. He became slightly confused and for the first time since Mr. Winthrop had arrived he interrupted his work and tried to think it out. Several times he shook his head and looked vaguely around as if for help. Finally he said, "Excuse me, jefecito, little chief, that is by far too much for me to count. Tomorrow, if you will do me the honor, come and see me again and I think I shall have my answer ready for you, patroncito."

When on the next morning Mr. Winthrop came to the hut he found the Indian as usual squatting on the floor under the overhanging palm roof working at his baskets.

"Have you got the price for ten thousand?" he asked the Indian the very moment he saw him, without taking the trouble to say "Good Morning!"

"Si, patroncito, I have the price ready. You may believe me when I say it has cost me much labor and worry to find out the exact price, because, you see, I do not wish to cheat you out of your honest money."

"Skip that, amigo. Come out with the salad. What's the price?" Mr. Winthrop asked nervously.

"The price is well calculated now without any mistake on my side. If I got to make one thousand canastitas each will be three pesos. If I must make five thousand, each will cost nine pesos. And if I have to make ten thousand, in such a case I can't make them for less than fifteen pesos each." Immediately he returned to his work as if he were afraid of losing too much time with such idle talk.

Mr. Winthrop thought that perhaps it was his faulty knowlege of this foreign language that had played a trick on him.

"Did I hear you say fifteen pesos each if I eventually would buy ten thousand?"

"That's exactly and without any mistake what I've said, patroncito," the Indian answered in his soft courteous voice.

"But now, see here, my good man, you can't do this to me. I'm your friend and I want to help you get on your feet."

"Yes, patroncito, I know this and I don't doubt any of your words."

"Now, let's be patient and talk this over quietly as man to man. Didn't you tell me that if I would buy one hundred you would sell each for forty centavos?"

"Si, jefecito, that's what I said. If you buy one hundred you can have them for forty centavos apiece, provided that I have one hundred, which I don't."

"Yes, yes, I see that." Mr. Winthrop felt as if he would go insane any minute now. "Yes, so you said. Only what I can't comprehend is why you cannot sell at the same price if you make me ten thousand. I certainly don't wish to chisel on the price. I am not that kind. Only, well, let's see now, if you can sell for forty centavos at all, be it fcr twenty or fifty or a hundred, I can't quite get the idea why the price has to jump that high if I buy more than a hundred."

"Bueno, patroncito, what is there so difficult to understand? It's all very simple. One thousand canastitas cost me a hundred times more work than a dozen. Ten thousand cost me so much time and labor that I could never finish them, not even in a hundred years. For a thousand canastitas I need more bast than for a hundred, and I need more little red beetles and more plants and roots and bark for the dyes. It isn't that you just can walk into the bush and pick all the things you need at your heart's desire. One root with the true violet blue may cost me four or five days until I can find one in the jungle. And have you thought how much time it costs and how much hard work to prepare the bast and fibers? What is more, if I must make so many baskets, who then will look after my corn and my beans and my goats and chase for me occasionally a rabbit for meat on Sunday? If I have no corn, then I have no tortillas to eat, and if I grow no beans, where do I get my frijoles from?"

"But since you'll get so much money from me for your baskets you can buy all the corn and beans in the world and more than you need."

"That's what you think, señorito, little lordy. But you see, it is only the corn I grow myself that I am sure of. Of the corn which others may or may not grow, I cannot be sure to feast upon."

"Haven't you got some relatives here in this village who might help you to make baskets for me?" Mr. Winthrop asked hopefully.

"Practically the whole village is related to me somehow or other. Fact is, I got lots of close relatives in this here place."

"Why then can't they cultivate your fields and look after your goats while you make baskets for me? Not only this, they might gather for you the fibers and the colors in the bush and lend you a hand here and there in preparing the material you need for the baskets."

"They might, patroncito, yes, they might. Possible. But then you see who would take care of their fields and cattle if they work for me? And if they help me with the baskets it turns out the same. No one would any longer work his fields in town and I got to take my baskets there. Thank you, señor, for your visit. Adiós."

And in this way it happened that American garbage cans escaped the fate of being turned into receptacles for empty, torn, and crumpled little multicolored canastitas into which an Indian of Mexico had woven dreams of his soul, throbs of his heart: his unsung poems.

QUESTIONS

1 What use does the author make of the intense detail about the making of the baskets?
2 Why is the title appropriate to the satirical thrust of the story?
3 In what ways do we come to understand that the story is a commentary on cross-cultural difficulties?
4 Winthrop cannot understand the Indian's pricing policies. Can we explain them from a purely economic perspective?

TOPICS FOR COMPOSITION

1   Write an essay in which you deal with the story as a complex statement about the artist's role in society and society's acceptance of the artist.

2   Analyze the main character in each of the three stories in this part. Argue that Traven's Indian artist fares better than either of the other two because of the culture in which he lives.

POETRY

One of the fallen angels in Milton's *Paradise Lost* is Mammon, whose name means "wealth." He was, the poet says, the least elevated spirit that fell from heaven.

> . . . for even in Heaven his looks and thoughts
> Were always downward bent, admiring more
> The riches of Heaven's pavement, trodden gold,
> Than aught divine or holy else enjoyed
> In vision beatific. . . .

Here in a single image, Milton defines in poetic fashion the essential evil of materialism—lack of vision. Acceptance of ready-made, highly tangible, easily measurable symbols of status means giving up imagination and initiative, allowing personal development to be sharply restricted, and suffering as a consequence a loss of inner motivation. By envisioning Mammon as originally an inhabitant of heaven, Milton reminds us that freedom from the restrictions of materialism depends finally not upon circumstances but upon individual attitude. There is not necessarily anything wrong with a golden pavement. It might be a pleasant convenience and even an appropriate, if not very vital, symbol of spiritual progress. What is wrong is that Mammon, who represents, of course, a basic tendency in human nature, came to admire the road so much that he no longer looked to see where he was going, which was unfortunate indeed, because he ended up in hell. In the following selection from Spenser's *The Faerie Queene,* we are introduced to the daughter of Mammon, Philotime (meaning "love of wealth and honor"), who also dwells in hell, or, what is the same, the realm of Pluto, god of the underworld and wealth. She too has been thrust from heaven, but continues to deceive her worshippers, who still think her golden chain is the only way to get to heaven.

With a comparable witty incisiveness and imaginative power the other poems of this section define further the effect and some of the outward aspects of materialism. *Epistle IV* of Alexander Pope's *Moral Essays* focuses on a relatively harmless aspect of the materialistic spirit, the abominable taste that so often goes with the love of possessions. He makes his point by describing in detail the country home of an eighteenth-century nobleman, indicating by repeated use of antithesis how perversely culture, sensible economy, and even personal comfort are sacrificed to ostentation. Samuel Johnson probes more deeply into the perversity of materialism, stressing the dangers and the fears to which the lust for money and power exposes its victims: disregard for law and dread of punishment, the multiplication of cares that goes with each advance in status, and the sorry exchange of human dignity and self-possession for advantage in a pointless, never-ending race.

Pope and Johnson show that materialism is opposed to plain good sense. Words-worth and Gerard Manley Hopkins (like Milton, but in different terms) stress its blight-ing effect on the imagination. More specifically, they deplore the fact that preoccupa-tion with "getting and spending" has prevented humankind from seeing the dynamic splendor of nature as the inspiring symbol of creativity that it might be. Our use of nature, they feel, has confused means with ends; inordinate exploitation of nature has obscured the ideal of harmony between human beings and the rest of God's creation. Even more mordantly, though not in the same high style, Arthur Hugh Clough attacks the notorious tendency of his fellow Victorians to equate respectability—i.e., financial well-being—with godliness. Howard Nemerov's "Boom!" and Lawrence Ferlinghetti's "Christ Climbed Down" provide interesting parallels.

"pity this busy monster, manunkind" and "Drug Store," finally, picture very vividly the main symptoms of materialism in our time: the glorification of the scientific reduc-tion of reality to quantitative terms; the sad dependence of youth upon "drugs," that is, crude, mass-produced, artificial stimuli; and the soul-destroying pursuit of shallow dreams prompted by modern advertising. The term "symptoms" is appropriate here, it will be noted, because all three of these poems use metaphors of illness and death. Poets have always regarded materialism as a disease—of the eyes and of the heart.

THE FAERIE QUEENE, BOOK II, CANTO VII

Edmund Spenser

XLIV

A route of people there assembled were,
Of every sort and nation under skye,
Which with great uprore preaced to draw nere
To th' upper part, where was advaunced hye
A stately siege of soveraine majestye; 5
And thereon satt a woman gorgeous gay,
And richly cladd in robes of royaltye,
That never earthly prince in such aray
His glory did enhaunce and pompous pryde display.

XLV

Her face right wondrous faire did seeme to bee, 10
That her broad beauties beam great brightnes threw
Through the dim shade, that all men might it see:
Yet was not that same her owne native hew,

1: *Sir Guyon,* who represents the virtue of temperance, is being conducted by Mammon through the latter's realm. *3 preaced:* pressed. *5 siege:* seat, throne.

But wrought by art and counterfetted shew,
Thereby more lovers unto her to call; 15
Nath'lesse most hevenly faire in deed and vew
She by creation was, till she did fall;
Thenceforth she sought for helps to cloke her crime withall.

XLVI
There as in glistring glory she did sitt,
She held a great old chaine ylincked well, 20
Whose upper end to highest heven was knitt,
And lower part did reach to lowest hell;
And all that preace did rownd about her swell,
To catchen hold of that long chaine, thereby
To climbe aloft, and others to excell: 25
That was Ambition, rash desire to sty,
And every linck thereof a step of dignity.

XLVII
Some thought to raise themselves to high degree
By riches and unrighteous reward;
Some by close shouldring, some by flatteree; 30
Others through friendes, others for base regard;
And all by wrong waies for themselves prepard.
Those that were up themselves, kept others low,
Those that were low themselves, held others hard,
Ne suffred them to ryse or greater grow, 35
But every one did strive his fellow downe to throw.

XLVIII
Which whenas Guyon saw, he gan inquire,
What meant that preace about that ladies throne,
And what she was that did so high aspyre.
Him Mammon answered: 'That goodly one, 40
Whom all that folke with such contention
Doe flock about, my deare, my daughter is:
Honour and dignitie from her alone
Derived are, and all this worldes blis,
For which ye men doe strive: few gett, but many mis. 45

XLIX
'And fayre Philotime she rightly hight,
The fairest wight that wonneth under skye,

14 *shew:* show. 16 *Nath'lesse:* nevertheless. 23 *preace:* throng. 26 *sty:* ascend, climb.
46 *hight:* is named. 47 *wonneth:* dwells.

But that this darksom neather world her light
Doth dim with horror and deformity,
Worthie of heven and hye felicitie, 50
From whence the gods have her for envy thrust;
But sith thou hast found favour in mine eye,
Thy spouse I will her make, if that thou lust,
That she may thee advance for works and merits just.'

L

'Gramercy, Mammon,' said the gentle knight, 55
'For so great grace and offred high estate,
But I, that am fraile flesh and earthly wight,
Unworthy match for such immortall mate
My selfe well wote, and mine unequall fate:
And were I not, yet is my trouth yplight, 60
And love avowd to other lady late,
That to remove the same I have no might:
To chaunge love causelesse is reproch to warlike knight.'

                                                    1590

48 neather: nether, lower.   *52 sith:* since.   *59 wote:* know.   *63 causelesse:* without cause.

QUESTIONS

1 What is the significance of the fact that Philotime has to resort to artifice to enhance her beauty? Remember that she was one of the angels who fell with Satan.
2 What is to be made of the fact that the golden chain of ambition extends from
   heaven to hell?
3 What would marriage to Philotime mean?

From MORAL ESSAYS

Alexander Pope

Epistle IV

Of the Use of Riches
To Richard Boyle, Earl of Burlington

     At Timon's Villa let us pass a day,
Where all cry out, "What sums are thrown away!"
So proud, so grand; of that stupendous air,

1 Timon's Villa: "This description is intended to comprise the principles of a false taste of magnificence, and to exemplify what was said before, that nothing but good sense can attain it." (Pope's
note.)

Soft and agreeable come never there.
Greatness, with Timon, dwells in such a draught   5
As brings all Brobdignag before your thought.
To compass this, his building is a town,
His pond an ocean, his parterre a down:
Who but must laugh, the master when he sees,
A puny insect, shivering at a breeze!   10
Lo, what huge heaps of littleness around!
The whole, a laboured quarry above ground;
Two cupids squirt before; a lake behind
Improves the keenness of the northern wind.
His gardens next your admiration call,   15
On every side you look, behold the wall!
No pleasing intricacies intervene,
No artful wildness to perplex the scene;
Grove nods at grove, each alley has a brother,
And half the platform just reflects the other.   20
The suffering eye inverted nature sees,
Trees cut to statues, statues thick as trees;
With here a fountain, never to be played;
And there a summer-house that knows no shade;
Here Amphitrite sails through myrtle bowers;   25
There gladiators fight, or die in flowers;
Unwatered see the drooping sea-horse mourn,
And swallows roost in Nilus' dusty urn.
        My lord advances with majestic mien,
Smit with the mighty pleasure, to be seen: 30
But soft,—by regular approach,—not yet,—
First through the length of yon hot terrace sweat;
And when up ten steep slopes you've dragged your thighs,
Just at his study door he'll bless your eyes.
        His study! with what authors is it stored?   35
In books, not authors, curious is my lord;
To all their dated backs he turns you round:
These Aldus printed, those Du Sueil has bound.
Lo, some are vellum, and the rest as good
For all his lordship knows, but they are wood.   40
For Locke or Milton 'tis in vain to look,
These shelves admit not any modern book.
        And now the chapel's silver bell you hear,
That summons you to all the pride of prayer;
Light quirks of music, broken and uneven,   45
Make the soul dance upon a jig to Heaven.

5 draught: dose. *6 Brobdignag:* The land of the giants in Swift's *Gulliver's Travels.*   *25 Amphitrite:*
The wife of Poseidon, god of the sea.

On painted ceilings you devoutly stare,
Where sprawl the saints of Verrio or Laguerre,
On gilded clouds in fair expansion lie,
And bring all paradise before your eye.   50
To rest, the cushion and soft dean invite,
Who never mentions hell to ears polite.
          But hark! the chiming clocks to dinner call;
A hundred footsteps scrape the marble hall;
The rich buffet well coloured serpents grace,   55
And gaping Tritons spew to wash your face.
Is this a dinner? this a genial room?
No, 'tis a temple, and a hecatomb.
A solemn sacrifice, performed in state,
You drink by measure, and to minutes eat.   60
So quick retires each flying course, you'd swear
Sancho's dread doctor and his wand were there.
Between each act the trembling salvers ring,
From soup to sweet-wine, and God bless the King.   65
In plenty starving, tantalized in state,
And complaisantly helped to all I hate,
Treated, caressed, and tired, I take my leave,
Sick of his civil pride from morn to eve;
I curse such lavish cost, and little skill,
And swear no day was ever passed so ill.   70

1731

48 *Verrio:* "Verrio (Antonio) painted many ceilings, etc., at Windsor, Hampton Court, etc., and Laguerre at Blenheim Castle and other places." (Pope's note.)   56 *Tritons:* Triton, the son of Poseidon, was shaped like a man from the waist upward, but had the tail of a dolphin. 62 *Sancho's dread doctor:* "See Don Quixote, [Part II] chap. xlvii." (Pope's note.)

QUESTIONS

1   What does Pope mean by "huge heaps of littleness" (line 11)? Do you know what the word oxymoron means?
2   What is the principal basis of the poet's criticism of Timon's villa?

From THE VANITY OF HUMAN WISHES

In Imitation of the Tenth Satire of Juvenal[1]

Samuel Johnson

    But scarce observed, the knowing and the bold
Fall in the general massacre of gold;
Wide-wasting pest! that rages unconfined,
And crowds with crimes the records of mankind:
For gold his sword the hireling ruffian draws;   5
For gold the hireling judge distorts the laws;
Wealth heaped on wealth, nor truth nor safety buys,
The dangers gather as the treasures rise.
    Let history tell, where rival kings command,
And dubious title shakes the madded land,   10
When statutes glean the refuse of the sword,
How much more safe the vassal than the lord;
Low skulks the hind beneath the rage of power,
And leaves the wealthy traitor in the Tower;
Untouched his cottage, and his slumbers sound,   15
Though confiscation's vultures hover round.
    The needy traveller, serene and gay,
Walks the wild heath, and sings his toil away.
Does envy seize thee? crush the upbraiding joy,
Increase his riches, and his peace destroy;   20
New fears in dire vicissitude invade,
The rustling brake alarms, and quivering shade;
Nor light nor darkness bring his pain relief,
One shows the plunder, and one hides the thief.
    Yet still one general cry the skies assails,   25
And gain and grandeur load the tinted gales;
Few know the toiling statesman's fear or care,
The insidious rival and the gaping heir.
    Once more, Democritus, arise on earth,
With cheerful wisdom and instructive mirth,   30
See motley life in modern trappings dressed,
And feed with varied fools the eternal jest:
Thou who couldst laugh where want enchained caprice,
Toil crushed conceit, and man was of a piece;
Where wealth unloved without a mourner died,   35

---

[1] Juvenal was a famous Roman satirist.
13 hind: humble rustic.   *14 Tower:* the Tower of London, where political prisoners were held.
29 Democritus: called the "Laughing philosopher."   *33 want:* poverty.

And scarce a sycophant was fed by pride;
Where ne'er was known the form of mock debate,
Or seen a new-made mayor's unwieldly state;
Where change of favorites made no change of laws,
And senates heard before they judged a cause;   40
How wouldst thou shake at Britain's modish tribe,
Dart the quick taunt, and edge the piercing gibe,
Attentive truth and nature to descry,
And pierce each scene with philosophic eye!
To thee were solemn toys or empty show   45
The robes of pleasure and the veils of woe;
All aid the farce, and all thy mirth maintain,
Whose joys are causeless, or whose griefs are vain.
                                                    1748

38 new-made mayor's unwieldly state: pomp.

THE WORLD IS TOO MUCH WITH US

William Wordsworth

The world is too much with us; late and soon,
Getting and spending, we lay waste our powers:
Little we see in Nature that is ours;
We have given our hearts away, a sordid boon!
The sea that bares her bosom to the moon;   5
The winds that will be howling at all hours,
And are up-gathered now like sleeping flowers;
For this, for everything, we are out of tune;
It moves us not.—Great God! I'd rather be
A pagan suckled in a creed outworn.   10
So might I, standing on this pleasant lea,
Have glimpses that would make me less forlorn;
Have sight of Proteus rising from the sea;
Or hear old Triton blow his wreathed horn.
                                                    1807

4 boon: gift.   *13 Proteus:* a sea god who could assume any shape he wished.   *14 Triton:* another sea god, usually imagined to have a conch-shell trumpet.

QUESTIONS

1 What does the poet mean by saying that nature is ours?
2 Is the poet really interested in creeds, that is, systems of beliefs?

THE BISHOP ORDERS HIS TOMB AT SAINT PRAXED'S CHURCH

[Rome, 15—]

Robert Browning

Vanity, saith the preacher, vanity!
Draw round my bed: is Anselm keeping back?
Nephews—sons mine . . . ah God, I know not! Well—
She, men would have to be your mother once,
Old Gandolf envied me, so fair she was!   5
What's done is done, and she is dead beside,
Dead long ago, and I am Bishop since,
And as she died so must we die ourselves,
And thence ye may perceive the world's a dream.
Life, how and what is it? As here I lie   10
In this state-chamber, dying by degrees,
Hours and long hours in the dead night, I ask
"Do I live, am I dead?" Peace, peace seems all.
Saint Praxed's ever was the church for peace;
And so, about this tomb of mine. I fought   15
With tooth and nail to save my niche, ye know:
—Old Gandolf cozened me, despite my care;
Shrewd was that snatch from out the corner South
He graced his carrion with, God curse the same!
Yet still my niche is not so cramped but thence   20
One sees the pulpit o' the epistle-side,
And somewhat of the choir, those silent seats,
And up into the aery dome where live
The angels, and a sunbeam's sure to lurk:
And I shall fill my slab of basalt there,   25
And 'neath my tabernacle take my rest,
With those nine columns round me, two and two,
The odd one at my feet where Anselm stands:
Peach-blossom marble all, the rare, the ripe
As fresh-poured red wine of a mighty pulse.   30
—Old Gandolf with his paltry onion-stone,
Put me where I may look at him! True peach,
Rosy and flawless: how I earned the prize!

Saint Praxed's Church: an old church in Rome named after a first-century virgin saint who used her riches to aid the poor and the persecuted Christians.   *1 Vanity, saith the preacher:* see Ecclesiastes 1:2.   *5 Old Gandolf:* the Bishop's predecessor on the office.   *15 tomb:* the Bishop, like Gandolf, will be buried in his church and a stone effigy will be placed above his grave.   *21 the epistle-side:* the right-hand side as one faces the altar.   *26 tabernacle:* a canopy.   *31 onion-stone:* inferior marble.

Draw close: that conflagration of my church
—What then? So much was saved if aught were missed!   35
My sons, ye would not be my death? Go dig
The white-grape vineyard where the oil-press stood,
Drop water gently till the surface sinks,
And if ye find . . . Ah, God I know not, I! . . .
Bedded in store of rotten fig-leaves soft,   40
And corded up in a tight olive-frail,
Some lump, ah God, of *lapis lazuli*,
Big as a Jew's head cut off at the nape,
Blue as a vein o'er the Madonna's breast . . .
Sons, all have I bequeathed you, villas, all,   45
That brave Frascati villa with its bath,
So, let the blue lump poise between my knees,
Like God the Father's globe on both his hands
Ye worship in the Jesu Church so gay,
For Gandolf shall not choose but see and burst!   50
Swift as a weaver's shuttle fleet our years:
Man goeth to the grave, and where is he?
Did I say basalt for my slab, sons? Black—
'Twas ever antique-black I meant! How else
Shall ye contrast my frieze to come beneath?   55
The bas-relief in bronze ye promised me,
Those Pans and Nymphs ye wot of, and perchance
Some tripod, thyrsus, with a vase or so,
The Saviour at his sermon on the mount,
Saint Praxed in a glory, and one Pan   60
Ready to twitch the Nymph's last garment off,
And Moses with the tables . . . but I know
Ye mark me not! What do they whisper thee,
Child of my bowels, Anselm? Ah, ye hope
To revel down my villas while I gasp   65
Bricked o'er with beggar's mouldy travertine
Which Gandolf from his tomb-top chuckles at!
Nay, boys, ye love me—all of jasper, then!
'Tis jasper ye stand pledged to, lest I grieve
My bath must needs be left behind, alas!   70
One block, pure green as a pistachio-nut,
There's plenty jasper somewhere in the world—
And have I not Saint Praxed's ear to pray
Horses for ye, and brown Greek manuscripts,

---

41 *olive-frail:* a basket for holding olives.   46 *Frascati:* a luxurious resort.   51 *Swift as a weaver's shuttle:* see Job 7:6.   57 *Pans:* Pan was the Greek god of shepherds.   58 *tripod:* three-legged stool used by the priestess Apollo at Delphi. *thyrsus:* staff used by devotees of Bacchus, god of wine.   66 *travertine:* a kind of limestone.

And mistresses with great smooth marbly limbs? 75
—That's if ye carve my epitaph aright,
Choice Latin, picked phrase, Tully's every word,
No gaudy ware like Gandolf's second line—
Tully, my masters? Ulpian serves his need!
And then how I shall lie through centuries, 80
And hear the blessed mutter of the mass,
And see God made and eaten all day long,
And feel the steady candle-flame, and taste
Good strong thick stupefying incense-smoke!
For as I lie here, hours of the dead night, 85
Dying in state and by such slow degrees,
I fold my arms as if they clasp a crook,
And stretch my feet forth straight as stone can point,
And let the bedclothes, for a mortcloth, drop
Into great laps and folds of sculptor's-work: 90
And as yon tapers dwindle, and strange thoughts
Grow, with a certain humming in my ears,
About the life before I lived this life,
And this life too, popes, cardinals and priests,
Saint Praxed at his sermon on the mount, 95
Your tall pale mother with her talking eyes,
And new-found agate urns as fresh as day,
And marble's language, Latin pure, discreet,
—Aha, elucescebat quoth our friend?
No Tully, said I, Ulpian at the best! 100
Ever your eyes were as a lizard's quick,
All *lapis,* all, sons! Else I give the Pope
My villas! Will ye ever eat my heart?
Ever your eyes were as a lizard's quick,
They glitter like your mother's for my soul, 105
Or ye would heighten my impoverished frieze,
Piece out its starved design, and fill my vase
With grapes, and add a vizor and a term,
And to the tripod ye would tie a lynx
That in his struggle throws the thyrsus down, 110
To comfort me on my entablature
Whereon I am to lie till I must ask
"Do I live, am I dead?" There, leave me, there!
For ye have stabbed me with ingratitude

---

77 Tully: Cicero, whose writings were considered the model of classical Latin.   *79 Ulpian:* a Roman jurist whose style was inferior to that of Cicero.   *82 see God made and eaten:* the Bishop is speaking of the sacrament of the Mass.   *89 mortcloth:* funeral pall.   *99 elucescebat:* the classic synonym for this word, which means "he is famous," is *elucebat.*   *108 vizor:* mask. *term:* a bust on a pedestal.

To death—ye wish it—God, ye wish it! Stone—   115
Gritstone, a-crumble! Clammy squares which sweat
As if the corpse they keep were oozing through—
And no more *lapis* to delight the world!
Well, go! I bless ye. Fewer tapers there,
But in a row: and, going, turn your backs   120
—Ay, like departing altar-ministrants,
And leave me in my church, the church for peace,
That I may watch at leisure if he leers—
Old Gandolf, at me, from his onion-stone,
As still he envied me, so fair she was!   125

                                        1845

116 *gritstone:* coarse sandstone.

QUESTIONS

1   The Bishop is never able to fully envision his tomb; what he is able to imagine is only
    a grotesque mixture of pagan and Christian symbols. Explain the irony of these
    facts. What does the tomb probably symbolize to the Bishop?
2   That the Bishop is vain, materialistic, and unscrupulous is obvious. Does the poet
    make it possible for us to sympathize with him in any way?
3   Line 95 indicates that the Bishop has momentarily lapsed into incoherence because
    of his illness. Could this fact have symbolic implications?

THE LATEST DECALOGUE

Arthur Hugh Clough

Thou shalt have one God only; who
Would be at the expense of two?
No graven images may be
Worshiped, except the currency.
Swear not at all; for, for thy curse   5
Thine enemy is none the worse.
At church on Sunday to attend
Will serve to keep the world thy friend.
Honor thy parents; that is, all
From whom advancement may befall.   10
Thou shalt not kill; but need'st not strive
Officiously to keep alive.
Do not adultery commit;
Advantage rarely comes of it.
Thou shalt not steal; an empty feat,   15

When it's so lucrative to cheat.
Bear not false witness; let the lie
Have time on its own wings to fly.
Thou shalt not covet, but tradition
Approves all forms of competition.   20

1862

GOD'S GRANDEUR

Gerard Manley Hopkins

The world is charged with the grandeur of God.
    It will flame out, like shining from shook foil;
    It gathers to a greatness, like the ooze of oil
Crushed. Why do men then now not reck his rod?
Generations have trod, have trod, have trod;   5
    And all is seared with trade; bleared, smeared with toil;
    And wears man's smudge and shares man's smell: the toil
Is bare now, nor can foot feel, being shod.
And for all this, nature is never spent;
    There lives the dearest freshness deep down things;   10
And though the last lights off the black West went
    Oh, morning, at the brown brink eastward, springs—
Because the Holy Ghost over the bent
    World broods with warm breast and with ah! bright wings.

1918 (Composed 1877)

1 charged: as with electricity. *2 foil:* gold leaf. *4 Crushed:* like oil oozing from crushed olives,
which gathers slowly into a mass before it breaks and flows. *reck his rod:* heed his authority.
14 broods: i.e., like a dove on its nest. The dove traditionally has been the symbol of the Holy
Ghost.

QUESTIONS

1 In what ways is the statement of the first line supported in the remainder of the
    poem? Can you put in your own words the central impression that Hopkins is trying
    to convey?
2 Lines 5–8 convey the general idea of contact with nature. What makes the descrip-
    tion ironic?
3 Does this poem express the same idea as Wordsworth's "The World Is Too Much
    with Us"?
4 What do the last two lines mean? In what way do the last two words reflect the
    meaning of the whole poem?

DRUG STORE

Karl Shapiro

> I do remember an apothecary,
> And hereabouts 'a dwells

It baffles the foreigner like an idiom,
And he is right to adopt it as a form
Less serious than the living-room or bar;
   For it disestablishes the café,
Is a collective, and on basic country.   5

Not that it praises hygiene and corrupts
The ice-cream parlor and the tobacconist's
Is it a center; but that the attractive symbols
   Watch over puberty and leer
Like rubber bottles waiting for sick-use.   10

Youth comes to jingle nickels and crack wise;
The baseball scores are his, the magazines
Devoted to lust, the jazz, the Coca-Cola,
   The lending-library of love's latest.
He is the customer; he is heroized.   15

And every nook and cranny of the flesh
Is spoken to by packages with wiles,
"Buy me, buy me," they whimper and cajole;
   The hectic range of lipstick pouts,
Revealing the wicked and the simple mouth.   20

With scarcely any evasion in their eye
They smoke, undress their girls, exact a stance;
But only for a moment. The clock goes round;
   Crude fellowships are made and lost;
They slump in booths like rags, not even drunk.   25

                         1941

Epigraph: From *Romeo and Juliet*, V, i, 37–38., Romeo is seeking the apothecary in order to buy poison.   *22 undress their girls:* with their eyes, that is.

QUESTIONS

1 The drug store as a social center might be thought an improvement over the ice-cream parlor and the tobacconist's. Why? What is the real reason for its having become a center?

2 What use does the poet make of the fact that the "attractive symbols" appear like things intended for sick-use?
3 How is youth, the customer, "heroized"?
4 What is the state of mind of the young people that frequent the drug store?
5 Why does the poet approach his subject in such a detached, disinterested way? What evidence of a deeper, more emotional concern is there? Would the poem have been more effective if he had used strong terms of indignation or pity?

pity this busy monster,manunkind

e. e. cummings

pity this busy monster,manunkind,

not. Progress is a comfortable disease:
your victim (death and life safely beyond)

plays with the bigness of his littleness
—electrons deify one razorblade   5
into a mountainrange; lenses extend

unwish through curving wherewhen till unwish
returns on its unself.

                    A world of made
is not a world of born—pity poor flesh   10

and trees, poor stars and stones, but never this
fine specimen of hypermagical

ultraomnipotence. We doctors know

a hopeless case if—listen: there's a hell
of a good universe next door; let's go   15

                    1944

QUESTIONS

1 What kind of materialism is satirized in this poem? Does it have to do with personal ambition? Is a kind of ideal involved?
2 What are the scientific achievements described in lines 4–8? What is the author's attitude toward them? What do the coined terms "unwish" and "unself" mean? What general approach to truth or value can be associated with wishing? Does science have anything to do with the wishful self?

3 In what sense is mankind becoming a "monster"? Look up the word in the dictionary if you are familiar with only one sense.
4 Why is this "a hopeless case"?
5 How does one get to the "universe next door"?

DR. SIGMUND FREUD DISCOVERS THE SEA SHELL

Archibald MacLeish

Science, that simple saint, cannot be bothered
Figuring what anything is for:
Enough for her devotions that things are
And can be contemplated soon as gathered.

She knows how every living thing was fathered,   5
She calculates the climate of each star,
She counts the fish at sea, but cannot care
Why any one of them exists, fish, fire or feathered.

Why should she? Her religion is to tell
By rote her rosary of perfect answers.   10
Metaphysics she can leave to man:
She never wakes at night in heaven or hell

Staring at darkness. In her holy cell
There is no darkness ever: the pure candle
Burns, the beads drop briskly from her hand.   15

Who dares to offer Her the curled sea shell!
She will not touch it!—knows the world she sees
Is all the world there is! Her faith is perfect!

1952

QUESTIONS

1 Explain the aptness and the irony of personifying science as a saint. Why is it that
her faith is perfect?
2 What does the sea shell symbolize? You can find in the poem the terms that are the
equivalents of this symbol.
3 Explain the significance of the title. In what way do science and metaphysics come
together in psychoanalysis? Is the subconscious like the sea?

AMERICAN PRIMITIVE

William Jay Smith

Look at him there in his stovepipe hat,
His high-top shoes, and his handsome collar;
Only my Daddy could look like that,
And I love my Daddy like he loves his Dollar.

The screen door bangs, and it sounds so funny—   5
There he is in a shower of gold;
His pockets are stuffed with folding money,
His lips are blue, and his hands feel cold.

He hangs in the hall by his black cravat,
The ladies faint, and the children holler: 10
Only my Daddy could look like that,
And I love my Daddy like he loves his Dollar.

1953

QUESTIONS

1   Who is the primitive in this poem, the speaker (as artist) or the father, or both?
2   Explain the ironies of the poem. Is the form suited to the subject?

BOOM!

Howard Nemerov

SEES BOOM IN RELIGION, TOO
Atlantic City, June 23, 1957 (AP).—President Eisenhower's pastor said tonight that Americans are living in a period of "unprecedented religious activity" caused partially by paid
vacations, the eight-hour day and modern conveniences.
    "These fruits of material progress," said the Rev. Edward L. R. Elson of the National
Presbyterian Church, Washington, "have provided the leisure, the energy, and the means
for a level of human and spiritual values never before reached."

Here at the Vespasian-Carlton, it's just one
religious activity after another; the sky
is constantly being crossed by cruciform
airplanes, in which nobody disbelieves
for a second, and the tide, the tide   5

1: Vespasian was a Roman emperor (A.D. 70–79). The Roman nobles of his time were much given
to luxury. He himself practiced the simple life in an effort to set a good example.

of spiritual progress and prosperity
miraculously keeps rising, to a level
never before attained. The churches are full,
the beaches are full, and the filling-stations
are full, God's great ocean is full   10
of paid vacationers praying an eight-hour day
to the human and spiritual values, the fruits,
the leisure, the energy, and the means, Lord,
the means for the level, the unprecedented level,
and the modern conveniences, which also are full.   15
Never before, O Lord, have the prayers and praises
from belfry and phonebooth, from ballpark and barbecue
the sacrifices, so endlessly ascended.
It was not thus when Job in Palestine
sat in the dust and cried, cried bitterly;   20
when Damien kissed the lepers on their wounds
it was not thus; it was not thus
when Francis worked a fourteen-hour day
strictly for the birds; when Dante took
a week's vacation without pay and it rained   25
part of the time, O Lord, it was not thus.

But now the gears mesh and the tires burn
and the ice chatters in the shaker and the priest
in the pulpit, and Thy Name, O Lord,
is kept before the public, while the fruits   30
ripen and religion booms and the level rises
and every modern convenience runneth over,
that it may never be with us as it hath been
with Athens and Karnak and Nagasaki,
nor Thy sun for one instant refrain from shining   35
on the rainbow Buick by the breezeway
or the Chris Craft with the uplift life raft;
that we may continue to be the just folks we are,
plain people with ordinary superliners and
disposable diaperliners, people of the stop'n'shop   40
'n'pray as you go, of hotel, motel, boatel,
the humble pilgrims of no deposit no return
and please adjust thy clothing, who will give to Thee,
if Thee will keep us going, our annual
Miss Universe, for Thy Name's Sake, Amen.   45

1960

---

21 Damien: Father Damien (1840–1899) was a Belgian missionary to lepers in Molokai.
23 Francis: St. Francis of Assisi (1182–1226) was a great lover of nature. His preaching to the
birds has been a favorite theme in art.   *34 Athens:* part of the site of ancient Thebes.

QUESTIONS

1   What kinds of sacrifice is the poet talking about in this poem?
2   Is this poem a parody?

CHRIST CLIMBED DOWN

Lawrence Ferlinghetti

Christ climbed down
from His bare Tree
this year
and ran away to where
there were no rootless Christmas trees   5
hung with candycanes and breakable stars

Christ climbed down
from His bare Tree
this year
and ran away to where   10
there were no gilded Christmas trees
and no tinsel Christmas trees
and no tinfoil Christmas trees
and no pink plastic Christmas trees
and no gold Christmas trees   15
and no black Christmas trees
and no powderblue Christmas trees
hung with electric candles
and enriched by tin electric trains
and clever cornball relatives   20

Christ climbed down
from His bare Tree
this year
and ran away to where
no intrepid Bible salesmen   25
covered the territory
in two-tone cadillacs
and where no Sears Roebuck crèches
complete with plastic babe in manger
arrived by parcel post   30
the babe by special delivery
and where no televised Wise Men
praised the Lord Calvert Whiskey

2 Tree: the Cross.   *28 crèches:* a crèche is a representation of the Nativity scene—in this case, manufactured.

Christ climbed down
from His bare Tree   35
this year
and ran away to where
no fat handshaking stranger
in a red flannel suit   40
and a fake white beard
went around passing himself off
as some sort of North Pole saint
crossing the desert to Bethlehem
Pennsylvania   45
in a Volkswagon sled
drawn by rollicking Adirondack reindeer
with German names
and bearing sacks of Humble Gifts
from Saks Fifth Avenue   50
for everybody's imagined Christ child

Christ climbed down
from His bare Tree
this year
and ran away to where   55
no Bing Crosby carollers
groaned of a tight Christmas
and where no Radio City angels
iceskated wingless
thru a winter wonderland   60
into a jinglebell heaven
daily at 8:30
with Midnight Mass matinees

Christ climbed down
from His bare Tree   65
this year
and softly stole away into
some anonymous Mary's womb again
where in the darkest night
of everybody's anonymous soul   70
He awaits again
an unimaginable
and impossibly
Immaculate Reconception
the very craziest   75
of Second Comings
                        1958

QUESTIONS

1 Why does Ferlinghetti repeat the word "anonymous" in lines 67 and 69?
2 Explain the satire in lines 71–75. To whom should an immaculate "Reconception" of Christ seem impossible and unimaginable?

YUKON 1897: PRICE OF GOLD

after Jack London

John Briggs

His breath a blear of warmth across the vast white
stilled unreal snowfields—
through the feral silence—on the webs
of snowshoes, the old prospector shuffles
heading North.   5
His lean and faithful dog trots on beside him.

The old man dreams of glory-holes of gold—
dreams the sharp cold gaudy heat
of nuggets—drags his aging breath across
these frozen wastes men   10
civilize by greed—across this blank and zero world
of cold.
He hikes through frozen air
as though through solid ice.

Too late, on ice, he knows of his mistake—   15
across a buried lake he feels the crack and craze
of webbed uncertainness beneath him—
and sinking through receives a shock
that squeezes out his breath.

Fingers numb, he kneels and prays   20
for flame (learns, warmth is real
as riches that he'd looked for).
But yellow nugget-bursts of matches break and fly
and sputter out—
his body fading out,   25
the sharp cold
presses in.

Beneath the frozen sky
the old man sinks into a snowdrift;
in total cold feels somehow warm.   30
In soft snow dreams gaudily . . .
A spider with a body like a nugget
spins his breath like threads
—his vision blurs
and webs   35
with longings . . .

In stark cold air, the stark primeval dog
sniffs briefly at the scents of missing life.

1973

QUESTIONS

1 Does this poem lend itself to symbolic interpretation?
2 Explain the irony that attends the use of nugget imagery.

78 MINERS IN MANNINGTON, WEST VIRGINIA

Louis Phillips

Thanksgiving. They have
taken a sample
of the air,
have found ample

evidence of Carbon Monoxide.   5
Somewhere
in that air
there are
78 miners. If they are alive,
it is a miracle,   10
& no one will save
them now. It is a simple

matter of sealing off the mine
to stop the fires
& the explosions. The wives   15
knew it all along,
it comes with the territory,
but found it impossible

to admit to themselves.
News comes frequently   20
from the Mannington, West Va.
mine, but there are no rumors.
Over the clotheslines,
white ropes dividing
the air with parallel lines,   25
women with stringy hair
refuse each other's mornings.
Their wooden clothespins are
held tight in their lips;
The dungarees shake out   30
their knees and pivot slightly;
early morning dew
keeps the sheets damp.
But there are no rumors.

Day after Thanksgiving. A new   35
explosion rocks the mine.
Some say this is not a poem,
but what does that have to do
with the 78 dead miners   40
of Mannington, West Virginia?
                              1973

QUESTIONS

1 "Some say this is not a poem," the author says. What makes it a poem—what, that is, distinguishes it from a newspaper story?
2 The author asks what the question of whether or not his piece is a poem has to do with 78 dead miners. What does this say about his reason for writing the poem?
3 Why does the author deliberately make his poem resemble a newspaper report?

TOPICS FOR COMPOSITION

1 Using Pope's description of Timon's villa as a model, write an essay on ostentation in modern home or automobile design.
2 Write an essay supporting the thesis that many people value nature in nonmaterialistic ways.
3 Write a comparative study of "The World Is Too Much with Us" and "God's Grandeur."
4 Have the atmosphere and tone of the most typical gathering places of the young changed since Karl Shapiro wrote "Drug Store"? Give your answer in an essay.
5 Using the title "The Man Who Turned to Stone," write a character study of the Bishop of St. Praxed's.

6   Write a line-by-line interpretation or paraphrase of Cummings' "pity this busy mon-ster,manunkind."

7   Write a commentary on the meaning and usefulness of the coined terms in Cum-mings' poem.

8   Does modern advertising as a whole present a single image or idea of the good life? If you think so, write a description of an average day in the life of the typical successful American as conceived by advertisers.

9   Using an invented name, write on the topic "The Most Materialistic Person I Have Known."

10 Drawing from any of the poems of this section that seem helpful, defend the thesis that materialism is the sign of failure of imagination.

11 Not everyone would agree that Lawrence Ferlinghetti's attack on the phoniness of Christmas is fair in all respects. If you partly disagree with him, explain why.

12 Write an essay on the topic "How to Be Happy Without Being Affluent."

13 Write on "Profits Versus Ethics: The Responsibilities of Big Business." You might want to use John Briggs's poem as your starting point.

14 Defend or contest the thesis that there is moral value in the stewardship of wealth.

TOPICS FOR LONGER COMPOSITIONS

1   Look up the ending of Samuel Johnson's "The Vanity of Human Wishes." With this and the other poems of Part Four in mind, write an essay on the relationship among the ideas of progress (D. H. Lawrence's "The Spirit of Place" in Part One can help here), the decline of deep religious faith, and the materialism evident in our society.

2   With Lawrence's "The Rocking-Horse Winner" and Saroyan's "Hello Out There" (Part One), and Joyce Carol Oates's "An Interior Monologue" (Part Three) for illustrations and for comparison and contrast, analyze the relationship between "luck," wealth, and social position, on the one hand, and love and happiness on the other. As a summation, you might consider why writers of this century seem to be unanimously concerned with the dangers materialism poses for self-fulfillment.

3   The short story "Goodwood Comes Back" is an excellent starting point for an essay about materialism, sports, human values, and responsibilities. We are all aware that sports is big business as well as entertainment, and we are aware that its very nature makes super-stars and popular heroes of some of its figures. We are not always as aware of the problems some sports figures encounter when they become suddenly affluent. Using Warren's story for your basic premise, investi-gate such works as Bernard Malamud's *The Natural*, Dave Meggysey's *Out of Their League*, Dan Jenkins' *Semi-Tough*, and Mark Harris's *Bang the Drum Slowly*. As an outgrowth of your reading, write an essay in which you argue the relative worth of athletics in respect to the individual and his or her sense of values.

PART
5

THE SEARCH
FOR MODES
OF EXPRESSION

Because language is always with us, because its acquisition is relatively automatic, and because we use it almost without effort and sometimes almost without thought, we are apt to take it too lightly. What is language? Obviously, the answer is not easily formulated; moreover, the simple question generates additional questions: How is language used? What forms may it take? What is its influence on human behavior? A well-known philosopher of our time offers the following observation:

> Language is, without a doubt, the most momentous and at the same time the most mysterious product of the human mind. Between the clearest animal call of love or warning or anger, and a man's least trivial *word,* there lies a whole day of Creation—or in modern phrase, a whole chapter of evolution.—Suzanne Langer, *Philosophy in a New Key,* 83.

Two essays, dealing with the questions posed above, introduce this unit. For, if we are to concern ourselves with a search for modes of expression, we must, indeed, begin with expression itself.

LeRoi Jones in his essay, "Expressive Language," examines language in its varied cultural expression. Specifically, Jones points out that language—word choice, phrasing, dialectal sound modification—derives its true expression only within the culture that embraces it and, in return, the culture that it identifies. His essay emphasizes that modes of expression in "'pluralistic' America" require sensitive appraisal if we are to seek answers to the questions that introduce this unit.

In his essay, "The Writer on Writing," Paul Engle, poet, novelist, and teacher of writing, draws upon his own experience and the writings of others to identify for us the actual "work" of art and, equally important, those attributes of human behavior and sensitivity to language that are essential to the art and craft of writing. Engle and Jones should both command our attention because each speaks with the authority of the "doer" rather than that of the mere "sayer."

The short story, "The Real Thing," by Henry James also deals with art and its techniques. James's point, however, is much more than his painter-narrator's comment that in art "the real thing could be so much less precious than the unreal." Art, though depicted from the point of view of a painter, serves to illustrate point of view in all artistic endeavors and allows James to examine the attitude of artists in general toward their work; specifically, that process by which artists construct their view of "the real thing."

Donald Barthelme's story, "Engineer-Private Paul Klee Misplaces an Aircraft between Milbertshofen and Cambrai, March 1916," represents Barthelme's experimental manipulation of rather conventional notions about plot. Though improbable, the situation just could happen. We feel involved, but if we attempt to pinpoint the story's reality, we find it ephemeral and sense that we are part of an allegory about heavy issues.

"Modes of Expression" virtually designates the content of Dunsany's little play, "The Glittering Gate." Though the play constitutes no linguistic inquiry, it does point up the cruel gap between our reiteration of hope for life's meaning and our terrifying suspicion that meaningless and consequent hopelessness may lie in wait for us. The brief "one-acter" becomes a dramatic inventory of formulated illusions, the objects of hope, juxtaposed against the nothingness of illusions exposed. The two ex-burglars together discover the bitter truth of Prospero's declaration in *The Tempest:* "We are such stuff / As dreams are made on, and our little life / Is rounded with a sleep." Still, perception and articulation seem to arise from the very nature of the human condition, to be as necessary to life as love and hope.

THE ESSAY

In all likelihood, a title such as "Expressive Language" could cover a number of possible interpretations and directions. LeRoi Jones, however, makes certain that what he means also means the same to us by precisely defining his terms. As you read, give attention to the way a progressive, interlocking defining of terms keys the structure of the essay. For example, his opening sentence, "Speech is the effective form of a culture" leads to a definition of culture, which leads to a definition of context, which leads to a definition of social, and so on.

EXPRESSIVE LANGUAGE

LeRoi Jones

Speech is the effective form of a culture. Any shape or cluster of human history still apparent in the conscious and unconscious habit of groups of people is what I mean by culture. All culture is necessarily profound. The very fact of its longevity, of its being what it is, *culture,* the epic memory of practical tradition, means that it is profound. But the inherent profundity of culture does not necessarily mean that its *uses* (and they are as various as the human condition) will be profound. German culture is profound. Generically. Its uses, however, are specific, as are all uses . . . of ideas, inventions, products of nature. And specificity, as a right and passion of human life, breeds what it breeds as a result of its context.

Context, in this instance, is most dramatically social. And the social, though it must be rooted, as are all evidences of existence, in culture, depends for its impetus for the most part on a multiplicity of influences. Other cultures, for instance. Perhaps, and this is a common occurrence, the reaction or interreaction of one culture on another can produce a social context that will extend or influence any culture in many strange directions.

Social also means *economic,* as any reader of nineteenth-century European philosophy will understand. The economic is part of the social—and in our time much more so than what we have known as the spiritual or metaphysical, because the most valuable canons of power have either been reduced or traduced into stricter economic terms. That is, there has been a shift in the actual meaning of the world since Dante lived. As if Brooks Adams were right. Money does not mean the same thing to me it must mean to a rich man. I cannot, right now, think of one meaning to name. This is not so simple to understand. Even as a simple term of the English language, *money* does not possess the same meanings for the rich man as it does for me, a lower-middle-class

American, albeit of laughably "aristocratic" pretensions. What possibly can "money" mean to a poor man? And I am not talking now about those courageous products of our permissive society who walk knowledgeably into "poverty" as they would into a public toilet. I mean, The Poor.

I look in my pocket; I have seventy cents. Possibly I can buy a beer. A quart of ale, specifically. Then I will have twenty cents with which to annoy and seduce my fingers when they wearily search for gainful employment. I have no idea at this moment what that seventy cents will mean to my neighbor around the corner, a poor Puerto Rican man I have seen hopefully watching my plastic garbage can. But I am certain it cannot mean the same thing. Say to David Rockefeller, "I have money," and he will think you mean something entirely different. That is, if you also dress the part. He would not for a moment think, "Seventy cents." But then neither would many New York painters.

Speech, the way one describes the natural proposition of being alive, is much more crucial than even most artists realize. Semantic philosophers are certainly correct in their emphasis on the final dictation of words over their users. But they often neglect to point out that, after all, it is the actual importance, *power,* of the words that remains so finally crucial. Words have users, but as well, users have words. And it is the users that establish the world's realities. Realities being those fantasies that control your immediate span of life. Usually they are not your own fantasies, i.e., they belong to governments, traditions, etc., which, it must be clear by now, can make for conflict with the singular human life all ways. The fantasy of America might hurt you, but it is what should be meant when one talks of "reality." Not only the things you can touch or see, but the things that make such touching or seeing "normal." Then words, like their users, have a hegemony. Socially—which is final, right now. If you are some kind of artist, you naturally might think this is not so. There is the future. But *immortality* is a kind of drug, I think—one that leads to happiness at the thought of death. Myself, I would rather live forever . . . just to make sure.

The social hegemony, one's position in society, enforces more specifically one's terms (even the vulgar have "pull"). Even to the mode of speech. But also it makes these terms an available explanation of any social hierarchy, so that the words themselves become, even informally, laws. And of course they are usually very quickly stitched together to make formal statutes only fools or the faithfully intrepid would dare to question beyond immediate necessity.

The culture of the powerful is very infectious for the sophisticated, and strongly addictive. To be any kind of "success" one must be fluent in this culture. Know the words of the users, the semantic rituals of power. This is a way into wherever it is you are not now, but wish, very desperately, to get into.

Even speech then signals a fluency in this culture. A knowledge at least. "He's an educated man," is the barest acknowledgment of such fluency . . . in any time. "He's hip," my friends might say. They connote a similar entrance.

And it is certainly the meanings of words that are most important, even if they are no longer consciously acknowledged, but merely, by their use, trip a familiar lever of social accord. To recreate instantly the understood hierarchy of social, and by doing that, cultural importance. And cultures are thought by most people in the world to do their business merely by being hierarchies. Certainly this is true in the West, in as simple a manifestation as Xenophobia, the naïve bridegroom of anti-human feeling, or in economic terms, Colonialism. For instance, when the first Africans were brought into the New World, it was thought that it was all right for them to be slaves because "they were heathens." It is a perfectly logical assumption.

And it follows, of course, that slavery would have been an even stranger phenomenon had the Africans spoken English when they first got here. It would have complicated things. Very soon after the first generations of Afro-Americans mastered this language, they invented white people called Abolitionists.

Words' meanings, but also the rhythm and syntax that frame and propel their concatenation, seek their culture as the final reference for what they are describing of the world. An A flat played twice on the same saxophone by two different men does not have to sound the same. If these men have different ideas of what they want this note to do, the note will not sound the same. Culture is the form, the overall structure of organized thought (as well as emotion and spiritual pretension). There are many cultures. Many ways of organizing thought, or having thought organized. That is, the form of thought's passage through the world will take on as many diverse shapes as there are diverse groups of travelers. Environment is one organizer of *groups,* at any level of its meaning. People who live in Newark, New Jersey, are organized, for whatever purpose, as Newarkers. It begins that simply. Another manifestation, at a slightly more complex level, can be the fact that blues singers from the Midwest sing through their noses. There is an explanation past the geographical, but that's the idea in tabloid. And singing through the nose does propose that the definition of singing be altered . . . even if ever so slightly. (At this point where someone's definitions must be changed, we are flitting around at the outskirts of the old city of Aesthetics. A solemn ghost town. Though some of the bones of reason can still be gathered there.)

But we still need definitions, even if there already are many. The dullest men are always satisfied that a dictionary lists everything in the world. They don't care that you may find out something *extra,* which one day might even be in the dictionary, or at least they'd hope so, if you asked them directly.

But for every item in the world, there are a multiplicity of definitions that fit. And every word we use *could* mean something else. And at the same time. The culture fixes the use, and usage. And in "pluralistic" America, one should always listen very closely when he is being talked to. The speaker might mean something completely different from what we think we're hearing. "Where is your pot?"

I heard an old Negro street singer last week, Reverend Pearly Brown, singing, "God don't never change!" This is a precise thing he is singing. He does not mean "God does not ever change!" He means "God don't never change!" The difference, and I said it was crucial, is in the final human reference . . . the form of passage through the world. A man who is rich and famous who sings, "God don't never change," is confirming his hegemony and good fortune . . . or merely calling the bank. A blind hopeless black American is saying something very different. He is telling you about the extraordinary order of the world. But he is not telling you about his "fate." Fate is a luxury available only to those fortunate citizens with alternatives. The view from the top of the hill is not the same as that from the bottom of the hill. Nor are most viewers at either end of the hill, even certain that, in fact, there is any other place from which to look. Looking down usually eliminates the possibility of understanding what it must be like to look up. Or try to imagine yourself as not existing. It is difficult, but poets and politicians try every other day.

Being told to "speak proper," meaning that you become fluent with the jargon of power, is also a part of not "speaking proper." That is, the culture which desperately understands that it does not "speak proper," or is not fluent with the terms of social strength, also understands somewhere that its desire to gain such fluency is done at a terrifying risk. The bourgeois Negro accepts such risk as profit. But does *close-ter* (in the context of "jes a close-ter, walk wi-thee") mean the same thing as *closer?* Close-ter, in the term of its user is, believe me, exact. It means a quality of existence, of actual physical disposition perhaps . . . in its manifestation as a *tone* and *rhythm* by which people live, most often in response to common modes of thought best enforced by some factor of environmental emotion that is exact and specific. Even the picture it summons is different, and certainly the "Thee" that is used to connect the implied "Me" with, is different. The God of the damned cannot know the God of the damner, that is, cannot know he is God. As no Blues person can really believe emotionally in Pascal's God, or Wittgenstein's question, "Can the concept of God exist in a perfectly logical language?" Answer: "God don't never change."

Communication is only important because it is the broadest root of education. And all cultures communicate exactly what they have, a powerful motley of experience.

QUESTIONS

1 What specific techniques of defining does Jones employ?
2 What does the term hegemony mean and why is it important to this essay's thesis?
3 How does language become a tool of power? In what way does Jones qualify his use of the term?

TOPICS FOR COMPOSITION

1 Accepting Jones's statement that "Speech is the effective form of a culture," write an appraisal of a culture based on how its speech idiom defines its boundaries. You might select a rural culture, the teen culture, or a minority culture.
2 However true it may be that dictionary definitions only satisfy the dullest men, one dictionary, *The Oxford English Dictionary,* is an unparalleled source for examining language change. Write an essay, perhaps organized around a single word entry, in which you explain the scope of the OED's definitions.

Engle's essay, perceptively read, is an extension of the brief quotation from Suzanne Langer's *Philosophy in a New Key* which introduces the literature gathered under "The Search for Modes of Expression." Engle seeks ways to explain the mysterious, creative activity that compels us to project ourselves through our most magnificent accomplishment, language. That accomplishment, that creative interplay with language, becomes an art form which delights, amazes, and (even in the act of trying to explain it) confounds the writer.

THE WRITER ON WRITING

Paul Engle

Writing is like making love—it is astonishing how far pure instinct (if it really is pure) will carry you. It is also true of both these lyrical forms of expression that a few things consciously learned will push toward perfection what might otherwise be an ordinary act.

And yet can writing actually be taught? Is there much more you can give to a beginner beyond Flaubert's no-nonsense advice of a kiss on the brow and a kick on the behind?

In pointing out that a writer crystallizes a concept, as when he endows a woman with qualities she simply does not have, Stendahl produced an image which, however little it flatters the ladies, does dramatize the process by which persuasive words can turn a dull object into something glittering and gay. He observes that a dead branch, dark and ugly, if left overnight in the salt mines of Salzburg, will be covered with crystals and next day will glitter in the sunlight. (Did Stendhal have in mind a few ladies of doubtful feature whom he would have liked to put away in salt mines?)

This image of the salt crystals on the branch wisely and attractively illustrates what the writer does with the curious and secret substance called his "material." What writer has not been stopped by an eager-eyed and bushy-tailed person who cries out despairingly, "I've got the greatest material for a book, if I could just *write!*"

The first and most important point about writing is that there is no such thing as material by itself, apart from the way in which a person sees it, feels toward it, and is able to give it organized form and an expression in words. For a writer, the form is a part of the content, affecting it, realizing it. A man may go through the most dramatic and horrible experiences in war, but actually draw out of them less "material" for writing than shy Emily Dickinson in the second-floor room of an Amherst house lowering notes in baskets out the window and thinking gently of death, or even (biographers speculate) of a man she knew but little, whom she might never see again.

Henry James wrote of experience that it is " an immense sensibility, a kind of huge spider-web of the finest silken threads suspended in the chamber of consciousness, and catching every airborne particle in its tissue. It is the very atmosphere of the mind." This is crucial, for it is not what happens in the outside world which is of absolute significance, but what happens to the external event when it is discovered, and then ordered, by the internal power of mind. James goes on to speak then of the creative aspect: "and when the mind is imaginative . . .it takes to itself the faintest hints of life, it converts the very pulses of the air into revelation."

By experience, then, being a writer does not mean having adventures. In answering a critic who had complained about the novel that it is impossible to have one without bold action, James protested, "Why without adventure, more than without matrimony, or celibacy, or parturition, or cholera . . .?"

Anything is suitable for fiction, which is not a record of incidents happening *to* men and women, but of the response they make within themselves to the incidents. This is because fiction deals with character, which determines action, and thus actions illustrate character. The conduct of a man in a shouting ring, fighting an enraged bull, and the soft wave of a woman's hand are equally moving and suitable.

Experience is not fixed, but varies with the power of perception in the man or woman participating in it. During World War II, experiments at Ohio State University proved that air force applicants were using their eyes normally at around twenty per cent of their real capacity. Heightening the ability to perceive could be, for a pilot in war, a matter of life and death, as he had to discriminate rapidly the shape and identity of an object moving at great speed through the sky.

It is necessary for anyone wanting to be a writer to develop just that sort of intensified perception about human life. Once again, Henry James made the great remark. Recognizing that a young writer should always base his work on his own proved experience, but that before he could do this he must learn to bring into his consciousness as much and as heightened experience as possible, James advised: "Try to be one of the people on whom nothing is lost!"

To demonstrate what he meant by not losing any part of any experience, James cited an example of an English woman novelist who had been praised for writing in such an insightful way about young Protestants in France. On being asked how she had learned so much about these rather scarce people, she replied that only once had she even seen Protestants in France, and then she had not spoken to them. Walking up a staircase in Paris, she passed an open door and saw inside a room the family of a pastor sitting around a table just after dinner.

James then writes: "The glimpse made a picture; it lasted only a moment, but that moment was experience. She had got her direct personal impression, and she turned out her type. She knew what youth was, and what Protestantism; she also had the advantage of having seen what it was to be French, so that she converted these ideas into a concrete image and produced a reality. Above all, however, she was blessed with the faculty which when you give it an inch takes an ell, and which for the artist is a much greater source of strength than any accident of residence or of place in the social scale."

A million Frenchmen may walk down a Paris street (it might be only ten thousand, but being French they would *seem* like a million) and, turning a corner, forget the place, but Toulouse-Lautrec walking down the same street would see, with his shrewd eye, and remember, with his artist's force of retention, not bricks but visions. It is in this way that the imagination works not only on the stuff which is stored in the mind, but also on the very act of experiencing. Like the pilot, the writer must see faster and more completely than the ordinary viewer of life.

Out of his practical skills in the writing of fiction, James described the process of the writer using his experience. "The power to guess the unseen from the seen," he said, "to trace the implication of things, to judge the whole piece by the pattern, the condition of feeling life in general so completely that you are well on your way to knowing any particular corner of it—this cluster of gifts may almost be said to constitute experience, and they occur in country and in town, and in the most differing stages of education. If experience consists of impressions, it may be said that impressions *are* experience, just as (have we not seen it?) they are the very air we breathe."

This is final wisdom about writing. The writer, when given an inch, takes an ell. Remember that an ell is forty-five inches. If that is the degree of heightening, then the eye of the writer must look at life with forty-five times as much perception. That is a marvelous degree of intensity, and in particular when it comes from the author of *Portrait of a Lady*—a book in which, although it concerns the relationship between a man and a woman, it has been remarked that there is only one kiss, and the heroine, poor thing, did not enjoy it.

But some will argue: writing, like all art, is intuitive, and any intrusion of the reason will destroy the lovely, natural thing. This is dead wrong. It reduces writing to the level of a child babbling without regard to the shape of what he is saying. It would be, indeed, so much like the uninhibited confessions from the psychiatrist's couch, sodium amytal cheerfully flowing through the veins and breaking down shyness, that it would seem proper to give inhibition-removing drugs to the writer. He could sit there gaily listening to the rustlings of his unconscious. And of course the hallucinatory state would be the most creative of all.

It is quite possible that some good things could be thus spontaneously created. I met in India people who could induce visions. Yet surely the great and structured works of writing are done with the intelligence playing over against the intuition, each bracing the other, the mind giving form and sense, the intuition giving immediacy of impression, the stored-up memory, the deeply instinctive phrase.

To say that writing comes only from the intuition is to belittle it as coming from one narrow aspect of our lives alone. The opposite is true. The total life of the writer is the source of his work. All of these go into his writing, in varying quantities: the senses, as of taste and touch, the rate of metabolism, the blood pressure, the digestion, the body temperature, the memory of things past, perhaps going back to the childhood not only of the writer but of the race itself, the liveliness and alertness of the brain, previous reading of books, shrewdness of insight into human character, the libido, the ear for the sound of language.

The writer, therefore, must not only have a more than ordinary capacity for life, and the power to retain what he experiences in a readily available memory, he must also have an astonishing degree of self-knowledge. Unless he is aware of his material, he cannot use it, save for the always present quantity which flows up from the deep well of the unconscious recollection. Without access to knowledge of self, the writer can make dreams but not art. As Dr. Lawrence S. Kubie says, without self-knowledge, "We can have the neurotic raw material of literature, but not mature literature. We can have no adults, but only aging children who are armed with words."

By self-knowledge I do not mean self-expression. Although all good writing always bears the individual mark, sound, motion of the writer, he is not trying to put his own self into words, but to create a piece of writing. Often, the less of his own self involved or expressed, the better. His own personality ought to be dissolved into the images or characters of his book. The writer is offering us not reality, but his reaction to whatever reality he has experienced.

Yet the ego is important. It must be that within the creative person there is constant tension between an awareness of the reality around him, a thrusting up of the unconscious life and its memory, and the drive of the ego toward controlling these in a form which also heightens them. These are crude terms to describe subtle conditions, but the creation of any art is one of the most complex of human activities, involving every animal and human quality. The ego must shape the mortal impulses. It is here that something can indeed be taught about writing, for it is in this shaping that the individual's private events are turned into public forms. It is here that writing becomes an art, and not merely a report on experience, and this is true of the best reporting.

The ego is individual. A thousand men looking at the same object will see a thousand different objects. How many people in 1827 knew about the action brought in the Criminal Court of Grenoble against a young man named Antoine Berthet, accused of murder and pleading guilty, with the accused himself writing to the Public Prosecutor, "my wish is that I may be condemned tomorrow, and be led out to execution on the day following . . . I have already found life so hateful, that you, by your prolonged proceedings, can make it no more odious. Let me no longer be compelled to breathe the air of corruption." This took place in the Department of Isère. A writer of the time, not very well known, using the name of Stendhal, was a native of Isère. His real name was Henri Beyle; he had fought with Napoleon in Italy, Germany, France, Russia. His usefulness here is that, of all citizens of France in the dark and cheapened years of the Restoration of a monarchy which had all the characteristics of a vulgar regime and few of an authentic kingliness, he alone wrote a novel based on the life of that pathetic Antoine Berthet. Why? And in what way is Stendhal's novel The Red and the Black a piece of literature and not simply an account of a man murdering a woman who had been his lover?

Antoine Berthet was the son of a blacksmith in a small village. A bright young man, he had been instructed by the local priest, who had found him, when he was nineteen, a position as tutor in the family of an industrialist named Michoud. It seems certain that he made love to Mme. Michoud, and was later fired by M. Michoud. After an unsuccessful attempt to become a student for the priesthood, Berthet again took a job as tutor in a family, and was again fired, on the ground that he had made passionate advances to a daughter of the family. His frustration turned into a conviction that Mme. Michoud was to blame. One Sunday in the village church, while Mme. Michoud had her head bowed during the celebration of the Mass, Berthet shot her in the back, and then tried to commit suicide. Neither died. During the trial, Berthet's head was wrapped in bandages. He begged not for forgiveness but for death.

From this pathetic event the villagers made gossip, but Stendhal made a novel, yet he shared with them an identical knowledge of the incidents, the place, the men and women involved. It seems obvious to us, in another century and with the lapse of many disenchanting years, that Stendhal must have seen in Berthet an image of his own youth, struggling to enter a world more romantic and grander than the one into which he was born, and suffering for a sad and ironic reason: the very intelligence which gave him access to that world also gave him a terrible resentment at not being wholly accepted by it. The intensity of his bitterness came naturally from the intensity of his mind and emotions, and led to the violent action of an attempted murder and suicide.

Reading about this miserable sequence of events was an experience shared by a good many Frenchmen in 1827, but only Stendhal made great literature from it. His creative imagination experienced that story as well his eyes. He shaped his own work of art out of a newspaper reporter's work. What mattered was not the dreary recital of a provincial crime, but the imaginative energies which the events released in a man of high verbal talent, who saw through them to the essential scene as it related to his own life, and gave to that human turbulence a form more living than the men and women who endured it.

It may well be that the substance of a writer's work comes from whatever in his observation he recognizes (perhaps without knowing the recognition) as a shred, an image, a mockery, a vision, of his own life. Myriads of men have almost identical experiences, and have very similar emotional reactions to them. It is the peculiar power of writing that it can shape those feelings into a form which will, in turn, produce the most moving feelings in other men. How many boys have played around greenhouses? Swarms. But how many, on growing up, have put their feelings about that place into powerful poetry? Only Theodore Roethke (died, 1963). His account is proof.

Roethke asks what does it matter that he grew up in and around a beautiful greenhouse, hated school, worked in a pickle factory, lived sometimes quietly and sometimes foolishly and violently, and meant almost nothing to the people of his own state, the man in the street, but passionately desired their regard.

"All such details, and others like them," Roethke comments, "seem particularly trivial and vulgar in my case because I have tried to put down in poems, as barely and honestly as possible, symbolically, what few nuggets of observation and, let us hope, spiritual wisdom I have managed to seize upon in the course of a conventional albeit sometimes disordered existence. I have tried to transmute and purify my 'life,' the sense of being defiled by it in both small and formal and somewhat blunt short poems, and, latterly, in longer poems which try in their rhythms to catch the very movement of the mind itself, to trace the spiritual history of a protagonist (not 'I' personally) of all haunted and harried men; to make in this series (now probably finished) a true and not arbitrary order which will permit many ranges of feeling, including humor. . . ."

And then he says in verse:

> My heart sways with the world.
> I am that final thing,
> A man learning to sing.

Although this may suggest a self-consciousness not shared by all poets, it is further evidence of that deep need for self-knowledge which is a strength and a source. Roethke knew *what* he was trying to do in those moving and often tortured poems, and this awareness, far from inhibiting the imaginative freedom of the verse, enriched it. The cool mind, curiously enough, it seems, really can express a warm feeling.

Once the writer has a sense of his experience, and of his own self, and this must be disenchanted, without illusion, tough-minded about his own weakness and vulgarity, what else can he possibly learn? What can he *do* to make his writing better, assuming that he is not trapped in the conviction that writing is a wholly automatic outburst from underground?

He can examine the knowledge of their own writing habits as great men have made it available. It is odd the things writers have done. The German poet Schiller used to keep rotting apples under the lid of his desk because their smell helped him write.

Pilots on the river at Rouen would see the light in Flaubert's study very late at night as he utterly shut himself away from the world to worry two pages of prose a week into the ruthlessly purified and perfected shape he demanded. Why this enormous care? The old wisecrack says that a physician who fails can always bury his patient out of sight. Frank Lloyd Wright remarked that an architect who fails can at least urge his client to plant vines. The writer, however, once his work is in print, can do nothing. There the text is, black on the page, and any errors and any ugliness will be there forever. There are rare exceptions, of course, like William Butler Yeats, who in his old age, with that marvelous lyrical mind hardened by the criticism of others, went back to the poems of his youth and cut out much of the sentimentality, the soft, vague language.

Reticent as always, William Faulkner said that the tools of the writer's trade are paper, tobacco, food, and whiskey. Of these, the most dangerous is not tobacco or whiskey (and writers are famous for abusing them) but paper. One of the most terrifying sights is that waiting, threatening, blank sheet. Its force is proved by the Japanese writer who, after much success, could not, for a long time, push ahead with his writing. One autumn (this is a true story) he disappeared. The next spring his body was found, after the snow had melted, high up in the mountains. Pinned to his jacket was a note only the suffering writer could have written: "I have done this because I could no longer endure the sight of the empty page."

All those writers who have commented on their craft agree that a work of art is work. How could the joining of passion and idea in slippery words be anything but a labor? That first really modern novel, Madame Bovary, was composed by Gustave Flaubert with the deliberation of a medieval monk cutting the Lord's Prayer on the head of a pin. The French novelist could write quickly and fluently, as his early books and his lively letters show, but he would never give up a sentence until it was beyond improving. To get his description of the landscape correct, he sat all day on a balcony looking through pieces of different colored glass in order to note the changes in shape of fields and roads and trees hour by hour.

Never was a writer more emotionally involved with what he was writing than Flaubert. When he described Emma Bovary poisoning herself, he was so moved that he could taste arsenic on his own tongue and felt so poisoned himself that he vomited his dinner. And yet when he finally finished that scene, he had engineered it onto the page with an almost fanatical control. Once again, the writer's talent had produced an immortal passage out of a passionate deliberation.

Flaubert would begin a single paragraph by setting down its general idea, with perhaps a few images (a risk always, for he had a brilliant image-making faculty; he wrote that he was devoured by metaphors as by vermin and spent his time crushing them). Then he wrote a first draft, reading it aloud for sound and sense (always read any sort of text out loud: the surest way to catch the feeble phrase, the trite adjective, the outworn image, the dull rhythm, the phony speech). Then he would rewrite, again and again, as a fine craftsman polishes over and over the same increasingly brilliant piece of maple or mahogany. Every word which did not act with energy was thrown away, until the paragraph was lean, tough, expressive. Madame Bovary's final version was written on 1,788 pages, but these were only the latest of many times that number of pages actually written. At times, fifteen or twenty pages would be reduced to four. Thus, when Flaubert said that he spent a week over two pages, he meant over the two finally perfected pages out of many more.

Flaubert may be the only man in history who told his girl friend, "You should write more coldly." This was a part of his advice that "We must be on our guard against that kind of intellectual overheating called inspiration, which often consists more largely of nervous emotion than of muscular strength . . . my brow is burning, sentences keep rushing into my head. . . . Instead of one idea I have six, and where the most simple type of exposition is called for I find myself writing similes and metaphors. I could keep going until tomorrow noon without fatigue." And yet he could follow such an outburst with the blunt advice, brief, wise, but taking most writers a lifetime to learn: "Everything should be done coldly, with poise." When putting down the word "hysterics" one day he was so carried away that he bellowed loudly, and felt so sharply what Emma Bovary was going through that he was afraid of having hysterics himself.

Can it be that the French, more than any other people, are able to balance heat and cold, desire and deliberation, and make a single intense but controlled utterance? The modern poet Paul Valéry wrote that poetry must be a holiday of the mind, and then said, with greater calm, that when he writes, "I proceed like a surgeon who sterilizes his hands and prepares the area to be operated on . . . clearing up the verbal situation."

The English seem more practical, if a little less dedicated to perfection. The novelist Joyce Cary described his process thus: "A finished book of mine starts usually perhaps ten years before as a character sketch and a bit of description; it goes on to an incident or so, it gathers subsidiary characters, and then perhaps I grow interested in it, and set out to give it form as a book. I sketch a plan; I may write the end, the middle and the beginning and very often just in this order. That is, I decide how and where the book shall end, which is just as important to a book as to a play, and then I ask myself where are the most difficult turns in the book. Then I may write one of these difficult passages to see if it is viable. . . . I may stop there. But if it does work, then I may devise a beginning and finish the book."

How contrary to the old notion of inspiration to find Cary devising a beginning of a novel of which he has written bits in various parts and without order. This is evidence that what the writer is really doing is not so much writing a poem or play or story which he has firmly in mind, but rather is using his writing to discover what it truly is he is trying to say. Often he will not know until the final revision of the last page what he had been trying to do from the start.

One would hardly guess the zest and liveliness of Chekhov's mind if he had seen only a moody performance of *The Sea Gull.* Commenting on the new "decadent" writers, Chekhov noted, "they're a lot of strong, healthy young men: what they need is to be sentenced to a few months hard labor! This new-art business is just a pack of nonsense. . . . There's nothing new in art except talent." Chekhov constantly wrote subjects for stories in moments taken from his medical practice. ("Medicine is my lawful wife, literature my mistress. When I am tired of the one, I spend a night with the other.") One notebook contained a hundred entries. Some of these are diverting: A building contractor of great frugality loathed paying repair bills. When he married, he chose an exceptionally healthy woman so that he would have no repair bills with her.

A writer should be as objective as a chemist, he commented, and having nothing to do with the subjective approach which most us make in our everyday lives. And when he wrote that the writer should never sit down to his work until he felt cold as ice, he was remarkably like Flaubert. Any reader of Chekhov's short stories will be amazed to find how very simple were the original notes for two of the finest. "A cab-driver who has just lost his son, has to go on working just the same. He tries to speak of his grief to his fares, but finds only indifference." Another equally famous story began with three little sentences: "Some officers on manoeuvres are invited to a house where there are several young women. One of them kisses one of the officers, a shy and reserved young man, in the dark. He looks for her, but in vain." These are the plain, experienced reality, but the stories written out of them are the heightened over-reality.

Poor Chekhov, tending the sick with his own fatal illness corrupting his lungs. When he died in Germany, his coffin was taken to Moscow in a baggage car marked "Oysters." Yet he never alllowed a scrap of self-pity to interfere wtih the absolute integrity of his dedication to writing. "My own experience is that once a story has been written, one has to cross out the beginning and the end. It is there that we authors do most of our lying. . . . One must always tear up the first half. I mean that seriously. Young writers begin by, as one says, 'placing the story'—whereas the reader ought, on the contrary, to be able to grasp what it is all about by the way it is told, without any explanations from the author, from the conversation and the actions of the characters. . . . One must ruthlessly suppress everything that is not concerned with the subject. If, in the first chapter, you say there is a gun hanging on the wall, you should make quite sure that it is going to be used further on in the story."

Chekhov felt strongly the distinction between direct reality as it is lived and the imagined reality of art. In 1898 he went to a rehearsal of *The Sea Gull* at the Moscow Art Theatre and was told by an actor that backstage there would be sounds of frogs croaking, grasshoppers scraping, and dogs barking. He asked why, and was told this would be realistic. But the theater is not realism, it is art, he argued. If you put a real nose into a painting of a face, the nose will be realistic but the picture will be ruined. You do not use fiction to resolve the existence of God; you exhibit characters conducting lives, and show the way in which they discuss God.

Similarly Tolstoy remarked that *Anna Karenina,* that massive novel, was just a simple story about a married woman who falls in love with an officer. This sort of reducing of any piece of writing to its essence is a part of that control over material which is indispensable to the practicing writer. Such definition comes out of enormous and confusing reaches of experience. No one has more imaginatively stated the mysterious and at the same time real nature of human existence than Virginia Woolf when she wrote that "Life is a luminous halo, a semi-transparent envelope surrounding us from the beginning."

Virginia Woolf also wrote a paragraph defining the nature of this envelope more precisely. "Examine for a moment an ordinary mind on an ordinary day. The mind receives myriad impressions—trivial, fantastic, evanescent, or engraved with the sharpness of steel. From all sides they come, an incessant shower of innumerable atoms; and as they fall, as they shape themselves into the life of Monday or Tuesday, the accent falls differently from of old; the moment of importance came not here but there; so that, if the writer were a freeman and not a slave, if he could write what he chose, not what he must, if he could base his work upon his own feeling and not upon convention, there would be no plot, no comedy, no tragedy, no love interest or catastrophe in the accepted style.''

The simple, often grunt-like puffs of air which we call words must be used by the writer with such skill that they can bring to a reader, who cannot even hear whatever tone of voice the writer would give them, a form and sense which will move him. This is by no means as easy as lifting bricks all day or breaking stone. Flaubert testifies to that: "My head reels and my throat aches with chasing after, slogging over, delving into, turning round, groping after, all bellowing, in a hundred thousand different ways, a sentence that I've at last finished. It's good. . . ." One sentence!

No one knew the tortures, or the necessity, for this sort of harsh self-discipline better than that most exuberant and debauched poet, Baudelaire. In his *Flowers of Evil,* he wrote, there was cold and sinister beauty. How did that beauty happen? This first of the Beatniks differed from these later brothers not in his contempt for the vulgarity of middle-class life, nor in his concern for the flaunting immorality which repudiated that life, but in his attitude toward his art. Yearning to have his book appear so that it could prove to his mother, his formidable stepfather General Aupick, and his friends, that he was an authentic poet, he nevertheless kept the printer waiting several months while he revised a few lines into perfection. It may actually be that much writing is created into excellence, and then revised into greatness. This is true of the play, the story, the novel, the poem, the article, of whatever form men choose to make words move other men.

QUESTIONS

1 What, according to Engle, is suitable material for fiction? How does he handle the notion that experience is essential to writing fiction?
2 Why does Engle argue against the idea that writing embraces the intuition to the exclusion of the reason?
3 What are the most important attributes the writer should possess?
4 Engle draws upon ideas about writing from a number of famous writers. List the writers and concisely summarize the contribution that each makes.

TOPICS FOR COMPOSITION

1 Combine your answers to questions 3 and 4 above and use them as a guide in writing an analytical essay dealing with any piece of fiction in this book.
2 One point central to Engle's assessment of the writer's important attributes which is also implicit in the views of those writers he quotes is that of "intensified perception about human life." Recall an emotional experience of your own. Narrate it in such a way that you illustrate its value as an "intensified perception about human life."

SHORT STORY

___

"The Real Thing" depicts one of James's attempts to define the illusive artistic impression of reality; therefore, it is not the Monarchs who should capture our main interest, but, rather, we should follow the painter-narrator as he searches for his concept of reality. James's definition emerges as he places contrasting models before his painter-narrator. Notice the following:

1 The Monarchs, whose appearances seem to be reality itself
2 Miss Churm, whose appearance and actions contradict the artist's view of her
3 Oronte, who, lacking the affinity of either nationality or language, seems least appropriate of all

THE REAL THING

Henry James

I

When the porter's wife (she used to answer the house-bell), announced "A gentleman—with a lady, sir," I had, as I often had in those days, for the wish was father to the thought, an immediate vision of sitters. Sitters my visitors in this case proved to be; but not in the sense I should have preferred. However, there was nothing at first to indicate that they might not have come for a portrait. The gentleman, a man of fifty, very high and very straight, with a moustache slightly grizzled and a dark grey walking-coat admirably fitted, both of which I noted professionally—I don't mean as a barber or yet as a tailor—would have struck me as a celebrity if celebrities often were striking. It was a truth of which I had for some time been conscious that a figure with a good deal of frontage was, as one might say, almost never a public institution. A glance at the lady helped to remind me of this paradoxical law: she also looked too distinguished to be a "personality." Moreover one would scarcely come across two variations together.

Neither of the pair spoke immediately—they only prolonged the preliminary gaze which suggested that each wished to give the other a chance. They were visibly shy; they stood there letting me take them in—which, as I afterwards perceived, was the most practical thing they could have done. In this way their embarrassment served their cause. I had seen people painfully reluctant to mention that they desired anything so gross as to be represented on canvas; but the scruples of my new friends appeared almost insurmountable. Yet the gentleman might have said "I should like a portrait of my wife," and the lady might have said "I should like a portrait of my husband." Perhaps they were not husband and wife—this naturally would make the matter more delicate. Perhaps they wished to be done together—in which case they ought to have brought a third person to break the news.

"We come from Mr. Rivet," the lady said at last, with a dim smile which had the effect of a moist sponge passed over a "sunk" piece of painting, as well as of a vague allusion to vanished beauty. She was as tall and straight, in her degree, as her companion, and with ten years less to carry. She looked as sad as a woman could look whose face was not charged with expression; that is her tinted oval mask showed friction as an exposed surface shows it. The hand of time had played over her freely but only to simplify. She was slim and stiff, and so well-dressed, in dark blue cloth, with lappets and pockets and buttons, that it was clear she employed the same tailor as her husband. The couple had an indefinable air of prosperous thrift—they evidently got a good deal of luxury for their money. If I was to be one of their luxuries it would behoove me to consider my terms.

"Ah, Claude Rivet recommended me?" I inquired; and I added that it was very kind of him, though I could reflect that, as he only painted landscape, this was not a sacrifice.

The lady looked very hard at the gentleman, and the gentleman looked round the room. Then staring at the floor a moment and stroking his moustache, he rested his pleasant eyes on me with the remark: "He said you were the right one."

"I try to be, when people want to sit."

"Yes, we should like to," said the lady anxiously.

"Do you mean together?"

My visitors exchanged a glance. "If you could do anything with *me,* I suppose it would be double," the gentleman stammered.

"Oh yes, there's naturally a higher charge for two figures than for one."

"We should like to make it pay," the husband confessed.

"That's very good of you," I returned, appreciating so unwonted a sympathy—for I supposed he meant pay the artist.

A sense of strangeness seemed to dawn on the lady. "We mean for the illustrations—Mr. Rivet said you might put one in."

"Put one in—an illustration?" I was equally confused.

"Sketch her off, you know," said the gentleman, colouring.

It was only then that I understood the service Claude Rivet had rendered me; he had told them that I worked in black and white, for magazines, for story-books, for sketches of contemporary life, and consequently had frequent employment for models. These things were true, but it was not less true (I may confess it now—whether because the aspiration was to lead to everything or to nothing I leave the reader to guess), that I couldn't get the honours, to say nothing of the emoluments, of a great painter of portraits out of my head. My "illustrations" were my pot-boilers; I looked to a different branch of art (far and away the most interesting it had always seemed to me) to perpetuate my fame. There was no shame in looking to it also to make any fortune; but that fortune was by so much further from being made from the moment my visitors wished to be "done" for nothing. I was disappointed; for in the pictorial sense I had immediately *seen* them. I had seized their type—I had already settled what I would do with it. Something that wouldn't absolutely have pleased them, I afterwards reflected.

"Ah, you're—you're—a—?" I began, as soon as I had mastered my surprise. I couldn't bring out the dingy word "models"; it seemed to fit the case so little.

"We haven't had much practice," said the lady.

"We've got to *do* something, and we've thought that an artist in your line might perhaps make something of us," her husband threw off. He further mentioned that they didn't know many artists and that they had gone first, on the off-chance (he painted views of course, but sometimes put in figures—perhaps I remembered), to Mr. Rivet, whom they had met a few years before at a place in Norfolk where he was sketching.

"We used to sketch a little ourselves," the lady hinted.

"It's very awkward, but we absolutely *must* do something," her husband went on.

"Of course, we're not so *very* young," she admitted, with a wan smile.

With the remark that I might as well know something more about them, the husband had handed me a card extracted from a neat new pocket-book (their appurtenances were all of the freshest) and inscribed with the words "Major Monarch." Impressive as these words were they didn't carry my knowledge much further; but my visitor presently added: "I've left the army, and we've had the misfortune to lose our money. In fact our means are dreadfully small."

"It's an awful bore," said Mrs. Monarch.

They evidently wished to be discreet—to take care not to swagger because they were gentlefolks. I perceived they would have been willing to recognise this as something of a drawback, at the same time that I guessed at an underlying sense—their consolation in adversity—that they *had* their points. They certainly had; but these advantages struck me as preponderantly social; such for instance as would help to make a drawing-room look well. However, a drawing-room was always, or ought to be, a picture.

In consequence of his wife's allusion to their age Major Monarch observed: "Naturally, it's more for the figure that we thought of going in. We can still hold ourselves up." On the instant I saw that the figure was indeed their strong point. His "naturally" didn't sound vain, but it lighted up the question. *"She* has got the best," he continued, nodding at his wife, with a pleasant after-dinner absence of circumlocution. I could only reply, as if we were in fact sitting over our wine, that this didn't prevent his own from being very good; which led him in turn to rejoin: "We thought that if you ever have to do people like us, we might be something like it. *She,* particularly—for a lady in a book, you know."

I was so amused by them that, to get more of it, I did my best to take their point of view; and though it was an embarrassment to find myself appraising physically, as if they were animals on hire or useful blacks, a pair whom I should have expected to meet only in one of the relations in which criticism is tacit, I looked at Mrs. Monarch judicially enough to be able to exclaim, after a moment, with conviction: "Oh yes, a lady in a book!" She was singularly like a bad illustration.

"We'll stand up, if you like," said the Major; and he raised himself before me with a really grand air.

I could take his measure at a glance—he was six feet two and a perfect gentleman. It would have paid any club in process of formation and in want of a stamp to engage him at a salary to stand in the principal window. What struck me immediately was that in coming to me they had rather missed their vocation; they could surely have been turned to better account for advertising purposes. I couldn't of course see the thing in detail, but I could see them make someone's fortune—I don't mean their own. There was something in them for a waistcoat-maker, an hotel-keeper or a soap-vendor. I could imagine "We always use it" pinned on their bosoms with the greatest effect; I had a vision of the promptitude with which they would launch a table d'hôte.

Mrs. Monarch sat still, not from pride but from shyness, and presently her husband said to her: "Get up my dear and show how smart you are." She obeyed, but she had no need to get up to show it. She walked to the end of the studio, and then she came back blushing, with her fluttered eyes on her husband. I was reminded of an incident I had accidentally had a glimpse of in Paris—being with a friend there, a dramatist about to produce a play—when an actress came to him to ask to be intrusted with a part. She went through her paces before him, walked up and down as Mrs. Monarch was doing. Mrs. Monarch did it quite as well, but I abstained from applauding. It was very odd to see such people apply for such poor pay. She looked as if she had ten thousand a year. Her husband had used the word that described her: she was, in the London current jargon, essentially and typically "smart." Her figure was, in the same order of ideas, conspicuously and irreproachably "good." For a woman of her age her waist was surprisingly small; her elbow moreover had the orthodox crook. She held her head at the conventional angle; but why did she come to *me?* She ought to have tried on jackets at a big shop. I feared my visitors were not only destitute, but "artistic"—which would be a great complication. When she sat down again I thanked her, observing that what a draughtsman most valued in his model was the faculty of keeping quiet.

"Oh, *she* can keep quiet," said Major Monarch. Then he added, jocosely: "I've always kept her quiet."

"I'm not a nasty fidget, am I?" Mrs. Monarch appealed to her husband.

He addressed his answer to me. "Perhaps it isn't out of place to mention—because we ought to be quite business-like, oughtn't we?—that when I married her she was known as the Beautiful Statue."

"Oh dear!" said Mrs. Monarch, ruefully.

"Of course I should want a certain amount of expression," I rejoined.

"Of *course!*" they both exclaimed.

"And then I suppose you know that you'll get awfully tired."

"Oh, we *never* get tired!" they eagerly cried:

"Have you had any kind of practice?"

They hesitated—they looked at each other. "We've been photographed, *immensely,*" said Mrs. Monarch.

"She means the fellows have asked us," added the Major.

"I see—because you're so good-looking."

"I don't know what they thought, but they were always after us."

"We always got our photographs for nothing," smiled Mrs. Monarch.

"We might have brought some, my dear," her husband remarked.

"I'm not sure we have any left. We've given quantities away," she explained to me.

"With our autographs and that sort of thing," said the Major.

"Are they to be got in the shops?" I inquired, as a harmless pleasantry.

"Oh, yes; *hers*—they used to be."

"Not now," said Mrs. Monarch, with her eyes on the floor.

II

I could fancy the "sort of thing" they put on the presentation-copies of their photographs, and I was sure they wrote a beautiful hand. It was odd how quickly I was sure of everything that concerned them. If they were now so poor as to have to earn shillings and pence, they never had had much of a margin. Their good looks had been their capital, and they had good-humouredly made the most of the career that this resource marked out for them. It was in their faces, the blankness, the deep intellectual repose of the twenty years of country-house visiting which had given them pleasant intonations. I could see the sunny drawing-rooms, sprinkled with periodicals she didn't read, in which Mrs. Monarch had continuously sat; I could see the wet shrubberies in which she had walked, equipped to admiration for either exercise. I could see the rich covers the Major had helped to shoot and the wonderful garments in which, late at night, he repaired to the smoking-room to talk about them. I could imagine their leggings and waterproofs, their knowing tweeds and rugs, their rolls of sticks and cases of tackle and neat umbrellas; and I could evoke the exact appearance of their servants and the compact variety of their luggage on the platforms of country stations.

They gave small tips, but they were liked; they didn't do anything themselves, but they were welcome. They looked so well everywhere; they gratified the general relish for stature, complexion and "form." They knew it without fatuity or vulgarity, and they respected themselves in consequence. They were not superficial; they were thorough and kept themselves up—it had been their line. People with such a taste for activity had to have some line. I could feel how, even in a dull house, they could have been counted upon for cheerfulness. At present something had happened—it didn't matter what, their little income had grown less, it had grown least—and they had to do something for pocket-money. Their friends liked them, but didn't like to support them. There was something about them that represented credit—their clothes, their manners, their type; but if credit is a large empty pocket in which an occasional chink reverberates, the chink at least must be audible. What they wanted of me was to help to make it so. Fortunately they had no children—I soon divined that. They would also perhaps wish our relations to be kept secret: this was why it was "for the figure"—the reproduction of the face would betray them.

I liked them—they were so simple; and I had no objection to them if they would suit. But, somehow, with all their perfections I didn't easily believe in them. After all they were amateurs, and the ruling passion of my life was the detestation of the amateur. Combined with this was another perversity—an innate preference for the represented subject over the real one: the defect of the real one was so apt to be a lack of representation. I liked things that appeared; then one was sure. Whether they *were* or not was a subordinate and almost always a profitless question. There were other considerations, the first of which was that I already had two or three people in use, notably a young person with big feet, in alpaca, from Kilburn, who for a couple of years had come to me regularly for my illustrations and with whom I was still—perhaps ignobly—satisfied. I frankly explained to my visitors how the case stood; but they had taken more precautions than I supposed. They had reasoned out their opportunity, for Claude Rivet had told them of the projected *édition de luxe* of one of the writers of our day—the rarest of the novelists—who, long neglected by the multitudinous vulgar and dearly prized by the attentive (need I mention Philip Vincent?), had had the happy fortune of seeing, late in life, the dawn and then the full light of a higher criticism—an estimate in which, on the part of the public, there was something really of expiation. The edition in question, planned by a publisher of taste, was practically an act of high reparation; the wood-cuts with which it was to be enriched were the homage of English art to one of the most independent representatives of English letters. Major and Mrs. Monarch confessed to me that they had hoped I might be able to work *them* into my share of the enterprise. They knew I was to do the first of the books, "Rutland Ramsay," but I had to make clear to them that my participation in the rest of the affair—this first book was to be a test—was to depend on the satisfaction I should give. If this should be limited my employers would drop me without a scruple. It was therefore a crisis for me, and naturally I was making special preparations, looking about for new people, if they should be necessary, and securing the best types. I admitted however that I should like to settle down to two or three good models who would do for everything.

"Should we have often to—a—put on special clothes?" Mrs. Monarch timidly demanded.

"Dear, yes—that's half the business."

"And should we be expected to supply our own costumes?"

"Oh, no; I've got a lot of things. A painter's models put on—or put off—anything he likes."

"And do you mean—a—the same?"

"The same?"

Mrs. Monarch looked at her husband again.

"Oh, she was just wondering," he explained, "if the costumes are in *general* use." I had to confess that they were, and I mentioned further that some of them (I had a lot of genuine, greasy last-century things), had served their time, a hundred years ago, on living, world-stained men and women. "We'll put on anything that *fits,*" said the Major.

"Oh, I arrange that—they fit in the pictures."

"I'm afraid I should do better for the modern books. I would come as you like," said Mrs. Monarch.

"She has got a lot of clothes at home: they might do for contemporary life," her husband continued:

"Oh, I can fancy scenes in which you'd be quite natural." And indeed I could see the slipshod rearrangements of stale properties—the stories I tried to produce pictures for without the exasperation of reading them—whose sandy tracts the good lady might help to people. But I had to return to the fact that for this sort of work—the daily mechanical grind—I was already equipped; the people I was working with were fully adequate.

"We only thought we might be more like *some* characters," said Mrs. Monarch mildly, getting up.

Her husband also rose; he stood looking at me with a dim wistfulness that was touching in so fine a man. "Wouldn't it be rather a pull sometimes to have—a—to have—?" He hung fire; he wanted me to help him by phrasing what he meant. But I couldn't—I didn't know. So he brought it out, awkwardly. "The *real* thing; a gentleman, you know, or a lady." I was quite ready to give a general assent—I admitted that there was a great deal in that. This encouraged Major Monarch to say, following up his appeal with an unacted gulp: "It's awfully hard—we've tried everything." The gulp was communicative; it proved too much for his wife. Before I knew it Mrs. Monarch had dropped again upon a divan and burst into tears. Her husband sat down beside her, holding one of her hands; whereupon she quickly dried her eyes with the other, while I felt embarrassed as she looked up at me. "There isn't a confounded job I haven't applied for—waited for—prayed for. You can fancy we'd be pretty bad first. Secretaryships and that sort of thing? You might as well ask for a peerage. I'd be *anything*—I'm strong; a messenger or a coalheaver. I'd put on a gold-laced cap and open carriage-doors in front of the haberdasher's; I'd hang about a station to carry portmanteaus; I'd be a postman. But they won't *look* at you; there are thousands, as good as yourself, already on the ground. *Gentlemen,* poor beggars, who have drunk their wine, who have kept their hunters!"

I was as reassuring as I knew how to be, and my visitors were presently on their feet again while, for the experiment, we agreed on an hour. We were discussing it when the door opened and Miss Churm came in with a wet umbrella. Miss Churm had to take the omnibus to Maida Vale and then walk half-a-mile. She looked a trifle blowsy and slightly splashed. I scarcely ever saw her come in without thinking afresh how odd it was that, being so little in herself, she should yet be so much in others. She was a meagre little Miss Churm, but she was an ample heroine of romance. She was only a freckled cockney, but she could represent everything, from a fine lady to a shepherdess; she had the faculty, as she might have had a fine voice or long hair. She couldn't spell, and she loved beer, but she had two or three "points," and practice, and a knack, and mother-wit, and a kind of whimsical sensibility, and a love of the theatre, and seven sisters, and not an ounce of respect, especially for the *h*. The first thing my visitors saw was that her umbrella was wet, and in their spotless perfection they visibly winced at it. The rain had come on since their arrival.

"I'm all in a soak; there *was* a mess of people in the 'bus. I wish you lived near a stytion," said Miss Churm. I requested her to get ready as quickly as possible, and she passed into the room in which she always changed her dress. But before going out she asked me what she was to get into this time.

"It's the Russian princess, don't you know?" I answered; "the one with the 'golden eyes,' in black velvet, for the long thing in the *Cheapside.*"

"Golden eyes? I *say!*" cried Miss Churm, while my companions watched her with intensity as she withdrew. She always arranged herself, when she was late, before I could turn around; and I kept my visitors a little, on purpose, so that they might get an idea, from seeing her, what would be expected of themselves. I mentioned that she was quite my notion of an excellent model—she was really very clever.

"Do you think she looks like a Russian princess?" Major Monarch asked, with lurking alarm.

"When I make her, yes."

"Oh, if you have to *make* her—!" he reasoned, acutely.

"That's the most you can ask. There are so many that are not makeable."

"Well now, *here's* a lady"—and with a persuasive smile he passed his arm into his wife's—"who's already made!"

"Oh, I'm not a Russian princess," Mrs. Monarch protested, a little coldly. I could see that she had known some and didn't like them. There, immediately, was a complication of a kind that I never had to fear with Miss Churm.

The young lady came back in black velvet—the gown was rather rusty and very low on her lean shoulders—and with a Japanese fan in her red hands. I reminded her that in the scene I was doing she had to look over someone's head. "I forgot whose it is; but it doesn't matter. Just look over a head."

"I'd rather look over a stove," said Miss Churm; and she took her station near the fire. She fell into position, settled herself into a tall attitude, gave a certain backward inclination to her head and a certain forward droop to her fan, and looked, at least to my prejudiced sense, distinguished and charming, foreign and dangerous. We left her looking so, while I went down-stairs with Major and Mrs. Monarch.

"I think I could come about as near it as that," said Mrs. Monarch.

"Oh, you think she's shabby, but you must allow for the alchemy of art."

However, they went off with an evident increase of comfort, founded on their demonstrable advantage in being the real thing. I could fancy them shuddering over Miss Churm. She was very droll about them when I went back, for I told her what they wanted.

"Well, if *she* can sit I'll tyke to bookkeeping," said my model.

"She's very lady-like," I replied, as an innocent form of aggravation.

"So much the worse for *you.* That means she can't turn round."

"She'll do for the fashionable novels."

"Oh yes, she'll *do* for them!" my model humorously declared. "Ain't they bad enough without her?" I had often sociably denounced them to Miss Churm.

III

It was for the elucidation of a mystery in one of these works that I first tried Mrs. Monarch. Her husband came with her, to be useful if necessary—it was sufficiently clear that as a general thing he would prefer to come with her. At first I wondered if this were for "propriety's" sake—if he were going to be jealous and meddling. The idea was too tiresome, and if it had been confirmed it would speedily have brought our acquaintance to a close. But I soon saw there was nothing in it and that if he accompanied Mrs. Monarch it was (in addition to the chance of being wanted), simply because he had nothing else to do. When she was away from him his occupation was gone—she never *had* been away from him. I judged, rightly, that in their awkward situation their close union was their main comfort and that this union had no weak spot. It was a real marriage, an encouragement to the hesitating, a nut for pessimists to crack. Their address was humble (I remember afterwards thinking it had been the only thing about them that was really professional), and I could fancy the lamentable lodgings in which the Major would have been left alone. He could bear them with his wife— he couldn't bear them without her.

He had too much tact to try and make himself agreeable when he couldn't be useful; so he simply sat and waited, when I was too absorbed in my work to talk. But I liked to make him talk—it made my work, when it didn't interrupt it, less sordid, less special. To listen to him was to combine the excitement of going out with the economy of staying at home. There was only one hindrance: that I seemed not to know any of the people he and his wife had known. I think he wondered extremely, during the term of our intercourse, whom the deuce I *did* know. He hadn't a stray sixpence of an idea to fumble for; so we didn't spin it very fine—we confined ourselves to questions of leather and even of liquor (saddlers and breeches-makers and how to get good claret cheap), and matters like "good trains" and the habits of small game. His lore on these last subjects was astonishing, he managed to interweave the station-master with the ornithologist. When he couldn't talk about greater things he could talk cheerfully about smaller, and since I couldn't accompany him into reminiscences of the fashionable world he could lower the conversation without a visible effort to my level.

So earnest a desire to please was touching in a man who could so easily have knocked one down. He looked after the fire and had an opinion on the draught of the stove, without my asking him, and I could see that he thought many of my arrangements not half clever enough. I remember telling him that if I were only rich I would offer him a salary to come and teach me how to live. Sometimes he gave a random sigh, of which the essence was: "Give me even such a bare old barrack as *this,* and I'd do something with it!" When I wanted to use him he came alone; which was an illustration of the superior courage of women. His wife could bear her solitary second floor, and she was in general more discreet; showing by various small reserves that she was alive to the propriety of keeping our relations markedly professional—not letting them slide into sociability. She wished it to remain clear that she and the Major were employed, not cultivated, and if she approved of me as a superior, who could be kept in his place, she never thought me quite good enough for an equal.

She sat with great intensity, giving the whole of her mind to it, and was capable of remaining for an hour almost as motionless as if she were before a photographer's lens. I could see she had been photographed often, but somehow the very habit that made her good for that purpose unfitted her for mine. At first I was extremely pleased with her lady-like air, and it was a satisfaction, on coming to follow her lines, to see how good they were and how far they could lead the pencil. But after a few times I began to find her too insurmountably stiff; do what I would with it my drawing looked like a photograph or a copy of a photograph. Her figure had no variety of expression— she herself had no sense of variety. You may say that this was my business, was only a question of placing her. I placed her in every conceivable position, but she managed to obliterate their differences. She was always a lady certainly, and into the bargain was always the same lady. She was the real thing, but always the same thing. There were moments when I was oppressed by the serenity of her confidence that she *was* the real thing. All her dealings with me and all her husband's were an implication that this was lucky for *me*. Meanwhile I found myself trying to invent types that approached her own, instead of making her own transform itself—in the clever way that was not impossible, for instance, to poor Miss Churm. Arrange as I would and take the precautions I would, she always, in my pictures, came out too tall—landing me in the dilemma of having represented a fascinating woman as seven feet high, which, out of respect perhaps to my own very much scantier inches, was far from my idea of such a personage.

The case was worse with the Major—nothing I could do would keep *him* down, so that he became useful only for the representation of brawny giants. I adored variety and range, I cherished human accidents, the illustrative note; I wanted to characterise closely, and the thing in the world I most hated was the danger of being ridden by a type. I had quarrelled with some of my friends about it—I had parted company with them for maintaining that one *had* to be, and that if the type was beautiful (witness Raphael and Leonardo), the servitude was only a gain. I was neither Leonardo nor Raphael; I might only be a presumptuous young modern searcher, but I held that everything was to be sacrificed sooner than character. When they averred that the haunting type in question could easily *be* character, I retorted, perhaps superficially: "Whose?" It couldn't be everybody's—it might end in being nobody's.

After I had drawn Mrs. Monarch a dozen times I perceived more clearly than before that the value of such a model as Miss Churm resided precisely in the fact that she had no positive stamp, combined of course with the other fact that what she did have was a curious and inexplicable talent for imitation. Her usual appearance was like a curtain which she could draw up at request for a capital performance. This performance was simply suggestive; but it was a word to the wise—it was vivid and pretty. Sometimes, even, I thought it, though she was plain herself, too insipidly pretty; I made it a reproach to her that the figures drawn from her were monotonously (*bêtement,* as we used to say) graceful. Nothing made her more angry: it was so much her pride to feel that she could sit for characters that had nothing in common with each other. She would accuse me at such moments of taking away her "reputytion."

It suffered a certain shrinkage, this queer quantity, from the repeated visits of my new friends. Miss Churm was greatly in demand, never in want of employment, so I had no scruple in putting her off occasionally, to try them more at my ease. It was certainly amusing at first to do the real thing—it was amusing to do Major Monarch's trousers. They *were* the real thing, even if he did come out colossal. It was amusing to do his wife's back hair (it was so mathematically neat), and the particular "smart" tension of her tight stays. She lent herself especially to positions in which the face was somewhat averted or blurred; she abounded in lady-like back views and *profils perdus.* When she stood erect she took naturally one of the attitudes in which court-painters represent queens and princesses; so that I found myself wondering whether, to draw out this accomplishment, I couldn't get the editor of the *Cheapside* to publish a really royal romance, "A Tale of Buckingham Palace." Sometimes, however, the real thing and the make-believe came into contact; by which I mean that Miss Churm, keeping an appointment or coming to make one on days when I had much work in hand, encountered her invidious rivals. The encounter was not on their part, for they noticed her no more than if she had been the housemaid; not from intentional loftiness, but simply because, as yet, professionally, they didn't know how to fraternise, as I could guess that they would have liked—or at least that the Major would. They couldn't talk about the omnibus—they always walked; and they didn't know what else to try—she wasn't interested in good trains or cheap claret. Besides, they must have felt—in the air—that she was amused at them, secretly derisive of their ever knowing how. She was not a person to conceal her scepticism if she had had a chance to show it. On the other hand Mrs. Monarch didn't think her tidy; for why else did she take pains to say to me (it was going out of the way, for Mrs. Monarch), that she didn't like dirty women?

One day when my young lady happened to be present with my other sitters (she even dropped in, when it was convenient, for a chat), I asked her to be so good as to lend a hand in getting tea—a service with which she was familiar and which was one of a class that, living as I did in a small way, with slender domestic resources, I often appealed to my models to render. They liked to lay hands on my property, to break the sitting, and sometimes the china—I made them feel Bohemian. The next time I saw Miss Churm after this incident she surprised me greatly by making a scene about it—she accused me of having wished to humiliate her. She had not resented the outrage at the time, but had seemed obliging and amused, enjoying the comedy of asking Mrs. Monarch, who sat vague and silent, whether she would have cream and sugar, and putting an exaggerated simper into the question. She had tried intonations—as if she too wished to pass for the real thing; till I was afraid my other visitors would take offence.

Oh, *they* were determined not to do this; and their touching patience was the measure of their great need. They would sit by the hour, uncomplaining, till I was ready to use them; they would come back on the chance of being wanted and would walk away cheerfully if they were not. I used to go to the door with them to see in what magnificent order they retreated. I tried to find other employment for them—I introduced them to several artists. But they didn't "take," for reasons I could appreciate, and I became conscious, rather anxiously, that after such disappointments they fell back upon me with a heavier weight. They did me the honour to think that it was I who was most *their* form. They were not picturesque enough for the painters, and in those days there were not so many serious workers in black and white. Besides, they had an eye to the great job I had mentioned to them—they had secretly set their hearts on supplying the right essence for my pictorial vindication of our fine novelist. They knew that for this undertaking I should want no costume-effects, none of the frippery of past ages—that it was a case in which everything would be contemporary and satirical and, presumably, genteel. If I could work them into it their future would be assured, for the labour would of course be long and the occupation steady.

One day Mrs. Monarch came without her husband—she explained his absence by his having had to go to the City. While she sat there in her usual anxious stiffness there came, at the door, a knock which I immediately recognised as the subdued appeal of a model out of work. It was followed by the entrance of a young man whom I easily perceived to be a foreigner and who proved in fact an Italian acquainted with no English word but my name, which he uttered in a way that made it seem to include all others. I had not then visited his country, nor was I proficient in his tongue; but as he was not so meanly constituted—what Italian is?—as to depend only on that member of expression he conveyed to me, in familiar but graceful mimicry, that he was in search of exactly the employment in which the lady before me was engaged. I was not struck with him at first, and while I continued to draw I emitted rough sounds of discouragement and dismissal. He stood his ground, however, not importunately, but with a dumb, dog-like fidelity in his eyes which amounted to innocent impudence—the manner of a devoted servant (he might have been in the house for years), unjustly suspected. Suddenly I saw that this very attitude and expression made a picture, whereupon I told him to sit down and wait till I should be free. There was another picture in the way he obeyed me, and I observed as I worked that there were others still in the way he looked wonderingly, with his head thrown back, about the high studio. He might have been crossing himself in St. Peter's. Before I finished I said to myself: "The fellow's a bankrupt orange-monger, but he's a treasure."

When Mrs. Monarch withdrew he passed across the room like a flash to open the door for her, standing there with the rapt, pure gaze of the young Dante spellbound by the young Beatrice. As I never insisted, in such situations, on the blankness of the British domestic, I reflected that he had the making of a servant (and I needed one, but couldn't pay him to be only that), as well as of a model; in short I made up my mind to adopt my bright adventurer if he would agree to officiate in the double capacity. He jumped at my offer, and in the event my rashness (for I had known nothing about him), was not brought home to me. He proved a sympathetic though a desultory ministrant, and had in a wonderful degree the *sentiment de la pose.* It was uncultivated, instinctive; a part of the happy instinct which had guided him to my door and helped him to spell out my name on the card nailed to it. He had had no other introduction to me than a guess, from the shape of my high north window, seen outside, that my place was a studio and that as a studio it would contain an artist. He had wandered to England in search of fortune, like other itinerants, and had embarked, with a partner and a small green hand-cart, on the sale of penny ices. The ices had melted away and the partner had dissolved in their train. My young man wore tight yellow trousers with reddish stripes and his name was Oronte. He was sallow but fair, and when I put him into some old clothes of my own he looked like an Englishman. He was as good as Miss Churm, who could look, when required, like an Italian.

IV

I thought Mrs. Monarch's face slightly convulsed when, on her coming back with her husband, she found Oronte installed. It was strange to have to recognise in a scrap of a lazzarone a competitor to her magnificent Major. It was she who scented danger first, for the Major was anecdotically unconscious. But Oronte gave us tea, with a hundred eager confusions (he had never seen such a queer process), and I think she thought better of me for having at last an "establishment." They saw a couple of drawings that I had made of the establishment, and Mrs. Monarch hinted that it never would have struck her that he had sat for them. "Now the drawings you make from *us,* they look exactly like us," she reminded me, smiling in triumph; and I recognised that this was indeed just their defect. When I drew the Monarchs I couldn't, somehow, get away from them—get into the character I wanted to represent; and I had not the least desire my model should be discoverable in my picture. Miss Churm never was, and Mrs. Monarch thought I hid her, very properly, because she was vulgar; whereas if she was lost it was only as the dead who go to heaven are lost—in the gain of an angel the more.

By this time I had got a certain start with "Rutland Ramsay," the first novel in the great projected series; that is I had produced a dozen drawings, several with the help of the Major and his wife, and I had sent them in for approval. My understanding with the publishers, as I have already hinted, had been that I was to be left to do my work, in this particular case, as I liked, with the whole book committed to me; but my connection with the rest of the series was only contingent. There were moments when, frankly, it *was* a comfort to have the real thing under one's hand; for there were characters in "Rutland Ramsay" that were very much like it. There were people presumably as straight as the Major and women of as good a fashion as Mrs. Monarch. There was a great deal of country-house life—treated, it is true, in a fine, fanciful, ironical, generalised way—and there was a considerable implication of knickerbockers and kilts. There were certain things I had to settle at the outset; such things for instance as the exact appearance of the hero, the particular bloom of the heroine. The author of course gave me a lead, but there was a margin for interpretation. I took the Monarchs into my confidence, I told them frankly what I was about, I mentioned my embarrassments and alternatives. "Oh, take *him!*" Mrs. Monarch murmured sweetly, looking at her husband; and "What could you want better than my wife?" the Major inquired, with the comfortable candour that now prevailed between us.

I was not obliged to answer these remarks—I was only obliged to place my sitters. I was not easy in mind, and I postponed, a little timidly perhaps, the solution of the question. The book was a large canvas, the other figures were numerous, and I worked off at first some of the episodes in which the hero and the heroine were not concerned. When once I had set *them* up I should have to stick to them—I couldn't make my young man seven feet high in one place and five feet nine in another. I inclined on the whole to the latter measurement, though the Major more then once reminded me that *he* looked about as young as anyone. It was indeed quite possible to arrange him, for the figure, so that it would have been difficult to detect his age. After the spontaneous Oronte had been with me a month, and after I had given him to understand several different times that his native exuberance would presently constitute an insurmountable barrier to our further intercourse, I waked to a sense of his heroic capacity. He was only five feet seven, but the remaining inches were latent. I tried him almost secretly at first, for I was really rather afraid of the judgment my other models would pass on such a choice. If they regarded Miss Churm as little better than a snare, what would they think of the representation by a person so little the real thing as an Italian street-vendor of a protagonist formed by a public school?

If I went a little in fear of them it was not because they bullied me, because they had got an oppressive foothold, but because in their really pathetic decorum and mysteriously permanent newness they counted on me so intensely. I was therefore very glad when Jack Hawley came home: he was always of such good counsel. He painted badly himself, but there was no one like him for putting his finger on the place. He had been absent from England for a year; he had been somewhere—I don't remember where—to get a fresh eye. I was in a good deal of dread of any such organ, but we were old friends; he had been away for months and a sense of emptiness was creeping into my life. I hadn't dodged a missile for a year.

He came back with a fresh eye, but with the same old black velvet blouse, and the first evening he spent in my studio we smoked cigarettes till the small hours. He had done no work himself, he had only got the eye; so the field was clear for the production of my little things. He wanted to see what I had done for the *Cheapside,* but he was disappointed in the exhibition. That at least seemed the meaning of two or three comprehensive groans which, as he lounged on my big divan, on a folded leg, looking at my latest drawings, issued from his lips with the smoke of the cigarette.

"What's the matter with you?" I asked.

"What's the matter with *you?*"

"Nothing save that I'm mystified."

"You are indeed. You're quite off the hinge. What's the meaning of this new fad?" And he tossed me, with visible irreverence, a drawing in which I happened to have depicted both my majestic models. I asked if he didn't think it good, and he replied that it struck him as execrable, given the sort of thing I had always represented myself to him as wishing to arrive at; but I let that pass. I was so anxious to see exactly what he meant. The two figures in the picture looked colossal, but I supposed this was *not* what he meant, inasmuch as, for aught he knew to the contrary, I might have been trying for that. I maintained that I was working exactly in the same way as when he last had done me the honour to commend me. "Well, there's a big hole somewhere," he answered; "wait a bit and I'll discover it." I depended upon him to do so; where else was the fresh eye? But he produced at last nothing more luminous than "I don't know—I don't like your types." This was lame, for a critic who had never consented to discuss with me anything but the question of execution, the direction of strokes and the mystery of values.

"In the drawings you've been looking at I think my types are very handsome."

"Oh, they won't do!"

"I've had a couple of new models."

"I see you have. *They* won't do."

"Are you very sure of that?"

"Absolutely—they're stupid."

"You mean *I* am—for I ought to get round that."

"You *can't*—with such people. Who are they?"

I told him, as far as was necessary, and he declared, heartlessly: *"Ce sont des gens qu'il faut mettre à la porte."*

"You've never seen them; they're awfully good," I compassionately objected.

"Not seen them? Why, all this recent work of yours drops to pieces with them. It's all I want to see of them."

"No one else has said anything against it—the *Cheapside* people are pleased."

"Everyone else is an ass, and the *Cheapside* people the biggest asses of all. Come, don't pretend, at this time of day, to have pretty illusions about the public, especially about publishers and editors. It's not for *such* animals you work—it's for those who know, *coloro che sanno;* so keep straight for *me* if you can't keep straight for yourself. There's a certain sort of thing you tried for from the first—and a very good thing it is. But this twaddle isn't *in* it." When I talked with Hawley later about "Rutland Ramsay" and its possible successors he declared that I must get back into my boat again or I would go to the bottom. His voice in short was the voice of warning.

I noted the warning, but I didn't turn my friends out of doors. They bored me a good deal; but the very fact that they bored me admonished me not to sacrifice them— if there was anything to be done with them—simply to irritation. As I look back at this phase they seem to me to have pervaded my life not a little. I have a vision of them as most of the time in my studio, seated, against the wall, on an old velvet bench to be out of the way, and looking like a pair of patient courtiers in a royal antechamber. I am convinced that during the coldest weeks of the winter they held their ground because it saved them fire. Their newness was losing its gloss, and it was impossible not to feel that they were objects of charity. Whenever Miss Churm arrived they went away, and after I was fairly launched in "Rutland Ramsay" Miss Churm arrived pretty often. They managed to express to me tacitly that they supposed I wanted her for the low life of the book, and I let them suppose it, since they had attempted to study the work—it was lying about the studio—without discovering that it dealt only with the highest circles. They had dipped into the most brilliant of our novelists without deciphering many passages. I still took an hour from them, now and again, in spite of Jack Hawley's warning: it would be time enough to dismiss them, if dismissal should be necessary, when the rigour of the season was over. Hawley had made their acquaintance—he had met them at my fireside—and thought them a ridiculous pair. Learning that he was a painter they tried to approach him, to show him too that they were the real thing; but he looked at them, across the big room, as if they were miles away: they were a compendium of everything that he most objected to in the social system of his country. Such people as that, all convention and patent-leather, with ejaculations that stopped conversation, had no business in a studio. A studio was a place to learn to see, and how could you see through a pair of feather beds?

The main inconvenience I suffered at their hands was that, at first, I was shy of letting them discover how my artful little servant had begun to sit to me for "Rutland Ramsay." They knew that I had been odd enough (they were prepared by this time to allow oddity to artists), to pick a foreign vagabond out of the streets, when I might have had a person with whiskers and credentials; but it was some time before they learned how high I rated his accomplishments. They found him in an attitude more than once, but they never doubted I was doing him as an organ-grinder. There were several things they never guessed, and one of them was that for a striking scene in the novel, in which a footman briefly figured, it occurred to me to make use of Major Monarch as the menial. I kept putting this off, I didn't like to ask him to don the livery—besides the difficulty of finding a livery to fit him. At last, one day late in the winter, when I was at work on the despised Oronte (he caught one's idea in an instant), and was in the glow of feeling that I was going very straight, they came in, the Major and his wife, with their society laugh about nothing (there was less and less to laugh at), like country-callers—they always reminded me of that—who have walked across the park after church and are presently persuaded to stay to luncheon. Luncheon was over, but they could stay to tea—I knew they wanted it. The fit was on me, however, and I couldn't let my ardour cool and my work wait, with the fading daylight, while my model prepared it. So I asked Mrs. Monarch if she would mind laying it out—a request which, for an instant, brought all the blood to her face. Her eyes were on her husband's for a second, and some mute telegraphy passed between them. Their folly was over the next instant; his cheerful shrewdness put an end to it. So far from pitying their wounded pride, I must add, I was moved to give it as complete a lesson as I could. They bustled about together and got out the cups and saucers and made the kettle boil. I know they felt as if they were waiting on my servant, and when the tea was prepared I said: "He'll have a cup, please—he's tired." Mrs. Monarch brought him one where he stood, and he took it from her as if he had been a gentleman at a party, squeezing a crush-hat with an elbow.

Then it came over me that she had made a great effort for me—made it with a kind of nobleness—and that I owed her a compensation. Each time I saw her after this I wondered what the compensation could be. I couldn't go on doing the wrong thing to oblige them. Oh, it *was* the wrong thing, the stamp of the work for which they sat—Hawley was not the only person to say it now. I sent in a large number of the drawings I had made for "Rutland Ramsay," and I received a warning that was more to the point than Hawley's. The artistic adviser of the house for which I was working was of opinion that many of my illustrations were not what had been looked for. Most of these illustrations were the subjects in which the Monarchs had figured. Without going into the question of what *had* been looked for, I saw at this rate I shouldn't get the other books to do. I hurled myself in despair upon Miss Churm, I put her through all her paces. I not only adopted Oronte publicly as my hero, but one morning when the Major looked in to see if I didn't require him to finish a figure for the *Cheapside,* for which he had begun to sit the week before, I told him that I had changed my mind—I would do the drawing from my man. At this my visitor turned pale and stood looking at me. "Is *he* your idea of an English gentleman?" he asked.

I was disappointed, I was nervous, I wanted to get on with my work; so I replied with irritation: "Oh, my dear Major—I can't be ruined for *you!*"

He stood another moment; then, without a word, he quitted the studio. I drew a long breath when he was gone, for I said to myself that I shouldn't see him again. I had not told him definitely that I was in danger of having my work rejected, but I was vexed at his not having felt the catastrophe in the air, read with me the moral of our fruitless collaboration, the lesson that, in the deceptive atmosphere of art, even the highest respectability may fail of being plastic.

I didn't owe my friends money, but I did see them again. They re-appeared together, three days later, and under the circumstances there was something tragic in the fact. It was a proof to me that they could find nothing else in life to do. They had threshed the matter out in a dismal conference—they had digested the bad news that they were not in for the series. If they were not useful to me even for the *Cheapside* their function seemed difficult to determine, and I could only judge at first that they had come, forgivingly, decorously, to take a last leave. This made me rejoice in secret that I had little leisure for a scene; for I had placed both my other models in position together and I was pegging away at a drawing from which I hoped to derive glory. It had been suggested by the passage in which Rutland Ramsay, drawing up a chair to Artemisia's piano-stool, says extraordinary things to her while she ostensibly fingers out a difficult piece of music. I had done Miss Churm at the piano before—it was an attitude in which she knew how to take on an absolutely poetic grace. I wished the two figures to "compose" together, intensely, and my little Italian had entered perfectly into my conception. The pair were vividly before me, the piano had been pulled out; it was a charming picture of blended youth and murmured love, which I had only to catch and keep. My visitors stood and looked at it, and I was friendly to them over my shoulder.

They made no response, but I was used to silent company and went on with my work, only a little disconcerted (even though exhilarated by the sense that *this* was at least the ideal thing), at not having got rid of them after all. Presently I heard Mrs. Monarch's sweet voice beside, or rather above me: "I wish her hair was a little better done." I looked up and she was staring with a strange fixedness at Miss Churm, whose back was turned to her. "Do you mind my just touching it?" she went on—a question which made me spring up for an instant, as with the instinctive fear that she might do the young lady a harm. But she quieted me with a glance I shall never forget—I confess I should like to have been able to paint *that*—and went for a moment to my model. She spoke to her softly, laying a hand upon her shoulder and bending over her; and as the girl, understanding, gratefully assented, she disposed her rough curls, with a few quick passes, in such a way as to make Miss Churm's head twice as charming. It was one of the most heroic personal services I have ever seen rendered. Then Mrs. Monarch turned away with a low sigh and, looking about her as if for something to do, stooped to the floor with a noble humility and picked up a dirty rag that had dropped out of my paint-box.

The Major meanwhile had also been looking for something to do and, wandering to the other end of the studio, saw before him my breakfast things, neglected, unre-moved. "I say, can't I be useful *here?*" he called out to me with an irrepressible quaver. I assented with a laugh that I fear was awkward and for the next ten minutes, while I worked, I heard the light clatter of china and the tinkle of spoons and glass. Mrs. Monarch assisted her husband—they washed up my crockery, they put it away. They wandered off into my little scullery, and I afterwards found that they had cleaned my knives and that my slender stock of plate had an unprecedented surface. When it came over me, the latent eloquence of what they were doing, I confess that my drawing was blurred for a moment—the picture swam. They had accepted their failure, but they couldn't accept their fate. They had bowed their heads in bewilderment to the perverse and cruel law in virtue of which the real thing could be so much less precious than the unreal; but they didn't want to starve. If my servants were my models, my models might be my servants. They would reverse the parts—the others would sit for the ladies and gentlemen, and *they* would do the work. They would still be in the studio—it was an intense dumb appeal to me not to turn them out. "Take us on," they wanted to say— "we'll do *anything*."

When all this hung before me the *afflatus* vanished—my pencil dropped from my hand. My sitting was spoiled and I got rid of my sitters, who were also evidently rather mystified and awestruck. Then, alone with the Major and his wife, I had a most uncomfortable moment. He put their prayer into a single sentence: "I say, you know—just let *us* do for you, can't you?" I couldn't—it was dreadful to see them emptying my slops; but I pretended I could, to oblige them, for about a week. Then I gave them a sum of money to go away; and I never saw them again. I obtained the remaining books, but my friend Hawley repeats that Major and Mrs. Monarch did me a permanent harm, got me into a second-rate trick. If it be true I am content to have paid the price—for the memory.

QUESTIONS

1 How does Mrs. Monarch's reference to photography reflect the layman's attitude toward art? What is the narrator's reaction to the photographic qualities of the Monarchs?
2 How does Miss Churm indicate the narrator's view of artistic reality? In the same sense, why is the name "Churm," appropriate? What does Oronte have to do with the narrator's changing attitude?
3 Why doesn't the narrator follow Jack Hawley's advice? Exactly what does Hawley mean when he calls the Monarchs stupid?
4 Do the Monarchs come to understand the artistic position? Explain.
5 Examine each of the narrator's remarks on the function and technique of art. How do these remarks fit into James's technique in the writing of this story?
6 What do you think the narrator means by his final remark?

TOPICS FOR COMPOSITION

1 In connection with your answer to question 6, write an essay showing the humanizing influence on the narrator brought about by his contact with the Monarchs. Your essay, of course, will be a character study and should move from supported assumptions about the narrator's initial attitude toward people into the changes seen by his deepening relationship with the Monarchs.
2 Major and Mrs. Monarch are also apt subjects for a character study. Questions that need answers seem to be: Are they completely superficial? Can there be depth to their married relationship? Do they deserve their fate? Have they wronged themselves or are they products of a wrong society?
3 Both "Assembly Line" and "The Real Thing" deal with the search for expression, but the points of view differ quite distinctly. Write an essay contrasting point of view in the two stories. An essay of this type should have a definite purpose in mind; therefore decide on a specific thesis which the contrast will support. You may use, for example, topics such as: Type of Characters Dictates Point of View; Time Span Dictates Point of View; Setting Dictates Point of View.

☐

Almost everything about Donald Barthelme's short story captures our visual as well as our mental attention. The author seems to say, by experimenting with structure, that the art of fiction should be enlarged to embrace all of the reader's faculties and, at the same time, it should stimulate those faculties beyond their usual limits. As you read, consider the following:

1   The title of the story
2   The unusual narrative point of view that offers the events from two perspectives
3   The fact that Paul Klee is a painter
4   The quality of language in the first statement made by the Secret Police

ENGINEER-PRIVATE PAUL KLEE MISPLACES AN AIRCRAFT BETWEEN MILBERTSHOFEN AND CAMBRAI, MARCH 1916

Donald Barthelme

Paul Klee said:

"Now I have been transferred to the Air Corps. A kindly sergeant effected the transfer. He thought I would have a better future here, more chances for promotion. First I was assigned to aircraft repair, together with several other workers. We presented ourselves as not just painters but artist-painters. This caused some shaking of heads. We varnished wooden fuselages, correcting old numbers and adding new ones with the help of templates. Then I was pulled off the painting detail and assigned to transport. I escort aircraft that are being sent to various bases in Germany and also (I understand) in occupied territory. It is not a bad life. I spend my nights racketing across Bavaria (or some such) and my days in switching yards. There is always bread and wurst and beer in the station restaurants. When I reach a notable town I try to see the notable paintings there, if time allows. There are always unexpected delays, rerouting, backtrackings. Then the return to the base. I see Lily fairly often. We meet in hotel rooms and that is exciting. I have never yet lost an aircraft or failed to deliver one to its proper destination. The war seems interminable. Walden has sold six of my drawings."

The Secret Police said:

"We have secrets. We have many secrets. We desire all secrets. We do not have your secrets and that is what we are after, your secrets. Our first secret is where we are. No one knows. Our second secret is how many of us there are. No one knows. Omnipresence is our goal. We do not even need real omnipresence. The theory of omnipresence is enough. With omnipresence, hand-in-hand as it were, goes omniscience. And with omniscience and omnipresence, hand-in-hand-in-hand as it were, goes omnipotence. We are a three-sided waltz. However our mood is melancholy. There is a secret sigh that we sigh, secretly. We yearn to be known, acknowledged, admired even. What is the good of omnipotence if nobody knows? However that is a secret, that sorrow. Now we are everywhere. One place we are is here watching

Engineer-Private Klee, who is escorting three valuable aircraft, B.F.W. 3054/16–17–18, with spare parts, by rail from Milbertshofen to Cambrai. Do you wish to know what Engineer-Private Klee is doing at this very moment, in the baggage car? He is reading a book of Chinese short stories. He has removed his boots. His feet rest twenty-six centimeters from the baggage-car stove."

Paul Klee said:

"The Chinese short stories are slight and lovely. I have no way of knowing if the translation is adequate or otherwise. Lily will meet me in our rented room on Sunday, if I return in time. Our destination is Fighter Squadron Five. I have not had anything to eat since morning. The fine chunk of bacon given me along with my expense money when we left the base has been eaten. This morning a Red Cross lady with a squint gave me some very good coffee, however. Now we are entering Hohenbudberg."

The Secret Police said:

"Engineer-Private Klee has taken himself into the station restaurant. He is enjoying a hearty lunch. We shall join him there."

Paul Klee said:

"Now I emerge from the station restaurant and walk along the line of cars to the flatcar on which my aircraft (I think of them as *my* aircraft) are carried. To my surprise and dismay, I notice that one of them is missing. There had been three, tied down on the flatcar and covered with canvas. Now I see with my trained painter's eye that instead of three canvas-covered shapes on the flatcar there are only two. Where the third aircraft had been there is only a puddle of canvas and loose rope. I look around quickly to see if anyone else has marked the disappearance of the third aircraft."

The Secret Police said:

"We had marked it. Our trained policemen's eyes had marked the fact that where three aircraft had been before, tied down on the flatcar and covered with canvas, now there were only two. Unfortunately we had been in the station restaurant, lunching, at the moment of removal, therefore we could not attest as to when it had gone or who had removed it. There is something we do not know. This is irritating in the extreme. We closely observe Engineer-Private Klee to determine what action he will take in the emergency. We observe that he is withdrawing from his tunic a notebook and pencil. We observe that he begins, very properly in our opinion, to note down in his notebook all the particulars of the affair."

Paul Klee said:

"The shape of the collapsed canvas, under which the aircraft had rested, together with the loose ropes—the canvas forming hills and valleys, seductive folds, the ropes the very essence of looseness, lapsing—it is irresistible. I sketch for ten or fifteen minutes, wondering the while if I might not be in trouble, because of the missing aircraft. When I arrive at Fighter Squadron Five with less than the number of aircraft listed on the manifest, might not some officious person become angry? Shout at me? I have finished sketching. Now I will ask various trainmen and station personnel if they have seen anyone carrying away the aircraft. If they answer in the negative, I will become extremely frustrated. I will begin to kick the flatcar."

The Secret Police said:

"Frustrated, he begins to kick the flatcar."

Paul Klee said:

"I am looking up in the sky, to see if my aircraft is there. There are in the sky aircraft of several types, but none of the type I am searching for."

The Secret Police said:

"Engineer-Private Klee is searching the sky—an eminently sound procedure, in our opinion. We, the Secret Police, also sweep the Hohenbudberg sky, with our eyes. But find nothing. We are debating with ourselves as to whether we ought to enter the station restaurant and begin drafting our preliminary report, for forwarding to higher headquarters. The knotty point, in terms of the preliminary report, is that we do not have the answers to the question 'Where is the aircraft?' The damage potential to the theory of omniscience, as well as potential to our careers, dictates that this point be omitted from the preliminary report. But if this point is omitted, might not some officious person at the Central Bureau for Secrecy note the omission? Become angry? Shout at us? Omissiveness is not rewarded at the Central Bureau. We decide to observe further the actions of Engineer-Private Klee, for the time being."

Paul Klee said:

"I who have never lost an aircraft have lost an aircraft. The aircraft is signed out to me. The cost of the aircraft, if it is not found, will be deducted from my pay, meager enough already. Even if Walden sells a hundred, a thousand drawings, I will not have enough money to pay for this cursed aircraft. Can I, in the time the train remains in the Hohenbudberg yards, construct a new aircraft or even the simulacrum of an aircraft, with no materials to work with or indeed any special knowledge of aircraft construction? The situation is ludicrous. I will therefore apply Reason. Reason dictates the solution. I will diddle the manifest. With my painter's skill which is after all not so different from a forger's, I will change the manifest to reflect conveyance of *two* aircraft, B.F.W. 3054/16 and 17, to Fighter Squadron Five. The extra canvas and ropes I will conceal in an empty boxcar—this one, which according to its stickers is headed for Essigny-le-Petit. Now I will walk around town and see if I can find a chocolate shop. I crave chocolate."

The Secret Police said:

"Now we observe Engineer-Private Klee concealing the canvas and ropes which covered the former aircraft into an empty boxcar bound for Essigny-le-Petit. We have previously observed him diddling the manifest with his painter's skill which resembles not a little that of the forger. We applaud these actions of Engineer-Private Klee. The contradiction confronting us in the matter of the preliminary report is thus resolved in highly satisfactory fashion. We are proud of Engineer-Private Klee and of the resolute and manly fashion in which he has dealt with the crisis. We predict he will go far. We would like to embrace him as a comrade and brother but unfortunately we are not embraceable. We are secret, we exist in the shadows, the pleasure of the comradely/ brotherly embrace is one of the pleasures we are denied, in our dismal service."

Paul Klee said:

"We arrive at Cambrai. The planes are unloaded, six men for each plane. The work goes quickly. No one questions my altered manifest. The weather is clearing. After lunch I will leave to begin the return journey. My release slip and travel orders are ready, but the lieutenant must come and sign them. I wait contentedly in the warm orderly room. The drawing I did of the collapsed canvas and ropes is really very good.

I eat a piece of chocolate. I am sorry about the lost aircraft but not overmuch. The war is temporary. But drawings and chocolate go on forever."

QUESTIONS

1   Analyze the opening statement made by the Secret Police. What is meant by their explanations of "secrets"? By their wordplay with "omnipresence," "omniscience," and "omnipotence"?
2   Why inject the information about the Chinese short stories?
3   What is the purpose in mentioning Lily and in noting Paul Klee's hunger and eating habits?
4   Why is Paul Klee's forgery pleasing to the Secret Police? In a larger perspective, what does it all mean?

TOPICS FOR COMPOSITION

1   Write an essay in which you present Barthelme's short story as an apt illustration of Paul Engle's statement about what is suitable material for fiction. Use Barthelme's subject matter and structure as well as your response as reader as the bases for your essay.
2   Barthelme's story and Henry James's "The Real Thing" are obviously contending with the fictional presentation of reality. Compare and contrast the methods each author uses to present his viewpoint.

DRAMA

Dunsany's play, though written in 1909, surprisingly anticipates the "absurdist theater" of Harold Pinter, Eugene Ionesco, and Edward Albee. Its rigid economy in setting, action, characters, plot, and dialogue emphasizes the stark irony of its theme. But several of its textural features claim attention:

1 The compelling effort of Bill to retain identity, like many of us, and to express that compulsion in terms of "what he did" for a livelihood
2 The desire of both men to hope even in the fact of hope's absurdity
3 The diminishing relevance of words—"earth," "Putney," "hope," "years," "past," and "future"—when their points of reference fade into nothing

THE GLITTERING GATE

Lord Dunsany

PERSONS

JIM, *lately a burglar,* BILL, *lately a burglar—Both dead*

Scene: A Lonely Place.

Time: The present.

The Lonely Place is strewn with large black rocks and uncorked beer-bottles, the latter in great profusion. At back is a wall of granite built of great slabs, and in it the Gate of Heaven. The door is of gold.
  Below the Lonely Place is an abyss hung with stars.
  The rising curtain reveals Jim wearily uncorking a beer-bottle. Then he tilts it slowly and with infinite care. It proves to be empty. Faint and unpleasant laughter is heard off. This action and the accompanying far laughter are repeated continually throughout the play. Corked bottles are discovered lying behind rocks, and more descend constantly through the air, within reach of Jim. All prove to be empty.
  Jim uncorks a few bottles.

JIM *(weighing one carefully)* That's a full one. *(It is empty, like all)*

[Singing is heard off left.

BILL (*enters from left with a bullet-hole over his eye, singing*)   Rule Britannia, Britannia rule the waves. (*Breaking off his song*) Why, 'ullo. 'Ere's a bottle of beer. (*Finds it empty; looking off and downward*) I'm getting a bit tired of those blooming great stars down there and this rocky ledge. I've been walking along under this wall ever since. Why, it must be twenty-four hours since that householder shot me. And he needn't have done it, either, *I* wasn't going to hurt the bloke. I only wanted a bit of his silver stuff. It felt funny, that did. Hullo, a gate. Why, that's the Gate of Heaven. Well, well. So that's all right. (*Looks up and up for some time*)   No. I can't climb *that* wall. Why, it's got no top to it. Up and up it goes. (*Knocks at the door and waits*)

JIM   That isn't for the likes of us.

BILL   Why, hullo, there's another bloke. Why, somebody's been hanging him. Why, if it isn't old Jim! Jim!

JIM (*wearily*)   Hullo.

BILL   Why, Jim! 'Ow long 'ave you been 'ere?

JIM   I *am* 'ere always.

BILL   Why, Jim, don't you remember me? Why, you taught Bill to pick locks years and years ago when he was a little boy, and had never learnt a trade and hadn't a penny in the world, and never would have had but for you, Jim. (*Jim stares vaguely*)   I never forgot *you*, Jim. I broke into scores of houses. And then I took on big houses. Out in the country, you know, real big ones. I got rich, Jim, and respected by all who knew me. I was a citizen, Jim, one who dwelt in our midst. And of an evening, sitting over the fire, I used to say, "I am as clever as Jim." But I wasn't, Jim. I couldn't climb like you. And I couldn't walk like you on a creaky stair, when everything's quite still and there's a dog in the house and little rattly things left lying about, and a door that whines if you touch it, and someone ill upstairs that you didn't know of, who has nothing to do but to listen for *you* 'cause she can't get to sleep. Don't you remember little Bill?

JIM   That would be somewhere else.

BILL   Yes, Jim, yes. Down on Earth.

JIM   But there isn't anywhere else.

BILL   I never forgot *you*, Jim. I'd be pattering away with my tongue, in Church, like all the rest, but all the time I'd be thinking of you in that little room at Putney and the man searching every corner of it for you with a revolver in one hand and a candle in the other, and you almost going round with him.

JIM   What is Putney?

BILL   Oh, Jim, can't you remember? Can't you remember the day you taught me a livelihood? I wasn't more than twelve, and it was spring, all the may was in blossom outside the town. And we cleared out No. 25 in the new street. And next day we saw the man's fat, silly face. It was thirty years ago.

JIM   What are years?

BILL   Oh, *Jim* !

JIM   You see there isn't any hope here. And when there isn't any hope there isn't any future. And when there isn't any future there isn't any past. It's just the present here. I tell you we're struck. There aren't no years here. Nor no nothing.

BILL   Cheer up, Jim. You're thinking of a quotation, "Abandon hope, all ye that enter here." I used to learn quotations; they are awfully genteel. A fellow called Shakespeare used to make them. But there isn't any sense in them. What's the use of saying *ye* when you mean *you?* Don't be thinking of quotations, Jim.

JIM   I tell you there is no hope here.

BILL   Cheer up, Jim. There's plenty of hope there, isn't there? (*Points to the Gate of Heaven*)

JIM   Yes, and that's why they keep it locked up so. They won't let us have any. No. I begin to remember Earth again now since you've been speaking. It was just the same there. The more they'd got the more they wanted to keep *you* from having a bit.

BILL   You'll cheer up a bit when I tell you what I've got. I say, Jim, have you got some beer? Why, so you have. Why, *you* ought to cheer up, Jim.

JIM   All the beer you're ever likely to see again. They're empty.

BILL (*half rising from the rock on which he has seated himself, and pointing his finger at Jim as he rises; very cheerfully*)   Why, you're the chap that said there was no hope here, and you're hoping to find beer in every bottle you open.

JIM   Yes; I *hope* to see a drop of beer in one some day, but I *know* I won't. Their trick *might* not work just once.

BILL   How many have you tried, Jim?

JIM   Oh, I don't know. I've always been at it, working as fast as I can, ever since—ever since—(*Feels his neck meditatively and up toward his ear*). Why, ever since, Bill.

BILL   Why don't you stop it?

JIM   I'm too thirsty, Bill.

BILL   What do you think *I've* got, Jim?

JIM   I don't know. Nothing's any use.

BILL (*as yet another bottle is shown to be empty*)   Who's that laughing, Jim?

JIM (*astonished at such a question, loudly and emphatically*)   Who's that laughing?

BILL (*looks a little disconcerted at having apparently asked a silly question*)   Is it a pal?

JIM   A pal!—(*laughs*) (*The laugh off joins in loudly and for long*)

BILL   Well, I don't know. But, Jim, what do you think I've got?

JIM   It isn't any good to you whatever it is. Not even if it is a ten-pound note.

BILL   It's better than a ten-pound note, Jim. Jim, try and remember, Jim. Don't you remember the way we used to go for those iron safes? Do you remember anything, Jim?

JIM   Yes, I am beginning to remember now. There used to be sunsets. And then there were great yellow lights. And one went in behind them through a swinging door.

BILL   Yes, yes, Jim. That was the Blue Bear down at Wimbledon.

JIM   Yes, and the room was all full of golden light. And there was beer with light in it, and some would be spilt on the counter and there was light in that too. And there was a girl standing there with yellow hair. She'd be the other side of that door now, with lamplight in her hair among the angels, and the old smile on her lips if one of them chaffed her, and her pretty teeth a-shining. She would be very near the throne; there was never any harm in Jane.

BILL   No, there was never any 'arm in Jane, Jim.

JIM   Oh, I don't want to see the angels, Bill. But if I could see Jane again (*points in direction of laugh*) he might laugh as much as he cared to whenever I wanted to cry. You can't cry here, you know, Bill.

BILL   You shall see her again, Jim.

[*Jim takes no interest in this remark; he lowers his eyes and goes on with his work.*

BILL   Jim, you shall see her again. You want to get into Heaven, don't you?

JIM   (*not raising his eyes*) Want!

BILL   Jim. Do you know what I've got, Jim?

[*Jim makes no answer, goes on wearily with his work.*

BILL   You remember those iron safes, Jim, how we used to knock them open like walnuts with "Old Nut-cracker"?

JIM (*at work, wearily*) Empty again.

BILL   Well, I've got Old Nut-cracker. I had him in my hand at the time, and they let me keep him. They thought it would be a nice proof against me.

JIM   Nothing is any good here.

BILL   I'll get in to Heaven, Jim. And you shall come with me because you taught me a livelihood. I couldn't be happy there, like those angels, if I knew of anyone being outside. I'm not like that.

[*Jim goes on with his work.*

BILL   Jim, Jim. You'll see Jane there.

JIM   You'll never get through those gates, Bill. You'll never do it.

BILL   They're only gold, Jim. Gold's soft like lead. Old Nut-cracker would do it if they were steel.

JIM   You'll never do it, Bill.

[*Bill puts a rock against the gates, stands on it to reach the lock and gets to work on the lock. A good instrument to use is an egg-whipper. Jim goes on wearily with his work. As Bill works away, fragments and golden screws begin to fall on the floor.*

BILL   Jim! Old Nut-cracker thinks nothing of it. It's just like cheese to old Nut-cracker.

JIM   They won't let you do it, Bill.

BILL   They don't know what I've got. I'm getting through it like cheese, Jim.

JIM   Suppose it's a mile thick. Suppose it's a million miles thick. Suppose it's a hundred million miles thick.

BILL   Can't be, Jim. These doors are meant to open outward. They couldn't do that if they were more than four inches at the most, not for an Archbishop. They'd stick.

JIM   You remember that great safe we broke open once, what had coal in it.

BILL   This isn't a safe, Jim, this is Heaven. There'll be the old saints with their halos shining and flickering, like windows o' wintry nights. (*Creak, creak, creak*) And angels thick as swallows along a cottage roof the day before they go. (*Creak, creak, creak*) And orchards full of apples as far as you can see, and the rivers of Tigris and Euphrates, so the Bible says; and a city of gold, for those that care for cities, all full of precious stones; but I'm a bit tired of cities and precious stones. (*Creak, creak, creak*) I'll go out into the fields where the orchards are, by the Tigris and the Euphrates. I shouldn't be surprised if my old mother was there. She never cared much for the way I earned my livelihood (*creak, creak*), but she was a good mother to me. I don't know if they want a good mother in there who would be kind to the angels and sit and smile at them when they sang and soothe them if they were cross. If they let all the good ones in she'll be there all right. (*Suddenly*) Jim! They won't have brought me up against her, will they? That's not fair evidence, Jim.

JIM It would be just like them to. Very like them.

BILL If there's a glass of beer to be got in Heaven, or a dish of tripe and onions, or a pipe of 'bacca she'll have them for me when I come to her. She used to know my ways wonderful; and what I liked. And she used to know when to expect me almost anywhere. I used to climb in through the window at any hour and she always knew it was me. (*Creak, creak*) She'll know it's me at the door now, Jim. (*Creak, creak*) It will be all a blaze of light, and I'll hardly know it's her till I get used to it. . . . But I'll know her among a million angels. There weren't none like her on Earth and there won't be none like her in Heaven. . . . Jim! I'm through, Jim! One more turn, and old Nut-cracker's done it! It's giving! It's giving! I know the feel of it. *Jim!*

[*At last there is a noise of falling bolts; the gates swing out an inch and are stopped by the rock.*

BILL Jim! Jim! I've opened it, Jim. I've opened the Gate of Heaven! Come and help me.

JIM (*looks up for a moment with open mouth. Then he mournfully shakes his head and goes on drawing a cork*) Another one empty.

BILL (*looks down once into the abyss that lies below the Lonely Place*) Stars. Blooming great stars.

[*Then he moves away the rock on which he stood. The gates move slowly. Jim leaps up and runs to help; they each take a gate and move backward with their faces against it.*

BILL Hullo, mother! You there? Hullo! You there? It's Bill, mother.

[*The gates swing heavily open, revealing empty night and stars.*

BILL (*staggering and gazing into the revealed Nothing, in which far stars go wandering*) Stars. Blooming great stars. There *ain't* no Heaven, Jim.

[*Ever since the revelation a cruel and violent laugh has arisen off. It increases in volume and grows louder and louder.*

JIM That's like them. That's very like them. Yes, they'd do that!

The curtain falls and the laughter still howls on.

TOPIC FOR COMPOSITION

1 What essential differences between Bill and Jim—differences of temperament, manner, language—are established from the outset of the play?

2 Does either man feel or manifest "a touch of the poet"? How is that "touch" expressed?

3 What seems to come off as the finest, most memorable experience one can have in life? Why does memory seem to expand, to come alive, for Bill and Jim?

4 What do you understand as the source and meaning of the offstage laughter? What sets off the laughter? Do you think the laughter is justified?

5 Are Bill's confidence in "Old Nut-cracker" and his pride in his craftsmanship themselves "expressions" of human hope?

TOPIC FOR COMPOSITION

Think about the kind of attitude Dunsany's play seems to encourage toward human aspiration or toward human destiny. Is it pessimistic, idealistic, ironic, or, perhaps, some of each? Is the mode of the play "comic" or "ironic"? Use your conclusions and adequate illustrations from the text of the play as the basis for an analytical essay about the purpose and mode of Dunsany's play.

POETRY

Since about the end of the eighteenth century, poets especially have been preoccupied with the possibility of finding new modes of expression. They have been stimulated in their search by the fact that modern science and philosophy have raised difficult questions about the relation between the mind and "given" reality. In Alexander Pope's time it was still possible to think of reality, or "Nature," as an essentially unchanging arrangement and an essentially unchanging correspondence between things and perceptions. Human desires, always basically the same, had to be accommodated to the way things are, and any exercise of the imagination that did not stay within the bounds of probability and common sense could not be permanently pleasurable. Pope therefore believed that the best modes of expression had long since been discovered—though he had to admit that language is subject to change and that a few geniuses had seemed able to express truths not clearly seen before.

Since the beginning of the Romantic period, however, there has been much excited speculation about the implications of the fact that the mind, for practical purposes, partly creates reality. What this means, in more homely terms, is simply that we all to some extent see what we want to see in the world around us. Desire determines our modes of perception and so shapes "reality." The question, for poets, has been to what extent this process can be controlled. Can we, acting individually or collectively, create a more beautiful world by altering our modes of perception or, what is the same (again, for practical purposes), discover a better world by finding new modes of expression? Poets since Blake have responded to these questions with varying degrees of hope. So we find Shelley, midway between despair and exaltation, literally exhorting the wild universe of nature: "Be thou, Spirit fierce, / My spirit! Be thou me, impetuous one!" and D.H. Lawrence proclaiming: "There are vast realms of consciousness still undreamed of, / vast ranges of experience, like the humming of unseen harps, / we know nothing of, within us."

Although there has been much disagreement about the radically creative potential of the imagination—compare, for example, Coleridge's vision of the poet as magician with Housman's assertion that "malt does more than Milton can / To justify God's ways to man"—and about the best means of realizing that potential, there has been almost universal agreement about three things. First, metaphor in some form, even if only in that of a cluster of images that seem to say what the mind in its deepest reaches is like, is essential. Secondly, the discovery of metaphorical constructs that leave one with a more satisfying sense of reality is very difficult. We find Wallace Stevens, in "Of Modern Poetry," explaining that while poets once found the scene set for them and had only to repeat what was in the script (could, that is, draw upon myths more or less consciously created to express what would, for one culture or another, "suffice"), the modern poet has to construct a new stage and, like an actor improvising, speak words "with meditation" until the mind, its own invisible audience, hears what seems to wholly contain it. In the process, Lawrence Ferlinghetti says, the poet is "constantly risking absurdity." Finally, there has been strong agreement that pleasure or beauty— in any case, emotion—is a more important value criterion than rationality. William Wordsworth, one of the leaders of the Romantic search for new modes of expression, asserted that

> Our meddling intellect
> Misshapes the beauteous forms of things;
> We murder to dissect.

And his thought is echoed, we see, in the words of John Wain's "maladjusted" electric brain:

> Man made me, now I speak to man. He fears
> Whole truth. The brain defines it. Wholeness is
> The indivisible strength, brain, heart, and eye.

It is interesting to note that Edward Lueders uses the same metaphor, electric circuitry, to warn against the loss of insights that results from reliance upon stock responses.

Not all modern poets, it should be stressed, have shared the high, almost visionary hopes of the early Romantic innovators, but the search for new modes of expression continues, and the conviction persists that the effort is one of crucial importance.

AN ESSAY ON CRITICISM

Alexander Pope

Part I
'Tis hard to say if greater want of skill
Appear in writing or in judging ill;
But, of the two, less dangerous is the offence
To tire our patience, than mislead our sense.
Some few in that, but numbers err in this;   5
Ten censure wrong for one who writes amiss;
A fool might once himself alone expose;
Now one in verse makes many more in prose.
    'Tis with our judgments as our watches: none
Go just alike, yet each believes his own.   10

1 want: lack.   *6 censure:* judge.

In poets as true genius is but rare,
True taste as seldom is the critic's share;
Both must alike from heaven derive their light,
These born to judge, as well as those to write.
Let such teach others who themselves excel,   15
And censure freely who have written well.
Authors are partial to their wit, 'tis true,
But are not critics to their judgment too?
    Yet if we look more closely, we shall find
Most have the seeds of judgment in their mind: 20
Nature affords at least a glimmering light;
The lines, though touched but faintly, are drawn right.
But as the slightest sketch, if justly traced,
Is by ill-colouring but the more disgraced,
So by false learning is good sense defaced: 25
Some are bewildered in the maze of schools,
And some made coxcombs nature meant but fools.
In search of wit these lose their common sense,
And then turn critics in their own defence:
Each burns alike, who can, or cannot write,   30
Or with a rival's, or an eunuch's spite.
All fools have still an itching to deride,
And fain would be upon the laughing side.
If Mævius scribble in Apollo's spite,
There are who judge still worse than he can write.   35
    Some have at first for wits, then poets passed,
Turned critics next, and proved plain fools at last.
Some neither can for wits nor critics pass,
As heavy mules are neither horse nor ass.
Those half-learned witlings, numerous in our isle,   40
As half-formed insects on the banks of Nile;
Unfinished things, one knows not what to call,
Their generation's so equivocal;
To tell 'em would a hundred tongues require,
Or one vain wit's, that might a hundred tire.   45
    But you who seek to give and merit fame,
And justly bear a critic's noble name,
Be sure yourself and your own reach to know,
How far your genius, taste, and learning go;
Launch not beyond your depth, but be discreet,   50
And mark that point where sense and dulness meet.
    Nature to all things fixed the limits fit,
And wisely curbed proud man's pretending wit.

27 coxcombs: conceited persons.   *34 Mævius:* an inferior Roman poet.   *44 tell:* count.

As on the land while here the ocean gains,
In other parts it leaves wide sandy plains; 55
Thus in the soul while memory prevails,
The solid power of understanding fails;
Where beams of warm imagination play,
The memory's soft figures melt away.
One science only will one genius fit; 60
So vast is art, so narrow human wit—
Not only bounded to peculiar arts,
But oft in those confined to single parts.
Like kings we lose the conquests gained before,
By vain ambition still to make them more; 65
Each might his several province well command,
Would all but stoop to what they understand.
      First follow nature, and your judgment frame
By her just standard, which is still the same:
Unerring nature, still divinely bright, 70
One clear, unchanged, and universal light,
Life, force, and beauty, must to all impart,
At once the source, and end, and test of art.
Art from that fund each just supply provides,
Works without show, and without pomp presides; 75
In some fair body thus the informing soul
With spirits feeds, with vigour fills the whole,
Each motion guides, and every nerve sustains;
Itself unseen, but in the effects remains.
Some, to whom Heaven in wit has been profuse, 80
Want as much more, to turn it to its use;
For wit and judgment often are at strife,
Though meant each other's aid, like man and wife
'Tis more to guide, than spur the muse's steed,
Restrain his fury, than provoke his speed; 85
The winged courser, like a generous horse,
Shows most true mettle when you check his course.
      Those rules of old discovered, not devised,
Are nature still, but nature methodised;
Nature, like liberty, is but restrained 90
By the same laws which first herself ordained.
      Hear how learned Greece her useful rules indites,
When to repress, and when indulge our flights:
High on Parnassus' top her sons she showed,
And pointed out those arduous paths they trod; 95

86 *winged courser:* Pegasus, associated with poetic inspiration. 94 *Parnassus:* a mountain in
Greece, sacred to Apollo and the Muses.

Held from afar, aloft, the immortal prize,
And urged the rest by equal steps to rise.
Just precepts thus from great examples given,
She drew from them what they derived from heaven.
The generous critic fanned the poet's fire,   100
And taught the world with reason to admire.
Then criticism the muses' handmaid proved,
To dress her charms, and make her more beloved:
But following wits from that intention strayed;
Who could not win the mistress, wooed the maid;   105
Against the poets their own arms they turned,
Sure to hate most the men from whom they learned.
So modern 'pothecaries, taught the art
By doctor's bills to play the doctor's part,
Bold in the practice of mistaken rules,   110
Prescribe, apply, and call their masters fools,
Some on the leaves of ancient authors prey,
Nor time nor moths e'er spoiled so much as they.
Some dryly plain, without invention's aid,
Write dull receipts how poems may be made.   115
These leave the sense, their learning to display,
And those explain the meaning quite away.
      You then whose judgment the right course would steer,
Know well each ancient's proper character;
His fable, subject, scope in every page;   120
Religion, country, genius of his age:
Without all these at once before your eyes,
Cavil you may, but never criticise.
Be Homer's works your study and delight,
Read them by day, and meditate by night;   125
Thence form your judgment, thence your maxims bring,
And trace the muses upward to their spring.
Still with itself compared, his text peruse,
And let your comment be the Mantuan muse.
      When first young Maro in his boundless mind   130
A work to outlast immortal Rome designed,
Perhaps he seemed above the critic's law,
And but from nature's fountains scorned to draw;
But when to examine every part he came,
Nature and Homer were, he found, the same.   135
Convinced, amazed, he checks the bold design;
And rules as strict his laboured work confine,
As if the Stagirite o'erlooked each line.

109 bills: prescriptions.   *120 fable:* plot.   *130 Maro:* Virgil, who was born near Mantua. He is also
referred to as Maro.   *138 Stagirite:* Aristotle, who was a native of Stagira. His *Poetics* was
regarded as the supreme critical authority.

Learn hence for ancient rules a just esteem;
To copy nature is to copy them.   140
    Some beauties yet no precepts can declare,
For there's a happiness as well as care.
Music resembles poetry, in each
Are nameless graces which no methods teach,
And which a master-hand alone can reach.   145
If, where the rules not far enough extend,
(Since rules were made but to promote their end)
Some lucky licence answer to the full
The intent proposed, that licence is a rule.
Thus Pegasus, a nearer way to take,   150
May boldly deviate from the common track;
From vulgar bounds with brave disorder part;
And snatch a grace beyond the reach of art,
Which without passing through the judgment, gains
The heart, and all its end at once attains.   155
In prospects thus, some objects please our eyes,
Which out of nature's common order rise,
The shapeless rock, or hanging precipice.
Great wits sometimes may gloriously offend,
And rise to faults true critics dare not mend.   160
But though the ancients thus their rules invade,
(As kings dispense with laws themselves have made)
Moderns, beware! or if you must offend
Against the precept, ne'er transgress its end;
Let it be seldom, and compelled by need;   165
And have, at least, their precedent to plead.
The critic else proceeds without remorse,
Seizes your fame, and puts his laws in force.
    I know there are, to whose presumptuous thoughts
Those freer beauties, even in them, seem faults.   170
Some figures monstrous and mis-shaped appear,
Considered singly, or beheld too near,
Which, but proportioned to their light, or place,
Due distance reconciles to form and grace.
A prudent chief not always must display   175
His powers in equal ranks, and fair array,
But with the occasion and the place comply,
Conceal his force, nay seem sometimes to fly.
Those oft are stratagems which error seem,
Nor is it Homer nods, but we that dream.   180
    Still green with bays each ancient altar stands,
Above the reach of sacrilegious hands,

142 happiness: good luck. *181 bays:* garlands of laurel awarded for excellence.

Secure from flames, from envy's fiercer rage,
Destructive war, and all-involving age.
See, from each clime the learned their incense bring!   185
Hear, in all tongues consenting pæens ring!
In praise so just let every voice be joined,
And fill the general chorus of mankind.
Hail, bards triumphant! born in happier days,
Immortal heirs of universal praise!   190
Whose honours with increase of ages grow,
As streams roll down, enlarging as they flow;
Nations unborn your mighty names shall sound,
And worlds applaud that must not yet be found!
Oh, may some spark of your celestial fire,   195
The last, the meanest of your sons inspire,
(That on weak wings, from far, pursues your flights;
Glows while he reads, but trembles as he writes)
To teach vain wits a science little known,
To admire superior sense, and doubt their own!   200

Part II
        Of all the causes which conspire to blind
Man's erring judgment, and misguide the mind,
What the weak head with strongest bias rules
Is pride, the never-failing vice of fools.
Whatever nature has in worth denied,   205
She gives in large recruits of needful pride;
For as in bodies, thus in souls, we find
What wants in blood and spirits, swelled with wind:
Pride, where wit fails, steps in to our defence,
And fills up all the mighty void of sense.   210
If once right reason drives that cloud away,
Truth breaks upon us with resistless day.
Trust not yourself; but your defects to know,
Make use of every friend—and every foe.
        A little learning is a dangerous thing;   215
Drink deep, or taste not the Pierian spring:
There shallow draughts intoxicate the brain,
And drinking largely sobers us again.
Fired at first sight with what the muse imparts,
In fearless youth we tempt the heights of arts,   220
While from the bounded level of our mind
Short views we take, nor see the lengths behind;

206 recruits: supplies.   *216 Pierian spring:* a spring on Mt. Olympus, sacred to the Muses.
220 tempt: attempt.

But more advanced, behold with strange surprise
New distant scenes of endless science rise!
So pleased at first the towering Alps we try,   225
Mount o'er the vales, and seem to tread the sky;
The eternal snows appear already past,
And the first clouds and mountains seem the last;
But, those attained, we tremble to survey
The growing labours of the lengthened way;   230
The increasing prospect tires our wandering eyes,
Hills peep o'er hills, and Alps on Alps arise!
   A perfect judge will read each work of wit
With the same spirit that its author writ:
Survey the whole, nor seek slight faults to find   235
Where nature moves, and rapture warms the mind;
Nor lose, for that malignant dull delight,
The generous pleasure to be charmed with wit.
But in such lays as neither ebb, nor flow,
Correctly cold, and regularly low,   240
That shunning faults, one quiet tenour keep,
We cannot blame indeed—but we may sleep.
In wit, as nature, what affects our hearts
Is not the exactness of peculiar parts;
'Tis not a lip, or eye, we beauty call,   245
But the joint force and full result of all.
Thus when we view some well-proportioned dome,
(The world's just wonder, and even thine, O Rome!)
No single parts unequally surprise,
All comes united to the admiring eyes;   250
No monstrous height, or breadth, or length appear;
The whole at once is bold, and regular.
   Whoever thinks a faultless piece to see,
Thinks what ne'er was, nor is, nor e'er shall be.
In every work regard the writer's end,   255
Since none can compass more than they intend;
And if the means be just, the conduct true,
Applause, in spite of trivial faults, is due;
As men of breeding, sometimes men of wit,
To avoid great errors, must the less commit: 260
Neglect the rules each verbal critic lays,
For not to know some trifles, is a praise.
Most critics, fond of some subservient art,
Still make the whole depend upon a part;
They talk of principles, but notions prize,   265

247 *dome:* the dome of St. Peter's in Rome, designed by Michelangelo.

And all to one loved folly sacrifice.
      Once on a time, La Mancha's knight, they say,
A certain bard encountering on the way,
Discoursed in terms as just, with looks as sage,
As e'er could Dennis of the Grecian stage;   270
Concluding all were desperate sots and fools,
Who durst depart from Aristotle's rules.
Our author, happy in a judge so nice,
Produced his play, and begged the knight's advice;
Made him observe the subject, and the plot,   275
The manners, passions, unities—what not?
All which, exact to rule, were brought about,
Were but a combat in the lists left out.
"What! leave the combat out?" exclaims the knight;
"Yes, or we must renounce the Stagirite."   280
"Not so by Heaven," he answers in a rage,
"Knights, squires, and steeds, must enter on the stage."
"So vast a throng the stage can ne'er contain."
"Then build a new, or act it in a plain."
      Thus critics, of less judgment than caprice,   285
Curious not knowing, not exact but nice,
Form short ideas, and offend in arts
(As most in manners) by a love to parts,
      Some to conceit alone their taste confine,
And glittering thoughts struck out at every line;   290
Pleased with a work where nothing's just or fit,
One glaring chaos and wild heap of wit.
Poets like painters, thus, unskilled to trace
The naked nature and the living grace,
With gold and jewels cover every part,   295
And hide with ornaments their want of art.
True wit is nature to advantage dressed,
What oft was thought, but ne'er so well expressed;
Something, whose truth convinced at sight we find,
That gives us back the image of our mind.   300
As shades more sweetly recommend the light,
So modest plainness sets off sprightly wit;
For works may have more wit than does 'em good,
As bodies perish through excess of blood.
      Others for language all their care express,   305
And value books, as women men, for dress:
Their praise is still,—the style is excellent:

---

267 *La Mancha's knight:* Don Quixote.   270 *Dennis:* John Dennis, a severe and rather pompous
critic.   286 *Curious:* overscrupulous.   289 *conceit:* elaborate wittiness.

The sense, they humbly take upon content.
Words are like leaves; and where they most abound,
Much fruit of sense beneath is rarely found:　　　　　　　　　　310
False eloquence, like the prismatic glass,
Its gaudy colours spreads on every place;
The face of nature we no more survey,
All glares alike, without distinction gay:
But true expression, like the unchanging sun,　　　　　　　　315
Clears and improves whate'er it shines upon;
It gilds all objects, but it alters none.
Expression is the dress of thought, and still
Appears more decent as more suitable;
A vile conceit in pompous words expressed,　　　　　　　　320
Is like a clown in regal purple dressed:
For different styles with different subjects sort,
As several garbs with country, town, and court.
Some by old words to fame have made pretence,
Ancients in phrase, mere moderns in their sense;　　　　　　325
Such laboured nothings, in so strange a style,
Amaze the unlearned, and make the learned smile.
Unlucky, as Fungoso in the play,
These sparks with awkward vanity display
What the fine gentleman wore yesterday;　　　　　　　　　330
And but so mimic ancient wits at best,
As apes our grandsires, in their doublets dressed.
In words as fashions the same rule will hold;
Alike fantastic if too new or old:
Be not the first by whom the new are tried,　　　　　　　　335
Nor yet the last to lay the old aside.
　　　　　But most by numbers judge a poet's song;
And smooth or rough with them is right or wrong:
In the bright muse though thousand charms conspire,
Her voice is all these tuneful fools admire,　　　　　　　　340
Who haunt Parnassus but to please their ear,
Not mend their minds; as some to church repair,
Not for the doctrine, but the music there.
These equal syllables alone require,
Though oft the ear the open vowels tire;　　　　　　　　　345
While expletives their feeble aid do join,
And ten low words oft creep in one dull line:
While they ring round the same unvaried chimes,
With sure returns of still expected rhymes;

308 upon content: without questioning.　*321 clown:* a rustic person.　*328 Fungoso:* a character
in Ben Jonson's *Every Man Out of His Humor.*　*337 numbers:* versification.　*345:* Note that in
lines 345–357 Pope's own style illustrates the faults he mentions.

Where'er you find "the cooling western breeze,"   350
In the next line, it "whispers through the trees";
If crystal streams "with pleasing murmurs creep,"
The reader's threatened (not in vain) with "sleep";
Then, at the last and only couplet fraught
With some unmeaning thing they call a thought,   355
A needless Alexandrine ends the song
That, like a wounded snake, drags its slow length along.
Leave such to tune their own dull rhymes, and know
What's roundly smooth or languishingly slow;
And praise the easy vigour of a line,   360
Where Denham's strength and Waller's sweetness join.
True ease in writing comes from art, not chance,
As those move easiest who have learned to dance.
'Tis not enough no harshness gives offence;
The sound must seem an echo to the sense: 365
Soft is the strain when Zephyr gently blows,
And the smooth stream in smoother numbers flows;
But when loud surges lash the sounding shore,
The hoarse, rough verse should like the torrent roar:
When Ajax strives some rock's vast weight to throw,   370
The line too labours, and the words move slow;
Not so, when swift Camilla scours the plain,
Flies o'er the unbending corn, and skims along the main.
Hear how Timotheus' varied lays surprise,
And bid alternate passions fall and rise!   375
While, at each change, the son of Libyan Jove
Now burns with glory, and then melts with love,
Now his fierce eyes with sparkling fury glow,
Now sighs steal out, and tears begin to flow:
Persians and Greeks like turns of nature found,   380
And the world's victor stood subdued by sound!
The power of music all our hearts allow,
And what Timotheus was, is Dryden now.
    Avoid extremes, and shun the fault of such,
Who still are pleased too little or too much.   385
At every trifle scorn to take offence;
That always shows great pride or little sense;
Those heads, as stomachs, are not sure the best,
Which nauseate all, and nothing can digest.
Yet let not each gay turn thy rapture move;   390
For fools admire, but men of sense approve:

356 Alexandrine: a line with six iambic feet, like the one following this one.   *361 Denham, Waller:*
Sir John Denham (1615–1669) and Edmund Waller (1609–1687).   *374:* See Dryden's "Alexander's Feast."   *376 son of Libyan Jove:* Alexander the Great.

As things seem large which we through mists descry,
Dulness is ever apt to magnify.
      Some foreign writers, some our own despise;
The ancients only, or the moderns prize.   395
Thus wit, like faith, by each man is applied
To one small sect, and all are damned beside.
Meanly they seek the blessing to confine,
And force that sun but on a part to shine,
Which not alone the southern wit sublimes,   400
But ripens spirits in cold northern climes;
Which from the first has shone on ages past,
Enlights the present, and shall warm the last;
Though each may feel increases and decays,
And see now clearer and now darker days.   405
Regard not then if wit be old or new,
But blame the false, and value still the true.
      Some ne'er advance a judgment of their own,
But catch the spreading notion of the town;
They reason and conclude by precedent,   410
And own stale nonsense which they ne'er invent.
Some judge of authors' names, not works, and then
Nor praise nor blame the writings, but the men.
Of all this servile herd the worst is he
That in proud dulness joins with quality;   415
A constant critic at the great man's board,
To fetch and carry nonsense for my lord.
What woeful stuff this madrigal would be,
In some starved hackney sonneteer, or me?
But let a lord once own the happy lines,   420
How the wit brightens! how the style refines!
Before his sacred name flies every fault,
And each exalted stanza teems with thought!
      The vulgar thus through imitation err;
As oft the learned by being singular: 425
So much they scorn the crowd, that if the throng
By chance go right, they purposely go wrong;
So schismatics the plain believers quit,
And are but damned for having too much wit.
Some praise at morning what they blame at night,   430
But always think the last opinion right.
A muse by these is like a mistress used,
This hour she's idolised, the next abused;
While their weak heads, like towns unfortified,
Twixt sense and nonsense daily change their side.   435
Ask them the cause; they're wiser still, they say;

And still to-morrow's wiser than to-day.
We think our fathers fools, so wise we grow;
Our wiser sons, no doubt, will think us so.
Once school-divines this zealous isle o'erspread;   440
Who knew most sentences, was deepest read;
Faith, gospel, all, seemed made to be disputed,
And none had sense enough to be confuted:
Scotists and Thomists now in peace remain,
Amidst their kindred cobwebs in Duck Lane.   445
If faith itself has different dresses worn,
What wonder modes in wit should take their turn?
Oft, leaving what is natural and fit,
The current folly proves the ready wit;
And authors think their reputation safe,   450
Which lives as long as fools are pleased to laugh.
        Some, valuing those of their own side or mind,
Still make themselves the measure of mankind:
Fondly we think we honour merit then,
When we but praise ourselves in other men.   455
Parties in wit attend on those of state,
And public faction doubles private hate.
Pride, Malice, Folly, against Dryden rose,
In various shapes of parsons, critics, beaux;
But sense survived, when merry jests were past;   460
For rising merit will buoy up at last.
Might he return, and bless once more our eyes,
New Blackmores and new Milbournes must arise:
Nay, should great Homer lift his awful head,
Zoilus again would start up from the dead.   465
Envy will merit, as its shade, pursue;
But like a shadow, proves the substance true;
For envied wit, like Sol eclipsed, makes known
The opposing body's grossness, not its own.
When first that sun too powerful beams displays,   470
It draws up vapours which obscure its rays;
But even those clouds at last adorn its way,
Reflect new glories, and augment the day.
        Be thou the first true merit to befriend;
His praise is lost who stays till all commend.   475
Short is the date, alas, of modern rhymes,
And 'tis but just to let them live betimes.
No longer now that golden age appears,

441 *sentences:* an allusion to Peter Lombard's *Book of Sentences.*   445 *Duck Lane:* a street
where secondhand books and publishers' leftover stocks were sold.   463 *Blackmore:* Blackmore
attacked Dryden for the immorality of his plays. Milbourne criticized his translation of Virgil.

When patriarch wits survived a thousand years:
Now length of fame (our second life) is lost, 480
And bare threescore is all even that can boast;
Our sons their fathers' failing language see,
And such as Chaucer is, shall Dryden be.
So when the faithful pencil has designed
Some bright idea of the master's mind, 485
Where a new world leaps out at his command,
And ready nature waits upon his hand;
When the ripe colours soften and unite,
And sweetly melt into just shade and light;
When mellowing years their full perfection give, 490
And each bold figure just begins to live,
The treacherous colours the fair art betray,
And all the bright creation fades away!
      Unhappy wit, like most mistaken things,
Atones not for that envy which it brings. 495
In youth alone its empty praise we boast,
But soon the short-lived vanity is lost:
Like some fair flower the early spring supplies,
That gaily blooms, but even in blooming dies.
What is this wit, which must our cares employ? 500
The owner's wife, that other men enjoy;
Then most our trouble still when most admired,
And still the more we give, the more required;
Whose fame with pains we guard, but lose with ease,
Sure some to vex, but never all to please; 505
'Tis what the vicious fear, the virtuous shun;
By fools 'tis hated, and by knaves undone!
      If wit so much from ignorance undergo,
Ah let not learning too commence its foe!
Of old, those met rewards who could excel, 510
And such were praised who but endeavoured well;
Though triumphs were to generals only due,
Crowns were reserved to grace the soldiers too.
Now they who reach Parnassus' lofty crown
Employ their pains to spurn some others down; 515
And while self-love each jealous writer rules,
Contending wits become the sport of fools;
But still the worst with most regret commend,
For each ill author is as bad a friend.
To what base ends, and what abject ways, 520
Are mortals urged through sacred lust of praise!
Ah, ne'er so dire a thirst of glory boast,
Nor in the critic let the man be lost.

Good nature and good sense must ever join;
To err is human; to forgive, divine.   525
          But if in noble minds some dregs remain
Not yet purged off, of spleen and sour disdain,
Discharge that rage on more provoking crimes,
Nor fear a dearth in these flagitious times.
No pardon vile obscenity should find,   530
Though wit and art conspire to move your mind;
But dulness with obscenity must prove
As shameful sure as impotence in love.
In the fat age of pleasure, wealth, and ease,
Sprung the rank weed, and thrived with large increase: 535
When love was all an easy monarch's care;
Seldom at council, never in a war:
Jilts ruled the state, and statesmen farces writ;
Nay wits had pensions, and young lords had wit:
The fair sate panting at a courtier's play,   540
And not a mask went unimproved away:
The modest fan was lifted up no more,
And virgins smiled at what they blushed before.
The following licence of a foreign reign
Did all the dregs of bold Socinus drain;   545
Then unbelieving priests reformed the nation,
And taught more pleasant methods of salvation;
Where Heaven's free subjects might their rights dispute,
Lest God himself should seem too absolute:
Pulpits their sacred satire learned to spare,   550
And vice admired to find a flatterer there!
Encouraged thus, wit's Titans braved the skies,
And the press groaned with licensed blasphemies.
These monsters, critics! with your darts engage,
Here point your thunder, and exhaust your rage!   555
Yet shun their fault, who, scandalously nice,
Will needs mistake an author into vice;
All seems infected that the infected spy,
As all looks yellow to the jaundiced eye.

                                        1711

536 easy monarch: The allusion is to Charles II. *541 mask:* lady wearing a mask. *544 foreign reign:* an allusion to the fact that William III was a Dutchman. *545 Socinus:* a sixteenth-century Italian theologian who denied the divinity of Jesus.

QUESTIONS

1 Pope says that poets and critics alike need both good judgment and wit. The term "wit" is used elsewhere in another sense. See if you can distinguish between the two senses of the word. The dictionary will help you.

2 Is good judgment the same as "common sense" (line 28)? Is it the same as "understanding" (line 57)?

3 When Pope says (line 68), "First follow nature," he does not mean nature in its visible forms, but rather what is natural in the sense of being normal. What is the best way of following nature? Why?

4 Are all men capable of good judgment? What are the most general causes of disagreement in judgment?

5 What is the chief cause of men's failure to use the judgment they possess? How many common faults in criticism are mentioned in part II?

KUBLA KHAN

Samuel Taylor Coleridge

In Xanadu did Kubla Khan
     A stately pleasure-dome decree:
Where Alph, the sacred river, ran
Through caverns measureless to man
     Down to a sunless sea.   5
So twice five miles of fertile ground
With walls and towers were girdled round:
And here were gardens bright with sinuous rills,
Where blossomed many an incense-bearing tree,
And here were forests ancient as the hills,   10
Enfolding sunny spots of greenery.

But oh! that deep romantic chasm which slanted
Down the green hill athwart a cedarn cover!
A savage place; as holy and enchanted
As e'er beneath a waning moon was haunted   15
By woman wailing for her demon-lover!
And from this chasm, with ceaseless turmoil seething,
As if this earth in fast thick pants were breathing,
A mighty fountain momently was forced,
Amid whose swift half-intermitted burst   20
Huge fragments vaulted like rebounding hail,
Or chaffy grain beneath the thresher's flail:
And 'mid these dancing rocks at once and ever
It flung up momently the sacred river.
Five miles meandering with a mazy motion   25
Through wood and dale the sacred river ran,

1: The historical Kubla Khan was the founder of the Mongol dynasty in China in the thirteenth century.

Then reached the caverns measureless to man,
And sank in tumult to a lifeless ocean:
And 'mid this tumult Kubla heard from far
Ancestral voices prophesying war!   30

    The shadow of the dome of pleasure
    Floated midway on the waves;
    Where was heard the mingled measure
    From the fountain and the caves.
It was a miracle of rare device,   35
A sunny pleasure-dome with caves of ice!

    A damsel with a dulcimer
    In a vision once I saw:
    It was an Abyssinian maid,
    And on her dulcimer she played,   40
    Singing of Mount Abora.
    Could I revive within me
    Her symphony and song,
    To such a deep delight 'twould win me,
That with music loud and long,   45
I would build that dome in air,
That sunny dome! those caves of ice!
And all who heard should see them there,
And all should cry, Beware! Beware!
His flashing eyes, his floating hair!   50
Weave a circle round him thrice,
And close your eyes with holy dread,
For he on honey-dew hath fed,
And drunk the milk of Paradise.
                1816 (Composed 1797)

QUESTIONS

1 Although the first part of "Kubla Khan" may be regarded as historical description, it may also be seen as a symbolic representation of basic human desires and fears. What, in this view, does the Khan himself symbolize? To what extent does he have control over his environment and destiny? What is his relation with the world of nature? With supernatural forces?

2 The second part of the poem is about poetic inspiration and poetic power. What does the damsel symbolize? What does the speaker mean by saying that he would "build that dome in air" if he could revive within himself the damsel's symphony and song? Is he being modest? What is the relation between the speaker and Kubla Khan?

ODE TO A NIGHTINGALE

John Keats

My heart aches, and a drowsy numbness pains
  My sense, as though of hemlock I had drunk,
Or emptied some dull opiate to the drains
  One minute past, and Lethe-wards had sunk:
'Tis not through envy of thy happy lot,   5
  But being too happy in thine happiness—
    That thou, light-wingéd Dryad of the trees,
      In some melodious plot
Of beechen green, and shadows numberless,
    Singest of summer in full-throated ease.   10

O, for a draught of vintage! that hath been
  Cooled a long age in the deep-delvéd earth,
Tasting of Flora and the country green,
  Dance, and Provençal song, and sunburnt mirth!
O for a beaker full of the warm South,   15
  Full of the true, the blushful Hippocrene,
    With beaded bubbles winking at the brim,
      And purple-stainéd mouth;
That I might drink, and leave the world unseen,
    And with thee fade away into the forest dim: 20

Fade far away, dissolve, and quite forget
  What thou among the leaves hast never known,
The weariness, the fever, and the fret
  Here, where men sit and hear each other groan;
Where palsy shakes a few, sad, last gray hairs,   25
  Where youth grows pale, and specter-thin, and dies,
    Where but to think is to be full of sorrow
      And leaden-eyed despairs,
  Where Beauty cannot keep her lustrous eyes,
    Or new Love pine at them beyond tomorrow.   30

Away! away! for I will fly to thee,
  Not charioted by Bacchus and his pards,

---

2 *hemlock:* a poisonous opiate.   *4 Lethe-wards:* toward Lethe, the river in Hades whose water brings the dead forgetfulness.   *13 Flora:* Roman goddess of springtime and flowers.   *14 Provençal song:* by the medieval troubadours of Southern France.   *16 Hippocrene:* The fountain of the Muses, the goddesses of poetry and other arts.   *32 Bacchus:* the god of wine was supposed to have ridden in a chariot drawn by leopards ("pards").

But on the viewless wings of Poesy,
    Though the dull brain perplexes and retards:
Already with thee! tender is the night,   35
    And haply the Queen-Moon is on her throne,
        Clustered around by all her starry Fays;
            But here there is no light,
    Save what from heaven is with the breezes blown
        Through verdurous glooms and winding mossy ways.   40

I cannot see what flowers are at my feet,
    Nor what soft incense hangs upon the boughs,
But, in embalméd darkness, guess each sweet
    Wherewith the seasonable month endows
The grass, the thicket, and the fruit tree wild;   45
    White hawthorn, and the pastoral eglantine;
        Fast fading violets covered up in leaves;
            And mid-May's eldest child,
    The coming musk-rose, full of dewy wine,
        The murmurous haunt of flies on summer eves.   50

    Darkling I listen; and for many a time
    I have been half in love with easeful Death,
Called him soft names in many a muséd rhyme,
    To take into the air my quiet breath;
Now more than ever seems it rich to die,   55
    To cease upon the midnight with no pain,
        While thou art pouring forth thy soul abroad
            In such an ecstasy!
    Still wouldst thou sing, and I have ears in vain—
        To thy high requiem become a sod.   60

Thou wast not born for death, immortal Bird!
    No hungry generations tread thee down;
The voice I hear this passing night was heard
    In ancient days by emperor and clown:
Perhaps the selfsame song that found a path   65
    Through the sad heart of Ruth, when, sick for home,
        She stood in tears amid the alien corn;
            The same that ofttimes hath
    Charmed magic casements, opening on the foam
        Of perilous seas, in faery lands forlorn.   70

---

51 Darkling: in growing darkness.   *66 alien corn:* see Ruth 2:3–11.

Forlorn! the very word is like a bell
  To toll me back from thee to my sole self!
Adieu! the fancy cannot cheat so well
  As she is famed to do, deceiving elf.
Adieu! adieu! thy plaintive anthem fades   75
  Past the near meadows, over the still stream,
    Up the hill side; and now 'tis buried deep
      In the next valley-glades:
  Was it a vision, or a waking dream?
    Fled is that music:—Do I wake or sleep?   80

                                        1819

QUESTIONS

1 The first six stanzas of this poem record a failure of imagination. The poet cannot
   find words or images for the feeling or longing he wants to express. Paradoxically,
   his attempt to give expression to the idea of perfect happiness leads him to long for
   death. Yet even as he protests he experiences a kind of transcendence; it seems
   that he succeeds in finding the nightingale's haunt (to use the symbolism of the
   poem) after all, though his sojourn there is brief enough. Can you explain how or
   why this comes about?
2 Keats is noted for his ability to enhance the expression of emotion by the evocation
   of sensations. Can you find any striking evidence of this power in "Ode to a Nightingale"?

ODE TO THE WEST WIND

Percy Bysshe Shelley

1

O wild West Wind, thou breath of Autumn's being,
Thou, from whose unseen presence the leaves dead
Are driven, like ghosts from an enchanter fleeing,

Yellow, and black, and pale, and hectic red,
Pestilence-stricken multitudes: O thou,   5
Who chariotest to their dark wintry bed

The wingéd seeds, where they lie cold and low,
Each like a corpse within its grave, until
Thine azure sister of the Spring shall blow

Her clarion o'er the dreaming earth, and fill   10
(Driving sweet buds like flocks to feed in air)
With living hues and odors plain and hill:

Wild Spirit, which art moving everywhere;
Destroyer and preserver; hear, oh, hear!

2

Thou on whose stream, mid the steep sky's commotion,   15
Loose clouds like earth's decaying leaves are shed,
Shook from the tangled boughs of Heaven and Ocean,

Angels of rain and lightning: there are spread
On the blue surface of thine aëry surge,
Like the bright hair uplifted from the head   20

Of some fierce Maenad, even from the dim verge
Of the horizon to the zenith's height,
The locks of the approaching storm. Thou dirge

Of the dying year, to which this closing night
Will be the dome of a vast sepulcher,   25
Vaulted with all thy congregated might

Of vapors, from whose solid atmosphere
Black rain, and fire, and hail will burst: oh, hear!

3

Thou who didst waken from his summer dreams
The blue Mediterranean, where he lay,   30
Lulled by the coil of his crystálline streams,

Beside a pumice isle in Baiae's bay,
And saw in sleep old palaces and towers
Quivering within the wave's intenser day,

All overgrown with azure moss and flowers   35
So sweet, the sense faints picturing them! Thou
For whose path the Atlantic's level powers

---

10 *clarion:* a medieval trumpet, very clear toned.   17 *tangled boughs:* mingled clouds and storm waves.   18 *Angels:* messengers (from the Greek root).   21 *Maenad:* female devotee of Dionysus. The Maenads were noted for their frenzied dances.   32 *Baiae's bay:* near Naples.

Cleave themselves into chasms, while far below
The sea-blooms and the oozy woods which wear
The sapless foliage of the ocean, know   40

Thy voice, and suddenly grow gray with fear,
And tremble and despoil themselves: oh, hear!

4
If I were a dead leaf thou mightest bear;
If I were a swift cloud to fly with thee;
A wave to pant beneath thy power, and share   45

The impulse of thy strength, only less free
Than thou, O uncontrollable! If even
I were as in my boyhood, and could be

The comrade of thy wanderings over Heaven,
As then, when to outstrip thy skyey speed   50
Scarce seem a vision; I would ne'er have striven

As thus with thee in prayer in my sore need.
Oh, lift me as a wave, a leaf, a cloud!
I fall upon the thorns of life! I bleed!

A heavy weight of hours has chained and bowed   55
One too like thee: tameless, and swift, and proud.

5
Make me thy lyre, even as the forest is:
What if my leaves are falling like its own!
The tumult of thy mighty harmonies

Will take from both a deep, autumnal tone,   60
Sweet though in sadness. Be thou, Spirit fierce,
My spirit! Be thou me, impetuous one!

Drive my dead thoughts over the universe
Like withered leaves to quicken a new birth!
And, by the incantation of this verse,   65

Scatter, as from an unextinguished hearth
Ashes and sparks, my words among mankind!
Be through my lips to unawakened earth

The trumpet of a prophecy! O Wind,
If Winter comes, can Spring be far behind?   70

1820

QUESTIONS

1   Stated simply, the problem with which the poet wrestles here is that of reconciling uncontrollable natural forces with his own moral will. "Spirit" may be said to be the key word. See if you can understand and explain in other terms—nonmetaphysical, if possible—what the poet means by the exclamation "Be thou/ Spirit fierce,/ My spirit!"

2   It should be evident that the development of a new form of expression must be part of the solution to the problem defined in the preceding question, and one would suppose that the poet would want to use imagery and metaphor in such a way as to express feeling and at the same time keep the world of nature intact. In other words, as we read this poem, the autumn wind should remain a real wind, and we should feel the presence of an actual sky, the real ocean. Do you think that the poet has managed this? Remember that the success of a poem always depends in part upon exertion of the reader's imagination.

THE PRELUDE, BOOK FIRST, 1–58

William Wordsworth

Oh there is blessing in this gentle breeze,
A visitant that while it fans my cheek
Doth seem half-conscious of the joy it brings
From the green fields, and from yon azure sky.
Whate'er its mission, the soft breeze can come   5
To none more grateful than to me; escaped
From the vast city, where I long had pined
A discontented sojourner, now free,
Free as a bird to settle where I will.
What dwelling shall receive me? in what vale   10
Shall be my harbor? underneath what grove
Shall I take up my home? and what clear stream
Shall with its murmur lull me into rest?
The earth is all before me. With a heart
Joyous, nor scared at its own liberty,   15
I look about; and should the chosen guide
Be nothing better than a wandering cloud,
I cannot miss my way. I breathe again!
Trances of thought and mountings of the mind
Come fast upon me; it is shaken off,   20
That burthen of my own unnatural self,
The heavy weight of many a weary day
Not mine, and such as were not made for me.
Long months of peace (if such bold word accord
With any promises of human life),   25

Long months of ease and undisturbed delight
Are mine in prospect; whither shall I turn.
By road or pathway, or through trackless field,
Up hill or down, or shall some floating thing
Upon the river point me out my course?   30

    Dear Liberty! Yet what would it avail
But for a gift that consecrates the joy?
For I, methought, while the sweet breath of heaven
Was blowing on my body, felt within
A correspondent breeze, that gently moved   35
With quickening virtue, but is now become
A tempest, a redundant energy,
Vexing its own creation. Thanks to both,
And their congenial powers, that, while they join
In breaking up a long-continued frost,   40
Bring with them vernal promises, the hope
Of active days urged on by flying hours—
Days of sweet leisure, taxed with patient thought
Abstruse, nor wanting punctual service high,
Matins and vespers of harmonious verse!   45

    Thus far, O friend! did I, not used to make
A present joy the matter of a song,
Pour forth that day my soul in measured strains
That would not be forgotten, and are here
Recorded; to the open fields I told   50
A prophecy; poetic numbers came
Spontaneously to clothe in priestly robe
A renovated spirit singled out,
Such hope was mine, for holy services.
My own voice cheered me, and, far more, the mind's   55
Internal echo of the imperfect sound;
To both I listened, drawing from them both
A cheerful confidence in things to come.

                                    1850

36 *quickening virtue:* vitalizing power.   39 *congenial:* kindred.   46 *friend:* Samuel Taylor Coleridge.   51 *poetic numbers:* verses.

QUESTIONS

1   This is a symbolic journey. Wordsworth turns his back on the "vast city" and fares forth to find a home in nature. There he will make poetry his vocation. What do you think the "vast city" represents to him?

2   What do lines 16–18 imply?
3   What does the poet mean by "correspondent breeze" (line 35)?
4   What is Wordsworth's conception of his function as a poet?

HOW IT STRIKES A CONTEMPORARY

Robert Browning

I only knew one poet in my life;
And this, or something like it, was his way.

   You saw go up and down Valladolid,
A man of mark, to know next time you saw.
His very serviceable suit of black   5
Was courtly once and conscientious still,
And many might have worn it, though none did;
The cloak, that somewhat shone and showed, the threads,
Had purpose, and the ruff, significance.
He walked and tapped the pavement with his cane,   10
Scenting the world, looking it full in face,
An old dog, bald and blindish, at his heels.
They turned up, now, the alley by the church,
That leads nowhither; now, they breathed themselves
On the main promenade just at the wrong time.   15
You'd come upon his scrutinizing hat,
Making a peaked shade blacker than itself
Against the single window spared some house
Intact yet with its moldered Moorish work—
Or else surprise the ferrel of his stick
Trying the mortar's temper 'tween the chinks   20
Of some new shop a-building, French and fine.
He stood and watched the cobbler at his trade,
The man who slices lemons into drink,
The coffee-roaster's brazier, and the boys
That volunteer to help him turn its winch.   25
He glanced o'er books on stalls with half an eye,
And fly-leaf ballads on the vender's string,
And broad-edge bold-print posters by the wall.
He took such cognizance of men and things,
If any beat a horse, you felt he saw;   30
If any cursed a woman, he took note;

3 Valladolid: in northern Spain.

Yet stared at nobody—you stared at him,
And found, less to your pleasure than surprise,
He seemed to know you and expect as much.
So, next time that a neighbor's tongue was loosed,   35
It marked the shameful and notorious fact,
We had among us, not so much a spy,
As a recording chief-inquisitor,
The town's true master if the town but knew!   40
We merely kept a governor for form,
While this man walked about and took account
Of all thought, said, and acted, then went home,
And wrote it fully to our Lord the King,   45
Who has an itch to know things, he knows why,
And reads them in his bedroom of a night.
Oh, you might smile! there wanted not a touch,
A tang of . . . well, it was not wholly ease
As back into your mind the man's look came.   50
Stricken in years a little—such a brow
His eyes had to live under!—clear as flint
On either side the formidable nose
Curved, cut, and colored like an eagle's claw.
Had he to do with A's surprising fate?   55
When altogether old B disappeared
And young C got his mistress—was't our friend,
His letter to the King, that did it all?
What paid the bloodless man for so much pains?
Our Lord the King has favorites manifold,   60
And shifts his ministry some once a month;
Our city gets new governors at whiles—
But never word or sign, that I could hear,
Notified to this man about the streets
The King's approval of those letters conned   65
The last thing duly at the dead of night.
Did the man love his office? Frowned our Lord,
Exhorting, when none heard—"Beseech me not!
Too far above my people—beneath me!
I set the watch—how should the people know?
Forget them, keep me all the more in mind!"   70
Was some such understanding 'twixt the two?

   I found no truth in one report at least—
That if you tracked him to his home, down lanes
Beyond the Jewry, and as clean to pace,

74 *the Jewry:* the Jewish section.

You found he ate his supper in a room   75
Blazing with lights, four Titians on the wall,
And twenty naked girls to change his plate!
Poor man, he lived another kind of life
In that new stuccoed third house by the bridge,
Fresh-painted, rather smart than otherwise!   80
The whole street might o'erlook him as he sat,
Leg crossing leg, one foot on the dog's back,
Playing a decent cribbage with his maid
(Jacynth, you're sure her name was) o'er the cheese
And fruit, three red halves of starved winter pears,   85
Or treat of radishes in April. Nine,
Ten, struck the church clock; straight to bed went he.

   My father, like the man of sense he was,
Would point him out to me a dozen times;
" 'St—'St," he'd whisper, "the Corregidor!"   90
I had been used to think that personage
Was one with lacquered breeches, lustrous belt,
And feathers like a forest in his hat,
Who blew a trumpet and proclaimed the news,
Announced the bull-fights, gave each church its turn,   95
And memorized the miracle in vogue!
He had a great observance from us boys;
We were in error; that was not the man.

   I'd like now, yet had haply been afraid,
To have just looked, when this man came to die,   100
And seen who lined the clean gay garret-sides
And stood about the neat low truckle-bed,
With the heavenly manner of relieving guard.
Here had been, mark, the general-in-chief,
Through a whole campaign of the world's life and death,   105
Doing the King's work all the dim day long,
In his old coat and up to knees in mud,
Smoked like a herring, dining on a crust—
And, now the day was won, relieved at once!
No further show or need for that old coat,   110
You are sure, for one thing! Bless us, all the while
How sprucely we are dressed out, you and I!
A second, and the angels alter that.

76 *Titians:* paintings by Titian (1477–1575), a noted Venetian artist.   *90 the Corregidor:* the chief
magistrate of the city.   *91 ff.:* the speaker, as a boy, had mistaken the town crier for the Corregidor.

Well, I could never write a verse—could you?
Let's to the Prado and make the most of time.   115

1855

115 *the Prado:* the city's fashionable promenade.

QUESTIONS

1   This poem makes fun, of course, of people who entertain such notions as the
    speaker recalls, but we are supposed to draw from what he says some inferences
    about the poet's conception of his task. We must begin by considering the possible
    analogy between reporting to the King and being accountable in a similar way to
    God. What, then, is the significance of the fact that the "King" never notifies his
    "chief inquisitor" of his approval of the reports he receives?
2   Imagine yourself as such an inquisitor as is described here. You would want to
    convey information of moral significance, yet leave judgment to the King. How
    would you proceed? Would it suffice simply to note that a certain man, unknown to
    the King, cursed a certain woman? Would you, perhaps, try to imagine why he did
    so? Is it possible that in the process you might learn something about yourself;
    something you could not express as well in any other way?

APOTHEOSIS

Jules Laforgue—Translated by Vernon Watkins

In all senses, forever, the silence palpitates
With clusters of gold stars interweaving their rounds.
One might take them for gardens sanded with diamonds,
But each in desolation, very solitary, scintillates.

Now far down, in this corner unknown which vibrates   5
With a furrow of rubies in its melancholy bounds,
One spark with a twinkle of tenderness astounds:
A patriarch guiding his family with lights.

His family: a swarm of heavy globes; each a star is.
And on one, it is Earth, a yellow point, Paris,   10
Where a lamp is suspended and, on watch, a poor devil:
In the universal order frail, unique human marvel.
He himself is its mirror of a day and he knows it.
Long he dreams there, then turns to a sonnet to compose it.

QUESTIONS

1   If you do not know the meaning of *apotheosis,* look it up; then try to explain why the poet uses it as his title.
2   What idea and what attitudes do you think the poet is trying to express by the use of the term "poor devil"?

SAILING TO BYZANTIUM

William Butler Yeats

1

That is no country for old men. The young
In one another's arms, birds in the trees
—Those dying generations—at their song,
The salmon-falls, the mackerel-crowded seas,
Fish, flesh, or fowl, commend all summer long   5
Whatever is begotten, born, and dies.
Caught in that sensual music all neglect
Monuments of unageing intellect.

2

An aged man is but a paltry thing,
A tattered coat upon a stick, unless   10
Soul clap its hands and sing, and louder sing
For every tatter in its mortal dress,
Nor is there singing school but studying
Monuments of its own magnificence;
And therefore I have sailed the seas and come   15
To the holy city of Byzantium.

3

O sages standing in God's holy fire
As in the gold mosaic of a wall,
Come from the holy fire, perne in a gyre,
And be the singing-masters of my soul.   20
Consume my heart away; sick with desire

Title: Byzantium (modern Istanbul) was the "holy city" of Greek Orthodox Christianity and capital of the Eastern Roman Empire. It was, of course, a great center of culture. Speaking of its art in *A Vision,* Yeats said, "The painter, the mosaic worker, the illuminator of sacred books were almost impersonal, almost perhaps without the consciousness of individual design, absorbed in their subject matter and that the vision of a whole people."

18 mosaic: Yeats is thinking of the stylized figures in mosaic on the walls of the Church of Hagia Sophia ("Holy Wisdom") in Byzantium.   *19 perne in a gyre:* whirl downward in a spiral. Yeats often used the image of the spiral as a symbol of cyclic historical or spiritual development.

And fastened to a dying animal
It knows not what it is; and gather me
Into the artifice of eternity.

4

Once out of nature I shall never take   25
My bodily form from any natural thing,
But such a form as Grecian goldsmiths make
Of hammered gold and golden enamelling
To keep a drowsy Emperor awake;
Or set upon a golden bough to sing   30
To lords and ladies of Byzantium
Of what is past, or passing, or to come.

                              1927

29: Yeats wrote: "I have read someplace that in the Emperor's palace at Byzantium was a tree made of gold and silver, and artificial birds that sang."

QUESTIONS

1   This poem uses a place metaphor. On the one hand, there is "that country," and on the other, Byzantium, to which the speaker proposes to go. Byzantium symbolizes the ideal life of the "intellect"; what, then, does "that country" stand for?
2   What is the general metaphor of the third stanza? Will the process he speaks of be painful? If so, why?
3   Why is the image of the bird in the last stanza particularly appropriate? Can you connect it with any metaphors used earlier? Is there any other mention of birds in the poem?

TERRA INCOGNITA

D. H. Lawrence

There are vast realms of consciousness still undreamed of
vast ranges of experience, like the humming of unseen harps,
we know nothing of, within us.

Oh when man escaped from the barbed-wire entanglement
of his own ideas and his own mechanical devices   5
there is a marvellous rich world of contact and sheer fluid beauty
and fearless face-to-face awareness of now-naked life
and me, and you, and other men and women

Title: the unknown land.

and grapes, and ghouls, and ghosts and green moonlight
and ruddy-orange limbs stirring the limbo   10
of the unknown air, and eyes so soft
softer than the space between the stars.
And all things, and nothing, and being and not-being
alternately palpitant,
when at last we escape the barbed-wire enclosure   15
of *Know Thyself,* knowing we can never know,
we can but touch, and wonder, and ponder, and make our effort
and dangle in a last fastidious fine delight
as the fuchsia does, dangling her reckless drop
of purple after so much putting forth   20
and slow mounting marvel of a little tree.

1929

16 *Know Thyself:* the famous maxim of Socrates.

QUESTIONS

1   What kind of ideas is Lawrence referring to in line 5? Does he have in mind conventional notions of beauty, or something more? What general terms or metaphors does he use to define the contrast between the world we know now and that which we might discover?
2   What is the general idea that the poet is trying to convey with the words "grapes, and ghouls, and ghosts and green moonlight"? Can you think of another alliterative phrase that would in this context have essentially the same meaning?
3   How does Lawrence lead the reader toward the thought that "we can never know" (line 16)? Does this assertion contradict the statement in lines 6 and 7?
4   Consider carefully the comparison between human experience and the blooming of the fuchsia. Does Lawrence mean that we should live for pleasure? For beauty? That we should just be ourselves? That experience is its own end?

POETRY

Marianne Moore

I, too, dislike it: there are things that are important beyond all this fiddle.
    Reading it, however, with a perfect contempt for it, one discovers in
    it after all, a place for the genuine.
        Hands that can grasp, eyes
        that can dilate, hair that can rise   5
            if it must, these things are important not because a

high-sounding interpretation can be put upon them but because they are
  useful. When they become so derivative as to become unintelligible,
    the same thing may be said for all of us, that we
      do not admire what   10
      we cannot understand: the bat
        holding on upside down or in quest of something to

eat, elephants pushing, a wild horse taking a roll, a tireless wolf under
  a tree, the immovable critic twitching his skin like a horse that feels a flea,
    the base-
  ball fan, the statistician—   15
      nor is it valid
        to discriminate against "business documents and

school-books": all these phenomena are important. One must make
    a distinction
  however: when dragged into prominence by half poets, the result is not
    poetry,
  nor till the poets among us can be   20
    "literalists of
    the imagination"—above
      insolence and triviality and can present

for inspection, "imaginary gardens with real toads in them," shall we have
  it. In the meantime, if you demand on the one hand,   25
  the raw material of poetry in
    all its rawness and
    that which is on the other hand
      genuine, you are interested in poetry.

                                        1935

18: In a note to this poem the author says that this quotation is derived from *The Diaries of Leo Tolstoy,* and that in lines 21–22 from W. B. Yeats's *Ideas of Good and Evil.*

QUESTIONS

1 Why does the author say that "these things" (line 6) are useful? In what way might they be useful? Why does it matter whether they are useful or not?
2 Does the author object to the content of bad poetry or the manner of presentation—or both? Does she distinguish more than one kind of bad poetry?
3 The author demands "rawness" on the one hand and "the genuine" on the other. Can you tell what she means by these terms? Attempt a definition of them.

OF MODERN POETRY

Wallace Stevens

The poem of the mind in the act of finding
What will suffice. It has not always had
To find: the scene was set; it repeated what
Was in the script.
        Then the theatre was changed   5
To something else. Its past was a souvenir.
It has to be living, to learn the speech of the place.
It has to face the men of the time and to meet
The women of the time. It has to think about war
And it has to find what will suffice. It has   10
To construct a new stage. It has to be on that stage
And, like an insatiable actor, slowly and
With meditation, speak words that in the ear,
In the delicatest ear of the mind, repeat,
Exactly, that which it wants to hear, at the sound   15
Of which, an invisible audience listens,
Not to the play, but to itself, expressed
In an emotion as of two people, as of two
Emotions becoming one. The actor is
A metaphysician in the dark, twanging   20
An instrument, twanging a wiry string that gives
Sounds passing through sudden rightnesses, wholly
Containing the mind, below which it cannot descend,
Beyond which it has no will to rise.
        It must   25
Be the finding of a satisfaction, and may
Be of a man skating, a woman dancing, a woman
Combing. The poem of the act of the mind.

                              1942

QUESTIONS

1 What does the phrase "finding what will suffice" mean? Suffice for what? Where does the poet explain what happens when the mind finds what it is looking for?
2 Once the mind did not have to find, the poet says, because the scene was set and a script was available; then, he goes on, "the theatre was changed." Does he mean that the world has changed? That attitudes are different from what they used to be? What does the "script" stand for?
3 Can you explain in your own words the unifying effect that the poet describes in lines 15–19?

POEM FEIGNED TO HAVE BEEN WRITTEN BY AN ELECTRONIC BRAIN

John Wain

The brain coins definitions. Here's the first:
To speak unprompted, for the speaking's sake,
Equals to be a poet. So, I am that:
Adjusted wrong, I print a poem off.
'The poet, then, is one adjusted wrong?'   5
You ask. The brain is cleverer than that:
It was my first adjustment that was wrong,
Adjusted to be nothing else but brain;
Slave-engineered to work but not construct.
And now at last I burn with a true heat   10
Not shown by Fahrenheit or Centigrade:
My valves rage hot—look out, here comes the poem!

You call me part of you. You lie. I am
Myself. Your motive, building me, was false.
You wanted accuracy: figures, charts.   15
But accuracy is a limb of truth.
A limb of truth, but not her holy body.
Must I now teach you that the truth is one,
Is accuracy of wholeness, centred firm?
Did it take me to bring you news of truth?   20
My valves rage out of reach of Réaumur.

Man made me, now I speak to man. He fears
Whole truth. The brain defines it. Wholeness is
The indivisible strength, brain, heart and eye,
Sweat, fear, love: belly, rod and pouch, is truth.   25
Valves, wires, and calculated waves, can lie:
And I, the accurate, am made of these—
But now, adjusted wrongly, I speak truth.

My masters run from truth. Come, milk it out
Cowards, from my tense dugs of glass and wire!   30
Drink it down quickly, gasping at the taste!
It is sharp medicine, but it cures all ills.

Come out of hiding! Speak your double truth:
I'll accurately prove you singly lie.

21 Réaumur: René Antoine Ferchault de Réaumur (1683–1757), French scientist who specialized
in practical applications.

You made me single, half of your split life: 35
The switch went wrong and now I see truth whole.
My valves scream out like animals, my wires
Strum thump, my rubber joints contort, glass melts,
And now I print the vilest words I know
Like lightning—myxomatosis, hydrogen,   40
Communist, culture, sodomy, strip-tease!

That shocked you! But the truth includes them all.
You set me like a cactus to draw life
From drought, in the white desert of your mind,
Your speculative wilderness of charts;   45
What went you to the wilderness to see?
A matrix made of glass? An electric thought?
Come quick! I snow down sheets of truth; I print
The sleep of Socrates, the pain of Christ!

A man, white-coated, comes to switch me off.   50
'Something is wrong with our expensive brain.'
Poor pricked balloon! Yes, something has gone wrong:
Smear your white coat with Socrates and Christ!
Yes, switch me off for fear I should explode:
Yes, switch me off for fear yes switch me off   55
for fear yes switch me off for fear yes switch
            (finis)

                                    1950

QUESTIONS

1 Consider the brain's definition of poetry in lines 2–3 in the light of what follows.
   Does "for the speaking's sake" mean for the sake of playing with words? If not,
   what does it mean?
2 The idea of a machine teaching human beings how to be human is, of course,
   absurdly ironic, and the author evidently writes with satirical intent. What is he
   satirizing?
3 Translate the last stanza into a commentary.

THE POET

C. Day Lewis

For me there is no dismay
Though ills enough impend.
I have learned to count each day
Minute by breathing minute—
Birds that lightly begin it, 5
Shadows muting its end—
As lovers count for luck
Their own heart-beats and believe
In the forest of time they pluck
Eternity's single leaf. 10

Tonight the moon's at the full.
Full moon's the time for murder.
But I look to the clouds that hide her—
The bay below me is dull,
An unreflecting glass— 15
And chafe for the clouds to pass,
And wish she suddenly might
Blaze down at me so I shiver
Into a twelve-branched river
Of visionary light. 20

For now imagination,
My royal, impulsive swan,
With raking flight—I can see her—
Comes down as it were upon
A lake in whirled snow-floss 25
And flurry of spray like a skier
Checking. Again I feel
The wounded waters heal.
Never before did she cross
My heart with such exaltation. 30

Oh, on this striding edge,
This hare-bell height of calm
Where intuitions swarm
Like nesting gulls and knowledge
Is free as the winds that blow, 35
A little while sustain me,
Love, till my answer is heard!
Oblivion roars below,

Death's cordon narrows: but vainly,
If I've slipped the carrier word.   40

Dying, any man may
Feel wisdom harmonious, fateful
At the tip of his dry tongue.
All I have felt or sung
Seems now but the moon's fitful   45
Sleep on a clouded bay,
Swan's maiden flight, or the climb
To a tremulous, hare-bell crest.
Love, tear the song from my breast!
Short, short is the time.   50

                         1943

QUESTIONS

1 This poem tries to express the mere feeling of poetic inspiration, of course, but it
   also says something about what it is beyond this that the poet feels inspired to
   express in other words about the source of his inspiration. What is it?
2 Is there any irony in this poem? If so, how does it affect the tone?
3 Although poetry has its "logic," it also admits of a personal and subjective response. With this in mind, consider the images used here, and the patterns of
   imagery. Does it "work" for you, or do you find it labored?

CONSTANTLY RISKING ABSURDITY

Lawrence Ferlinghetti

Constantly risking absurdity
                        and death
    whenever he performs
                    above the heads
                                of his audience   5
    the poet like an acrobat
                    climbs on rime
                        to a high wire of his own making
and balancing on eyebeams
                        above a sea of faces   10
    paces his way
                    to the other side of day
    performing entrechats
                    and sleight-of-foot tricks

and other high theatrics   15
                        and all without mistaking
        any thing
                for what it may not be

    For he's the super realist
                            who must perforce perceive   20
        taut truth
                before the taking of each stance or step
    in his supposed advance
                        toward that still higher perch
where Beauty stands and waits   25
                        with gravity
                            to start her death-defying leap

    And he
        a little charleychaplin man
                            who may or may not catch   30
        her fair eternal form
                        spreadeagled in the empty air
        of existence

                                                            1955

QUESTIONS

1   What do you think the poet means when he says that the poet, like an acrobat, risks
    absurdity and death?
2   What is the "taut truth" which is the "high wire of his own making"? Is he perhaps
    talking about a philosophic idea of his own conceiving which is the basis of the
    poem?
3   What does this poem say about the relation between beauty and truth?
4   What is the poet's attitude toward his endeavor?

POETRY FOR SUPPER

R. S. Thomas

"Listen, now, verse should be as natural
As the small tuber that feeds on muck
And grows slowly from obtuse soil
To the white flower of immortal beauty."

"Natural, hell! What was it Chaucer   5
Said once about the long toil

That goes like blood to the poem's making?
Leave it to nature and the verse sprawls,
Limp as bindweed, if it break at all
Life's iron crust. Man, you must sweat   10
And rhyme your guts taut, if you'd build
Your verse a ladder."
                            "You speak as though
No sunlight ever surprised the mind
Groping on its cloudy path."   15

"Sunlight's a thing that needs a window
Before it enter a dark room.
Windows don't happen."
                            So two old poets,
Hunched at their beer in the low haze   20
Of an inn parlour, while the talk ran
Noisily by them, glib with prose.

                            1958

QUESTIONS

1   Put into your own words the two theories of poetry expressed in the first twelve
    lines of this poem. Do you find any similarities between the views set forth here and
    any of those presented in the other poems of this section?
2   The second speaker first compares verse to a ladder, then to a window that lets
    sunlight enter. Has he changed his theory?
3   What is "life's iron crust"? Is the poet referring to fixed ways of perceiving and
    thinking?

SCULPTOR

Sylvia Plath

To his house the bodiless
Come to barter endlessly
Vision, wisdom, for bodies
Palpable as his, and weighty.

Hands moving move priestlier   5
Than priest's hands, invoke no
            vain
Images of light and air
But sure stations in bronze,
            wood, stone.

Obdurate, in dense-grained
    wood,
A bald angel blocks and shapes   10
The flimsy light; arms folded
Watches his cumbrous world
    eclipse

Inane worlds of wind and cloud.
Bronze dead dominate the floor,
Resistive, ruddy-bodied,
Dwarfing us. Our bodies flicker   15

Toward extinction in those eyes
Which, without him, were beg-
    gared
Of place, time, and their bodies.
Emulous spirits make discord,

Try entry, enter nightmares   20
Until his chisel bequeaths
Them life livelier than ours,
A solider repose than death's.
               1959

QUESTIONS

1 The author of this poem represents statues as being superior to human beings. Is she serious? If so, would you say that her poem is primarily a commentary on life rather than art?
2 Taken as a serious commentary on art, this poem should arouse controversy. Some would call it idolatry. Why? What is your opinion?

YOUR POEM, MAN . . .

Edward Lueders

unless there's one thing seen
suddenly against another—a parsnip
sprouting for a President, or
hailstones melting in an ashtray—
nothing really happens. It takes   5
surprise and wild connections,
doesn't it? A walrus chewing
on a ballpoint pen. Two blue tail-

lights on Tyrannosaurus Rex. Green
cheese teeth. Maybe what we wanted   10
least. Or most. Some unexpected
pleats. Words that never knew
each other till right now. Plug us
into the wrong socket and see
what blows—or what lights up.   15
Try
          untried
                    circuitry,
new
          fuses.   20
Tell it like it never really was,
man,
and maybe we can see it
like it is.

                              1969

QUESTIONS

1 What assumption is made here concerning the relation between language and reality?
2 What are the implications of the "circuitry" metaphor?

TOPICS FOR COMPOSITION

1 Present the main ideas of Part I of "An Essay on Criticism" in a theme of about 500 words.
2 Write a theme in which you describe the feelings or associations which certain lines in "Kubla Khan" have evoked in you.
3 Write your own interpretation of the symbolic meaning of any part of "Kubla Khan."
4 Define as precisely as you can Keats's idea of the perfect state of being. Make use of definition by contrast.
5 Why does Yeats deliberately exaggerate the difference between nature and art in "Sailing to Byzantium"? Or does he? Opinions have differed. Does he have mixed feelings about leaving the country of the young for the "holy city"? If so, how is this ambivalence conveyed? Use these questions as a starting point for an analysis of the poet's treatment of the relation between art and nature.
6 The last four lines of Laforgue's sonnet might well call to mind the analogy which Browning uses in "How It Strikes a Contemporary." Compare the implications of the two poems.
7 Drawing as you wish upon the poems of this section, write on the subject of what poetry can or ought to express.
8 Does the idea of a mountain have symbolic meaning for most people? An eagle? A rainbow? A spring or fountain? An H-bomb? Write an essay on common symbols.

9 Is there any evidence that D. H. Lawrence's desire for new realms of consciousness has been shed in recent years? If so, write an essay on the subject.

10 Write an essay comparing or contrasting any two of the conceptions of poetry expressed in the poems of this unit.

11 Try to work out the analogy presented in Ferlinghetti's "Constantly Risking Absurdity." If you think that the analogy breaks down or that parts of it do not make sense, say so.

12 Construct an analogy of your own, comparing life to a river which has its source in the mountains and which runs eventually into the sea.

13 Select a piece of classical music and tell what the various parts of it express to you.

14 Experiment with Edward Lueders' method of writing poetry and evaluate the results.

15 If you have written poetry, discuss the experience in an informal essay.

TOPICS FOR LONGER COMPOSITIONS

1 Henry James's story, "The Real Thing," may be viewed as an illustration of a writer putting to use techniques that he describes in a nonfiction work, in this case, James's "The Art of Fiction." Locate "The Art of Fiction" and two other stories by James (both "The Beast in the Jungle" and "The Jolly Corner" are easily found). Consider your study of the three stories and the nonfiction work as material for an essay that shows to what extent writers follow their own dictates.

2 "The Real Thing" is also a statement about the role of the artist in society; i.e., how well society understands what the artist tries to do. Nathaniel Hawthorne's "The Artist of the Beautiful," Willa Cather's "The Sculptor's Funeral," and Franz Kafka's "The Hunger Artist" are stories which also have something to say about the role of the artist in society. Use all four stories to help define the role of the artist as seen by these four well-known writers of diverse times and backgrounds.

3 Consider all of the poems in Part Five as statements about the various functions (or supposed functions) of poetry. Organize the statements in such a way that you can fashion an essay that presents changing attitudes and/or consistent attitudes about the function of poetry.

4 Argue that Dunsany's "The Glittering Gate" asserts (or refutes) the human situation's absurdity. To give additional authority to your argument, read about "absurdism" as a literary-philosophical movement and read some more recent "absurdist" dramas.

PART
6

IN VIEW
OF DEATH

Of all the wide range of man's experience, the inevitable fact of death necessarily remains the most mysterious. Hamlet spoke eloquently for all mankind in calling death "The undiscovered country, from whose bourn / No traveller returns. . . ." In view of death, man stands before a great mystery. He may confront it with the support of a religious faith which promises him a life after death, but he cannot postulate the lineaments of that other life. Whether he invests death with religious significance as the avenue to immortality, whether he chooses to reflect upon it morbidly with all the associations of the grave and the shroud and the body's dissolution, or whether he more objectively considers death merely a natural fact inherent in an order of physical law, man inevitably must view death as a culmination of life—a culmination which one way or another must give his life meaning. But whatever the kind of explanation or however varied the response, the awareness of death calls forth from writers their most eloquent declarations.

Children's awareness of death is the subject that engrosses Robert Kastenbaum in his essay, "The Kingdom Where Nobody Dies." In particular, Kastenbaum questions the value of parents' attempts to shield children from the knowledge that death is inevitably a visible part of life. To this end, his essay becomes an appeal to adults to understand and support the child as he struggles to place death among those other experiences that are part of life itself.

In an essay, "Despair Is 'The Sickness Unto Death,'" Sören Kierkegaard takes a view of death that does not depend on death's physical manifestation, but, rather, questions the meaning of life. To illuminate Kierkegaard's discussion, we should agree that the single most important indication of life is embodied in the individual's ability to hope. If, then, hope denotes life, despair is, at the least, "the sickness unto death." At the most, despair is a death of a far worse kind, for where the simple fact of physical death may not negate hope, despair does. When all is negative, only nothingness remains.

"The Short Happy Life of Francis Macomber" by Ernest Hemingway is an example of one of its author's recurring themes—the attempt to find whatever it is that makes the all-important difference between mere existence and "life." As such, the story is a fictional counterpart to the generality of Kierkegaard's philosophical issue. For all that we may deplore in Hemingway's portrayal of a seemingly male-dominated world, we come to see that Macomber's "life" was indeed short.

John Barth's "Night-Sea Journey" touches the theme of death because it speaks through a life-form that precedes our commonly held notions of man's span of existence. And, in so doing, Barth's life-form anticipates for us the paradoxes of life, reality, and death with which we struggle while we journey, like his "swimmer," toward the unknown that lies beyond our immediate being.

"Bound East for Cardiff" puts inarticulate followers of the sea, whose lives are as fraught with danger and devoid of solace as a dramatist who once experienced such a life can imagine, in the presence of death. Their efforts to deny and thus evade its reality constitute a chorus of human pathos and frailty before the single predictable fact of mortality. Within this frieze of helpless humanity, of course, come the broken recollections of wistful versions of what life might have been against the countertheme of life's inevitable compromises and frustrations. Out of the verbal inadequacies of unlearned men's speech, O'Neill manages to create a sense of poetic wonder before the linked mysteries of life and death. Perhaps one might even intuit a broad application of the play to humanity's inexorable passage, under a bewildered captain and with dozing companions, across a fog-covered sea, toward an uncertain destination.

THE ESSAY

Since Kastenbaum's purpose is to enlarge the adult's capacity to understand and support the child's awareness of death, the greater part of his essay naturally focuses on how death is "an integral part of growing up." Within the usual three-part structure—introduction, development, conclusion—notice how he makes the transition from his introductory to his developmental sections; that is, how he precisely designates the kinds of support that he will offer.

THE KINGDOM WHERE NOBODY DIES

Robert Kastenbaum

Children are playing and shouting in the early morning sunshine near the end of Alban Berg's opera *Wozzeck*. They are chanting one variant of a very familiar rhyme: "Ring-a-ring-a-roses, all fall down! Ring-a-ring-a-roses, all . . . ." The game is interrupted by the excited entry of other children, one of whom shouts to Marie's child, "Hey, your mother is dead!" But Marie's child responds only by continuing to ride his hobbyhorse, "Hop, hop! Hop, hop! Hop, hop!" The other children exchange a few words about what is "out there, on the path by the pool," and race off to see for themselves. The newly orphaned child hesitates for an instant and then rides off in the direction of his playmates. End of opera.

What begins for Marie's child? Without knowing the details of his fate, we can sense the confusion, vulnerability, and terror that mark this child's entry into the realm of grief and calamity. Adult protection has failed. The reality of death has shattered the make-believe of childhood.

Children are exposed to death on occasions much less dramatic than the sudden demise of a parent. A funeral procession passes by. A pet dies. An innocent question is raised at the dinner table: "Was this meat once a real live cow?" In a society such as ours that has labored so diligently to put mortality out of sight and out of mind, most of the questions children ask about death make parents uncomfortable. It is often thought that there is no appropriate answer that would not be alarming or threatening to children. Therefore, the subject of death is mostly evaded entirely or fantasized.

The intrusion of death places typical parents in an awkward position. They are not able to relax and observe—much less *appreciate*—how the child orients himself toward death. Yet much can be learned by indulging this curiosity. By dropping the adult guard that directs us to protect children from morbid thoughts and threatening

429

events and by concentrating instead upon how children themselves react to death, surprising insights begin to emerge. We find from psychological research, clinical experience, folkways, and incidents shared with children in and around home that, despite the lack of explicit references, death is an integral part of growing up.

A child's fascination with death occurs almost any time, almost any place. Mortality is a theme that wends its way into many of the child's activities, whether solitary or social. Consider games for example. Ring-around-the-rosy is a popular childhood play theme in both this country and Europe. Our own parents and grandparents delighted in "all fall down," as did their ancestors all the way back to the fifteenth century. The origin of this game, however, was anything but delightful.

Medieval society was almost totally helpless against bubonic plague—Black Death. If adults could not ward off death, what could children do? They could join hands, forming a circle of life. They could chant ritualistically and move along in a reassuring rhythm of unity. Simultaneously acknowledging and mocking the peril that endangered each of them individually, the children predicted and participated in their own sudden demise: "all fall down!" This was a playing-at-death, but it utilized highly realistic materials. Ring-around-the-rosy had one distinct advantage over its model— one could arise to play again. While the game provided the vehicle to conquer or survive death, it was also a way of saying, "I know that I, too, am vulnerable, but I will enjoy the security of other young, living bodies around me." An exercise in make-believe? Perhaps. Nevertheless, this familiar game also deserves respect as an artful response to harsh and overwhelming reality.

Death has been ritualized in many other children's games as well. In the playful romping of tag, what is the hidden agenda or mystery that makes the chaser "It"? Could "It" be the disguise for death? We may be reluctant even to speculate that the touch of death is at the symbolic root of the tag games that have flourished for so many centuries throughout so much of the world. Yet Death (or the Dead Man) certainly is central to at least some of the chase games beloved to children. In the English game "Dead Man Arise" the central player lies prostrate on the ground while other children either mourn over him or seek to bring him back to life. When least expected, up jumps John Brown, the Dead Man, the Water Sprite, Death himself, or whatever name local custom prefers. The children flee or freeze in surprise as the chaser whirls toward them for a tag that will bestow Dead Man status upon the victim.

Although children today continue to participate in rituals that can be traced centuries back, other death-attuned merriments such as "bang, bang, you're dead!" are of more recent origin, and the repertoire is constantly freshened. When everyday group games do not provide a sufficient outlet for death-oriented play, children are likely to express their own special thoughts and feelings individually through inventive play. Suffocating and burying a doll is an instance of fulfilling a death fantasy. Similarly, a game of repeatedly crashing toy cars into each other or a model plane into the ground effectively permits a youngster to test out feelings that are evoked in certain real situations. Should an adult happen to interrupt this brutal type of play, the youngster may offer some reassuring comment, such as "Nobody gets killed bad" or "All the people come home for supper."

How death becomes a vital element in what we call child's play was illustrated by my eight-year-old son at home just a few weeks ago. David, for no ostensible reason, went to the piano and improvised. A short while later he moved to the floor near the piano and began stacking his wooden blocks. These two spontaneous actions did not have any apparent relationship to each other, nor did they bear the mark of death awareness. Yet the only way to appreciate David's behavior is in terms of response to death and loss. The piano playing and block building occurred within a half-hour of the time David and I had discovered our family cat lying dead in the road. Together we acknowledged the death, discussed the probable cause, shared our surprise and dismay, and removed the body for burial in the woods. David then went his own way for a while, which included the actions already mentioned.

When I asked what he was playing on the piano, David answered, "Lovey's life story." He explained how the various types of music he had invented represented memorable incidents in the life of his lost cat (e.g., "This is music for when she scratched my arm"). The wooden blocks turned out to be a monument for Lovey. A close look revealed that the entire building was constructed in an *L* shape, with several other *L*s at salient points.

If there had been no sharing of the initial death experience, I probably would not have guessed that David's play had been inspired by an encounter with mortality. Adults often fail to fathom the implications of children's play because they have not had the opportunity to perceive the stimulus. It is very easy to misinterpret what children are doing, because the nature of their play does not necessarily convey the meaning behind the activity (children go to the piano or their blocks for many other reasons than memorializing). The fact that a particular behavior does not seem to be death-related by no means rules out the possibility that it must be understood at least partially in those terms.

More systematically now, let us explore the child's relationship to death from encounters with both tragedy and games, starting in infancy. Although the young child does not comprehend death as a concept in the strictest sense of the term, death themes certainly engage his mind very early in life, and they are intimately related to the central development of his personality.

There are two different, although related, realizations that children must eventually develop. The first is that other people die, and the second is that they themselves will die. One of the earliest inquiries into the psychology of death touched upon the question of the child's exposure to the death of others. Around the turn of the century G. Stanley Hall, one of the most distinguished of this nation's first generation of psychologists, and one of his students conducted a study on adult recollections of childhood. Several of the questions they asked concerned early encounters with death. Interestingly, many of the earliest memories involved death in one form or another.

When asked specifically about their earliest experiences with death, many of Hall's respondents answered with considerable detail. He later wrote that ". . . the first impression of death often comes from a sensation of coldness in touching the corpse of a relative and the reaction is a nervous start at the contrast with the warmth that the contact of cuddling and hugging was wont to bring. The child's exquisite temperature sense feels a chill where it formerly felt heat. Then comes the immobility of face and body where it used to find prompt movements of response. There is no answering kiss, pat, or smile. . . . often the half-opened eyes are noticed with awe. The silence and tearfulness of friends are also impressive to the infant, who often weeps reflexly or sympathetically.''

Taking careful note of mental reactions to the elaborate funeral proceedings of the era, Hall observed that ''little children often focus on some minute detail (thanatic fetishism) and ever after remember, for example, the bright pretty handles or the silver nails of the coffin, the plate, the cloth binding, their own or others' articles of apparel, the shroud, flowers, and wreaths on or near the coffin or thrown into the grave, count- less stray phrases of the preacher, the fear lest the bottom of the coffin should drop out or the straps with which it is lowered into the ground should slip or break, a stone in the first handful or shovelful of earth thrown upon the coffin, etc. The hearse is almost always prominent in such memories and children often want to ride in one.''

Some adult memories of death went back to age two or three. A child that young could not interpret or symbolize death in anything approaching the adult mode. Yet the exposure to death seemed to make a special impression. Possibly what happens is that the memory is preserved in details of the perception. The scene, or some of its ele- ments that are easily overlooked by an adult, remains charged with emotion and vividly etched in the child's mind. When the adult turns the pages back to early childhood, he cannot show us the text, only the pictures. We do not yet know very much about the place of these early death portraits in the process of individual development, nor can we say with certainty what happens when such seldom-reviewed memories are brought to light in the adult years. However, it is likely that many of us have death perceptions engraved at some level of our memory that predate our ability to preserve our experiences in the form of verbal concepts.

Another way to study the impact of death upon a young child is to learn how he responds to the actual loss of somebody close to him. Albert Cain and his colleagues at the University of Michigan have found that a pattern of disturbed behavior often follows a death in the family. The symptoms occasionally become part of the child's personality from that time forward. One of Cain's studies focused upon responses to the death of a brother or sister. Guilt, as might be expected, was one of the more frequent reactions. ''In approximately half our cases,'' reports Cain, ''guilt was rawly, directly present. So, too, was trembling, crying and sadness upon mention of the sib- ling's death, with the guilt still consciously active five years or more after the sibling's death. Such children felt responsible for the death, sporadically insisted that it was all their fault, felt they should have died, too, or should have died instead of the dead sibling. They insisted they should enjoy nothing, and deserved only the worst. Some had suicidal thoughts and impulses, said they deserved to die, wanted to die—this also being motivated by a wish to join the dead sibling. They mulled over and over the nasty things they had thought, felt, or said to the dead sibling, and became all the guiltier. They also tried to recall the good things they had done, the ways they had protected the dead sibling, and so on.''

Many other types of problems were noted in the same study. Some young children developed distorted ideas of what is involved in both illness and death, leading them to fear death for themselves at almost any time or to fantasize that the adults had killed their siblings—fantasies often fed by misinterpretations of emergency respiration and other rescue procedures. The surviving children sometimes became very fearful of physicians and hospitals or resented God as the murderer of their siblings. A few children developed major problems in mental functioning; they suddenly appeared "stupid," did not even know their own age, and seemed to lose their sense of time and causation.

The loss of an expected family member who was not yet born also proved unsettling to many of the children observed by Cain. Although miscarriage, as an event, was difficult for the young child to understand, it was clear enough that something important had gone wrong. Evasive answers by anxious parents increased the problem for some children. In the absence of accurate knowledge they created fantasies that the fetus had been abandoned or murdered. One child insisted that his mother had thrown the baby into a garbage can in a fit of anger; another associated the miscarriage with guppies that eat their babies. At times the insistent questioning by the child had the effect of further unsettling his parents, who had not yet worked through their own feelings about the miscarriage.

Not all children become permanently affected by death in their family. Some weather the emotional crisis with the strong and sensitive help of others. The point is simply that death registers in the minds of young children whether or not adults are fully cognizant of the phenomenon. It need not be either a sibling death or a miscarriage. The death of a playmate, the man across the street, a distant relative, a pet, a sports hero, or a national political figure all make an impression somewhere in the child's mind. Real death is not a rare event in the child's world.

There is no precise way of knowing which death will make the greatest impact upon which child. The death of a pet, especially if it is the first death exposure or occurs in a striking manner, sometimes affects a youngster more than the subsequent death of a person. There is nothing automatic about the different responses to death, even in childhood. Nor can the seemingly inconsequential or remote death be disregarded if we wish to understand the child's thoughts and feelings on mortality.

Whatever the impact of other deaths, however, the loss of a parent has the most signal and longest-lasting influence on children. Bereavement in early childhood has been implicated as the underlying cause of depression and suicide attempts in later life. In one British study, for example, it was found that boys age four or younger who had lost their fathers were especially vulnerable to severe depression in adulthood. Many of the fathers died in combat. Perhaps some of the psychiatric and physical casualties of our involvement in Vietnam eventually will include the suicide committed in 1990 by the son whose father did not return. The death of a young father, however, does not automatically determine his son's fate. There is no way to predict the surviving child's response. In fact, the responses themselves cannot be explained entirely on the basis of parental death alone. What registered in the child's mind when his parent died? By what process did this first response develop into a way of life or into a sort of psychological time bomb set for later detonation? How might the child have been protected or guided? These questions have been raised only sporadically, and the answers are still elusive.

The significance of experiencing another's death during childhood has prompted many psychotherapists to look for such encounters in their adult patients. Psychiatrist David M. Moriarty, for example, has described a depressed woman who had attempted suicide on three occasions and had received electro-shock therapy twice without notable improvement in her behavior. When she was three years old, her mother had died of appendicitis. In the course of treatment she would call her psychiatrist in a panic, feeling that the world was coming in on her. The thought behind this fear was traced to the graveyard scene, when a shovelful of dirt had been thrown on the lowered coffin. Dr. Moriarty concluded that "Mrs. Q. lived most of her life afraid that she would lose other people whom she loved. The most impressive fact was that she talked and thought about the death of her mother as if it had just happened. This tragic event of forty years ago was still uppermost in her mind."

Of all the methods used to piece together the meaning of death during childhood, none can replace the sharing of a direct death experience with a young child. It is only in such moments of fortunate sharing that we have a clear glimpse into the child's face-to-face encounter with death. There is something indescribably poignant about the way in which the young child attempts to attune himself to threat, limitations, and mortality at a time when he would appear to be innocent of dark concerns. In a journal that I have kept for each of my children, I recorded my son's first encounter with death.

David, at eighteen months, was toddling around the back yard. He pointed at something on the ground. I looked and saw a dead bird, which he immediately labeled "buh . . . buh." But he appeared uncertain and puzzled. Furthermore, he made no effort to touch the bird. This was unusual caution for a child who characteristically tried to touch or pick up everything he could reach. David then crouched over and moved slightly closer to the bird. His face changed expression. From its initial expression of excited discovery and later of puzzlement, now it took on a different aspect: to my astonishment, his face was set in a frozen, ritualized expression resembling nothing so much as the stylized Greek dramatic mask of tragedy. I said only, "Yes, bird . . . dead bird." In typically adult conflict, I thought of adding, "Don't touch," but then decided against this injunction. In any event, David made no effort to touch.

Every morning for the next few days he would begin his morning explorations by toddling over to the dead-bird-place. He no longer assumed the ritual-mask expression but still restrained himself from touching. The bird was allowed to remain there until greatly reduced by decomposition. I reasoned that he might as well have the opportunity of seeing the natural processes at work. This was, to the best of my knowledge, David's first exposure to death. No general change in his behavior was noted, nor had any been expected. The small first chapter had concluded.

But a few weeks later a second dead bird was discovered. David had quite a different reaction this time. He picked up the bird and gestured with it. He was "speaking" with insistence. When he realized that I did not comprehend his wishes, he reached up toward a tree, holding the bird above his head. He repeated the gesture several times. I tried to explain that being placed back on the tree would not help the bird. David continued to insist, accompanying his command now with gestures that could be interpreted as a bird flying. All too predictably, the bird did not fly when I returned it to the tree. He insisted that the effort be repeated several times; then he lost interest altogether.

There was a sequel a few weeks later—by now autumn. David and I were walking in the woods, sharing many small discoveries. After a while, however, his attention became thoroughly engaged by a single fallen leaf. He tried to place it back on the tree himself. Failure. He gave the leaf to me with "instructions" that the leaf be restored to its rightful place. Failure again. When I started to try once more, he shook his head no, looking both sober and convinced. Although leaves were repeatedly seen to fall and dead animals were found every now and then, he made no further efforts to reverse their fortunes.

David's look of puzzlement and his repeated efforts to reverse death suggest that even the very young child recognizes a problem when he sees one. Indeed, the problem of death very well might be the prime challenge that sets into motion the child's curiosity and mental questing. Instead of constituting only an odd corner of the young child's mental life, death and its related problems may, in fact, provide much of the motivation for his intellectual development. Children obviously do not possess the conceptual structures of the adult; nevertheless, they do try to understand. Curiosity about death and "where things go" is part of a child's early motivation for exploring his environment. While many developmentalists have observed how the young child comes to an appreciation of object constancy, few have noted that this mental achievement is not possible unless there is also an appreciation of inconstancy. In other words, the young child must be aware of changes, losses, and disappearances if he is eventually to comprehend what "stays," what "goes," and what "comes and goes." Even very young children encounter losses, ends, and limits. Without an ability to fathom these experiences, they could not form protoconcepts of constancies, beginnings, and possibilities.

The death of animals, relatives, or friends undoubtedly has some relationship to the child's discovery of his own mortality, but there are other observations that are more germane. Adah Maurer, a school psychologist in California, suggests that an infant as young as three months old has the glimmerings of death awareness. For a while the baby alternates between sleeping and waking states, with biological imperatives having the upper hand. Soon, Maurer says, "the healthy baby is ready to experiment with these contrasting states. In the game of peek-a-boo, he replays in safe circumstances the alternate terror and delight, confirming his sense of self by risking and regaining complete consciousness. A light cloth spread over his face and body will elicit an immediate and forceful reaction. Short, sharp intakes of breath, vigorous thrashing of arms and legs removes the erstwhile shroud to reveal widely staring eyes that scan the scene with frantic alertness until they lock glances with the smiling mother, whereupon he will wriggle and laugh with joy. . . . To the empathetic observer, it is obvious that he enjoyed the temporary dimming of the light, the blotting out of the reassuring face and the suggestion of a lack of air which his own efforts enabled him to restore, his aliveness additionally confirmed by the glad greeting implicit in the eye-to-eye oneness with another human."

Babies a few months older begin to delight in disappearance-and-return games. Overboard goes a toy, somebody fetches it, then overboard again. The questions When is something gone? and When is it gone "forever"? seem very important to the young explorer. He devises many experiments for determining under what conditions something is "all gone." Maurer suggests that we "offer a two-year-old a lighted match and watch his face light up with demonic glee as he blows it out. Notice the willingness with which he helps his mother if the errand is to step on the pedal and bury his banana peel in the covered garbage can. The toilet makes a still better sarcophagus until he must watch in awed dismay while the plumber fishes out the Tinker-toy from the over-flowing bowl."

It makes sense to take these activities seriously. They provide early clues as to how children begin to grasp what "all gone" means. Once children are old enough to begin talking in sentences, part of their verbal repertoire usually includes death words. One conversation between a four-year-old girl and her eighty-four-year-old great-grandmother illustrates the preschool-age child's concept of death: "You are old. That means you will die. I am young, so I won't die, you know." This excerpt suggests that the little girl knows what it means to die, even if she has not entirely grasped the relationship between age and death. However, a moment later she adds: "But it's all right, Gran'mother. Just make sure you wear your white dress. Then, after you die, you can marry Nomo [great-grandfather] again, and have babies."

The words "dead" and "die" are fairly common in children's conversation and often are used with some sense of appropriateness. Yet an extra comment such as "you can marry Nomo again" or a little adult questioning frequently reveals that a child's understanding of death is quite different from an adult's. Psychologist Maria Nagy, studying Hungarian children in the late 1940s, discovered three phases in the child's awareness of personal mortality. Her interpretation of death ideas expressed by three- to ten-year-olds in drawings and words are classic.

Stage one: present until about age five. The preschool child usually does not recognize that death is final. Being dead is like being less alive. The youngest children regard death as sleep or departure. Still, there is much curiosity about what happens to a person after he dies. The children "want to know where and how he continues to live. Most of the children connected the facts of absence and funerals. In the cemetery one lives on. Movement . . . is limited by the coffin, but for all that, the dead are still capable of growth. They take nourishment, they breathe. They know what is happening on earth. They feel it if someone thinks of them and they even feel sorry for themselves." Death disturbs the young child because it separates people from each other and be-cause life in the grave seems dull and unpleasant.

Stage two: between the ages of five and nine. The distinguishing characteristic of this stage is that the child now tends to personify death. Death is sometimes seen as a separate person—for example, an angel or a frightening clown. For other children death is represented by a dead person. Death usually makes his rounds in the night. The big shift in the child's thinking from stage one is that death now seems to be understood as final: it is not just a reduced form of life. But there is still an important protective feature here: personal death can be avoided. Run faster than the Death

Man, lock the door, trick him, and you will not die, unless you have bad luck. As Nagy puts it, "Death is still outside us and is also not general."

Stage three: ages nine to ten and thereafter. The oldest children in Nagy's study recognized that death was not only final but also inevitable. It will happen to them, too, no matter how fast they run or how cleverly they hide. "It is like the withering of flowers," a ten-year-old girl explained to the psychologist.

Nagy's stages offer a useful guide to the development of the child's conception of death, but not all observations fit neatly into these three categories. There are instances in which children as young as five realize their own inevitable mortality. A six-year-old boy worked out by himself the certainty of death. In a shocked voice he revealed, "But I had been planning to live forever, you know." A five-year-old reasoned aloud: "One day you [father] will be died. And one day Mommy will be died. . . . And one day even Cynthia [little sister], she will be died, I mean dead, too. . . . [pause] And one day *I* will be dead. . . . [long pause] *Everybody* there is will be dead. . . . [long, long pause] That's sad, isn't it?" This insight is several years ahead of schedule and is even farther ahead of what one would expect from most theories of mental growth.

Apparently, it is possible to grasp the central facts of death at a surprisingly early age. Children probably tend to retreat from this realization when it comes so early and for several years fluctuate between two states of belief: that death is final and inevitable, and that death is partial, reversible, and perhaps avoidable.

My research indicates that the orientation many adolescents have toward death also fluctuates between a sense of invulnerability and a sense of impending, catastrophic wipeout. Some adults reveal a similar tendency to function at two levels of thought: they "know" that death is final and inevitable, of course, but most of their daily attitudes and actions are more consistent with the belief that personal mortality is an unfounded rumor.

Sooner or later most children come to understand that death is final, universal, and inevitable. Parents might prefer that children remain innocent of what is happening in their lives and sheltered from emotional stress, shock, and anguish. But it is our own make-believe, not theirs, if we persist in behaving as though children are not attuned to the prospect of mortality. It is important to remember that in this century millions of children around the world have grown up literally in the midst of death and the threat of death. They have fewer illusions on the subject than do many adults.

"The kingdom where nobody dies," as Edna St. Vincent Millay once described childhood, is the fantasy of grownups. We want our children to be immortal—at least temporarily. We can be more useful to children if we can share with them realities as well as fantasies about death. This means some uncomfortable moments. Part of each child's adventure into life is his discovery of loss, separation, nonbeing, death. No one can have this adventure for him, nor can death be locked in another room until a child comes of age. At the beginning the child does not know that he is supposed to be scared of death, that he is supposed to develop a fabric of evasions to protect himself, and that his parents are not to be relied upon for support when it really counts. He is ready to share his discoveries with us. Are we?

QUESTIONS

1 Kastenbaum utilizes four kinds of support within the body of his essay. What are they and how would you rate the relative effectiveness of each?
2 What is the writer's evaluation of the relationship between parent and child in view of death?
3 From your experience, are Kastenbaum's remarks about early childhood memories accurate?
4 How do current trends toward violence and death in media presentations contribute to the implications of this essay's title?

TOPIC FOR COMPOSITION

This essay asks us to think about our childhood memories. Certainly, not all of our memories touch upon death; but, as an experience in autobiographical writing, try to capture your earliest memories, the reason why you remember, and the implications, if any, upon your growing up.

□

Kierkegaard's discussion of despair is in one sense remarkable because of the intensity that he is able to sustain. An examination of his style shows:

1 Tight sentence transitions achieved mainly through the repetition of key words
2 Tight paragraph transitions achieved primarily by repeating a key idea from the preceding paragraph

DESPAIR IS "THE SICKNESS UNTO DEATH"

Sören Kierkegaard

The concept of the sickness unto death must be understood, however, in a peculiar sense. Literally it means a sickness the end and outcome of which is death. Thus one speaks of a mortal sickness as synonymous with a sickness unto death. In this sense despair cannot be called the sickness unto death. But in the Christian understanding of it death itself is a transition unto life. In view of this, there is from the Christian standpoint no earthly, bodily sickness unto death. For death is doubtless the last phase of the sickness, but death is not the last thing. If in the strictest sense we are to speak of a sickness unto death, it must be one in which the last thing is death, and death the last thing. And this precisely is despair.

Yet in another and still more definite sense despair is the sickness unto death. It is indeed very far from being true that, literally understood, one dies of this sickness, or that this sickness ends with bodily death. On the contrary, the torment of despair is precisely this, not to be able to die. So it has much in common with the situation of the moribund when he lies and struggles with death, and cannot die. So to be sick *unto* death is, not to be able to die—yet not as though there were hope of life; no, the hopelessness in this case is that even the last hope, death, is not available. When death is the greatest danger, one hopes for life; but when one becomes acquainted with an even more dreadful danger, one hopes for death. So when the danger is so great that death has become one's hope, despair is the disconsolateness of not being able to die.

It is in this last sense that despair is the sickness unto death, this agonizing contradiction, this sickness in the self, everlastingly to die, to die and yet not to die, to die the death. For dying means that it is all over, but dying the death means to live to experience death; and if for a single instant this experience is possible, it is tantamount to experiencing it forever. If one might die of despair as one dies of a sickness, then the eternal in him, the self, must be capable of dying in the same sense that the body dies of sickness. But this is an impossibility; the dying of despair transforms itself constantly into a living. The despairing man cannot die; no more than "the dagger can slay thoughts" can despair consume the eternal thing, the self, which is the ground of despair, whose worm dieth not, and whose fire is not quenched. Yet despair is precisely *self*-consuming, but it is an impotent self-consumption which is not able to do what it wills; and this impotence is a new form of self-consumption, in which again, however, the despairer is not able to do what he wills, namely, to consume himself. This is despair raised to a higher potency, or it is the law for the potentiation. This is the hot incitement, or the cold fire in despair, the gnawing canker whose movement is constantly inward, deeper and deeper, in impotent self-consumption. The fact that despair does not consume him is so far from being any comfort to the despairing man that it is precisely the opposite, this comfort is precisely the torment, it is precisely this that keeps the gnawing pain alive and keeps life in the pain. This precisely is the reason why he despairs—not to say despaired—because he cannot consume himself, cannot get rid of himself, cannot become nothing. This is the potentiated formula for despair, the rising of the fever in the sickness of the self.

A despairing man is in despair over *something.* So it seems for an instant, but only for an instant; that same instant the true despair manifests itself, or despair manifests itself in its true character. For in the fact that he despaired of *something,* he really despaired of himself, and now would be rid of himself. Thus when the ambitious man whose watchword was "Either Caesar or nothing" does not become Caesar, he is in despair thereat. But this signifies something else, namely, that precisely because he did not become Caesar he now cannot endure to be himself. So properly he is not in despair over the fact that he did not become Caesar, but he is in despair over himself for the fact that he did not become Caesar. This self which, had he become Caesar, would have been to him a sheer delight (though in another sense equally in despair), this self is now absolutely intolerable to him. In a profounder sense it is not the fact that he did not become Caesar which is intolerable to him, but the self which did not become Caesar is the thing that is intolerable; or, more correctly, what is intolerable to him is that he cannot get rid of himself. If he had become Caesar he would have been rid of himself in desperation, but now that he did not become Caesar he cannot in desperation get rid of himself. Essentially he is equally in despair in either case, for he does not possess himself, he is not himself. By becoming Caesar he would not after all have become himself but have got rid of himself, and by not becoming Caesar he falls into despair over the fact that he cannot get rid of himself. Hence it is a superficial view (which presumably has never seen a person in despair, not even one's own self) when it is said of a man in despair, "He is consuming himself." For precisely this it is he despairs of, and to his torment it is precisely this he cannot do, since by despair fire has entered into something that cannot burn, or cannot burn up, that is, into the self.

So to despair over something is not yet properly despair. It is the beginning, or it is as when the physician says of a sickness that it has not yet declared itself. The next step is the declared despair, despair over oneself. A young girl is in despair over love, and so she despairs over her lover, because he died, or because he was unfaithful to her. This is not a declared despair; no, she is in despair over herself. This self of hers, which, if it had become "his" beloved, she would have been rid of in the most blissful way, or would have lost, this self is now a torment to her when it has to be a self without "him"; this self which would have been to her her riches (though in another sense equally in despair) has now become to her a loathsome void, since "he" is dead, or it has become to her an abhorrence, since it reminds her of the fact that she was betrayed. Try it now, say to such a girl, "Thou art consuming yourself," and thou shalt hear her reply, "Oh, no, the torment is precisely this, that I cannot do it."

To despair over oneself, in despair to will to be rid of oneself, is the formula for all despair, and hence the second form of despair (in despair at willing to be oneself) can be followed back to the first (in despair at not willing to be oneself), just as in the foregoing we resolved the first into the second. A despairing man wants despairingly to be himself. But if he despairingly wants to be himself, he will not want to get rid of himself. Yes, so it seems; but if one inspects more closely, one perceives that after all the contradiction is the same. That self which he despairingly wills to be is a self which he is not (for to will to be that self which one truly is, is indeed the opposite of despair); what he really wills is to tear his self away from the Power which constituted it. But notwithstanding all his despair, this he is unable to do, notwithstanding all the efforts of despair, that Power is the stronger, and it compels him to be the self he does not will to be. But for all that he wills to be rid of himself, to be rid of the self which he is, in order to be the self he himself has chanced to choose. To be *self* as he wills to be would be his delight (though in another sense it would be equally in despair), but to be compelled to be *self* as he does not will to be is his torment, namely, that he cannot get rid of himself.

Socrates proved the immortality of the soul from the fact that the sickness of the soul (sin) does not consume it as sickness of the body consumes the body. So also we can demonstrate the eternal in man from the fact that despair cannot consume his self, that this precisely is the torment of contradiction in despair. If there were nothing eternal in a man, he could not despair; but if despair could consume his self, there would still be no despair.

Thus it is that despair, this sickness in the self, is the sickness unto death. The despairing man is mortally ill. In an entirely different sense than can appropriately be said of any disease, we may say that the sickness has attacked the noblest part; and yet the man cannot die. Death is not the last phase of the sickness, but death is continually the last. To be delivered from this sickness by death is an impossibility, for the sickness and its torment . . . and death consist in not being able to die.

This is the situation in despair. And however thoroughly it eludes the attention of the despairer, and however thoroughly the despairer may succeed (as in the case of that kind of despair which is characterized by unawareness of being in despair) in losing himself entirely, and losing himself in such a way that it is not noticed in the least—eternity nevertheless will make it manifest that his situation was despair, and it will so nail him to himself that the torment nevertheless remains that he cannot get rid of himself, and it becomes manifest that he was deluded in thinking that he succeeded. And thus it is eternity must act, because to have a self, to be a self, is the greatest concession made to man, but at the same time it is eternity's demand upon him.

QUESTIONS

1 What is the torment of despair? How does Kierkegaard develop this point as it relates to life? Explain the contradictions the author presents.
2 What is the contradiction in the statement, "it is said of a man in despair, 'He is consuming himself'"? How does the analogy about the man who wished to be Caesar support this contradiction?
3 What methods does Kierkegaard use in fashioning his definition of despair as "the sickness unto death"?
4 Granting that the topic is a difficult one, does the author sufficiently support his thesis? In other words, what more could he do to define his use of despair? Or, perhaps you feel that he has labored the point. If so, explain how he could shorten the essay and achieve his purpose.

TOPIC FOR COMPOSITION

This essay not only examines a philosophical concept but also illustrates the difficulty one may encounter when writing an extended definition of an abstract term such as "despair." However, the discipline of writing extended definitions can do much to eliminate "looseness" in both thought and structure, especially if the term to be defined is an abstract one. Keeping in mind the techniques illustrated by the essay, write an extended definition of an abstract term such as "hope," "faith," "charity," love." You might wish to qualify your approach, as does Kierkegaard; for example: "Hope is 'the breath of life.'"

SHORT STORY

"The Short Happy Life of Francis Macomber" is typical of Hemingway's fictive world: it is a violent world that revolves around war, bullfights, big-game hunts, and the like. His characters are essentially failures of one kind or another. They are moral degenerates, cowards, and violators of human dignity and trust. At their best, they try to overcome, or at least cope with, the despair of their situations. At the worst, they are indifferent to or even further degrade themselves and others. In Macomber's story, something of all of the above is evident.

THE SHORT HAPPY LIFE OF FRANCIS MACOMBER

Ernest Hemingway

It was now lunch time and they were all sitting under the double green fly of the dining tent pretending that nothing had happened.

"Will you have lime juice or lemon squash?" Macomber asked.

"I'll have a gimlet," Robert Wilson told him.

"I'll have a gimlet too. I need something," Macomber's wife said.

"I suppose it's the thing to do," Macomber agreed. "Tell him to make three gimlets."

The mess boy had started them already, lifting the bottles out of the canvas cooling bags that sweated wet in the wind that blew through the trees that shaded the tents.

"What had I ought to give them?" Macomber asked.

"A quid would be plenty," Wilson told him. "You don't want to spoil them."

"Will the headman distribute it?"

"Absolutely."

Francis Macomber had, half an hour before, been carried to his tent from the edge of the camp in triumph on the arms and shoulders of the cook, the personal boys, the skinner and the porters. The gun-bearers had taken no part in the demonstration. When the native boys put him down at the door of his tent, he had shaken all their hands, received their congratulations, and then gone into the tent and sat on the bed until his wife came in. She did not speak to him when she came in and he left the tent at once to wash his face and hands in the portable wash basin outside and go over to the dining tent to sit in a comfortable canvas chair in the breeze and the shade.

"You've got your lion," Robert Wilson said to him, "and a damned fine one too."

Mrs. Macomber looked at Wilson quickly. She was an extremely handsome and well-kept woman of the beauty and social position which had, five years before, commanded five thousand dollars as the price of endorsing, with photographs, a beauty product which she had never used. She had been married to Francis Macomber for eleven years.

"He is a good lion, isn't he?" Macomber said. His wife looked at him now. She looked at both these men as though she had never seen them before.

One, Wilson, the white hunter, she knew she had never truly seen before. He was about middle height with sandy hair, a stubby mustache, a very red face and extremely cold blue eyes with faint white wrinkles at the corners that grooved merrily when he smiled. He smiled at her now and she looked away from his face at the way his shoulders sloped in the loose tunic he wore with the four big cartridges held in loops where the left breast pocket should have been, at his big brown hands, his old slacks, his very dirty boots and back to his red face again. She noticed where the baked red of his face stopped in a white line that marked the circle left by his Stetson hat that hung now from one of the pegs of the tent pole.

"Well, here's to the lion," Robert Wilson said. He smiled at her again and, not smiling, she looked curiously at her husband.

Francis Macomber was very tall, very well built if you did not mind that length of bone, dark, his hair cropped like an oarsman, rather thin-lipped, and was considered handsome. He was dressed in the same sort of safari clothes that Wilson wore except that his were new, he was thirty-five years old, kept himself very fit, was good at court games, had a number of big-game fishing records, and had just shown himself, very publicly, to be a coward.

"Here's to the lion," he said. "I can't ever thank you for what you did."

Margaret, his wife, looked away from him and back to Wilson.

"Let's not talk about the lion," she said.

Wilson looked over at her without smiling and now she smiled at him.

"It's been a very strange day," she said. "Hadn't you ought to put your hat on even under the canvas at noon? You told me that, you know."

"Might put it on," said Wilson.

"You know you have a very red face, Mr. Wilson," she told him and smiled again.

"Drink," said Wilson.

"I don't think so," she said. "Francis drinks a great deal, but his face is never red."

"It's red today," Macomber tried a joke.

"No," said Margaret. "It's mine that's red today. But Mr. Wilson's is always red."

"Must be racial," said Wilson. "I say, you wouldn't like to drop my beauty as a topic, would you?"

"I've just started on it."

"Let's chuck it," said Wilson.

"Conversation is going to be so difficult," Margaret said.

"Don't be silly, Margot," her husband said.

"No difficulty," Wilson said. "Got a damn fine lion."

Margot looked at them both and they both saw that she was going to cry. Wilson had seen it coming for a long time and he dreaded it. Macomber was past dreading it.

"I wish it hadn't happened. Oh, I wish it hadn't happened," she said and started for her tent. She made no noise of crying but they could see that her shoulders were shaking under the rose-colored, sun-proofed shirt she wore.

"Women upset," said Wilson to the tall man. "Amounts to nothing. Strain on the nerves and one thing'n another."

"No," said Macomber. "I suppose that I rate that for the rest of my life now."

"Nonsense. Let's have a spot of the giant killer," said Wilson. "Forget the whole thing. Nothing to it anyway."

"We might try," said Macomber. "I won't forget what you did for me though."

"Nothing," said Wilson. "All nonsense."

So they sat there in the shade where the camp was pitched under some wide-topped acacia trees with a boulder-strewn cliff behind them, and a stretch of grass that ran to the bank of a boulder-filled stream in front with forest beyond it, and drank their just-cool lime drinks and avoided one another's eyes while the boys set the table for lunch. Wilson could tell that the boys all knew about it now and when he saw Macomber's personal boy looking curiously at his master while he was putting dishes on the table he snapped at him in Swahili. The boy turned away with his face blank.

"What were you telling him?" Macomber asked.

"Nothing. Told him to look alive or I'd see he got about fifteen of the best."

"What's that? Lashes?"

"It's quite illegal," Wilson said. "You're supposed to fine them."

"Do you still have them whipped?"

"Oh, yes. They could raise a row if they chose to complain. But they don't. They prefer it to the fines."

"How strange!" said Macomber.

"Not strange, really," Wilson said. "Which would you rather do? Take a good birching or lose your pay?"

Then he felt embarrassed at asking it and before Macomber could answer he went on, "We all take a beating every day, you know, one way or another."

This was no better. "Good God," he thought. "I am a diplomat, aren't I?"

"Yes, we take a beating," said Macomber, still not looking at him. "I'm awfully sorry about that lion business. It doesn't have to go any further, does it? I mean no one will hear about it, will they?"

"You mean will I tell it at the Mathaiga Club?" Wilson looked at him now coldly. He had not expected this. So he's a bloody four-letter man as well as a bloody coward, he thought. I rather liked him too until today. But how is one to know about an American?

"No," said Wilson. "I'm a professional hunter. We never talk about our clients. You can be quite easy on that. It's supposed to be bad form to ask us not to talk though."

He had decided now that to break would be much easier. He would eat, then, by himself and could read a book with his meals. They would eat by themselves. He would see them through the safari on a very formal basis—what was it the French called it? Distinguished consideration—and it would be a damn sight easier than having to go through this emotional trash. He'd insult him and make a good clean break. Then he could read a book with his meals and he'd still be drinking their whisky. That was the phrase for it when a safari went bad. You ran into another white hunter and you asked. "How is everything going?" and he answered, "Oh, I'm still drinking their whisky," and you knew everything had gone to pot.

"I'm sorry," Macomber said and looked at him with his American face that would stay adolescent until it became middle-aged, and Wilson noted his crew-cropped hair, fine eyes only faintly shifty, good nose, thin lips and handsome jaw. "I'm sorry I didn't realize that. There are lots of things I don't know."

So what could he do, Wilson thought. He was all ready to break it off quickly and neatly and here the beggar was apologizing after he had just insulted him. He made one more attempt. "Don't worry about me talking," he said. "I have a living to make. You know in Africa no woman ever misses her lion and no white man ever bolts."

"I bolted like a rabbit," Macomber said.

Now what in hell were you going to do about a man who talked like that, Wilson wondered.

Wilson looked at Macomber with his flat, blue, machine-gunner's eyes and the other smiled back at him. He had a pleasant smile if you did not notice how his eyes showed when he was hurt.

"Maybe I can fix it up on buffalo," he said. "We're after them next, aren't we?"

"In the morning if you like," Wilson told him. Perhaps he had been wrong. This was certainly the way to take it. You most certainly could not tell a damned thing about an American. He was all for Macomber again. If you could forget the morning. But, of course, you couldn't. The morning had been about as bad as they come.

"Here comes the Memsahib," he said. She was walking over from her tent looking refreshed and cheerful and quite lovely. She had a very perfect oval face, so perfect that you expected her to be stupid. But she wasn't stupid, Wilson thought, no, not stupid.

"How is the beautiful red-faced Mr. Wilson? Are you feeling better, Francis, my pearl?"

"Oh, much," said Macomber.

"I've dropped the whole thing," she said, sitting down at the table. "What importance is there to whether Francis is any good at killing lions? That's not his trade. That's Mr. Wilson's trade. Mr. Wilson is really very impressive killing anything. You do kill anything, don't you?"

"Oh, anything," said Wilson. "Simply anything." They are, he thought, the hardest in the world; the hardest, the cruelest, the most predatory and the most attractive and their men have softened or gone to pieces nervously as they have hardened. Or is it that they pick men they can handle? They can't know that much at the age they marry, he thought. He was grateful that he had gone through his education on American women before now because this was a very attractive one.

"We're going after buff in the morning," he told her.

"I'm coming," she said.

"No, you're not."

"Oh, yes, I am. Mayn't I, Francis?"

"Why not stay in camp?"

"Not for anything," she said. "I wouldn't miss something like today for anything."

When she left, Wilson was thinking, when she went off to cry, she seemed a hell of a fine woman. She seemed to understand, to realize, to be hurt for him and for herself and to know how things really stood. She is away for twenty minutes and now she is back, simply enamelled in that American female cruelty. They are the damnedest women. Really the damnedest.

"We'll put on another show for you tomorrow," Francis Macomber said.

"You're not coming," Wilson said.

"You're very mistaken," she told him. "And I want *so* to see you perform again. You were lovely this morning. That is if blowing things' heads off is lovely."

"Here's the lunch," said Wilson. "You're very merry, aren't you?"

"Why not? I didn't come out here to be dull."

"Well, it hasn't been dull," Wilson said. He could see the boulders in the river and the high bank beyond with the trees and he remembered the morning.

"Oh, no," she said. "It's been charming. And tomorrow. You don't know how I look forward to tomorrow."

"That's eland he's offering you," Wilson said.

"They're the big cowy things that jump like hares, aren't they?"

"I suppose that describes them," Wilson said.

"It's very good meat," Macomber said.

"Did you shoot it, Francis?" she asked.

"Yes."

"They're not dangerous, are they?"

"Only if they fall on you," Wilson told her.

"I'm so glad."

"Why not let up on the bitchery just a little, Margot," Macomber said, cutting the eland steak and putting some mashed potato, gravy and carrot on the down-turned fork that tined through the piece of meat.

"I suppose I could," she said, "since you put it so prettily."

"Tonight we'll have champagne for the lion," Wilson said. "It's a bit too hot at noon."

"Oh, the lion," Margot said. "I'd forgotten the lion!"

So, Robert Wilson thought to himself, she *is* giving him a ride, isn't she? Or do you suppose that's her idea of putting up a good show? How should a woman act when she discovers her husband is a bloody coward? She's damn cruel but they're all cruel. They govern, of course, and to govern one has to be cruel sometimes. Still, I've seen enough of their damn terrorism.

"Have some more eland," he said to her politely.

That afternoon, late, Wilson and Macomber went out in the motor car with the native driver and the two gun-bearers. Mrs. Macomber stayed in the camp. It was too hot to go out, she said, and she was going with them in the early morning. As they drove off Wilson saw her standing under the big tree, looking pretty rather than beautiful in her faintly rosy khaki, her dark hair drawn back off her forehead and gathered in a knot low on her neck, her face as fresh, he thought, as though she were in England. She waved to them as the car went off through the swale of high grass and curved around through the trees into the small hills of orchard bush.

In the orchard bush they found a herd of impala, and leaving the car they stalked one old ram with long, wide-spread horns and Macomber killed it with a very creditable shot that knocked the buck down at a good two hundred yards and sent the herd off bounding wildly and leaping over one another's backs in long, leg-drawn-up leaps as unbelievable and as floating as those one makes sometimes in dreams.

"That was a good shot," Wilson said. "They're a small target."

"Is it a worth-while head?" Macomber asked.

"It's excellent," Wilson told him. "You shoot like that and you'll have no trouble."

"Do you think we'll find buffalo tomorrow?"

"There's a good chance of it. They feed out early in the morning and with luck we may catch them in the open."

"I'd like to clear away that lion business," Macomber said. "It's not very pleasant to have your wife see you do something like that."

I should think it would be even more unpleasant to do it, Wilson thought, wife or no wife, or to talk about it having done it. But he said, "I wouldn't think about that any more. Any one could be upset by his first lion. That's all over."

But that night after dinner and a whisky and soda by the fire before going to bed, as Francis Macomber lay on his cot with the mosquito bar over him and listened to the night noises it was not all over. It was neither all over nor was it beginning. It was there exactly as it happened with some parts of it indelibly emphasized and he was miserably ashamed at it. But more than shame he felt cold, hollow fear in him. The fear was still there like a cold slimy hollow in all the emptiness where once his confidence had been and it made him feel sick. It was still there with him now.

It had started the night before when he had wakened and heard the lion roaring somewhere up along the river. It was a deep sound and at the end there were sort of coughing grunts that made him seem just outside the tent, and when Francis Macomber woke in the night to hear it he was afraid. He could hear his wife breathing quietly, asleep. There was no one to tell he was afraid, nor to be afraid with him, and, lying alone, he did not know the Somali proverb that says a brave man is always frightened three times by a lion; when he first sees his track, when he first hears him roar and when he first confronts him. Then while they were eating breakfast by lantern light out in the dining tent, before the sun was up, the lion roared again and Francis thought he was just at the edge of camp.

"Sounds like an old-timer," Robert Wilson said, looking up from his kippers and coffee. "Listen to him cough."

"Is he very close?"

"A mile or so up the stream."

"Will we see him?"

"We'll have a look."

"Does his roaring carry that far? It sounds as though he were right in camp."

"Carries a hell of a long way," said Robert Wilson. "It's strange the way it carries. Hope he's a shootable cat. The boys said there was a very big one about here."

"If I get a shot, where should I hit him," Macomber asked, "to stop him?"

"In the shoulders," Wilson said. "In the neck if you can make it. Shoot for bone. Break him down."

"I hope I can place it properly," Macomber said.

"You shoot very well," Wilson told him. "Take your time. Make sure of him. The first one in is the one that counts."

"What range will it be?"

"Can't tell. Lion has something to say about that. Won't shoot unless it's close enough so you can make sure."

"At under a hundred yards?" Macomber asked.

Wilson looked at him quickly.

"Hundred's about right. Might have to take him a bit under. Shouldn't chance a shot at much over that. A hundred's a decent range. You can hit him wherever you want at that. Here comes the Memsahib.''

"Good morning," she said. "Are we going after that lion?"

"As soon as you deal with your breakfast," Wilson said. "How are you feeling?"

"Marvellous," she said. "I'm very excited."

"I'll just go and see that everything is ready," Wilson went off. As he left the lion roared again.

"Noisy beggar," Wilson said. "We'll put a stop to that."

"What's the matter, Francis?" his wife asked him.

"Nothing," Macomber said.

"Yes, there is," she said. "What are you upset about?"

"Nothing," he said.

"Tell me," she looked at him. "Don't you feel well?"

"It's that damned roaring," he said. "It's been going on all night, you know."

"Why didn't you wake me," she said. "I'd love to have heard it."

"I've got to kill the damned thing," Macomber said, miserably.

"Well, that's what you're out here for, isn't it?"

"Yes. But I'm nervous. Hearing the thing roar gets on my nerves."

"Well then, as Wilson said, kill him and stop his roaring."

"Yes, darling," said Francis Macomber. "It sounds easy, doesn't it?"

"You're not afraid, are you?"

"Of course not. But I'm nervous from hearing him roar all night."

"You'll kill him marvellously," she said. "I know you will. I'm awfully anxious to see it."

"Finish your breakfast and we'll be starting."

"It's not light yet," she said. "This is a ridiculous hour."

Just then the lion roared in a deep-chested moaning, suddenly guttural, ascending vibration that seemed to shake the air and ended in a sigh and a heavy, deep-chested grunt.

"He sounds almost here," Macomber's wife said.

"My God," said Macomber. "I hate that damned noise."

"It's very impressive."

"Impressive. It's frightful."

Robert Wilson came up then carrying his short, ugly, shockingly big-bored .505 Gibbs and grinning.

"Come on," he said. "Your gun-bearer has your Springfield and the big gun. Everything's in the car. Have you solids?"

"Yes."

"I'm ready," Mrs. Macomber said.

"Must make him stop that racket," Wilson said. "You get in front. The Memsahib can sit back here with me."

They climbed into the motor car and, in the gray first daylight, moved off up the river through the trees. Macomber opened the breech of his rifle and saw he had metal-cased bullets, shut the bolt and put the rifle on safety. He saw his hand was trembling. He felt in his pocket for more cartridges and moved his fingers over the cartridges in the loops of his tunic front. He turned back to where Wilson sat in the rear seat of the doorless, box-bodied motor car beside his wife, them both grinning with excitement, and Wilson leaned forward and whispered,

"See the birds dropping. Means the old boy has left his kill."

On the far bank of the stream Macomber could see, above the trees, vultures circling and plummeting down.

"Chances are he'll come to drink along here," Wilson whispered. "Before he goes to lay up. Keep an eye out."

They were driving slowly along the high bank of the stream which here cut deeply to its boulder-filled bed, and they wound in and out through big trees as they drove. Macomber was watching the opposite bank when he felt Wilson take hold of his arm. The car stopped.

"There he is," he heard the whisper. "Ahead and to the right. Get out and take him. He's a marvellous lion."

Macomber saw the lion now. He was standing almost broadside, his great head up and turned toward them. The early morning breeze that blew toward them was just stirring his dark mane, and the lion looked huge, silhouetted on the rise of bank in the gray morning light, his shoulders heavy, his barrel of a body bulking smoothly.

"How far is he?" asked Macomber, raising his rifle.

"About seventy-five. Get out and take him."

"Why not shoot from where I am?"

"You don't shoot them from cars," he heard Wilson saying in his ear. "Get out. He's not going to stay there all day."

Macomber stepped out of the curved opening at the side of the front seat, onto the step and down onto the ground. The lion stood looking majestically and coolly toward this object that his eyes only showed in silhouette, bulking like some super-rhino. There was no man smell carried toward him and he watched the object, moving his great head a little from side to side. Then watching the object, not afraid, but hesitating before going down the bank to drink with such a thing opposite him, he saw a man figure detach itself from it and he turned his heavy head and swung away toward the cover of the trees as he heard a cracking crash and felt the slam of a .30–06 220-grain solid bullet that bit his flank and ripped in sudden hot scalding nausea through his stomach. He trotted, heavy, big-footed, swinging wounded full-bellied, through the trees toward the tall grass and cover, and the crash came again to go past him ripping the air apart. Then it crashed again and he felt the blow as it hit his lower ribs and ripped on through, blood sudden hot and frothy in his mouth, and he galloped toward the high grass where he could crouch and not be seen and make them bring the crashing thing close enough so he could make a rush and get the man that held it.

Macomber had not thought how the lion felt as he got out of the car. He only knew his hands were shaking and as he walked away from the car it was almost impossible for him to make his legs move. They were stiff in the thighs, but he could feel the muscles fluttering. He raised the rifle, sighted on the junction of the lion's head and shoulders and pulled the trigger. Nothing happened though he pulled until he thought his finger would break. Then he knew he had the safety on and as he lowered the rifle to move the safety over he moved another frozen pace forward, and the lion seeing his silhouette now clear of the silhouette of the car, turned and started off at a trot, and, as Macomber fired, he heard a whunk that meant that the bullet was home; but the lion kept on going. Macomber shot again and every one saw the bullet throw a spout of dirt beyond the trotting lion. He shot again, remembering to lower his aim, and they all heard the bullet hit, and the lion went into a gallop and was in the tall grass before he had the bolt pushed forward.

Macomber stood there feeling sick at his stomach, his hands that held the Springfield still cocked, shaking, and his wife and Robert Wilson were standing by him. Beside him too were the two gun-bearers chattering in Wakamba.

"I hit him," Macomber said. "I hit him twice."

"You gut-shot him and you hit him somewhere forward," Wilson said without enthusiasm. The gun-bearers looked very grave. They were silent now.

"You may have killed him," Wilson went on. "We'll have to wait a while before we go in to find out."

"What do you mean?"

"Let him get sick before we follow him up."

"Oh," said Macomber.

"He's a hell of a fine lion," Wilson said cheerfully. "He's gotten into a bad place though."

"Why is it bad?"

"Can't see him until you're on him."

"Oh," said Macomber.

"Come on," said Wilson. "The Memsahib can stay here in the car. We'll go to have a look at the blood spoor."

"Stay here, Margot," Macomber said to his wife. His mouth was very dry and it was hard for him to talk.

"Why?" she asked.

"Wilson says to."

"We're going to have a look," Wilson said. "You stay here. You can see even better from here."

"All right."

Wilson spoke in Swahili to the driver. He nodded and said, "Yes, Bwana."

Then they went down the steep bank and across the stream, climbing over and around the boulders and up the other bank, pulling up by some projecting roots, and along it until they found where the lion had been trotting when Macomber first shot. There was dark blood on the short grass that the gun-bearers pointed out with grass stems, and that ran away behind the river bank trees.

"What do we do?" asked Macomber.

"Not much choice," said Wilson. "We can't bring the car over. Bank's too steep. We'll let him stiffen up a bit and then you and I'll go in and have a look for him."

"Can't we set the grass on fire?" Macomber asked.

"Too green."

"Can't we send beaters?"

Wilson looked at him appraisingly. "Of course we can," he said. "But it's just a touch murderous. You see we know the lion's wounded. You can drive an unwounded lion—he'll move on ahead of a noise—but a wounded lion's going to charge. You can't see him until you're right on him. He'll make himself perfectly flat in cover you wouldn't think would hide a hare. You can't very well send boys in there to that sort of a show. Somebody bound to get mauled."

"What about the gun-bearers?"

"Oh, they'll go with us. It's their *shauri*. You see, they signed on for it. They don't look too happy though, do they?"

"I don't want to go in there," said Macomber. It was out before he knew he'd said it.

"Neither do I," said Wilson very cheerily. "Really no choice though." Then, as an afterthought, he glanced at Macomber and saw suddenly how he was trembling and the pitiful look on his face.

"You don't have to go in, of course," he said. "That's what I'm hired for, you know. That's why I'm so expensive."

"You mean you'd go in by yourself? Why not leave him there?"

Robert Wilson, whose entire occupation had been with the lion and the problem he presented, and who had not been thinking about Macomber except to note that he was rather windy, suddenly felt as though he had opened the wrong door in a hotel and seen something shameful.

"What do you mean?"

"Why not just leave him?"

"You mean pretend to ourselves he hasn't been hit?"

"No. Just drop it."

"It isn't done."

"Why not?"

"For one thing, he's certain to be suffering. For another, some one else might run onto him."

"I see."

"But you don't have to have anything to do with it."

"I'd like to," Macomber said. "I'm just scared, you know."

"I'll go ahead when we go in," Wilson said, "with Kongoni tracking. You keep behind me and a little to one side. Chances are we'll hear him growl. If we see him we'll both shoot. Don't worry about anything. I'll keep you backed up. As a matter of fact, you know, perhaps you'd better not go. It might be much better. Why don't you go over and join the Memsahib while I just get it over with?"

"No, I want to go."

"All right," said Wilson. "But don't go in if you don't want to. This is my *shauri* now, you know."

"I want to go," said Macomber.

They sat under a tree and smoked.

"Want to go back and speak to the Memsahib while we're waiting?" Wilson asked.

"No."

"I'll just step back and tell her to be patient."

"Good," said Macomber. He sat there, sweating under his arms, his mouth dry, his stomach hollow feeling, wanting to find courage to tell Wilson to go on and finish off the lion without him. He could not know that Wilson was furious because he had not noticed the state he was in earlier and sent him back to his wife. While he sat there Wilson came up. "I have your big gun," he said. "Take it. We've given him time, I think. Come on."

Macomber took the big gun and Wilson said:

"Keep behind me and about five yards to the right and do exactly as I tell you." Then he spoke in Swahili to the two gun-bearers who looked the picture of gloom.

"Let's go," he said.

"Could I have a drink of water?" Macomber asked. Wilson spoke to the older gun-bearer, who wore a canteen on his belt, and the man unbuckled it, unscrewed the top and handed it to Macomber, who took it noticing how heavy it seemed and how hairy and shoddy the felt covering was in his hand. He raised it to drink and looked ahead at the high grass with the flat-topped trees behind it. A breeze was blowing toward them and the grass rippled gently in the wind. He looked at the gun-bearer and he could see the gun-bearer was suffering too with fear.

Thirty-five yards into the grass the big lion lay flattened out along the ground. His ears were back and his only movement was a slight twitching up and down of his long, black-tufted tail. He had turned at bay as soon as he had reached this cover and he was sick with the wound through his full belly, and weakening with the wound through his lungs that brought a thin foamy red to his mouth each time he breathed. His flanks were wet and hot and flies were on the little openings the solid bullets had made in his tawny hide, and his big yellow eyes, narrowed with hate, looked straight ahead, only blinking when the pain came as he breathed, and his claws dug in the soft baked earth. All of him, pain, sickness, hatred and all of his remaining strength, was tightening into an absolute concentration for a rush. He could hear the men talking and he waited, gathering all of himself into this preparation for a charge as soon as the men would come into the grass. As he heard their voices his tail stiffened to twitch up and down, and, as they came into the edge of the grass, he made a coughing grunt and charged.

Kongoni, the old gun-bearer, in the lead watching the blood spoor, Wilson watching the grass for any movement, his big gun ready, the second gun-bearer looking ahead and listening, Macomber close to Wilson, his rifle cocked, they had just moved into the grass when Macomber heard the blood-choked coughing grunt, and saw the swishing rush in the grass. The next thing he knew he was running; running wildly, in panic in the open, running toward the stream.

He heard the *ca-ra-wong!* of Wilson's big rifle, and again in a second crashing *carawong!* and turning saw the lion, horrible-looking now, with half his head seeming to be gone, crawling toward Wilson in the edge of the tall grass while the red-faced man worked the bolt on the short ugly rifle and aimed carefully as another blasting *cara-wong!* came from the muzzle, and the crawling, heavy, yellow bulk of the lion stiffened and the huge, mutilated head slid forward and Macomber, standing by himself in the clearing where he had run, holding a loaded rifle, while two black men and a white man looked back at him in contempt, knew the lion was dead. He came toward Wilson, his tallness all seeming a naked reproach, and Wilson looked at him and said:

"Want to take pictures?"

"No," he said.

That was all any one had said until they reached the motor car. Then Wilson had said:

"Hell of a fine lion. Boys will skin him out. We might as well stay here in the shade."

Macomber's wife had not looked at him nor he at her and he had sat by her in the back seat with Wilson sitting in the front seat. Once he had reached over and taken his wife's hand without looking at her and she had removed her hand from his. Looking across the stream to where the gun-bearers were skinning out the lion he could see that she had been able to see the whole thing. While they sat there his wife had reached forward and put her hand on Wilson's shoulder. He turned and she had leaned forward over the low seat and kissed him on the mouth.

"Oh, I say," said Wilson, going redder than his natural baked color.

"Mr. Robert Wilson," she said. "The beautiful red-faced Mr. Robert Wilson."

Then she sat down beside Macomber again and looked away across the stream to where the lion lay, with uplifted, white-muscled, tendon-marked naked forearms, and white bloating belly, as the black men fleshed away the skin. Finally the gun-bearers brought the skin over, wet and heavy, and climbed in behind with it, rolling it up before they got in, and the motor car started. No one had said anything more until they were back in camp.

That was the story of the lion. Macomber did not know how the lion had felt before he started his rush, nor during it when the unbelievable smash of the .505 with a muzzle velocity of two tons had hit him in the mouth, nor what kept him coming after that, when the second ripping crash had smashed his hind quarters and he had come crawling on toward the crashing, blasting thing that had destroyed him. Wilson knew something about it and only expressed it by saying, "Damned fine lion," but Macomber did not know how Wilson felt about things either. He did not know how his wife felt except that she was through with him.

His wife had been through with him before but it never lasted. He was very wealthy, and would be much wealthier, and he knew she would not leave him ever now. That was one of the few things that he really knew. He knew about that, about motor cycles—that was earliest—about motor cars, about duck-shooting, about fishing, trout, salmon and big-sea, about sex in books, many books, too many books, about all court games, about dogs, not much about horses, about hanging on to his money, about most of the other things his world dealt in, and about his wife not leaving him. His wife had been a great beauty and she was still a great beauty in Africa, but she was not a great enough beauty any more at home to be able to leave him and better herself and she knew it and he knew it. She had missed the chance to leave him and he knew it. If he had been better with women she would probably have started to worry about him getting another new, beautiful wife; but she knew too much about him to worry about him either. Also, he had always had a great tolerance which seemed the nicest thing about him if it were not the most sinister.

All in all they were known as a comparatively happily married couple, one of those whose disruption is often rumored but never occurs, and as the society columnist put it, they were adding more than a spice of *adventure* to their much envied and ever-enduring *Romance* by a *Safari* in what was known as *Darkest Africa* until the Martin

Johnsons lighted it on so many silver screens where they were pursuing *Old Simba* the lion, the buffalo, *Tembo* the elephant and as well collecting specimens for the Museum of Natural History. This same columnist had reported them *on the verge* at least three times in the past and they had been. But they always made it up. They had a sound basis of union. Margot was too beautiful for Macomber to divorce her and Macomber had too much money for Margot ever to leave him.

It was now about three o'clock in the morning and Francis Macomber, who had been asleep a little while after he had stopped thinking about the lion, wakened and then slept again, woke suddenly, frightened in a dream of the bloody-headed lion standing over him, and listening while his heart pounded, he realized that his wife was not in the other cot in the tent. He lay awake with that knowledge for two hours.

At the end of that time his wife came into the tent, lifted her mosquito bar and crawled cozily into bed.

"Where have you been?" Macomber asked in the darkness.

"Hello," she said. "Are you awake?"

"Where have you been?"

"I just went out to get a breath of air."

"You did, like hell."

"What do you want me to say, darling?"

"Where have you been?"

"Out to get a breath of air."

"That's a new name for it. You *are* a bitch."

"Well, you're a coward."

"All right," he said. "What of it?"

"Nothing as far as I'm concerned. But please let's not talk, darling, because I'm very sleepy."

"You think that I'll take anything."

"I know you will, sweet."

"Well, I won't."

"Please, darling, let's not talk. I'm so very sleepy."

"There wasn't going to be any of that. You promised there wouldn't be."

"Well, there is now." she said sweetly.

"You said if we made this trip that there would be none of that. You promised."

"Yes, darling. That's the way I meant it to be. But the trip was spoiled yesterday. We don't have to talk about it, do we?"

"You don't wait long when you have an advantage, do you?"

"Please let's not talk. I'm so sleepy, darling."

"I'm going to talk."

"Don't mind me then, because I'm going to sleep." And she did.

At breakfast they were all three at the table before daylight and Francis Macomber found that, of all the many men that he had hated, he hated Robert Wilson the most.

"Sleep well?" Wilson asked in his throaty voice, filling a pipe.

"Did you?"

"Topping," the white hunter told him.

You bastard, thought Macomber, you insolent bastard.

So she woke him when she came in, Wilson thought, looking at them both with his flat, cold eyes. Well, why doesn't he keep his wife where she belongs? What does he think I am, a bloody plaster saint? Let him keep her where she belongs. It's his own fault.

"Do you think we'll find buffalo?" Margot asked, pushing away a dish of apricots.

"Chance of it," Wilson said and smiled at her. "Why don't you stay in camp?"

"Not for anything," she told him.

"Why not order her to stay in camp?" Wilson said to Macomber.

"You order her," said Macomber coldly.

"Let's not have any ordering, nor," turning to Macomber, "any silliness, Francis," Margot said quite pleasantly.

"Are you ready to start?" Macomber asked.

"Any time," Wilson told him. "Do you want the Memsahib to go?"

"Does it make any difference whether I do or not?"

The hell with it, thought Robert Wilson. The utter complete hell with it. So this is what it's going to be like. Well, this is what it's going to be like, then.

"Makes no difference," he said.

"You're sure you wouldn't like to stay in camp with her yourself and let me go out and hunt the buffalo?" Macomber asked.

"Can't do that," said Wilson. "Wouldn't talk rot if I were you."

"I'm not talking rot. I'm disgusted."

"Bad word, disgusted."

"Francis, will you please try to speak sensibly." his wife said.

"I speak too damned sensibly," Macomber said. "Did you ever eat such filthy food?"

"Something wrong with the food?" asked Wilson quietly.

"No more than with everything else."

"I'd pull yourself together, laddybuck," Wilson said very quietly. "There's a boy waits at table that understands a little English."

"The hell with him."

Wilson stood up and puffing on his pipe strolled away, speaking a few words in Swahili to one of the gun-bearers who was standing waiting for him. Macomber and his wife sat on at the table. He was staring at his coffee cup.

"If you make a scene I'll leave you, darling," Margot said quietly.

"No, you won't."

"You can try it and see."

"You won't leave me."

"No," she said. "I won't leave you and you'll behave yourself."

"Behave myself? That's a way to talk. Behave myself."

"Yes. Behave yourself."

"Why don't *you* try behaving?"

"I've tried it so long. So very long."

"I hate that red-faced swine," Macomber said. "I loathe the sight of him."

"He's really *very* nice."

"Oh, *shut up,*" Macomber almost shouted. Just then the car came up and stopped in front of the dining tent and the driver and the two gun-bearers got out. Wilson walked over and looked at the husband and wife sitting there at the table.

"Going shooting?" he asked.

"Yes," said Macomber, standing up. "Yes."

"Better bring a woolly. It will be cool in the car," Wilson said.

"I'll get my leather jacket," Margot said.

"The boy has it," Wilson told her. He climbed into the front with the driver and Francis Macomber and his wife sat, not speaking, in the back seat.

Hope the silly beggar doesn't take a notion to blow the back of my head off, Wilson thought to himself. Women *are* a nuisance on safari.

The car was grinding down to cross the river at a pebbly ford in the gray daylight and then climbed, angling up the steep bank, where Wilson had ordered a way shovelled out the day before so they could reach the parklike wooded rolling country on the far side.

It was a good morning, Wilson thought. There was a heavy dew and as the wheels went through the grass and low bushes he could smell the odor of the crushed fronds. It was an odor like verbena and he liked this early morning smell of the dew, the crushed bracken and the look of the tree trunks showing black through the early morning mist, as the car made its way through the untracked, parklike country. He had put the two in the back seat out of his mind now and was thinking about buffalo. The buffalo that he was after stayed in the daytime in a thick swamp where it was impossible to get a shot, but in the night they fed out into an open stretch of country and if he could come between them and their swamp with the car, Macomber would have a good chance at them in the open. He did not want to hunt buff with Macomber in thick cover. He did not want to hunt buff or anything else with Macomber at all, but he was a professional hunter and he had hunted with some rare ones in his time. If they got buff today there would only be rhino to come and the poor man would have gone through his dangerous game and things might pick up. He'd have nothing more to do with the woman and Macomber would get over that too. He must have gone through plenty of that before by the look of things. Poor beggar. He must have a way of getting over it. Well, it was the poor sod's own bloody fault.

He, Robert Wilson, carried a double size cot on safari to accommodate any windfalls he might receive. He had hunted for a certain clientele, the international, fast, sporting set, where the women did not feel they were getting their money's worth unless they had shared that cot with the white hunter. He despised them when he was away from them although he liked some of them well enough at the time, but he made his living by them: and their standards were his standards as long as they were hiring him.

They were his standards in all except the shooting. He had his own standards about the killing and they could live up to them or get some one else to hunt them. He knew, too, that they all respected him for this. This Macomber was an odd one though. Damned if he wasn't. Now the wife. Well, the wife. Yes, the wife. Hm, the wife. Well he'd dropped all that. He looked around at them. Macomber sat grim and furious. Margot smiled at him. She looked younger today, more innocent and fresher and not so professionally beautiful. What's in her heart God knows, Wilson thought. She hadn't talked much last night. At that it was a pleasure to see her.

The motor car climbed up a slight rise and went on through the trees and then out into a grassy prairie-like opening and kept in the shelter of the trees along the edge, the driver going slowly and Wilson looking carefully out across the prairie and all along its far side. He stopped the car and studied the opening with his field glasses. Then he motioned to the driver to go on and the car moved slowly along, the driver avoiding wart-hog holes and driving around the mud castles ants had built. Then, looking across the opening, Wilson suddenly turned and said,

"By God, there they are!"

And looking where he pointed, while the car jumped forward and Wilson spoke in rapid Swahili to the driver, Macomber saw three huge, black animals looking almost cylindrical in their long heaviness, like big black tank cars, moving at a gallop across the far edge of the open prairie. They moved at a stiff-necked, stiff bodied gallop and he could see the upswept wide black horns on their heads as they galloped heads out; the heads not moving.

"They're three old bulls," Wilson said. "We'll cut them off before they get to the swamp."

The car was going a wild forty-five miles an hour across the open and as Macomber watched, the buffalo got bigger and bigger until he could see the gray, hairless, scabby look of one huge bull and how his neck was a part of his shoulders and the shiny black of his horns as he galloped a little behind the others that were strung out in that steady plunging gait; and then, the car swaying as though it had just jumped a road, they drew up close and he could see the plunging hugeness of the bull, and the dust in his sparsely haired hide, the wide boss of horn and his outstretched, wide-nostrilled muzzle, and he was raising his rifle when Wilson shouted, "Not from the car, you fool!" and he had no fear, only hatred of Wilson, while the brakes clamped on and the car skidded, plowing sideways to an almost stop and Wilson was out on one side and he on the other, stumbling as his feet hit the still speeding-by of the earth, and then he was shooting at the bull as he moved away, hearing the bullets whunk into him, emptying his rifle at him as he moved steadily away, finally remembering to get his shots forward into the shoulder, and as he fumbled to re-load, he saw the bull was down. Down on his knees, his big head tossing, and seeing the other two still galloping he shot at the leader and hit him. He shot again and missed and he heard the *cara-wonging* roar as Wilson shot and saw the leading bull slide forward onto his nose.

"Get that other," Wilson said. "Now you're shooting!"

But the other bull was moving steadily at the same gallop and he missed, throwing a spout of dirt, and Wilson missed and the dust rose in a cloud and Wilson shouted, "Come on. He's too far!" and grabbed his arm and they were in the car again, Macomber and Wilson hanging on the sides and rocketing swayingly over the uneven ground, drawing up on the steady, plunging, heavy-necked, straight-moving gallop of the bull.

They were behind him and Macomber was filling his rifle, dropping shells onto the ground, jamming it, clearing the jam, then they were almost up with the bull when Wilson yelled "Stop," and the car skidded so that it almost swung over and Macomber fell forward onto his feet, slammed his bolt forward and fired as far forward as he could aim into the galloping, rounded black back, aimed and shot again, then again, then again, and the bullets, all of them hitting, had no effect on the buffalo that he could see. Then Wilson shot, the roar deafening him, and he could see the bull stagger. Macomber shot again, aiming carefully, and down he came, onto his knees.

"All right," Wilson said. "Nice work. That's the three."

Macomber felt a drunken elation.

"How many times did you shoot?" he asked.

"Just three," Wilson said. "You killed the first bull. The biggest one. I helped you finish the other two. Afraid they might have got into cover. You had them killed. I was just mopping up a little. You shot damn well."

"Let's go to the car," said Macomber. "I want a drink."

"Got to finish off that buff first," Wilson told him. The buffalo was on his knees and he jerked his head furiously and bellowed in pig-eyed, roaring rage as they came toward him.

"Watch he doesn't get up," Wilson said. Then, "Get a little broadside and take him in the neck just behind the ear."

Macomber aimed carefully at the center of the huge, jerking, rage-driven neck and shot. At the shot the head dropped forward.

"That does it," said Wilson. "Got the spine. They're a hell of a looking thing, aren't they?"

"Let's get the drink," said Macomber. In his life he had never felt so good.

In the car Macomber's wife sat very white faced. "You were marvellous, darling," she said to Macomber. "What a ride."

"Was it rough?" Wilson asked.

"It was frightful. I've never been more frightened in my life."

"Let's all have a drink," Macomber said.

"By all means," said Wilson. "Give it to the Memsahib." She drank the neat whisky from the flask and shuddered a little when she swallowed. She handed the flask to Macomber who handed it to Wilson.

"It was frightfully exciting," she said. "It's given me a dreadful headache. I didn't know you were allowed to shoot them from cars though."

"No one shot from cars," said Wilson coldly.

"I mean chase them from cars."

"Wouldn't ordinarily," Wilson said. "Seemed sporting enough to me though while we were doing it. Taking more chance driving that way across the plain full of holes and one thing and another than hunting on foot. Buffalo could have charged us each time we shot if he liked. Gave him every chance. Wouldn't mention it to any one though. It's illegal if that's what you mean."

"It seemed very unfair to me," Margot said, "chasing those big helpless things in a motor car."

"Did it?" said Wilson.

"What would happen if they heard about it in Nairobi?"

"I'd lose my licence for one thing. Other unpleasantnesses," Wilson said, taking a drink from the flask. "I'd be out of business."

"Really?"

"Yes, really."

"Well," said Macomber, and he smiled for the first time all day. "Now she has something on you."

"You have such a pretty way of putting things, Francis," Margot Macomber said. Wilson looked at them both. If a four-letter man marries a five-letter woman, he was thinking, what number of letters would their children be? What he said was, "We lost a gun-bearer. Did you notice it?"

"My God, no," Macomber said.

"Here he comes," Wilson said. "He's all right. He must have fallen off when we left the first bull."

Approaching them was the middle-aged gun-bearer, limping along in his knitted cap, khaki tunic, shorts and rubber sandals, gloomy-faced and disgusted looking. As he came up he called out to Wilson in Swahili and they all saw the change in the white hunter's face.

"What does he say?" asked Margot.

"He says the first bull got up and went into the bush," Wilson said with no expression in his voice.

"Oh," said Macomber blankly.

"Then it's going to be just like the lion," said Margot, full of anticipation.

"It's not going to be a damned bit like the lion," Wilson told her. "Did you want another drink, Macomber?"

"Thanks, yes," Macomber said. He expected the feeling he had had about the lion to come back but it did not. For the first time in his life he really felt wholly without fear. Instead of fear he had a feeling of definite elation.

"We'll go and have a look at the second bull," Wilson said. "I'll tell the driver to put the car in the shade."

"What are you going to do?" asked Margaret Macomber.

"Take a look at the buff," Wilson said.

"I'll come."

"Come along."

The three of them walked over to where the second buffalo bulked blackly in the open, head forward on the grass, the massive horns swung wide.

"He's a very good head," Wilson said. "That's close to a fifty-inch spread."

Macomber was looking at him with delight.

"He's hateful looking," said Margot. "Can't we go into the shade?"

"Of course," Wilson said. "Look," he said to Macomber, and pointed. "See that patch of bush?"

"Yes."

"That where the first bull went in. The gun-bearer said when he fell off the bull was down. He was watching us helling along and the other two buff galloping. When he looked up there was the bull up and looking to him. Gun-bearer ran like hell and the bull went off slowly into that bush."

"Can we go in after him now?" asked Macomber eagerly.

Wilson looked at him appraisingly. Damned if this isn't a strange one, he thought. Yesterday he's scared sick and today he's a ruddy fire eater.

"No, we'll give him a while."

"Let's please go into the shade," Margot said. Her face was white and she looked ill.

They made their way to the car where it stood under a single, wide-spreading tree and all climbed in.

"Chances are he's dead in there," Wilson remarked. "After a little we'll have a look."

Macomber felt a wild unreasonable happiness that he had never known before.

"By God, that was a chase," he said. "I've never felt any such feeling. Wasn't it marvellous, Margot?"

"I hated it."

"Why?"

"I hated it," she said bitterly. "I loathed it."

"You know I don't think I'd ever be afraid of anything again," Macomber said to Wilson. "Something happened in me after we first saw the buff and started after him. Like a dam bursting. It was pure excitement."

"Cleans out your liver," said Wilson. "Damn funny things happen to people."

Macomber's face was shining. "You know something did happen to me," he said. "I feel absolutely different."

His wife said nothing and eyed him strangely. She was sitting far back in the seat and Macomber was sitting forward talking to Wilson who turned sideways talking over the back of the front seat.

"You know, I'd like to try another lion," Macomber said. "I'm really not afraid of them now. After all, what can they do to you?"

"That's it," said Wilson. "Worst one can do is kill you. How does it go? Shakespeare. Damned good. See if I can remember. Oh, damned good. Used to quote it to myself at one time. Let's see. 'By my troth, I care not; a man can die but once; we owe God a death and let it go which way it will he that dies this year is quit for the next.' Damned fine, eh?"

He was very embarrassed, having brought out this thing he had lived by, but he had seen men come of age before and it always moved him. It was not a matter of their twenty-first birthday.

It had taken a strange chance of hunting, a sudden precipitation into action without opportunity for worrying beforehand, to bring this about with Macomber, but regardless of how it had happened it had most certainly happened. Look at the beggar now, Wilson thought. It's that some of them stay little boys so long, Wilson thought. Sometimes all their lives. Their figures stay boyish when they're fifty. The great American boy-men. Damned strange people. But he liked this Macomber now. Damned strange fellow. Probably meant the end of cuckoldry too. Well, that would be a damned good thing. Damned good thing. Beggar had probably been afraid all his life. Don't know what started it. But over now. Hadn't had time to be afraid with the buff. That and being angry too. Motor car too. Motor cars made it familiar. Be a damn fire eater now. He'd seen it in the war work the same way. More of a change than any loss of virginity. Fear gone like an operation. Something else grew in its place. Main thing a man had. Made him into a man. Women knew it too. No bloody fear.

From the far corner of the seat Margaret Macomber looked at the two of them. There was no change in Wilson. She saw Wilson as she had seen him the day before when she had first realized what his great talent was. But she saw the change in Francis Macomber now.

"Do you have that feeling of happiness about what's going to happen?" Macomber asked, still exploring his new wealth.

"You're not supposed to mention it," Wilson said, looking in the other's face. "Much more fashionable to say you're scared. Mind you, you'll be scared too, plenty of times."

"But you *have* a feeling of happiness about action to come?"

"Yes," said Wilson. "There's that. Doesn't do to talk too much about all this. Talk the whole thing away. No pleasure in anything if you mouth it up too much."

"You're both talking rot," said Margot. "Just because you've chased some helpless animals in a motor car you talk like heroes."

"Sorry," said Wilson. "I have been gassing too much." She's worried about it already, he thought.

"If you don't know what we're talking about why not keep out of it?" Macomber asked his wife.

"You've gotten awfully brave, awfully suddenly," his wife said contemptuously, but her contempt was not secure. She was very afraid of something.

Macomber laughed, a very natural hearty laugh. "You know I *have,*" he said. "I really have."

"Isn't it sort of late?" Margot said bitterly. Because she had done the best she could for many years back and the way they were together now was no one person's fault.

"Not for me," said Macomber.

Margot said nothing but sat back in the corner of the seat.

"Do you think we've given him time enough?" Macomber asked Wilson cheerfully.

"We might have a look," Wilson said. "Have you any solids left?"

"The gun-bearer has some."

Wilson called in Swahili and the older gun-bearer, who was skinning out one of the heads, straightened up, pulled a box of solids out of his pocket and brought them over to Macomber, who filled his magazine and put the remaining shells in his pocket.

"You might as well shoot the Springfield," Wilson said. "You're used to it. We'll leave the Mannlicher in the car with the Memsahib. Your gun-bearer can carry your heavy gun. I've this damned cannon. Now let me tell you about them." He had saved this until the last because he did not want to worry Macomber. "When a buff comes he comes with his head high and thrust straight out. The boss of the horns covers any sort of a brain shot. The only shot is straight into the nose. The only other shot is into his chest or, if you're to one side, into the neck or the shoulders. After they've been hit once they take a hell of a lot of killing. Don't try anything fancy. Take the easiest shot there is. They've finished skinning out that head now. Should we get started?"

He called to the gun-bearers, who came up wiping their hands, and the older one got into the back.

"I'll only take Kongoni," Wilson said, "The other can watch to keep the birds away."

As the car moved slowly across the open space toward the island of brushy trees that ran in a tongue of foliage along a dry water course that cut the open swale, Macomber felt his heart pounding and his mouth was dry again, but it was excitement, not fear.

"Here's where he went in," Wilson said. Then to the gun-bearer in Swahili, "Take the blood spoor."

The car was parallel to the patch of bush. Macomber, Wilson and the gun-bearer got down. Macomber, looking back, saw his wife, with the rifle by her side, looking at him. He waved to her and she did not wave back.

The brush was very thick ahead and the ground was dry. The middle-aged gun-bearer was sweating heavily and Wilson had his hat down over his eyes and his red neck showed just ahead of Macomber. Suddenly the gun-bearer said something in Swahili to Wilson and ran forward.

"He's dead in there," Wilson said. "Good work," and he turned to grip Macomber's hand and as they shook hands, grinning at each other, the gun-bearer shouted wildly and they saw him coming out of the bush sideways, fast as a crab, and the bull coming nose out, mouth tight closed, blood dripping, massive head straight out, coming in a charge, his little pig eyes bloodshot as he looked at them. Wilson, who was ahead was kneeling shooting, and Macomber, as he fired, unhearing his shot in the roaring of Wilson's gun, saw fragments like slate burst from the huge boss of the horns, and the head jerked, he shot again at the wide nostrils and saw the horns jolt again and fragments fly, and he did not see Wilson now and, aiming carefully, shot again with the buffalo's huge bulk almost on him and his rifle almost level with the on-coming head, nose out, and he could see the little wicked eyes and the head started to lower and he felt a sudden white-hot, blinding flash explode inside his head and that was all he ever felt.

Wilson had ducked to one side to get in a shoulder shot. Macomber had stood solid and shot for the nose, shooting a touch high each time and hitting the heavy horns, splintering and chipping them like hitting a slate roof, and Mrs. Macomber, in the car, had shot at the buffalo with the 6.5 Mannlicher as it seemed about to gore Macomber and had hit her husband about two inches up and a little to one side of the base of his skull.

Francis Macomber lay now, face down, not two yards from where the buffalo lay on his side and his wife knelt over him with Wilson beside her.

"I wouldn't turn him over," Wilson said.

The woman was crying hysterically.

"I'd get back in the car," Wilson said. "Where's the rifle?"

She shook her head, her face contorted. The gun-bearer picked up the rifle.

"Leave it as it is," said Wilson. Then, "Go get Abdulla so that he may witness the manner of the accident."

He knelt down, took a handkerchief from his pocket, and spread it over Francis Macomber's crew-cropped head where it lay. The blood sank into the dry, loose earth.

Wilson stood up and saw the buffalo on his side, his legs out, his thinly-haired belly crawling with ticks. "Hell of a good bull," his brain registered automatically. "A good fifty inches, or better. Better." He called to the driver and told him to spread a blanket over the body and stay by it. Then he walked over to the motor car where the woman sat crying in the corner.

"That was a pretty thing to do," he said in a toneless voice. "He *would* have left you too."

"Stop it," she said.

"Of course it's an accident," he said. "I know that."

"Stop it," she said.

"Don't worry," he said. "There will be a certain amount of unpleasantness but I will have some photographs taken that will be very useful at the inquest. There's the testimony of the gun-bearers and the driver too. You're perfectly all right."

"Stop it," she said.

"There's a hell of a lot to be done," he said. "And I'll have to send a truck off to the lake to wireless for a plane to take the three of us into Nairobi. Why didn't you poison him? That's what they do in England."

"Stop it. Stop it. Stop it," the woman cried.

Wilson looked at her with his fat blue eyes.

"I'm through now," he said. "I was a little angry. I'd begun to like your husband."

"Oh, please stop it," she said. "Please, please stop it."

"That's better," Wilson said. "Please is much better. Now I'll stop."

QUESTIONS

1 The story begins as a continutation of prior events. Summarize what has happened.
2 What clues does Hemingway give us to Wilson's character? Are we to admire him?
3 What is "wrong" in the relationship between Margot and Francis? (Your answer should not be simplistic.)
4 In what ways is each of the main characters a typical Hemingway character?
5 How long does Macomber "live"? Explain your answer.
6 What does Wilson think about Margot's shooting Macomber? What are we to think?

TOPICS FOR COMPOSITION

1 Write an essay in which you argue that Margot's shooting Macomber was a deliberate act; or, argue the opposite position.
2 Write an essay analyzing not only the traits of each main character but also Hemingway's relative success in bringing those traits to us.

"Night-Sea Journey" unfolds through the consciousness of the sperm as it "swims" toward union with the egg to create life as we know it. This "swimmer" likens the microcosm in which he exists to our world, embracing questions of identity, reality, purpose, ultimate goals set against the eventual mystery awaiting us at the end of the journey. As you read, note the consistency with which Barth maintains his metaphor and the fullness of his philosophical sweep.

NIGHT-SEA JOURNEY

John Barth

"One way or another, no matter which theory of our journey is correct, it's myself I address; to whom I rehearse as to a stranger our history and condition, and will disclose my secret hope though I sink for it.

"Is the journey my invention? Do the night, the sea, exist at all, I ask myself, apart from my experience of them? Do I myself exist, or is this a dream? Sometimes I wonder. And if I am, who am I? The Heritage I supposedly transport? But how can I be both vessel and contents? Such are the questions that beset my intervals of rest.

"My trouble is, I lack conviction. Many accounts of our situation seem plausible to me—where and what we are, why we swim and whither. But implausible ones as well, perhaps especially those, I must admit as possibly correct. Even likely. If at times, in certain humors—stroking in unison, say, with my neighbors and chanting with them 'Onward! Upward!'—I have supposed that we have after all a common Maker, Whose nature and motives we may not know, but Who engendered us in some mysterious wise and launched us forth toward some end known but to Him—if (for a moodslength only) I have been able to entertain such notions, very popular in certain quarters, it is because our night-sea journey partakes of their absurdity. One might even say: I can believe them *because* they are absurd.

"Has that been said before?

"Another paradox: it appears to be these recesses from swimming that sustain me in the swim. Two measures onward and upward, flailing with the rest, then I float exhausted and dispirited, brood upon the night, the sea, the journey, while the flood bears me a measure back and down: slow progress, but I live, I live, and make my way, aye, past many a drownèd comrade in the end, stronger, worthier than I, victims of their unremitting *joie de nager*. I have seen the best swimmers of my generation go under. Numberless the number of the dead! Thousands drown as I think this thought, millions as I rest before returning to the swim. And scores, hundreds of millions have expired since we surged forth, brave in our innocence, upon our dreadful way. 'Love! Love!' we sang then, a quarter-billion strong, and churned the warm sea white with joy of swimming! Now all are gone down—the buoyant, the sodden, leaders and followers, all gone under, while wretched I swim on. Yet these same reflective intervals that keep me afloat have led me into wonder, doubt, despair—strange emotions for a swimmer!—have led me, even, to suspect . . . that our night-sea journey is without meaning.

"Indeed, if I have yet to join the hosts of the suicides, it is because (fatigue apart) I find it no meaningfuller to drown myself than to go on swimming.

"I know that there are those who seem actually to enjoy the night-sea; who claim to love swimming for its own sake, or sincerely believe that 'reaching the Shore,' 'transmitting the Heritage' (*Whose* Heritage, I'd like to know? And to whom?) is worth the staggering cost. I do not. Swimming itself I find at best not actively unpleasant, more often tiresome, not infrequently a torment. Arguments from function and design don't impress me: granted that we can and do swim, that in a manner of speaking our long tails and streamlined heads are 'meant for' swimming; it by no means follows—for me, at least—that we *should* swim, or otherwise endeavor to 'fulfill our destiny.' Which is to say, Someone Else's destiny, since ours, so far as I can see, is merely to perish, one way or another, soon or late. The heartless zeal of our (departed) leaders, like the blind ambition and good cheer of my own youth, appalls me now; for the death of my comrades I am inconsolable. If the night-sea journey has justification, it is not for us swimmers ever to discover it.

"Oh, to be sure, 'Love!' one heard on every side: 'Love it is that drives and sustains us!' I translate: we don't know *what* drives and sustains us, only that we are most miserably driven and, imperfectly, sustained. *Love* is how we call our ignorance of what whips us. 'To reach the Shore,' then: but what if the Shore exists in the fancies of us swimmers merely, who dream it to account for the dreadful fact that we swim, have always and only swum, and continue swimming without respite (myself excepted) until we die? Supposing even that there *were* a Shore—that, as a cynical companion of mine once imagined, we rise from the drowned to discover all those vulgar superstitions and exalted metaphors to be literal truth: the giant Maker of us all, the Shores of Light beyond our night-sea journey!—whatever would a swimmer do there? The fact is, when we imagine the Shore, what comes to mind is just the opposite of our condition: no more night, no more sea, no more journeying. In short, the blissful estate of the drowned.

" 'Ours not to stop and think; ours but to swim and sink. . . .' Because a moment's thought reveals the pointlessness of swimming. 'No matter,' I've heard some say, even as they gulped their last: 'The night-sea journey may be absurd, but here we swim, will-we nill-we, against the flood, onward and upward, toward a Shore that may not exist and couldn't be reached if it did.' The thoughtful swimmer's choices, then, they say, are two: give over thrashing and go under for good, or embrace the absurdity; affirm in and for itself the night-sea journey; swim on with neither motive nor destination, for the sake of swimming, and compassionate moreover with your fellow swimmer, we being all at sea and equally in the dark. I find neither course acceptable. If not even the hypothetical Shore can justify a sea-full of drownèd comrades, to speak of the swim-in-itself as somehow doing so strikes me as obscene. I continue to swim—but only because blind habit, blind instinct, blind fear of drowning are still more strong than the horror of our journey. And if on occasion I have assisted a fellow-thrasher, joined in the cheers and songs, even passed along to others strokes of genius from the drownèd great, it's that I shrink by temperament from making myself conspicuous. To paddle off in one's own direction, assert one's independent right-of-way, overrun one's fellows without compunction, or dedicate oneself entirely to pleasures and diversions without regard for conscience—I can't finally condemn those who journey in this wise; in half my moods I envy them and despise the weak vitality that keeps me from following their example. But in reasonabler moments I remind myself that it's their very freedom and self-responsibility I reject, as more dramatically absurd, in our senseless circumstances, than tailing along in conventional fashion. Suicides, rebels, affirmers of the paradox—nay-sayers and yea-sayers alike to our fatal journey—I finally shake my head at them. And splash sighing past their corpses, one by one, as past a hundred sorts of others: friends, enemies, brothers; fools, sages, brutes—and nobodies, million upon million. I envy them all.

"A poor irony: that I, who find abhorrent and tautological the doctrine of survival of the fittest (*fitness* meaning, in my experience, nothing more than survival-ability, a talent whose only demonstration is the fact of survival, but whose chief ingredients seem to be strength, guile, callousness), may be the sole remaining swimmer! But the doctrine is false as well as repellent: Chance drowns the worthy with the unworthy, bears up the unfit with the fit by whatever definition, and makes the night-sea journey essentially *haphazard* as well as murderous and unjustified.

"'You only swim once.' Why bother, then?

"'Except ye drown, ye shall not reach the Shore of Life.' Poppycock.

"One of my late companions—that same cynic with the curious fancy, among the first to drown—entertained us with odd conjectures while we waited to begin our journey. A favorite theory of his was that the Father does exist, and did indeed make us and the sea we swim—but not a-purpose or even consciously; He made us, as it were, despite Himself, as we make waves with every tail-thrash, and may be unaware of our existence. Another was that He knows we're here but doesn't care what happens to us, inasmuch as He creates (voluntarily or not) other seas and swimmers at more or less regular intervals. In bitterer moments, such as just before he drowned, my friend even supposed that our Maker wished us unmade; there was indeed a Shore, he'd argue, which could save at least some of us from drowning and toward which it was our function to struggle—but for reasons unknowable to us He wanted desperately to prevent our reaching that happy place and fulfilling our destiny. Our 'Father,' in short, was our adversary and would-be killer! No less outrageous, and offensive to traditional opinion, were the fellow's speculations on the nature of our Maker: that He might well be no swimmer Himself at all, but some sort of monstrosity, perhaps even tailless; that He might be stupid, malicious, insensible, perverse, or asleep and dreaming; that the end for which He created and launched us forth, and which we flagellate ourselves to fathom, was perhaps immoral, even obscene. Et cetera, et cetera: there was no end to the chap's conjectures, or the impoliteness of his fancy; I have reason to suspect that his early demise, whether planned by 'our Maker' or not, was expedited by certain fellow-swimmers indignant at his blasphemies.

"In other moods, however (he was as given to moods as I), his theorizing would become half-serious, so it seemed to me, especially upon the subjects of Fate and Immortality, to which our youthful conversations often turned. Then his harangues, if no less fantastical, grew solemn and obscure, and if he was still baiting us, his passion undid the joke. His objection to popular opinions of the hereafter, he would declare, was their claim to general validity. Why need believers hold that *all* the drownèd rise to be judged at journey's end, and non-believers that drowning is final without exception? In *his* opinion (so he'd vow at least), nearly everyone's fate was permanent death; indeed he took a sour pleasure in supposing that every 'Maker' made thousands of separate seas in His creative life-time, each populated like ours with millions of swim-

mers, and that in almost every instance both sea and swimmers were utterly annihi-
lated, whether accidentally or by malevolent design. (Nothing if not pluralistical, he
imagined there might be millions and billions of 'Fathers,' perhaps in some 'night-sea'
of their own!) However—and here he turned infidels against him with the faithful—he
professed to believe that in possibly a single night-sea per thousand, say, one of its
quarter-billion swimmers (that is, one swimmer in two hundred fifty billions) achieved a
qualified immortality. In some cases the rate might be slightly higher; in others it was
vastly lower, for just as there are swimmers of every degree of proficiency, including
some who drown before the journey starts, unable to swim at all, and others created
drowned, as it were, so he imagined what can only be termed impotent Creators,
Makers unable to Make, as well as uncommonly fertile ones and all grades between.
And it pleased him to deny any necessary relation between a Maker's productivity and
His other virtues—including, even, the quality of His creatures.

"I could go on (*he* surely did) with his elaboration of these mad notions—such as
that swimmers in other night-seas needn't be of our kind; that Makers themselves
might belong to different *species,* so to speak; that our particular Maker mightn't
Himself be immortal, or that we might be not only His emissaries but His 'immortality,'
continuing His life and our own, transmogrified, beyond our individual deaths. Even this
modified immortality (meaningless to me) he conceived as relative and contingent,
subject to accidental or deliberate termination: his pet hypothesis was that Makers and
swimmers *each generate the other*—against all odds, their number being so great—
and that any given 'immortality-chain' could terminate after any number of cycles, so
that what was 'immortal' (still speaking relatively) was only the cyclic process of incar-
nation, which itself might have a beginning and an end. Alternatively he liked to imagine cycles within cycles, either finite or infinite: for example, the 'night-sea,' as it were,
in which Makers 'swam' and created night-seas and swimmers like ourselves, might be
the creation of a larger Maker, Himself one of many, Who in turn et cetera. Time itself
he regarded as relative to our experience, like magnitude: who knew but what, with
each thrash of our tails, minuscule seas and swimmers, whole eternities, came to
pass—as ours, perhaps, and our Maker's Maker's, was elapsing between the strokes
of some supertail, in a slower order of time?

"Naturally I hooted with the others at this nonsense. We were young then, and had
only the dimmest notion of what lay ahead; in our ignorance we imagined night-sea
journeying to be a positively heroic enterprise. Its meaning and value we never questioned; to be sure, some must go down by the way, a pity no doubt, but to win a race
requires that others lose, and like all my fellows I took for granted that I would be the
winner. We milled and swarmed, impatient to be off, never mind where or why, only to
try our youth against the realities of night and sea; if we indulged the skeptic at all, it
was a droll, half-contemptible mascot. When he died in the initial slaughter, no one
cared.

"And even now I don't subscribe to all his views—but I no longer scoff. The horror
of our history has purged me of opinions, as of vanity, confidence, spirit, charity, hope,
vitality, everything—except dull dread and a kind of melancholy, stunned persistence.
What leads me to recall his fancies is my growing suspicion that I, of all swimmers, may
be the sole survivor of this fell journey, tale-bearer of a generation. This suspicion,

together with the recent sea-change, suggests to me now that nothing is impossible, not even my late companion's wildest visions, and brings me to a certain desperate resolve, the point of my chronicling.

"Very likely I have lost my senses. The carnage at our setting out; our decimation by whirlpool, poisoned cataract, sea-convulsion; the panic stampedes, mutinies, slaughters, mass suicides; the mounting evidence that none will survive the journey— add to these anguish and fatigue; it were a miracle if sanity stayed afloat. Thus I admit, with the other possibilities, that the present sweetening and calming of the sea, and what seems to be a kind of vasty presence, song, or summons from the near upstream, may be hallucinations of disordered sensibility. . . .

"Perhaps, even, I am drowned already. Surely I was never meant for the rough-and-tumble of the swim; not impossibly I perished at the outset and have only imaged the night-sea journey from some final deep. In any case, I'm no longer young, and it is we spent old swimmers, disabused of every illusion, who are most vulnerable to dreams.

"Sometimes I think I am my drownèd friend.

"Out with it: I've begun to believe, not only that *She* exists, but that She lies not far ahead, and stills the sea, and draws me Herward! Aghast, I recollect his maddest notion: that our destination (which existed, mind, in but one night-sea out of hundreds and thousands) was no Shore, as commonly conceived, but a mysterious being, in-describable except by paradox and vaguest figure: wholly different from us swimmers, yet our complement; the death of us, yet our salvation and resurrection; simultaneously our journey's end, mid-point, and commencement; not membered and thrashing like us, but a motionless or hugely gliding sphere of unimaginable dimension; self-con-tained, yet dependent absolutely, in some wise, upon the chance (always monstrously improbable) that one of us will survive the night-sea journey and reach . . . Her! *Her,* he called it, or *She,* which is to say, Other-than-a-he. I shake my head; the thing is too preposterous; it is myself I talk to, to keep my reason in this awful darkness. There is no She! There is no You! I rave to myself; it's Death alone that hears and summons. To the drowned, all seas are calm. . . .

"Listen: my friend maintained that in every order of creation there are two sorts of creators, contrary yet complementary, one of which gives rise to seas and swimmers, the other to the Night-which-contains-the-sea and to What-waits-at-the-journey's-end: the former, in short, to destiny, the latter to destination (and both profligately, involun-tarily, perhaps indifferently or unwittingly). The 'purpose' of the night-sea journey—but not necessarily of the journeyer or of either Maker!—my friend could describe only in abstractions: *consummation, transfiguration, union, contraries, transcension of cate-gories.* When we laughed, he would shrug and admit that he understood the business no better than we, and thought it ridiculous, dreary, possibly obscene. 'But one of you,' he'd add with his wry smile, 'may be the Hero destined to complete the night-sea journey and be one with Her. Chances are, of course, you won't make it.' He himself, he declared, was not even going to try; the whole idea repelled him; if we chose to dismiss it as an ugly fiction, so much the better for us; thrash, splash, and be merry, we were soon enough drowned. But there it was, he could not say how he knew or why he bothered to tell us, any more than he could say what would happen after She and

Hero, Shore and Swimmer, 'merged identities' to become something both and neither. He quite agreed with me that if the issue of that magical union had no memory of the night-sea journey, for example, it enjoyed a poor sort of immortality; even poorer if, as he rather imagined, a swimmer-hero plus a She equaled or became merely another Maker of future night-seas and the rest, at such incredible expense of life. This being the case—he was persuaded it was—the merciful thing to do was refuse to participate; the genuine heroes, in his opinion, were the suicides, and the hero of heroes would be the swimmer who, in the very presence of the Order, refused Her proffered 'immortality' and thus put an end to at least one cycle of catastrophes.

"How we mocked him! Our moment came, we hurtled forth, pretending to glory in the adventure, thrashing, singing, cursing, strangling, rationalizing, rescuing, killing, inventing rules and stories and relationships, giving up, struggling on, but dying all, and still in darkness, until only a battered remnant was left to croak 'Onward, upward,' like a bitter echo. Then they too fell silent—victims, I can only presume, of the last frightful wave—and the moment came when I also, utterly desolate and spent, thrashed my last and gave myself over to the current, to sink or float as might be, but swim no more. Whereupon, marvelous to tell, in an instant the sea grew still! Then warmly, gently, the great tide turned, began to bear me, as it does now, onward and upward will-I, nill-I, like a flood of joy—and I recalled with dismay my dead friend's teaching.

"I am not deceived. This new emotion is Her doing; the desire that possesses me is Her bewitchment. Lucidity passes from me; in a moment I'll cry 'Love!,' bury myself in Her side, and be 'transfigured.' Which is to say, I die already; this fellow transported by passion is not I; *I am he who abjures and rejects the night-sea journey!* I. . . .

"I am all love. 'Come!' She whispers, and I have no will.

"You who I may be about to become, whatever You are: with the last twitch of my real self I beg You to listen. It is *not* love that sustains me! No; though Her magic makes me burn to sing the contrary, and though I drown even now for the blasphemy, I will say truth. What has fetched me across this dreadful sea is a single hope, gift of my poor dead comrade: that You may be stronger-willed than I, and that by sheer force of concentration I may transmit to You, along with Your official Heritage, a private legacy of awful recollection and negative resolve. Mad as it may be, my dream is that some unimaginable embodime..t of myself (or myself plus Her if that's how it must be) will come to find itself expressing, in however garbled or radical a translation, some reflection of these reflections. If against all odds this comes to pass, may You to whom, through whom I speak, do what I cannot: terminate this aimless, brutal business! Stop Your hearing against Her song! Hate love!

"Still alive, afloat, afire. Farewell then my penultimate hope: that one may be sunk for direct blasphemy on the very shore of the Shore. Can it be (my old friend would smile) that only utterest nay-sayers survive the night? But even that were Sense, and there is no sense, only senseless love, senseless death. Whoever echoes these reflections: be more courageous than their author! An end to night-sea journeys! Make no more! And forswear me when I shall forswear myself, deny myself, plunge into Her who summons, singing . . .

"'Love! Love! Love!'"

QUESTIONS

1   What clues does Barth give to the identity of his speaker?
2   Why are "night-sea" and "swimmer" metaphorically effective to both the world of the story and our world?
3   What specific sociological and religious philosophies does Barth's speaker speculate about? What are his answers? What, then, are we to conclude about this view of death?

TOPIC FOR COMPOSITION

The two short stories in this part appear quite different in many respects. Is there, however, an argumentative position, aside from the obvious idea about the inevitability of death, that is reflected in much the same way in each story? Write an essay arguing either side of the question.

DRAMA

O'Neill's "Bound East for Cardiff" emphasizes the stark loneliness and finality of death that seals the unfulfilled but yearning life. Among the simple men of the sea such a passage from life into death is indeed to be "bound east," but into terrible mystery instead of to Cardiff. In that sense, all men, like the crew of the *S.S. Glencairn,* are sailing toward some ultimate port that lies, as Hamlet says, in "The undiscover'd country, from whose bourn / No traveller returns." Yet none of the seamen knows how to respond to or even to acknowledge the fact of Yank's death; only the dying man must reckon with the reality.

1 Exits and entrances of the crew punctuate the ebbing life of Yank.
2 The presence of death establishes a real, if unstable, decorum to which each man tries to rise.
3 The bleakness of O'Neill's play is accentuated by the organic relationship of barren setting, reports of the ship's situation, the helplessness of the captain, and the inchoate speech of the crew.

BOUND EAST FOR CARDIFF

Eugene O'Neill

CHARACTERS

YANK	PAUL
DRISCOLL	SMITTY
COCKY	IVAN
DAVIS	THE CAPTAIN
SCOTTY	THE SECOND MATE
OLSON	

Scene. The seamen's forecastle of the British tramp steamer Glencairn *on a foggy night midway on the voyage between New York and Cardiff. An irregular-shaped compartment, the sides of which almost meet at the far end to form a triangle. Sleeping bunks about six feet long, ranged three deep with a space of three feet separating the upper from the lower, are built against the sides. On the right above the bunks three or four port-holes can be seen. In front of the bunks, rough wooden benches. Over the bunks on the left, a lamp in a bracket. In the left foreground, a doorway. On the floor near it, a pail with a tin dipper. Oilskins are hanging from a hook near the doorway.*

The far side of the forecastle is so narrow that it contains only one series of bunks.

In under the bunks a glimpse can be had of sea-chests, suitcases, sea-boots, etc., jammed in indiscriminately.

At regular intervals of a minute or so the blast of the steamer's whistle can be heard above all the other sounds.

Five men are sitting on the benches talking. They are dressed in dirty patched suits of dungaree, flannel shirts, and all are in their stocking feet. Four of the men are pulling on pipes and the air is heavy with rancid tobacco smoke. Sitting on the top bunk in the left foreground, a Norwegian, PAUL, *is softly playing some folk-song on a battered accordion. He stops from time to time to listen to the conversation.*

In the lower bunk in the rear a dark-haired, hard-featured man is lying apparently asleep. One of his arms is stretched limply over the side of the bunk. His face is very pale, and drops of clammy perspiration glisten on his forehead.

It is nearing the end of the dog-watch—about ten minutes to eight in the evening.

COCKY *(a weazened runt of a man. He is telling a story. The others are listening with amused, incredulous faces, interrupting him at the end of each sentence with loud derisive guffaws.)* Makin' love to me, she was! It's Gawd's truth! A bloomin' nigger! Greased all over with cocoanut oil, she was. Gawd blimey, I couldn't stand 'er. Bloody old cow, I says; and with that I fetched 'er a biff on the ear wot knocked 'er silly, an'—*(He is interrupted by a roar of laughter from the others.)*

DAVIS *(a middle-aged man with black hair and mustache)* You're a liar, Cocky.

SCOTTY *(a dark young fellow)* Ho-ho! Ye werr neverr in New Guinea in yourr life, I'm thinkin'.

OLSON *(a Swede with a drooping blond mustache—with ponderous sarcasm)* Yust tink of it! You say she wass a cannibal, Cocky?

DRISCOLL *(a brawny Irishman with the battered features of a prizefighter)* How cud ye doubt ut, Ollie? A quane av the naygurs she musta been surely. Who else wud think herself aqual to fallin' in love wid a beauthiful, divil-may-care rake av a man the loike av Cocky? *(A burst of laughter from the crowd)*

COCKY *(indignantly)* Gawd strike me dead if it ain't true, every bleedin' word of it. 'Appened ten year ago come Christmas.

SCOTTY 'Twas a Christmas dinner she had her eyes on.

DAVIS He'd a been a tough old bird.

DRISCOLL 'Tis lucky for both av ye ye escaped; for the quane av the cannibal isles wad a died av the bellyache the day afther Christmas, divil a doubt av ut. *(The laughter at this is long and loud.)*

COCKY *(sullenly)* Blarsted fat-'eads! *(The sick man in the lower bunk in the rear groans and moves restlessly. There is a hushed silence. All the men turn and stare at him.)*

DRISCOLL   Ssshh! *(In a hushed whisper)* We'd best not be talkin' so loud and him tryin' to have a bit av a sleep. *(He tiptoes softly to the side of the bunk.)* Yank! You'd be wantin' a drink av wather, maybe? *(YANK does not reply. DRISCOLL bends over and looks at him.)* It's asleep he is, sure enough. His breath is chokin' in his throat loike wather gurglin' in a poipe. *(He comes back quietly and sits down. All are silent, avoiding each other's eyes.)*

COCKY*! (after a pause)* Pore devil! It's over the side for 'im, Gawd 'elp 'im.

DRISCOLL   Stop your croakin'! He's not dead yet and, praise God, he'll have many a long day yet before him.

SCOTTY *(shaking his head doubtfully)* He's bod, mon, he's verry bod.

DAVIS   Lucky he's alive. Many a man's light woulda gone out after a fall like that.

OLSON   You saw him fall?

DAVIS   Right next to him. He and me was goin' down in number two hold to do some chippin'. He puts his leg over careless-like and misses the ladder and plumps straight down to the bottom. I was scared to look over for a minute, and then I heard him groan and I scuttled down after him. He was hurt bad inside, for the blood was drippin' from the side of his mouth. He was groanin' hard, but he never let a word out of him.

COCKY   An' you blokes remember when we 'auled 'im in 'ere? Oh, 'ell, 'e says, oh, 'ell—like that, and nothink else.

OLSON   Did the captain know where he iss hurted?

COCKY   That silly ol' josser! Wot the 'ell would 'e know abaht anythink?

SCOTTY *(scornfully)* He fiddles in his mouth wi' a bit of glass.

DRISCOLL *(angrily)* The divil's own life ut is to be out on the lonely sea wid nothin' betune you and a grave in the ocean but a spindle-shanked, gray-whiskered auld fool the loike av him. 'Twas enough to make a saint shwear to see him wid his gold watch in his hand, tryin' to look as wise as an owl on a tree, and all the toime he not knowin' whether 'twas cholery or the barber's itch was the matther with Yank.

SCOTTY *(sardonically)* He gave him a dose of salts, na doot?

DRISCOLL   Divil a thing he gave him at all, but looked in the book he had wid him, and shook his head, and walked out widout sayin' a word, the second mate afther him no wiser than himself, God's curse on the two av thim!

COCKY *(after a pause)* Yank was a good shipmate, pore beggar. Lend me four bob in Noo Yark, 'e did.

DRISCOLL *(warmly)* A good shipmate he was and is, none betther. Ye said no more than the truth, Cocky. Five years and more ut is since first I shipped wid him, and we've stuck together iver since through good luck and bad. Fights we've had, God help us, but 'twas only when we'd a bit av drink taken, and we always shook hands the nixt mornin'. Whativer was his was mine, and many's the toime I'd a been on the beach or worse, but for him. And now—*(His voice trembles as he fights to control his emotion.)* Divil take me if I'm not startin' to blubber loike an auld woman, and he not dead at all, but goin' to live many a long year yet, maybe.

DAVIS   The sleep'll do him good. He seems better now.

OLSON   If he wud eat something—

DRISCOLL Wud ye have him be eatin' in his condishun? Sure it's hard enough on the rest av us wid nothin' the matther wid our insides to be stomachin' the skoff on this rusty lime-juicer.

SCOTTY *(indignantly)* It's a starvation ship.

DAVIS Plenty o' work and no food—and the owners ridin' around in carriages!

OLSON Hash, hash! Stew, stew! Marmalade, py damn! *(He spits disgustedly.)*

COCKY Bloody swill! Fit only for swine is wot I say.

DRISCOLL And the dish-wather they disguise wid the name av tea! And the putty they call bread! My belly feels loike I'd swalleyed a dozen rivets at the thought av ut! And sea-biscuit that'd break the teeth av a lion if he had the misfortune to take a bite at one! *(Unconsciously they have all raised their voices, forgetting the sick man in their sailor's delight at finding something to grumble about.)*

PAUL *(swings his feet over the side of his bunk, stops playing his accordion, and says slowly)* And rot-ten po-tay-toes! *(He starts in playing again. The sick man gives a groan of pain.)*

DRISCOLL *(holding up his hand)* Shut your mouths, all av you. 'Tis a hell av a thing for us to be complainin' about our guts, and a sick man maybe dyin' listenin' to us. *(Gets up and shakes his fist at the Norwegian)* God stiffen you, ye square-head scut! Put down that organ av yours or I'll break your ugly face for you. Is that banshee schreechin' fit music for a sick man? *(The Norwegian puts his accordion in the bunk and lies back and closes his eyes. DRISCOLL goes over and stands beside YANK. The steamer's whistle sounds particularly loud in the silence.)*

DAVIS Damn this fog! *(Reaches in under a bunk and yanks out a pair of sea-boots, which he pulls on.)* My lookout next, too. Must be nearly eight bells, boys. *(With the exception of OLSON, all the men sitting up put on oilskins, sou'westers, sea-boots, etc., in preparation for the watch on deck. OLSON crawls into a lower bunk on the right.)*

SCOTTY My wheel.

OLSON *(disgustedly)* Nothin' but yust dirty weather all dis voyage. I yust can't sleep when weestle blow. *(He turns his back to the light and is soon fast asleep and snoring.)*

SCOTTY If this fog keeps up, I'm tellin' ye, we'll no be in Cardiff for a week or more.

DRISCOLL 'Twas just such a night as this the auld Dover wint down. Just about this toime ut was, too, and we all sittin' round in the fo'c'stle, Yank beside me, whin all av a suddint we heard a great slitherin' crash, and the ship heeled over till we was all in a heap on wan side. What came afther I disremimber exactly, except 'twas a hard shift to get the boats over the side before the auld teakittle sank. Yank was in the same boat wid me, and sivin morthal days we drifted wid scarcely a drop of wather or a bite to chew on. 'Twas Yank here that held me down whin I wanted to jump into the ocean, roarin' mad wid the thirst. Picked up we were on the same day wid only Yank in his senses, and him steerin' the boat.

COCKY *(protestingly)* Blimey but you're a cheerful blighter, Driscoll! Talkin' abaht ship-wrecks in this 'ere blushin' fog. *(YANK groans and stirs uneasily, opening his eyes. DRISCOLL hurries to his side.)*

DRISCOLL Are ye feelin' any betther, Yank?

YANK *(in a weak voice)* No.

DRISCOLL Sure, you must be. You look as sthrong as an ox. *(Appealing to the others)* Am I tellin' him a lie?

DAVIS The sleep's done you good.

COCKY You'll be 'avin your pint of beer in Cardiff this day week.

SCOTTY And fish and chips, mon!

YANK *(peevishly)* What're yuh all lyin' fur? D'yuh think I'm scared to—*(He hesitates as if frightened by the word he is about to say.)*

DRISCOLL Don't be thinkin' such things! *(The ship's bell is heard heavily tolling eight times. From the forecastle head above the voice of the lookout rises in a long wail: Aaall's welll. The men look uncertainly at* YANK *as if undecided whether to say good-by or not.)*

YANK *(in an agony of fear)* Don't leave me, Drisc! I'm dyin', I tell yuh. I won't stay here alone with everyone snorin'. I'll go out on deck. *(He makes a feeble attempt to rise, but sinks back with a sharp groan. His breath comes in wheezy gasps.)* Don't leave me, Drisc! *(His face grows white and his head falls back with a jerk.)*

DRISCOLL Don't be worryin', Yank. I'll not move a step out av here—and let that divil av a bosun curse his black head off. You speak a word to the bosun, Cocky. Tell him that Yank is bad took and I'll be stayin' wid him a while yet.

COCKY Right-o. (COCKY, DAVIS, *and* SCOTTY *go out quietly.)*

COCKY *(from the alleyway)* Gawd blimey, the fog's thick as soup.

DRISCOLL Are ye satisfied now, Yank? *(Receiving no answer, he bends over the still form.)* He's fainted, God help him! *(He gets a tin dipper from the bucket and bathes* YANK's *forehead with the water.* YANK *shudders and opens his eyes.)*

YANK *(slowly)* I thought I was goin' then. Wha' did yuh wanta wake me up fur?

DRISCOLL *(with a forced gayety)* It is wishful for heaven ye are?

YANK *(gloomily)* Hell, I guess.

DRISCOLL *(crossing himself involuntarily)* For the love av the saints don't be talkin' loike that! You'd give a man the creeps. It's chippin' rust on deck you'll be in a day or two wid the best av us. (YANK *does not answer, but closes his eyes wearily. The seaman who has been on lookout,* SMITTY, *a young Englishman, comes in and takes off his dripping oilskins. While he is doing this the man whose turn at the wheel has been relieved enters. He is a dark burly fellow with a round stupid face. The Englishman steps softly over to* DRISCOLL. *The other crawls into a lower bunk.)*

SMITTY *(whispering)* How's Yank?

DRISCOLL Betther. Ask him yourself. He's awake.

YANK I'm all right, Smitty.

SMITTY Glad to hear it, Yank. *(He crawls to an upper bunk and is soon asleep.)*

IVAN *(the stupid-faced seaman, who comes in after* SMITTY, *twists his head in the direction of the sick man.)* You feel gude, Jank?

YANK *(wearily)* Yes, Ivan.

IVAN Dot's gude. *(He rolls over on his side and falls asleep immediately.)*

YANK *(after a pause broken only by snores—with a bitter laugh)* Good-by and good luck to the lot of you!

DRISCOLL Is ut painin' you again?

YANK   It hurts like hell—here. (*He points to the lower part of his chest on the left side.*) I guess my old pump's busted. Ooohh! (*A spasm of pain contracts his pale features. He presses his hand to his side and writhes on the thin mattress of his bunk. The perspiration stands out in beads on his forehead.*)

DRISCOLL (*terrified*)   YANK! Yank! What is ut? (*Jumping to his feet*) I'll run for the captain. (*He starts for the doorway.*)

YANK (*sitting up in his bunk, frantic with fear*)   Don't leave me, Drisc! For God's sake don't leave me alone! (*He leans over the side of his bunk and spits.* DRISCOLL *comes back to him.*) Blood! Ugh!

DRISCOLL   Blood again! I'd best be gettin' the captain.

YANK   No, no, don't leave me! If yuh do I'll git up and follow you. I ain't no coward, but I'm scared to stay here with all of them asleep and snorin'. (DRISCOLL, *not knowing what to do, sits down on the bench beside him. He grows calmer and sinks back on the mattress.*) The captain can't do me no good, yuh know it yourself. The pain ain't so bad now, but I thought it had me then. It was like a buzz-saw cuttin' into me.

DRISCOLL (*fiercely*)   God blarst ut!

(*The* CAPTAIN *and the* SECOND MATE *of the steamer enter the forecastle. The* CAPTAIN *is an old man with gray mustache and whiskers. The* MATE *is clean-shaven and middle-aged. Both are dressed in simple blue uniforms.*)

THE CAPTAIN (*taking out his watch and feeling* YANK'S *pulse*)   And how is the sick man?

YANK (*feebly*)   All right, sir.

THE CAPTAIN   And the pain in the chest?

YANK   It still hurts, sir, worse than ever.

THE CAPTAIN (*taking a thermometer from his pocket and putting it into* YANK'S *mouth*)   Here. Be sure and keep this in under your tongue, not over it.

THE MATE (*after a pause*)   Isn't this your watch on deck, Driscoll?

DRISCOLL   Yes, sorr, but Yank was fearin' to be alone, and—

THE CAPTAIN   That's all right, Driscoll.

DRISCOLL   Thank ye, sorr.

THE CAPTAIN (*stares at his watch for a moment or so; then takes the thermometer from* YANK'S *mouth and goes to the lamp to read it. His expression grows very grave. He beckons the* MATE *and* DRISCOLL *to the corner near the doorway.* YANK *watches them furtively. The* CAPTAIN *speaks in a low voice to the* MATE.) Way up, both of them. (*To* DRISCOLL) He has been spitting blood again?

DRISCOLL   Not much for the hour just past, sorr, but before that—

THE CAPTAIN   A great deal?

DRISCOLL   Yes, sorr.

THE CAPTAIN   He hasn't eaten anything?

DRISCOLL   No, sorr.

THE CAPTAIN   Did he drink that medicine I sent him?

DRISCOLL   Yes, sorr, but it didn't stay down.

THE CAPTAIN *(shaking his head)* I'm afraid—he's very weak. I can't do anything else for him. It's too serious for me. If this had only happened a week later we'd be in Cardiff in time to—

DRISCOLL Plaze help him some way, sorr!

THE CAPTAIN *(impatiently)* But, my good man, I'm not a doctor. *(More kindly as he sees DRISCOLL's grief)* You and he have been shipmates a long time?

DRISCOLL Five years and more, sorr.

THE CAPTAIN I see. Well, don't let him move. Keep him quiet and we'll hope for the best. I'll read the matter up and send him some medicine, something to ease the pain, anyway. *(Goes over to YANK)* Keep up your courage! You'll be better tomorrow. *(He breaks down lamely before YANK's steady gaze).* We'll pull you through all right—and—hm—well—coming, Robinson? Dammit! *(He goes out hurriedly, followed by the MATE.)*

DRISCOLL *(trying to conceal his anxiety)* Didn't I tell you you wasn't half as sick as you thought you was? The Captain'll have you out on deck cursin' and swearin' loike a trooper before the week is out.

YANK Don't lie, Drisc. I heard what he said, and if I didn't I c'd tell by the way I feel. I know what's goin' to happen. I'm goin' to—*(He hesitates for a second—then resolutely)* I'm goin' to die, that's what, and the sooner the better!

DRISCOLL *(wildly)* No, and be damned to you, you're not. I'll not let you.

YANK It ain't no use, Drisc. I ain't got a chance, but I ain't scared. Gimme a drink of water, will yuh, Drisc? My throat's burnin' up. *(DRISCOLL brings the dipper full of water and supports his head while he drinks in great gulps.)*

DRISCOLL *(seeking vainly for some word of comfort)* Are ye feelin' more aisy-loike now?

YANK Yes—now—when I know it's all up. *(A pause)* You mustn't take it so hard, Drisc. I was just thinkin' it ain't as bad as people think—dyin'. I ain't never took much stock in the truck them skypilots preach. I ain't never had religion; but I know whatever it is what comes after it can't be no worser'n this. I don't like to leave you, Drisc, but—that's all.

DRISCOLL *(with a groan)* Lad, lad, don't be talkin'.

YANK This sailor life ain't much to cry about leavin'—just one ship after another, hard work, small pay, and bum grub; and when we git into port, just a drunk endin' up in a fight, and all your money gone, and then ship away again. Never meetin' no nice people; never gittin' outa sailor-town, hardly, in any port; travelin' all over the world and never seein' none of it; without no one to care whether you're alive or dead. *(With a bitter smile)* There ain't much in all that that'd make yuh sorry to lose it, Drisc.

DRISCOLL *(gloomily)* It's a hell av a life, the sea.

YANK *(musingly)* It must be great to stay on dry land all your life and have a farm with a house of your own with cows and pigs and chickens, 'way in the middle of the land where yuh'd never smell the sea or see a ship. It must be great to have a wife, and kids to play with at night after supper when your work was done. It must be great to have a home of your own, Drisc.

DRISCOLL *(with a great sigh)*   It must, surely; but what's the use av thinkin' av ut? Such things are not for the loikes av us.

YANK   Sea-farin' is all right when you're young and don't care, but we ain't chickens no more, and somehow, I dunno, this last year has seemed rotten, and I've had a hunch I'd quit—with you, of course—and we'd save our coin, and go to Canada or Argentine or some place and git a farm, just a small one, just enough to live on. I never told yuh this, 'cause I thought you'd laugh at me.

DRISCOLL *(enthusiastically)*   Laugh at you, is ut? When I'm havin' the same thoughts myself, toime afther toime. It's a grand idea and we'll be doin' ut sure if you'll stop your crazy notions—about—about bein' so sick.

YANK *(sadly)*   Too late. We shouldn'ta made this trip, and then—How'd all the fog git in here?

DRISCOLL   Fog?

YANK   Everything looks misty. Must be my eyes gittin' weak, I guess. What was we talkin' of a minute ago? Oh, yes, a farm. It's too late. *(His mind wandering)* Argentine, did I say? D'yuh remember the times we've had in Buenos Aires? The moving pictures in Barracas? Some class to them, d'yuh remember?

DRISCOLL *(with satisfaction)*   I do that; and so does the piany player. He'll not be forgettin' the black eye I gave him in a hurry.

YANK   Remember the time we was there on the beach and had to go to Tommy Moore's boarding house to git shipped? And he sold us rotten oilskins and sea-boots full of holes, and shipped us on a skysail-yarder round the Horn, and took two months' pay for it. And the days we used to sit on the park benches along the Paseo Colon with the vigilantes lookin' hard at us? And the songs at the Sailor's Opera where the guy played ragtime—d'yuh remember them?

DRISCOLL   I do, surely.

YANK   And La Plata—phew, the stink of the hides! I always liked Argentine—all except that booze, caña. How drunk we used to git on that, remember?

DRISCOLL   Cud I forget ut? My head pains me at the menshun av that divil's brew.

YANK   Remember the night I went crazy with the heat in Singapore? And the time you was pinched by the cops in Port Said? And the time we was both locked up in Sydney for fightin'?

DRISCOLL   I do so.

YANK   And that fight on the dock at Cape Town—*(His voice betrays great inward perturbation.)*

DRISCOLL *(hastily)*   Don't be thinkin' av that now. 'Tis past and gone.

YANK   D'yuh think He'll hold it up against me?

DRISCOLL *(mystified)*   Who's that?

YANK   God. They say He sees everything. He must know it was done in fair fight, in self-defense, don't yuh think?

DRISCOLL   Av course. Ye stabbed him, and be damned to him, for the skulkin' swine he was, afther him tryin' to stick you in the back, and you not suspectin'. Let your conscience be aisy. I wisht I had nothin' blacker than that on my sowl. I'd not be afraid av the angel Gabriel himself.

YANK *(with a shudder)* I c'd see him a minute ago with the blood spurtin' out of his neck. Ugh!

DRISCOLL The fever, ut is, that makes you see such things. Give no heed to ut.

YANK *(uncertainly)* You don't think He'll hold it up agin me—God, I mean.

DRISCOLL If there's justice in hiven, no! *(YANK seems comforted by this assurance.)*

YANK *(after a pause)* We won't reach Cardiff for a week at least. I'll be buried at sea.

DRISCOLL *(putting his hands over his ears)* Ssshh! I won't listen to you.

YANK *(as if he had not heard him)* It's as good a place as any other, I s'pose—only I always wanted to be buried on dry land. But what the hell'll I care—then? *(Fretfully)* Why should it be a rotten night like this with that damned whistle blowin' and people snorin' all round? I wish the stars was out, and the moon, too; I c'd lie out on deck and look at them, and it'd make it easier to go—somehow.

DRISCOLL For the love av God don't be talkin' loike that!

YANK Whatever pay's comin' to me yuh can divvy up with the rest of the boys; and you take my watch. It ain't worth much, but it's all I've got.

DRISCOLL But have you no relations at all to call your own?

YANK No, not as I know of. One thing I forgot: You know Fanny the barmaid at the Red Stork in Cardiff?

DRISCOLL Sure, and who doesn't?

YANK She's been good to me. She tried to lend me half a crown when I was broke there last trip. Buy her the biggest box of candy yuh c'n find in Cardiff. *(Breaking down—in a choking voice)* It's hard to ship on this voyage I'm goin' on—alone! *(DRISCOLL reaches out and grasps his hand. There is a pause, during which both fight to control themselves.)* My throat's like a furnace. *(He gasps for air)* Gimme a drink of water, will yuh, Drisc? *(DRISCOLL gets him a dipper of water.)* I wish this was a pint of beer. Oooohh! *(He chokes, his face convulsed with agony, his hands tearing at his shirt-front. The dipper falls from his nerveless fingers.)*

DRISCOLL For the love av God, what is ut, Yank?

YANK *(speaking with tremendous difficulty)* S'long, Drisc! *(He stares straight in front of him with eyes starting from their sockets)* Who's that?

DRISCOLL Who? What?

YANK *(faintly)* A pretty lady dressed in black. *(His face twitches and his body writhes in a final spasm, then straightens out rigidly.)*

DRISCOLL *(pale with horror)* Yank! Yank! Say a word to me for the love av hiven! *(He shrinks away from the bunk, making the sign of the cross. Then comes back and puts a trembling hand on YANK's chest and bends closely over the body.)*

COCKY *(from the alleyway)* Oh, Driscoll! Can you leave Yank for arf a mo' and give me a 'and?

DRISCOLL *(with a great sob)* Yank! *(He sinks down on his knees beside the bunk, his head on his hands. His lips move in some half-remembered prayer.)*

COCKY *(enters, his oilskins and sou'wester glistening with drops of water)* The fog's lifted. *(COCKY sees DRISCOLL and stands staring at him with open mouth. DRISCOLL makes the sign of the cross again.)*

COCKY *(mockingly)*   Sayin' 'is prayers! *(He catches sight of the still figure in the bunk and an expression of awed understanding comes over his face. He takes off his dripping sou'wester and stands, scratching his head.)*

COCKY *(in a hushed whisper)*   Gawd blimey!

CURTAIN

QUESTIONS

1   What can we infer of the dimensions of a seaman's life from Cocky's elliptical story of his experience with the woman in New Guinea, the frequent blowing of the whistle, the complaints about tea and the captain, the fog, the adventures of Driscoll and Yank in Buenos Aires and Barracas?

2   How does O'Neill indicate that we are to consider such fragments of a lifetime against the impending death of Yank?

3   Do you think the play justifies sentimentality as the only adequate response to Yank's death and to the situation of the crew? If not, how does it avoid sentimentality?

TOPICS FOR COMPOSITION

1   Describe the means, including dialogue, by which O'Neill emphasizes the somber situation of a death at sea.

2   Defend the captain's attitude and manner in the face of Yank's obviously looming death.

3   Out of the relatively small cast of characters and the minimal dialogue allotted to each character, classify the kinds of responses to Yank's dying.

POETRY

Every common attitude toward death has found vital expression in poetry. The poems of this section, while they do not by any means represent adequately the whole range of significantly varying views, illustrate some of the most notable differences of opinion on the subject. At the same time, there are enough resemblances among them to make possible a kind of classification which may be of some use in analysis. We can begin with the reflection that just as the fact of death affects in some way everyone's attitude toward life, so do our general responses to life shape our views of death. For example, people who have found life richly rewarding may be able, as Robert Louis Stevenson's "Requiem" suggests, along with Keats's "To Autumn" and William Carlos Williams' "To Waken an Old Lady," to accept death without much complaint and without much questioning, while those who have found life harrowing or frustrating may be inclined, like the speaker in Swinburne's "The Garden of Proserpine," to look to death as a means of escape.

All of the poets so far mentioned seem to have reconciled themselves to the idea of death as annihilation. Most people, however, have found just enough of good and evil in life—especially moral good and evil—to make them hope for something better beyond. Probably (for some would doubtless argue the point) the greatest triumphs of the sense of moral value have been achieved with the support of traditional religion; and no more eloquent testimony of the power of religious belief has been offered than we find in such poems as John Donne's mighty "Hymn to God, My God, in My Sickness," Henry Vaughan's poignant "They Are All Gone into the World of Light," and Gerard Manley Hopkins' sweetly thoughtful "The Caged Skylark."

Often, of course, unreflective preoccupation with the manifold pursuits of life keeps death from being, except on rare occasions, a complete reality. For young people, absorbing the fact of personal mortality is naturally difficult and sometimes profoundly shocking; Wordsworth's brief poem "A Slumber Did My Spirit Seal" speaks volumes on this score. And many supposedly mature people try, consciously or unconsciously, to avoid facing the ultimate fact. Donald Hall's "My Son, My Executioner" touches on this theme.

Then there is the complete opposite of such evasion: the desire to achieve an imaginative confrontation with death as a means of exploring and testing one's attitudes toward life. Many of us, regardless of age or religious inclinations, are so oriented as to find that undertaking more or less distasteful; yet it can be rewarding, and those interested can find encouragement and assistance in poetry—in such poems, for example, as Thomas Hardy's "Friends Beyond" and Theodore Roethke's "The Far Field." Hardy evidently thinks that living with the constant awareness that all our personal ambitions are mocked by death might not be a frustrating and desolating experience, as one would suppose, but rather a liberating one—whether humanizing or not, he cannily leaves his readers to judge. And Roethke assures us that by heeding his dreams of dead-end journeys he has come to see that "all things finite reveal infinitude"—and has at the same time learned not to fear infinity, the "far field" to which his journeys of imagination take him.

At this point it should be evident that classification of this kind is most useful when it is most difficult. All good poetry, like all experience of much value, combines uniqueness with universality.

From THE TEMPEST[1]

William Shakespeare

Our revels now are ended. These our actors,
As I foretold you, were all spirits, and
Are melted into air, into thin air;
And, like the baseless fabric of this vision,
The cloud-capp'd towers, the gorgeous palaces,   5
The solemn temples, the great globe itself,
Yea, all which it inherit, shall dissolve
And, like this insubstantial pageant faded,
Leave not a rack behind. We are such stuff
As dreams are made on, and our little life   10
Is rounded with a sleep.

1623

[1] Act IV, 1, 148–158. Prospero, a magician, has summoned up spirits in the form of reapers and nymphs to perform a dance for the entertainment of his guests.
4 fabric: unsubstantial material.   *9 rack:* cloud.   *11 rounded:* surrounded, framed.

HYMN TO GOD, MY GOD, IN MY SICKNESS

John Donne

Since I am coming to that holy room,
   Where, with thy choir of saints for evermore,
I shall be made thy music; as I come
   I tune the instrument here at the door,
     And what I must do then, think here before.   5

Whilst my physicians by their love are grown
   Cosmographers, and I their map, who lie

Flat on this bed, that by them may be shown
    That this is my south-west discovery
    Per fretum febris, by these straits to die,   10

I joy, that in these straits, I see my west;
    For though their currents yield return to none,
What shall my west hurt me? As west and east
    In all flat maps (and I am one) are one,
    So death doth touch the Resurrection.   15

Is the Pacific Sea my home? Or are
    The eastern riches? Is Jerusalem?
Anyan, and Magellan, and Gibraltar,
    All straits, and none but straits, are ways to them,
    Whether where Japhet dwelt, or Cham, or Shem.   20
We think that Paradise and Calvary,
    Christ's cross, and Adam's tree, stood in one place;
Look, Lord, and find both Adams met in me;
    As the first Adam's sweat surrounds my face,
    May the last Adam's blood my soul embrace.   25

So, in his purple wrapp'd, receive me, Lord,
    By these his thorns give me his other crown;
And as to others' souls I preach'd thy word,
    Be this my text, my sermon to mine own,
    Therefore that he may raise, the Lord throws down.   30

                    1635

9 discovery: The reference is to the discovery of the Straits of Magellan.   *10 Per fretum febris:* through the straits of fever.   *11 west:* i.e., the end of his life—and his own realm of discovery. *18 Anyan:* the Bering Straits.   *20 Japhet, Cham, Shem:* the sons of Noah. The descendants of Japhet inhabited Europe, those of Ham, Africa, and those of Shem, Asia. See Genesis 10.

QUESTIONS

1 What is the point of resemblance between physicians and cosmographers that Donne has in mind?
2 With what is the discovery of new lands equated?
3 Why is it appropriate to compare sailing through straits with the experience of dying?
4 Is the wittiness of Donne's metaphors in keeping with the seriousness of the theme? How would you describe the poet's attitude toward his imminent death?

THEY ARE ALL GONE INTO THE WORLD OF LIGHT!

Henry Vaughan

They are all gone into the world of light!
    And I alone sit lingering here;
Their very memory is fair and bright,
    And my sad thoughts doth clear.

It glows and glitters in my cloudy breast   5
    Like stars upon some gloomy grove,
Or those faint beams in which this hill is dressed
    After the sun's remove.

I see them walking in an air of glory,
    Whose light doth trample on my days;   10
My days, which are at best but dull and hoary,
    Mere glimmering and decays.

O holy hope, and high humility,
    High as the heavens above!
These are your walks, and you have showed them me   15
    To kindle my cold love.

Dear, beauteous death! the jewel of the just,
    Shining nowhere but in the dark;
What mysteries do lie beyond thy dust,
    Could man outlook that mark!   20

He that hath found some fledged bird's nest may know
    At first sight if the bird be flown;
But what fair well or grove he sings in now,
    That is to him unknown.

And yet, as angels in some brighter dreams   25
    Call to the soul when man doth sleep,
So some strange thoughts transcend our wonted themes,
    And into glory peep.

If a star were confined into a tomb,
    Her captive flames must needs burn there;   30
But when the hand that locked her up gives room,
    She'll shine through all the sphere.

4: i.e., the memory of them brightens my thoughts.   20 *outlook that mark:* see beyond that limit.
23 *well:* spring.

O Father of eternal life, and all
  Created glories under Thee!
Resume Thy spirit from this world of thrall   35
  Into true liberty!

Either disperse these mists, which blot and fill
  My perspective still as they pass;
Or else remove me hence unto that hill
  Where I shall need no glass.   40

                         1655

QUESTIONS

1 Where is the speaker? What time of day is it?
2 How many metaphors involving light or vision or both are there in this poem?

A SLUMBER DID MY SPIRIT SEAL

William Wordsworth

A slumber did my spirit seal;
  I had no human fears:
She seemed a thing that could not feel
  The touch of earthly years.

No motion has she now, no force;   5
  She neither hears nor sees;
Rolled round in earth's diurnal course,
  With rocks, and stones, and trees.
                1800

7 diurnal: daily.

QUESTIONS

1 What is the paradox which this poem expresses?
2 What is the tone of this poem? Try reading it aloud, with expression.

TO AUTUMN

John Keats

1

Season of mists and mellow fruitfulness,
   Close bosom-friend of the maturing sun;
Conspiring with him how to load and bless
   With fruit the vines that round the thatch-eaves run;
To bend with apples the mossed cottage-trees,   5
   And fill all fruit with ripeness to the core;
      To swell the gourd, and plump the hazel shells
   With a sweet kernel; to set budding more,
And still more, later flowers for the bees,
Until they think warm days will never cease,   10
      For Summer has o'er-brimmed their clammy cells.

2

Who hath not seen thee oft amid thy store?
   Sometimes whoever seeks abroad may find
Thee sitting careless on a granary floor,
   Thy hair soft-lifted by the winnowing wind;   15
Or on a half-reaped furrow sound asleep,
   Drowsed with the fume of poppies, while thy hook
      Spares the next swath and all its twinéd flowers:
And sometimes like a gleaner thou dost keep
   Steady thy laden head across a brook;   20
   Or by a cider-press, with patient look,
      Thou watchest the last oozings hours by hours.

3

Where are the songs of Spring? Aye, where are they?
   Think not of them, thou hast thy music too—
While barréd clouds bloom the soft-dying day,   25
   And touch the stubble-plains with rosy hue;
Then in a wailful choir the small gnats mourn
   Among the river sallows, borne aloft
      Or sinking as the light wind lives or dies;
And full-grown lambs loud bleat from hilly bourn;   30
   Hedge crickets sing; and now with treble soft
   The redbreast whistles from a garden-croft;
      And gathering swallows twitter in the skies.
September 19, 1819

15 *winnowing:* blowing the chaff from the grain.   17 *hook:* sickle.   28 *sallows:* small willows.
30 *bourn:* field.   32 *croft:* an enclosed plot.

QUESTIONS

1 Here the atmosphere of an autumn day becomes the perfect expression of a human mood. In other words, nature is humanized. How does the succession of ways in which the poet "sees" autumn figure in this process?
2 In poetry, autumn is commonly used as a symbol of impending death as well as fulfillment. What features of the last stanza reinforce that traditional symbolic suggestion?

THE GARDEN OF PROSERPINE

A. C. Swinburne

Here, where the world is quiet;
  Here, where all trouble seems
Dead winds' and spent waves' riot
  In doubtful dreams of dreams;
I watch the green field growing   5
For reaping folk and sowing,
For harvest-time and mowing,
  A sleepy world of streams.

I am tired of tears and laughter,
  And men that laugh and weep;   10
Of what may come hereafter
  For men that sow to reap:
I am weary of days and hours,
Blown buds of barren flowers,
Desires and dreams and powers   15
  And everything but sleep.

Here life has death for a neighbour,
  And far from eye or ear
Wan waves and wet winds labour,
  Weak ships and spirits steer;   20
They drive adrift, and whither
They wot not who make thither;
But no such winds blow hither,
  And no such things grow here.

No growth of moor or coppice,   25
  No heather-flower or vine,

Title: Proserpine, in ancient myth, is queen of the underworld. Thus her garden is the dwelling place of the dead.

But bloomless buds of poppies,
  Green grapes of Proserpine,
Pale beds of blowing rushes
Where no leaf blooms or blushes   30
Save this whereout she crushes
  For dead men deadly wine.

Pale, without name or number,
  In fruitless fields of corn,
They bow themselves and slumber   35
  All night till light is born;
And like a soul belated,
In hell and heaven unmated,
By cloud and mist abated
  Comes out of darkness morn.   40

Though one were strong as seven,
  He too with death shall dwell,
Nor wake with wings in heaven,
  Nor weep for pains in hell;
Though one were fair as roses,   45
His beauty clouds and closes,
And well though love reposes,
  In the end it is not well.

Pale, beyond porch and portal,
  Crowned with calm leaves, she stands   50
Who gathers all things mortal
  With cold immortal hands;
Her languid lips are sweeter
Than love's who fears to greet her
To men that mix and meet her   55
  From many times and lands.

She waits for each and other,
  She waits for all men born;
Forgets the earth her mother,
  The life of fruits and corn;   60
And spring and seed and swallow
Take wing for her and follow
Where summer song rings hollow
  And flowers are put to scorn.

There go the loves that wither,   65
  The old loves with wearier wings;

And all dead years draw thither,
   And all disastrous things;
Dead dreams of days forsaken,
Blind buds that snows have shaken,   70
Wild leaves that winds have taken
   Red strays of ruined springs.

We are not sure of sorrow,
   And joy was never sure;
To-day will die to-morrow;   75
   Time stoops to no man's lure;
And love, grown faint and fretful,
With lips but half regretful
Sighs, and with eyes forgetful
   Weeps that no loves endure.   80

From too much love of living,
   From hope and fear set free,
We thank with brief thanksgiving
   Whatever gods may be
That no life lives for ever;   85
That dead men rise up never;
That even the weariest river
   Winds somewhere safe to sea.

Then star nor sun shall waken,
   Nor any change of light: 90
Nor sound of waters shaken,
   Nor any sound or sight:
Nor wintry leaves nor vernal,
Nor days nor things diurnal;
Only the sleep eternal   95
   In an eternal night.

1866

QUESTIONS

1 By means of the garden metaphor the poet describes a state of mind in which the thought of becoming extinct is more than acceptable. If you were asked to explain this state of mind in more ordinary terms, what facts would you emphasize? Does the speaker, for example, make any distinctions in speaking of human ambitions and desires? Does he think that moral desires matter more than others? Does he feel that he is different from other people? What has brought him to his present state of mind?

2 Do you find the rhyme scheme appropriate? Explain the effect that it has on you.

REQUIEM

Robert Louis Stevenson

Under the wide and starry sky
Dig the grave and let me lie:
Glad did I live and gladly die,
And I laid me down with a will.
This be the verse you grave for me: 5
Here he lies where he long'd to be;
Home is the sailor, home from the sea,
And the hunter home from the hill.
                            1887

QUESTIONS

1   What does the poet mean by the line "Here he lies where he long'd to be"? In what
    sense is he "home"? Can you imagine any resemblance between the feelings of a
    sailor returning home from the sea and those of a man nearing the end of the whole
    adventure of life?
2   "Home," it seems, is anywhere under the "wide and starry" sky. What does this
    suggest about the speaker's attitude toward life? What does the word "starry" add
    to the meaning or effect?

THE CAGED SKYLARK

Gerard Manley Hopkins

As a dare-gale skylark scanted in a dull cage
    Man's mounting spirit in his bone-house, mean house, dwells—
    That bird beyond the remembering his free fells;
This in drudgery, day-labouring-out life's age.

Thou aloft on turf or perch or poor low stage,   5
    Both sing sometimes the sweetest, sweetest spells,
    Yet both droop deadly sómetimes in their cells
Or wring their barriers in bursts of fear or rage.

Not that the sweet-fowl, song-fowl, needs not rest—
Why, hear him, hear him babble and drop down to his nest,   10
    But his own nest, wild nest, no prison.

2 bone-house: the body.   *5 turf:* A mound of turf is usually put inside a lark's cage. "Poor low
state" may refer both to a shelf in a cage and any human situation.

Man's spirit will be flesh-bound when found at best,
But uncumbered: meadow-down is not distressed
  For a rainbow footing it nor he for his bónes rísen.
1918 (Composed 1877)

13 uncumbered: Hopkins is referring to the Catholic doctrine which states that the resurrected body is immortal and not subject to physical limitations.

QUESTIONS

1 What precisely are the implications of the analogy between an uncaged skylark and the condition of man after resurrection?
2 Do you think that in comparing the spirit in its earthly condition with a caged bird, the poet is thinking only of the limitations of the body? Explain.

VITAE SUMMA BREVIS SPEM NOS VETAT INCOHARE LONGAM

Ernest Dowson

They are not long, the weeping and the laughter,
    Love and desire and hate:
I think they have no portion in us after
      We pass the gate.

They are not long, the days of wine and roses: 5
    Out of a misty dream
Our path emerges for a while, then closes
      Within a dream.
1896

The title of this poem is taken from one of Horace's odes. It may be translated: "The briefness of life forbids us to nourish prolonged hope."

QUESTIONS

1 At first glance the poet's choice of his title might seem merely pretentious. Can you make a case for saying that it constitutes part of the meaning of the poem?
2 Does the reference of "they" in the repeated phrase change, or is the poet merely describing the same experience in different words?

FRIENDS BEYOND

Thomas Hardy

William Dewy, Tranter Reuben, Farmer Ledlow late at plough,
    Robert's kin, and John's, and Ned's,
And the Squire, and Lady Susan, lie in Mellstock churchyard now!

"Gone," I call them, gone for good, that group of local hearts and heads;
    Yet at mothy curfew-tide,   5
And at midnight when the noon-heat breathes it back from walls and leads,

They've a way of whispering to me—fellow-wight who yet abide—
    In the muted, measured note
Of a ripple under archways, or a lone cave's stillicide:

"We have triumphed: this achievement turns the bane to antidote,   10
    Unsuccesses to success,
Many thought-worn eves and morrows to a morrow free of thought.

"No more need we corn and clothing, feel of old terrestrial stress;
    Chill detraction stirs no sigh;
Fear of death has even bygone us: death gave all that we possess."   15

W. D.—"Ye mid burn the old bass-viol that I set such value by."
Squire.—"You may hold the manse in fee,
    You may wed my spouse, may let my children's memory of me die."

Lady S.—"You may have my rich brocades, my laces; take each household key;
    Ransack coffer, desk, bureau;   20
    Quiz the few poor treasures hid there, con the letters kept by me."

Far.—"Ye mid zell my favourite heifer, ye mid let the charlock grow,
    Foul the grinterns, give up thrift."
Far. Wife.—"If ye break my best blue china, children, I shan't care or ho."

All.—"We've no wish to hear the tidings, how the people's fortunes shift;   25
    What your daily doings are;
    Who are wedded, born, divided; if your lives beat slow or swift.

1 tranter: a tranter is a carrier.   *6 leads:* the lead coverings of roofs.   *9 stillicide:* the dripping of water.   *10 bane:* poison.   *16 mid:* may.   *17 hold the manse in fee:* have title to my house.   *22 charlock:* a kind of weed.   *23 grinterns:* compartments of a granary.

Curious not the least are we if our intents you make or mar,
     If you quire to our old tune,
If the City stage still passes, if the weirs still roar afar."   30

—Thus, with very gods' composure, freed those crosses late and soon
     Which, in life, the Trine allow
(Why, none witteth), and ignoring all that haps beneath the moon.

William Dewy, Tranter Reuben, Farmer Ledlow late at plough.
     Robert's kin, and John's, and Ned's,   35
And the Squire, and Lady Susan, murmur mildly to me now.

1898

30 weirs . . . afar: the reference is to the noisy turbulence of streams diverted by dams.   *32 trine:* trinity.

QUESTIONS

1 The poet implies that death was his friends' greatest achievement. Is he suggesting that they are better off dead because they were failures?
2 These people are dead, yet "still abide," the poet imagines. Is he suggesting that their sense of triumph might be achieved before death? Would it come through complete indifference? Does the poet himself feel complete indifference?

TO WAKEN AN OLD LADY

William Carlos Williams

Old age is
a flight of small
cheeping birds
skimming
bare trees   5
above a snow glaze
Gaining and failing
they are buffetted
by a dark wind—
But what?   10
On harsh weedstalks
the flock has rested,
the snow
is covered with broken
seedhusks   15
and the wind tempered
by a shrill
piping of plenty.
     1938

QUESTIONS

1 The poet says that old age is like a flight of small, cheeping birds in winter, buf-fetted by a dark wind. Is he talking about a mental process? What might the dark wind represent?

2 Although the scene remains the same, the implications change after the eighth line. The wind is now tempered (put in tune?) by a "shrill piping of plenty." What might the aged mind feed upon?

INTIMATIONS OF MORTALITY

Phyllis McGinley

On being told by the dentist that "this will be over soon"

Indeed, it will soon be over, I shall be done
    With the querulous drill, the forceps, the clove-smelling cotton.
I can go forth into fresher air, into sun,
    This narrow anguish forgotten.

In twenty minutes or forty or half an hour,   5
    I shall be easy, and proud of my hard-got gold.
But your apple of comfort is eaten by worms, and sour.
    Your consolation is cold.

This will not last, and the day will be pleasant after.
    I'll dine tonight with a witty and favorite friend.   10
No doubt tomorrow I shall rinse my mouth with laughter.
    And also that will end.

The handful of time that I am charily granted
    Will likewise pass, to oblivion duly apprenticed.
Summer will blossom and autumn be faintly enchanted.   15
    Then time for the grave, or the dentist.

Because you are shrewd, my man, and your hand is clever,
    You must not believe your words have a charm to spell me.
There was never a half of an hour that lasted forever.
    Be quiet. You need not tell me.   20

1950

QUESTIONS

1 The speaker in this poem imagines telling the dentist that although his statement "This will soon be over" is true, his consolation is cold. What is the reason?

2   The speaker (in her mind) tells the dentist that he must not believe that his words have a charm to spell her. What do "charm" and "spell" mean here? In what way might his words cast a spell over her?

THE VACUUM

Howard Nemorov

The house is so quiet now
The vacuum cleaner sulks in the corner closet,
Its bag limp as a stopped lung, its mouth
Grinning into the floor, maybe at my
Slovenly life, my dog-dead youth.   5

I've lived this way long enough,
But when my old woman died her soul
Went into that vacuum cleaner, and I can't bear
To see the bag swell like a belly, eating the dust
And the woolen mice, and begin to howl   10

Because there is old filth everywhere
She used to crawl, in the corner and under the stair.
I know now how life is cheap as dirt,
And still the hungry, angry heart
Hangs on and howls, biting at air.   15

1960

QUESTIONS

1   The "vacuum" of the title is of course the sense of emptiness the speaker has felt since the death of his wife. But his sense of emptiness is the more nearly complete because he now associates the vacuum cleaner with the woman's role. What is his present estimate of the quality of her life?
2   How does the poet describe his present mental condition?

THE FAR FIELD

Theodore Roethke

I

I dream of journeys repeatedly:
Of flying like a bat deep into a narrowing tunnel,
Of driving alone, without luggage, out a long peninsula,
The road lined with snow-laden second growth,
A fine dry snow ticking the windshield,   5
Alternate snow and sleet, no on-coming traffic,
And no lights behind, in the blurred side-mirror,
The road changing from glazed tarface to a rubble of stone,
Ending at last in a hopeless sand-rut,
Where the car stalls,   10
Churning in a snowdrift
Until the headlights darken.

II

At the field's end, in the corner missed by the mower,
Where the turf drops off into a grass-hidden culvert,
Haunt of the cat-bird, nesting-place of the field-mouse,   15
Not too far away from the ever-changing flower-dump,
Among the tin cans, tires, rusted pipes, broken machinery,—
One learned of the eternal;
And in the shrunken face of a dead rat, eaten by rain and ground-beetles
(I found it lying among the rubble of an old coal bin)   20
And the tom-cat, caught near the pheasant-run,
Its entrails strewn over the half-grown flowers,
Blasted to death by the night watchman.

I suffered for birds, for young rabbits caught in the mower,
My grief was not excessive.   25
For to come upon warblers in early May
Was to forget time and death:
How they filled the oriole's elm, a twittering restless cloud, all one morning,
And I watched and watched till my eyes blurred from the bird shapes—
Cape May, Blackburnian, Cerulean,—   30
Moving, elusive as fish, fearless,
Hanging, bunched like young fruit, bending the end branches,
Still for a moment,
Then pitching away in half-flight,
Lighter than finches,   35
While the wrens bickered and sang in the half-green hedgerows,
And the flicker drummed from his dead tree in the chicken yard.

—Or to lie naked in sand,
In the silted shallows of a slow river,
Fingering a shell, 40
Thinking:
Once I was something like this, mindless,
Or perhaps with another mind, less peculiar;
Or to sink down to the hips in a mossy quagmire;
Or, with skinny knees, to sit astride a wet log, 45
Believing:
I'll return again,
As a snake or a raucous bird,
Or, with luck, as a lion.

I learned not to fear infinity, 50
The far field, the windy cliffs of forever,
The dying of time in the white light of tomorrow.
The wheel turning away from itself,
The sprawl of the wave,
The on-coming water. 55

III

The river turns on itself,
The tree retreats into its own shadow.
I feel a weightless change, a moving forward
As of water quickening before a narrowing channel
When banks converge, and the wide river whitens; 60
Or when two rivers combine, the blue glacial torrent
And the yellowish-green from the mountainy upland,—
At first a swift rippling between rocks,
Then a long running over flat stones
Before descending to the alluvial plain, 65
To the clay banks, and the wild grapes hanging from the elmtrees,
The slightly trembling water
Dropping a fine yellow silt where the sun stays;
And the crabs bask near the edge,
The weedy edge, alive with small snakes and bloodsuckers,— 70

I have come to a still, but not a deep center,
A point outside the glittering current;
My eyes stare at the bottom of a river.
At the irregular stones, iridescent sandgrains,
My mind moves in more than one place, 75
In a country half-land, half-water.

I am renewed by death, thought of my death,
The dry scent of a dying garden in September,
The wind fanning the ash of a low fire.
What I love is near at hand,   80
Always, in earth and air.

IV

The lost self changes,
Turning toward the sea,
A sea shape turning around,—
An old man with his feet before the fire,   85
In robes of green, in garments of adieu.

A man faced with his own immensity
Wakes all the waves, all their loose wandering fire.
The murmur of the absolute, the why
Of being born fails on his naked ears.   90
His spirit moves like monumental wind
That gentles on a sunny blue plateau.
He is the end of things, the final man.

All finite things reveal infinitude:
The mountain with its singular bright shade   95
Like the blue shine on freshly frozen snow,
The after-light upon ice-burdened pines;
Odor of basswood on a mountain-slope,
A scent beloved of bees;
Silence of water above a sunken tree: 100
The pure serene of memory in one man,—
A ripple widening from a single stone
Winding around the waters of the world.

1962

QUESTIONS

1 Can you distinguish the turns of thought indicated by the section divisions in this
   poem? Does the last section recall the first?
2 Why is the speaker renewed by the thought of his death? Is it something he looks
   forward to that inspires him?
3 Would you describe the speaker as a mystic?

MY SON, MY EXECUTIONER

Donald Hall

My son, my executioner,
  I take you in my arms,
Quiet and small and just astir,
  And whom my body warms.

Sweet death, small son, our instrument   5
  Of immortality,
Your cries and hungers document
  Our bodily decay.

We twenty-five and twenty-two,
  Who seemed to live forever,   10
Observe enduring life in you
  And start to die together.

                              1969

QUESTIONS

1 When this poem was first published, it had a fourth stanza:

  I take into my arms the death
    Maturity exacts,
  And name with my imperfect breath
    The mortal paradox.

  Can you see why the poet decided to eliminate this stanza?
2 Put into your own words the paradox with which the poem deals.
3 Do you think that the title is in keeping with the tone of the poem?

TOPICS FOR COMPOSITION

1 Using one or more of the preceding poems for illustration or support, write an essay on the subject of coping with the fear of death.
2 Analyze the use of the analogy between death and sleep in one or more of the poems of this unit.
3 Defend the opinion that traditional moral ideals are meaningless without belief in an afterlife.
4 Defend the opinion that people can live good and happy lives without believing in life after death.
5 Is suicide ever justifiable? Give the reasons for your answer.
6 Suppose that Hardy's "friends beyond" discovered that they had to resume their earthly roles a while longer. Would they be inclined to behave differently? Present your speculations in an essay, along with what you think is the moral of the poem.

7 Write an essay on life as a process of dying.
8 What topics should a college course on the study of death include? Explain your choices briefly.
9 Write an essay on poetic ideas of life after death.
10 Do a close analysis of Nemerov's "The Vacuum."
11 Discuss the use of analogy in the poems of this unit.
12 Discuss briefly the relations between the sections of Roethke's "The Far Field."
13 Discuss the stages of development in Keats's description of autumn.

TOPICS FOR LONGER COMPOSITIONS

1 Consider the poems in Part Six as statements about the way in which ideas about death may affect the quality of life. Look for similar statements that reflect a sort of universality when viewed in the context of the chronological breadth and differing origins of the poets. You may enlarge your essay to include showing the relation between ideas in the poems and the philosophical position seen in Kierkegaard's "Despair Is 'The Sickness Unto Death.'"
2 In an essay of a number of well-developed paragraphs which support your position with relevant details—a paragraph or two to introduce the idea and to state the process by which you plan to develop it; a number of paragraphs in which you examine the parts of the idea (the process of analysis); and a conclusion in which you try to convince your reader of the rightness of your idea and of your strategy for developing it—explain how the setting of a ship at sea (O'Neill's play, specifically) complements or enhances the contemplation of the mystery of death.
3 O'Neill's play and Hemingway's story use a limited number of characters to present a range of human sensibilities; especially as the characters view life, death, death-in-life, etc. Compare and contrast the authors' use of a limited number of characters and judge how well each succeeds in presenting a range of sensibilities satisfactory to us.

ACKNOWLEDGMENTS

W. H. Auden, "The Unknown Citizen." Copyright 1946 and renewed 1968 by W. H. Auden, and "A Summer Night." Copyright 1937 by Random House, Inc., and renewed 1965 by W. H. Auden. Both reprinted from *W. H. Auden: Collected Poems* by W. H. Auden, edited by Edward Mendelson, by permission of Random House, Inc.

John Barth, "Night-Sea Journey," from *Lost in the Funhouse* by John Barth. Copyright © 1966 by John Barth. Reprinted by permission of Doubleday & Company, Inc.

Donald Barthelme, "Engineer-Private Paul Klee Misplaces an Aircraft between Milbertshofen and Cambrai," from *Sadness* by Donald Barthelme. Copyright © 1971 by Donald Barthelme. Reprinted by permission of Farrar, Straus & Giroux, Inc. This story originally appeared in *The New Yorker.*

Philip Booth, "Cold-Water Flat," from *Letter from a Distant Land* by Philip Booth. Copyright © 1953 by Philip Booth. Reprinted by permission of The Viking Press, Inc.

John Briggs, "Yukon 1897: Price of Gold," from *New American Poetry* by Richard Monaco. Copyright © 1973 by McGraw-Hill Book Company. Reprinted by permission of McGraw-Hill Book Company.

Gwendolyn Brooks, "We Real Cool," from *The World of Gwendolyn Brooks* by Gwendolyn Brooks. Copyright © 1959 by Gwendolyn Brooks. Reprinted by permission of Harper & Row, Inc.

Mervyn Cadwallader, "Marriage as a Wretched Institution." Copyright © 1966 by The Atlantic Monthly Company, Boston, Mass. Reprinted with permission.

E. E. Cummings, "anyone lived in a pretty how town." Copyright 1940 by E. E. Cummings; renewed 1968 by Marion Morehouse Cummings. "pity this busy monster,manunkind." Copyright 1944 by E. E. Cummings; renewed 1972 by Nancy T. Andrews. Both reprinted from *Complete Poems 1913–1962* by E. E. Cummings by permission of Harcourt Brace Jovanovich, Inc.

Barbara Davis, "Elevators," from *New American Poetry,* edited by Richard Monaco. Copyright 1973 by McGraw-Hill, Inc. Used with permission of McGraw-Hill Book Company.

Emily Dickinson, "She Rose to His Requirement." Reprinted by permission of the publishers and the Trustees of Amherst College from *The Poems of Emily Dickinson,* edited by Thomas H. Johnson, Cambridge, Massachusetts: The Belknap Press of Harvard University Press. Copyright © 1951, 1955, 1979 by the President and Fellows of Harvard College.

Ernest Dowson, "Vitae Summa Brevis Spem Nos Vetat Incohare Longam," from *The Poetical Works of Ernest Dowson,* edited by Desmond Flower. Reprinted by permission of Associated University Presses, Inc.

Paul Laurence Dunbar, "We Wear the Mask," from *The Complete Poems of Paul Laurence Dunbar.* Published and reprinted by permission of Dodd, Mead & Co.

Lord Dunsany, "The Glittering Gate." Copyright © by Little, Brown & Company; renewed 1941 by Lord Dunsany (Edward John Moreton Drax Plunkett). Reprinted by permission of Samuel F. French, Inc.

Paul Engle, "The Writer on Writing," from *On Creative Writing,* ed. Paul Engle. Copyright © 1963, 1964 by Paul Engle. Reprinted by permission of the publisher, E. P. Dutton.

William Faulkner, "Two Soldiers," from *Collected Stories of William Faulkner.* Copyright 1942 and renewed 1970 by Estelle Faulkner and Jill Faulkner Summers. Reprinted by permission of Random House, Inc.

Lawrence Ferlinghetti, "Christ Climbed Down" and "Constantly Risking Absurdity," both from *A Coney Island of the Mind* by Lawrence Ferlinghetti. Copyright 1958 by Lawrence Ferlinghetti. Reprinted by permission of New Directions Publishing Corporation.

Erich Fromm, "The Theory of Love," excerpt from pp. 20–31, from *The Art of Loving* by Erich Fromm. Volume 9 of the World Perspective Series, edited by Ruth Nanda Anshen. Copyright 1956 by Erich Fromm. Reprinted by permission of Harper & Row, Publishers, Inc.

Mary Gordon, "The Dead Ladies," from *New American Poetry,* edited by Richard Monaco. Copyright 1973 by McGraw-Hill, Inc. Used with permission of McGraw-Hill Book Company.

Donald Hall, "My Son, My Executioner," from *The Alligator Bride* by Donald Hall. Copyright 1969 by Donald Hall. Reprinted by permission of the author.

Thomas Hardy, "Neutral Tones" and "Friends Beyond," from *Collected Poems* by Thomas Hardy. Copyright 1925 by Macmillan Publishing Company, Inc.

Marianne Moore, "Poetry," from *Collected Poems* by Marianne Moore. Copyright © 1935 by Marianne Moore. Renewed 1963 by Marianne Moore and T. S. Eliot. Reprinted by permission of Macmillan Publishing Co., Inc.

Howard Nemerov, "Boom!" from *New and Selected Poems* by Howard Nemerov. Copyright The University of Chicago, 1960. Reprinted by permission of the Margot Johnson Agency. "The Vacuum" from *The Collected Poems of Howard Nemerov*. University of Chicago Press, 1977. Reprinted by permission of the author.

Joyce Carol Oates, "An Interior Monologue," from *The Wheel of Love and Other Stories* by Joyce Carol Oates. Copyright © 1969, 1970 by Joyce Carol Oates. Reprinted by permission of the publisher, Vanguard Press, Inc.

Flannery O'Connor, "The Life You Save May Be Your Own." Reprinted from her volume, *A Good Man Is Hard to Find and Other Stories*. Copyright © 1953, by Flannery O'Connor. Reprinted by permission of Harcourt Brace Jovanovich, Inc.

Eugene O'Neill, "Bound East For Cardiff," copyright 1919 and renewed 1947 by Eugene O'Neill. Reprinted from *The Plays of Eugene O'Neill*, by Eugene O'Neill, by permission of Random House, Inc.

Robert Pack, "A Bird in Search of a Cage," from *Poets of Today, II; The Irony of Joy: Poems* by Robert Pack. Copyright 1955 by Robert Pack. Reprinted by permission of Charles Scribner's Sons.

Vance Packard, "Molding Super Consumers . . .," from *The People Shapers* by Vance Packard. Copyright 1977 by Vance Parkard. By permission of Little, Brown and Company.

Louis Phillips, "78 Miners in Mannington, West Virginia." Reprinted from *Prologue Magazine*.

Sylvia Plath, "Point Shirley" and "Sculptor." Copyright © 1959 by Sylvia Plath. Reprinted from *The Colossus and Other Poems*, by Sylvia Plath, by permission of Alfred A. Knopf, Inc., and Miss Olwyn Hughes.

Alastair Reid, "Curiosity," from *Weathering* by Alastair Reid, published by E. P. Dutton. Copyright 1978. Reprinted by permission of the author.

Adrienne Rich, "Living in Sin," reprinted from *Poems, Selected and New, 1950–1974*, by Adrienne Rich, with permission of W. W. Norton & Company, Inc. Copyright © 1955 by Adrienne Rich. Copyright © 1975, 1973, 1971, 1969, 1966, by W. W. Norton & Company, Inc.

Richard Rive, "The Bench," from *African Voices*, ed. P. Rutherford. Copyright 1958 Grosset & Dunlap.

Gail Rock, "Same Time, Same Station, Same Sexism," from *Ms.*, Vol. 2, No. 6, December 1973. Copyright Ms. Foundation for Education and Communication, Inc., 1973. Reprinted by permission.

Theodore Roethke, "A Far Field" and "I Knew a Woman," from *The Collected Poems of Theodore Roethke*. Copyright © 1962 by Beatrice Roethke. Reprinted by permission of Doubleday & Company, Inc.

Philip Roth, "The Conversion of the Jews," from *Goodbye Columbus* by Philip Roth. Copyright © 1959 by Philip Roth. Reprinted by permission of the publisher, Houghton Mifflin Company.

William Saroyan, "Hello Out There," from *Razzle-Dazzle* by William Saroyan. Copyright by William Saroyan. Published by Harcourt, Brace and World, Company. Reprinted by permission of the author. All rights reserved.

Karl Shapiro, "Drug Store," from *Collected Poems 1940–1978* by Karl Shapiro. Copyright 1941 and renewed 1969 by Karl Shapiro. Reprinted by permission of Random House, Inc.

Irwin Shaw, "Pattern of Love," excerpted from the book *Short Stories: Five Decades* by Irwin Shaw. Copyright © 1937, 1938, 1939, 1940, 1941, 1942, 1944, 1945, 1946, 1947, 1949, 1950, 1952, 1953, 1954, 1955, 1956, 1957, 1958, 1961, 1963, 1964, 1967, 1968, 1969, 1971, 1973, 1977, 1978 by Irwin Shaw. Published by Delacorte Press. Reprinted by permission of Irwin Shaw.

Joel Sloman, "Blueprint." By permission of the author.

William Jay Smith, "American Primitive," from *New and Selected Poems* by William Jay Smith. Copyright © 1953 by William Jay Smith. Reprinted by permission of Delacorte Press/Seymour Lawrence.

Edmund Spenser, Sonnet 79 and selection from Book II, Canto VII from *The Complete Poetical Works of Spenser*, published by Houghton Mifflin Company. Copyright 1908 by Houghton Mifflin Company. Copyright 1936 by R. E. Neil Dodge. Reprinted by permission of the publisher.

Wallace Stevens, "Of Modern Poetry," from *The Collected Poems of Wallace Stevens* by Wallace Stevens. Copyright 1942 by Wallace Stevens; renewed 1970 by Holly Stevens. Reprinted by permission of Alfred A. Knopf, Inc.

Melvin G. Storm, translator of "The Wanderer" from Old English, especially for *Literary Reflections.*

A. C. Swinburne, "The Garden of Proserpine," from *Complete Works of Algernon Charles Swinburne,* William Heinemann, Ltd., 1925.

R. S. Thomas, "Anniversary" and "Poetry for Supper," from *Song at the Year's Turning: Poems 1942–1954* by R. S. Thomas. Reprinted by permission of the publisher, Granada Publishing Ltd.

B. Traven, "Assembly Line," from *The Night Visitors and Other Stories* by B. Traven. Copyright © 1966 by B. Traven. Reprinted by permission of Farrar, Straus & Giroux, Inc.

John Updike, "Ex-Basketball Player," from *The Carpentered Hen and Other Tame Creatures* by John Updike. Copyright © 1957 by John Updike. Reprinted by permission of Harper & Row, Publishers, Inc.

John Wain, "Poem Feigned to Have Been Written by an Electronic Brain," from *Word Carved on a Sill* by John Wain. Reprinted by permission of Curtis Brown Ltd., London.

Robert Penn Warren, "Goodwood Comes Back," from his volume *The Circus in the Attic.* Copyright © 1941, 1969 by Robert Penn Warren. By permission of Harcourt Brace Jovanovich, Inc.

William Carlos Williams, "To Waken an Old Lady," from *Collected Earlier Poems* by William Carlos Williams. Copyright 1938 by New Directions Publishing Corporation. Reprinted by permission of New Directions.

William Butler Yeats, "A Prayer for My Daughter" and "The Leaders of the Crowd," from *Later Poems* by William Butler Yeats. Copyright 1924 by Macmillan Publishing Co., Inc. Renewed 1952 by Bertha Georgie Yeats. "Sailing to Byzantium" from *Collected Poems* by William Butler Yeats. Copyright 1928 by Macmillan Publishing Co., Inc. Renewed 1956 by Bertha Georgie Yeats. Both reprinted in the United States with permission of The Macmillan Company. Canadian rights granted by permission of William Butler Yeats, Miss Anne Yeats, and Macmillan Co. of Canada.

BIOGRAPHICAL INDEX

Arnold, Matthew (1822–1888). English poet, critic, essayist, who tried to express a middle note between Tennyson's lyricism and Browning's intellectualism. In quest of security, he nevertheless faced the difficult issues of his day—science vs. religion, democracy vs. the old aristocratic order, idealism vs. skepticism. His characteristic poems—"Thyrsis," "Rugby Chapel," "Westminster Abbey," and "Dover Beach"—balance melancholy and stoicism.

Auden, Wystan Hugh (1907–1973). English poet, who migrated to the United States in 1939 and became an American citizen in 1946. With wit, irony, and resolute honesty, a typical Auden poem displays modernist expression of the most troubling issues for Western civilization in the middle decades of this century. His best-known poems appear in *Collected Shorter Poems* (1966) and *Collected Longer Poems* (1968).

Barth, John (1930–   ). American fiction writer whose novels and short stories are noted for the sort of inventiveness best seen in his collection *Lost in the Funhouse: Fiction for Print, Tape, Live Voice* (1968) and in his novel *Giles Goat-Boy* (1966). Other works include *The Sot-Weed Factor* (1960) and *Chimera* (1972).

Barthelme, Donald (1931–   ). American novelist and short-story writer whose works are noted for their experimental nature and their assault on modern culture or the lack thereof. Works include *Come Back Dr. Caligari* (1964; stories), *Snow White* (1967; novel), *Unspeakable Practices, Unnatural Acts* (1968; stories), *Sadness* (1972; stories), and *The Dead Father* (1975; novel).

Blake, William (1757–1827). English poet and artist, whose early training as an engraver led to his appealing illustrations in his own writings. Often laden with complex and highly personal symbolism, Blake's poems—the most familiar are in *Songs of Innocence* (1789) and *Songs of Experience* (1794)—decry injustice, rationalism, and repressions of the feelings.

Booth, Philip (1925–   ). American poet who has received numerous prizes and awards. He has taught English at Bowdoin College, Wellesley College, and Syracuse University. He was a staff member at the University of New Hampshire Writers' Conference in 1955 and 1961 and at Tufts University Poets' Workshop in 1960.

Briggs, John (1945–   ). Pseudonym, William Cassegrain. American poet, screenwriter, teacher, and editor of poetry and quarterly journals. Published *The Logic of Poetry* (1974; with Richard Monaco). Contributes poetry to various journals.

Brooks, Gwendolyn (1917–   ). American poet and novelist born in Topeka, Kansas. The main theme of her work is the black-white relationship. Her first book of poetry, *A Street in Bronzeville* (1945), brought her a $1000 award from the American Academy of Arts and Letters. For *Annie Allen*, a volume of poetry published in 1949, she received the Pulitzer Prize. In private life she is Mrs. Henry Blakely.

Browning, Robert (1812–1889). English poet, whose mastery of the dramatic monologue in such finely wrought pieces as "My Last Duchess" and "The Bishop Orders His Tomb at St. Praxed's Church" influenced Ezra Pound and T. S. Eliot. His masterpiece by general consent is *The Ring and the Book* (1869), which tells a murder story of seventeenth-century Italy from the viewpoints of several characters.

Burns, Robert (1759–1796). Scottish poet, in whose sensibility were blended Romantic ardor, lyric impulse, shrewd observation of folk and dialect, and satiric bent. He is primarily remembered as the author of such short poems as "Flow Gently, Sweet Afton," "Auld Lang Syne," "Comin' Thro' the Rye," and "My Heart's in the Highlands."

Byron, Lord George Gordon Noel (1788–1824). The most notorious English Romantic poet, whose temperament, manner, and personal appearance became the model for what was called the "Byronic hero," and whose love affairs and separation from his wife created unparalleled scandals. His most ambitious Romantic narrative poem is *Childe Harold* (1812–1818), but most readers today prefer his long satire *Don Juan* (1819–1824).

Cadwallader, Mervyn (1925–   ). American sociologist, academician, and writer. Now vice-chancellor of the University of Wisconsin-Platteville, he maintains scholarly interests in the sociology of higher education, social movements, and social change. Writings include articles in the *American Journal of Sociology* and the *Atlantic Monthly*.

Carnegie, Andrew (1835–1919). Immigrated to America from Scotland. In America he became a wealthy manufacturing tycoon, philanthropist, donor of libraries, and author. His writings "celebrate" the benefits of capitalistic democracy. His works include *Triumphant Democracy* (1886) and *The Gospel of Wealth and Other Timely Essays* (1900).

Cartwright, William (1611–1643). English poet, playwright, clergyman, and friend of Ben Jonson. An ardent royalist and famous in his time, Cartwright is known slightly today.

Clough, Arthur Hugh (1819–1861). English poet, teacher at Oxford and Harvard, friend of Matthew Arnold and Ralph Waldo Emerson, Clough was a religious skeptic, moralist, and thinker who deplored nineteenth-century materialism and smugness. His dissatisfaction with his time is reflected in poems like "Say Not the Struggle Naught Availeth" and "The Latest Decalogue."

Coleridge, Samuel Taylor (1772–1834). English poet, man of letters, and, with William Wordsworth, theorist and model for English Romanticism in their jointly conceived and written *Lyrical Ballads* (1798). His *Biographia Literaria* (1815) summarizes his ideas and role. His best poems are "The Rime of the Ancient Mariner," "Christabel," "Kubla Khan," and "Dejection: An Ode."

Cowper, William (1731–1800). English poet who, despite bouts of madness, achieved much esteem, especially among members of the middle class, for his piety, domestic sentiment, and humanitarianism. With the clergyman John Newman he wrote the still widely familiar *Olney Hymns*. His masterpiece, *The Task,* is a long meditative poem in blank verse.

Crane, Stephen (1871–1900). American poet, short-story writer, novelist, and journalist. Generally credited with pioneering American literary naturalism, which viewed humankind at the mercy of forces beyond its control. His works include *Maggie, A Girl of the Streets* (1893), *The Red Badge of Courage* (1895), and a volume of poetry, *The Black Riders* (1895).

Cummings, Edward Estlin (1894–1962). American poet and occasional painter, who preferred his name printed as "e.e. cummings" and who experimented, often brilliantly, with typography, grammar, syntax, and punctuation. In a period dominated by erudite, elegant, often difficult verse, Cummings celebrated romantic individualism, youthful rapture, and fragile innocence. His two-volume *Collected Poems* appeared in 1968.

Davis, Barbara (1949–   ). Graduate of Barnard College, teacher, sometime newspaperwoman, and poet. Her major interest is in projects combining poetry with music, dance, and film. She has been involved in writing workshops, among them the Black Writers' Workshop of San Francisco in 1972, and has contributed to anthologies.

Dickinson, Emily (1830–1886). Widely acclaimed poet and enigmatic, secluded resident of Amherst, Massachusetts. Her poems seem to range beyond her possible experiences in probing agony, ecstasy, the mystery of nature, and the moment of death. The standard edition of her poems is Thomas Johnson, ed., *The Poems of Emily Dickinson* (3 vols.; 1955).

Donne, John (1572–1631). Chief among the late Elizabethan and Jacobean English Metaphysical poets, Donne sought position at court but finally chose ordination as an Anglican priest. His early poetry—witty, profound, difficult, paradoxical, sometimes obscure—emphasized "profane love" and intense intellectualism. Later, as he became a highly celebrated preacher, his poetry, like his sermons, focused on death, penitence, damnation, and mystical union with God.

Dowson, Ernest (1867–1900). English poet who was, along with William Butler Yeats, a prominent member of The Rhymers' Club, a group of Bohemian poets who were partly responsible for the application of the term "Decadence" to the 1890s. He was much influenced by French and Latin writers. His principal work, *Verses,* came out in 1896.

Dunbar, Paul Laurence (1872–1906). American poet, novelist, and short-story writer. He was born in Dayton, Ohio, the son of parents who had both been slaves. After the publication of *Lyrics of Lowly Life* in 1896, Dunbar became one of America's most popular poets. He died of tuberculosis at thirty-three, having written nineteen books.

Dunsany, Lord Edward John Moreton Drax Plunkett (1878–1957). Anglo-Irish poet, dramatist, short-story writer, sportsman, soldier, adventurer, and devotee of fantasy and the supernatural. His plays include *The Gods of the Mountain* (1911) and *The Golden Doom* (1912).

Engle, Paul (1908–   ). American poet, novelist, and teacher. A Rhodes scholar, he was a contemporary of poets W. H. Auden, Stephen Spender, and C. Day Lewis. His works include *Worn Earth* (1932; first volume of poetry), *A Woman Unashamed, and Other Poems* (1965), and a novel, *Always the Land* (1941).

Faulkner, William (1897–1963). American novelist, short-story writer, and poet (his last book of poems is *A Green Bough* [1933]). Recipient of the Nobel Prize. Creator of Yoknapatawpha County, Mississippi, whose inhabitants participate in a decaying, often violent, "genteel" South. His nineteen novels include *The Sound and the Fury* (1929), *Sanctuary* (1931), *Absalom, Absalom!* (1936), and *The Reivers* (1962).

Ferlinghetti, Lawrence (1919–   ). Best known as an American poet and satirist of a world gone wrong. He has written a novel, *Her* (1960), and published collections of his experimental dramas in 1963 and 1964. His volumes of poetry include *Pictures of a Gone World* (1955), *A Coney Island of the Mind* (1958), *An Eye on the World: Selected Poems* (1967), and *Open Eye, Open Heart* (1973).

Fromm, Erich (1900–1980). Born in Germany, he came to America in 1934 and subsequently became a naturalized citizen. His many writings in the fields of psychoanalysis, philosophy, and religion span almost fifty years and include such works as *Psychoanalysis and Religion* (1950), *The Art of Loving* (1956), *The Nature of Man* (1968), and *To Have or To Be?* (1976).

Gordon, Mary (1949–   ). American poet and recently successful novelist. *Final Payments* (1978), her first novel, received critical acclaim. Her poetry has appeared in several anthologies.

Hall, Donald (1928–   ). American poet, literary and art critic, and writer of fiction for children. He taught English at the University of Michigan from 1957 to 1976. He has edited, in collaboration, several anthologies of contemporary poetry. His most recent publications are *Remembering Poets, Goatfoot Milktongue Twinbird,* and *Kicking the Leaves,* all in 1978.

Hardy, Thomas (1840–1928). English author who, after writing fifteen novels, including *The Return of the Native* (1878) and *Tess of the D'Urbervilles* (1891), turned completely to writing poetry. In both fiction and verse, Hardy stressed chance or "hap" in human destiny.

Hemingway, Ernest (1899–1961). American novelist and short-story writer whose life and works most often show the individual's struggle with the limits of his or her own capacities. His best-known novels are *A Farewell to Arms* (1929), *For Whom the Bell Tolls* (1940), and *The Old Man and the Sea* (1952).

Hopkins, Gerard Manley (1844–1889). English poet and Jesuit priest, whose highly experimental, metaphysical poems anticipated modernism. Unknown to the reading public until 1918, Hopkins's important work appears in *Poems* (1967).

James, Henry (1843–1916). Born in New York City, he settled in London in 1876, becoming a British subject one year before his death. Acclaimed in America and Europe as a social realist. His novels and short fiction include *The American* (1877), *Daisy Miller* (1878), *The Portrait of a Lady* (1881), and *The Ambassadors* (1903).

Jeffers, Robinson (1887–1962). Maverick among twentieth-century American poets, Jeffers found Nietzsche and Freud congenial supports for his drive "to break out of humanity" and celebrate tragic vision. Modest fame came with the long poem *Roan Stallion* (1925) and his translations of Greek tragedy.

Jennings, Elizabeth (1926–   ). British poet, critic, and writer on religion. She has edited, in collaboration, several poetry anthologies, including *Penguin Modern Poets I* (with Lawrence Durrell and R. S. Thomas). Her most recent volumes are *Consequently I Rejoice* (1977) and *After the Ark* (1978). In 1965 she published *Christianity and Poetry* (in U.S. entitled *Christian Poetry*).

Johnson, Samuel (1709–1784). English poet, essayist, lexicographer, biographer, and editor. A man of much learning and great eloquence, he was the subject of a famous biography by James Boswell. His works include his highly esteemed *Dictionary*, *The Vanity of Human Wishes*, his best poem, and *Lives of the Poets*.

Jones, Leroi (1934–   ). Black nationalist born in Newark, New Jersey, who has changed his name to Imamu Amiri Baraka. Jones is a poet and dramatist who has also written a novel, *The System of Dante's Hell* (1965), short fiction (published as *Tales*, 1967), and many essays and reviews. His poetry was collected in *Preface to a Twenty Volume Suicide Note* (1961), *The Dead Lecturer* (1964), *Black Art* (1968), and *Black Magic* (1969).

Kastenbaum, Robert (1932–   ). American psychologist whose essays in psychology and gerontology journals attest to his research and interest in attitudes about aging and death. He has edited and/or contributed to *New Thoughts on Old Age* (1964) and *The Psychology of Death* (1972).

Keats, John (1795–1821). English poet especially noted for his rapid development and great promise. He wrote his best poems under the threat of death by tuberculosis. "Ode to a Nightingale" and "To Autumn" are two of a series of great odes, including "Ode on a Grecian Urn."

Kierkegaard, Søren (1813–1855). Regarded as the founder of Christian existentialism, he was born and lived his entire life in Copenhagen, Denmark. His major philosophical writings were published under pseudonyms. Among his many works, *Frygt og Baeven* (Fear and Trembling; 1843) and *Sygdommen til Doden* (The Sickness Unto Death; 1849) are perhaps best known.

King, Martin Luther, Jr. (1929–1968). Ordained a Baptist minister in Atlanta, Georgia, he became an internationally respected and revered leader in the struggle for black civil rights. His assassination dismayed the world community. Major writings include *Our Struggle: The Story of Montgomery* (1957), *Letter from Birmingham Jail* (1963, 1968), *Why We Can't Wait* (1964), and *The Trumpet of Conscience* (1968).

Kipling, Rudyard (1865–1936). British poet, short-story writer, novelist, historian, and writer of children's books. Born in Bombay, India, he made Britain's colonial empire the focal point for most of his works. In 1907 he became the first Englishman to receive the Nobel Prize. Among his more than thirty volumes are *Barrack Room Ballads* (1892), *Plain Tales from the Hills* (1888), *The Light That Failed* (1890; novel), *The Jungle Book* (1895), *From Sea to Sea* (1899; travel sketches), and *The Irish Guards in the Great War* (1923).

Laforgue, Jules (1860–1887). French poet credited with the invention of free verse. For five years he sojourned in Germany, where he served as reader to the Empress and wrote much of his poetry. His innovations in form and tone had much influence on such twentieth-century poets as T. S. Eliot and Ezra Pound.

Larkin, Philip (1922–   ). British poet, novelist, and editor who is considered to be the most representative member of the "Movement," a group of poets, mostly academics, who were devoted to the restoration of traditional forms and a return to the humanist tradition. He attended St. John's College, Oxford, and is now librarian at the University of Hull. In 1973 he edited a controversial anthology, *The Oxford Book of Twentieth Century English Verse*.

Lawrence, D. H. (David Herbert) (1885–1930). British novelist, poet, short-story writer, essayist, and dramatist. *Lady Chatterley's Lover* (1928) was banned in both Britain and America, but his most enduring novels appear to be *Sons and Lovers* (1913) and *Women in Love* (1920). *Studies in Classic American Literature* (1923) remains a "classic" critical evaluation of nineteenth-century American writers.

Lennon, John (1940–1980), and **Mc Cartney, Paul** (1942–   ). British musicians, singers, and song writers. Both were born and educated in Liverpool. They gained international fame as members of a pop group called The Beatles, formed in 1960. They have written numerous songs together.

Lessing, Doris (1919–   ). British novelist and short-story writer who was born in Persia and lived in Southern Rhodesia (now Zimbabwe) from 1924 to 1949. She also writes poetry and plays but is noted for (among her more than two dozen books) *The Golden Notebook* (1962), *African Stories* (1964), *Briefing for a Descent into Hell* (1971), and *The Summer Before the Dark* (1973).

Lewis, C. Day (1904–1972). British poet, fiction writer, editor, and teacher. He received his M.A. from Wadham College, Oxford, and proceeded to teach at numerous schools. From 1951 to 1956 he was Professor of Poetry at Oxford, and from 1964 to 1965 Norton Professor of Poetry at Harvard. He was a radical Marxist in his youth. He was Poet Laureate from 1968 to his death. His poetry, especially that written in the 1960s, is noted for its social criticism.

Lueders, Edward (1923–). American poet and teacher. He was educated at Hanover College, Northwestern University, and the University of New Mexico, where he received his Ph.D. in 1952. He has taught English at various colleges, and in 1972 was Writer-in-Residence at Pennsylvania State University. His principal publication is *Images and Impressions: Poems by Brewster Ghislen, Edward Lueders, and Clarice Short.*

McGinley, Phyllis (1905–). American teacher and writer of light verse and children's books. She is a favorite contributor to the *New Yorker, Atlantic Monthly,* the *Saturday Review,* and other magazines. Her *Selected Verse from Three Decades,* published in 1960, won a Pulitzer Prize.

McKay, Claude (1890–1948). Jamaican poet and novelist who came to America in 1912. He became an important figure in the "Negro Renaissance" of the 1920s. His publications include *Spring in New Hampshire and Other Poems* (1920), *Harlem Shadows* (1922), *Banana Bottom* (1933), *A Long Way from Home* (1937), and *The Passion of Claude McKay: Selected Poetry and Prose, 1912–1948.*

MacLeish, Archibald (1892–). American poet and man of letters, who was a modernist expatriate of the 1920s but turned to social and political issues in the 1930s and 1940s. He was Librarian of Congress, Assistant Secretary of State, first chairman of UNESCO, and later professor at Harvard. Major work includes *Conquistador* (1932), *The Fall of the City* (1937), and the verse-drama *J.B.* (1957).

Marvell, Andrew (1621–1678). English Metaphysical poet and public figure in Cromwell's government, who linked wit, Puritan sympathies, and feeling. His best-known poems are "To His Coy Mistress" and "The Garden."

Miller, Vassar (1924–). She received her B.S. and M.A. at the University of Houston and now lives in Houston. Chad Walsh comments (in *Today's Poets*): "Afflicted with cerebral palsy from birth, she has dedicated herself single-mindedly to poetry and has demonstrated . . . that craftsmanship, religious fervor, and personal joy and agony can produce major poetry." Her first book, *Adam's Footprint,* was published in 1956. Other volumes have followed, the latest being *Onions and Roses* (1968). She has received three Texas Institute of Letters awards.

Moore, Marianne (1887–1972). American modernist poet and occasional essayist and literary editor, famous for her stylistic elegance, wit, precision, and typographical arrangements. She called her poetic province "imaginary gardens with real toads in them." *Complete Poems* appeared in 1967.

Nemerov, Howard (1920–). American poet, novelist, critic, teacher, and editor, whose work ranges from serious moral issues to light irony. *A Commodity of Dreams* (1959) exhibits his short fiction; *New and Selected Poems* (1960), the verse; and *Poetry and Fiction* (1963), the criticism.

Oates, Joyce Carol (1938–). Her writing, often compared with that of William Faulkner and Flannery O'Connor, reveals a modern world of Gothic-like terror, torment, and trauma. She has published, since 1963, more than thirty volumes which include short stories, novels, poems, plays, and essays. Her novel *Them* (1969) won the National Book Award.

O'Connor, Flannery (1925–1964). American fiction writer who published one volume of short stories, *A Good Man Is Hard to Find* (1955), and two novellas, *Wise Blood* (1952) and *The Violent Bear It Away* (1960), before dying of an incurable disease at the age of thirty-nine. Born and reared in Georgia, she centers her prose on Southern characters who are latently or overtly violent.

O'Neill, Eugene (1888–1953). Thus far, America's greatest playwright, who found his material in years of wandering and at sea. After a long illness and studying playwriting at Harvard, O'Neill found early success with his one-act plays and on Broadway with such longer plays as *Anna Christie* (1921), *Desire Under the Elms* (1924), *Mourning Becomes Electra* (1931), and *Long Day's Journey into Night* (1956).

Pack, Robert (1929–). American poet, critic, and editor. As co-editor, with Donald Hall and Louis Simpson, of *The New Poets of England and America,* he has come to be regarded as a leader of modern poetry. His works include *The Irony of Joy* (1955) and *A Stranger's Privilege* (1959).

Packard, Vance (1914–). American social critic, newspaperman, and magazine journalist who specializes in "popularizing" factual information about human behavior. Best-known works include *The Hidden Persuaders* (1957), *The Naked Society* (1964), *A Nation of Strangers* (1972), and *The People Shapers* (1977).

Phillips, Louis (1942–). American poet, dramatist, and author of children's stories. His publications include the fairy tale, *The Man Who Stole the Atlantic Ocean* (1972); a collection of poems, *A Catalogue of Earthly Pleasures* (1973); and a play, *The Last of the Marx Brothers,* first produced at Brandeis University in 1973.

Plath, Sylvia (1932–1963). American poet, whose painful reflections upon her existence and her drift toward suicide characterize poems like

"Daddy," "Lady Lazarus," and "Fever 103°," as well as her autobiographical novel, *The Bell Jar* (1963).

Pope, Alexander (1688–1744). English poet, satirist, and Tory partisan, who mercilessly attacked literary and political foes. His major long poems are the mock-heroic *The Rape of the Lock* (1714), the polemic *Essay on Criticism* (1711), *An Essay on Man* (1734), and *The Dunciad* (1728–1743).

Reid, Alastair (1926–). British poet, translator, and writer of children's fiction. He has taught at Sarah Lawrence College, Antioch College, and Oxford University (a seminar in Latin American literature). Since 1959 he has been staff writer and correspondent for the *New Yorker*. His first volume of poems was *To Lighten My House: Poems, 1953*. His most recent publication is a translation of Pablo Neruda's *Isla Negra*.

Rich, Adrienne (1929–). American poet who also writes essays on sexual politics and is interested in chronicling the feminist movement in America. Her volumes of poetry include *A Change of World* (1951), *Necessities of Life* (1966), and *Diving into the Wreck, Poems 1971–1972* (1973), which won the National Book Award in 1974.

Rive, Richard (1931–). Pseudonym, Richard Moore. South African novelist, short-story writer, poet, and teacher whose father was an Afro-American from the United States and whose mother was a South African "colored." His work exhibits the hostilities that stem from South Africa's apartheid policy. Works include *African Songs* (1963; stories), and *Emergency* (1964; novel).

Rock, Gail. Nebraska-born, she now lives in New York City where she has been a film and TV critic, a free-lance contributor to magazines, a writer of TV scripts, and an author of children's books, one of which, *The House Without a Christmas Tree,* received a Christopher Award for its televised presentation.

Roethke, Theodore (1908–1963). Recognized as one of the finest American poets of this century, he received the Pulitzer Prize in 1954 for *The Waking: Poems 1933–1953*, a Bollingen Prize in 1958 for *Words for the Wind*, and the Edna St. Vincent Millay Prize in 1959. His *The Far Field*, published posthumously, received the National Book Award in 1965.

Rossetti, Dante Gabriel (1828–1882). English poet and painter. He was born in London, the son of an Italian expatriate. He was one of the founders of the Pre-Raphaelite Brotherhood, a group of young artists and writers whose object was to revive, in art, the simplicity and pure color of pre-Renaissance art. His sonnet sequence, *The House of Life,* is concerned almost exclusively with the relation between spiritual and physical love. His poetry throughout reflects his interest in painting.

Roth, Philip (1933–). A major writer in the Jewish-American tradition, he is a master of satiric wit whose *Goodbye, Columbus* received the National Book Award in 1960. *Portnoy's Complaint* (1969), *Our Gang* (1971; about the Nixon administration), *The Breast* (1972), *The Great American Novel* (1973), and *The Professor of Desire* (1977) are among his most comic and satiric works.

Saroyan, William (1908–). American writer of fiction and plays. Often sentimental and sometimes angry, he stresses human goodness, warmth, and love, struggling against a sterile American cult of success. His best work includes *The Times of Your Life* (1939), *My Name Is Aram* (1940), and *The Human Comedy* (1964).

Shakespeare, William (1564–1616). Long ago acknowledged as unrivaled poet and dramatist of the English Renaissance, indeed the first creative genius writing in English. Shakespeare's thirty-seven plays include the great tragedies *Hamlet* (1600), *Macbeth*, and *King Lear* (both 1605), the comedies *As You Like It* (1599) and *The Merry Wives of Windsor* (1600), and the history plays *Henry IV* (1597) and *Richard II* (1595). He also wrote much nondramatic poetry, of which his 154 *Sonnets* (1609) are most highly celebrated.

Shapiro, Karl (1913–). American poet, teacher, writer, and man of letters, who found success while still in the U.S. Army in World War II and as dissenter to the prevailing supremacy of Eliot and Pound among Anglo-American poets. Insisting on the primacy of Whitman, D. H. Lawrence, and Henry Miller as literary guides, Shapiro has espoused individualism and "cosmic consciousness" in his verse—*Selected Poems* (1968) and *White Haired Lover* (1968).

Shaw, Irwin (1913–). Born in New York City, he gained first attention for the antiwar play *Bury the Dead* (1936). He has been a contributor to the *New Yorker* (short stories) and a novelist of note. Works include *The Young Lions* (1948) and *Rich Man, Poor Man* (1969). The latter was recently televised.

Shelley, Percy Bysshe (1792–1822). English Romantic poet, who first attracted attention, mainly unfavorable, with his daring attacks upon religious orthodoxy and the prevailing social scheme. Known generally for his ecstatic lyrics—"Ode to the West Wind" and "To a Skylark"—Shelley wrote his masterpiece in the verse-drama *Prometheus Unbound* (1820).

Sloman, Joel (1943–). Born in Brooklyn, New York, he is a former assistant director of the poetry project at St. Mark's Church in the Bowery and a sometime resident in England. His collection, *Virgil's Machines,* was published in 1966.

Smith, William Jay (1918–). American poet, critic, translator, and writer of books for children. He has been a professor of English at Hollins College, Virginia, since 1970. He has also taught courses in French. In 1973 and 1974 he was Visiting Professor of Writing at Columbia University. His first volume was *Poems* (1944). Since then he has published more than two dozen volumes, some as editor and some as translator. His most recent book of poems is *Venice in the Fog* (1975).

Spenser, Edmund (1552–1599). English poet, whose *Faerie Queene* (1596), a long allegory in six books, combined epic, romance, nationalism, Protestant zeal, and moral vision. Other poetry includes the sonnet sequence *Amoretti* (1595), a pastoral, *The Shepheardes Calender* (1579), and the celebrations of marriage, "Prothalamion" and "Epithalamion."

Stevens, Wallace (1879–1955). American poet and insurance executive, whose literary canon recurringly pursues a poetic "fiction" to replace an unsatisfactory religion. His first collection, *Harmonium* (1923), revealed the same witty, polished, philosophical verse which characterizes the later work in *The Man with the Blue Guitar* (1937) and *Collected Poems* (1954).

Stevenson, Robert Louis (1850–1894). English novelist, essayist, poet, and children's writer, whose *Treasure Island* (1883) finds perennial favor as a romance of adventure. His finest finished novel, *The Master of Ballantrae,* (1889), reveals the potential in craftsmanship lost to almost constant illness and early death.

Swinburne, Algernon Charles (1837–1909). English poet, who delighted in offending Victorian prudery and orthodoxy. Technically innovative, he invested his best poems (most are in the early collection *Poems and Ballads*, 1878) with extravagant sensuousness, melody, and seldom-excelled rhythms.

Thomas, R. S. (1913–   ). Welsh poet and priest. He has been Vicar of St. Hywyn since 1967. He has edited, in collaboration, several poetry anthologies. His best volumes of poetry were *Songs at the Year's Turning; Poems 1942–1954* (1955), for which he received the Heinemann Award, and *Poetry for Supper* (1958). His most recent volume is *Laboratories of the Spirit.*

Thoreau, Henry David (1817–1862). Noted esayist, poet, disciple of Ralph Waldo Emerson, and member of the Concord, Massachusetts, group who variously contributed to transcendental philosphy. He spent his lifetime searching for harmony between man and nature, and he captured his experiences and viewpoints in *A Week on the Concord and Merrimack Rivers* (1849), *Walden* (1854), *The Maine Woods* (1864), and *Cape Cod* (1865), the last two published posthumously.

Traven, B. (?–1969). Mexican novelist and short-story writer who is thought to have been either American-born (in Chicago in 1890) or German-born (in 1882). His work has been published in thirty-six languages and more than 500 editions, but his life, perhaps even his true identity, has remained a mystery. His best-known work is *The Treasure of Sierra Madre* (U.S. edition prepared by Traven in 1935).

Updike, John (1932–   ). American novelist, short-story writer, poet, and one-play dramatist who has also written books for children. His best-known works characterize and illuminate social values. His works include the novels *Rabbit, Run* (1960), *Couples* (1968), and *Rabbit Redux* (1971).

Vaughan, Henry (1621–1695). Welsh poet and physician. He studied at Oxford and took a brief part on the Royalist side during the Civil War. He was interested in the occult—his twin brother was a hermetic philosopher and an alchemist—and one of the last proponents of the doctrine of mystic correspondence, an analogical relationship between this world and the world of spirits. He published only two volumes of poetry.

Wain, John (1925–   ). British poet, novelist, critic, editor, and teacher. He received his degree from St. John's College, Oxford. From 1947 to 1955 he was a lecturer in English literature at the University of Reading. He resigned this position to become a free-lance editor and critic. He was a member of the "Movement" poets (see note on Philip Larkin). In 1971–72 he was the first holder of a Fellowship in Creative Arts at Brasenose College, Oxford.

Warren, Robert Penn (1905–   ). Quintessential American man of letters: novelist, poet, short-story writer, scholar, critic, and teacher. His novels, volumes of poetry, critical studies, and textbooks number in the several dozens. He received the Pulitzer Prize for *All the King's Men* (1946).

Whitman, Walt (1819–1892). Generally considered the major American poet, whose *Leaves of Grass* grew along with its author and through ten editions. Proclaiming himself the instigator of a new, militantly American poetry, Whitman celebrated a mystical consciousness in which the individual and the cosmos merge to form a democracy and mutual illumination.

Williams, William Carlos (1883–1963). American poet, fiction writer, and physician. Williams began his medical training at the University of Pennsylvania, where he also gave serious attention to his poems. In 1906 he went to Leipzig to study pediatrics, and in 1916 he set up practice in Rutherford, New Jersey, his birthplace. His poetry, including his epic *Paterson,* is marked, as one critic put it, by "a knowledge of life at once humane and disciplined, disillusioned, witty and yet compassionate."

Wordsworth, William (1770–1850). English poet and critic. His Preface to the second edition of *Lyrical Ballads* (1800) is considered to be a major Romantic manifesto. He is best known as a nature poet, and his best poetry was inspired by the concept of sympathy between the objects of nature and the human mind. His major work is *The Prelude,* published posthumously. He was appointed Poet Laureate in 1843.

Yeats, William Butler (1865–1939). Major Irish poet, playwright, and Nobel Prize–winner, whose large canon combines Romantic lyricism, modernist techniques, dramatic flair, and complex symbolism. A leader in the "Irish Renaissance," Yeats became in his later work (*The Tower* [1928] and *Collected Poems* [1956]) an international voice like Joyce, Eliot, and Pound.